2004 SEAK, Inc.

National Guide to Expert Witness Fees and Billing Procedures

Alex Babitsky, MBA
Steven Babitsky, JD
James J. Mangraviti, Jr., JD

SEAK, Inc.
Excellence in Education Since 1980

Falmouth, Massachusetts
www.seak.com

2004 SEAK, Inc.
National Guide to Expert Witness Fees and Billing Procedures

ISBN: 1-892904-25-X

CONTENTS

Acknowledgments

The authors wish to acknowledge the 1,030 experts across the country who provided the information that forms the basis of this book. The authors would also like to thank Jon Cahill, Jeanne Lovering, Dee Netzel, Helen Stahl, and Mary Frances Mangraviti for their invaluable assistance in making this book a reality.

Related Products by SEAK, Inc.

TEXTS
Cross-Examination: The Comprehensive Guide for Experts
Writing and Defending Your IME Report
Writing and Defending Your Expert Report
The Comprehensive Forensic Services Manual
How to Excel During Depositions
The Successful Physician Negotiator
The Comprehensive IME System

TRAINING SEMINARS
Trick and Difficult Question Workshop
Practice Management Workshop for Experts
Advanced Cross-Examination Workshop
Expert Report Writing Workshop
Testifying Skills Workshop
Law School for Experts
How to Be an Effective Medical Witness
SEAK Law School for Physicians ™
Malpractice Survival Training for Physicians
SEAK Negotiating Skills for Physicians ™
SEAK Business School for Physicians ™
National Expert Witness and Litigation Seminar
Medical Witness Summit

AUDIOTAPE PROGRAMS
Law School for Experts
Marketing Your Forensic Practice
Achieving Success as a Medical Witness

VIDEOTAPES
The Expert Deposition: How to Be an Effective and Ethical Witness
Winning Over the Jury: Techniques for Experts That Work
Symptom Magnification, Malingering, and Deception
Cross-Examination of the Expert
The Most Difficult Questions for Experts: With Answers

DIRECTORIES
SEAK, Inc. National Directory of Independent Medical Examiners (www.imenet.com)
SEAK, Inc. National Directory of Experts (www.seakexperts.com)
SEAK, Inc. National Directory of Physicians' Counsel (www.counselforphysicians.com)

For more information, call SEAK at (508) 457-1111. Inquiries may also be addressed to SEAK, Inc. at P.O. Box 729, Falmouth, MA 02541. Fax (508) 540-8304; e-mail address: seakinc@aol.com; Internet address: www.seak.com

About the Authors

Alex Babitsky, MBA, is the Directory Manager of SEAK, Inc. Mr. Babitsky received his BS degree from the University of Massachusetts and his MBA from Northeastern University. Mr. Babitsky deals with expert witnesses and the attorneys who retain them on a daily basis as the Product Manager of SEAK's annual *National Directory of Experts* (www.seakexperts.com) and SEAK's annual *National Directory of Independent Medical Examiners* (www.imenet.com). These two publications currently have a combined distribution of over 70,000 copies per edition. Mr. Babitsky regularly consults with experts of all fields on the subject of expert witness marketing and has designed dozens of display advertisements for expert witnesses.

Steven Babitsky, JD, is the President of SEAK, Inc. He was a personal injury trial attorney for twenty years and is the former managing partner of the firm Kistin, Babitsky, Latimer & Beitman. Mr. Babitsky is the co-author of the texts *Cross-Examination: The Comprehensive Guide for Experts, Writing and Defending Your Expert Report: The Step-by-Step Guide with Models, How to Excel During Cross-Examination: Techniques for Experts That Work, The Comprehensive Forensic Services Manual: The Essential Resources for All Experts,* and *How to Excel During Depositions: Techniques for Experts That Work.* Attorney Babitsky is the co-developer and trainer for the "How to Be an Effective Medical Witness" seminar, the seminar leader for SEAK's Annual National Expert Witness Seminar, and the scriptwriter for the videos "How to Be an Effective Medical Witness" and "The Expert Medical Deposition: How to Be an Effective and Ethical Witness." Mr. Babitsky trains hundreds of experts every year.

James J. Mangraviti, Jr., JD, has trained hundreds of expert witnesses across the United States and Canada. He is a former trial lawyer with experience in defense and plaintiff personal injury law and insurance law. He currently serves as Vice President and General Counsel of SEAK, Inc. Mr. Mangraviti received his BA degree in mathematics *summa cum laude* from Boston College and his JD degree *cum laude* from Boston College Law School. His publications include the texts *SEAK Law School for Physicians, Law School for the Safety and Health Professional, Writing and Defending Your Independent Medical Examination Report, The Successful Physician Negotiator: How to Get What You Deserve, How to Excel During Cross-Examination: Techniques for Experts That Work, How to Excel During Depositions: Techniques for Experts That Work, The Comprehensive Forensic Services Manual: The Essential Resources for All Experts,* and *Writing and Defending Your Expert Report: The Step-by-Step Guide with Models*, and *Cross-Examination: The Comprehensive Guide for Experts.*

Preface

Over the past several years we at SEAK, Inc. have continued to travel across the United States to train thousands of professionals in testifying skills and in how to be more effective and ethical expert witnesses. As part of this training, we often facilitate a discussion regarding expert witness fees and billing procedures. This usually includes an oral survey of the attendees in our workshop. This survey is invariably one of the most popular sections of our workshop because it allows our attendees to see what other experts are charging and it helps them determine whether they should amend their rates or their billing procedures.

This book has been written to provide detailed expert witness fee and billing information on a national basis and from a large sample size. It is our hope that this information will be useful to both experts and the trial attorneys who employ them. As always, your feedback is welcome.

Alex Babitsky, MBA
Steven Babitsky, JD
James J. Mangraviti, Jr., JD

SEAK, Inc.
P.O. Box 729
Falmouth, MA 02541
Phone: (508) 457-1111
Fax: (508) 540-8304
www.seak.com

Chapter 1 Introduction and Summary of Findings

Introduction

The authors hope that the information contained herein will be useful to both experts and attorneys. The responses regarding the more populous states and the more common areas of expertise are numerous enough to obtain a very good understanding of current fee and billing practices. For those interested in less common areas of expertise and less populous states, the authors suggest considering both the direct on-point data contained herein and data from similar specialties.

Source of Data

Over the period of June to December 2003, the authors provided detailed one-page questionnaires to approximately 8,500 expert witnesses. The experts were offered the chance to win free SEAK, Inc., continuing education products if they filled out the questionnaire. 1,030 usable questionnaires were returned. The authors then compiled and analyzed the reported data. The results are reported herein. The authors believe this to be the largest and most detailed fee and billing survey of expert witnesses ever reported. The authors requested the following information from surveyed experts.

1. *Area of expertise.* All respondents were asked to provide an "area of expertise/specialty." The authors, where possible, attempted to combine similar areas into the same standard category. For example, the authors combined "Law Enforcement" and "Police" into the category of "Law Enforcement." Based on the reported information, the authors categorized each expert as either a "medical" or "non-medical" expert.

2. *State.* Experts were asked their state. For those experts who reported "national," an investigation was done to attempt to determine their primary state.

3. *Number of years testifying.*

4. *Hourly fees for in-court testimony, file reviews/preparation, and depositions.* Where a flat day rate or a half-day rate was provided, the authors attempted, where possible, to translate this into an hourly rate.

5. *Minimum charge for depositions and trial and the number of hours in each minimum.* Where a flat day rate or a half-day rate was provided, the authors attempted, where possible, to translate this into the appropriate number of hours.

6. *Whether the expert has a cancellation policy whereby he retains all or a portion of a deposition or trial appearance fee for a cancellation made within a certain specified time prior to the scheduled date.*

7. *Whether the expert requires an up-front retainer and the amount and type of this retainer.* Some experts reported that their retainer is a percentage of the estimated fee, as opposed to a fixed dollar amount. These amounts are reported in the listings of individual responses by state, but are not part of the calculations for the statistics regarding retainers.

8. *Whether the expert requires deposition payment in advance.*

9. *The procedure for handling the situation where the time for the expert's deposition exceeds prepayment by opposing counsel.* The experts were asked to circle either "Get payment before

proceeding further," "Proceed without immediate payment," or "Other________." The statistics reported reflect only those that circled "Get payment before proceeding further" or "Proceed without immediate payment."

10. *Does the expert mark up out-of-pocket expenses with an administrative, handling, or other fee? If so, how much is the fee?* The statistics reported reflect only those whose fee is expressed as a percentage. Some experts reported this fee as a fixed amount or an hourly charge.

11. *For what out-of-pocket expenses does the expert charge?* The expert was asked to circle the following expenses: "Mileage," "Airline Tickets," "Photocopies," "Telephone Calls," "Lab/Testing," "Photographs," "Demonstrative Aids," and "Other_____________." The statistics reported do not reflect the "other" responses.

12. *Does the expert bill travel time portal-to-portal?*

13. *Does the expert require first-class airfare?*

14. *Is it the expert's policy to require retaining counsel to sign a written retainer agreement? If so, what terms and conditions are contained in the written agreement?* The expert was asked to choose from the following expenses: "Lawyer is responsible for fee, not lawyer's client," "Interest for delinquent accounts," "Out-of-pocket expense policies," "Retainer/prepayment requirements," "In-court testimony minimum fees," "Retaining counsel will pay for all deposition charges," "Fee schedules," "Attorney's fees if forced to sue for collection," "Portal-to-portal travel time," "Deposition minimum fees," "Payment for preparation times," "First-class air travel," and "Other_____________." The statistics reported do not reflect the "other" responses.

15. *Is the majority of the expert's work for plaintiffs, defendants, or neither?*

16. *Has a retaining lawyer failed to pay any of the expert's bills in the last five years?*

17. *Has opposing counsel failed to pay any of the expert's deposition fees in the last five years?*

Summary of Findings

Fees by State

Expert witness fees vary significantly from state to state. A state-by-state summary of fees and billings for all responding experts in all 50 states is provided in Chapter 3. Nine states had more than 30 experts respond to our survey. These were: California (159 responding experts), Florida (92 responding experts), Illinois (45 responding experts), Massachusetts (41 responding experts), New Jersey (38 responding experts), New York (74 responding experts), Ohio (38 responding experts), Pennsylvania (49 responding experts), and Texas (81 responding experts). The national average for hourly fees for in-court testimony is $385. The average hourly fee for in-court testimony for each of the above 9 large sample-size states is as follows.

- California $365
- Florida $493
- Illinois $384
- Massachusetts $357
- New Jersey $484
- New York $453
- Ohio $539
- Pennsylvania $455
- Texas $331
- National $385

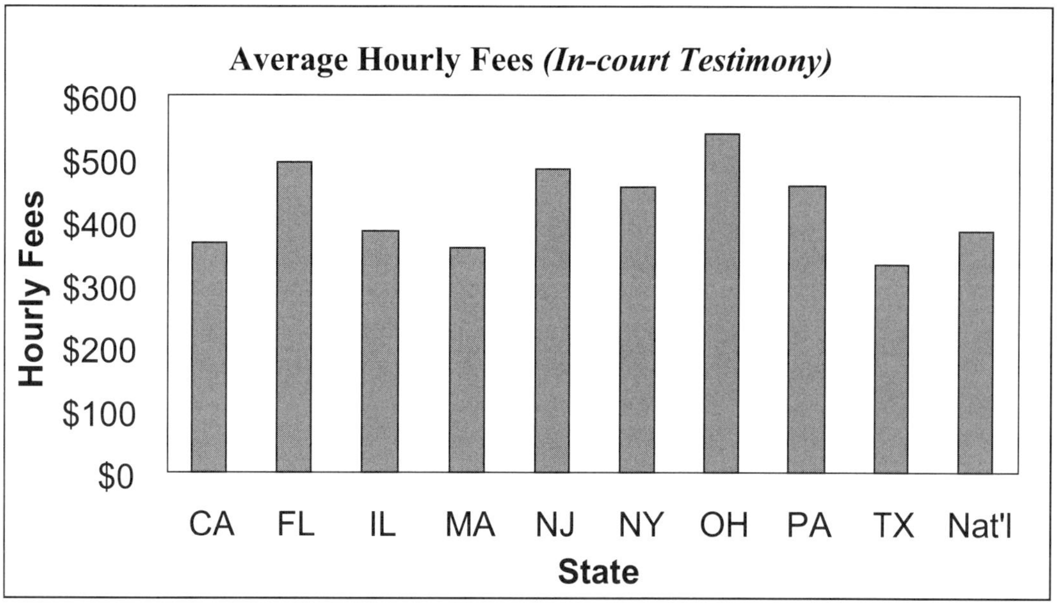

The fees for the lowest state (Texas) are 63% less than those of the highest state (Ohio).

Fees by Area of Expertise

The survey includes responses from over 300 areas of expertise, from Accident Reconstruction to Wound Care. There was significant variation in fees amongst different areas of expertise. Medical experts are on average much better compensated than non-medical experts. The average hourly fee for in-court testimony for all non-medical experts is $248. The average hourly fee for in-court testimony for all medical experts is $555. Medical experts on average earn *more than double* (124% more) what non-medical experts earn. Forty-five percent of all responding experts were medical experts and 55% of all responding experts were non-medical experts. Fee and billings statistics for over 300 areas of expertise are presented in Chapter 4.

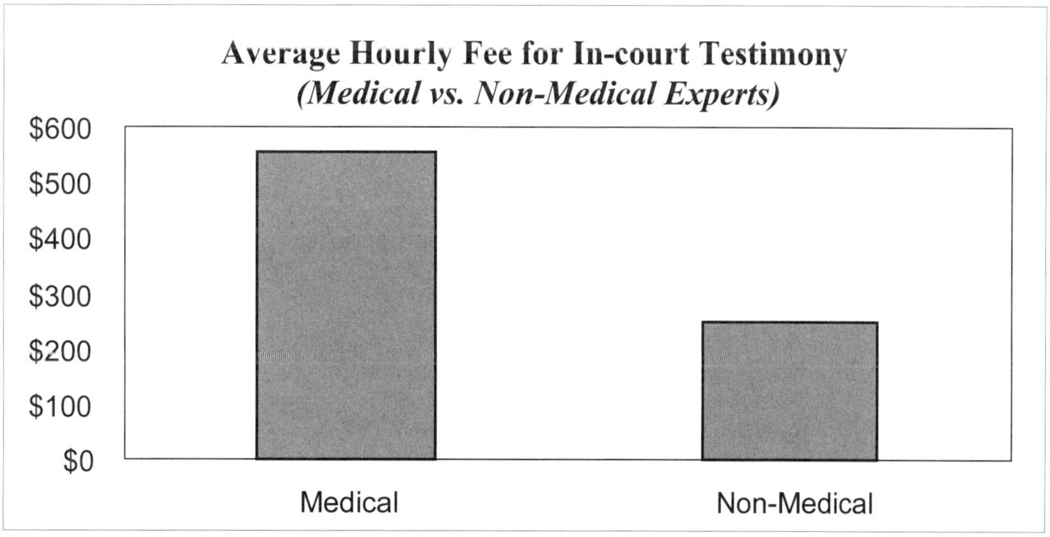

Number of Years of Experience

The majority of all experts (58%) have been testifying for 15 years or less. Medical experts tend to have less experience testifying than non-medical experts. The median number of years of testifying was 15 for all experts, 15 for all non-medical experts, and 12 for all medical experts.

Surprisingly, less experienced experts generally charge more than experienced experts. The median hourly rate for all experts for in-court testimony was $300. The median hourly rate for experts who have been testifying 1-5 years was $350 and the median hourly rate for experts who have been testifying 26+ years was $275.

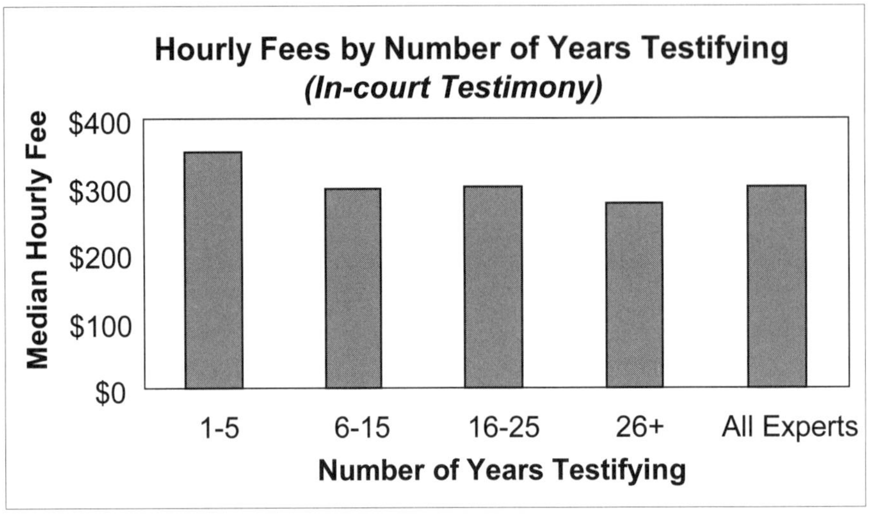

Fees for Trial, File Review, and Depositions

On average, experts charge significantly more for their time while testifying at trial and deposition than they charge for their time while conducting file reviews and preparing. The average hourly fee for all experts was $385 for in-court testimony, $353 for depositions, and $254 for file reviews and preparation. The average hourly fee for trial testimony is *52% higher* than the average hourly fee for file reviews and preparation.

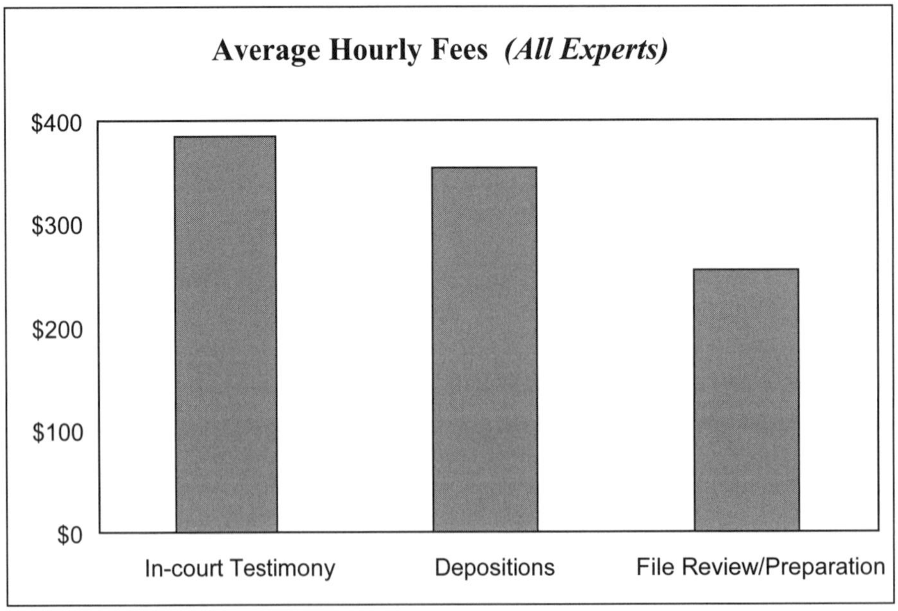

Minimum Fees for Depositions and Trials
A majority of all experts (58%) charge a minimum number of hours for depositions and trial testimony. Medical experts are far more likely to charge such a minimum. For example, 72% of medical experts have a minimum deposition charge. Only 46% of non-medical experts have a minimum deposition charge. The median minimum charge for all experts was 3 hours for depositions and 4 hours for trials.

Cancellation Fees for Depositions and Trials
45% of all experts have a cancellation policy whereby they retain all or a portion of a deposition or trial appearance fee for cancellations made within a certain specified time prior to the scheduled date. Medical experts are far more likely to have such a cancellation policy. 69% of medical experts have such a policy, whereas only 25% of non-medical experts have such a policy. This may be reflective of a physician's inability to fill up her calendar with patients after cancellation is made on short notice.

Depositions
20% of all experts report opposing counsel having failed to pay them for at least part of the expert's deposition fee in the last five years. To avoid this situation, 48% of experts require advance payment from opposing counsel for depositions. When the time of the deposition exceeds that prepayment amount, the vast majority of experts (77%) proceed with the deposition. However, a sizeable minority (23%) obtain payment before proceeding further. 38% of experts who require written retainer agreements include a clause in that agreement whereby retaining counsel agrees to pay for all deposition charges.

Retainers
The vast majority of all experts (73%) obtain some sort of up-front retainer. The median amount of this retainer is $1,500. Non-medical experts are significantly more likely to require a retainer than medical experts. 79% of non-medical experts require an up-front retainer, whereas only 65% of all medical experts require an up-front retainer.

Requiring a replenishable retainer is one way to guarantee payment by retaining counsel. Of those experts requiring retainers, 69% use one-time retainers and 31% use replenishable retainers.

A problem commonly faced by experts is being named as an expert in a case for the sole purpose of "conflicting the expert out" and denying the opposing sides the expert. One way to mitigate this problem is to require a nonrefundable retainer prior to reviewing any documents or doing any work on a case. 44% of all experts who require a retainer have their retainer be non-refundable.

Out-of-Pocket Expenses
A significant minority of all experts (19%) mark up their out-of-pocket expenses with an administrative, handling, or other fee. Non-medical experts (23%) are far more likely than medical experts (14%) to mark up their expenses. The median markup for all experts is 15%. In terms of which out-of-pocket expenses are billed for:

- 68% of all experts bill for mileage,
- 83% bill for airline tickets,
- 44% bill for photocopies,
- 38% bill for telephone calls,
- 41% bill for lab/testing,
- 45% bill for photos, and

- 48% bill for demonstrative aids.

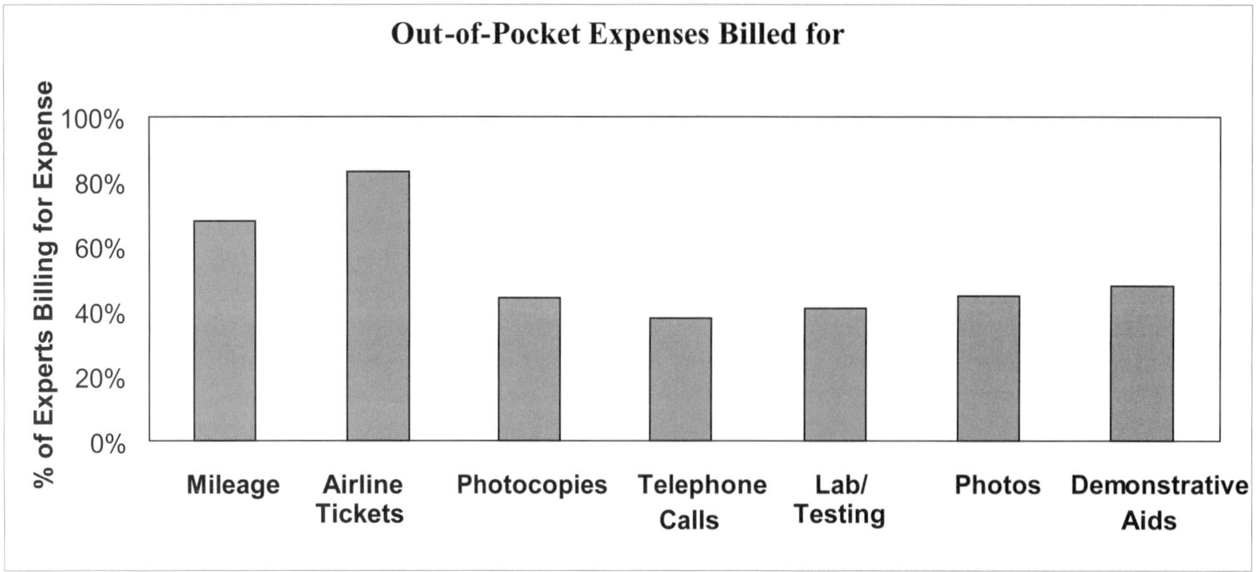

Other out-of-pocket expenses reported as billed-for include:

- all travel costs,
- auto rental,
- car service,
- colleagues' opinions,
- computer research,
- equipment rentals,
- evidence storage,
- express packages,
- faxes,
- hotel,
- limousines,
- meals,
- parking,
- per diem travel expenses,
- postage,
- printing of reports,
- research publications,
- supplies,
- tolls, and
- transcriptions.

10% of all experts require first-class airfare. Medical experts are far more likely (13%) than non-medical experts (8%) to require first-class airfare.

Travel Time
86% of all experts bill their travel time portal-to-portal. 62% of experts who require counsel to sign a written retainer agreement have a clause in their agreement that requires portal-to-portal travel time charges.

First-class Airfare
10% of all experts require that they fly first class. This is far more common amongst medical experts (13%) than non-medical experts (8%).

Written Fee Agreements
A little less than half (46%) of all experts require retaining counsel to sign a written retention agreement. Non-medical experts are much more likely to require retaining counsel to sign a written fee agreement (58%) than medical experts (31%). Of the experts who require counsel to sign a written fee agreement:

- 66% include a clause stating that retaining counsel, not counsel's client, is responsible for paying the expert's fee,
- 55% include a clause authorizing interest for overdue accounts,
- 78% contain the expert's out-of-pocket expense policies,
- 83% contain retainer/prepayment requirements,
- 59% contain in-court minimum fees,
- 38% contain a clause whereby retaining counsel agrees to be responsible for paying all deposition fees,
- 82% contain the expert's fee schedules,
- 48% contain a clause authorizing attorney's fees if the expert is forced to sue for collection,
- 62% contain a clause agreeing to travel time being billed portal-to-portal,
- 52% have a clause establishing minimum fees for depositions,
- 65% require payment for preparation time, and
- 10% contain a clause requiring first-class airfare for the expert.

Other clauses reported to be used by responding experts include:

- a clause requiring that any disputes under the agreement be arbitrated,
- limitation of liability clauses (e.g., if the expert is sued, damages are limited to the expert's fee),
- indemnification/hold-harmless clauses,
- choice of jurisdiction clauses (e.g., any suit arising out of this agreement must be filed in the expert's home jurisdiction),
- right to increase fees after a certain period of time, such as one year,
- clauses dealing with cancellation fees/policies,
- clauses requiring retaining counsel to be cooperative,
- clauses stating that the expert does not guarantee a result,
- clauses requiring mediation of disputes, and
- clauses stating that the expert reserves the right to stop work if he is not paid.

Majority of Experts' Work
The majority of experts (57%) reported working equally for plaintiffs and defendants. Twenty-three percent of experts reported themselves as working a majority of the time for plaintiffs and

20% reported working a majority of the time for defendants. Defense experts on average charge more than plaintiffs' experts. Plaintiffs' and defendants' experts on average charge more than experts who testify equally for each side.

The median hourly fee for trial testimony was exactly the same ($300) for all three types of experts. However, the average hourly fee for trial testimony for plaintiffs ($405) and defense experts ($415) was significantly higher than those of experts who testify equally for both sides ($364). Defense experts charge on average greater fees for trial testimony ($415), file review ($272), and depositions ($370) than plaintiffs' experts charge for trial testimony ($405), file review ($244), and depositions ($342).

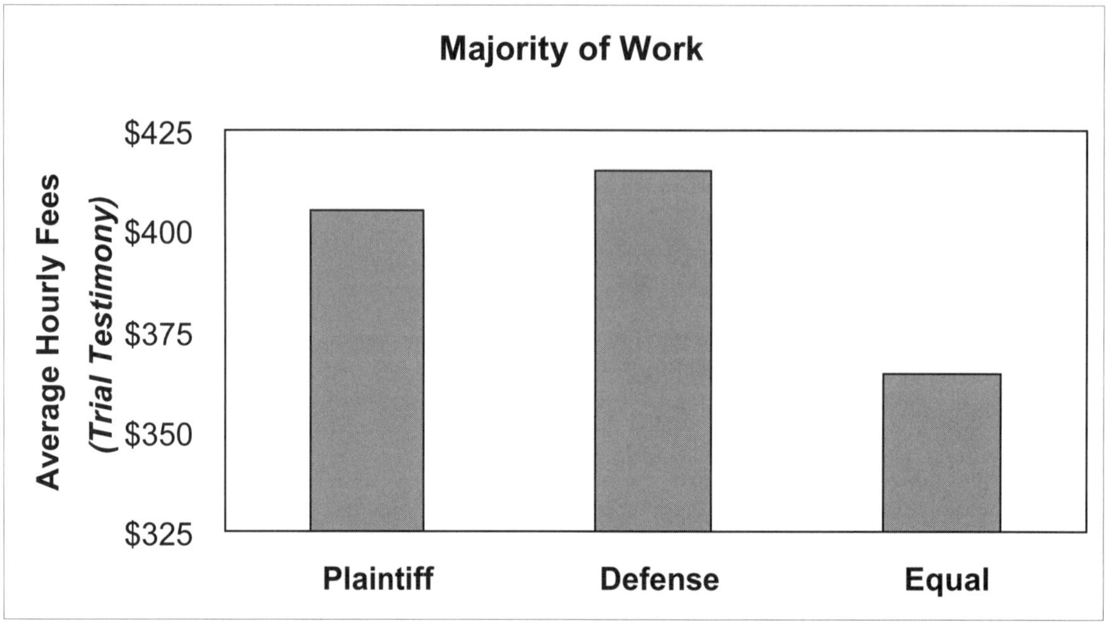

Collections Troubles

A significant number of experts reported retaining or opposing counsel failing to pay one or more of their bills in the preceding five years. Experts were far more likely to report collection difficulties with retaining counsel than with opposing counsel. Forty-six percent of all experts reported having retaining counsel fail to pay a bill in the last 5 years, whereas only 20% of experts reported that opposing counsel failed to pay a bill in the last 5 years.

Chapter 2 National Summary Data

All Experts

Responding Experts: 1,030
Years Testifying: *High:* 75 *Low:* 1 *Average:* 15.6 *Median:* 15

In-court Testimony (hourly):	*High:* $7,500	*Low:* $75	*Average:* $385	*Median:* $300
File Review/Prep (hourly):	*High:* $1,000	*Low:* $0	*Average:* $254	*Median:* $240
Depositions (hourly):	*High:* $3,000	*Low:* $0	*Average:* $353	*Median:* $300

Min. Charge for Depositions: 58% **Hours in Minimum:** *High:* 12 *Low:* 1 *Average:* 3.1 *Median:* 3

Min. Charge for Trial: 58% **Hours in Minimum:** *High:* 20 *Low:* 1 *Average:* 4.2 *Median:* 4

Cancellation Fee for Depositions or Trial: 45% **Deposition Payment in Advance:** 48%

Up-front Retainer: 73% **Retainer Amount:** *High:* $15,000 *Low:* $150 *Average:* $1,967 *Median:* $1,500
Type of Retainer: *Refundable:* 54% *Partially Refundable:* 2% *Non-Refundable:* 44%
One Time: 69% *Replenishable:* 31%

Depositions That Exceed Paid-for Time: *Get payment before proceeding:* 23% *Proceed without immediate payment:* 77%

Out-of-Pocket Expenses Marked Up: 19% **Markup Amount:** *High:* 40% *Low:* 3% *Average:* 14% *Median:* 15%
Out-of-Pockets Billed for: *Mileage:* 68% *Airline Tickets:* 83% *Photocopies:* 44% *Telephone Calls:* 38% *Lab/Testing:* 41% *Photos:* 45% *Demonstrative Aids:* 48% **Travel Billed Portal-to-Portal:** 86% **First-class Airfare Required:** 10%

Require Signed Written Fee Agreement: 46% **Terms Contained in Fee Agreement:** *Lawyer is responsible for fee, not lawyer's client:* 66% *Interest for delinquent accounts:* 55% *Out-of-pocket expense policies:* 78% *Retainer/prepayment requirements:* 83% *In-court testimony minimum fees:* 59% *Retaining counsel will pay for all deposition charges:* 38% *Fee schedules:* 82% *Attorney's fees if forced to sue for collection:* 48% *Portal-to-portal travel time:* 62% *Deposition minimum fees:* 52% *Payment for preparation time:* 65% *First-class air travel:* 10%

Majority of Work: *Plaintiffs:* 23% *Neither:* 57% *Defendants:* 20%
Type of Expert: *Medical:* 45% *Non-Medical:* 55%
Retaining Counsel Failed to Pay in Last 5 Years: 46% **Opposing Counsel Failed to Pay in Last 5 Years:** 20%

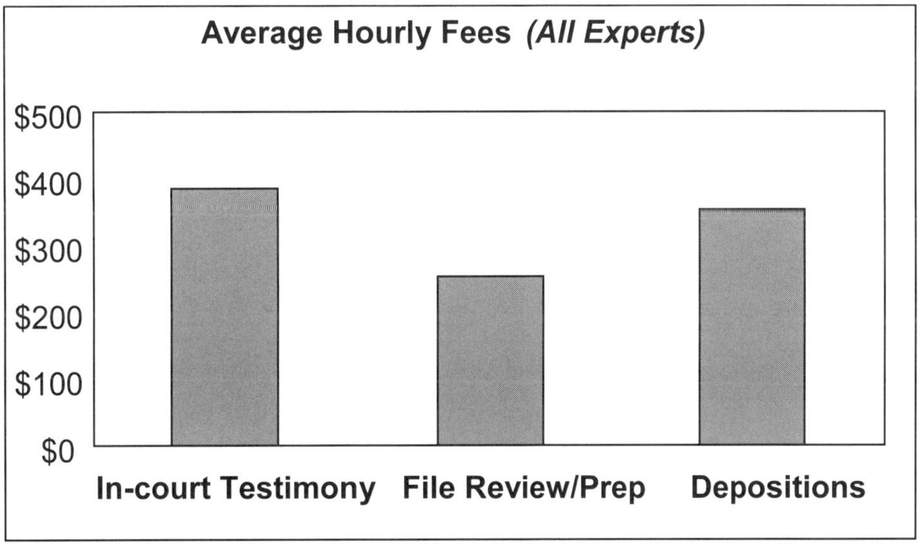

All Medical Experts

Responding Experts: 466
Years Testifying: *High:* 75 *Low:* 1 *Average:* 14 *Median:* 12

In-court Testimony (hourly):	*High:* $7,500	*Low:* $100	*Average:* $555	*Median:* $500
File Review/Prep (hourly):	*High:* $1,000	*Low:* $0	*Average:* $319	*Median:* $300
Depositions (hourly):	*High:* $3,000	*Low:* $85	*Average:* $465	*Median:* $400

Min. Charge for Depositions: 72% **Hours in Minimum:** *High:* 10 *Low:* 1 *Average:* 2.5 *Median:* 2

Min. Charge for Trial: 73% **Hours in Minimum:** *High:* 20 *Low:* 1 *Average:* 4 *Median:* 4

Cancellation Fee for Depositions or Trial: 69% **Deposition Payment in Advance:** 59%

Up-front Retainer: 65% **Retainer Amount:** *High:* $10,000 *Low:* $150 *Average:* $1,441 *Median:* $1000

Type of Retainer: *Refundable:* 49% *Partially Refundable:* 2% *Non-Refundable:* 49%
One Time: 70% *Replenishable:* 30%

Depositions That Exceed Paid-for Time: *Get payment before proceeding:* 23% *Proceed without immediate payment:* 77%

Out-of-Pocket Expenses Marked Up: 14% **Markup Amount:** *High:* 22% *Low:* 6% *Average:* 14% *Median:* 15%
Out-of-Pockets Billed for: *Mileage:* 60% *Airline Tickets:* 75% *Photocopies:* 35% *Telephone Calls:* 36% *Lab/Testing:* 25% *Photos:* 24% *Demonstrative Aids:* 28% **Travel Billed Portal-to-Portal**: 82% **First-class Airfare Required:** 13%

Require Signed Written Fee Agreement: 31% **Terms Contained in Fee Agreement:** *Lawyer is responsible for fee, not lawyer's client:* 73% *Interest for delinquent accounts:* 41% *Out-of-pocket expense policies:* 61% *Retainer/prepayment requirements:* 81% *In-court testimony minimum fees:* 75% *Retaining counsel will pay for all deposition charges:* 47% *Fee schedules:* 83% *Attorney's fees if forced to sue for collection:* 38% *Portal-to-portal travel time:* 64% *Deposition minimum fees:* 66% *Payment for preparation time:* 65% *First-class air travel:* 15%

Majority of Work: *Plaintiffs:* 22% *Neither:* 52% *Defendants:* 26%
Retaining Counsel Failed to Pay in Last 5 Years: 40% **Opposing Counsel Failed to Pay in Last 5 Years:** 21%

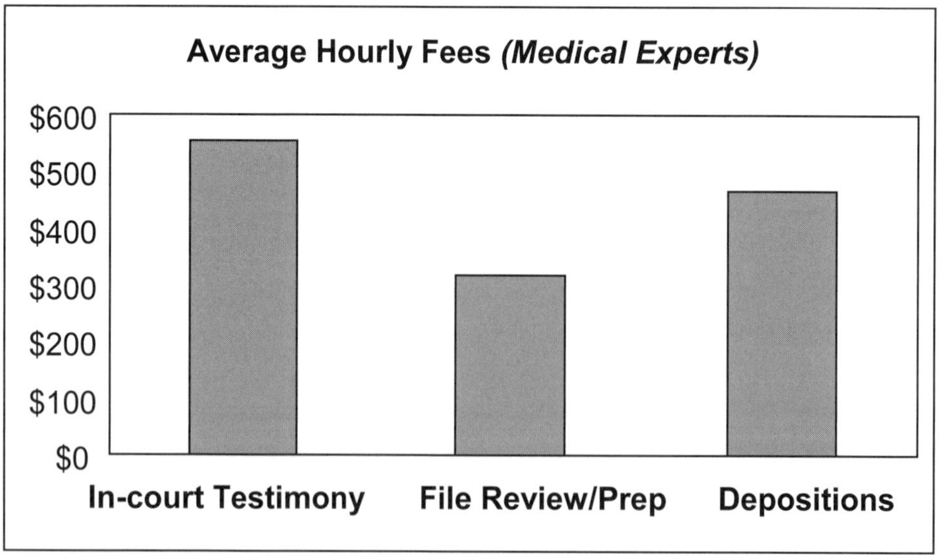

All Non-Medical Experts

Responding Experts: 563
Years Testifying: *High:* 50 *Low:* 1 *Average:* 16.7 *Median:* 15

In-court Testimony (hourly):	*High:* $2000	*Low:* $75	*Average:* $248	*Median:* $230
File Review/Prep (hourly):	*High:* $675	*Low:* $25	*Average:* $201	*Median:* $185
Depositions (hourly):	*High:* $1000	*Low:* $0	*Average:* $241	*Median:* $225

Min. Charge for Depositions: 46% **Hours in Minimum:** *High:* 12 *Low:* 1 *Average:* 3.9 *Median:* 4

Min. Charge for Trial: 45% **Hours in Minimum:** *High:* 12 *Low:* 1 *Average:* 4.5 *Median:* 4

Cancellation Fee for Depositions or Trial: 25% **Deposition Payment in Advance:** 39%

Up-front Retainer: 79% **Retainer Amount:** *High:* $15,000 *Low:* $150 *Average:* $2,330 *Median:* $1,938

Type of Retainer: *Refundable:* 57% *Partially Refundable:* 2% *Non-Refundable:* 41%
One Time: 67% *Replenishable:* 33%

Depositions That Exceed Paid-for Time: *Get payment before proceeding:* 23% *Proceed without immediate payment:* 77%

Out-of-Pocket Expenses Marked Up: 23% **Markup Amount:** *High:* 40% *Low:* 3% *Average:* 14% *Median:* 15%
Out-of-Pockets Billed for: *Mileage:* 76% *Airline Tickets:* 90% *Photocopies:* 51% *Telephone Calls:* 40% *Lab/Testing:* 55% *Photos:* 62% *Demonstrative Aids:* 64% **Travel Billed Portal-to-Portal:** 89% **1st-class Airfare Required:** 8%

Require Signed Written Fee Agreement: 58% **Terms Contained in Fee Agreement:** *Lawyer is responsible for fee, not lawyer's client:* 64% *Interest for delinquent accounts:* 62% *Out-of-pocket expense policies:* 86% *Retainer/prepayment requirements:* 85% *In-court testimony minimum fees:* 53% *Retaining counsel will pay for all deposition charges:* 34% *Fee schedules:* 82% *Attorney's fees if forced to sue for collection:* 51% *Portal-to-portal travel time:* 62% *Deposition minimum fees:* 46% *Payment for preparation time:* 65% *First-class air travel:* 7%

Majority of Work: *Plaintiffs:* 24% *Neither:* 61% *Defendants:* 15%
Retaining Counsel Failed to Pay in Last 5 Years: 50% **Opposing Counsel Failed to Pay in Last 5 Years:** 19%

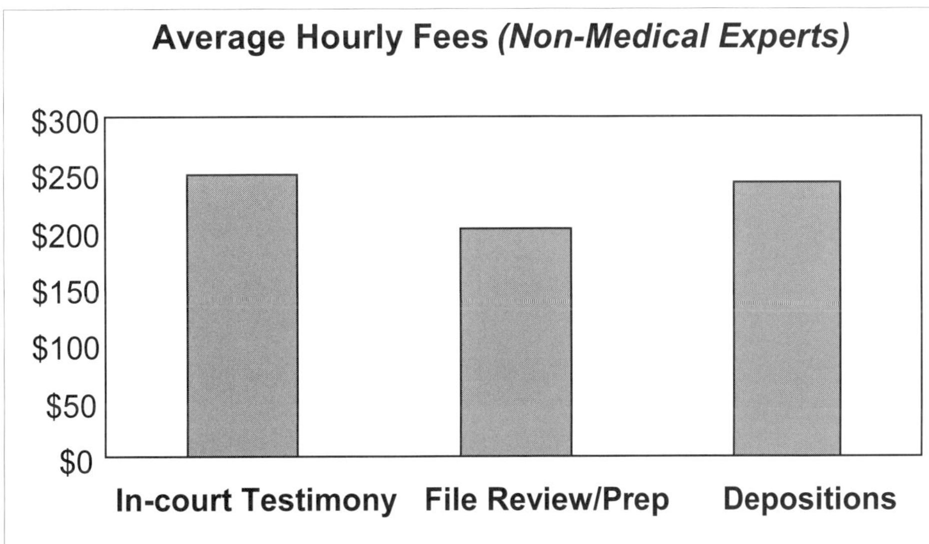

Fees by Number of Years Testifying

Experts Who Have Testified 1–5 Years

Responding Experts: 170 **Percentage of all Responding Experts:** 17%

In-court Testimony (hourly)	*Average:* $398	*Median:* $350
File Review/Prep (hourly)	*Average:* $264	*Median:* $250
Depositions (hourly)	*Average:* $358	*Median:* $300

Experts Who Have Testified 6–15 Years

Responding Experts: 409 **Percentage of all Responding Experts:** 41%

In-court Testimony (hourly)	*Average:* $388	*Median:* $295
File Review/Prep (hourly)	*Average:* $250	*Median:* $220
Depositions (hourly)	*Average:* $330	*Median:* $278

Experts Who Have Testified 16–25 Years

Responding Experts: 274 **Percentage of all Responding Experts:** 28%

In-court Testimony (hourly)	*Average:* $375	*Median:* $300
File Review/Prep (hourly)	*Average:* $251	*Median:* $250
Depositions (hourly)	*Average:* $348	*Median:* $300

Experts Who Have Testified 26+ Years

Responding Experts: 86 **Percentage of all Responding Experts:** 14%

In-court Testimony (hourly)	*Average:* $348	*Median:* $275
File Review/Prep (hourly)	*Average:* $247	*Median:* $210
Depositions (hourly)	*Average:* $329	*Median:* $275

All Experts

Responding Experts: 1,030

In-court Testimony (hourly)	*Average:* $385	*Median:* $300
File Review/Prep (hourly)	*Average:* $254	*Median:* $240
Depositions (hourly)	*Average:* $353	*Median:* $300

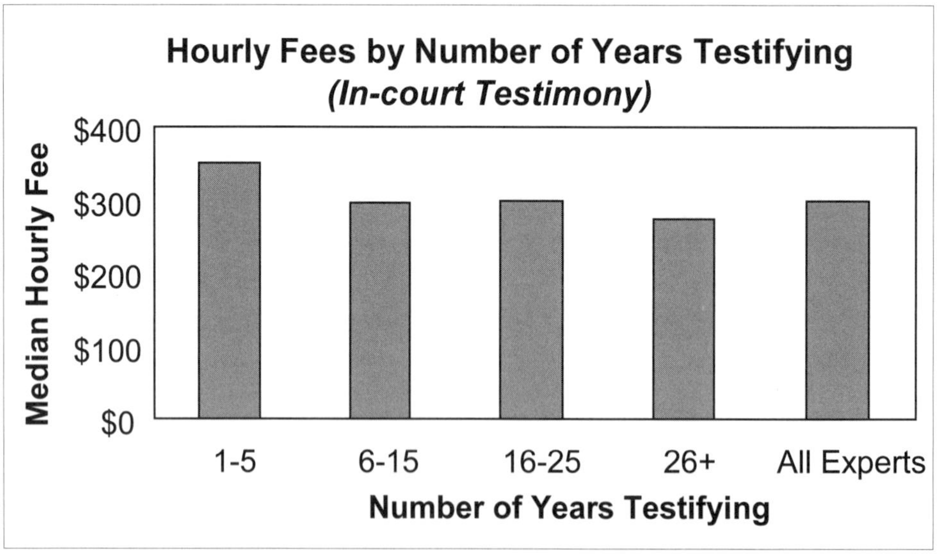

Fees by Majority of Work

Experts Who Testify Mostly for Plaintiffs

Responding Experts: 233 **Percentage of all Responding Experts:** 23%

In-court Testimony (hourly)	*Average:* $405	*Median:* $300
File Review/Prep (hourly)	*Average:* $244	*Median:* $200
Depositions (hourly)	*Average:* $342	*Median:* $300

Retaining Counsel Failed to Pay in Last 5 Years: 50% **Opposing Counsel Failed to Pay in Last 5 Years:** 19%

Experts Who Testify Mostly for Defendants

Responding Experts: 204 **Percentage of all Responding Experts:** 20%

In-court Testimony (hourly)	*Average:* $415	*Median:* $300
File Review/Prep (hourly)	*Average:* $272	*Median:* $250
Depositions (hourly)	*Average:* $370	*Median:* $300

Retaining Counsel Failed to Pay in Last 5 Years: 43% **Opposing Counsel Failed to Pay in Last 5 Years:** 19%

Experts Who Testify Equally for Defendants and Plaintiffs

Responding Experts: 575 **Percentage of all Responding Experts:** 57%

In-court Testimony (hourly)	*Average:* $364	*Median:* $300
File Review/Prep (hourly)	*Average:* $252	*Median:* $225
Depositions (hourly)	*Average:* $331	*Median:* $295

Retaining Counsel Failed to Pay in Last 5 Years: 45% **Opposing Counsel Failed to Pay in Last 5 Years:** 20%

All Experts

Responding Experts: 1,030

In-court Testimony (hourly)	*Average:* $385	*Median:* $300
File Review/Prep (hourly)	*Average:* $254	*Median:* $240
Depositions (hourly)	*Average:* $353	*Median:* $300

Retaining Counsel Failed to Pay in Last 5 Years: 46% **Opposing Counsel Failed to Pay in Last 5 Years:** 20%

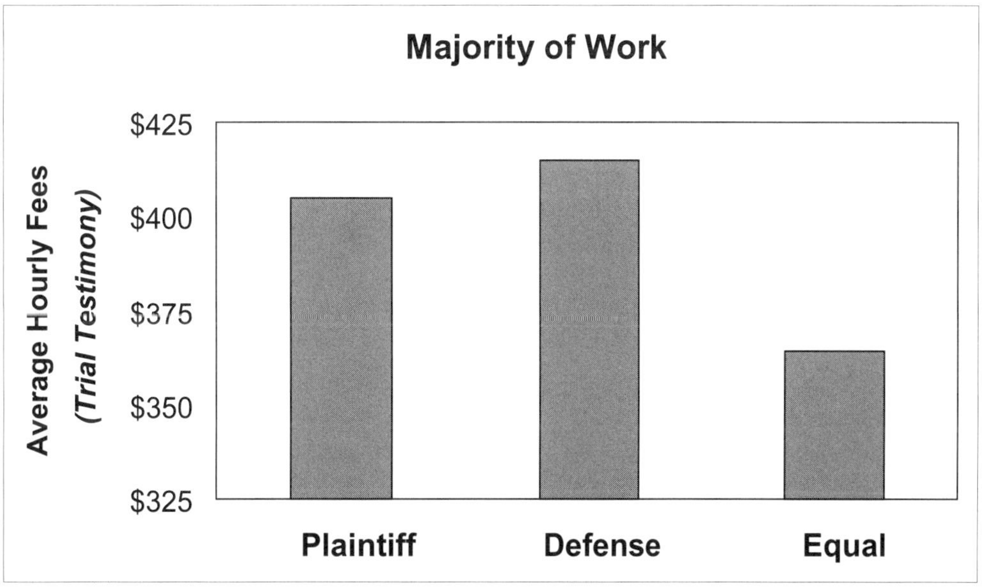

Chapter 3 State-by-State Summary of Expert Fees and Billing Procedures

Alabama

Responding Experts: 8

Per-hour Fees

	High	*Low*	*Average*	*Median*
In-court Testimony	$500	$115	$258	$250
File Review/Prep	$300	$115	$168	$150
Depositions	$500	$115	$249	$250

Depositions

Min. Charge for Deps: 50% **Hours in Minimum:** *High:* 4 *Low:* 1 *Average:* 2 *Median:* 1.5
Cancellation Fee for Deps or Trial: 38% **Deposition Payment in Advance:** 13%
Exceeding Paid-for Time: *Get payment before proceeding:* 0% *Proceed without immediate payment:* 100%

Retainers

Required: 50% **Amounts:** *High:* $1,200 *Low:* $1,000 *Average:* $1,100 *Median:* $1,100

Expenses

Out-of-Pocket Expenses Marked Up: 25% **Out-of-Pockets Billed for:** *Mileage:* 63% *Airline Tickets:* 63% *Photocopies:* 75% *Telephone Calls:* 75% *Lab/Testing:* 50% *Photos:* 75% *Demonstrative Aids:* 50%
Travel Billed Portal-to-Portal: 88% **1st-class Airfare Required:** 13%

Fee Agreement

Require Signed Written Fee Agreement: 38% **Terms:** *Lawyer is responsible for fee, not lawyer's client:* 100% *Interest for delinquent accounts:* 67% *Out-of-pocket expense policies:* 100% *Retainer/prepayment requirements:* 100% *In-court testimony minimum fees:* 100% *Retaining counsel will pay for all deposition charges:* 33% *Fee schedules:* 100% *Attorney's fees if forced to sue for collection:* 67% *Portal-to-portal travel time:* 100% *Deposition minimum fees:* 66% *Payment for preparation time:* 33% *First-class air travel:* 0%

Majority of Work: *Plaintiffs:* 43% *Neither:* 43% *Defendants:* 14%
Counsel Failed to Pay in Last 5 Years: *Retaining:* 63% *Opposing:* 29%

Alaska

Responding Experts: 2

Per-hour Fees

	High	*Low*	*Average*	*Median*
In-court Testimony	$350	$295	$323	$323
File Review/Prep	$350	$295	$323	$323
Depositions	$350	$295	$323	$323

Depositions

Min. Charge for Deps: 0% **Hours in Minimum:** *High:* N/A *Low:* N/A *Average:* N/A *Median:* N/A
Cancellation Fee for Deps or Trial: 0% **Deposition Payment in Advance:** 0%
Exceeding Paid-for Time: *Get payment before proceeding:* 0% *Proceed without immediate payment:* 100%

Retainers

Required: 100% **Amounts:** *High:* $5,000 *Low:* $2,500 *Average:* $3,750 *Median:* $3,750

Expenses

Out-of-Pocket Expenses Marked Up: 0% **Out-of-Pockets Billed for:** *Mileage:* 0% *Airline Tickets:* 100% *Photocopies:* 0% *Telephone Calls:* 0% *Lab/Testing:* 0% *Photos:* 0% *Demonstrative Aids:* 50%
Travel Billed Portal-to-Portal: 100% **1st-class Airfare Required:** 50%

Fee Agreement

Require Signed Written Fee Agreement: 50% **Terms:** *Lawyer is responsible for fee, not lawyer's client:* 0% *Interest for delinquent accounts:* 100% *Out-of-pocket expense policies:* 100% *Retainer/prepayment requirements:* 100% *In-court testimony minimum fees:* 0% *Retaining counsel will pay for all deposition charges:* 0% *Fee schedules:* 100% *Attorney's fees if forced to sue for collection:* 100% *Portal-to-portal travel time:* 100% *Deposition minimum fees:* 0% *Payment for preparation time:* 100% *First-class air travel:* 0%

Majority of Work: *Plaintiffs:* 0% *Neither:* 100% *Defendants:* 0%
Counsel Failed to Pay in Last 5 Years: *Retaining:* 50% *Opposing:* 0%

Arizona

Responding Experts: 10

Per-hour Fees

	High	*Low*	*Average*	*Median*
In-court Testimony	$2,000	$125	$476	$288
File Review/Prep	$400	$100	$220	$230
Depositions	$1,000	$125	$378	$288

Depositions

Min. Charge for Deps: 60% **Hours in Minimum:** *High:* 4 *Low:* 1 *Average:* 3.1 *Median:* 4
Cancellation Fee for Deps or Trial: 50% **Deposition Payment in Advance:** 60%
Exceeding Paid-for Time: *Get payment before proceeding:* 17% *Proceed without immediate payment:* 83%

Retainers

Required: 80% **Amounts:** *High:* $3,000 *Low:* $500 *Average:* $1,875 *Median:* $1,875

Expenses

Out-of-Pocket Expenses Marked Up: 40% **Out-of-Pockets Billed for:** *Mileage:* 80% *Airline Tickets:* 100% *Photocopies:* 50% *Telephone Calls:* 40% *Lab/Testing:* 60% *Photos:* 60% *Demonstrative Aids:* 70%
Travel Billed Portal-to-Portal: 100% **1st-class Airfare Required:** 0%

Fee Agreement

Require Signed Written Fee Agreement: 70% **Terms:** *Lawyer is responsible for fee, not lawyer's client:* 100% *Interest for delinquent accounts:* 71% *Out-of-pocket expense policies:* 86% *Retainer/prepayment requirements:* 86% *In-court testimony minimum fees:* 71% *Retaining counsel will pay for all deposition charges:* 43% *Fee schedules:* 71% *Attorney's fees if forced to sue for collection:* 43% *Portal-to-portal travel time:* 43% *Deposition minimum fees:* 71% *Payment for preparation time:* 71% *First-class air travel:* 0%

Majority of Work: *Plaintiffs:* 10% *Neither:* 80% *Defendants:* 10%

Counsel Failed to Pay in Last 5 Years: *Retaining:* 40% *Opposing:* 40%

Arkansas

Responding Experts: 7

Per-hour Fees

	High	*Low*	*Average*	*Median*
In-court Testimony	$500	$75	$235	$200
File Review/Prep	$300	$75	$166	$175
Depositions	$300	$75	$221	$200

Depositions

Min. Charge for Deps: 57% **Hours in Minimum:** *High:* 4 *Low:* 1 *Average:* 3.25 *Median:* 4
Cancellation Fee for Deps or Trial: 29% **Deposition Payment in Advance:** 29%
Exceeding Paid-for Time: *Get payment before proceeding:* 0% *Proceed without immediate payment:* 100%

Retainers

Required: 57% **Amounts:** *High:* $2,500 *Low:* $800 *Average:* $1,450 *Median:* $1,250

Expenses

Out-of-Pocket Expenses Marked Up: 29% **Out-of-Pockets Billed For:** *Mileage:* 86% *Airline Tickets:* 100% *Photocopies:* 43% *Telephone Calls:* 14% *Lab/Testing:* 57% *Photos:* 57% *Demonstrative Aids:* 29%
Travel Billed Portal-to-Portal: 71% **1st-class Airfare Required:** 0%

Fee Agreements

Require Signed Written Fee Agreement: 57% **Terms:** *Lawyer is responsible for fee, not lawyer's client:* 50% *Interest for delinquent accounts:* 25% *Out-of-pocket expense policies:* 75% *Retainer/prepayment requirements:* 25% *In-court testimony minimum fees:* 75% *Retaining counsel will pay for all deposition charges:* 25% *Fee schedules:* 100% *Attorney's fees if forced to sue for collection:* 50% *Portal-to-portal travel time:* 25% *Deposition minimum fees:* 50% *Payment for preparation time:* 75% *First-class air travel:* 0%

Majority of Work: *Plaintiffs:* 57% *Neither:* 28% *Defendants:* 14%

Counsel Failed to Pay in Last 5 Years: *Retaining:* 29% *Opposing:* 14%

California

Responding Experts: 159

Per-hour Fees

	High	*Low*	*Average*	*Median*
In-court Testimony	$2,000	$125	$365	$300
File Review/Prep	$975	$150	$285	$250
Depositions	$975	$100	$345	$300

Depositions

Min. Charge for Deps: 55% **Hours in Minimum:** *High:* 4 *Low:* 1 *Average:* 2.6 *Median:* 2
Cancellation Fee for Deps or Trial: 37% **Deposition Payment in Advance:** 50%
Exceeding Paid-for Time: *Get payment before proceeding:* 26% *Proceed without immediate payment:* 74%

Retainers

Required: 85% **Amounts:** *High:* $15,000 *Low:* $150 *Average:* $2,134 *Median:* $1,500

Expenses

Out-of-Pocket Expenses Marked Up: 25% **Out-of-Pockets Billed for:** *Mileage:* 66% *Airline Tickets:* 84% *Photocopies:* 38% *Telephone Calls:* 33% *Lab/Testing:* 47% *Photos:* 48% *Demonstrative Aids:* 50%
Travel Billed Portal-to-Portal: 91% **1st-class Airfare Required:** 14%

Fee Agreement

Require Signed Written Fee Agreement: 56% **Terms:** *Lawyer is responsible for fee, not lawyer's client:* 63% *Interest for delinquent accounts:* 65% *Out-of-pocket expense policies:* 76% *Retainer/prepayment requirements:* 86% *In-court testimony minimum fees:* 58% *Retaining counsel will pay for all deposition charges:* 23% *Fee schedules:* 73% *Attorney's fees if forced to sue for collection:* 60% *Portal-to-portal travel time:* 64% *Deposition minimum fees:* 48% *Payment for preparation time:* 61% *First-class air travel:* 14%

Majority of Work: *Plaintiffs:* 21% *Neither:* 60% *Defendants:* 19%

Counsel Failed to Pay in Last 5 Years: *Retaining:* 58% *Opposing:* 14%

Colorado

Responding Experts: 22

Per-hour Fees

	High	*Low*	*Average*	*Median*
In-court Testimony	$500	$125	$264	$250
File Review/Prep	$415	$100	$234	$223
Depositions	$425	$150	$260	$250

Depositions

Min. Charge for Deps: 32% **Hours in Minimum:** *High:* 4 *Low:* 1 *Average:* 3 *Median:* 4
Cancellation Fee for Deps or Trial: 23% **Deposition Payment in Advance:** 23%
Exceeding Paid-for Time: *Get payment before proceeding:* 25% *Proceed without immediate payment:* 75%

Retainers

Required: 65% **Amounts:** *High:* $5,000 *Low:* $160 *Average:* $1,751 *Median:* $1,500

Expenses

Out-of-Pocket Expenses Marked Up: 18% **Out-of-Pockets Billed for:** *Mileage:* 64% *Airline Tickets:* 88% *Photocopies:* 36% *Telephone Calls:* 27% *Lab/Testing:* 59% *Photos:* 59% *Demonstrative Aids:* 59%
Travel Billed Portal-to-Portal: 81% **1st-class Airfare Required:** 5%

Fee Agreement

Require Signed Written Fee Agreement: 55% **Terms:** *Lawyer is responsible for fee, not lawyer's client:* 50% *Interest for delinquent accounts:* 67% *Out-of-pocket expense policies:* 83% *Retainer/prepayment requirements:* 50% *In-court testimony minimum fees:* 17% *Retaining counsel will pay for all deposition charges:* 33% *Fee schedules:* 92% *Attorney's fees if forced to sue for collection:* 33% *Portal-to-portal travel time:* 50% *Deposition minimum fees:* 8% *Payment for preparation time:* 66% *First-class air travel:* 8%

Majority of Work: *Plaintiffs:* 27% *Neither:* 50% *Defendants:* 23%

Counsel Failed to Pay in Last 5 Years: *Retaining:* 36% *Opposing:* 23%

Connecticut

Responding Experts: 28

Per-hour Fees

	High	*Low*	*Average*	*Median*
In-court Testimony	$1,000	$113	$355	$300
File Review/Prep	$465	$100	$251	$250
Depositions	$800	$113	$335	$300

Depositions

Min. Charge for Deps: 54% **Hours in Minimum:** *High:* 8 *Low:* 1 *Average:* 3.8 *Median:* 4
Cancellation Fee for Deps or Trial: 30% **Deposition Payment in Advance:** 43%
Exceeding Paid-for Time: *Get payment before proceeding:* 25% *Proceed without immediate payment:* 75%

Retainers

Required: 64% **Amounts:** *High:* $4,000 *Low:* $500 *Average:* $1,629 *Median:* $1,200

Expenses

Out-of-Pocket Expenses Marked Up: 29% **Out-of-Pockets Billed for:** *Mileage:* 50% *Airline Tickets:* 68% *Photocopies:* 32% *Telephone Calls:* 18% *Lab/Testing:* 39% *Photos:* 29% *Demonstrative Aids:* 36%
Travel Billed Portal-to-Portal: 86% **1st-class Airfare Required:** 7%

Fee Agreement

Require Signed Written Fee Agreement: 61% **Terms:** *Lawyer is responsible for fee, not lawyer's client:* 59% *Interest for delinquent accounts:* 35% *Out-of-pocket expense policies:* 59% *Retainer/prepayment requirements:* 43% *In-court testimony minimum fees:* 59% *Retaining counsel will pay for all deposition charges:* 24% *Fee schedules:* 88% *Attorney's fees if forced to sue for collection:* 35% *Portal-to-portal travel time:* 65% *Deposition minimum fees:* 59% *Payment for preparation time:* 59% *First-class air travel:* 6%

Majority of Work: *Plaintiffs:* 30% *Neither:* 44% *Defendants:* 26%
Counsel Failed to Pay in Last 5 Years: *Retaining:* 50% *Opposing* 15%

Delaware

Responding Experts: 2

Per-hour Fees

	High	*Low*	*Average*	*Median*
In-court Testimony	$660	$275	$468	$468
File Review/Prep	$395	$225	$310	$310
Depositions	$1,000	$275	$638	$638

Depositions

Min. Charge for Deps: 100% **Hours in Minimum:** *High:* 4 *Low:* 1 *Average:* 2.5 *Median:* 2.5
Cancellation Fee for Deps or Trial: 100% **Deposition Payment in Advance:** 100%
Exceeding Paid-for Time: *Get payment before proceeding:* 50% *Proceed without immediate payment:* 50%

Retainers

Required: 100% **Amounts:** *High:* $1,000 *Low:* $800 *Average:* $900 *Median:* $900

Expenses

Out-of-Pocket Expenses Marked Up: 0% **Out-of-Pockets Billed for:** *Mileage:* 100% *Airline Tickets:* 100% *Photocopies:* 0% *Telephone Calls:* 0% *Lab/Testing:* 50% *Photos:* 50% *Demonstrative Aids:* 50%
Travel Billed Portal-to-Portal: 100% **1st-class Airfare Required:** 50%

Fee Agreement

Require Signed Written Fee Agreement: 50% **Terms:** *Lawyer is responsible for fee, not lawyer's client:* 100% *Interest for delinquent accounts:* 100% *Out-of-pocket expense policies:* 100% *Retainer/prepayment requirements:* 100% *In-court testimony minimum fees:* 100% *Retaining counsel will pay for all deposition charges:* 0% *Fee schedules:* 100% *Attorney's fees if forced to sue for collection:* 0% *Portal-to-portal travel time:* 0% *Deposition minimum fees:* 100% *Payment for preparation time:* 100% *First-class air travel:* 0%

Majority of Work: *Plaintiffs:* 0% *Neither:* 100% *Defendants:* 0%
Counsel Failed to Pay in Last 5 Years: *Retaining:* 50% *Opposing:* 50%

District of Columbia

Responding Experts: 3

Per-hour Fees

	High	*Low*	*Average*	*Median*
In-court Testimony	$450	$350	$400	$400
File Review/Prep	$450	$350	$383	$350
Depositions	$450	$350	$400	$400

Depositions

Min. Charge for Deps: 33% **Hours in Minimum:** *High:* 2 *Low:* 2 *Average:* 2 *Median:* 2
Cancellation Fee for Deps or Trial: 100% **Deposition Payment in Advance:** 67%
Exceeding Paid-for Time: *Get payment before proceeding:* 100% *Proceed without immediate payment:* 0%

Retainers

Required: 67% **Amounts:** *High:* $1,500 *Low:* $1,500 *Average:* $1,500 *Median:* $1,500

Expenses

Out-of-Pocket Expenses Marked Up: 0% **Out-of-Pockets Billed for:** *Mileage:* 67% *Airline Tickets:* 100% *Photocopies:* 0% *Telephone Calls:* 33% *Lab/Testing:* 33% *Photos:* 33% *Demonstrative Aids:* 0%
Travel Billed Portal-to-Portal: 67% **1st-class Airfare Required:** 33%

Fee Agreement

Require Signed Written Fee Agreement: 33% **Terms:** *Lawyer is responsible for fee, not lawyer's client:* 100% *Interest for delinquent accounts:* 100% *Out-of-pocket expense policies:* 100% *Retainer/prepayment requirements:* 100% *In-court testimony minimum fees:* 0% *Retaining counsel will pay for all deposition charges:* 0% *Fee schedules:* 100% *Attorney's fees if forced to sue for collection:* 0% *Portal-to-portal travel time:* 100% *Deposition minimum fees:* 0% *Payment for preparation time:* 0% *First-class air travel:* 100%

Majority of Work: *Plaintiffs:* 0% *Neither:* 33% *Defendants:* 67%
Counsel Failed to Pay in Last 5 Years: *Retaining:* 33% *Opposing:* 67%

Florida

Responding Experts: 92

Per-hour Fees

	High	*Low*	*Average*	*Median*
In-court Testimony	$1,500	$125	$493	$375
File Review/Prep	$650	$75	$273	$233
Depositions	$1,400	$115	$398	$315

Depositions

Min. Charge for Deps: 70% **Hours in Minimum:** *High:* 8 *Low:* 1 *Average:* 2.1 *Median:* 2
Cancellation Fee for Deps or Trial: 53% **Deposition Payment in Advance:** 71%
Exceeding Paid-for Time: *Get payment before proceeding:* 17% *Proceed without immediate payment:* 83%

Retainers

Required: 86% **Amounts:** *High:* $7,500 *Low:* $250 *Average:* $1,627 *Median:* $1,200

Expenses

Out-of-Pocket Expenses Marked Up: 20% **Out-of-Pockets Billed for:** *Mileage:* 64% *Airline Tickets:* 91% *Photocopies:* 53% *Telephone Calls:* 45% *Lab/Testing:* 36% *Photos:* 48% *Demonstrative Aids:* 51%
Travel Billed Portal-to-Portal: 90% **1st-class Airfare Required:** 12%

Fee Agreement

Require Signed Written Fee Agreement: 51% **Terms:** *Lawyer is responsible for fee, not lawyer's client:* 68% *Interest for delinquent accounts:* 57% *Out-of-pocket expense policies:* 75% *Retainer/prepayment requirements:* 89% *In-court testimony minimum fees:* 57% *Retaining counsel will pay for all deposition charges:* 45% *Fee schedules:* 79% *Attorney's fees if forced to sue for collection:* 51% *Portal-to-portal travel time:* 68% *Deposition minimum fees:* 47% *Payment for preparation time:* 64% *First-class air travel:* 6%

Majority of Work: *Plaintiffs:* 25% *Neither:* 57% *Defendants:* 18%
Counsel Failed to Pay in Last 5 Years: *Retaining:* 39% *Opposing:* 28%

Georgia

Responding Experts: 24

Per-hour Fees

	High	*Low*	*Average*	*Median*
In-court Testimony	$850	$100	$311	$300
File Review/Prep	$500	$100	$235	$200
Depositions	$800	$100	$330	$300

Depositions

Min. Charge for Deps: 63% **Hours in Minimum:** *High:* 8 *Low:* 1 *Average:* 2.8 *Median:* 2
Cancellation Fee for Deps or Trial: 38% **Deposition Payment in Advance:** 48%
Exceeding Paid-for Time: *Get payment before proceeding:* 50% *Proceed without immediate payment:* 50%

Retainers

Required: 75% **Amounts:** *High:* $8,000 *Low:* $400 *Average:* $2,161 *Median:* $1,300

Expenses

Out-of-Pocket Expenses Marked Up: 17% **Out-of-Pockets Billed for:** *Mileage:* 71% *Airline Tickets:* 75% *Photocopies:* 63% *Telephone Calls:* 38% *Lab/Testing:* 33% *Photos:* 50% *Demonstrative Aids:* 50%
Travel Billed Portal-to-Portal: 91% **1st-class Airfare Required:** 23%

Fee Agreement

Require Signed Written Fee Agreement: 54% **Terms:** *Lawyer is responsible for fee, not lawyer's client:* 69% *Interest for delinquent accounts:* 62% *Out-of-pocket expense policies:* 77% *Retainer/prepayment requirements:* 85% *In-court testimony minimum fees:* 62% *Retaining counsel will pay for all deposition charges:* 54% *Fee schedules:* 62% *Attorney's fees if forced to sue for collection:* 54% *Portal-to-portal travel time:* 62% *Deposition minimum fees:* 46% *Payment for preparation time:* 54% *First-class air travel:* 15%

Majority of Work: *Plaintiffs:* 21% *Neither:* 58% *Defendants:* 21%
Counsel Failed to Pay in Last 5 Years: *Retaining:* 33% *Opposing:* 22%

Hawaii

Responding Experts: 4

Per-hour Fees

	High	*Low*	*Average*	*Median*
In-court Testimony	$400	$240	$240	$218
File Review/Prep	$250	$90	$175	$180
Depositions	$400	$100	$234	$218

Depositions

Min. Charge for Deps: 25% **Hours in Minimum:** *High:* 4 *Low:* 4 *Average:* 4 *Median:* 4
Cancellation Fee for Deps or Trial: 0% **Deposition Payment in Advance:** 0%
Exceeding Paid-for Time: *Get payment before proceeding:* N/A *Proceed without immediate payment:* N/A

Retainers

Required: 100% **Amounts:** *High:* $4,000 *Low:* $180 *Average:* $1,727 *Median:* $1,000

Expenses

Out-of-Pocket Expenses Marked Up: 25% **Out-of-Pockets Billed for:** *Mileage:* 25% *Airline Tickets:* 75% *Photocopies:* 75% *Telephone Calls:* 50% *Lab/Testing:* 50% *Photos:* 50% *Demonstrative Aids:* 50%
Travel Billed Portal-to-Portal: 100% **1st-class Airfare Required:** 25%

Fee Agreements

Require Signed Written Fee Agreement: 25% **Terms:** *Lawyer is responsible for fee, not lawyer's client:* 0% *Interest for delinquent accounts:* 0% *Out-of-pocket expense policies:* 100% *Retainer/prepayment requirements:* 100% *In-court testimony minimum fees:* 0% *Retaining counsel will pay for all deposition charges:* 0% *Fee schedules:* 100% *Attorney's fees if forced to sue for collection:* 0% *Portal-to-portal travel time:* 0% *Deposition minimum fees:* 0% *Payment for preparation time:* 100% *First-class air travel:* 0%

Majority of Work: *Plaintiffs:* 0% *Neither:* 100% *Defendants:* 0%
Counsel Failed to Pay in Last 5 Years: *Retaining:* 50% *Opposing:* 0%

Idaho

Responding Experts: 1

Per-hour Fees

	High	*Low*	*Average*	*Median*
In-court Testimony	$135	$135	$135	$135
File Review/Prep	$150	$150	$150	$150
Depositions	$135	$135	$135	$135

Depositions

Min. Charge for Deps: 100% **Hours in Minimum:** *High:* 1 *Low:* 1 *Average:* 1 *Median:* 1
Cancellation Fee for Deps or Trial: 0% **Deposition Payment in Advance:** 0%
Exceeding Paid-for Time: *Get payment before proceeding:* N/A *Proceed without immediate payment:* N/A

Retainers

Required: 100% **Amounts:** *High:* $500 *Low:* $500 *Average:* $500 *Median:* $500

Expenses

Out-of-Pocket Expenses Marked Up: 0% **Out-of-Pockets Billed for:** *Mileage:* 100% *Airline Tickets:* 0% *Photocopies:* 100% *Telephone Calls:* 100% *Lab/Testing:* 0% *Photos:* 100% *Demonstrative Aids:* 0%
Travel Billed Portal-to-Portal: 100% **1st-class Airfare Required:** 0%

Fee Agreement

Require Signed Written Fee Agreement: 0% **Terms:** *Lawyer is responsible for fee, not lawyer's client:* N/A *Interest for delinquent accounts:* N/A *Out-of-pocket expense policies:* N/A *Retainer/prepayment requirements:* N/A *In-court testimony minimum fees:* N/A *Retaining counsel will pay for all deposition charges:* N/A *Fee schedules:* N/A *Attorney's fees if forced to sue for collection:* N/A *Portal-to-portal travel time:* N/A *Deposition minimum fees:* N/A *Payment for preparation time:* N/A *First-class air travel:* N/A

Majority of Work: *Plaintiffs:* 0% *Neither:* 0% *Defendants:* 100%
Counsel Failed to Pay in Last 5 Years: *Retaining:* 100% *Opposing:* 0%

Illinois

Responding Experts: 45

Per-hour Fees

	High	*Low*	*Average*	*Median*
In-court Testimony	$2,750	$100	$384	$300
File Review/Prep	$500	$75	$269	$275
Depositions	$1,000	$100	$338	$300

Depositions

Min. Charge for Deps: 66% **Hours in Minimum:** *High:* 6 *Low:* 1 *Average:* 3 *Median:* 3
Cancellation Fee for Deps or Trial: 48% **Deposition Payment in Advance:** 56%
Exceeding Paid-for Time: *Get payment before proceeding:* 24% *Proceed without immediate payment:* 76%

Retainers

Required: 68% **Amounts:** *High:* $7,500 *Low:* $300 *Average:* $1,953 *Median:* $1,450

Expenses

Out-of-Pocket Expenses Marked Up: 30% **Out-of-Pockets Billed for:** *Mileage:* 80% *Airline Tickets:* 89% *Photocopies:* 44% *Telephone Calls:* 47% *Lab/Testing:* 38% *Photos:* 47% *Demonstrative Aids:* 51%
Travel Billed Portal-to-Portal: 89% **1st-class Airfare Required:** 7%

Fee Agreement

Require Signed Written Fee Agreement: 40% **Terms:** *Lawyer is responsible for fee, not lawyer's client:* 67% *Interest for delinquent accounts:* 39% *Out-of-pocket expense policies:* 83% *Retainer/prepayment requirements:* 83% *In-court testimony minimum fees:* 56% *Retaining counsel will pay for all deposition charges:* 50% *Fee schedules:* 89% *Attorney's fees if forced to sue for collection:* 50% *Portal-to-portal travel time:* 78% *Deposition minimum fees:* 56% *Payment for preparation time:* 44% *First-class air travel:* 17%

Majority of Work: *Plaintiffs:* 20% *Neither:* 64% *Defendants:* 16%
Counsel Failed to Pay in Last 5 Years: *Retaining:* 47% *Opposing:* 27%

Indiana

Responding Experts: 17

Per-hour Fees

	High	*Low*	*Average*	*Median*
In-court Testimony	$1,700	$100	$506	$500
File Review/Prep	$900	$100	$333	$250
Depositions	$1,200	$100	$432	$500

Depositions

Min. Charge for Deps: 88% **Hours in Minimum:** *High:* 8 *Low:* 1 *Average:* 2.7 *Median:* 2
Cancellation Fee for Deps or Trial: 63% **Deposition Payment in Advance:** 63%
Exceeding Paid-for Time: *Get payment before proceeding:* 11% *Proceed without immediate payment:* 89%

Retainers

Required: 71% **Amounts:** *High:* $1,500 *Low:* $350 *Average:* $822 *Median:* $850

Expenses

Out-of-Pocket Expenses Marked Up: 19% **Out-of-Pockets Billed for:** *Mileage:* 88% *Airline Tickets:* 88% *Photocopies:* 59% *Telephone Calls:* 41% *Lab/Testing:* 18% *Photos:* 29% *Demonstrative Aids:* 35%
Travel Billed Portal-to-Portal: 82% **1st-class Airfare Required:** 29%

Fee Agreement

Require Signed Written Fee Agreement: 29% **Terms:** *Lawyer is responsible for fee, not lawyer's client:* 80% *Interest for delinquent accounts:* 40% *Out-of-pocket expense policies:* 60% *Retainer/prepayment requirements:* 80% *In-court testimony minimum fees:* 100% *Retaining counsel will pay for all deposition charges:* 80% *Fee schedules:* 80% *Attorney's fees if forced to sue for collection:* 40% *Portal-to-portal travel time:* 40% *Deposition minimum fees:* 80% *Payment for preparation time:* 60% *First-class air travel:* 0%

Majority of Work: *Plaintiffs:* 41% *Neither:* 53% *Defendants:* 6%

Counsel Failed to Pay in Last 5 Years: *Retaining:* 47% *Opposing:* 29%

Iowa

Responding Experts: 6

Per-hour Fees

	High	*Low*	*Average*	*Median*
In-court Testimony	$2,000	$95	$739	$470
File Review/Prep	$600	$75	$268	$250
Depositions	$800	$85	$388	$425

Depositions

Min. Charge for Deps: 100% **Hours in Minimum:** *High:* 4 *Low:* 1 *Average:* 2 *Median:* 1
Cancellation Fee for Deps or Trial: 33% **Deposition Payment in Advance:** 83%
Exceeding Paid-for Time: *Get payment before proceeding:* 20% *Proceed without immediate payment:* 80%

Retainers

Required: 50% **Amounts:** *High:* $8,000 *Low:* $2,000 *Average:* $5,000 *Median:* $5,000

Expenses

Out-of-Pocket Expenses Marked Up: 50% **Out-of-Pockets Billed for:** *Mileage:* 50% *Airline Tickets:* 50% *Photocopies:* 50% *Telephone Calls:* 50% *Lab/Testing:* 0% *Photos:* 17% *Demonstrative Aids:* 33%
Travel Billed Portal-to-Portal: 100% **1st-class Airfare Required:** 50%

Fee Agreement

Require Signed Written Fee Agreement: 50% **Terms:** *Lawyer is responsible for fee, not lawyer's client:* 100% *Interest for delinquent accounts:* 67% *Out-of-pocket expense policies:* 100% *Retainer/prepayment requirements:* 67% *In-court testimony minimum fees:* 67% *Retaining counsel will pay for all deposition charges:* 33% *Fee schedules:* 100% *Attorney's fees if forced to sue for collection:* 67% *Portal-to-portal travel time:* 100% *Deposition minimum fees:* 100% *Payment for preparation time:* 100% *First-class air travel:* 33%

Majority of Work: *Plaintiffs:* 50% *Neither:* 17% *Defendants:* 33%

Counsel Failed to Pay in Last 5 Years: *Retaining:* 17% *Opposing:* 50%

Kansas

Responding Experts: 6

Per-hour Fees

	High	*Low*	*Average*	*Median*
In-court Testimony	$1,000	$200	$433	$350
File Review/Prep	$350	$100	$221	$200
Depositions	$500	$200	$333	$300

Depositions

Min. Charge for Deps: 67% **Hours in Minimum:** *High:* 2 *Low:* 1 *Average:* 1.8 *Median:* 2
Cancellation Fee for Deps or Trial: 50% **Deposition Payment in Advance:** 0%
Exceeding Paid-for Time: *Get payment before proceeding:* N/A *Proceed without immediate payment:* N/A

Retainers

Required: 17% **Amounts:** *High:* $700 *Low:* $700 *Average:* $700 *Median:* $700

Expenses

Out-of-Pocket Expenses Marked Up: 17% **Out-of-Pockets Billed for:** *Mileage:* 67% *Airline Tickets:* 50% *Photocopies:* 50% *Telephone Calls:* 33% *Lab/Testing:* 17% *Photos:* 17% *Demonstrative Aids:* 17%
Travel Billed Portal-to-Portal: 67% **1st-class Airfare Required:** 0%

Fee Agreement

Require Signed Written Fee Agreement: 0% **Terms:** *Lawyer is responsible for fee, not lawyer's client:* N/A *Interest for delinquent accounts:* N/A *Out-of-pocket expense policies:* N/A *Retainer/prepayment requirements:* N/A *In-court testimony minimum fees:* N/A *Retaining counsel will pay for all deposition charges:* N/A *Fee schedules:* N/A *Attorney's fees if forced to sue for collection:* N/A *Portal-to-portal travel time:* N/A *Deposition minimum fees:* N/A *Payment for preparation time:* N/A *First-class air travel:* N/A

Majority of Work: *Plaintiffs:* 50% *Neither:* 17% *Defendants:* 33%
Counsel Failed to Pay in Last 5 Years: *Retaining:* 50% *Opposing:* 33%

Kentucky

Responding Experts: 4

Per-hour Fees

	High	*Low*	*Average*	*Median*
In-court Testimony	$500	$150	$249	$173
File Review/Prep	$600	$100	$261	$173
Depositions	$650	$150	$286	$172

Depositions

Min. Charge for Deps: 75% **Hours in Minimum:** *High:* 4 *Low:* 1 *Average:* 2 *Median:* 1
Cancellation Fee for Deps or Trial: 50% **Deposition Payment in Advance:** 0%
Exceeding Paid-for Time: *Get payment before proceeding:* N/A *Proceed without immediate payment:* N/A

Retainers

Required: 33% **Amounts:** *High:* N/A *Low:* N/A *Average:* N/A *Median:* N/A

Expenses

Out-of-Pocket Expenses Marked Up: 25% **Out-of-Pockets Billed for:** *Mileage:* 50% *Airline Tickets:* 50% *Photocopies:* 25% *Telephone Calls:* 25% *Lab/Testing:* 25% *Photos:* 50% *Demonstrative Aids:* 50%
Travel Billed Portal-to-Portal: 75% **1st-class Airfare Required:** 0%

Fee Agreement

Require Signed Written Fee Agreement: 75% **Terms:** *Lawyer is responsible for fee, not lawyer's client:* 67% *Interest for delinquent accounts:* 33% *Out-of-pocket expense policies:* 67% *Retainer/prepayment requirements:* 33% *In-court testimony minimum fees:* 33% *Retaining counsel will pay for all deposition charges:* 33% *Fee schedules:* 67% *Attorney's fees if forced to sue for collection:* 33% *Portal-to-portal travel time:* 33% *Deposition minimum fees:* 33% *Payment for preparation time:* 67% *First-class air travel:* 0%

Majority of Work: *Plaintiffs:* 50% *Neither:* 50% *Defendants:* 0%
Counsel Failed to Pay in Last 5 Years: *Retaining:* 25% *Opposing:* 25%

Louisiana

Responding Experts: 16

Per-hour Fees

	High	*Low*	*Average*	*Median*
In-court Testimony	$1,300	$150	$321	$228
File Review/Prep	$350	$125	$182	$175
Depositions	$900	$125	$316	$225

Depositions

Min. Charge for Deps: 47% **Hours in Minimum:** *High:* 8 *Low:* 1 *Average:* 3.1 *Median:* 2
Cancellation Fee for Deps or Trial: 31% **Deposition Payment in Advance:** 56%
Exceeding Paid-for Time: *Get payment before proceeding:* 29% *Proceed without immediate payment:* 71%

Retainers

Required: 60% **Amounts:** *High:* $5,000 *Low:* $550 *Average:* $2,194 *Median:* $1,250

Expenses

Out-of-Pocket Expenses Marked Up: 25% **Out-of-Pockets Billed for:** *Mileage:* 69% *Airline Tickets:* 81% *Photocopies:* 38% *Telephone Calls:* 38% *Lab/Testing:* 44% *Photos:* 50% *Demonstrative Aids:* 62%
Travel Billed Portal-to-Portal: 80% **1st-class Airfare Required:** 19%

Fee Agreement

Require Signed Written Fee Agreement: 50% **Terms:** *Lawyer is responsible for fee, not lawyer's client:* 75% *Interest for delinquent accounts:* 38% *Out-of-pocket expense policies:* 88% *Retainer/prepayment requirements:* 88% *In-court testimony minimum fees:* 50% *Retaining counsel will pay for all deposition charges:* 50% *Fee schedules:* 88% *Attorney's fees if forced to sue for collection:* 50% *Portal-to-portal travel time:* 63% *Deposition minimum fees:* 63% *Payment for preparation time:* 75% *First-class air travel:* 0%

Majority of Work: *Plaintiffs:* 6% *Neither:* 75% *Defendants:* 19%

Counsel Failed to Pay in Last 5 Years: *Retaining:* 38% *Opposing:* 20%

Maine

Responding Experts: 2

Per-hour Fees

	High	*Low*	*Average*	*Median*
In-court Testimony	$300	$200	$250	$250
File Review/Prep	$300	$150	$225	$225
Depositions	$300	$200	$250	$250

Depositions

Min. Charge for Deps: 50% **Hours in Minimum:** *High:* 1 *Low:* 1 *Average:* 1 *Median:* 1
Cancellation Fee for Deps or Trial: 50% **Deposition Payment in Advance:** 100%
Exceeding Paid-for Time: *Get payment before proceeding:* 0% *Proceed without immediate payment:* 100%

Retainers

Required: 100% **Amounts:** *High:* $7,500 *Low:* $3,000 *Average:* $5,250 *Median:* $5,250

Expenses

Out-of-Pocket Expenses Marked Up: 0% **Out-of-Pockets Billed for:** *Mileage:* 100% *Airline Tickets:* 100% *Photocopies:* 50% *Telephone Calls:* 100% *Lab/Testing:* 50% *Photos:* 50% *Demonstrative Aids:* 50%
Travel Billed Portal-to-Portal: 100% **1st-class Airfare Required:** 0%

Fee Agreement

Require Signed Written Fee Agreement: 100% **Terms:** *Lawyer is responsible for fee, not lawyer's client:* 50% *Interest for delinquent accounts:* 0% *Out-of-pocket expense policies:* 100% *Retainer/prepayment requirements:* 100% *In-court testimony minimum fees:* 100% *Retaining counsel will pay for all deposition charges:* 0% *Fee schedules:* 50% *Attorney's fees if forced to sue for collection:* 0% *Portal-to-portal travel time:* 50% *Deposition minimum fees:* 0% *Payment for preparation time:* 50% *First-class air travel:* 0%

Majority of Work: *Plaintiffs:* 0% *Neither:* 100% *Defendants:* 0%

Counsel Failed to Pay in Last 5 Years: *Retaining:* 0% *Opposing:* 0%

Maryland

Responding Experts: 20

Per-hour Fees

	High	*Low*	*Average*	*Median*
In-court Testimony	$900	$150	$369	$350
File Review/Prep	$600	$150	$301	$300
Depositions	$600	$150	$354	$350

Depositions

Min. Charge for Deps: 55% **Hours in Minimum:** *High:* 5 *Low:* 2 *Average:* 3.2 *Median:* 3
Cancellation Fee for Deps or Trial: 55% **Deposition Payment in Advance:** 30%
Exceeding Paid-for Time: *Get payment before proceeding:* 20% *Proceed without immediate payment:* 80%

Retainers

Required: 74% **Amounts:** *High:* $10,000 *Low:* $600 *Average:* $2,954 *Median:* $1,250

Expenses

Out-of-Pocket Expenses Marked Up: 5% **Out-of-Pockets Billed for:** *Mileage:* 60% *Airline Tickets:* 75% *Photocopies:* 45% *Telephone Calls:* 35% *Lab/Testing:* 35% *Photos:* 45% *Demonstrative Aids:* 50%
Travel Billed Portal-to-Portal: 95% **1st-class Airfare Required:** 10%

Fee Agreement

Require Signed Written Fee Agreement: 50% **Terms:** *Lawyer is responsible for fee, not lawyer's client:* 80% *Interest for delinquent accounts:* 90% *Out-of-pocket expense policies:* 80% *Retainer/prepayment requirements:* 100% *In-court testimony minimum fees:* 70% *Retaining counsel will pay for all deposition charges:* 60% *Fee schedules:* 90% *Attorney's fees if forced to sue for collection:* 70% *Portal-to-portal travel time:* 60% *Deposition minimum fees:* 60% *Payment for preparation time:* 70% *First class air travel:* 20%

Majority of Work: *Plaintiffs:* 25% *Neither:* 60% *Defendants:* 15%
Counsel Failed to Pay in Last 5 Years: *Retaining:* 40% *Opposing:* 25%

Massachusetts

Responding Experts: 41

Per-hour Fees

	High	*Low*	*Average*	*Median*
In-court Testimony	$2,000	$115	$357	$293
File Review/Prep	$800	$100	$260	$250
Depositions	$800	$100	$310	$285

Depositions

Min. Charge for Deps: 61% **Hours in Minimum:** *High:* 8 *Low:* 1 *Average:* 3.3 *Median:* 3.5
Cancellation Fee for Deps or Trial: 37% **Deposition Payment in Advance:** 60%
Exceeding Paid-for Time: *Get payment before proceeding:* 39% *Proceed without immediate payment:* 61%

Retainers

Required: 74% **Amounts:** *High:* $10,000 *Low:* $500 *Average:* $2,594 *Median:* $2,000

Expenses

Out-of-Pocket Expenses Marked Up: 10% **Out-of-Pockets Billed for:** *Mileage:* 63% *Airline Tickets:* 83% *Photocopies:* 44% *Telephone Calls:* 46% *Lab/Testing:* 44% *Photos:* 51% *Demonstrative Aids:* 46%
Travel Billed Portal-to-Portal: 85% **1st-class Airfare Required:** 11%

Fee Agreement

Require Signed Written Fee Agreement: 41% **Terms:** *Lawyer is responsible for fee, not lawyer's client:* 78% *Interest for delinquent accounts:* 50% *Out-of-pocket expense policies:* 78% *Retainer/prepayment requirements:* 89% *In-court testimony minimum fees:* 67% *Retaining counsel will pay for all deposition charges:* 39% *Fee schedules:* 78% *Attorney's fees if forced to sue for collection:* 44% *Portal-to-portal travel time:* 78% *Deposition minimum fees:* 67% *Payment for preparation time:* 78% *First-class air travel:* 11%

Majority of Work: *Plaintiffs:* 10% *Neither:* 75% *Defendants:* 15%
Counsel Failed to Pay in Last 5 Years: *Retaining:* 50% *Opposing:* 21%

Michigan

Responding Experts: 22

Per-hour Fees

	High	*Low*	*Average*	*Median*
In-court Testimony	$600	$125	$315	$300
File Review/Prep	$400	$100	$221	$220
Depositions	$750	$100	$302	$275

Depositions

Min. Charge for Deps: 73% **Hours in Minimum:** *High:* 6 *Low:* 1 *Average:* 2.6 *Median:* 2.5
Cancellation Fee for Deps or Trial: 48% **Deposition Payment in Advance:** 50%
Exceeding Paid-for Time: *Get payment before proceeding:* 10% *Proceed without immediate payment:* 90%

Retainers

Required: 73% **Amounts:** *High:* $3,000 *Low:* $250 *Average:* $1,165 *Median:* $825

Expenses

Out-of-Pocket Expenses Marked Up: 36% **Out-of-Pockets Billed for:** *Mileage:* 59% *Airline Tickets:* 68% *Photocopies:* 36% *Telephone Calls:* 36% *Lab/Testing:* 32% *Photos:* 32% *Demonstrative Aids:* 46%
Travel Billed Portal-to-Portal: 76% **1st-class Airfare Required:** 15%

Fee Agreement

Require Signed Written Fee Agreement: 36% **Terms:** *Lawyer is responsible for fee, not lawyer's client:* 75% *Interest for delinquent accounts:* 75% *Out-of-pocket expense policies:* 75% *Retainer/prepayment requirements:* 100% *In-court testimony minimum fees:* 63% *Retaining counsel will pay for all deposition charges:* 50% *Fee schedules:* 88% *Attorney's fees if forced to sue for collection:* 25% *Portal-to-portal travel time:* 88% *Deposition minimum fees:* 63% *Payment for preparation time:* 75% *First-class air travel:* 38%

Majority of Work: *Plaintiffs:* 14% *Neither:* 67% *Defendants:* 19%
Counsel Failed to Pay in Last 5 Years: *Retaining:* 27% *Opposing:* 18%

Minnesota

Responding Experts: 5

Per-hour Fees

	High	*Low*	*Average*	*Median*
In-court Testimony	$500	$150	$259	$225
File Review/Prep	$500	$150	$259	$225
Depositions	$500	$150	$259	$225

Depositions

Min. Charge for Deps: 40% **Hours in Minimum:** *High:* 6 *Low:* 4 *Average:* 5 *Median:* 5
Cancellation Fee for Deps or Trial: 40% **Deposition Payment in Advance:** 40%
Exceeding Paid-for Time: *Get payment before proceeding:* 50% *Proceed without immediate payment:* 50%

Retainers

Required: 80% **Amounts:** *High:* $5,000 *Low:* $600 *Average:* $2,367 *Median:* $1,500

Expenses

Out-of-Pocket Expenses Marked Up: 40% **Out-of-Pockets Billed for:** *Mileage:* 80% *Airline Tickets:* 80% *Photocopies:* 60% *Telephone Calls:* 0% *Lab/Testing:* 60% *Photos:* 60% *Demonstrative Aids:* 100%
Travel Billed Portal-to-Portal: 80% **1st-class Airfare Required:** 0%

Fee Agreement

Require Signed Written Fee Agreement: 60% **Terms:** *Lawyer is responsible for fee, not lawyer's client:* 33% *Interest for delinquent accounts:* 67% *Out-of-pocket expense policies:* 100% *Retainer/prepayment requirements:* 100% *In-court testimony minimum fees:* 0% *Retaining counsel will pay for all deposition charges:* 0% *Fee schedules:* 100% *Attorney's fees if forced to sue for collection:* 33% *Portal-to-portal travel time:* 33% *Deposition minimum fees:* 0% *Payment for preparation time:* 33% *First-class air travel:* 0%

Majority of Work: *Plaintiffs:* 40% *Neither:* 40% *Defendants:* 20%
Counsel Failed to Pay in Last 5 Years: *Retaining:* 40% *Opposing:* 40%

Mississippi

Responding Experts: 10

Per-hour Fees

	High	*Low*	*Average*	*Median*
In-court Testimony	$1,250	$75	$260	$125
File Review/Prep	$375	$25	$162	$113
Depositions	$750	$90	$199	$125

Depositions

Min. Charge for Deps: 50% **Hours in Minimum:** *High:* 8 *Low:* 2 *Average:* 4.8 *Median:* 4
Cancellation Fee for Deps or Trial: 70% **Deposition Payment in Advance:** 70%
Exceeding Paid-for Time: *Get payment before proceeding:* 0% *Proceed without immediate payment:* 100%

Retainers

Required: 40% **Amounts:** *High:* $3,000 *Low:* $500 *Average:* $1,750 *Median:* $1,750

Expenses

Out-of-Pocket Expenses Marked Up: 0% **Out-of-Pockets Billed for:** *Mileage:* 90% *Airline Tickets:* 90% *Photocopies:* 10% *Telephone Calls:* 40% *Lab/Testing:* 30% *Photos:* 40% *Demonstrative Aids:* 50%
Travel Billed Portal-to-Portal: 70% **1st-class Airfare Required:** 20%

Fee Agreement

Require Signed Written Fee Agreement: 20% **Terms:** *Lawyer is responsible for fee, not lawyer's client:* 100% *Interest for delinquent accounts:* 50% *Out-of-pocket expense policies:* 50% *Retainer/prepayment requirements:* 50% *In-court testimony minimum fees:* 50% *Retaining counsel will pay for all deposition charges:* 0% *Fee schedules:* 100% *Attorney's fees if forced to sue for collection:* 50% *Portal-to-portal travel time:* 0% *Deposition minimum fees:* 50% *Payment for preparation time:* 80% *First-class air travel:* 0%

Majority of Work: *Plaintiffs:* 0% *Neither:* 70% *Defendants:* 30%
Counsel Failed to Pay in Last 5 Years: *Retaining:* 30% *Opposing:* 30%

Missouri

Responding Experts: 22

Per-hour Fees

	High	*Low*	*Average*	*Median*
In-court Testimony	$1,500	$100	$357	$235
File Review/Prep	$500	$75	$224	$210
Depositions	$750	$100	$285	$230

Depositions

Min. Charge for Deps: 53% **Hours in Minimum:** *High:* 8 *Low:* 1 *Average:* 3.3 *Median:* 3.5
Cancellation Fee for Deps or Trial: 56% **Deposition Payment in Advance:** 37%
Exceeding Paid-for Time: *Get payment before proceeding:* 43% *Proceed without immediate payment:* 57%

Retainers

Required: 50% **Amounts:** *High:* $2,500 *Low:* $375 *Average:* $1,128 *Median:* $1,000

Expenses

Out-of-Pocket Expenses Marked Up: 32% **Out-of-Pockets Billed for:** *Mileage:* 84% *Airline Tickets:* 84% *Photocopies:* 42% *Telephone Calls:* 42% *Lab/Testing:* 53% *Photos:* 47% *Demonstrative Aids:* 68%
Travel Billed Portal-to-Portal: 79% **1st-class Airfare Required:** 21%

Fee Agreement

Require Signed Written Fee Agreement: 53% **Terms:** *Lawyer is responsible for fee, not lawyer's client:* 70% *Interest for delinquent accounts:* 70% *Out-of-pocket expense policies:* 60% *Retainer/prepayment requirements:* 80% *In-court testimony minimum fees:* 50% *Retaining counsel will pay for all deposition charges:* 70% *Fee schedules:* 60% *Attorney's fees if forced to sue for collection:* 50% *Portal-to-portal travel time:* 70% *Deposition minimum fees:* 50% *Payment for preparation time:* 80% *First-class air travel:* 10%

Majority of Work: *Plaintiffs:* 6% *Neither:* 66% *Defendants:* 28%
Counsel Failed to Pay in Last 5 Years: *Retaining:* 44% *Opposing:* 22%

Montana

Responding Experts: 5

Per-hour Fees

	High	*Low*	*Average*	*Median*
In-court Testimony	$500	$110	$334	$360
File Review/Prep	$300	$100	$210	$240
Depositions	$500	$100	$280	$260

Depositions

Min. Charge for Deps: 20% **Hours in Minimum:** *High:* 1 *Low:* 1 *Average:* 1 *Median:* 1
Cancellation Fee for Deps or Trial: 40% **Deposition Payment in Advance:** 0%
Exceeding Paid-for Time: *Get payment before proceeding:* N/A *Proceed without immediate payment:* N/A

Retainers

Required: 60% **Amounts:** *High:* $6,000 *Low:* $500 *Average:* $3,333 *Median:* $3,500

Expenses

Out-of-Pocket Expenses Marked Up: 0% **Out-of-Pockets Billed for:** *Mileage:* 100% *Airline Tickets:* 100% *Photocopies:* 40% *Telephone Calls:* 40% *Lab/Testing:* 40% *Photos:* 20% *Demonstrative Aids:* 20%
Travel Billed Portal-to-Portal: 100% **1st-class Airfare Required:** 0%

Fee Agreement

Require Signed Written Fee Agreement: 60% **Terms:** *Lawyer is responsible for fee, not lawyer's client:* 67% *Interest for delinquent accounts:* 67% *Out-of-pocket expense policies:* 67% *Retainer/prepayment requirements:* 100% *In-court testimony minimum fees:* 67% *Retaining counsel will pay for all deposition charges:* 33% *Fee schedules:* 67% *Attorney's fees if forced to sue for collection:* 33% *Portal-to-portal travel time:* 33% *Deposition minimum fees:* 33% *Payment for preparation time:* 33% *First-class air travel:* 33%

Majority of Work: *Plaintiffs:* 25% *Neither:* 75% *Defendants:* 0%
Counsel Failed to Pay in Last 5 Years: *Retaining:* 20% *Opposing:* 0%

Nebraska

Responding Experts: 2

Per-hour Fees

	High	*Low*	*Average*	*Median*
In-court Testimony	$350	$250	$300	$300
File Review/Prep	$250	$175	$213	$213
Depositions	$350	$250	$300	$300

Depositions

Min. Charge for Deps: 50% **Hours in Minimum:** *High:* 1 *Low:* 1 *Average:* 1 *Median:* 1
Cancellation Fee for Deps or Trial: 50% **Deposition Payment in Advance:** 50%
Exceeding Paid-for Time: *Get payment before proceeding:* 0% *Proceed without immediate payment:* 100%

Retainers

Required: 50% **Amounts:** *High:* $900 *Low:* $900 *Average:* $900 *Median:* $900

Expenses

Out-of-Pocket Expenses Marked Up: 0% **Out-of-Pockets Billed for:** *Mileage:* 100% *Airline Tickets:* 100% *Photocopies:* 50% *Telephone Calls:* 100% *Lab/Testing:* 50% *Photos:* 0% *Demonstrative Aids:* 0%
Travel Billed Portal-to-Portal: 100% **1st-class Airfare Required:** 0%

Fee Agreement

Require Signed Written Fee Agreement: 50% **Terms:** *Lawyer is responsible for fee, not lawyer's client:* 100% *Interest for delinquent accounts:* 0% *Out-of-pocket expense policies:* 100% *Retainer/prepayment requirements:* 0% *In-court testimony minimum fees:* 0% *Retaining counsel will pay for all deposition charges:* 0% *Fee schedules:* 100% *Attorney's fees if forced to sue for collection:* 0% *Portal-to-portal travel time:* 100% *Deposition minimum fees:* 0% *Payment for preparation time:* 100% *First-class air travel:* 0%

Majority of Work: *Plaintiffs:* 0% *Neither:* 0% *Defendants:* 100%
Counsel Failed to Pay in Last 5 Years: *Retaining:* 50% *Opposing:* 50%

Nevada

Responding Experts: 9

Per-hour Fees

	High	*Low*	*Average*	*Median*
In-court Testimony	$700	$165	$407	$400
File Review/Prep	$500	$140	$288	$250
Depositions	$750	$165	$402	$300

Depositions

Min. Charge for Deps: 56% **Hours in Minimum:** *High:* 4 *Low:* 1 *Average:* 2.4 *Median:* 2
Cancellation Fee for Deps or Trial: 44% **Deposition Payment in Advance:** 44%
Exceeding Paid-for Time: *Get payment before proceeding:* 25% *Proceed without immediate payment:* 75%

Retainers

Required: 78% **Amounts:** *High:* $2,500 *Low:* $500 *Average:* $1,458 *Median:* $1,500

Expenses

Out-of-Pocket Expenses Marked Up: 13% **Out-of-Pockets Billed for:** *Mileage:* 78% *Airline Tickets:* 89% *Photocopies:* 56% *Telephone Calls:* 44% *Lab/Testing:* 44% *Photos:* 33% *Demonstrative Aids:* 33%
Travel Billed Portal-to-Portal: 89% **1st-class Airfare Required:** 11%

Fee Agreement

Require Signed Written Fee Agreement: 33% **Terms:** *Lawyer is responsible for fee, not lawyer's client:* 67% *Interest for delinquent accounts:* 33% *Out-of-pocket expense policies:* 100% *Retainer/prepayment requirements:* 100% *In-court testimony minimum fees:* 67% *Retaining counsel will pay for all deposition charges:* 0% *Fee schedules:* 67% *Attorney's fees if forced to sue for collection:* 33% *Portal-to-portal travel time:* 0% *Deposition minimum fees:* 67% *Payment for preparation time:* 67% *First-class air travel:* 0%

Majority of Work: *Plaintiffs:* 0% *Neither:* 88% *Defendants:* 12%
Counsel Failed to Pay in Last 5 Years: *Retaining:* 88% *Opposing:* 25%

New Hampshire

Responding Experts: 7

Per-hour Fees

	High	*Low*	*Average*	*Median*
In-court Testimony	$500	$100	$248	$210
File Review/Prep	$250	$75	$191	$200
Depositions	$500	$100	$248	$210

Depositions

Min. Charge for Deps: 67% **Hours in Minimum:** *High:* 8 *Low:* 2 *Average:* 4.5 *Median:* 4
Cancellation Fee for Deps or Trial: 57% **Deposition Payment in Advance:** 71%
Exceeding Paid-for Time: *Get payment before proceeding:* 25% *Proceed without immediate payment:* 75%

Retainers

Required: 83% **Amounts:** *High:* $3,000 *Low:* $250 *Average:* $1,250 *Median:* $750

Expenses

Out-of-Pocket Expenses Marked Up: 17% **Out-of-Pockets Billed for:** *Mileage:* 71% *Airline Tickets:* 71% *Photocopies:* 43% *Telephone Calls:* 29% *Lab/Testing:* 29% *Photos:* 29% *Demonstrative Aids:* 43%
Travel Billed Portal-to-Portal: 86% **1st-class Airfare Required:** 0%

Fee Agreement

Require Signed Written Fee Agreement: 43% **Terms:** *Lawyer is responsible for fee, not lawyer's client:* 33% *Interest for delinquent accounts:* 0% *Out-of-pocket expense policies:* 67% *Retainer/prepayment requirements:* 100% *In-court testimony minimum fees:* 37% *Retaining counsel will pay for all deposition charges:* 67% *Fee schedules:* 100% *Attorney's fees if forced to sue for collection:* 33% *Portal-to-portal travel time:* 100% *Deposition minimum fees:* 33% *Payment for preparation time:* 33% *First-class air travel:* 0%

Majority of Work: *Plaintiffs:* 42% *Neither:* 29% *Defendants:* 29%
Counsel Failed to Pay in Last 5 Years: *Retaining:* 57% *Opposing:* 0%

New Jersey

Responding Experts: 38

Per-hour Fees

	High	*Low*	*Average*	*Median*
In-court Testimony	$3,000	$100	$484	$300
File Review/Prep	$1,000	$100	$307	$300
Depositions	$2,000	$100	$395	$300

Depositions

Min. Charge for Deps: 53% **Hours in Minimum:** *High:* 10 *Low:* 1 *Average:* 3.5 *Median:* 3.5
Cancellation Fee for Deps or Trial: 60% **Deposition Payment in Advance:** 53%
Exceeding Paid-for Time: *Get payment before proceeding:* 28% *Proceed without immediate payment:* 72%

Retainers

Required: 78% **Amounts:** *High:* $6,500 *Low:* $150 *Average:* $1,946 *Median:* $1,500

Expenses

Out-of-Pocket Expenses Marked Up: 3% **Out-of-Pockets Billed for:** *Mileage:* 42% *Airline Tickets:* 71% *Photocopies:* 40% *Telephone Calls:* 34% *Lab/Testing:* 37% *Photos:* 40% *Demonstrative Aids:* 34%
Travel Billed Portal-to-Portal: 81% **1st-class Airfare Required:** 11%

Fee Agreement

Require Signed Written Fee Agreement: 47% **Terms:** *Lawyer is responsible for fee, not lawyer's client:* 61% *Interest for delinquent accounts:* 61% *Out-of-pocket expense policies:* 67% *Retainer/prepayment requirements:* 78% *In-court testimony minimum fees:* 67% *Retaining counsel will pay for all deposition charges:* 22% *Fee schedules:* 78% *Attorney's fees if forced to sue for collection:* 39% *Portal-to-portal travel time:* 56% *Deposition minimum fees:* 50% *Payment for preparation time:* 61% *First-class air travel:* 11%

Majority of Work: *Plaintiffs:* 27% *Neither:* 59% *Defendants:* 14%

Counsel Failed to Pay in Last 5 Years: *Retaining:* 53% *Opposing:* 29%

New Mexico

Responding Experts: 6

Per-hour Fees

	High	*Low*	*Average*	*Median*
In-court Testimony	$500	$200	$321	$300
File Review/Prep	$400	$125	$216	$190
Depositions	$500	$200	$321	$300

Depositions

Min. Charge for Deps: 67% **Hours in Minimum:** *High:* 4 *Low:* 1 *Average:* 2.25 *Median:* 2
Cancellation Fee for Deps or Trial: 60% **Deposition Payment in Advance:** 50%
Exceeding Paid-for Time: *Get payment before proceeding:* 50% *Proceed without immediate payment:* 50%

Retainers

Required: 50% **Amounts:** *High:* $3,000 *Low:* $500 *Average:* $2,000 *Median:* $2,500

Expenses

Out-of-Pocket Expenses Marked Up: 17% **Out-of-Pockets Billed for:** *Mileage:* 83% *Airline Tickets:* 83% *Photocopies:* 50% *Telephone Calls:* 67% *Lab/Testing:* 50% *Photos:* 17% *Demonstrative Aids:* 67%
Travel Billed Portal-to-Portal: 100% **1st-class Airfare Required:** 17%

Fee Agreement

Require Signed Written Fee Agreement: 33% **Terms:** *Lawyer is responsible for fee, not lawyer's client:* 100% *Interest for delinquent accounts:* 50% *Out-of-pocket expense policies:* 100% *Retainer/prepayment requirements:* 100% *In-court testimony minimum fees:* 100% *Retaining counsel will pay for all deposition charges:* 50% *Fee schedules:* 100% *Attorney's fees if forced to sue for collection:* 50% *Portal-to-portal travel time:* 100% *Deposition minimum fees:* 100% *Payment for preparation time:* 100% *First-class air travel:* 50%

Majority of Work: *Plaintiffs:* 50% *Neither:* 50% *Defendants:* 0%

Counsel Failed to Pay in Last 5 Years: *Retaining:* 67% *Opposing:* 0%

New York

Responding Experts: 74

Per-hour Fees

	High	Low	Average	Median
In-court Testimony	$1,500	$95	$453	$300
File Review/Prep	$850	$95	$288	$263
Depositions	$1,500	$125	$399	$300

Depositions

Min. Charge for Deps: 63% **Hours in Minimum:** *High:* 10 *Low:* 1 *Average:* 4.15 *Median:* 4
Cancellation Fee for Deps or Trial: 51% **Deposition Payment in Advance:** 46%
Exceeding Paid-for Time: *Get payment before proceeding:* 28% *Proceed without immediate payment:* 72%

Retainer

Required: 75% **Amounts:** *High:* $10,000 *Low:* $150 *Average:* $1,873 *Median:* $1,325

Expenses

Out-of-Pocket Expenses Marked Up: 14% **Out-of-Pockets Billed for:** *Mileage:* 65% *Airline Tickets:* 82% *Photocopies:* 26% *Telephone Calls:* 26% *Lab/Testing:* 34% *Photos:* 39% *Demonstrative Aids:* 45%
Travel Billed Portal-to-Portal: 79% **1st-class Airfare Required:** 11%

Fee Agreement

Require Signed Written Fee Agreement: 33% **Terms:** *Lawyer is responsible for fee, not lawyer's client:* 58% *Interest for delinquent accounts:* 42% *Out-of-pocket expense policies:* 88% *Retainer/prepayment requirements:* 83% *In-court testimony minimum fees:* 50% *Retaining counsel will pay for all deposition charges:* 54% *Fee schedules:* 79% *Attorney's fees if forced to sue for collection:* 38% *Portal-to-portal travel time:* 63% *Deposition minimum fees:* 54% *Payment for preparation time:* 75% *First-class air travel:* 0%

Majority of Work: *Plaintiffs:* 28% *Neither:* 51% *Defendants:* 21%

Counsel Failed to Pay in Last 5 Years: *Retaining:* 43% *Opposing:* 12%

North Carolina

Responding Experts: 19

Per-hour Fees

	High	Low	Average	Median
In-court Testimony	$875	$150	$294	$250
File Review/Prep	$350	$125	$209	$185
Depositions	$600	$150	$265	$250

Depositions

Min. Charge for Deps: 63% **Hours in Minimum:** *High:* 8 *Low:* 1 *Average:* 3.2 *Median:* 2
Cancellation Fee for Deps or Trial: 53% **Deposition Payment in Advance:** 47%
Exceeding Paid-for Time: *Get payment before proceeding:* 0% *Proceed without immediate payment:* 100%

Retainers

Required: 79% **Amounts:** *High:* $3,000 *Low:* $200 *Average:* $1,621 *Median:* $1,500

Expenses

Out-of-Pocket Expenses Marked Up: 16% **Out-of-Pockets Billed for:** *Mileage:* 84% *Airline Tickets:* 89% *Photocopies:* 68% *Telephone Calls:* 63% *Lab/Testing:* 47% *Photos:* 47% *Demonstrative Aids:* 47%
Travel Billed Portal-to-Portal: 100% **1st-class Airfare Required:** 5%

Fee Agreement

Require Signed Written Fee Agreement: 53% **Terms:** *Lawyer is responsible for fee, not lawyer's client:* 82% *Interest for delinquent accounts:* 73% *Out-of-pocket expense policies:* 82% *Retainer/prepayment requirements:* 82% *In-court testimony minimum fees:* 73% *Retaining counsel will pay for all deposition charges:* 46% *Fee schedules:* 91% *Attorney's fees if forced to sue for collection:* 73% *Portal-to-portal travel time:* 55% *Deposition minimum fees:* 36% *Payment for preparation time:* 55% *First-class air travel:* 0%

Majority of Work: *Plaintiffs:* 11% *Neither:* 61% *Defendants:* 28%

Counsel Failed to Pay in Last 5 Years: *Retaining:* 63% *Opposing:* 26%

North Dakota

Responding Experts: 2

Per-hour Fees

	High	*Low*	*Average*	*Median*
In-court Testimony	$225	$225	$225	$225
File Review/Prep	$250	$225	$238	$238
Depositions	$350	$225	$238	$288

Depositions

Min. Charge for Deps: 0% **Hours in Minimum:** *High:* N/A *Low:* N/A *Average:* N/A *Median:* N/A
Cancellation Fee for Deps or Trial: 50% **Deposition Payment in Advance:** 0%
Exceeding Paid-for Time: *Get payment before proceeding:* N/A *Proceed without immediate payment:* N/A

Retainers

Required: 50% **Amounts:** *High:* N/A *Low:* N/A *Average:* N/A *Median:* N/A

Expenses

Out-of-Pocket Expenses Marked Up: 0% **Out-of-Pockets Billed for:** *Mileage:* 100% *Airline Tickets:* 50% *Photocopies:* 50% *Telephone Calls:* 50% *Lab/Testing:* 50% *Photos:* 50% *Demonstrative Aids:* 50%
Travel Billed Portal-to-Portal: 100% **1st-class Airfare Required:** 0%

Fee Agreement

Require Signed Written Fee Agreement: 50% **Terms:** *Lawyer is responsible for fee, not lawyer's client:* 100% *Interest for delinquent accounts:* 100% *Out-of-pocket expense policies:* 100% *Retainer/prepayment requirements:* 50% *In-court testimony minimum fees:* 0% *Retaining counsel will pay for all deposition charges:* 0% *Fee schedules:* 100% *Attorney's fees if forced to sue for collection:* 100% *Portal-to-portal travel time:* 100% *Deposition minimum fees:* 0% *Payment for preparation time:* 100% *First-class air travel:* 0%

Majority of Work: *Plaintiffs:* 0% *Neither:* 100% *Defendants:* 0%
Counsel Failed to Pay in Last 5 Years: *Retaining:* 50% *Opposing:* 0%

Ohio

Responding Experts: 38

Per-hour Fees

	High	*Low*	*Average*	*Median*
In-court Testimony	$2,500	$100	$539	$372
File Review/Prep	$1,000	$75	$276	$238
Depositions	$1,250	$100	$385	$338

Depositions

Min. Charge for Deps: 63% **Hours in Minimum:** *High:* 8 *Low:* 1 *Average:* 3.2 *Median:* 3
Cancellation Fee for Deps or Trial: 60% **Deposition Payment in Advance:** 47%
Exceeding Paid-for Time: *Get payment before proceeding:* 13% *Proceed without immediate payment:* 87%

Retainers

Required: 74% **Amounts:** *High:* $8,750 *Low:* $250 *Average:* $1,922 *Median:* $1,000

Expenses

Out-of-Pocket Expenses Marked Up: 3% **Out-of-Pockets Billed for:** *Mileage:* 82% *Airline Tickets:* 90% *Photocopies:* 55% *Telephone Calls:* 53% *Lab/Testing:* 29% *Photos:* 37% *Demonstrative Aids:* 40%
Travel Billed Portal-to-Portal: 89% **1st-class Airfare Required:** 8%

Fee Agreement

Require Signed Written Fee Agreement: 40% **Terms:** *Lawyer is responsible for fee, not lawyer's client:* 73% *Interest for delinquent accounts:* 20% *Out-of-pocket expense policies:* 73% *Retainer/prepayment requirements:* 73% *In-court testimony minimum fees:* 67% *Retaining counsel will pay for all deposition charges:* 47% *Fee schedules:* 53% *Attorney's fees if forced to sue for collection:* 40% *Portal-to-portal travel time:* 60% *Deposition minimum fees:* 60% *Payment for preparation time:* 67% *First-class air travel:* 13%

Majority of Work: *Plaintiffs:* 16% *Neither:* 50% *Defendants:* 34%
Counsel Failed to Pay in Last 5 Years: *Retaining:* 42% *Opposing:* 13%

Oklahoma

Responding Experts: 7

Per-hour Fees

	High	Low	Average	Median
In-court Testimony	$750	$100	$254	$150
File Review/Prep	$350	$65	$191	$150
Depositions	$500	$100	$225	$150

Depositions

Min. Charge for Deps: 29% **Hours in Minimum:** *High:* 8 *Low:* 4 *Average:* 5.3 *Median:* 4
Cancellation Fee for Deps or Trial: 43% **Deposition Payment in Advance:** 50%
Exceeding Paid-for Time: *Get payment before proceeding:* 33% *Proceed without immediate payment:* 67%

Retainers

Required: 33% **Amounts:** *High:* $6,000 *Low:* $2,000 *Average:* $4,000 *Median:* $4,000

Expenses

Out-of-Pocket Expenses Marked Up: 29% **Out-of-Pockets Billed for:** *Mileage:* 100% *Airline Tickets:* 100% *Photocopies:* 71% *Telephone Calls:* 57% *Lab/Testing:* 57% *Photos:* 100% *Demonstrative Aids:* 86%
Travel Billed Portal-to-Portal: 83% **1st-class Airfare Required:** 29%

Fee Agreement

Require Signed Written Fee Agreement: 43% **Terms:** *Lawyer is responsible for fee, not lawyer's client:* 100% *Interest for delinquent accounts:* 100% *Out-of-pocket expense policies:* 100% *Retainer/prepayment requirements:* 100% *In-court testimony minimum fees:* 67% *Retaining counsel will pay for all deposition charges:* 67% *Fee schedules:* 100% *Attorney's fees if forced to sue for collection:* 100% *Portal-to-portal travel time:* 33% *Deposition minimum fees:* 67% *Payment for preparation time:* 67% *First-class air travel:* 67%

Majority of Work: *Plaintiffs:* 0% *Neither:* 71% *Defendants:* 29%
Counsel Failed to Pay in Last 5 Years: *Retaining:* 43% *Opposing:* 29%

Oregon

Responding Experts: 11

Per-hour Fees

	High	Low	Average	Median
In-court Testimony	$500	$100	$296	$260
File Review/Prep	$500	$100	$251	$250
Depositions	$500	$100	$291	$260

Depositions

Min. Charge for Deps: 46% **Hours in Minimum:** *High:* 8 *Low:* 4 *Average:* 4.8 *Median:* 4
Cancellation Fee for Deps or Trial: 46% **Deposition Payment in Advance:** 27%
Exceeding Paid-for Time: *Get payment before proceeding:* 0% *Proceed without immediate payment:* 100%

Retainers

Required: 67% **Amounts:** *High:* $7,500 *Low:* $500 *Average:* $3,188 *Median:* $2,375

Expenses

Out-of-Pocket Expenses Marked Up: 9% **Out-of-Pockets Billed for:** *Mileage:* 64% *Airline Tickets:* 82% *Photocopies:* 55% *Telephone Calls:* 36% *Lab/Testing:* 64% *Photos:* 55% *Demonstrative Aids:* 73%
Travel Billed Portal-to-Portal: 82% **1st-class Airfare Required:** 0%

Fee Agreement

Require Signed Written Fee Agreement: 27% **Terms:** *Lawyer is responsible for fee, not lawyer's client:* 67% *Interest for delinquent accounts:* 33% *Out-of-pocket expense policies:* 67% *Retainer/prepayment requirements:* 67% *In-court testimony minimum fees:* 0% *Retaining counsel will pay for all deposition charges:* 33% *Fee schedules:* 67% *Attorney's fees if forced to sue for collection:* 67% *Portal-to-portal travel time:* 33% *Deposition minimum fees:* 0% *Payment for preparation time:* 67% *First-class air travel:* 0%

Majority of Work: *Plaintiffs:* 9% *Neither:* 73% *Defendants:* 18%
Counsel Failed to Pay in Last 5 Years: *Retaining:* 36% *Opposing:* 0%

Pennsylvania

Responding Experts: 49

Per-hour Fees

	High	*Low*	*Average*	*Median*
In-court Testimony	$2,500	$110	$455	$250
File Review/Prep	$800	$100	$259	$250
Depositions	$300	$125	$492	$250

Depositions

Min. Charge for Deps: 63% **Hours in Minimum:** *High:* 10 *Low:* 1 *Average:* 4.2 *Median:* 4
Cancellation Fee for Deps or Trial: 49% **Deposition Payment in Advance:** 53%
Exceeding Paid-for Time: *Get payment before proceeding:* 40% *Proceed without immediate payment:* 60%

Retainers

Required: 49% **Amounts:** *High:* $5,000 *Low:* $200 *Average:* $1,742 *Median:* $1,000

Expenses

Out-of-Pocket Expenses Marked Up: 15% **Out-of-Pockets Billed for:** *Mileage:* 53% *Airline Tickets:* 84% *Photocopies:* 33% *Telephone Calls:* 34% *Lab/Testing:* 29% *Photos:* 32% *Demonstrative Aids:* 45%
Travel Billed Portal-to-Portal: 73% **1st-class Airfare Required:** 4%

Fee Agreement

Require Signed Written Fee Agreement: 39% **Terms:** *Lawyer is responsible for fee, not lawyer's client:* 63% *Interest for delinquent accounts:* 47% *Out-of-pocket expense policies:* 90% *Retainer/prepayment requirements:* 90% *In-court testimony minimum fees:* 84% *Retaining counsel will pay for all deposition charges:* 58% *Fee schedules:* 100% *Attorney's fees if forced to sue for collection:* 32% *Portal-to-portal travel time:* 63% *Deposition minimum fees:* 68% *Payment for preparation time:* 74% *First-class air travel:* 0%

Majority of Work: *Plaintiffs:* 33% *Neither:* 48% *Defendants:* 19%

Counsel Failed to Pay in Last 5 Years: *Retaining:* 38% *Opposing:* 19%

Puerto Rico

Responding Experts: 9

Per-hour Fees

	High	*Low*	*Average*	*Median*
In-court Testimony	$450	$75	$205	$200
File Review/Prep	$200	$50	$158	$200
Depositions	$600	$120	$263	$200

Depositions

Min. Charge for Deps: 78% **Hours in Minimum:** *High:* 8 *Low:* 1 *Average:* 4.1 *Median:* 4
Cancellation Fee for Deps or Trial: 56% **Deposition Payment in Advance:** 67%
Exceeding Paid-for Time: *Get payment before proceeding:* 0% *Proceed without immediate payment:* 100%

Retainers

Required: 89% **Amounts:** *High:* $7,500 *Low:* $600 *Average:* $2,700 *Median:* $1,250

Expenses

Out-of-Pocket Expenses Marked Up: 11% **Out-of-Pockets Billed for:** *Mileage:* 22% *Airline Tickets:* 44% *Photocopies:* 22% *Telephone Calls:* 22% *Lab/Testing:* 33% *Photos:* 11% *Demonstrative Aids:* 0%
Travel Billed Portal-to-Portal: 67% **1st-class Airfare Required:** 0%

Fee Agreement

Require Signed Written Fee Agreement: 56% **Terms:** *Lawyer is responsible for fee, not lawyer's client:* 40% *Interest for delinquent accounts:* 0% *Out-of-pocket expense policies:* 40% *Retainer/prepayment requirements:* 100% *In-court testimony minimum fees:* 80% *Retaining counsel will pay for all deposition charges:* 20% *Fee schedules:* 100% *Attorney's fees if forced to sue for collection:* 0% *Portal-to-portal travel time:* 40% *Deposition minimum fees:* 80% *Payment for preparation time:* 60% *First-class air travel:* 0%

Majority of Work: *Plaintiffs:* 22% *Neither:* 45% *Defendants:* 33%

Counsel Failed to Pay in Last 5 Years: *Retaining:* 44% *Opposing:* 22%

Rhode Island

Responding Experts: 4

Per-hour Fees

	High	*Low*	*Average*	*Median*
In-court Testimony	$400	$300	$363	$375
File Review/Prep	$400	$200	$300	$300
Depositions	$400	$300	$338	$325

Depositions

Min. Charge for Deps: 75% **Hours in Minimum:** *High:* 4 *Low:* 1 *Average:* 2.2 *Median:* 1.5
Cancellation Fee for Deps or Trial: 75% **Deposition Payment in Advance:** 50%
Exceeding Paid-for Time: *Get payment before proceeding:* 0% *Proceed without immediate payment:* 100%

Retainers

Required: 50% **Amounts:** *High:* N/A *Low:* N/A *Average:* N/A *Median:* N/A

Expenses

Out-of-Pocket Expenses Marked Up: 0% **Out-of-Pockets Billed for:** *Mileage:* 25% *Airline Tickets:* 75% *Photocopies:* 25% *Telephone Calls:* 25% *Lab/Testing:* 25% *Photos:* 25% *Demonstrative Aids:* 50%
Travel Billed Portal-to-Portal: 67% **1st-class Airfare Required:** 33%

Fee Agreement

Require Signed Written Fee Agreement: 50% **Terms:** *Lawyer is responsible for fee, not lawyer's client:* 50% *Interest for delinquent accounts:* 100% *Out-of-pocket expense policies:* 100% *Retainer/prepayment requirements:* 100% *In-court testimony minimum fees:* 100% *Retaining counsel will pay for all deposition charges:* 50% *Fee schedules:* 100% *Attorney's fees if forced to sue for collection:* 100% *Portal-to-portal travel time:* 50% *Deposition minimum fees:* 100% *Payment for preparation time:* 50% *First-class air travel:* 50%

Majority of Work: *Plaintiffs:* 0% *Neither:* 33% *Defendants:* 67%
Counsel Failed to Pay in Last 5 Years: *Retaining:* 100% *Opposing:* 50%

South Carolina

Responding Experts: 12

Per-hour Fees

	High	*Low*	*Average*	*Median*
In-court Testimony	$437	$150	$250	$250
File Review/Prep	$350	$150	$199	$188
Depositions	$350	$150	$228	$200

Depositions

Min. Charge for Deps: 50% **Hours in Minimum:** *High:* 4 *Low:* 4 *Average:* 4 *Median:* 4
Cancellation Fee for Deps or Trial: 33% **Deposition Payment in Advance:** 50%
Exceeding Paid-for Time: *Get payment before proceeding:* 50% *Proceed without immediate payment:* 50%

Retainers

Required: 75% **Amounts:** *High:* $3,500 *Low:* $700 *Average:* $1,933 *Median:* $2,000

Expenses

Out-of-Pocket Expenses Marked Up: 33% **Out-of-Pockets Billed for:** *Mileage:* 100% *Airline Tickets:* 100% *Photocopies:* 67% *Telephone Calls:* 33% *Lab/Testing:* 50% *Photos:* 58% *Demonstrative Aids:* 50%
Travel Billed Portal-to-Portal: 83% **1st-class Airfare Required:** 18%

Fee Agreement

Require Signed Written Fee Agreement: 33% **Terms:** *Lawyer is responsible for fee, not lawyer's client:* 75% *Interest for delinquent accounts:* 100% *Out-of-pocket expense policies:* 100% *Retainer/prepayment requirements:* 100% *In-court testimony minimum fees:* 50% *Retaining counsel will pay for all deposition charges:* 75% *Fee schedules:* 100% *Attorney's fees if forced to sue for collection:* 75% *Portal-to-portal travel time:* 50% *Deposition minimum fees:* 100% *Payment for preparation time:* 50% *First-class air travel:* 25%

Majority of Work: *Plaintiffs:* 50% *Neither:* 33% *Defendants:* 17%
Counsel Failed to Pay in Last 5 Years: *Retaining:* 17% *Opposing:* 8%

South Dakota

Responding Experts: 3

Per-hour Fees

	High	*Low*	*Average*	*Median*
In-court Testimony	$400	$275	$317	$275
File Review/Prep	$275	$250	$267	$275
Depositions	$400	$275	$317	$275

Depositions

Min. Charge for Deps: 67% **Hours in Minimum:** *High:* 8 *Low:* 1 *Average:* 4.5 *Median:* 4.5
Cancellation Fee for Deps or Trial: 100% **Deposition Payment in Advance:** 0%
Exceeding Paid-for Time: *Get payment before proceeding:* N/A *Proceed without immediate payment:* N/A

Retainers

Required: 0% **Amounts:** *High:* N/A *Low:* N/A *Average:* N/A *Median:* N/A

Expenses

Out-of-Pocket Expenses Marked Up: 33% **Out-of-Pockets Billed for:** *Mileage:* 67% *Airline Tickets:* 67% *Photocopies:* 0% *Telephone Calls:* 100% *Lab/Testing:* 0% *Photos:* 0% *Demonstrative Aids:* 33%
Travel Billed Portal-to-Portal: 100% **1st-class Airfare Required:** 0%

Fee Agreement

Require Signed Written Fee Agreement: 67% **Terms:** *Lawyer is responsible for fee, not lawyer's client:* 0% *Interest for delinquent accounts:* 0% *Out-of-pocket expense policies:* 100% *Retainer/prepayment requirements:* 0% *In-court testimony minimum fees:* 0% *Retaining counsel will pay for all deposition charges:* 0% *Fee schedules:* 100% *Attorney's fees if forced to sue for collection:* 0% *Portal-to-portal travel time:* 100% *Deposition minimum fees:* 0% *Payment for preparation time:* 100% *First-class air travel:* 0%

Majority of Work: *Plaintiffs:* 0% *Neither:* 100% *Defendants:* 0%

Counsel Failed to Pay in Last 5 Years: *Retaining:* 67% *Opposing:* 0%

Tennessee

Responding Experts: 10

Per-hour Fees

	High	*Low*	*Average*	*Median*
In-court Testimony	$1,000	$175	$405	$275
File Review/Prep	$500	$85	$224	$213
Depositions	$1,000	$175	$360	$275

Depositions

Min. Charge for Deps: 90% **Hours in Minimum:** *High:* 10 *Low:* 1 *Average:* 2.7 *Median:* 1.5
Cancellation Fee for Deps or Trial: 60% **Deposition Payment in Advance:** 30%
Exceeding Paid-for Time: *Get payment before proceeding:* 0% *Proceed without immediate payment:* 100%

Retainers

Required: 44% **Amounts:** *High:* $5,000 *Low:* $250 *Average:* $1,988 *Median:* $1,350

Expenses

Out-of-Pocket Expenses Marked Up: 11% **Out-of-Pockets Billed for:** *Mileage:* 60% *Airline Tickets:* 80% *Photocopies:* 30% *Telephone Calls:* 30% *Lab/Testing:* 20% *Photos:* 30% *Demonstrative Aids:* 50%
Travel Billed Portal-to-Portal: 90% **1st-class Airfare Required:** 11%

Fee Agreement

Require Signed Written Fee Agreement: 30% **Terms:** *Lawyer is responsible for fee, not lawyer's client:* 67% *Interest for delinquent accounts:* 67% *Out-of-pocket expense policies:* 100% *Retainer/prepayment requirements:* 67% *In-court testimony minimum fees:* 100% *Retaining counsel will pay for all deposition charges:* 67% *Fee schedules:* 100% *Attorney's fees if forced to sue for collection:* 67% *Portal-to-portal travel time:* 33% *Deposition minimum fees:* 100% *Payment for preparation time:* 67% *First-class air travel:* 0%

Majority of Work: *Plaintiffs:* 30% *Neither:* 50% *Defendants:* 20%

Counsel Failed to Pay in Last 5 Years: *Retaining:* 44% *Opposing:* 20%

Texas

Responding Experts: 81

Per-hour Fees

	High	*Low*	*Average*	*Median*
In-court Testimony	$2,000	$100	$331	$250
File Review/Prep	$750	$100	$238	$200
Depositions	$1,500	$0	$304	$250

Depositions

Min. Charge for Deps: 37% **Hours in Minimum:** *High:* 12 *Low:* 1 *Average:* 4.1 *Median:* 4
Cancellation Fee for Deps or Trial: 30% **Deposition Payment in Advance:** 35%
Exceeding Paid-for Time: *Get payment before proceeding:* 13% *Proceed without immediate payment:* 87%

Retainers

Required: 74% **Amounts:** *High:* $8,000 *Low:* $200 *Average:* $2,424 *Median:* $2,000

Expenses

Out-of-Pocket Expenses Marked Up: 10% **Out-of-Pockets Billed for:** *Mileage:* 68% *Airline Tickets:* 95% *Photocopies:* 42% *Telephone Calls:* 37% *Lab/Testing:* 44% *Photos:* 42% *Demonstrative Aids:* 53%
Travel Billed Portal-to-Portal: 84% **1st-class Airfare Required:** 6%

Fee Agreement

Require Signed Written Fee Agreement: 43% **Terms:** *Lawyer is responsible for fee, not lawyer's client:* 54% *Interest for delinquent accounts:* 57% *Out-of-pocket expense policies:* 89% *Retainer/prepayment requirements:* 80% *In-court testimony minimum fees:* 60% *Retaining counsel will pay for all deposition charges:* 29% *Fee schedules:* 80% *Attorney's fees if forced to sue for collection:* 46% *Portal-to-portal travel time:* 60% *Deposition minimum fees:* 40% *Payment for preparation time:* 66% *First-class air travel:* 3%

Majority of Work: *Plaintiffs:* 29% *Neither:* 52% *Defendants:* 19%
Counsel Failed to Pay in Last 5 Years: *Retaining:* 49% *Opposing:* 11%

Utah

Responding Experts: 5

Per-hour Fees

	High	*Low*	*Average*	*Median*
In-court Testimony	$1,000	$150	$442	$350
File Review/Prep	$500	$120	$276	$250
Depositions	$500	$150	$302	$300

Depositions

Min. Charge for Deps: 60% **Hours in Minimum:** *High:* 2 *Low:* 1 *Average:* 1.3 *Median:* 1
Cancellation Fee for Deps or Trial: 80% **Deposition Payment in Advance:** 40%
Exceeding Paid-for Time: *Get payment before proceeding:* 0% *Proceed without immediate payment:* 100%

Retainers

Required: 40% **Amounts:** *High:* $750 *Low:* $750 *Average:* $750 *Median:* $750

Expenses

Out-of-Pocket Expenses Marked Up: 60% **Out-of-Pockets Billed for:** *Mileage:* 80% *Airline Tickets:* 80% *Photocopies:* 60% *Telephone Calls:* 40% *Lab/Testing:* 40% *Photos:* 60% *Demonstrative Aids:* 20%
Travel Billed Portal-to-Portal: 75% **1st-class Airfare Required:** 0%

Fee Agreement

Require Signed Written Fee Agreement: 40% **Terms:** *Lawyer is responsible for fee, not lawyer's client:* 20% *Interest for delinquent accounts:* 20% *Out-of-pocket expense policies:* 20% *Retainer/prepayment requirements:* 20% *In-court testimony minimum fees:* 20% *Retaining counsel will pay for all deposition charges:* 20% *Fee schedules:* 20% *Attorney's fees if forced to sue for collection:* 20% *Portal-to-portal travel time:* 20% *Deposition minimum fees:* 20% *Payment for preparation time:* 40% *First-class air travel:* 0%

Majority of Work: *Plaintiffs:* 0% *Neither:* 60% *Defendants:* 40%
Counsel Failed to Pay in Last 5 Years: *Retaining:* 40% *Opposing:* 20%

Vermont

Responding Experts: 6

Per-hour Fees

	High	*Low*	*Average*	*Median*
In-court Testimony	$500	$85	$285	$275
File Review/Prep	$300	$85	$210	$213
Depositions	$500	$85	$285	$275

Depositions

Min. Charge for Deps: 83% **Hours in Minimum:** *High:* 8 *Low:* 1 *Average:* 4 *Median:* 3.5
Cancellation Fee for Deps or Trial: 60% **Deposition Payment in Advance:** 67%
Exceeding Paid-for Time: *Get payment before proceeding:* 33% *Proceed without immediate payment:* 67%

Retainers

Required: 67% **Amounts:** *High:* $1,500 *Low:* $1,500 *Average:* $1,500 *Median:* $1,500

Expenses

Out-of-Pocket Expenses Marked Up: 17% **Out-of-Pockets Billed for:** *Mileage:* 50% *Airline Tickets:* 67% *Photocopies:* 67% *Telephone Calls:* 50% *Lab/Testing:* 50% *Photos:* 67% *Demonstrative Aids:* 33%
Travel Billed Portal-to-Portal: 100% **1st-class Airfare Required:** 25%

Fee Agreement

Require Signed Written Fee Agreement: 33% **Terms:** *Lawyer is responsible for fee, not lawyer's client:* 100% *Interest for delinquent accounts:* 100% *Out-of-pocket expense policies:* 50% *Retainer/prepayment requirements:* 100% *In-court testimony minimum fees:* 50% *Retaining counsel will pay for all deposition charges:* 50% *Fee schedules:* 100% *Attorney's fees if forced to sue for collection:* 0% *Portal-to-portal travel time:* 100% *Deposition minimum fees:* 100% *Payment for preparation time:* 100% *First-class air travel:* 0%

Majority of Work: *Plaintiffs:* 33% *Neither:* 50% *Defendants:* 17%
Counsel Failed to Pay in Last 5 Years: *Retaining:* 0% *Opposing:* 0%

Virginia

Responding Experts: 18

Per-hour Fees

	High	*Low*	*Average*	*Median*
In-court Testimony	$7,500	$150	$790	$350
File Review/Prep	$450	$100	$276	$300
Depositions	$700	$150	$357	$325

Depositions

Min. Charge for Deps: 67% **Hours in Minimum:** *High:* 11 *Low:* 1 *Average:* 2.8 *Median:* 2
Cancellation Fee for Deps or Trial: 67% **Deposition Payment in Advance:** 50%
Exceeding Paid-for Time: *Get payment before proceeding:* 33% *Proceed without immediate payment:* 67%

Retainers

Required: 67% **Amounts:** *High:* $7,500 *Low:* $100 *Average:* $2,288 *Median:* $1,900

Expenses

Out-of-Pocket Expenses Marked Up: 39% **Out-of-Pockets Billed for:** *Mileage:* 89% *Airline Tickets:* 94% *Photocopies:* 61% *Telephone Calls:* 56% *Lab/Testing:* 56% *Photos:* 56% *Demonstrative Aids:* 50%
Travel Billed Portal-to-Portal: 94% **1st-class Airfare Required:** 6%

Fee Agreement

Require Signed Written Fee Agreement: 61% **Terms:** *Lawyer is responsible for fee, not lawyer's client:* 64% *Interest for delinquent accounts:* 46% *Out-of-pocket expense policies:* 73% *Retainer/prepayment requirements:* 91% *In-court testimony minimum fees:* 73% *Retaining counsel will pay for all deposition charges:* 73% *Fee schedules:* 82% *Attorney's fees if forced to sue for collection:* 46% *Portal-to-portal travel time:* 55% *Deposition minimum fees:* 73% *Payment for preparation time:* 55% *First-class air travel:* 9%

Majority of Work: *Plaintiffs:* 27% *Neither:* 67% *Defendants:* 6%
Counsel Failed to Pay in Last 5 Years: *Retaining:* 78% *Opposing:* 33%

Washington

Responding Experts: 18

Per-hour Fees

	High	*Low*	*Average*	*Median*
In-court Testimony	$750	$100	$319	$275
File Review/Prep	$400	$94	$204	$163
Depositions	$700	$94	$289	$240

Depositions

Min. Charge for Deps: 56% **Hours in Minimum:** *High:* 5 *Low:* 1 *Average:* 1.9 *Median:* 2
Cancellation Fee for Deps or Trial: 50% **Deposition Payment in Advance:** 28%
Exceeding Paid-for Time: *Get payment before proceeding:* 0% *Proceed without immediate payment:* 100%

Retainers

Required: 67% **Amounts:** *High:* $2,500 *Low:* $500 *Average:* $1,223 *Median:* $1,000

Expenses

Out-of-Pocket Expenses Marked Up: 24% **Out-of-Pockets Billed for:** *Mileage:* 67% *Airline Tickets:* 67% *Photocopies:* 61% *Telephone Calls:* 61% *Lab/Testing:* 44% *Photos:* 39% *Demonstrative Aids:* 50%
Travel Billed Portal-to-Portal: 89% **1st-class Airfare Required:** 6%

Fee Agreement

Require Signed Written Fee Agreement: 29% **Terms:** *Lawyer is responsible for fee, not lawyer's client:* 80% *Interest for delinquent accounts:* 60% *Out-of-pocket expense policies:* 80% *Retainer/prepayment requirements:* 100% *In-court testimony minimum fees:* 60% *Retaining counsel will pay for all deposition charges:* 0% *Fee schedules:* 80% *Attorney's fees if forced to sue for collection:* 20% *Portal-to-portal travel time:* 20% *Deposition minimum fees:* 40% *Payment for preparation time:* 40% *First-class air travel:* 0%

Majority of Work: *Plaintiffs:* 17% *Neither:* 61% *Defendants:* 22%
Counsel Failed to Pay in Last 5 Years: *Retaining:* 28% *Opposing:* 33%

West Virginia

Responding Experts: 6

Per-hour Fees

	High	*Low*	*Average*	*Median*
In-court Testimony	$600	$125	$310	$250
File Review/Prep	$450	$125	$252	$225
Depositions	$450	$125	$260	$250

Depositions

Min. Charge for Deps: 50% **Hours in Minimum:** *High:* 5 *Low:* 2 *Average:* 3.3 *Median:* 3
Cancellation Fee for Deps or Trial: 17% **Deposition Payment in Advance:** 33%
Exceeding Paid-for Time: *Get payment before proceeding:* 0% *Proceed without immediate payment:* 100%

Retainers

Required: 67% **Amounts:** *High:* $2,000 *Low:* $500 *Average:* $1,038 *Median:* $825

Expenses

Out-of-Pocket Expenses Marked Up: 0% **Out-of-Pockets Billed for:** *Mileage:* 50% *Airline Tickets:* 100% *Photocopies:* 67% *Telephone Calls:* 50% *Lab/Testing:* 83% *Photos:* 83% *Demonstrative Aids:* 83%
Travel Billed Portal-to-Portal: 83% **1st-class Airfare Required:** 0%

Fee Agreement

Require Signed Written Fee Agreement: 17% **Terms:** *Lawyer is responsible for fee, not lawyer's client:* 100% *Interest for delinquent accounts:* 100% *Out-of-pocket expense policies:* 100% *Retainer/prepayment requirements:* 100% *In-court testimony minimum fees:* 100% *Retaining counsel will pay for all deposition charges:* 100% *Fee schedules:* 100% *Attorney's fees if forced to sue for collection:* 100% *Portal-to-portal travel time:* 0% *Deposition minimum fees:* 100% *Payment for preparation time:* 100% *First-class air travel:* 0%

Majority of Work: *Plaintiffs:* 33% *Neither:* 33% *Defendants:* 33%
Counsel Failed to Pay in Last 5 Years: *Retaining:* 33% *Opposing:* 17%

Wisconsin

Responding Experts: 12

Per-hour Fees

	High	*Low*	*Average*	*Median*
In-court Testimony	$1,500	$145	$477	$388
File Review/Prep	$400	$85	$262	$275
Depositions	$1,000	$145	$418	$388

Depositions

Min. Charge for Deps: 58% **Hours in Minimum:** *High:* 4 *Low:* 1 *Average:* 2.4 *Median:* 2
Cancellation Fee for Deps or Trial: 33% **Deposition Payment in Advance:** 27%
Exceeding Paid-for Time: *Get payment before proceeding:* 0% *Proceed without immediate payment:* 100%

Retainers

Required: 50% **Amounts:** *High:* $1,000 *Low:* $350 *Average:* $890 *Median:* $1,000

Expenses

Out-of-Pocket Expenses Marked Up: 9% **Out-of-Pockets Billed for:** *Mileage:* 83% *Airline Tickets:* 75% *Photocopies:* 33% *Telephone Calls:* 25% *Lab/Testing:* 25% *Photos:* 33% *Demonstrative Aids:* 25%
Travel Billed Portal-to-Portal: 83% **1st-class Airfare Required:** 8%

Fee Agreement

Require Signed Written Fee Agreement: 17% **Terms:** *Lawyer is responsible for fee, not lawyer's client:* 100% *Interest for delinquent accounts:* 50% *Out-of-pocket expense policies:* 50% *Retainer/prepayment requirements:* 100% *In-court testimony minimum fees:* 100% *Retaining counsel will pay for all deposition charges:* 100% *Fee schedules:* 100% *Attorney's fees if forced to sue for collection:* 0% *Portal-to-portal travel time:* 100% *Deposition minimum fees:* 50% *Payment for preparation time:* 100% *First-class air travel:* 0%

Majority of Work: *Plaintiffs:* 8% *Neither:* 42% *Defendants:* 50%
Counsel Failed to Pay in Last 5 Years: *Retaining:* 17% *Opposing:* 25%

Wyoming

Responding Experts: 2

Per-hour Fees

	High	*Low*	*Average*	*Median*
In-court Testimony	$400	$400	$400	$400
File Review/Prep	$400	$400	$400	$400
Depositions	$400	$400	$400	$400

Depositions

Min. Charge for Deps: 100% **Hours in Minimum:** *High:* 2 *Low:* 1 *Average:* 1.5 *Median:* 1.5
Cancellation Fee for Deps or Trial: 100% **Deposition Payment in Advance:** 100%
Exceeding Paid-for Time: *Get payment before proceeding:* 0% *Proceed without immediate payment:* 100%

Retainers

Required: 100% **Amounts:** *High:* $800 *Low:* $400 *Average:* $600 *Median:* $600

Expenses

Out-of-Pocket Expenses Marked Up: 50% **Out-of-Pockets Billed for:** *Mileage:* 100% *Airline Tickets:* 50% *Photocopies:* 50% *Telephone Calls:* 50% *Lab/Testing:* 50% *Photos:* 50% *Demonstrative Aids:* 50%
Travel Billed Portal-to-Portal: 100% **1st-class Airfare Required:** 50%

Fee Agreement

Require Signed Written Fee Agreement: 50% **Terms:** *Lawyer is responsible for fee, not lawyer's client:* 100% *Interest for delinquent accounts:* 100% *Out-of-pocket expense policies:* 100% *Retainer/prepayment requirements:* 100% *In-court testimony minimum fees:* 0% *Retaining counsel will pay for all deposition charges:* 100% *Fee schedules:* 100% *Attorney's fees if forced to sue for collection:* 100% *Portal-to-portal travel time:* 100% *Deposition minimum fees:* 100% *Payment for preparation time:* 100% *First-class air travel:* 100%

Majority of Work: *Plaintiffs:* 0% *Neither:* 100% *Defendants:* 0%
Counsel Failed to Pay in Last 5 Years: *Retaining:* 0% *Opposing:* 0%

Chapter 4 Summary of Expert Fees and Billings by Area of Expertise

Accident Reconstruction, (All)

Responding Experts: *47*

Hourly Fees:					
	In-court Testimony:	*High:* $440	*Low:* $75	*Average:* $210	*Median:* $180
	File Review/Prep:	*High:* $500	*Low:* $75	*Average:* $180	*Median:* $150
	Depositions:	*High:* $400	*Low:* $75	*Average:* $209	*Median:* $178

Percent of Experts Having a Minimum Charge for Deps: 60% **Cancellation Fee for Deps or Trial:** 23%
Deposition Payment in Advance: 45% **Markup of Out-of-Pocket Expenses:** 24%

Up-front Retainer: 81% **Retainer Amount:** *High:* $5,000 *Low:* $300 *Average:* $1,500 *Median:* $1,000
Travel Billed Portal-to-Portal: 89% **1st-class Airfare Required:** 9%

Written Fee Agreement: 76% **Majority of Work:** *Plaintiffs:* 20% *Defendants:* 24% *Neither:* 56%
Retaining Counsel Failed to Pay Last 5 Years: 57% **Opposing Counsel Failed to Pay Last 5 Years:** 33%

Accident Reconstruction, Aircraft

Responding Experts: *1*

Hourly Fees:					
	In-court Testimony:	*High:* $150	*Low:* $150	*Average:* $150	*Median:* $150
	File Review/Prep:	*High:* $150	*Low:* $150	*Average:* $150	*Median:* $150
	Depositions:	*High:* $150	*Low:* $150	*Average:* $150	*Median:* $150

Percent of Experts Having a Minimum Charge for Deps: 0% **Cancellation Fee for Deps or Trial:** 0%
Deposition Payment in Advance: 0% **Markup of Out-of-Pocket Expenses:** 0%

Up-front Retainer: 100% **Retainer Amount:** *High:* $1,500 *Low:* $1,500 *Average:* $1,500 *Median:*$1,500
Travel Billed Portal-to-Portal: 0% **1st-class Airfare Required:** 0%

Written Fee Agreement: 0% **Majority of Work:** *Plaintiffs:* 0% *Defendants:* 0% *Neither:* 100%
Retaining Counsel Failed to Pay Last 5 Years: 0% **Opposing Counsel Failed to Pay Last 5 Years:** 0%

Accident Reconstruction, Collisions

Responding Experts: *1*

Hourly Fees:					
	In-court Testimony:	*High:* $100	*Low:* $100	*Average:* $100	*Median:* $100
	File Review/Prep:	*High:* $75	*Low:* $75	*Average:* $75	*Median:* $75
	Depositions:	*High:* $100	*Low:* $100	*Average:* $100	*Median:* $100

Percent of Experts Having a Minimum Charge for Deps: 0% **Cancellation Fee for Deps or Trial:** 100%
Deposition Payment in Advance: 0% **Markup of Out-of-Pocket Expenses:** 0%

Up-front Retainer: 0% **Retainer Amount:** *High:* N/A *Low:* N/A *Average:* N/A *Median:* N/A
Travel Billed Portal-to-Portal: 100% **1st-class Airfare Required:** N/A

Written Fee Agreement: 100% **Majority of Work:** *Plaintiffs:* 0% *Defendants:* 100% *Neither:* 0%
Retaining Counsel Failed to Pay Last 5 Years: 0% **Opposing Counsel Failed to Pay Last 5 Years:** 0%

Accidents, (All)

Responding Experts: *2*

Hourly Fees:					
	In-court Testimony:	*High:* $300	*Low:* $250	*Average:* $275	*Median:* $275
	File Review/Prep:	*High:* $300	*Low:* $100	*Average:* $200	*Median:* $200
	Depositions:	*High:* $300	*Low:* $150	*Average:* $225	*Median:* $225

Percent of Experts Having a Minimum Charge for Deps: 0% **Cancellation Fee for Deps or Trial:** 0%
Deposition Payment in Advance: 50% **Markup of Out-of-Pocket Expenses:** 0%

Up-front Retainer: 50% **Retainer Amount:** *High:* $1,000 *Low:* $1,000 *Average:* $1,000 *Median:* $1,000
Travel Billed Portal-to-Portal: 100% **1st-class Airfare Required:** 50%

Written Fee Agreement: 0% **Majority of Work:** *Plaintiffs:* 50% *Defendants:* 0% *Neither:* 50%
Retaining Counsel Failed to Pay Last 5 Years: 0% **Opposing Counsel Failed to Pay Last 5 Years:** 0%

Accidents, Chemical

Responding Experts: *1*

Hourly Fees: **In-court Testimony:** *High:* $250 *Low:* $250 *Average:* $250 *Median:* $250
File Review/Prep: *High:* $100 *Low:* $100 *Average:* $100 *Median:* $100
Depositions: *High:* $150 *Low:* $150 *Average:* $150 *Median:* $150

Percent of Experts Having a Minimum Charge for Deps: 0% **Cancellation Fee for Deps or Trial:** 0%
Deposition Payment in Advance: 100% **Markup of Out-of-Pocket Expenses:** 0%

Up-front Retainer: 0% **Retainer Amount:** *High:* N/A *Low:* N/A *Average:* N/A *Median:* N/A
Travel Billed Portal-to-Portal: 100% **1st-class Airfare Required:** 0%

Written Fee Agreement: 0% **Majority of Work:** *Plaintiffs:* 0% *Defendants:* 0% *Neither:* 100%
Retaining Counsel Failed to Pay Last 5 Years: 0% **Opposing Counsel Failed to Pay Last 5 Years:** 0%

Accidents, Industrial

Responding Experts: *1*

Hourly Fees: **In-court Testimony:** *High:* $300 *Low:* $300 *Average:* $300 *Median:* $300
File Review/Prep: *High:* $300 *Low:* $300 *Average:* $300 *Median:* $300
Depositions: *High:* $300 *Low:* $300 *Average:* $300 *Median:* $300

Percent of Experts Having a Minimum Charge for Deps: 0% **Cancellation Fee for Deps or Trial:** 0%
Deposition Payment in Advance: 0% **Markup of Out-of-Pocket Expenses:** 0%

Up-front Retainer: 100% **Retainer Amount:** *High:* $1,000 *Low:* $1,000 *Average:* $1,000 *Median:* $1,000
Travel Billed Portal-to-Portal: 100% **1st-class Airfare Required:** 100%

Written Fee Agreement: 0% **Majority of Work:** *Plaintiffs:* 100% *Defendants*: 0% *Neither:* 0%
Retaining Counsel Failed to Pay Last 5 Years: 0% **Opposing Counsel Failed to Pay Last 5 Years:** 0%

Accounting

Responding Experts: *15*

Hourly Fees: **In-court Testimony:** *High:* $675 *Low:* $85 *Average:* $320 *Median:* $300
File Review/Prep: *High:* $675 *Low:* $85 *Average:* $315 *Median:* $300
Depositions: *High:* $675 *Low:* $85 *Average:* $320 *Median:* $300

Percent of Experts Having a Minimum Charge for Deps: 13% **Cancellation Fee for Deps or Trial:** 0%
Deposition Payment in Advance: 21% **Markup of Out-of-Pocket Expenses:** 7%

Up-front Retainer: 80% **Retainer Amount:** *High:* $10,000 *Low:* $1,500 *Average:* $6,450 *Median:* $6,875
Travel Billed Portal-to-Portal: 93% **1st-class Airfare Required:** 7%

Written Fee Agreement: 53% **Majority of Work:** *Plaintiffs:* 27% *Defendants:* 13% *Neither:* 60%
Retaining Counsel Failed to Pay Last 5 Years: 53% **Opposing Counsel Failed to Pay Last 5 Years:** 0%

Actuary

Responding Experts: *1*

Hourly Fees: **In-court Testimony:** *High:* $415 *Low:* $415 *Average:* $415 *Median:* $415
File Review/Prep: *High:* $415 *Low:* $415 *Average:* $415 *Median:* $415
Depositions: *High:* $425 *Low:* $425 *Average:* $425 *Median:* $425

Percent of Experts Having a Minimum Charge for Deps: 0% **Cancellation Fee for Deps or Trial:** 0%
Deposition Payment in Advance: 0% **Markup of Out-of-Pocket Expenses:** 0%

Up-front Retainer: 0% **Retainer Amount:** *High:* N/A *Low:* N/A *Average:* N/A *Median:* N/A
Travel Billed Portal-to-Portal: 0% **1st-class Airfare Required:** 0%

Written Fee Agreement: 0% **Majority of Work:** *Plaintiffs:* 0% *Defendants:* 0% *Neither:* 100%
Retaining Counsel Failed to Pay Last 5 Years: 0% **Opposing Counsel Failed to Pay Last 5 Years:** 0%

Acupuncture

Responding Experts: *4*

Hourly Fees:

	High	Low	Average	Median
In-court Testimony:	$500	$300	$300	$300
File Review/Prep:	$340	$300	$300	$300
Depositions:	$800	$300	$450	$400

Percent of Experts Having a Minimum Charge for Deps: 100% **Cancellation Fee for Deps or Trial:** 100%
Deposition Payment in Advance: 100% **Markup of Out-of-Pocket Expenses:** 25%

Up-front Retainer: 75% **Retainer Amount:** *High:* $600 *Low:* $600 *Average:* $600 *Median:* $600
Travel Billed Portal-to-Portal: 50% **1st-class Airfare Required:** 0%

Written Fee Agreement: 50% **Majority of Work:** *Plaintiffs:* 0% *Defendants:* 50% *Neither:* 50%
Retaining Counsel Failed to Pay Last 5 Years: 25% **Opposing Counsel Failed to Pay Last 5 Years:** 0%

Addiction Medicine

Responding Experts: *1*

Hourly Fees:

	High	Low	Average	Median
In-court Testimony:	$300	$300	$300	$300
File Review/Prep:	$300	$300	$300	$300
Depositions:	$300	$300	$300	$300

Percent of Experts Having a Minimum Charge for Deps: 0% **Cancellation Fee for Deps or Trial:** 100%
Deposition Payment in Advance: 100% **Markup of Out-of-Pocket Expenses:** 0%

Up-front Retainer: 100% **Retainer Amount:** *High:* $2,000 *Low:* $2,000 *Average:* $2,000 *Median:* $2,000
Travel Billed Portal-to-Portal: 100% **1st-class Airfare Required:** 0%

Written Fee Agreement: 0% **Majority of Work:** *Plaintiffs:* 0% *Defendants:* 100% *Neither:* 0%
Retaining Counsel Failed to Pay Last 5 Years: 100% **Opposing Counsel Failed to Pay Last 5 Years:** 0%

Advertising

Responding Experts: *2*

Hourly Fees:

	High	Low	Average	Median
In-court Testimony:	$400	$350	$375	$375
File Review/Prep:	$400	$350	$375	$375
Depositions:	$400	$350	$375	$375

Percent of Experts Having a Minimum Charge for Deps: 0% **Cancellation Fee for Deps or Trial:** 0%
Deposition Payment in Advance: 0% **Markup of Out-of-Pocket Expenses:** 0%

Up-front Retainer: 50% **Retainer Amount:** *High:* $8,000 *Low:* $8,000 *Average:* $8,000 *Median:* $8,000
Travel Billed Portal-to-Portal: 50% **1st-class Airfare Required:** 50%

Written Fee Agreement: 0% **Majority of Work:** *Plaintiffs:* 0% *Defendants:* 0% *Neither:* 100%
Retaining Counsel Failed to Pay Last 5 Years: 0% **Opposing Counsel Failed to Pay Last 5 Years:** 50%

Air Quality

Responding Experts: *2*

Hourly Fees:

	High	Low	Average	Median
In-court Testimony:	$300	$150	$225	$225
File Review/Prep:	$300	$125	$213	$213
Depositions:	$300	$150	$225	$213

Percent of Experts Having a Minimum Charge for Deps: 0% **Cancellation Fee for Deps or Trial:** 0%
Deposition Payment in Advance: 100% **Markup of Out-of-Pocket Expenses:** 0%

Up-front Retainer: 0% **Retainer Amount:** *High:* N/A *Low:* N/A *Average:* N/A *Median:* N/A
Travel Billed Portal-to-Portal: 50% **1st-class Airfare Required:** 0%

Written Fee Agreement: 100% **Majority of Work:** *Plaintiffs:* 0% *Defendants:* 100% *Neither:* 0%
Retaining Counsel Failed to Pay Last 5 Years: 50% **Opposing Counsel Failed to Pay Last 5 Years:** 50%

Alcoholism

Responding Experts: *1*

Hourly Fees:

	High	*Low*	*Average*	*Median*
In-court Testimony:	$350	$350	$350	$350
File Review/Prep:	$150	$150	$150	$150
Depositions:	$175	$175	$175	$175

Percent of Experts Having a Minimum Charge for Deps: 100% **Cancellation Fee for Deps or Trial:** 100%
Deposition Payment in Advance: 0% **Markup of Out-of-Pocket Expenses:** 100%

Up-front Retainer: 100% **Retainer Amount:** *High:* $3,000 *Low:* $3,000 *Average:* $3,000 *Median:* $3,000
Travel Billed Portal-to-Portal: 100% **1st-class Airfare Required:** 0%

Written Fee Agreement: 100% **Majority of Work:** *Plaintiffs:* 0% *Defendants:* 0% *Neither:* 100%
Retaining Counsel Failed to Pay Last 5 Years: 0% **Opposing Counsel Failed to Pay Last 5 Years:** 100%

Allergy

Responding Experts: *2*

Hourly Fees:

	High	*Low*	*Average*	*Median*
In-court Testimony:	$500	$350	$425	$425
File Review/Prep:	$350	$300	$325	$325
Depositions:	$500	$350	$425	$425

Percent of Experts Having a Minimum Charge for Deps: 0% **Cancellation Fee for Deps or Trial:** 100%
Deposition Payment in Advance: 50% **Markup of Out-of-Pocket Expenses:** 0%

Up-front Retainer: 50% **Retainer Amount:** *High:* $1,000 *Low:* $1,000 *Average:* $1,000 *Median:* $1,000
Travel Billed Portal-to-Portal: 100% **1st-class Airfare Required:** 0%

Written Fee Agreement: 100% **Majority of Work:** *Plaintiffs:* 0% *Defendants:* 50% *Neither:* 50%
Retaining Counsel Failed to Pay Last 5 Years: 50% **Opposing Counsel Failed to Pay Last 5 Years:** 50%

Anesthesiology

Responding Experts: *8*

Hourly Fees:

	High	*Low*	*Average*	*Median*
In-court Testimony:	$1,000	$300	$580	$550
File Review/Prep:	$500	$275	$350	$325
Depositions:	$700	$300	$465	$450

Percent of Experts Having a Minimum Charge for Deps: 50% **Cancellation Fee for Deps or Trial:** 50%
Deposition Payment in Advance: 63% **Markup of Out-of-Pocket Expenses:** 0%

Up-front Retainer: 75% **Retainer Amount:** *High:* $3,500 *Low:* $750 *Average:* $1,500 *Median:* $1,150
Travel Billed Portal-to-Portal: 75% **1st-class Airfare Required:** 0%

Written Fee Agreement: 100% **Majority of Work:** *Plaintiffs:* 25% *Defendants:* 25% *Neither:* 50%
Retaining Counsel Failed to Pay Last 5 Years: 30% **Opposing Counsel Failed to Pay Last 5 Years:** 15%

Animation

Responding Experts: *1*

Hourly Fees:

	High	*Low*	*Average*	*Median*
In-court Testimony:	$225	$225	$225	$225
File Review/Prep:	$175	$175	$175	$175
Depositions:	$225	$225	$225	$225

Percent of Experts Having a Minimum Charge for Deps: 100% **Cancellation Fee for Deps or Trial:** 100%
Deposition Payment in Advance: 100% **Markup of Out-of-Pocket Expenses:** 100%

Up-front Retainer: 100% **Retainer Amount:** *High:* $3,000 *Low:* $3,000 *Average:* $3,000 *Median:* $3,000
Travel Billed Portal-to-Portal: 0% **1st-class Airfare Required:** 0%

Written Fee Agreement: 100% **Majority of Work:** *Plaintiffs:* 0% *Defendants:* 100% *Neither:* 0%
Retaining Counsel Failed to Pay Last 5 Years: 100% **Opposing Counsel Failed to Pay Last 5 Years:** 0%

Annuitist

Responding Experts: *1*

Hourly Fees: **In-court Testimony:** *High:* $275 *Low:* $275 *Average:* $275 *Median:* $275
File Review/Prep: *High:* $275 *Low:* $275 *Average:* $275 *Median:* $275
Depositions: *High:* $275 *Low:* $275 *Average:* $275 *Median:* $275
Percent of Experts Having a Minimum Charge for Deps: 100% **Cancellation Fee for Deps or Trial:** 0%
Deposition Payment in Advance: 0% **Markup of Out-of-Pocket Expenses:** 0%

Up-front Retainer: 0% **Retainer Amount:** *High:* N/A *Low:* N/A *Average:* N/A *Median:* N/A
Travel Billed Portal-to-Portal: 100% **1st-class Airfare Required:** 0%

Written Fee Agreement: 0% **Majority of Work:** *Plaintiffs:* 0% *Defendants:* 100% *Neither:* 0%
Retaining Counsel Failed to Pay Last 5 Years: 0% **Opposing Counsel Failed to Pay Last 5 Years:** 0%

Appraisal, (All)

Responding Experts: *20*

Hourly Fees: **In-court Testimony:** *High:* $500 *Low:* $100 *Average:* $240 *Median:* $200
File Review/Prep: *High:* $300 *Low:* $65 *Average:* $190 *Median:* $200
Depositions: *High:* $350 *Low:* $100 *Average:* $222 *Median:* $200
Percent of Experts Having a Minimum Charge for Deps: 68% **Cancellation Fee for Deps or Trial:** 41%
Deposition Payment in Advance: 50% **Markup of Out-of-Pocket Expenses:** 10%

Up-front Retainer: 84% **Retainer Amount:** *High:* $3,000 *Low:* $350 *Average:* $1,300 *Median:* $1,000
Travel Billed Portal-to-Portal: 94% **1st-class Airfare Required:** 16%

Written Fee Agreement: 58% **Majority of Work:** *Plaintiffs:* 11% *Defendants:* 16% *Neither:* 73%
Retaining Counsel Failed to Pay Last 5 Years: 40% **Opposing Counsel Failed to Pay Last 5 Years:** 10%

Appraisal, Art

Responding Experts: *2*

Hourly Fees: **In-court Testimony:** *High:* $350 *Low:* $300 *Average:* $325 *Median:* $325
File Review/Prep: *High:* $250 *Low:* $240 *Average:* $245 *Median:* $245
Depositions: *High:* $350 *Low:* $275 *Average:* $313 *Median:* $313
Percent of Experts Having a Minimum Charge for Deps: 100% **Cancellation Fee for Deps or Trial:** 100%
Deposition Payment in Advance: 100% **Markup of Out-of-Pocket Expenses:** 0%

Up-front Retainer: 100% **Retainer Amount:** *High:* $3,000 *Low:* $1,000 *Average:* $2,000 *Median:* $2,000
Travel Billed Portal-to-Portal: 100% **1st-class Airfare Required:** 50%

Written Fee Agreement: 100% **Majority of Work:** *Plaintiffs:* 0% *Defendants:* 0% *Neither:* 100%
Retaining Counsel Failed to Pay Last 5 Years: 100% **Opposing Counsel Failed to Pay Last 5 Years:** 0%

Appraisal, Coin

Responding Experts: *1*

Hourly Fees: **In-court Testimony:** *High:* $240 *Low:* $240 *Average:* $240 *Median:* $240
File Review/Prep: *High:* $240 *Low:* $240 *Average:* $240 *Median:* $240
Depositions: *High:* $240 *Low:* $240 *Average:* $240 *Median:* $240
Percent of Experts Having a Minimum Charge for Deps: 100% **Cancellation Fee for Deps or Trial:** N/A
Deposition Payment in Advance: 100% **Markup of Out-of-Pocket Expenses:** 0%

Up-front Retainer: 100% **Retainer Amount:** *High:* N/A *Low:* N/A *Average:* N/A *Median:* N/A
Travel Billed Portal-to-Portal: 100% **1st-class Airfare Required:** 100%

Written Fee Agreement: 100% **Majority of Work:** *Plaintiffs:* 0% *Defendants:* 0% *Neither:* 100%
Retaining Counsel Failed to Pay Last 5 Years: 100% **Opposing Counsel Failed to Pay Last 5 Years:** 0%

Appraisal, Equipment

Responding Experts: *1*

Hourly Fees: **In-court Testimony:** *High:* $200 *Low:* $200 *Average:* $200 *Median:* $200
File Review/Prep: *High:* $100 *Low:* $100 *Average:* $100 *Median:* $100
Depositions: *High:* $200 *Low:* $200 *Average:* $200 *Median:* $200

Percent of Experts Having a Minimum Charge for Deps: 100% **Cancellation Fee for Deps or Trial:** 100%
Deposition Payment in Advance: 0% **Markup of Out-of-Pocket Expenses:** 0%

Up-front Retainer: 100% **Retainer Amount:** *High:* $350 *Low:* $350 *Average:* $350 *Median:* $350
Travel Billed Portal-to-Portal: 100% **1st-class Airfare Required:** 0%

Written Fee Agreement: 0% **Majority of Work:** *Plaintiffs:* 100% *Defendants:* 0% *Neither:* 0%
Retaining Counsel Failed to Pay Last 5 Years: 0% **Opposing Counsel Failed to Pay Last 5 Years:** 0%

Appraisal, Gem & Jewelry

Responding Experts: *4*

Hourly Fees: **In-court Testimony:** *High:* $400 *Low:* $200 *Average:* $260 *Median:* $220
File Review/Prep: *High:* $250 *Low:* $150 *Average:* $200 *Median:* $195
Depositions: *High:* $350 *Low:* $240 *Average:* $250 *Median:* $220

Percent of Experts Having a Minimum Charge for Deps: 50% **Cancellation Fee for Deps or Trial:** 35%
Deposition Payment in Advance: 75% **Markup of Out-of-Pocket Expenses:** 0%

Up-front Retainer: 100% **Retainer Amount:** *High:* $1,500 *Low:* $1,500 *Average:* $1,500 *Median:* $1,500
Travel Billed Portal-to-Portal: 100% **1st-class Airfare Required:** 25%

Written Fee Agreement: 35% **Majority of Work:** *Plaintiffs:* 0% *Defendants:* 0% *Neither:* 100%
Retaining Counsel Failed to Pay Last 5 Years: 25% **Opposing Counsel Failed to Pay Last 5 Years:** 0%

Appraisal, Industrial

Responding Experts: *1*

Hourly Fees: **In-court Testimony:** *High:* $150 *Low:* $150 *Average:* $150 *Median:* $150
File Review/Prep: *High:* $150 *Low:* $150 *Average:* $150 *Median:* $150
Depositions: *High:* $150 *Low:* $150 *Average:* $150 *Median:* $150

Percent of Experts Having a Minimum Charge for Deps: 100% **Cancellation Fee for Deps or Trial:** 100%
Deposition Payment in Advance: 100% **Markup of Out-of-Pocket Expenses:** 100%

Up-front Retainer: 100% **Retainer Amount:** *High:* $500 *Low:* $500 *Average:* $500 *Median:* $500
Travel Billed Portal-to-Portal: 100% **1st-class Airfare Required:** 0%

Written Fee Agreement: 0% **Majority of Work:** *Plaintiffs:* N/A *Defendants:* N/A *Neither:* N/A
Retaining Counsel Failed to Pay Last 5 Years: 0% **Opposing Counsel Failed to Pay Last 5 Years:** 0%

Appraisal, Machinery & Equipment

Responding Experts: *1*

Hourly Fees: **In-court Testimony:** *High:* $300 *Low:* $300 *Average:* $300 *Median:* $300
File Review/Prep: *High:* $200 *Low:* $200 *Average:* $200 *Median:* $200
Depositions: *High:* $300 *Low:* $300 *Average:* $300 *Median:* $300

Percent of Experts Having a Minimum Charge for Deps: 0% **Cancellation Fee for Deps or Trial:** 0%
Deposition Payment in Advance: 0% **Markup of Out-of-Pocket Expenses:** 0%

Up-front Retainer: 0% **Retainer Amount:** *High:* N/A *Low:* N/A *Average:* N/A *Median:* N/A
Travel Billed Portal-to-Portal: 0% **1st-class Airfare Required:** 0%

Written Fee Agreement: 0% **Majority of Work:** *Plaintiffs:* 0% *Defendants:* 100% *Neither:* 0%
Retaining Counsel Failed to Pay Last 5 Years: 100% **Opposing Counsel Failed to Pay Last 5 Years:** 100%

Appraisal, Marine

Responding Experts: *1*

Hourly Fees:

	High	Low	Average	Median
In-court Testimony:	$125	$125	$125	$125
File Review/Prep:	$100	$100	$100	$100
Depositions:	$125	$125	$125	$125

Percent of Experts Having a Minimum Charge for Deps: 0% **Cancellation Fee for Deps or Trial:** 0%
Deposition Payment in Advance: 100% **Markup of Out-of-Pocket Expenses:** 0%

Up-front Retainer: 100% **Retainer Amount:** *High:* $1,000 *Low:* $1,000 *Average:* $1,000 *Median:* $1,000
Travel Billed Portal-to-Portal: 100% **1st-class Airfare Required:** 0%

Written Fee Agreement: 100% **Majority of Work:** *Plaintiffs:* 0% *Defendants:* 0% *Neither:* 100%
Retaining Counsel Failed to Pay Last 5 Years: 0% **Opposing Counsel Failed to Pay Last 5 Years:** 0%

Appraisal, Real Estate

Responding Experts: *7*

Hourly Fees:

	High	Low	Average	Median
In-court Testimony:	$500	$100	$225	$175
File Review/Prep:	$300	$65	$180	$190
Depositions:	$300	$100	$195	$175

Percent of Experts Having a Minimum Charge for Deps: 57% **Cancellation Fee for Deps or Trial:** 15%
Deposition Payment in Advance: 15% **Markup of Out-of-Pocket Expenses:** 0%

Up-front Retainer: 71% **Retainer Amount:** *High:* $500 *Low:* $500 *Average:* $500 *Median:* $500
Travel Billed Portal-to-Portal: 100% **1st-class Airfare Required:** 100%

Written Fee Agreement: 57% **Majority of Work:** *Plaintiffs:* 14% *Defendants:* 29% *Neither:* 57%
Retaining Counsel Failed to Pay Last 5 Years: 29% **Opposing Counsel Failed to Pay Last 5 Years:** 14%

Arborist

Responding Experts: *1*

Hourly Fees:

	High	Low	Average	Median
In-court Testimony:	$110	$110	$110	$110
File Review/Prep:	N/A	N/A	N/A	N/A
Depositions:	$350	$350	$350	$350

Percent of Experts Having a Minimum Charge for Deps: 100% **Cancellation Fee for Deps or Trial:** 100%
Deposition Payment in Advance: 100% **Markup of Out-of-Pocket Expenses:** 100%

Up-front Retainer: 100% **Retainer Amount:** *High:* $650 *Low:* $650 *Average:* $650 *Median:* $650
Travel Billed Portal-to-Portal: 100% **1st-class Airfare Required:** 0%

Written Fee Agreement: 100% **Majority of Work:** *Plaintiffs:* 0% *Defendants:* 0% *Neither:* 100%
Retaining Counsel Failed to Pay Last 5 Years: 0% **Opposing Counsel Failed to Pay Last 5 Years:** 0%

Architecture

Responding Experts: *9*

Hourly Fees:

	High	Low	Average	Median
In-court Testimony:	$500	$200	$310	$300
File Review/Prep:	$250	$150	$200	$200
Depositions:	$500	$200	$305	$285

Percent of Experts Having a Minimum Charge for Deps: 20% **Cancellation Fee for Deps or Trial:** 0%
Deposition Payment in Advance: 30% **Markup of Out-of-Pocket Expenses:** 45%

Up-front Retainer: 90% **Retainer Amount:** *High:* $3,000 *Low:* $500 *Average:* $1,750 *Median:* $1,625
Travel Billed Portal-to-Portal: 100% **1st-class Airfare Required:** 0%

Written Fee Agreement: 100% **Majority of Work:** *Plaintiffs:* 11% *Defendants:* 33% *Neither:* 56%
Retaining Counsel Failed to Pay Last 5 Years: 78% **Opposing Counsel Failed to Pay Last 5 Years:** 38%

Asthma

Responding Experts: *1*

Hourly Fees: **In-court Testimony:** *High:* $500 *Low:* $500 *Average:* $500 *Median:* $500
File Review/Prep: *High:* $300 *Low:* $300 *Average:* $300 *Median:* $300
Depositions: *High:* $500 *Low:* $500 *Average:* $500 *Median:* $500

Percent of Experts Having a Minimum Charge for Deps: 0% **Cancellation Fee for Deps or Trial:** 100%
Deposition Payment in Advance: 100% **Markup of Out-of-Pocket Expenses:** 0%

Up-front Retainer: 100% **Retainer Amount:** *High:* $1,000 *Low:* $1,000 *Average:* $1,000 *Median:* $1,000
Travel Billed Portal-to-Portal: 100% **1st-class Airfare Required:** 0%

Written Fee Agreement: 100% **Majority of Work:** *Plaintiffs:* 0% *Defendants:* 100% *Neither:* 0%
Retaining Counsel Failed to Pay Last 5 Years: 0% **Opposing Counsel Failed to Pay Last 5 Years:** 0%

Attachments

Responding Experts: *1*

Hourly Fees: **In-court Testimony:** *High:* $175 *Low:* $175 *Average:* $175 *Median:* $175
File Review/Prep: *High:* $175 *Low:* $175 *Average:* $175 *Median:* $175
Depositions: *High:* $175 *Low:* $175 *Average:* $175 *Median:* $175

Percent of Experts Having a Minimum Charge for Deps: 0% **Cancellation Fee for Deps or Trial:** 100%
Deposition Payment in Advance: 0% **Markup of Out-of-Pocket Expenses:** 100%

Up-front Retainer: 100% **Retainer Amount:** *High:* $850 *Low:* $850 *Average:* $850 *Median:* $850
Travel Billed Portal-to-Portal: 100% **1st-class Airfare Required:** 0%

Written Fee Agreement: 100% **Majority of Work:** *Plaintiffs:* 0% *Defendants:* 0% *Neither:* 100%
Retaining Counsel Failed to Pay Last 5 Years: 0% **Opposing Counsel Failed to Pay Last 5 Years:** 0%

Automotive, (All)

Responding Experts: *7*

Hourly Fees: **In-court Testimony:** *High:* $500 *Low:* $150 *Average:* $330 *Median:* $300
File Review/Prep: *High:* $450 *Low:* $150 *Average:* $270 *Median:* $250
Depositions: *High:* $500 *Low:* $150 *Average:* $330 *Median:* $300

Percent of Experts Having a Minimum Charge for Deps: 43% **Cancellation Fee for Deps or Trial:** 30%
Deposition Payment in Advance: 15% **Markup of Out-of-Pocket Expenses:** 57%

Up-front Retainer: 100% **Retainer Amount:** *High:* $5,000 *Low:* $750 *Average:* $3,075 *Median:* $3,000
Travel Billed Portal-to-Portal: 88% **1st-class Airfare Required:** 43%

Written Fee Agreement: 71% **Majority of Work:** *Plaintiffs:* 29% *Defendants:* 29% *Neither:* 43%
Retaining Counsel Failed to Pay Last 5 Years: 57% **Opposing Counsel Failed to Pay Last 5 Years:** 43%

Automotive, Collisions

Responding Experts: *1*

Hourly Fees: **In-court Testimony:** *High:* $150 *Low:* $150 *Average:* $150 *Median:* $150
File Review/Prep: *High:* $150 *Low:* $150 *Average:* $150 *Median:* $150
Depositions: *High:* $150 *Low:* $150 *Average:* $150 *Median:* $150

Percent of Experts Having a Minimum Charge for Deps: 100% **Cancellation Fee for Deps or Trial:** 0%
Deposition Payment in Advance: 0% **Markup of Out-of-Pocket Expenses:** 100%

Up-front Retainer: 100% **Retainer Amount:** *High:* $750 *Low:* $750 *Average:* $750 *Median:* $750
Travel Billed Portal-to-Portal: 100% **1st-class Airfare Required:** 0%

Written Fee Agreement: 100% **Majority of Work:** *Plaintiffs:* 100% *Defendants:* 0% *Neither:* 0%
Retaining Counsel Failed to Pay Last 5 Years: 100% **Opposing Counsel Failed to Pay Last 5 Years:** 100%

Automotive, Tires

Responding Experts: *1*

Hourly Fees: **In-court Testimony:** *High:* $450 *Low:* $450 *Average:* $450 *Median:* $450
File Review/Prep: *High:* $450 *Low:* $450 *Average:* $450 *Median:* $450
Depositions: *High:* $450 *Low:* $450 *Average:* $450 *Median:* $450
Percent of Experts Having a Minimum Charge for Deps: 0% **Cancellation Fee for Deps or Trial:** 0%
Deposition Payment in Advance: 0% **Markup of Out-of-Pocket Expenses:** 100%

Up-front Retainer: 100% **Retainer Amount:** *High:* $5,000 *Low:* $5,000 *Average:* $5,000 *Median:* $5,000
Travel Billed Portal-to-Portal: 100% **1st-class Airfare Required:** 100%

Written Fee Agreement: 0% **Majority of Work:** *Plaintiffs:* 0% *Defendants:* 100% *Neither:* 0%
Retaining Counsel Failed to Pay Last 5 Years: 0% **Opposing Counsel Failed to Pay Last 5 Years:** 0%

Aviation, (All)

Responding Experts: *4*

Hourly Fees: **In-court Testimony:** *High:* $150 *Low:* $150 *Average:* $150 *Median:* $150
File Review/Prep: *High:* $150 *Low:* $125 *Average:* $145 *Median:* $150
Depositions: *High:* $150 *Low:* $150 *Average:* $150 *Median:* $150
Percent of Experts Having a Minimum Charge for Deps: 50% **Cancellation Fee for Deps or Trial:** 0%
Deposition Payment in Advance: 0% **Markup of Out-of-Pocket Expenses:** 0%

Up-front Retainer: 0% **Retainer Amount:** *High:* N/A *Low:* N/A *Average:* N/A *Median:* N/A
Travel Billed Portal-to-Portal: 100% **1st-class Airfare Required:** 0%

Written Fee Agreement: 100% **Majority of Work:** *Plaintiffs:* 75% *Defendants:* 25% *Neither:* 0%
Retaining Counsel Failed to Pay Last 5 Years: 0% **Opposing Counsel Failed to Pay Last 5 Years:** 0%

Aviation, Air Traffic Control

Responding Experts: *1*

Hourly Fees: **In-court Testimony:** *High:* $150 *Low:* $150 *Average:* $150 *Median:* $150
File Review/Prep: *High:* $150 *Low:* $150 *Average:* $150 *Median:* $150
Depositions: *High:* $150 *Low:* $150 *Average:* $150 *Median:* $150
Percent of Experts Having a Minimum Charge for Deps: 100% **Cancellation Fee for Deps or Trial:** 0%
Deposition Payment in Advance: 0% **Markup of Out-of-Pocket Expenses:** 0%

Up-front Retainer: 0% **Retainer Amount:** *High:* N/A *Low:* N/A *Average:* N/A *Median:* N/A
Travel Billed Portal-to-Portal: 100% **1st-class Airfare Required:** 0%

Written Fee Agreement: 100% **Majority of Work:** *Plaintiffs:* 100% *Defendants:* 0% *Neither:* 0%
Retaining Counsel Failed to Pay Last 5 Years: 0% **Opposing Counsel Failed to Pay Last 5 Years:** 0%

Banking

Responding Experts: *4*

Hourly Fees: **In-court Testimony:** *High:* $500 *Low:* $170 *Average:* $355 *Median:* $375
File Review/Prep: *High:* $350 *Low:* $170 *Average:* $240 *Median:* $215
Depositions: *High:* $450 *Low:* $170 *Average:* $320 *Median:* $325
Percent of Experts Having a Minimum Charge for Deps: 50% **Cancellation Fee for Deps or Trial:** 0%
Deposition Payment in Advance: 0% **Markup of Out-of-Pocket Expenses:** 0%

Up-front Retainer: 100% **Retainer Amount:** *High:* $5,000 *Low:* $2,500 *Average:* $3,500 *Median:* $3,000
Travel Billed Portal-to-Portal: 75% **1st-class Airfare Required:** 0%

Written Fee Agreement: 75% **Majority of Work:** *Plaintiffs:* 25% *Defendants:* 0% *Neither:* 75%
Retaining Counsel Failed to Pay Last 5 Years: 50% **Opposing Counsel Failed to Pay Last 5 Years:** 50%

Biomechanics

Responding Experts: *4*

Hourly Fees: **In-court Testimony:** *High:* $400 *Low:* $150 *Average:* $250 *Median:* $230
File Review/Prep: *High:* $400 *Low:* $150 *Average:* $240 *Median:* $205
Depositions: *High:* $400 *Low:* $150 *Average:* $250 *Median:* $230
Percent of Experts Having a Minimum Charge for Deps: 50% **Cancellation Fee for Deps or Trial:** 75%
Deposition Payment in Advance: 75% **Markup of Out-of-Pocket Expenses:** 50%

Up-front Retainer: 100% **Retainer Amount:** *High:* $3,500 *Low:* $750 *Average:* $2,315 *Median:* $2,500
Travel Billed Portal-to-Portal: 75% **1st-class Airfare Required:** 0%

Written Fee Agreement: 100% **Majority of Work:** *Plaintiffs:* 0% *Defendants:* 50% *Neither:* 50%
Retaining Counsel Failed to Pay Last 5 Years: 50% **Opposing Counsel Failed to Pay Last 5 Years:** 25%

Biomedical, (All)

Responding Experts: *5*

Hourly Fees: **In-court Testimony:** *High:* $350 *Low:* $300 *Average:* $320 *Median:* $300
File Review/Prep: *High:* $350 *Low:* $200 *Average:* $260 *Median:* $250
Depositions: *High:* $350 *Low:* $200 *Average:* $290 *Median:* $300
Percent of Experts Having a Minimum Charge for Deps: 80% **Cancellation Fee for Deps or Trial:** 20%
Deposition Payment in Advance: 40% **Markup of Out-of-Pocket Expenses:** 20%

Up-front Retainer: 80% **Retainer Amount:** *High:* $2,500 *Low:* $500 *Average:* $1,670 *Median:* $2,000
Travel Billed Portal-to-Portal: 80% **1st-class Airfare Required:** 0%

Written Fee Agreement: 80% **Majority of Work:** *Plaintiffs:* 0% *Defendants:* 40% *Neither:* 60%
Retaining Counsel Failed to Pay Last 5 Years: 40% **Opposing Counsel Failed to Pay Last 5 Years:** 0%

Biomedical, Biotechnology

Responding Experts: *3*

Hourly Fees: **In-court Testimony:** *High:* $350 *Low:* $300 *Average:* $320 *Median:* $300
File Review/Prep: *High:* $250 *Low:* $200 *Average:* $235 *Median:* $250
Depositions: *High:* $350 *Low:* $200 *Average:* $285 *Median:* $300
Percent of Experts Having a Minimum Charge for Deps: 66% **Cancellation Fee for Deps or Trial:** 0%
Deposition Payment in Advance: 66% **Markup of Out-of-Pocket Expenses:** 33%

Up-front Retainer: 100% **Retainer Amount:** *High:* $2,000 *Low:* $500 *Average:* $1,250 *Median:* $1,250
Travel Billed Portal-to-Portal: 66% **1st-class Airfare Required:** 0%

Written Fee Agreement: 66% **Majority of Work:** *Plaintiffs:* 0% *Defendants:* 66% *Neither:* 33%
Retaining Counsel Failed to Pay Last 5 Years: 66% **Opposing Counsel Failed to Pay Last 5 Years:** 0%

Cardiology, (All)

Responding Experts: *8*

Hourly Fees: **In-court Testimony:** *High:* $500 *Low:* $375 *Average:* $430 *Median:* $400
File Review/Prep: *High:* $400 *Low:* $275 *Average:* $335 *Median:* $340
Depositions: *High:* $500 *Low:* $350 *Average:* $425 *Median:* $400
Percent of Experts Having a Minimum Charge for Deps: 50% **Cancellation Fee for Deps or Trial:** 50%
Deposition Payment in Advance: 13% **Markup of Out-of-Pocket Expenses:** 50%

Up-front Retainer: 50% **Retainer Amount:** *High:* $1,500 *Low:* $900 *Average:* $1,135 *Median:* $1,000
Travel Billed Portal-to-Portal: 63% **1st-class Airfare Required:** 0%

Written Fee Agreement: 75% **Majority of Work:** *Plaintiffs:* 25% *Defendants:* 25% *Neither:* 50%
Retaining Counsel Failed to Pay Last 5 Years: 38% **Opposing Counsel Failed to Pay Last 5 Years:** 0%

Cardiology, Pediatric

Responding Experts: *1*

Hourly Fees: **In-court Testimony:** *High:* $400 *Low:* $400 *Average:* $400 *Median:* $400
File Review/Prep: *High:* $375 *Low:* $375 *Average:* $375 *Median:* $375
Depositions: *High:* $400 *Low:* $400 *Average:* $400 *Median:* $400
Percent of Experts Having a Minimum Charge for Deps: 0% **Cancellation Fee for Deps or Trial:** 100%
Deposition Payment in Advance: 100% **Markup of Out-of-Pocket Expenses:** 0%

Up-front Retainer: 100% **Retainer Amount:** *High:* N/A *Low:* N/A *Average:* N/A *Median:* N/A
Travel Billed Portal-to-Portal: 100% **1st-class Airfare Required:** 0%

Written Fee Agreement: 0% **Majority of Work:** *Plaintiffs:* 100% *Defendants:* 0% *Neither:* 0%
Retaining Counsel Failed to Pay Last 5 Years: 0% **Opposing Counsel Failed to Pay Last 5 Years:** 0%

Cement

Responding Experts: *1*

Hourly Fees: **In-court Testimony:** *High:* $175 *Low:* $175 *Average:* $175 *Median:* $175
File Review/Prep: *High:* $150 *Low:* $150 *Average:* $150 *Median:* $150
Depositions: *High:* $175 *Low:* $175 *Average:* $175 *Median:* $175
Percent of Experts Having a Minimum Charge for Deps: 100% **Cancellation Fee for Deps or Trial:** 0%
Deposition Payment in Advance: 0% **Markup of Out-of-Pocket Expenses:** 100%

Up-front Retainer: 100% **Retainer Amount:** *High:* N/A *Low:* N/A *Average:* N/A *Median:* N/A
Travel Billed Portal-to-Portal: 100% **1st-class Airfare Required:** 0%

Written Fee Agreement: 100% **Majority of Work:** *Plaintiffs:* 0% *Defendants:* 0% *Neither:* 100%
Retaining Counsel Failed to Pay Last 5 Years: 100% **Opposing Counsel Failed to Pay Last 5 Years:** 100%

Chemicals, (All)

Responding Experts: *6*

Hourly Fees: **In-court Testimony:** *High:* $450 *Low:* $175 *Average:* $300 *Median:* $275
File Review/Prep: *High:* $300 *Low:* $150 *Average:* $220 *Median:* $200
Depositions: *High:* $350 *Low:* $175 *Average:* $270 *Median:* $240
Percent of Experts Having a Minimum Charge for Deps: 33% **Cancellation Fee for Deps or Trial:** 0%
Deposition Payment in Advance: 20% **Markup of Out-of-Pocket Expenses:** 16%

Up-front Retainer: 43% **Retainer Amount:** *High:* $3,000 *Low:* $200 *Average:* $2,500 *Median:* $2,500
Travel Billed Portal-to-Portal: 83% **1st-class Airfare Required:** 0%

Written Fee Agreement: 83% **Majority of Work:** *Plaintiffs:* 17% *Defendants:* 0% *Neither:* 83%
Retaining Counsel Failed to Pay Last 5 Years: 50% **Opposing Counsel Failed to Pay Last 5 Years:** 33%

Chemicals, Environmental

Responding Experts: *1*

Hourly Fees: **In-court Testimony:** *High:* $450 *Low:* $450 *Average:* $450 *Median:* $450
File Review/Prep: *High:* $225 *Low:* $225 *Average:* $225 *Median:* $225
Depositions: *High:* $225 *Low:* $225 *Average:* $225 *Median:* $225
Percent of Experts Having a Minimum Charge for Deps: 0% **Cancellation Fee for Deps or Trial:** 0%
Deposition Payment in Advance: 0% **Markup of Out-of-Pocket Expenses:** 0%

Up-front Retainer: 0% **Retainer Amount:** *High:* N/A *Low:* N/A *Average:* N/A *Median:* N/A
Travel Billed Portal-to-Portal: 0% **1st-class Airfare Required:** 0%

Written Fee Agreement: 100% **Majority of Work:** *Plaintiffs:* 0% *Defendants:* 0% *Neither:* 100%
Retaining Counsel Failed to Pay Last 5 Years: 100% **Opposing Counsel Failed to Pay Last 5 Years:** 100%

Child Custody

Responding Experts: *1*

Hourly Fees: **In-court Testimony:** *High:* $250 *Low:* $250 *Average:* $250 *Median:* $250
File Review/Prep: *High:* $250 *Low:* $250 *Average:* $250 *Median:* $250
Depositions: *High:* $250 *Low:* $250 *Average:* $250 *Median:* $250

Percent of Experts Having a Minimum Charge for Deps: 100% **Cancellation Fee for Deps or Trial:** 100%
Deposition Payment in Advance: 100% **Markup of Out-of-Pocket Expenses:** 0%

Up-front Retainer: 100% **Retainer Amount:** *High:* $5,000 *Low:* $5,000 *Average:* $5,000 *Median:* $5,000
Travel Billed Portal-to-Portal: 100% **1st-class Airfare Required:** 0%

Written Fee Agreement: 100% **Majority of Work:** *Plaintiffs:* 0% *Defendants:* 0% *Neither:* 100%
Retaining Counsel Failed to Pay Last 5 Years: 100% **Opposing Counsel Failed to Pay Last 5 Years:** 100%

Chiropractic

Responding Experts: *25*

Hourly Fees: **In-court Testimony:** *High:* $525 *Low:* $150 *Average:* $370 *Median:* $400
File Review/Prep: *High:* $400 *Low:* $85 *Average:* $225 *Median:* $200
Depositions: *High:* $525 *Low:* $85 *Average:* $320 *Median:* $350

Percent of Experts Having a Minimum Charge for Deps: 92% **Cancellation Fee for Deps or Trial:** 84%
Deposition Payment in Advance: 75% **Markup of Out-of-Pocket Expenses:** 18%

Up-front Retainer: 68% **Retainer Amount:** *High:* $3,500 *Low:* $150 *Average:* $635 *Median:* $500
Travel Billed Portal-to-Portal: 92% **1st-class Airfare Required:** 14%

Written Fee Agreement: 72% **Majority of Work:** *Plaintiffs:* 28% *Defendants:* 20% *Neither:* 52%
Retaining Counsel Failed to Pay Last 5 Years: 24% **Opposing Counsel Failed to Pay Last 5 Years:** 4%

Coatings

Responding Experts: *1*

Hourly Fees: **In-court Testimony:** *High:* $175 *Low:* $175 *Average:* $175 *Median:* $175
File Review/Prep: *High:* $150 *Low:* $150 *Average:* $150 *Median:* $150
Depositions: *High:* $175 *Low:* $175 *Average:* $175 *Median:* $175

Percent of Experts Having a Minimum Charge for Deps: 100% **Cancellation Fee for Deps or Trial:** 0%
Deposition Payment in Advance: 0% **Markup of Out-of-Pocket Expenses:** 100%

Up-front Retainer: 100% **Retainer Amount:** *High:* N/A *Low:* N/A *Average:* N/A *Median:* N/A
Travel Billed Portal-to-Portal: 100% **1st-class Airfare Required:** 0%

Written Fee Agreement: 100% **Majority of Work:** *Plaintiffs:* 0% *Defendants:* 0% *Neither:* 100%
Retaining Counsel Failed to Pay Last 5 Years: 100% **Opposing Counsel Failed to Pay Last 5 Years:** 100%

Coins

Responding Experts: *1*

Hourly Fees: **In-court Testimony:** *High:* $300 *Low:* $300 *Average:* $300 *Median:* $300
File Review/Prep: *High:* $250 *Low:* $250 *Average:* $250 *Median:* $250
Depositions: *High:* $250 *Low:* $250 *Average:* $250 *Median:* $250

Percent of Experts Having a Minimum Charge for Deps: 100% **Cancellation Fee for Deps or Trial:** 100%
Deposition Payment in Advance: 100% **Markup of Out-of-Pocket Expenses:** 0%

Up-front Retainer: 100% **Retainer Amount:** *High:* $500 *Low:* $500 *Average:* $500 *Median:* $500
Travel Billed Portal-to-Portal: 100% **1st-class Airfare Required:** 0%

Written Fee Agreement: 100% **Majority of Work:** *Plaintiffs:* 0% *Defendants:* 0% *Neither:* 100%
Retaining Counsel Failed to Pay Last 5 Years: 0% **Opposing Counsel Failed to Pay Last 5 Years:** 0%

Compliance
Responding Experts: *1*

Hourly Fees: **In-court Testimony:** *High:* $240 *Low:* $240 *Average:* $240 *Median:* $240
File Review/Prep: *High:* $120 *Low:* $120 *Average:* $120 *Median:* $120
Depositions: *High:* $240 *Low:* $240 *Average:* $240 *Median:* $240
Percent of Experts Having a Minimum Charge for Deps: 0% **Cancellation Fee for Deps or Trial:** 100%
Deposition Payment in Advance: 100% **Markup of Out-of-Pocket Expenses:** 0%

Up-front Retainer: 100% **Retainer Amount:** *High:* $1,000 *Low:* $1,000 *Average:* $1,000 *Median:* $1,000
Travel Billed Portal-to-Portal: 0% **1st-class Airfare Required:** 0%

Written Fee Agreement: 100% **Majority of Work:** *Plaintiffs:* 100% *Defendants:* 0% *Neither:* 0%
Retaining Counsel Failed to Pay Last 5 Years: 0% **Opposing Counsel Failed to Pay Last 5 Years:** 0%

Computers, (All)
Responding Experts: *6*

Hourly Fees: **In-court Testimony:** *High:* $400 *Low:* $200 *Average:* $270 *Median:* $235
File Review/Prep: *High:* $350 *Low:* $150 *Average:* $245 *Median:* $200
Depositions: *High:* $500 *Low:* $200 *Average:* $290 *Median:* $235
Percent of Experts Having a Minimum Charge for Deps: 33% **Cancellation Fee for Deps or Trial:** 0%
Deposition Payment in Advance: 50% **Markup of Out-of-Pocket Expenses:** 0%

Up-front Retainer: 66% **Retainer Amount:** *High:* $10,000 *Low:* $1,500 *Average:* $5,500 *Median:* $5,000
Travel Billed Portal-to-Portal: 83% **1st-class Airfare Required:** 17%

Written Fee Agreement: 50% **Majority of Work:** *Plaintiffs:* 0% *Defendants:* 17% *Neither:* 83%
Retaining Counsel Failed to Pay Last 5 Years: 67% **Opposing Counsel Failed to Pay Last 5 Years:** 16%

Computers, Software
Responding Experts: *2*

Hourly Fees: **In-court Testimony:** *High:* $350 *Low:* $220 *Average:* $285 *Median:* $285
File Review/Prep: *High:* $350 *Low:* $170 *Average:* $260 *Median:* $260
Depositions: *High:* $350 *Low:* $220 *Average:* $285 *Median:* $285
Percent of Experts Having a Minimum Charge for Deps: 50% **Cancellation Fee for Deps or Trial:** 0%
Deposition Payment in Advance: 100% **Markup of Out-of-Pocket Expenses:** 0%

Up-front Retainer: 100% **Retainer Amount:** *High:* $5,000 *Low:* $5,000 *Average:* $5,000 *Median:* $5,000
Travel Billed Portal-to-Portal: 100% **1st-class Airfare Required:** 0%

Written Fee Agreement: 100% **Majority of Work:** *Plaintiffs:* 0% *Defendants:* 50% *Neither:* 50%
Retaining Counsel Failed to Pay Last 5 Years: 100% **Opposing Counsel Failed to Pay Last 5 Years:** 50%

Concrete
Responding Experts: *2*

Hourly Fees: **In-court Testimony:** *High:* $300 *Low:* $190 *Average:* $245 *Median:* $245
File Review/Prep: *High:* $220 *Low:* $190 *Average:* $205 *Median:* $205
Depositions: *High:* $300 *Low:* $190 *Average:* $245 *Median:* $245
Percent of Experts Having a Minimum Charge for Deps: 0% **Cancellation Fee for Deps or Trial:** 0%
Deposition Payment in Advance: 0% **Markup of Out-of-Pocket Expenses:** 100%

Up-front Retainer: 100% **Retainer Amount:** *High:* N/A *Low:* N/A *Average:* N/A *Median:* N/A
Travel Billed Portal-to-Portal: 100% **1st-class Airfare Required:** 0%

Written Fee Agreement: 100% **Majority of Work:** *Plaintiffs:* 0% *Defendants:* 0% *Neither:* 100%
Retaining Counsel Failed to Pay Last 5 Years: 50% **Opposing Counsel Failed to Pay Last 5 Years:** 0%

Construction

Responding Experts: *30*

Hourly Fees: **In-court Testimony:** *High:* $550 *Low:* $100 *Average:* $275 *Median:* $250
File Review/Prep: *High:* $335 *Low:* $75 *Average:* $192 *Median:* $185
Depositions: *High:* $550 *Low:* $100 *Average:* $260 *Median:* $250

Percent of Experts Having a Minimum Charge for Deps: 53% **Cancellation Fee for Deps or Trial:** 27%
Deposition Payment in Advance: 50% **Markup of Out-of-Pocket Expenses:** 43%

Up-front Retainer: 89% **Retainer Amount:** *High:* $7,500 *Low:* $750 *Average:* $2,400 *Median:* $2,000
Travel Billed Portal-to-Portal: 90% **1st-class Airfare Required:** 7%

Written Fee Agreement: 100% **Majority of Work:** *Plaintiffs:* 20% *Defendants:* 17% *Neither:* 63%
Retaining Counsel Failed to Pay Last 5 Years: 53% **Opposing Counsel Failed to Pay Last 5 Years:** 17%

Corrosion

Responding Experts: *1*

Hourly Fees: **In-court Testimony:** *High:* $275 *Low:* $275 *Average:* $275 *Median:* $275
File Review/Prep: *High:* $225 *Low:* $225 *Average:* $225 *Median:* $225
Depositions: *High:* $275 *Low:* $275 *Average:* $275 *Median:* $275

Percent of Experts Having a Minimum Charge for Deps: 100% **Cancellation Fee for Deps or Trial:** 100%
Deposition Payment in Advance: 100% **Markup of Out-of-Pocket Expenses:** 100%

Up-front Retainer: 100% **Retainer Amount:** *High:* $1,000 *Low:* $1,000 *Average:* $1,000 *Median:* $1,000
Travel Billed Portal-to-Portal: 100% **1st-class Airfare Required:** 0%

Written Fee Agreement: 100% **Majority of Work:** *Plaintiffs:* 0% *Defendants:* 0% *Neither:* 100%
Retaining Counsel Failed to Pay Last 5 Years: 0% **Opposing Counsel Failed to Pay Last 5 Years:** 0%

Crime

Responding Experts: *1*

Hourly Fees: **In-court Testimony:** *High:* $275 *Low:* $275 *Average:* $275 *Median:* $275
File Review/Prep: *High:* $275 *Low:* $275 *Average:* $275 *Median:* $275
Depositions: *High:* $275 *Low:* $275 *Average:* $275 *Median:* $275

Percent of Experts Having a Minimum Charge for Deps: 100% **Cancellation Fee for Deps or Trial:** N/A
Deposition Payment in Advance: 0% **Markup of Out-of-Pocket Expenses:** 0%

Up-front Retainer: 0% **Retainer Amount:** *High:* N/A *Low:* N/A *Average:* N/A *Median:* N/A
Travel Billed Portal-to-Portal: 100% **1st-class Airfare Required:** 0%

Written Fee Agreement: 100% **Majority of Work:** *Plaintiffs:* 0% *Defendants:* 0% *Neither:* 100%
Retaining Counsel Failed to Pay Last 5 Years: 100% **Opposing Counsel Failed to Pay Last 5 Years:** 0%

Critical Care Medicine

Responding Experts: *2*

Hourly Fees: **In-court Testimony:** *High:* $900 *Low:* $240 *Average:* $570 *Median:* $570
File Review/Prep: *High:* $375 *Low:* $120 *Average:* $248 *Median:* $248
Depositions: *High:* $600 *Low:* $240 *Average:* $420 *Median:* $420

Percent of Experts Having a Minimum Charge for Deps: 0% **Cancellation Fee for Deps or Trial:** 100%
Deposition Payment in Advance: 50% **Markup of Out-of-Pocket Expenses:** 0%

Up-front Retainer: 100% **Retainer Amount:** *High:* $3,500 *Low:* $1,000 *Average:* $2,250 *Median:* $2,250
Travel Billed Portal-to-Portal: 50% **1st-class Airfare Required:** 0%

Written Fee Agreement: 100% **Majority of Work:** *Plaintiffs:* 50% *Defendants:* 50% *Neither:* 0%
Retaining Counsel Failed to Pay Last 5 Years: 0% **Opposing Counsel Failed to Pay Last 5 Years:** 0%

Damages, (All)

Responding Experts: *24*

Hourly Fees: **In-court Testimony:** *High:* $450 *Low:* $100 *Average:* $250 *Median:* $245
File Review/Prep: *High:* $450 *Low:* $100 *Average:* $225 *Median:* $225
Depositions: *High:* $450 *Low:* $100 *Average:* $245 *Median:* $245
Percent of Experts Having a Minimum Charge for Deps: 38% **Cancellation Fee for Deps or Trial:** 22%
Deposition Payment in Advance: 43% **Markup of Out-of-Pocket Expenses:** 4%

Up-front Retainer: 92% **Retainer Amount:** *High:* $15,000 *Low:* $800 *Average:* $4,770 *Median:* $4,000
Travel Billed Portal-to-Portal: 66% **1st-class Airfare Required:** 4%

Written Fee Agreement: 54% **Majority of Work:** *Plaintiffs:* 25% *Defendants:* 8% *Neither:* 67%
Retaining Counsel Failed to Pay Last 5 Years: 42% **Opposing Counsel Failed to Pay Last 5 Years:** 21%

Damages, Business

Responding Experts: *14*

Hourly Fees: **In-court Testimony:** *High:* $450 *Low:* $175 *Average:* $252 *Median:* $237
File Review/Prep: *High:* $450 *Low:* $160 *Average:* $230 *Median:* $218
Depositions: *High:* $450 *Low:* $160 *Average:* $250 *Median:* $238
Percent of Experts Having a Minimum Charge for Deps: 29% **Cancellation Fee for Deps or Trial:** 23%
Deposition Payment in Advance: 36% **Markup of Out-of-Pocket Expenses:** 0%

Up-front Retainer: 100% **Retainer Amount:** *High:* $10,000 *Low:* $800 *Average:* $3,925 *Median:* $3,500
Travel Billed Portal-to-Portal: 73% **1st-class Airfare Required:** 0%

Written Fee Agreement: 50% **Majority of Work:** *Plaintiffs:* 29% *Defendants:* 7% *Neither:* 64%
Retaining Counsel Failed to Pay Last 5 Years: 43% **Opposing Counsel Failed to Pay Last 5 Years:** 29%

Damages, Commercial

Responding Experts: *1*

Hourly Fees: **In-court Testimony:** *High:* $170 *Low:* $170 *Average:* $170 *Median:* $170
File Review/Prep: *High:* $170 *Low:* $170 *Average:* $170 *Median:* $170
Depositions: *High:* $170 *Low:* $170 *Average:* $170 *Median:* $170
Percent of Experts Having a Minimum Charge for Deps: 0% **Cancellation Fee for Deps or Trial:** 0%
Deposition Payment in Advance: 0% **Markup of Out-of-Pocket Expenses:** 0%

Up-front Retainer: 100% **Retainer Amount:** *High:* N/A *Low:* N/A *Average:* N/A *Median:* N/A
Travel Billed Portal-to-Portal: 100% **1st-class Airfare Required:** 0%

Written Fee Agreement: 100% **Majority of Work:** *Plaintiffs:* 0% *Defendants:* 0% *Neither:* 100%
Retaining Counsel Failed to Pay Last 5 Years: 0% **Opposing Counsel Failed to Pay Last 5 Years:** 0%

Damages, Economic

Responding Experts: *6*

Hourly Fees: **In-court Testimony:** *High:* $400 *Low:* $100 *Average:* $269 *Median:* $285
File Review/Prep: *High:* $315 *Low:* $100 *Average:* $218 *Median:* $238
Depositions: *High:* $315 *Low:* $100 *Average:* $243 *Median:* $265
Percent of Experts Having a Minimum Charge for Deps: 66% **Cancellation Fee for Deps or Trial:** 33%
Deposition Payment in Advance: 80% **Markup of Out-of-Pocket Expenses:** 17%

Up-front Retainer: 80% **Retainer Amount:** *High:* $15,000 *Low:* $900 *Average:* $7,000 *Median:* $5,000
Travel Billed Portal-to-Portal: 66% **1st-class Airfare Required:** 20%

Written Fee Agreement: 50% **Majority of Work:** *Plaintiffs:* 17% *Defendants:* 17% *Neither:* 66%
Retaining Counsel Failed to Pay Last 5 Years: 50% **Opposing Counsel Failed to Pay Last 5 Years:** 0%

Damages, Financial

Responding Experts: *1*

Hourly Fees: **In-court Testimony:** *High:* $240 *Low:* $240 *Average:* $240 *Median:* $240
File Review/Prep: *High:* $240 *Low:* $240 *Average:* $240 *Median:* $240
Depositions: *High:* $240 *Low:* $240 *Average:* $240 *Median:* $240
Percent of Experts Having a Minimum Charge for Deps: 0% **Cancellation Fee for Deps or Trial:** 0%
Deposition Payment in Advance: 0% **Markup of Out-of-Pocket Expenses:** 0%

Up-front Retainer: 100% **Retainer Amount:** *High:* $5,000 *Low:* $5,000 *Average:* $5,000 *Median:* $5,000
Travel Billed Portal-to-Portal: 100% **1st-class Airfare Required:** 0%

Written Fee Agreement: 0% **Majority of Work:** *Plaintiffs:* 100% *Defendants:* 0% *Neither:* 0%
Retaining Counsel Failed to Pay Last 5 Years: 0% **Opposing Counsel Failed to Pay Last 5 Years:** 0%

Demolition

Responding Experts: *1*

Hourly Fees: **In-court Testimony:** *High:* $350 *Low:* $350 *Average:* $350 *Median:* $350
File Review/Prep: *High:* $350 *Low:* $350 *Average:* $350 *Median:* $350
Depositions: *High:* $350 *Low:* $350 *Average:* $350 *Median:* $350
Percent of Experts Having a Minimum Charge for Deps: 100% **Cancellation Fee for Deps or Trial:** 0%
Deposition Payment in Advance: 0% **Markup of Out-of-Pocket Expenses:** 0%

Up-front Retainer: 100% **Retainer Amount:** *High:* $3,000 *Low:* $3,000 *Average:* $3,000 *Median:* $3,000
Travel Billed Portal-to-Portal: 0% **1st-class Airfare Required:** 0%

Written Fee Agreement: 0% **Majority of Work:** *Plaintiffs:* 100% *Defendants:* 0% *Neither:* 0%
Retaining Counsel Failed to Pay Last 5 Years: 0% **Opposing Counsel Failed to Pay Last 5 Years:** 0%

Dentistry

Responding Experts: *3*

Hourly Fees: **In-court Testimony:** *High:* $750 *Low:* $200 *Average:* $485 *Median:* $500
File Review/Prep: *High:* $250 *Low:* $150 *Average:* $200 *Median:* $200
Depositions: *High:* $500 *Low:* $200 *Average:* $370 *Median:* $400
Percent of Experts Having a Minimum Charge for Deps: 100% **Cancellation Fee for Deps or Trial:** 66%
Deposition Payment in Advance: 33% **Markup of Out-of-Pocket Expenses:** 0%

Up-front Retainer: 66% **Retainer Amount:** *High:* $1,000 *Low:* $200 *Average:* $600 *Median:* $600
Travel Billed Portal-to-Portal: 33% **1st-class Airfare Required:** 0%

Written Fee Agreement: 100% **Majority of Work:** *Plaintiffs:* 66% *Defendants:* 0% *Neither:* 34%
Retaining Counsel Failed to Pay Last 5 Years: 33% **Opposing Counsel Failed to Pay Last 5 Years:** 0%

Dermatology

Responding Experts: *2*

Hourly Fees: **In-court Testimony:** *High:* $750 *Low:* $500 *Average:* $625 *Median:* $625
File Review/Prep: *High:* $300 *Low:* $250 *Average:* $275 *Median:* $275
Depositions: *High:* $300 *Low:* $300 *Average:* $300 *Median:* $300
Percent of Experts Having a Minimum Charge for Deps: 50% **Cancellation Fee for Deps or Trial:** 100%
Deposition Payment in Advance: 50% **Markup of Out-of-Pocket Expenses:** 50%

Up-front Retainer: 50% **Retainer Amount:** *High:* N/A *Low:* N/A *Average:* N/A *Median:* N/A
Travel Billed Portal-to-Portal: 100% **1st-class Airfare Required:** 0%

Written Fee Agreement: 50% **Majority of Work:** *Plaintiffs:* 0% *Defendants:* 0% *Neither:* 100%
Retaining Counsel Failed to Pay Last 5 Years: 0% **Opposing Counsel Failed to Pay Last 5 Years:** 0%

Disability

Responding Experts: *2*

Hourly Fees: **In-court Testimony:** *High:* $1,450 *Low:* $1,450 *Average:* $1,450 *Median:* $1,450
File Review/Prep: *High:* $340 *Low:* $340 *Average:* $340 *Median:* $340
Depositions: *High:* $1,250 *Low:* $400 *Average:* $825 *Median:* $825

Percent of Experts Having a Minimum Charge for Deps: 50% **Cancellation Fee for Deps or Trial:** 100%
Deposition Payment in Advance: 100% **Markup of Out-of-Pocket Expenses:** 50%

Up-front Retainer: 50% **Retainer Amount:** *High:* N/A *Low:* N/A *Average:* N/A *Median:* N/A
Travel Billed Portal-to-Portal: 50% **1st-class Airfare Required:** 0%

Written Fee Agreement: 50% **Majority of Work:** *Plaintiffs:* 50% *Defendants:* 0% *Neither:* 50%
Retaining Counsel Failed to Pay Last 5 Years: 0% **Opposing Counsel Failed to Pay Last 5 Years:** 0%

Disability, Handicapped Vehicles

Responding Experts: *1*

Hourly Fees: **In-court Testimony:** *High:* $150 *Low:* $150 *Average:* $150 *Median:* $150
File Review/Prep: *High:* $150 *Low:* $150 *Average:* $150 *Median:* $150
Depositions: *High:* $150 *Low:* $150 *Average:* $150 *Median:* $150

Percent of Experts Having a Minimum Charge for Deps: 0% **Cancellation Fee for Deps or Trial:** 0%
Deposition Payment in Advance: 0% **Markup of Out-of-Pocket Expenses:** 0%

Up-front Retainer: 100% **Retainer Amount:** *High:* $1,500 *Low:* $1,500 *Average:* $1,500 *Median:* $1,500
Travel Billed Portal-to-Portal: 100% **1st-class Airfare Required:** 0%

Written Fee Agreement: 100% **Majority of Work:** *Plaintiffs:* 0% *Defendants:* 100% *Neither:* 0%
Retaining Counsel Failed to Pay Last 5 Years: 0% **Opposing Counsel Failed to Pay Last 5 Years:** 0%

Document Examiner

Responding Experts: *13*

Hourly Fees: **In-court Testimony:** *High:* $1,000 *Low:* $75 *Average:* $242 *Median:* $150
File Review/Prep: *High:* $300 *Low:* $50 *Average:* $153 *Median:* $150
Depositions: *High:* $800 *Low:* $100 *Average:* $290 *Median:* $175

Percent of Experts Having a Minimum Charge for Deps: 57% **Cancellation Fee for Deps or Trial:** 46%
Deposition Payment in Advance: 85% **Markup of Out-of-Pocket Expenses:** 8%

Up-front Retainer: 100% **Retainer Amount:** *High:* $2,250 *Low:* $180 *Average:* $740 *Median:* $500
Travel Billed Portal-to-Portal: 77% **1st-class Airfare Required:** 0%

Written Fee Agreement: 69% **Majority of Work:** *Plaintiffs:* 7% *Defendants:* 8% *Neither:* 85%
Retaining Counsel Failed to Pay Last 5 Years: 46% **Opposing Counsel Failed to Pay Last 5 Years:** 7%

Earthquakes

Responding Experts: *1*

Hourly Fees: **In-court Testimony:** *High:* $220 *Low:* $220 *Average:* $220 *Median:* $220
File Review/Prep: *High:* $220 *Low:* $220 *Average:* $220 *Median:* $220
Depositions: *High:* $220 *Low:* $220 *Average:* $220 *Median:* $220

Percent of Experts Having a Minimum Charge for Deps: 0% **Cancellation Fee for Deps or Trial:** 0%
Deposition Payment in Advance: 0% **Markup of Out-of-Pocket Expenses:** 100%

Up-front Retainer: 0% **Retainer Amount:** *High:* N/A *Low:* N/A *Average:* N/A *Median:* N/A
Travel Billed Portal-to-Portal: 100% **1st-class Airfare Required:** 0%

Written Fee Agreement: 100% **Majority of Work:** *Plaintiffs:* 0% *Defendants:* 0% *Neither:* 100%
Retaining Counsel Failed to Pay Last 5 Years: 0% **Opposing Counsel Failed to Pay Last 5 Years:** 0%

Economics

Responding Experts: *11*

Hourly Fees: **In-court Testimony:** *High:* $450 *Low:* $125 *Average:* $275 *Median:* $250
File Review/Prep: *High:* $450 *Low:* $150 *Average:* $260 *Median:* $225
Depositions: *High:* $500 *Low:* $125 *Average:* $300 *Median:* $290
Percent of Experts Having a Minimum Charge for Deps: 20% **Cancellation Fee for Deps or Trial:** 18%
Deposition Payment in Advance: 55% **Markup of Out-of-Pocket Expenses:** 18%

Up-front Retainer: 82% **Retainer Amount:** *High:* $10,000 *Low:* $500 *Average:* $3,125 *Median:* $1,750
Travel Billed Portal-to-Portal: 91% **1st-class Airfare Required:** 0%

Written Fee Agreement: 73% **Majority of Work:** *Plaintiffs:* 64% *Defendants:* 9% *Neither:* 27%
Retaining Counsel Failed to Pay Last 5 Years: 64% **Opposing Counsel Failed to Pay Last 5 Years:** 36%

Education, (All)

Responding Experts: *3*

Hourly Fees: **In-court Testimony:** *High:* $475 *Low:* $115 *Average:* $355 *Median:* $475
File Review/Prep: *High:* $350 *Low:* $150 *Average:* $285 *Median:* $350
Depositions: *High:* $475 *Low:* $115 *Average:* $355 *Median:* $475
Percent of Experts Having a Minimum Charge for Deps: 33% **Cancellation Fee for Deps or Trial:** 100%
Deposition Payment in Advance: 66% **Markup of Out-of-Pocket Expenses:** 0%

Up-front Retainer: 100% **Retainer Amount:** *High:* $6,500 *Low:* $750 *Average:* $4,580 *Median:* $6,500
Travel Billed Portal-to-Portal: 100% **1st-class Airfare Required:** 0%

Written Fee Agreement: 100% **Majority of Work:** *Plaintiffs:* 33% *Defendants:* 0% *Neither:* 66%
Retaining Counsel Failed to Pay Last 5 Years: 66% **Opposing Counsel Failed to Pay Last 5 Years:** 0%

Education, Physical

Responding Experts: *1*

Hourly Fees: **In-court Testimony:** *High:* $475 *Low:* $475 *Average:* $475 *Median:* $475
File Review/Prep: *High:* $350 *Low:* $350 *Average:* $350 *Median:* $350
Depositions: *High:* $475 *Low:* $475 *Average:* $475 *Median:* $475
Percent of Experts Having a Minimum Charge for Deps: 100% **Cancellation Fee for Deps or Trial:** 100%
Deposition Payment in Advance: 0% **Markup of Out-of-Pocket Expenses:** 0%

Up-front Retainer: 100% **Retainer Amount:** *High:* $750 *Low:* $750 *Average:* $750 *Median:* $750
Travel Billed Portal-to-Portal: 100% **1st-class Airfare Required:** 0%

Written Fee Agreement: 100% **Majority of Work:** *Plaintiffs:* 100% *Defendants:* 0% *Neither:* 0%
Retaining Counsel Failed to Pay Last 5 Years: 0% **Opposing Counsel Failed to Pay Last 5 Years:** 0%

Education, Schools

Responding Experts: *1*

Hourly Fees: **In-court Testimony:** *High:* $475 *Low:* $475 *Average:* $475 *Median:* $475
File Review/Prep: *High:* $350 *Low:* $350 *Average:* $350 *Median:* $350
Depositions: *High:* $475 *Low:* $475 *Average:* $475 *Median:* $475
Percent of Experts Having a Minimum Charge for Deps: 0% **Cancellation Fee for Deps or Trial:** 100%
Deposition Payment in Advance: 100% **Markup of Out-of-Pocket Expenses:** 0%

Up-front Retainer: 100% **Retainer Amount:** *High:* $6,500 *Low:* $6,500 *Average:* $6,500 *Median:* $6,500
Travel Billed Portal-to-Portal: 100% **1st-class Airfare Required:** 0%

Written Fee Agreement: 100% **Majority of Work:** *Plaintiffs:* 0% *Defendants:* 0% *Neither:* 100%
Retaining Counsel Failed to Pay Last 5 Years: 100% **Opposing Counsel Failed to Pay Last 5 Years:** 0%

Electrical, (All)

Responding Experts: *4*

Hourly Fees: **In-court Testimony:** *High:* $275 *Low:* $175 *Average:* $240 *Median:* $250
File Review/Prep: *High:* $250 *Low:* $150 *Average:* $200 *Median:* $200
Depositions: *High:* $275 *Low:* $175 *Average:* $240 *Median:* $250
Percent of Experts Having a Minimum Charge for Deps: 25% **Cancellation Fee for Deps or Trial:** 0%
Deposition Payment in Advance: 25% **Markup of Out-of-Pocket Expenses:** 100%

Up-front Retainer: 75% **Retainer Amount:** *High:* $2,500 *Low:* $750 *Average:* $1,920 *Median:* $2,500
Travel Billed Portal-to-Portal: 100% **1st-class Airfare Required:** 0%

Written Fee Agreement: 75% **Majority of Work:** *Plaintiffs:* 25% *Defendants:* 25% *Neither:* 50%
Retaining Counsel Failed to Pay Last 5 Years: 50% **Opposing Counsel Failed to Pay Last 5 Years:** 0%

Electrical, Power Systems

Responding Experts: *1*

Hourly Fees: **In-court Testimony:** *High:* $275 *Low:* $275 *Average:* $275 *Median:* $275
File Review/Prep: *High:* $250 *Low:* $250 *Average:* $250 *Median:* $250
Depositions: *High:* $275 *Low:* $275 *Average:* $275 *Median:* $275
Percent of Experts Having a Minimum Charge for Deps: 0% **Cancellation Fee for Deps or Trial:** 0%
Deposition Payment in Advance: 100% **Markup of Out-of-Pocket Expenses:** N/A

Up-front Retainer: 100% **Retainer Amount:** *High:* $750 *Low:* $750 *Average:* $750 *Median:* $750
Travel Billed Portal-to-Portal: 100% **1st-class Airfare Required:** 0%

Written Fee Agreement: 0% **Majority of Work:** *Plaintiffs:* 100% *Defendants:* 0% *Neither:* 0%
Retaining Counsel Failed to Pay Last 5 Years: 0% **Opposing Counsel Failed to Pay Last 5 Years:** 0%

Electronics

Responding Experts: *1*

Hourly Fees: **In-court Testimony:** *High:* $250 *Low:* $250 *Average:* $250 *Median:* $250
File Review/Prep: *High:* $250 *Low:* $250 *Average:* $250 *Median:* $250
Depositions: *High:* $250 *Low:* $250 *Average:* $250 *Median:* $250
Percent of Experts Having a Minimum Charge for Deps: 0% **Cancellation Fee for Deps or Trial:** 0%
Deposition Payment in Advance: 0% **Markup of Out-of-Pocket Expenses:** N/A

Up-front Retainer: 100% **Retainer Amount:** *High:* $5,000 *Low:* $5,000 *Average:* $5,000 *Median:* $5,000
Travel Billed Portal-to-Portal: 100% **1st-class Airfare Required:** 0%

Written Fee Agreement: 100% **Majority of Work:** *Plaintiffs:* 0% *Defendants:* 0% *Neither:* 100%
Retaining Counsel Failed to Pay Last 5 Years: 100% **Opposing Counsel Failed to Pay Last 5 Years:** 0%

Elevators & Escalators

Responding Experts: *1*

Hourly Fees: **In-court Testimony:** *High:* $275 *Low:* $275 *Average:* $275 *Median:* $275
File Review/Prep: *High:* $275 *Low:* $275 *Average:* $275 *Median:* $275
Depositions: *High:* $275 *Low:* $275 *Average:* $275 *Median:* $275
Percent of Experts Having a Minimum Charge for Deps: 0% **Cancellation Fee for Deps or Trial:** 0%
Deposition Payment in Advance: 0% **Markup of Out-of-Pocket Expenses:** 100%

Up-front Retainer: 100% **Retainer Amount:** *High:* $2,000 *Low:* $2,000 *Average:* $2,000 *Median:* $2,000
Travel Billed Portal-to-Portal: 100% **1st-class Airfare Required:** 0%

Written Fee Agreement: 100% **Majority of Work:** *Plaintiffs:* 100% *Defendants:* 0% *Neither:* 0%
Retaining Counsel Failed to Pay Last 5 Years: 100% **Opposing Counsel Failed to Pay Last 5 Years:** 0%

Emergency Medicine

Responding Experts: *18*

Hourly Fees: **In-court Testimony:** *High:* $1,000 *Low:* $250 *Average:* $470 *Median:* $500
File Review/Prep: *High:* $500 *Low:* $250 *Average:* $325 *Median:* $300
Depositions: *High:* $600 *Low:* $200 *Average:* $375 *Median:* $350
Percent of Experts Having a Minimum Charge for Deps: 76% **Cancellation Fee for Deps or Trial:** 50%
Deposition Payment in Advance: 28% **Markup of Out-of-Pocket Expenses:** 0%

Up-front Retainer: 60% **Retainer Amount:** *High:* $5,000 *Low:* $250 *Average:* $1,175 *Median:* $750
Travel Billed Portal-to-Portal: 72% **1st-class Airfare Required:** 0%

Written Fee Agreement: 67% **Majority of Work:** *Plaintiffs:* 17% *Defendants:* 33% *Neither:* 50%
Retaining Counsel Failed to Pay Last 5 Years: 35% **Opposing Counsel Failed to Pay Last 5 Years:** 10%

Employment, (All)

Responding Experts: *9*

Hourly Fees: **In-court Testimony:** *High:* $450 *Low:* $135 *Average:* $260 *Median:* $250
File Review/Prep: *High:* $350 *Low:* $85 *Average:* $200 *Median:* $195
Depositions: *High:* $500 *Low:* $135 *Average:* $290 *Median:* $250
Percent of Experts Having a Minimum Charge for Deps: 25% **Cancellation Fee for Deps or Trial:** 33%
Deposition Payment in Advance: 44% **Markup of Out-of-Pocket Expenses:** 0%

Up-front Retainer: 56% **Retainer Amount:** *High:* $2,500 *Low:* $250 *Average:* $1,350 *Median:* $1,500
Travel Billed Portal-to-Portal: 89% **1st-class Airfare Required:** 0%

Written Fee Agreement: 78% **Majority of Work:** *Plaintiffs:* 44% *Defendants:* 11% *Neither:* 45%
Retaining Counsel Failed to Pay Last 5 Years: 56% **Opposing Counsel Failed to Pay Last 5 Years:** 44%

Employment, Earning Capacity

Responding Experts: *4*

Hourly Fees: **In-court Testimony:** *High:* $350 *Low:* $250 *Average:* $285 *Median:* $270
File Review/Prep: *High:* $300 *Low:* $195 *Average:* $225 *Median:* $205
Depositions: *High:* $450 *Low:* $250 *Average:* $335 *Median:* $325
Percent of Experts Having a Minimum Charge for Deps: 33% **Cancellation Fee for Deps or Trial:** 25%
Deposition Payment in Advance: 50% **Markup of Out-of-Pocket Expenses:** 0%

Up-front Retainer: 25% **Retainer Amount:** *High:* $2,500 *Low:* $2,000 *Average:* $2,250 *Median:* $2,250
Travel Billed Portal-to-Portal: 100% **1st-class Airfare Required:** 0%

Written Fee Agreement: 75% **Majority of Work:** *Plaintiffs:* 75% *Defendants:* 0% *Neither:* 25%
Retaining Counsel Failed to Pay Last 5 Years: 25% **Opposing Counsel Failed to Pay Last 5 Years:** 50%

Employment, Wrongful Discharge

Responding Experts: *1*

Hourly Fees: **In-court Testimony:** *High:* $450 *Low:* $450 *Average:* $450 *Median:* $450
File Review/Prep: *High:* $350 *Low:* $350 *Average:* $350 *Median:* $350
Depositions: *High:* $500 *Low:* $500 *Average:* $500 *Median:* $500
Percent of Experts Having a Minimum Charge for Deps: 100% **Cancellation Fee for Deps or Trial:** 100%
Deposition Payment in Advance: 0% **Markup of Out-of-Pocket Expenses:** 100%

Up-front Retainer: 100% **Retainer Amount:** *High:* N/A *Low:* N/A *Average:* N/A *Median:* N/A
Travel Billed Portal-to-Portal: 100% **1st-class Airfare Required:** 0%

Written Fee Agreement: 100% **Majority of Work:** *Plaintiffs:* 100% *Defendants:* 0% *Neither:* 0%
Retaining Counsel Failed to Pay Last 5 Years: 100% **Opposing Counsel Failed to Pay Last 5 Years:** 100%

Endocrinology

Responding Experts: *1*

Hourly Fees: **In-court Testimony:** *High:* $400 *Low:* $400 *Average:* $400 *Median:* $400
File Review/Prep: *High:* $360 *Low:* $360 *Average:* $360 *Median:* $360
Depositions: *High:* $400 *Low:* $400 *Average:* $400 *Median:* $400
Percent of Experts Having a Minimum Charge for Deps: 100% **Cancellation Fee for Deps or Trial:** 100%
Deposition Payment in Advance: 100% **Markup of Out-of-Pocket Expenses:** N/A

Up-front Retainer: 100% **Retainer Amount:** *High:* N/A *Low:* N/A *Average:* N/A *Median:* N/A
Travel Billed Portal-to-Portal: 100% **1st-class Airfare Required:** 100%

Written Fee Agreement: 100% **Majority of Work:** *Plaintiffs:* 100% *Defendants:* 0% *Neither:* 0%
Retaining Counsel Failed to Pay Last 5 Years: 100% **Opposing Counsel Failed to Pay Last 5 Years:** 0%

Engineering, (All)

Responding Experts: *127*

Hourly Fees: **In-court Testimony:** *High:* $400 *Low:* $100 *Average:* $220 *Median:* $210
File Review/Prep: *High:* $350 *Low:* $80 *Average:* $185 *Median:* $180
Depositions: *High:* $220 *Low:* $94 *Average:* $220 *Median:* $210
Percent of Experts Having a Minimum Charge for Deps: 42% **Cancellation Fee for Deps or Trial:** 18%
Deposition Payment in Advance: 32% **Markup of Out-of-Pocket Expenses:** 38%

Up-front Retainer: 65% **Retainer Amount:** *High:* $4,000 *Low:* $160 *Average:* $1,900 *Median:* $2,000
Travel Billed Portal-to-Portal: 94% **1st-class Airfare Required:** 8%

Written Fee Agreement: 75% **Majority of Work:** *Plaintiffs:* 23% *Defendants:* 17% *Neither:* 60%
Retaining Counsel Failed to Pay Last 5 Years: 53% **Opposing Counsel Failed to Pay Last 5 Years:** 26%

Engineering, Aeronautical

Responding Experts: *1*

Hourly Fees: **In-court Testimony:** *High:* $290 *Low:* $290 *Average:* $290 *Median:* $290
File Review/Prep: *High:* $290 *Low:* $290 *Average:* $290 *Median:* $290
Depositions: *High:* $290 *Low:* $290 *Average:* $290 *Median:* $290
Percent of Experts Having a Minimum Charge for Deps: 100% **Cancellation Fee for Deps or Trial:** 0%
Deposition Payment in Advance: 0% **Markup of Out-of-Pocket Expenses:** 0%

Up-front Retainer: 0% **Retainer Amount:** *High:* N/A *Low:* N/A *Average:* N/A *Median:* N/A
Travel Billed Portal-to-Portal: 100% **1st-class Airfare Required:** 0%

Written Fee Agreement: 100% **Majority of Work:** *Plaintiffs:* 0% *Defendants:* 100% *Neither:* 0%
Retaining Counsel Failed to Pay Last 5 Years: 100% **Opposing Counsel Failed to Pay Last 5 Years:** 0%

Engineering, Agricultural

Responding Experts: *1*

Hourly Fees: **In-court Testimony:** *High:* $200 *Low:* $200 *Average:* $200 *Median:* $200
File Review/Prep: *High:* $200 *Low:* $200 *Average:* $200 *Median:* $200
Depositions: *High:* $200 *Low:* $200 *Average:* $200 *Median:* $200
Percent of Experts Having a Minimum Charge for Deps: 0% **Cancellation Fee for Deps or Trial:** 0%
Deposition Payment in Advance: 0% **Markup of Out-of-Pocket Expenses:** 0%

Up-front Retainer: 100% **Retainer Amount:** *High:* $1,000 *Low:* $1,000 *Average:* $1,000 *Median:* $1,000
Travel Billed Portal-to-Portal: 100% **1st-class Airfare Required:** 0%

Written Fee Agreement: 100% **Majority of Work:** *Plaintiffs:* 0% *Defendants:* 0% *Neither:* 100%
Retaining Counsel Failed to Pay Last 5 Years: 0% **Opposing Counsel Failed to Pay Last 5 Years:** 0%

Engineering, Biomechanical

Responding Experts: *1*

Hourly Fees:

	High	*Low*	*Average*	*Median*
In-court Testimony:	$200	$200	$200	$200
File Review/Prep:	$125	$125	$125	$125
Depositions:	$200	$200	$200	$200

Percent of Experts Having a Minimum Charge for Deps: 100% **Cancellation Fee for Deps or Trial:** 0%
Deposition Payment in Advance: N/A **Markup of Out-of-Pocket Expenses:** 0%

Up-front Retainer: 0% **Retainer Amount:** *High:* N/A *Low:* N/A *Average:* N/A *Median:* N/A
Travel Billed Portal-to-Portal: 100% **1st-class Airfare Required:** 0%

Written Fee Agreement: 100% **Majority of Work:** *Plaintiffs:* 0% *Defendants:* 0% *Neither:* 100%
Retaining Counsel Failed to Pay Last 5 Years: 0% **Opposing Counsel Failed to Pay Last 5 Years:** 0%

Engineering, Biomedical

Responding Experts: *3*

Hourly Fees:

	High	*Low*	*Average*	*Median*
In-court Testimony:	$400	$300	$350	$350
File Review/Prep:	$300	$250	$284	$300
Depositions:	$400	$300	$340	$325

Percent of Experts Having a Minimum Charge for Deps: 33% **Cancellation Fee for Deps or Trial:** 33%
Deposition Payment in Advance: 33% **Markup of Out-of-Pocket Expenses:** 0%

Up-front Retainer: 100% **Retainer Amount:** *High:* $3,000 *Low:* $2,000 *Average:* $2,500 *Median:* $2,500
Travel Billed Portal-to-Portal: 66% **1st-class Airfare Required:** 0%

Written Fee Agreement: 100% **Majority of Work:** *Plaintiffs:* 33% *Defendants:* 0% *Neither:* 66%
Retaining Counsel Failed to Pay Last 5 Years: 0% **Opposing Counsel Failed to Pay Last 5 Years:** 0%

Engineering, Chemical

Responding Experts: *1*

Hourly Fees:

	High	*Low*	*Average*	*Median*
In-court Testimony:	$250	$250	$250	$250
File Review/Prep:	$125	$125	$125	$125
Depositions:	$250	$250	$250	$250

Percent of Experts Having a Minimum Charge for Deps: 0% **Cancellation Fee for Deps or Trial:** 0%
Deposition Payment in Advance: 100% **Markup of Out-of-Pocket Expenses:** 100%

Up-front Retainer: 100% **Retainer Amount:** *High:* $2,000 *Low:* $2,000 *Average:* $2,000 *Median:* $2,000
Travel Billed Portal-to-Portal: 100% **1st-class Airfare Required:** 0%

Written Fee Agreement: 0% **Majority of Work:** *Plaintiffs:* 0% *Defendants:* 0% *Neither:* 100%
Retaining Counsel Failed to Pay Last 5 Years: 0% **Opposing Counsel Failed to Pay Last 5 Years:** 0%

Engineering, Civil

Responding Experts: *18*

Hourly Fees:

	High	*Low*	*Average*	*Median*
In-court Testimony:	$315	$100	$220	$230
File Review/Prep:	$250	$90	$180	$185
Depositions:	$315	$95	$215	$222

Percent of Experts Having a Minimum Charge for Deps: 42% **Cancellation Fee for Deps or Trial:** 11%
Deposition Payment in Advance: 22% **Markup of Out-of-Pocket Expenses:** 45%

Up-front Retainer: 65% **Retainer Amount:** *High:* $4,000 *Low:* $500 *Average:* $1,830 *Median:* $2,000
Travel Billed Portal-to-Portal: 100% **1st-class Airfare Required:** 5%

Written Fee Agreement: 72% **Majority of Work:** *Plaintiffs:* 12% *Defendants:* 53% *Neither:* 35%
Retaining Counsel Failed to Pay Last 5 Years: 50% **Opposing Counsel Failed to Pay Last 5 Years:** 11%

Engineering, Electrical

Responding Experts: *14*

Hourly Fees:					
	In-court Testimony:	*High:* $250	*Low:* $140	*Average:* $200	*Median:* $200
	File Review/Prep:	*High:* $210	*Low:* $125	*Average:* $180	*Median:* $180
	Depositions:	*High:* $235	*Low:* $150	*Average:* $200	*Median:* $200

Percent of Experts Having a Minimum Charge for Deps: 47% **Cancellation Fee for Deps or Trial:** 21%
Deposition Payment in Advance: 29% **Markup of Out-of-Pocket Expenses:** 21%

Up-front Retainer: 60% **Retainer Amount:** *High:* $3,200 *Low:* $750 *Average:* $1,940 *Median:* $2,000
Travel Billed Portal-to-Portal: 93% **1st-class Airfare Required:** 21%

Written Fee Agreement: 85% **Majority of Work:** *Plaintiffs:* 7% *Defendants:* 0% *Neither:* 93%
Retaining Counsel Failed to Pay Last 5 Years: 50% **Opposing Counsel Failed to Pay Last 5 Years:** 21%

Engineering, Environmental

Responding Experts: *1*

Hourly Fees:					
	In-court Testimony:	*High:* $200	*Low:* $200	*Average:* $200	*Median:* $200
	File Review/Prep:	*High:* $200	*Low:* $200	*Average:* $200	*Median:* $200
	Depositions:	*High:* $200	*Low:* $200	*Average:* $200	*Median:* $200

Percent of Experts Having a Minimum Charge for Deps: 0% **Cancellation Fee for Deps or Trial:** 0%
Deposition Payment in Advance: 0% **Markup of Out-of-Pocket Expenses:** 100%

Up-front Retainer: 0% **Retainer Amount:** *High:* N/A *Low:* N/A *Average:* N/A *Median:* N/A
Travel Billed Portal-to-Portal: 100% **1st-class Airfare Required:** 0%

Written Fee Agreement: 0% **Majority of Work:** *Plaintiffs:* 0% *Defendants:* 100% *Neither:* 0%
Retaining Counsel Failed to Pay Last 5 Years: 0% **Opposing Counsel Failed to Pay Last 5 Years:** 0%

Engineering, Forensic

Responding Experts: *1*

Hourly Fees:					
	In-court Testimony:	*High:* $195	*Low:* $195	*Average:* $195	*Median:* $195
	File Review/Prep:	*High:* $195	*Low:* $195	*Average:* $195	*Median:* $195
	Depositions:	*High:* $195	*Low:* $195	*Average:* $195	*Median:* $195

Percent of Experts Having a Minimum Charge for Deps: 100% **Cancellation Fee for Deps or Trial:** 0%
Deposition Payment in Advance: 100% **Markup of Out-of-Pocket Expenses:** 100%

Up-front Retainer: 100% **Retainer Amount:** *High:* $2,500 *Low:* $2,500 *Average:* $2,500 *Median:* $2,500
Travel Billed Portal-to-Portal: 100% **1st-class Airfare Required:** 0%

Written Fee Agreement: 100% **Majority of Work:** *Plaintiffs:* 0% *Defendants:* 0% *Neither:* 100%
Retaining Counsel Failed to Pay Last 5 Years: 100% **Opposing Counsel Failed to Pay Last 5 Years:** 100%

Engineering, Geotechnical

Responding Experts: *4*

Hourly Fees:					
	In-court Testimony:	*High:* $300	*Low:* $150	*Average:* $200	*Median:* $175
	File Review/Prep:	*High:* $185	*Low:* $120	*Average:* $165	*Median:* $175
	Depositions:	*High:* $300	*Low:* $150	*Average:* $200	*Median:* $175

Percent of Experts Having a Minimum Charge for Deps: 0% **Cancellation Fee for Deps or Trial:** 0%
Deposition Payment in Advance: 100% **Markup of Out-of-Pocket Expenses:** 50%

Up-front Retainer: 100% **Retainer Amount:** *High:* $1,000 *Low:* $1,000 *Average:* $1,000 *Median:* $1,000
Travel Billed Portal-to-Portal: 100% **1st-class Airfare Required:** 0%

Written Fee Agreement: 75% **Majority of Work:** *Plaintiffs:* 25% *Defendants:* 25% *Neither:* 50%
Retaining Counsel Failed to Pay Last 5 Years: 50% **Opposing Counsel Failed to Pay Last 5 Years:** 50%

Engineering, Highway

Responding Experts: *1*

Hourly Fees:					
	In-court Testimony:	*High:* $180	*Low:* $180	*Average:* $180	*Median:* $180
	File Review/Prep:	*High:* $180	*Low:* $180	*Average:* $180	*Median:* $180
	Depositions:	*High:* $180	*Low:* $180	*Average:* $180	*Median:* $180

Percent of Experts Having a Minimum Charge for Deps: 0% **Cancellation Fee for Deps or Trial:** 0%
Deposition Payment in Advance: 0% **Markup of Out-of-Pocket Expenses:** 0%

Up-front Retainer: 0% **Retainer Amount:** *High:* N/A *Low:* N/A *Average:* N/A *Median:* N/A
Travel Billed Portal-to-Portal: 0% **1st-class Airfare Required:** 0%

Written Fee Agreement: 100% **Majority of Work:** *Plaintiffs:* 100% *Defendants:* 0% *Neither:* 0%
Retaining Counsel Failed to Pay Last 5 Years: 100% **Opposing Counsel Failed to Pay Last 5 Years:** 100%

Engineering, Industrial

Responding Experts: *1*

Hourly Fees:					
	In-court Testimony:	*High:* $200	*Low:* $200	*Average:* $200	*Median:* $200
	File Review/Prep:	*High:* $200	*Low:* $200	*Average:* $200	*Median:* $200
	Depositions:	*High:* $200	*Low:* $200	*Average:* $200	*Median:* $200

Percent of Experts Having a Minimum Charge for Deps: 100% **Cancellation Fee for Deps or Trial:** 0%
Deposition Payment in Advance: 0% **Markup of Out-of-Pocket Expenses:** 0%

Up-front Retainer: 100% **Retainer Amount:** *High:* $1,600 *Low:* $1,600 *Average:* $1,600 *Median:* $1,600
Travel Billed Portal-to-Portal: 100% **1st-class Airfare Required:** 0%

Written Fee Agreement: 100% **Majority of Work:** *Plaintiffs:* 0% *Defendants:* 0% *Neither:* 100%
Retaining Counsel Failed to Pay Last 5 Years: 100% **Opposing Counsel Failed to Pay Last 5 Years:** 100%

Engineering, Marine

Responding Experts: *1*

Hourly Fees:					
	In-court Testimony:	*High:* $200	*Low:* $200	*Average:* $200	*Median:* $200
	File Review/Prep:	*High:* $150	*Low:* $150	*Average:* $150	*Median:* $150
	Depositions:	*High:* $150	*Low:* $150	*Average:* $150	*Median:* $150

Percent of Experts Having a Minimum Charge for Deps: 100% **Cancellation Fee for Deps or Trial:** 100%
Deposition Payment in Advance: 100% **Markup of Out-of-Pocket Expenses:** 0%

Up-front Retainer: 0% **Retainer Amount:** *High:* N/A *Low:* N/A *Average:* N/A *Median:* N/A
Travel Billed Portal-to-Portal: N/A **1st-class Airfare Required:** 100%

Written Fee Agreement: 0% **Majority of Work:** *Plaintiffs:* 0% *Defendants:* 100% *Neither:* 0%
Retaining Counsel Failed to Pay Last 5 Years: 0% **Opposing Counsel Failed to Pay Last 5 Years:** 0%

Engineering, Materials

Responding Experts: *1*

Hourly Fees:					
	In-court Testimony:	*High:* $270	*Low:* $270	*Average:* $270	*Median:* $270
	File Review/Prep:	*High:* $210	*Low:* $210	*Average:* $210	*Median:* $210
	Depositions:	*High:* $270	*Low:* $270	*Average:* $270	*Median:* $270

Percent of Experts Having a Minimum Charge for Deps: 100% **Cancellation Fee for Deps or Trial:** 0%
Deposition Payment in Advance: 0% **Markup of Out-of-Pocket Expenses:** 100%

Up-front Retainer: 0% **Retainer Amount:** *High:* N/A *Low:* N/A *Average:* N/A *Median:* N/A
Travel Billed Portal-to-Portal: 0% **1st-class Airfare Required:** 0%

Written Fee Agreement: 100% **Majority of Work:** *Plaintiffs:* 0% *Defendants:* 0% *Neither:* 100%
Retaining Counsel Failed to Pay Last 5 Years: 100% **Opposing Counsel Failed to Pay Last 5 Years:** 100%

Engineering, Mechanical

Responding Experts: *23*

Hourly Fees:

In-court Testimony:	*High:* $380	*Low:* $150	*Average:* $250	*Median:* $230
File Review/Prep:	*High:* $350	*Low:* $150	*Average:* $210	*Median:* $200
Depositions:	*High:* $380	*Low:* $150	*Average:* $250	*Median:* $230

Percent of Experts Having a Minimum Charge for Deps: 43% **Cancellation Fee for Deps or Trial:** 26%
Deposition Payment in Advance: 39% **Markup of Out-of-Pocket Expenses:** 43%

Up-front Retainer: 82% **Retainer Amount:** *High:* $3,000 *Low:* $600 *Average:* $1,890 *Median:* $2,000
Travel Billed Portal-to-Portal: 87% **1st-class Airfare Required:** 9%

Written Fee Agreement: 81% **Majority of Work:** *Plaintiffs:* 30% *Defendants:* 13% *Neither:* 57%
Retaining Counsel Failed to Pay Last 5 Years: 61% **Opposing Counsel Failed to Pay Last 5 Years:** 26%

Engineering, Metallurgical

Responding Experts: *1*

Hourly Fees:

In-court Testimony:	*High:* $125	*Low:* $125	*Average:* $125	*Median:* $125
File Review/Prep:	*High:* $80	*Low:* $80	*Average:* $80	*Median:* $80
Depositions:	*High:* $115	*Low:* $115	*Average:* $115	*Median:* $115

Percent of Experts Having a Minimum Charge for Deps: 0% **Cancellation Fee for Deps or Trial:** 0%
Deposition Payment in Advance: N/A **Markup of Out-of-Pocket Expenses:** 0%

Up-front Retainer: 0% **Retainer Amount:** *High:* N/A *Low:* N/A *Average:* N/A *Median:* N/A
Travel Billed Portal-to-Portal: 100% **1st-class Airfare Required:** 0%

Written Fee Agreement: 0% **Majority of Work:** *Plaintiffs:* 0% *Defendants:* 100% *Neither:* 0%
Retaining Counsel Failed to Pay Last 5 Years: 0% **Opposing Counsel Failed to Pay Last 5 Years:** 0%

Engineering, Petroleum

Responding Experts: *2*

Hourly Fees:

In-court Testimony:	*High:* $195	*Low:* $125	*Average:* $160	*Median:* $160
File Review/Prep:	*High:* $195	*Low:* $125	*Average:* $160	*Median:* $160
Depositions:	*High:* $195	*Low:* $125	*Average:* $160	*Median:* $160

Percent of Experts Having a Minimum Charge for Deps: 0% **Cancellation Fee for Deps or Trial:** 0%
Deposition Payment in Advance: 0% **Markup of Out-of-Pocket Expenses:** 0%

Up-front Retainer: 0% **Retainer Amount:** *High:* N/A *Low:* N/A *Average:* N/A *Median:* N/A
Travel Billed Portal-to-Portal: 100% **1st-class Airfare Required:** 0%

Written Fee Agreement: 100% **Majority of Work:** *Plaintiffs:* 0% *Defendants:* 50% *Neither:* 50%
Retaining Counsel Failed to Pay Last 5 Years: 0% **Opposing Counsel Failed to Pay Last 5 Years:** 0%

Engineering, Railway

Responding Experts: *1*

Hourly Fees:

In-court Testimony:	*High:* $250	*Low:* $250	*Average:* $250	*Median:* $250
File Review/Prep:	*High:* $170	*Low:* $170	*Average:* $170	*Median:* $170
Depositions:	*High:* $250	*Low:* $250	*Average:* $250	*Median:* $250

Percent of Experts Having a Minimum Charge for Deps: 100% **Cancellation Fee for Deps or Trial:** 100%
Deposition Payment in Advance: 100% **Markup of Out-of-Pocket Expenses:** 100%

Up-front Retainer: 100% **Retainer Amount:** *High:* $4,000 *Low:* $4,000 *Average:* $4,000 *Median:* $4,000
Travel Billed Portal-to-Portal: 100% **1st-class Airfare Required:** 100%

Written Fee Agreement: 100% **Majority of Work:** *Plaintiffs:* 100% *Defendants:* 0% *Neither:* 0%
Retaining Counsel Failed to Pay Last 5 Years: 0% **Opposing Counsel Failed to Pay Last 5 Years:** 0%

Engineering, Residential

Responding Experts: *1*

Hourly Fees: **In-court Testimony:** *High:* $250 *Low:* $250 *Average:* $250 *Median:* $250
File Review/Prep: *High:* $165 *Low:* $165 *Average:* $165 *Median:* $165
Depositions: *High:* $200 *Low:* $200 *Average:* $200 *Median:* $200
Percent of Experts Having a Minimum Charge for Deps: 0% **Cancellation Fee for Deps or Trial:** 100%
Deposition Payment in Advance: 100% **Markup of Out-of-Pocket Expenses:** 0%

Up-front Retainer: 100% **Retainer Amount:** *High:* N/A *Low:* N/A *Average:* N/A *Median:* N/A
Travel Billed Portal-to-Portal: 100% **1st-class Airfare Required:** 0%

Written Fee Agreement: 100% **Majority of Work:** *Plaintiffs:* 100% *Defendants:* 0% *Neither:* 0%
Retaining Counsel Failed to Pay Last 5 Years: 0% **Opposing Counsel Failed to Pay Last 5 Years:** 0%

Engineering, Safety

Responding Experts: *2*

Hourly Fees: **In-court Testimony:** *High:* $150 *Low:* $150 *Average:* $150 *Median:* $150
File Review/Prep: *High:* $150 *Low:* $125 *Average:* $137 *Median:* $137
Depositions: *High:* $150 *Low:* $150 *Average:* $150 *Median:* $150
Percent of Experts Having a Minimum Charge for Deps: 100% **Cancellation Fee for Deps or Trial:** 0%
Deposition Payment in Advance: 50% **Markup of Out-of-Pocket Expenses:** 50%

Up-front Retainer: 100% **Retainer Amount:** *High:* $1,000 *Low:* $500 *Average:* $750 *Median:* $750
Travel Billed Portal-to-Portal: 100% **1st-class Airfare Required:** 0%

Written Fee Agreement: 100% **Majority of Work:** *Plaintiffs:* 100% *Defendants:* 0% *Neither:* 0%
Retaining Counsel Failed to Pay Last 5 Years: 50% **Opposing Counsel Failed to Pay Last 5 Years:** 50%

Engineering, Structural

Responding Experts: *17*

Hourly Fees: **In-court Testimony:** *High:* $375 *Low:* $100 *Average:* $225 *Median:* $220
File Review/Prep: *High:* $350 *Low:* $100 *Average:* $190 *Median:* $150
Depositions: *High:* $350 *Low:* $175 *Average:* $220 *Median:* $220
Percent of Experts Having a Minimum Charge for Deps: 29% **Cancellation Fee for Deps or Trial:** 6%
Deposition Payment in Advance: 19% **Markup of Out-of-Pocket Expenses:** 41%

Up-front Retainer: 47% **Retainer Amount:** *High:* $4,000 *Low:* $1,250 *Average:* $2,700 *Median:* $2,750
Travel Billed Portal-to-Portal: 100% **1st-class Airfare Required:** 12%

Written Fee Agreement: 58% **Majority of Work:** *Plaintiffs:* 6% *Defendants:* 12% *Neither:* 82%
Retaining Counsel Failed to Pay Last 5 Years: 50% **Opposing Counsel Failed to Pay Last 5 Years:** 31%

Engineering, Traffic

Responding Experts: *3*

Hourly Fees: **In-court Testimony:** *High:* $250 *Low:* $180 *Average:* $215 *Median:* $210
File Review/Prep: *High:* $250 *Low:* $100 *Average:* $175 *Median:* $180
Depositions: *High:* $250 *Low:* $180 *Average:* $215 *Median:* $210
Percent of Experts Having a Minimum Charge for Deps: 0% **Cancellation Fee for Deps or Trial:** 0%
Deposition Payment in Advance: 66% **Markup of Out-of-Pocket Expenses:** 50%

Up-front Retainer: 100% **Retainer Amount:** *High:* $1,500 *Low:* $1,500 *Average:* $1,500 *Median:* $1,500
Travel Billed Portal-to-Portal: 100% **1st-class Airfare Required:** 0%

Written Fee Agreement: 100% **Majority of Work:** *Plaintiffs:* 33% *Defendants:* 33% *Neither:* 33%
Retaining Counsel Failed to Pay Last 5 Years: 100% **Opposing Counsel Failed to Pay Last 5 Years:** 33%

Engineering, Transportation

Responding Experts: *1*

Hourly Fees: **In-court Testimony:** *High:* $175 *Low:* $175 *Average:* $175 *Median:* $175
File Review/Prep: *High:* $130 *Low:* $130 *Average:* $130 *Median:* $130
Depositions: *High:* $175 *Low:* $175 *Average:* $175 *Median:* $175
Percent of Experts Having a Minimum Charge for Deps: 0% **Cancellation Fee for Deps or Trial:** 0%
Deposition Payment in Advance: 0% **Markup of Out-of-Pocket Expenses:** 100%

Up-front Retainer: 100% **Retainer Amount:** *High:* $1,500 *Low:* $1,500 *Average:* $1,500 *Median:* $1,500
Travel Billed Portal-to-Portal: 100% **1st-class Airfare Required:** 0%

Written Fee Agreement: 100% **Majority of Work:** *Plaintiffs:* 0% *Defendants:* 0% *Neither:* 100%
Retaining Counsel Failed to Pay Last 5 Years: 100% **Opposing Counsel Failed to Pay Last 5 Years:** 0%

Engineering, Wind

Responding Experts: *1*

Hourly Fees: **In-court Testimony:** *High:* $200 *Low:* $200 *Average:* $200 *Median:* $200
File Review/Prep: *High:* $100 *Low:* $100 *Average:* $100 *Median:* $100
Depositions: *High:* $200 *Low:* $200 *Average:* $200 *Median:* $200
Percent of Experts Having a Minimum Charge for Deps: 0% **Cancellation Fee for Deps or Trial:** 0%
Deposition Payment in Advance: 0% **Markup of Out-of-Pocket Expenses:** 0%

Up-front Retainer: 0% **Retainer Amount:** *High:* N/A *Low:* N/A *Average:* N/A *Median:* N/A
Travel Billed Portal-to-Portal: 0% **1st-class Airfare Required:** 0%

Written Fee Agreement: 100% **Majority of Work:** *Plaintiffs:* 0% *Defendants:* 0% *Neither:* 100%
Retaining Counsel Failed to Pay Last 5 Years: 0% **Opposing Counsel Failed to Pay Last 5 Years:** 0%

Environmental, (All)

Responding Experts: *13*

Hourly Fees: **In-court Testimony:** *High:* $600 *Low:* $150 *Average:* $305 *Median:* $250
File Review/Prep: *High:* $500 *Low:* $100 *Average:* $235 *Median:* $200
Depositions: *High:* $500 *Low:* $150 *Average:* $295 *Median:* $250
Percent of Experts Having a Minimum Charge for Deps: 23% **Cancellation Fee for Deps or Trial:** 23%
Deposition Payment in Advance: 9% **Markup of Out-of-Pocket Expenses:** 54%

Up-front Retainer: 38% **Retainer Amount:** *High:* $4,000 *Low:* $1,500 *Average:* $3,375 *Median:* $4,000
Travel Billed Portal-to-Portal: 92% **1st-class Airfare Required:** 0%

Written Fee Agreement: 92% **Majority of Work:** *Plaintiffs:* 31% *Defendants:* 15% *Neither:* 54%
Retaining Counsel Failed to Pay Last 5 Years: 42% **Opposing Counsel Failed to Pay Last 5 Years:** 0%

Environmental Health

Responding Experts: *2*

Hourly Fees: **In-court Testimony:** *High:* $250 *Low:* $225 *Average:* $238 *Median:* $238
File Review/Prep: *High:* $200 *Low:* $190 *Average:* $180 *Median:* $180
Depositions: *High:* $250 *Low:* $225 *Average:* $238 *Median:* $238
Percent of Experts Having a Minimum Charge for Deps: 0% **Cancellation Fee for Deps or Trial:** 0%
Deposition Payment in Advance: 0% **Markup of Out-of-Pocket Expenses:** 50%

Up-front Retainer: 0% **Retainer Amount:** *High:* N/A *Low:* N/A *Average:* N/A *Median:* N/A
Travel Billed Portal-to-Portal: 100% **1st-class Airfare Required:** 0%

Written Fee Agreement: 100% **Majority of Work:** *Plaintiffs:* 0% *Defendants:* 0% *Neither:* 100%
Retaining Counsel Failed to Pay Last 5 Years: 0% **Opposing Counsel Failed to Pay Last 5 Years:** 0%

Environmental Medicine

Responding Experts: *1*

Hourly Fees: **In-court Testimony:** *High:* $250 *Low:* $250 *Average:* $250 *Median:* $250
File Review/Prep: *High:* $225 *Low:* $225 *Average:* $225 *Median:* $225
Depositions: *High:* $250 *Low:* $250 *Average:* $250 *Median:* $250
Percent of Experts Having a Minimum Charge for Deps: 0% **Cancellation Fee for Deps or Trial:** 0%
Deposition Payment in Advance: 0% **Markup of Out-of-Pocket Expenses:** 100%

Up-front Retainer: 0% **Retainer Amount:** *High:* N/A *Low:* N/A *Average:* N/A *Median:* N/A
Travel Billed Portal-to-Portal: 0% **1st-class Airfare Required:** 0%

Written Fee Agreement: 100% **Majority of Work:** *Plaintiffs:* 0% *Defendants:* 0% *Neither:* 100%
Retaining Counsel Failed to Pay Last 5 Years: 100% **Opposing Counsel Failed to Pay Last 5 Years:** 0%

Environmental Toxicology

Responding Experts: *1*

Hourly Fees: **In-court Testimony:** *High:* $400 *Low:* $400 *Average:* $400 *Median:* $400
File Review/Prep: *High:* $225 *Low:* $225 *Average:* $225 *Median:* $225
Depositions: *High:* $400 *Low:* $400 *Average:* $400 *Median:* $400
Percent of Experts Having a Minimum Charge for Deps: 0% **Cancellation Fee for Deps or Trial:** 0%
Deposition Payment in Advance: 0% **Markup of Out-of-Pocket Expenses:** 100%

Up-front Retainer: 100% **Retainer Amount:** *High:* N/A *Low:* N/A *Average:* N/A *Median:* N/A
Travel Billed Portal-to-Portal: 100% **1st-class Airfare Required:** 0%

Written Fee Agreement: 100% **Majority of Work:** *Plaintiffs:* 0% *Defendants:* 0% *Neither:* 100%
Retaining Counsel Failed to Pay Last 5 Years: 100% **Opposing Counsel Failed to Pay Last 5 Years:** 0%

Environmental, Air Pollution

Responding Experts: *2*

Hourly Fees: **In-court Testimony:** *High:* $500 *Low:* $400 *Average:* $450 *Median:* $450
File Review/Prep: *High:* $350 *Low:* $250 *Average:* $300 *Median:* $300
Depositions: *High:* $500 *Low:* $400 *Average:* $450 *Median:* $450
Percent of Experts Having a Minimum Charge for Deps: 50% **Cancellation Fee for Deps or Trial:** 50%
Deposition Payment in Advance: 0% **Markup of Out-of-Pocket Expenses:** 100%

Up-front Retainer: 100% **Retainer Amount:** *High:* N/A *Low:* N/A *Average:* N/A *Median:* N/A
Travel Billed Portal-to-Portal: 100% **1st-class Airfare Required:** 0%

Written Fee Agreement: 100% **Majority of Work:** *Plaintiffs:* 100% *Defendants:* 0% *Neither:* 0%
Retaining Counsel Failed to Pay Last 5 Years: 100% **Opposing Counsel Failed to Pay Last 5 Years:** 0%

Environmental, Contaminated Soil

Responding Experts: *1*

Hourly Fees: **In-court Testimony:** *High:* $500 *Low:* $500 *Average:* $500 *Median:* $500
File Review/Prep: *High:* $400 *Low:* $400 *Average:* $400 *Median:* $400
Depositions: *High:* $500 *Low:* $500 *Average:* $500 *Median:* $500
Percent of Experts Having a Minimum Charge for Deps: 100% **Cancellation Fee for Deps or Trial:** 100%
Deposition Payment in Advance: 0% **Markup of Out-of-Pocket Expenses:** 100%

Up-front Retainer: 100% **Retainer Amount:** *High:* N/A *Low:* N/A *Average:* N/A *Median:* N/A
Travel Billed Portal-to-Portal: 100% **1st-class Airfare Required:** 0%

Written Fee Agreement: 100% **Majority of Work:** *Plaintiffs:* 100% *Defendants:* 0% *Neither:* 0%
Retaining Counsel Failed to Pay Last 5 Years: 100% **Opposing Counsel Failed to Pay Last 5 Years:** 0%

Environmental, Groundwater

Responding Experts: *1*

Hourly Fees: **In-court Testimony:** *High:* $600 *Low:* $600 *Average:* $600 *Median:* $600
File Review/Prep: *High:* $500 *Low:* $500 *Average:* $500 *Median:* $500
Depositions: *High:* $500 *Low:* $500 *Average:* $500 *Median:* $500
Percent of Experts Having a Minimum Charge for Deps: 100% **Cancellation Fee for Deps or Trial:** 100%
Deposition Payment in Advance: 100% **Markup of Out-of-Pocket Expenses:** 100%

Up-front Retainer: 100% **Retainer Amount:** *High:* N/A *Low:* N/A *Average:* N/A *Median:* N/A
Travel Billed Portal-to-Portal: N/A **1st-class Airfare Required:** N/A

Written Fee Agreement: 100% **Majority of Work:** *Plaintiffs:* 100% *Defendants:* 0% *Neither:* 0%
Retaining Counsel Failed to Pay Last 5 Years: N/A **Opposing Counsel Failed to Pay Last 5 Years:** N/A

Epidemiology

Responding Experts: *1*

Hourly Fees: **In-court Testimony:** *High:* $1,000 *Low:* $1,000 *Average:* $1,000 *Median:* $1,000
File Review/Prep: *High:* $650 *Low:* $650 *Average:* $650 *Median:* $650
Depositions: *High:* $650 *Low:* $650 *Average:* $650 *Median:* $650
Percent of Experts Having a Minimum Charge for Deps: 100% **Cancellation Fee for Deps or Trial:** 100%
Deposition Payment in Advance: 0% **Markup of Out-of-Pocket Expenses:** 0%

Up-front Retainer: 0% **Retainer Amount:** *High:* N/A *Low:* N/A *Average:* N/A *Median:* N/A
Travel Billed Portal-to-Portal: 100% **1st-class Airfare Required:** 0%

Written Fee Agreement: 100% **Majority of Work:** *Plaintiffs:* 0% *Defendants:* 0% *Neither:* 100%
Retaining Counsel Failed to Pay Last 5 Years: 100% **Opposing Counsel Failed to Pay Last 5 Years:** 100%

Ergonomics

Responding Experts: *1*

Hourly Fees: **In-court Testimony:** *High:* $275 *Low:* $150 *Average:* $213 *Median:* $213
File Review/Prep: *High:* $210 *Low:* $150 *Average:* $180 *Median:* $180
Depositions: *High:* $275 *Low:* $150 *Average:* $213 *Median:* $213
Percent of Experts Having a Minimum Charge for Deps: 0% **Cancellation Fee for Deps or Trial:** 0%
Deposition Payment in Advance: 50% **Markup of Out-of-Pocket Expenses:** 0%

Up-front Retainer: 100% **Retainer Amount:** *High:* $2,000 *Low:* $1,250 *Average:* $1,625 *Median:* $1,625
Travel Billed Portal-to-Portal: 100% **1st-class Airfare Required:** 0%

Written Fee Agreement: 100% **Majority of Work:** *Plaintiffs:* 0% *Defendants:* 50% *Neither:* 50%
Retaining Counsel Failed to Pay Last 5 Years: 50% **Opposing Counsel Failed to Pay Last 5 Years:** 50%

Explosions

Responding Experts: *1*

Hourly Fees: **In-court Testimony:** *High:* $250 *Low:* $250 *Average:* $250 *Median:* $250
File Review/Prep: *High:* $100 *Low:* $100 *Average:* $100 *Median:* $100
Depositions: *High:* $150 *Low:* $150 *Average:* $150 *Median:* $150
Percent of Experts Having a Minimum Charge for Deps: 0% **Cancellation Fee for Deps or Trial:** 0%
Deposition Payment in Advance: 100% **Markup of Out-of-Pocket Expenses:** 0%

Up-front Retainer: 0% **Retainer Amount:** *High:* N/A *Low:* N/A *Average:* N/A *Median:* N/A
Travel Billed Portal-to-Portal: 100% **1st-class Airfare Required:** 0%

Written Fee Agreement: 0% **Majority of Work:** *Plaintiffs:* 0% *Defendants:* 0% *Neither:* 100%
Retaining Counsel Failed to Pay Last 5 Years: 0% **Opposing Counsel Failed to Pay Last 5 Years:** 0%

Failure Analysis

Responding Experts: *6*

Hourly Fees: **In-court Testimony:** *High:* $400 *Low:* $180 *Average:* $265 *Median:* $250
File Review/Prep: *High:* $250 *Low:* $150 *Average:* $210 *Median:* $215
Depositions: *High:* $400 *Low:* $180 *Average:* $265 *Median:* $250
Percent of Experts Having a Minimum Charge for Deps: 33% **Cancellation Fee for Deps or Trial:** 33%
Deposition Payment in Advance: 17% **Markup of Out-of-Pocket Expenses:** 50%

Up-front Retainer: 83% **Retainer Amount:** *High:* $200 *Low:* $1,000 *Average:* $1,500 *Median:* $1,500
Travel Billed Portal-to-Portal: 100% **1st-class Airfare Required:** 33%

Written Fee Agreement: 100% **Majority of Work:** *Plaintiffs:* 17% *Defendants:* 0% *Neither:* 83%
Retaining Counsel Failed to Pay Last 5 Years: 66% **Opposing Counsel Failed to Pay Last 5 Years:** 17%

Family Practice

Responding Experts: *8*

Hourly Fees: **In-court Testimony:** *High:* $850 *Low:* $200 *Average:* $475 *Median:* $425
File Review/Prep: *High:* $500 *Low:* $125 *Average:* $280 *Median:* $275
Depositions: *High:* $600 *Low:* $200 *Average:* $405 *Median:* $425
Percent of Experts Having a Minimum Charge for Deps: 75% **Cancellation Fee for Deps or Trial:** 86%
Deposition Payment in Advance: 88% **Markup of Out-of-Pocket Expenses:** 0%

Up-front Retainer: 63% **Retainer Amount:** *High:* $1,000 *Low:* $500 *Average:* $840 *Median:* $1,000
Travel Billed Portal-to-Portal: 88% **1st-class Airfare Required:** 0%

Written Fee Agreement: 88% **Majority of Work:** *Plaintiffs:* 25% *Defendants:* 0% *Neither:* 75%
Retaining Counsel Failed to Pay Last 5 Years: 25% **Opposing Counsel Failed to Pay Last 5 Years:** 38%

Fasteners

Responding Experts: *1*

Hourly Fees: **In-court Testimony:** *High:* $175 *Low:* $175 *Average:* $175 *Median:* $175
File Review/Prep: *High:* $175 *Low:* $175 *Average:* $175 *Median:* $175
Depositions: *High:* $175 *Low:* $175 *Average:* $175 *Median:* $175
Percent of Experts Having a Minimum Charge for Deps: 0% **Cancellation Fee for Deps or Trial:** 100%
Deposition Payment in Advance: 0% **Markup of Out-of-Pocket Expenses:** 100%

Up-front Retainer: 100% **Retainer Amount:** *High:* $850 *Low:* $850 *Average:* $850 *Median:* $850
Travel Billed Portal-to-Portal: 100% **1st-class Airfare Required:** 0%

Written Fee Agreement: 100% **Majority of Work:** *Plaintiffs:* 0% *Defendants:* 0% *Neither:* 100%
Retaining Counsel Failed to Pay Last 5 Years: 0% **Opposing Counsel Failed to Pay Last 5 Years:** 0%

Finance

Responding Experts: *4*

Hourly Fees: **In-court Testimony:** *High:* $300 *Low:* $250 *Average:* $268 *Median:* $263
File Review/Prep: *High:* $300 *Low:* $185 *Average:* $235 *Median:* $225
Depositions: *High:* $300 *Low:* $200 *Average:* $245 *Median:* $238
Percent of Experts Having a Minimum Charge for Deps: 25% **Cancellation Fee for Deps or Trial:** 25%
Deposition Payment in Advance: 0% **Markup of Out-of-Pocket Expenses:** 25%

Up-front Retainer: 75% **Retainer Amount:** *High:* $8,750 *Low:* $5,000 *Average:* $6,250 *Median:* $5,000
Travel Billed Portal-to-Portal: 75% **1st-class Airfare Required:** 0%

Written Fee Agreement: 50% **Majority of Work:** *Plaintiffs:* 75% *Defendants:* 0% *Neither:* 25%
Retaining Counsel Failed to Pay Last 5 Years: 0% **Opposing Counsel Failed to Pay Last 5 Years:** 0%

Fingerprints

Responding Experts: *1*

Hourly Fees: **In-court Testimony:** *High:* $125 *Low:* $125 *Average:* $125 *Median:* $125
File Review/Prep: *High:* $125 *Low:* $125 *Average:* $125 *Median:* $125
Depositions: *High:* $125 *Low:* $125 *Average:* $125 *Median:* $125
Percent of Experts Having a Minimum Charge for Deps: 100% **Cancellation Fee for Deps or Trial:** 0%
Deposition Payment in Advance: 100% **Markup of Out-of-Pocket Expenses:** 0%

Up-front Retainer: 100% **Retainer Amount:** *High:* $500 *Low:* $500 *Average:* $500 *Median:* $500
Travel Billed Portal-to-Portal: 100% **1st-class Airfare Required:** 0%

Written Fee Agreement: 100% **Majority of Work:** *Plaintiffs:* 0% *Defendants:* 100% *Neither:* 0%
Retaining Counsel Failed to Pay Last 5 Years: 100% **Opposing Counsel Failed to Pay Last 5 Years:** 0%

Fire, (All)

Responding Experts: *15*

Hourly Fees: **In-court Testimony:** *High:* $300 *Low:* $100 *Average:* $196 *Median:* $200
File Review/Prep: *High:* $215 *Low:* $25 *Average:* $138 *Median:* $125
Depositions: *High:* $300 *Low:* $100 *Average:* $192 *Median:* $195
Percent of Experts Having a Minimum Charge for Deps: 47% **Cancellation Fee for Deps or Trial:** 14%
Deposition Payment in Advance: 40% **Markup of Out-of-Pocket Expenses:** 36%

Up-front Retainer: 69% **Retainer Amount:** *High:* $5,000 *Low:* $800 *Average:* $2,040 *Median:* $1,500
Travel Billed Portal-to-Portal: 94% **1st-class Airfare Required:** 13%

Written Fee Agreement: 93% **Majority of Work:** *Plaintiffs:* 7% *Defendants:* 28% *Neither:* 65%
Retaining Counsel Failed to Pay Last 5 Years: 60% **Opposing Counsel Failed to Pay Last 5 Years:** 13%

Fire Investigation

Responding Experts: *6*

Hourly Fees: **In-court Testimony:** *High:* $250 *Low:* $200 *Average:* $225 *Median:* $225
File Review/Prep: *High:* $200 *Low:* $125 *Average:* $160 *Median:* $150
Depositions: *High:* $250 *Low:* $195 *Average:* $215 *Median:* $215
Percent of Experts Having a Minimum Charge for Deps: 83% **Cancellation Fee for Deps or Trial:** 0%
Deposition Payment in Advance: 83% **Markup of Out-of-Pocket Expenses:** 67%

Up-front Retainer: 100% **Retainer Amount:** *High:* $5,000 *Low:* $5,000 *Average:* $5,000 *Median:* $5,000
Travel Billed Portal-to-Portal: 83% **1st-class Airfare Required:** 0%

Written Fee Agreement: 83% **Majority of Work:** *Plaintiffs:* 0% *Defendants:* 0% *Neither:* 100%
Retaining Counsel Failed to Pay Last 5 Years: 100% **Opposing Counsel Failed to Pay Last 5 Years:** 16%

Fire Protection

Responding Experts: *1*

Hourly Fees: **In-court Testimony:** *High:* $300 *Low:* $300 *Average:* $300 *Median:* $300
File Review/Prep: *High:* $200 *Low:* $200 *Average:* $200 *Median:* $200
Depositions: *High:* $300 *Low:* $300 *Average:* $300 *Median:* $300
Percent of Experts Having a Minimum Charge for Deps: 100% **Cancellation Fee for Deps or Trial:** 100%
Deposition Payment in Advance: 100% **Markup of Out-of-Pocket Expenses:** 100%

Up-front Retainer: N/A **Retainer Amount:** *High:* N/A *Low:* N/A *Average:* N/A *Median:* N/A
Travel Billed Portal-to-Portal: 100% **1st-class Airfare Required:** 0%

Written Fee Agreement: 100% **Majority of Work:** *Plaintiffs:* 100% *Defendants:* 0% *Neither:* 0%
Retaining Counsel Failed to Pay Last 5 Years: 100% **Opposing Counsel Failed to Pay Last 5 Years:** 0%

Fires, Electrical

Responding Experts: *1*

Hourly Fees:					
	In-court Testimony:	*High:* $300	*Low:* $300	*Average:* $300	*Median:* $300
	File Review/Prep:	*High:* $215	*Low:* $215	*Average:* $215	*Median:* $215
	Depositions:	*High:* $300	*Low:* $300	*Average:* $300	*Median:* $300

Percent of Experts Having a Minimum Charge for Deps: 100% **Cancellation Fee for Deps or Trial:** 100%
Deposition Payment in Advance: N/A **Markup of Out-of-Pocket Expenses:** N/A

Up-front Retainer: N/A **Retainer Amount:** *High:* N/A *Low:* N/A *Average:* N/A *Median:* N/A
Travel Billed Portal-to-Portal: 100% **1st-class Airfare Required:** 100%

Written Fee Agreement: 100% **Majority of Work:** *Plaintiffs:* N/A *Defendants:* N/A *Neither:* N/A
Retaining Counsel Failed to Pay Last 5 Years: 100% **Opposing Counsel Failed to Pay Last 5 Years:** 0%

Floors, Wood

Responding Experts: *1*

Hourly Fees:					
	In-court Testimony:	*High:* $115	*Low:* $115	*Average:* $115	*Median:* $115
	File Review/Prep:	*High:* $115	*Low:* $115	*Average:* $115	*Median:* $115
	Depositions:	*High:* $115	*Low:* $115	*Average:* $115	*Median:* $115

Percent of Experts Having a Minimum Charge for Deps: 0% **Cancellation Fee for Deps or Trial:** 0%
Deposition Payment in Advance: 0% **Markup of Out-of-Pocket Expenses:** 0%

Up-front Retainer: 0% **Retainer Amount:** *High:* N/A *Low:* N/A *Average:* N/A *Median:* N/A
Travel Billed Portal-to-Portal: 100% **1st-class Airfare Required:** 0%

Written Fee Agreement: 0% **Majority of Work:** *Plaintiffs:* 0% *Defendants:* 0% *Neither:* 100%
Retaining Counsel Failed to Pay Last 5 Years: 100% **Opposing Counsel Failed to Pay Last 5 Years:** 0%

Force Dynamics

Responding Experts: *1*

Hourly Fees:					
	In-court Testimony:	*High:* $395	*Low:* $395	*Average:* $395	*Median:* $395
	File Review/Prep:	*High:* $295	*Low:* $295	*Average:* $295	*Median:* $295
	Depositions:	*High:* $395	*Low:* $395	*Average:* $395	*Median:* $395

Percent of Experts Having a Minimum Charge for Deps: 0% **Cancellation Fee for Deps or Trial:** 0%
Deposition Payment in Advance: 100% **Markup of Out-of-Pocket Expenses:** 0%

Up-front Retainer: 100% **Retainer Amount:** *High:* $5,000 *Low:* $5,000 *Average:* $5,000 *Median:* $5,000
Travel Billed Portal-to-Portal: 100% **1st-class Airfare Required:** 0%

Written Fee Agreement: 100% **Majority of Work:** *Plaintiffs:* 100% *Defendants:* 0% *Neither:* 0%
Retaining Counsel Failed to Pay Last 5 Years: 100% **Opposing Counsel Failed to Pay Last 5 Years:** 0%

Forecasting

Responding Experts: *1*

Hourly Fees:					
	In-court Testimony:	*High:* $200	*Low:* $200	*Average:* $200	*Median:* $200
	File Review/Prep:	*High:* $150	*Low:* $150	*Average:* $150	*Median:* $150
	Depositions:	*High:* $200	*Low:* $200	*Average:* $200	*Median:* $200

Percent of Experts Having a Minimum Charge for Deps: 100% **Cancellation Fee for Deps or Trial:** 0%
Deposition Payment in Advance: 100% **Markup of Out-of-Pocket Expenses:** 0%

Up-front Retainer: 100% **Retainer Amount:** *High:* $1,500 *Low:* $1,500 *Average:* $1,500 *Median:* $1,500
Travel Billed Portal-to-Portal: 100% **1st-class Airfare Required:** 0%

Written Fee Agreement: 100% **Majority of Work:** *Plaintiffs:* 100% *Defendants:* 0% *Neither:* 0%
Retaining Counsel Failed to Pay Last 5 Years: 100% **Opposing Counsel Failed to Pay Last 5 Years:** 0%

Forensics

Responding Experts: *1*

Hourly Fees: **In-court Testimony:** *High:* $350 *Low:* $350 *Average:* $350 *Median:* $350
File Review/Prep: *High:* $350 *Low:* $350 *Average:* $350 *Median:* $350
Depositions: *High:* $350 *Low:* $350 *Average:* $350 *Median:* $350

Percent of Experts Having a Minimum Charge for Deps: 0% **Cancellation Fee for Deps or Trial:** 0%
Deposition Payment in Advance: 0% **Markup of Out-of-Pocket Expenses:** 0%

Up-front Retainer: 100% **Retainer Amount:** *High:* $4,250 *Low:* $4,250 *Average:* $4,250 *Median:* $4,250
Travel Billed Portal-to-Portal: 100% **1st-class Airfare Required:** 0%

Written Fee Agreement: 100% **Majority of Work:** *Plaintiffs:* 100% *Defendants:* 0% *Neither:* 0%
Retaining Counsel Failed to Pay Last 5 Years: 0% **Opposing Counsel Failed to Pay Last 5 Years:** 0%

Franchises

Responding Experts: *1*

Hourly Fees: **In-court Testimony:** *High:* $300 *Low:* $300 *Average:* $300 *Median:* $300
File Review/Prep: *High:* $275 *Low:* $275 *Average:* $275 *Median:* $275
Depositions: *High:* $300 *Low:* $300 *Average:* $300 *Median:* $300

Percent of Experts Having a Minimum Charge for Deps: 0% **Cancellation Fee for Deps or Trial:** 100%
Deposition Payment in Advance: 0% **Markup of Out-of-Pocket Expenses:** 100%

Up-front Retainer: 100% **Retainer Amount:** *High:* $5,000 *Low:* $5,000 *Average:* $5,000 *Median:* $5,000
Travel Billed Portal-to-Portal: 100% **1st-class Airfare Required:** 0%

Written Fee Agreement: 100% **Majority of Work:** *Plaintiffs:* 0% *Defendants:* 0% *Neither:* 100%
Retaining Counsel Failed to Pay Last 5 Years: 0% **Opposing Counsel Failed to Pay Last 5 Years:** 0%

Fraud, (All)

Responding Experts: *3*

Hourly Fees: **In-court Testimony:** *High:* $300 *Low:* $280 *Average:* $293 *Median:* $293
File Review/Prep: *High:* $300 *Low:* $280 *Average:* $293 *Median:* $293
Depositions: *High:* $300 *Low:* $280 *Average:* $293 *Median:* $293

Percent of Experts Having a Minimum Charge for Deps: 33% **Cancellation Fee for Deps or Trial:** 33%
Deposition Payment in Advance: 33% **Markup of Out-of-Pocket Expenses:** 0%

Up-front Retainer: 100% **Retainer Amount:** *High:* $3,000 *Low:* $2,500 *Average:* $2,750 *Median:* $2,750
Travel Billed Portal-to-Portal: 66% **1st-class Airfare Required:** 0%

Written Fee Agreement: 66% **Majority of Work:** *Plaintiffs:* 0% *Defendants:* 0% *Neither:* 100%
Retaining Counsel Failed to Pay Last 5 Years: 33% **Opposing Counsel Failed to Pay Last 5 Years:** 0%

Fraud, Securities

Responding Experts: *1*

Hourly Fees: **In-court Testimony:** *High:* $300 *Low:* $300 *Average:* $300 *Median:* $300
File Review/Prep: *High:* $300 *Low:* $300 *Average:* $300 *Median:* $300
Depositions: *High:* $300 *Low:* $300 *Average:* $300 *Median:* $300

Percent of Experts Having a Minimum Charge for Deps: 0% **Cancellation Fee for Deps or Trial:** 100%
Deposition Payment in Advance: 0% **Markup of Out-of-Pocket Expenses:** 0%

Up-front Retainer: 100% **Retainer Amount:** *High:* $3,000 *Low:* $3,000 *Average:* $3,000 *Median:* $3,000
Travel Billed Portal-to-Portal: 100% **1st-class Airfare Required:** 0%

Written Fee Agreement: 100% **Majority of Work:** *Plaintiffs:* 0% *Defendants:* 0% *Neither:* 100%
Retaining Counsel Failed to Pay Last 5 Years: 100% **Opposing Counsel Failed to Pay Last 5 Years:** 0%

Gastroenterology

Responding Experts: *5*

Hourly Fees: **In-court Testimony:** *High:* $600 *Low:* $500 *Average:* $530 *Median:* $500
File Review/Prep: *High:* $550 *Low:* $300 *Average:* $405 *Median:* $400
Depositions: *High:* $600 *Low:* $400 *Average:* $510 *Median:* $500
Percent of Experts Having a Minimum Charge for Deps: 40% **Cancellation Fee for Deps or Trial:** 40%
Deposition Payment in Advance: 40% **Markup of Out-of-Pocket Expenses:** 20%

Up-front Retainer: 80% **Retainer Amount:** *High:* $1,650 *Low:* $600 *Average:* $1,250 *Median:* $1,500
Travel Billed Portal-to-Portal: 100% **1st-class Airfare Required:** 40%

Written Fee Agreement: 60% **Majority of Work:** *Plaintiffs:* 0% *Defendants:* 40% *Neither:* 60%
Retaining Counsel Failed to Pay Last 5 Years: 60% **Opposing Counsel Failed to Pay Last 5 Years:** 20%

Genetics

Responding Experts: *2*

Hourly Fees: **In-court Testimony:** *High:* $350 *Low:* $250 *Average:* $300 *Median:* $300
File Review/Prep: *High:* $350 *Low:* $250 *Average:* $300 *Median:* $300
Depositions: *High:* $350 *Low:* $250 *Average:* $300 *Median:* $300
Percent of Experts Having a Minimum Charge for Deps: 0% **Cancellation Fee for Deps or Trial:** 0%
Deposition Payment in Advance: 0% **Markup of Out-of-Pocket Expenses:** 0%

Up-front Retainer: 0% **Retainer Amount:** *High:* N/A *Low:* N/A *Average:* N/A *Median:* N/A
Travel Billed Portal-to-Portal: 100% **1st-class Airfare Required:** 0%

Written Fee Agreement: 50% **Majority of Work:** *Plaintiffs:* 0% *Defendants:* 50% *Neither:* 50%
Retaining Counsel Failed to Pay Last 5 Years: 0% **Opposing Counsel Failed to Pay Last 5 Years:** 0%

Geology, (All)

Responding Experts: *6*

Hourly Fees: **In-court Testimony:** *High:* $350 *Low:* $150 *Average:* $265 *Median:* $250
File Review/Prep: *High:* $250 *Low:* $120 *Average:* $165 *Median:* $150
Depositions: *High:* $300 *Low:* $120 *Average:* $225 *Median:* $250
Percent of Experts Having a Minimum Charge for Deps: 50% **Cancellation Fee for Deps or Trial:** 0%
Deposition Payment in Advance: 17% **Markup of Out-of-Pocket Expenses:** 100%

Up-front Retainer: 33% **Retainer Amount:** *High:* $1,000 *Low:* $1,000 *Average:* $1,000 *Median:* $1,000
Travel Billed Portal-to-Portal: 100% **1st-class Airfare Required:** 0%

Written Fee Agreement: 100% **Majority of Work:** *Plaintiffs:* 16% *Defendants:* 0% *Neither:* 84%
Retaining Counsel Failed to Pay Last 5 Years: 0% **Opposing Counsel Failed to Pay Last 5 Years:** 0%

Geology, Hydro

Responding Experts: *3*

Hourly Fees: **In-court Testimony:** *High:* $350 *Low:* $290 *Average:* $315 *Median:* $300
File Review/Prep: *High:* $250 *Low:* $150 *Average:* $195 *Median:* $185
Depositions: *High:* $300 *Low:* $250 *Average:* $280 *Median:* $290
Percent of Experts Having a Minimum Charge for Deps: 33% **Cancellation Fee for Deps or Trial:** 0%
Deposition Payment in Advance: 33% **Markup of Out-of-Pocket Expenses:** 100%

Up-front Retainer: 0% **Retainer Amount:** *High:* N/A *Low:* N/A *Average:* N/A *Median:* N/A
Travel Billed Portal-to-Portal: 100% **1st-class Airfare Required:** 0%

Written Fee Agreement: 100% **Majority of Work:** *Plaintiffs:* 33% *Defendants:* 0% *Neither:* 66%
Retaining Counsel Failed to Pay Last 5 Years: 0% **Opposing Counsel Failed to Pay Last 5 Years:** 0%

Geriatrics

Responding Experts: *7*

Hourly Fees: **In-court Testimony:** *High:* $500 *Low:* $150 *Average:* $325 *Median:* $300
File Review/Prep: *High:* $350 *Low:* $75 *Average:* $225 *Median:* $250
Depositions: *High:* $500 *Low:* $125 *Average:* $315 *Median:* $300

Percent of Experts Having a Minimum Charge for Deps: 57% **Cancellation Fee for Deps or Trial:** 43%
Deposition Payment in Advance: 30% **Markup of Out-of-Pocket Expenses:** 0%

Up-front Retainer: 71% **Retainer Amount:** *High:* $1,500 *Low:* $500 *Average:* $900 *Median:* $750
Travel Billed Portal-to-Portal: 57% **1st-class Airfare Required:** 14%

Written Fee Agreement: 71% **Majority of Work:** *Plaintiffs:* 50% *Defendants:* 0% *Neither:* 50%
Retaining Counsel Failed to Pay Last 5 Years: 30% **Opposing Counsel Failed to Pay Last 5 Years:** 16%

Gerontology

Responding Experts: *1*

Hourly Fees: **In-court Testimony:** *High:* $150 *Low:* $150 *Average:* $150 *Median:* $150
File Review/Prep: *High:* $125 *Low:* $125 *Average:* $125 *Median:* $125
Depositions: *High:* $150 *Low:* $150 *Average:* $150 *Median:* $150

Percent of Experts Having a Minimum Charge for Deps: 0% **Cancellation Fee for Deps or Trial:** 0%
Deposition Payment in Advance: 0% **Markup of Out-of-Pocket Expenses:** 0%

Up-front Retainer: N/A **Retainer Amount:** *High:* N/A *Low:* N/A *Average:* N/A *Median:* N/A
Travel Billed Portal-to-Portal: 0% **1st-class Airfare Required:** 0%

Written Fee Agreement: N/A **Majority of Work:** *Plaintiffs:* 0% *Defendants:* 0% *Neither:* 100%
Retaining Counsel Failed to Pay Last 5 Years: 0% **Opposing Counsel Failed to Pay Last 5 Years:** 0%

Groundwater

Responding Experts: *1*

Hourly Fees: **In-court Testimony:** *High:* $350 *Low:* $350 *Average:* $350 *Median:* $350
File Review/Prep: *High:* $250 *Low:* $250 *Average:* $250 *Median:* $250
Depositions: *High:* $250 *Low:* $250 *Average:* $250 *Median:* $250

Percent of Experts Having a Minimum Charge for Deps: 100% **Cancellation Fee for Deps or Trial:** 0%
Deposition Payment in Advance: 100% **Markup of Out-of-Pocket Expenses:** 100%

Up-front Retainer: 0% **Retainer Amount:** *High:* N/A *Low:* N/A *Average:* N/A *Median:* N/A
Travel Billed Portal-to-Portal: 100% **1st-class Airfare Required:** 0%

Written Fee Agreement: 100% **Majority of Work:** *Plaintiffs:* 0% *Defendants:* 0% *Neither:* 100%
Retaining Counsel Failed to Pay Last 5 Years: 0% **Opposing Counsel Failed to Pay Last 5 Years:** 0%

Handwriting

Responding Experts: *1*

Hourly Fees: **In-court Testimony:** *High:* $125 *Low:* $125 *Average:* $125 *Median:* $125
File Review/Prep: *High:* $125 *Low:* $125 *Average:* $125 *Median:* $125
Depositions: *High:* $125 *Low:* $125 *Average:* $125 *Median:* $125

Percent of Experts Having a Minimum Charge for Deps: 100% **Cancellation Fee for Deps or Trial:** 0%
Deposition Payment in Advance: 100% **Markup of Out-of-Pocket Expenses:** 0%

Up-front Retainer: 100% **Retainer Amount:** *High:* $500 *Low:* $500 *Average:* $500 *Median:* $500
Travel Billed Portal-to-Portal: 100% **1st-class Airfare Required:** 0%

Written Fee Agreement: 100% **Majority of Work:** *Plaintiffs:* 0% *Defendants:* 0% *Neither:* 100%
Retaining Counsel Failed to Pay Last 5 Years: 0% **Opposing Counsel Failed to Pay Last 5 Years:** 0%

Hazardous Materials

Responding Experts: *2*

Hourly Fees: **In-court Testimony:** *High:* $375 *Low:* $250 *Average:* $312 *Median:* $312
File Review/Prep: *High:* $275 *Low:* $200 *Average:* $238 *Median:* $238
Depositions: *High:* $375 *Low:* $250 *Average:* $312 *Median:* $312

Percent of Experts Having a Minimum Charge for Deps: 100% **Cancellation Fee for Deps or Trial:** 50%
Deposition Payment in Advance: 10% **Markup of Out-of-Pocket Expenses:** 50%

Up-front Retainer: 100% **Retainer Amount:** *High:* $3,000 *Low:* $2,500 *Average:* $2,750 *Median:* $2,750
Travel Billed Portal-to-Portal: 100% **1st-class Airfare Required:** 0%

Written Fee Agreement: 100% **Majority of Work:** *Plaintiffs:* 0% *Defendants:* 0% *Neither:* 100%
Retaining Counsel Failed to Pay Last 5 Years: 100% **Opposing Counsel Failed to Pay Last 5 Years:** 50%

Healthcare, (All)

Responding Experts: *5*

Hourly Fees: **In-court Testimony:** *High:* $600 *Low:* $125 *Average:* $313 *Median:* $275
File Review/Prep: *High:* $350 *Low:* $125 *Average:* $225 *Median:* $185
Depositions: *High:* $550 *Low:* $125 *Average:* $295 *Median:* $250

Percent of Experts Having a Minimum Charge for Deps: 40% **Cancellation Fee for Deps or Trial:** 40%
Deposition Payment in Advance: 20% **Markup of Out-of-Pocket Expenses:** 0%

Up-front Retainer: 100% **Retainer Amount:** *High:* $8,750 *Low:* $500 *Average:* $3,280 *Median:* $3,000
Travel Billed Portal-to-Portal: 100% **1st-class Airfare Required:** 0%

Written Fee Agreement: 80% **Majority of Work:** *Plaintiffs:* 60% *Defendants:* 20% *Neither:* 20%
Retaining Counsel Failed to Pay Last 5 Years: 40% **Opposing Counsel Failed to Pay Last 5 Years:** 20%

Healthcare, Correctional

Responding Experts: *1*

Hourly Fees: **In-court Testimony:** *High:* $275 *Low:* $275 *Average:* $275 *Median:* $275
File Review/Prep: *High:* $185 *Low:* $185 *Average:* $185 *Median:* $185
Depositions: *High:* $250 *Low:* $250 *Average:* $250 *Median:* $250

Percent of Experts Having a Minimum Charge for Deps: 100% **Cancellation Fee for Deps or Trial:** 0%
Deposition Payment in Advance: 0% **Markup of Out-of-Pocket Expenses:** 0%

Up-front Retainer: 100% **Retainer Amount:** *High:* $3,000 *Low:* $3,000 *Average:* $3,000 *Median:* $3,000
Travel Billed Portal-to-Portal: 100% **1st-class Airfare Required:** 0%

Written Fee Agreement: 0% **Majority of Work:** *Plaintiffs:* 0% *Defendants:* 0% *Neither:* 100%
Retaining Counsel Failed to Pay Last 5 Years: 0% **Opposing Counsel Failed to Pay Last 5 Years:** 0%

Healthcare, Medical Staff Issues

Responding Experts: *1*

Hourly Fees: **In-court Testimony:** *High:* $315 *Low:* $315 *Average:* $315 *Median:* $315
File Review/Prep: *High:* $315 *Low:* $315 *Average:* $315 *Median:* $315
Depositions: *High:* $315 *Low:* $315 *Average:* $315 *Median:* $315

Percent of Experts Having a Minimum Charge for Deps: 100% **Cancellation Fee for Deps or Trial:** 100%
Deposition Payment in Advance: 100% **Markup of Out-of-Pocket Expenses:** 0%

Up-front Retainer: 100% **Retainer Amount:** *High:* $3,000 *Low:* $3,000 *Average:* $3,000 *Median:* $3,000
Travel Billed Portal-to-Portal: 100% **1st-class Airfare Required:** 0%

Written Fee Agreement: 100% **Majority of Work:** *Plaintiffs:* 100% *Defendants:* 0% *Neither:* 0%
Retaining Counsel Failed to Pay Last 5 Years: 100% **Opposing Counsel Failed to Pay Last 5 Years:** 100%

Healthcare, Operations

Responding Experts: *1*

Hourly Fees:					
	In-court Testimony:	*High:* $600	*Low:* $600	*Average:* $600	*Median:* $600
	File Review/Prep:	*High:* $350	*Low:* $350	*Average:* $350	*Median:* $350
	Depositions:	*High:* $550	*Low:* $550	*Average:* $550	*Median:* $550

Percent of Experts Having a Minimum Charge for Deps: 0% **Cancellation Fee for Deps or Trial:** 0%
Deposition Payment in Advance: 0% **Markup of Out-of-Pocket Expenses:** 0%

Up-front Retainer: 100% **Retainer Amount:** *High:* $8,750 *Low:* $8,750 *Average:* $8,750 *Median:* $8,750
Travel Billed Portal-to-Portal: 100% **1st-class Airfare Required:** 0%

Written Fee Agreement: 0% **Majority of Work:** *Plaintiffs:* 100% *Defendants:* 0% *Neither:* 0%
Retaining Counsel Failed to Pay Last 5 Years: 0% **Opposing Counsel Failed to Pay Last 5 Years:** 0%

Highways

Responding Experts: *2*

Hourly Fees:					
	In-court Testimony:	*High:* $200	*Low:* $180	*Average:* $190	*Median:* $190
	File Review/Prep:	*High:* $180	*Low:* $100	*Average:* $140	*Median:* $140
	Depositions:	*High:* $200	*Low:* $180	*Average:* $190	*Median:* $190

Percent of Experts Having a Minimum Charge for Deps: 50% **Cancellation Fee for Deps or Trial:** 0%
Deposition Payment in Advance: 0% **Markup of Out-of-Pocket Expenses:** 0%

Up-front Retainer: 0% **Retainer Amount:** *High:* N/A *Low:* N/A *Average:* N/A *Median:* N/A
Travel Billed Portal-to-Portal: 50% **1st-class Airfare Required:** 0%

Written Fee Agreement: 50% **Majority of Work:** *Plaintiffs:* 50% *Defendants:* 50% *Neither:* 0%
Retaining Counsel Failed to Pay Last 5 Years: 50% **Opposing Counsel Failed to Pay Last 5 Years:** 0%

Horses

Responding Experts: *1*

Hourly Fees:					
	In-court Testimony:	*High:* $250	*Low:* $250	*Average:* $250	*Median:* $250
	File Review/Prep:	*High:* $125	*Low:* $125	*Average:* $125	*Median:* $125
	Depositions:	*High:* $250	*Low:* $250	*Average:* $250	*Median:* $250

Percent of Experts Having a Minimum Charge for Deps: 0% **Cancellation Fee for Deps or Trial:** 0%
Deposition Payment in Advance: 0% **Markup of Out-of-Pocket Expenses:** 0%

Up-front Retainer: 100% **Retainer Amount:** *High:* $1,000 *Low:* $1,000 *Average:* $1,000 *Median:* $1,000
Travel Billed Portal-to-Portal: 100% **1st-class Airfare Required:** 0%

Written Fee Agreement: 100% **Majority of Work:** *Plaintiffs:* 0% *Defendants:* 0% *Neither:* 100%
Retaining Counsel Failed to Pay Last 5 Years: 0% **Opposing Counsel Failed to Pay Last 5 Years:** 0%

Horticulture

Responding Experts: *1*

Hourly Fees:					
	In-court Testimony:	*High:* $150	*Low:* $150	*Average:* $150	*Median:* $150
	File Review/Prep:	*High:* $150	*Low:* $150	*Average:* $150	*Median:* $150
	Depositions:	*High:* $150	*Low:* $150	*Average:* $150	*Median:* $150

Percent of Experts Having a Minimum Charge for Deps: 100% **Cancellation Fee for Deps or Trial:** 0%
Deposition Payment in Advance: 0% **Markup of Out-of-Pocket Expenses:** 0%

Up-front Retainer: 100% **Retainer Amount:** *High:* $1,000 *Low:* $1,000 *Average:* $1,000 *Median:* $1,000
Travel Billed Portal-to-Portal: 100% **1st-class Airfare Required:** 0%

Written Fee Agreement: 100% **Majority of Work:** *Plaintiffs:* 0% *Defendants:* 0% *Neither:* 100%
Retaining Counsel Failed to Pay Last 5 Years: 0% **Opposing Counsel Failed to Pay Last 5 Years:** 0%

Hospitality, (All)

Responding Experts: *4*

Hourly Fees: **In-court Testimony:** *High:* $415 *Low:* $275 *Average:* $360 *Median:* $375
File Review/Prep: *High:* $415 *Low:* $275 *Average:* $348 *Median:* $350
Depositions: *High:* $425 *Low:* $275 *Average:* $362 *Median:* $375
Percent of Experts Having a Minimum Charge for Deps: 25% **Cancellation Fee for Deps or Trial:** 25%
Deposition Payment in Advance: 50% **Markup of Out-of-Pocket Expenses:** 0%

Up-front Retainer: 100% **Retainer Amount:** *High:* $5,000 *Low:* $4,000 *Average:* $4,500 *Median:* $4,500
Travel Billed Portal-to-Portal: 100% **1st-class Airfare Required:** 0%

Written Fee Agreement: 75% **Majority of Work:** *Plaintiffs:* 50% *Defendants:* 0% *Neither:* 50%
Retaining Counsel Failed to Pay Last 5 Years: 50% **Opposing Counsel Failed to Pay Last 5 Years:** 0%

Hospitality, Hotels

Responding Experts: *3*

Hourly Fees: **In-court Testimony:** *High:* $415 *Low:* $350 *Average:* $389 *Median:* $400
File Review/Prep: *High:* $415 *Low:* $300 *Average:* $371 *Median:* $400
Depositions: *High:* $425 *Low:* $350 *Average:* $392 *Median:* $400
Percent of Experts Having a Minimum Charge for Deps: 33% **Cancellation Fee for Deps or Trial:** 33%
Deposition Payment in Advance: 33% **Markup of Out-of-Pocket Expenses:** 0%

Up-front Retainer: 100% **Retainer Amount:** *High:* $5,000 *Low:* $4,000 *Average:* $4,500 *Median:* $4,500
Travel Billed Portal-to-Portal: 100% **1st-class Airfare Required:** 0%

Written Fee Agreement: 66% **Majority of Work:** *Plaintiffs:* 33% *Defendants:* 0% *Neither:* 66%
Retaining Counsel Failed to Pay Last 5 Years: 33% **Opposing Counsel Failed to Pay Last 5 Years:** 0%

Human Factors

Responding Experts: *7*

Hourly Fees: **In-court Testimony:** *High:* $600 *Low:* $160 *Average:* $312 *Median:* $275
File Review/Prep: *High:* $600 *Low:* $110 *Average:* $270 *Median:* $210
Depositions: *High:* $600 *Low:* $160 *Average:* $312 *Median:* $275
Percent of Experts Having a Minimum Charge for Deps: 29% **Cancellation Fee for Deps or Trial:** 29%
Deposition Payment in Advance: 43% **Markup of Out-of-Pocket Expenses:** 0%

Up-front Retainer: 100% **Retainer Amount:** *High:* $6,000 *Low:* $160 *Average:* $1,980 *Median:* $1,400
Travel Billed Portal-to-Portal: 100% **1st-class Airfare Required:** 14%

Written Fee Agreement: 100% **Majority of Work:** *Plaintiffs:* 43% *Defendants:* 14% *Neither:* 43%
Retaining Counsel Failed to Pay Last 5 Years: 100% **Opposing Counsel Failed to Pay Last 5 Years:** 43%

Human Resources

Responding Experts: *4*

Hourly Fees: **In-court Testimony:** *High:* $300 *Low:* $150 *Average:* $238 *Median:* $250
File Review/Prep: *High:* $275 *Low:* $150 *Average:* $190 *Median:* $168
Depositions: *High:* $300 *Low:* $150 *Average:* $238 *Median:* $250
Percent of Experts Having a Minimum Charge for Deps: 75% **Cancellation Fee for Deps or Trial:** 25%
Deposition Payment in Advance: 25% **Markup of Out-of-Pocket Expenses:** 25%

Up-front Retainer: 75% **Retainer Amount:** *High:* $3,000 *Low:* $650 *Average:* $2,050 *Median:* $2,500
Travel Billed Portal-to-Portal: 100% **1st-class Airfare Required:** 0%

Written Fee Agreement: 75% **Majority of Work:** *Plaintiffs:* 0% *Defendants:* 25% *Neither:* 75%
Retaining Counsel Failed to Pay Last 5 Years: 75% **Opposing Counsel Failed to Pay Last 5 Years:** 25%

HVAC
Responding Experts: *1*

Hourly Fees:

	High	Low	Average	Median
In-court Testimony:	$250	$250	$250	$250
File Review/Prep:	$150	$150	$150	$150
Depositions:	$250	$250	$250	$250

Percent of Experts Having a Minimum Charge for Deps: 0% **Cancellation Fee for Deps or Trial:** 0%
Deposition Payment in Advance: 0% **Markup of Out-of-Pocket Expenses:** 0%

Up-front Retainer: 100% **Retainer Amount:** *High:* $1,500 *Low:* $1,500 *Average:* $1,500 *Median:* $1,500
Travel Billed Portal-to-Portal: 100% **1st-class Airfare Required:** 0%

Written Fee Agreement: 100% **Majority of Work:** *Plaintiffs:* 0% *Defendants:* 100% *Neither:* 0%
Retaining Counsel Failed to Pay Last 5 Years: 0% **Opposing Counsel Failed to Pay Last 5 Years:** 0%

Hydrology
Responding Experts: *2*

Hourly Fees:

	High	Low	Average	Median
In-court Testimony:	$250	$225	$238	$238
File Review/Prep:	$150	$150	$150	$150
Depositions:	$250	$225	$238	$238

Percent of Experts Having a Minimum Charge for Deps: 50% **Cancellation Fee for Deps or Trial:** 0%
Deposition Payment in Advance: 50% **Markup of Out-of-Pocket Expenses:** 50%

Up-front Retainer: 50% **Retainer Amount:** *High:* $2,000 *Low:* $2,000 *Average:* $2,000 *Median:* $2,000
Travel Billed Portal-to-Portal: 100% **1st-class Airfare Required:** 0%

Written Fee Agreement: 100% **Majority of Work:** *Plaintiffs:* 50% *Defendants:* 0% *Neither:* 50%
Retaining Counsel Failed to Pay Last 5 Years: 100% **Opposing Counsel Failed to Pay Last 5 Years:** 0%

Industrial
Responding Experts: *1*

Hourly Fees:

	High	Low	Average	Median
In-court Testimony:	$500	$500	$500	$500
File Review/Prep:	$250	$250	$250	$250
Depositions:	$500	$500	$500	$500

Percent of Experts Having a Minimum Charge for Deps: 100% **Cancellation Fee for Deps or Trial:** 100%
Deposition Payment in Advance: 100% **Markup of Out-of-Pocket Expenses:** 100%

Up-front Retainer: 100% **Retainer Amount:** *High:* $750 *Low:* $750 *Average:* $750 *Median:* $750
Travel Billed Portal-to-Portal: 100% **1st-class Airfare Required:** 100%

Written Fee Agreement: 100% **Majority of Work:** *Plaintiffs:* 100% *Defendants:* 0% *Neither:* 0%
Retaining Counsel Failed to Pay Last 5 Years: 100% **Opposing Counsel Failed to Pay Last 5 Years:** 0%

Infectious Diseases
Responding Experts: *2*

Hourly Fees:

	High	Low	Average	Median
In-court Testimony:	$750	$500	$625	$625
File Review/Prep:	$500	$500	$500	$500
Depositions:	$650	$500	$575	$575

Percent of Experts Having a Minimum Charge for Deps: 50% **Cancellation Fee for Deps or Trial:** 100%
Deposition Payment in Advance: 50% **Markup of Out-of-Pocket Expenses:** 0%

Up-front Retainer: 100% **Retainer Amount:** *High:* $1,500 *Low:* $500 *Average:* $1,000 *Median:* $1,000
Travel Billed Portal-to-Portal: 100% **1st-class Airfare Required:** 0%

Written Fee Agreement: 100% **Majority of Work:** *Plaintiffs:* 0% *Defendants:* 0% *Neither:* 100%
Retaining Counsel Failed to Pay Last 5 Years: 100% **Opposing Counsel Failed to Pay Last 5 Years:** 100%

Insurance, (All)

Responding Experts: *17*

Hourly Fees: **In-court Testimony:** *High:* $400 *Low:* $140 *Average:* $240 *Median:* $250
File Review/Prep: *High:* $400 *Low:* $125 *Average:* $217 *Median:* $220
Depositions: *High:* $400 *Low:* $125 *Average:* $232 *Median:* $250
Percent of Experts Having a Minimum Charge for Deps: 29% **Cancellation Fee for Deps or Trial:** 6%
Deposition Payment in Advance: 17% **Markup of Out-of-Pocket Expenses:** 6%

Up-front Retainer: 76% **Retainer Amount:** *High:* $10,000 *Low:* $500 *Average:* $2,812 *Median:* $2,500
Travel Billed Portal-to-Portal: 81% **1st-class Airfare Required:** 17%

Written Fee Agreement: 43% **Majority of Work:** *Plaintiffs:* 29% *Defendants:* 6% *Neither:* 65%
Retaining Counsel Failed to Pay Last 5 Years: 41% **Opposing Counsel Failed to Pay Last 5 Years:** 0%

Insurance, Disability

Responding Experts: *1*

Hourly Fees: **In-court Testimony:** *High:* $300 *Low:* $300 *Average:* $300 *Median:* $300
File Review/Prep: *High:* $250 *Low:* $250 *Average:* $250 *Median:* $250
Depositions: *High:* $300 *Low:* $300 *Average:* $300 *Median:* $300
Percent of Experts Having a Minimum Charge for Deps: 100% **Cancellation Fee for Deps or Trial:** 0%
Deposition Payment in Advance: 0% **Markup of Out-of-Pocket Expenses:** 0%

Up-front Retainer: 100% **Retainer Amount:** *High:* $10,000 *Low:* $10,000 *Average:* $10,000 *Median:* $10,000
Travel Billed Portal-to-Portal: 0% **1st-class Airfare Required:** 0%

Written Fee Agreement: 100% **Majority of Work:** *Plaintiffs:* 100% *Defendants:* 0% *Neither:* 0%
Retaining Counsel Failed to Pay Last 5 Years: 100% **Opposing Counsel Failed to Pay Last 5 Years:** 0%

Insurance, Health

Responding Experts: *2*

Hourly Fees: **In-court Testimony:** *High:* $300 *Low:* $300 *Average:* $300 *Median:* $300
File Review/Prep: *High:* $300 *Low:* $260 *Average:* $280 *Median:* $280
Depositions: *High:* $300 *Low:* $300 *Average:* $300 *Median:* $300
Percent of Experts Having a Minimum Charge for Deps: 0% **Cancellation Fee for Deps or Trial:** 0%
Deposition Payment in Advance: 0% **Markup of Out-of-Pocket Expenses:** 0%

Up-front Retainer: 50% **Retainer Amount:** *High:* $2,000 *Low:* $2,000 *Average:* $2,000 *Median:* $2,000
Travel Billed Portal-to-Portal: 50% **1st-class Airfare Required:** 50%

Written Fee Agreement: 50% **Majority of Work:** *Plaintiffs:* 50% *Defendants:* 0% *Neither:* 50%
Retaining Counsel Failed to Pay Last 5 Years: 0% **Opposing Counsel Failed to Pay Last 5 Years:** 0%

Insurance, Property & Casualty

Responding Experts: *1*

Hourly Fees: **In-court Testimony:** *High:* $300 *Low:* $300 *Average:* $300 *Median:* $300
File Review/Prep: *High:* $300 *Low:* $300 *Average:* $300 *Median:* $300
Depositions: *High:* $300 *Low:* $300 *Average:* $300 *Median:* $300
Percent of Experts Having a Minimum Charge for Deps: 100% **Cancellation Fee for Deps or Trial:** 0%
Deposition Payment in Advance: 0% **Markup of Out-of-Pocket Expenses:** 0%

Up-front Retainer: 100% **Retainer Amount:** *High:* $500 *Low:* $500 *Average:* $500 *Median:* $500
Travel Billed Portal-to-Portal: 100% **1st-class Airfare Required:** 0%

Written Fee Agreement: 0% **Majority of Work:** *Plaintiffs:* 0% *Defendants:* 0% *Neither:* 100%
Retaining Counsel Failed to Pay Last 5 Years: 100% **Opposing Counsel Failed to Pay Last 5 Years:** 0%

Internal Medicine

Responding Experts: *16*

Hourly Fees: **In-court Testimony:** *High:* $800 *Low:* $300 *Average:* $500 *Median:* $500
File Review/Prep: *High:* $450 *Low:* $200 *Average:* $315 *Median:* $300
Depositions: *High:* $600 *Low:* $250 *Average:* $415 *Median:* $400

Percent of Experts Having a Minimum Charge for Deps: 50% **Cancellation Fee for Deps or Trial:** 47%
Deposition Payment in Advance: 47% **Markup of Out-of-Pocket Expenses:** 7%

Up-front Retainer: 60% **Retainer Amount:** *High:* $2,000 *Low:* $600 *Average:* $1,445 *Median:* $1,500
Travel Billed Portal-to-Portal: 80% **1st-class Airfare Required:** 43%

Written Fee Agreement: 60% **Majority of Work:** *Plaintiffs:* 27% *Defendants:* 27% *Neither:* 46%
Retaining Counsel Failed to Pay Last 5 Years: 47% **Opposing Counsel Failed to Pay Last 5 Years:** 36%

Investments/Securities

Responding Experts: *3*

Hourly Fees: **In-court Testimony:** *High:* $500 *Low:* $200 *Average:* $300 *Median:* $200
File Review/Prep: *High:* $200 *Low:* $150 *Average:* $185 *Median:* $185
Depositions: *High:* $350 *Low:* $200 *Average:* $250 *Median:* $250

Percent of Experts Having a Minimum Charge for Deps: 0% **Cancellation Fee for Deps or Trial:** 0%
Deposition Payment in Advance: 33% **Markup of Out-of-Pocket Expenses:** 0%

Up-front Retainer: 100% **Retainer Amount:** *High:* $7,500 *Low:* $2,000 *Average:* $4,170 *Median:* $3,000
Travel Billed Portal-to-Portal: 33% **1st-class Airfare Required:** 0%

Written Fee Agreement: 33% **Majority of Work:** *Plaintiffs:* 33% *Defendants:* 0% *Neither:* 66%
Retaining Counsel Failed to Pay Last 5 Years: 66% **Opposing Counsel Failed to Pay Last 5 Years:** 33%

Jewelry

Responding Experts: *1*

Hourly Fees: **In-court Testimony:** *High:* $250 *Low:* $250 *Average:* $250 *Median:* $250
File Review/Prep: *High:* $250 *Low:* $250 *Average:* $250 *Median:* $250
Depositions: *High:* $250 *Low:* $250 *Average:* $250 *Median:* $250

Percent of Experts Having a Minimum Charge for Deps: 100% **Cancellation Fee for Deps or Trial:** 100%
Deposition Payment in Advance: 100% **Markup of Out-of-Pocket Expenses:** 100%

Up-front Retainer: 100% **Retainer Amount:** *High:* $1,000 *Low:* $1,000 *Average:* $1,000 *Median:* $1,000
Travel Billed Portal-to-Portal: 100% **1st-class Airfare Required:** 0%

Written Fee Agreement: 0% **Majority of Work:** *Plaintiffs:* 0% *Defendants:* 0% *Neither:* 100%
Retaining Counsel Failed to Pay Last 5 Years: 0% **Opposing Counsel Failed to Pay Last 5 Years:** 0%

Ladders

Responding Experts: *1*

Hourly Fees: **In-court Testimony:** *High:* $225 *Low:* $225 *Average:* $225 *Median:* $225
File Review/Prep: *High:* $185 *Low:* $185 *Average:* $185 *Median:* $185
Depositions: *High:* $225 *Low:* $225 *Average:* $225 *Median:* $225

Percent of Experts Having a Minimum Charge for Deps: 100% **Cancellation Fee for Deps or Trial:** 0%
Deposition Payment in Advance: 100% **Markup of Out-of-Pocket Expenses:** 0%

Up-front Retainer: 100% **Retainer Amount:** *High:* N/A *Low:* N/A *Average:* N/A *Median:* N/A
Travel Billed Portal-to-Portal: 0% **1st-class Airfare Required:** 0%

Written Fee Agreement: 100% **Majority of Work:** *Plaintiffs:* 100% *Defendants:* 0% *Neither:* 0%
Retaining Counsel Failed to Pay Last 5 Years: 100% **Opposing Counsel Failed to Pay Last 5 Years:** 0%

Land Surveying

Responding Experts: *1*

Hourly Fees: **In-court Testimony:** *High:* $275 *Low:* $275 *Average:* $275 *Median:* $275
File Review/Prep: *High:* $225 *Low:* $225 *Average:* $225 *Median:* $225
Depositions: *High:* $275 *Low:* $275 *Average:* $275 *Median:* $275
Percent of Experts Having a Minimum Charge for Deps: 100% **Cancellation Fee for Deps or Trial:** 0%
Deposition Payment in Advance: 0% **Markup of Out-of-Pocket Expenses:** 0%

Up-front Retainer: 100% **Retainer Amount:** *High:* $1,000 *Low:* $1,000 *Average:* $1,000 *Median:* $1,000
Travel Billed Portal-to-Portal: 100% **1st-class Airfare Required:** 0%

Written Fee Agreement: 100% **Majority of Work:** *Plaintiffs:* 0% *Defendants:* 100% *Neither:* 0%
Retaining Counsel Failed to Pay Last 5 Years: 0% **Opposing Counsel Failed to Pay Last 5 Years:** 0%

Law Enforcement

Responding Experts: *7*

Hourly Fees: **In-court Testimony:** *High:* $300 *Low:* $125 *Average:* $210 *Median:* $200
File Review/Prep: *High:* $250 *Low:* $100 *Average:* $175 *Median:* $200
Depositions: *High:* $300 *Low:* $125 *Average:* $210 *Median:* $200
Percent of Experts Having a Minimum Charge for Deps: 86% **Cancellation Fee for Deps or Trial:** 43%
Deposition Payment in Advance: 71% **Markup of Out-of-Pocket Expenses:** 29%

Up-front Retainer: 100% **Retainer Amount:** *High:* $5,000 *Low:* $1,250 *Average:* $2,395 *Median:* $1,800
Travel Billed Portal-to-Portal: 83% **1st-class Airfare Required:** 43%

Written Fee Agreement: 100% **Majority of Work:** *Plaintiffs:* 14% *Defendants:* 14% *Neither:* 72%
Retaining Counsel Failed to Pay Last 5 Years: 57% **Opposing Counsel Failed to Pay Last 5 Years:** 14%

Law, (All)

Responding Experts: *10*

Hourly Fees: **In-court Testimony:** *High:* $2,000 *Low:* $180 *Average:* $515 *Median:* $375
File Review/Prep: *High:* $450 *Low:* $180 *Average:* $335 *Median:* $350
Depositions: *High:* $800 *Low:* $100 *Average:* $380 *Median:* $350
Percent of Experts Having a Minimum Charge for Deps: 30% **Cancellation Fee for Deps or Trial:** 40%
Deposition Payment in Advance: 40% **Markup of Out-of-Pocket Expenses:** 0%

Up-front Retainer: 80% **Retainer Amount:** *High:* $8,000 *Low:* $500 *Average:* $3,625 *Median:* $3,000
Travel Billed Portal-to-Portal: 85% **1st-class Airfare Required:** 10%

Written Fee Agreement: 40% **Majority of Work:** *Plaintiffs:* 20% *Defendants:* 0% *Neither:* 80%
Retaining Counsel Failed to Pay Last 5 Years: 50% **Opposing Counsel Failed to Pay Last 5 Years:** 40%

Law, Employment

Responding Experts: *1*

Hourly Fees: **In-court Testimony:** *High:* $180 *Low:* $180 *Average:* $180 *Median:* $180
File Review/Prep: *High:* $180 *Low:* $180 *Average:* $180 *Median:* $180
Depositions: *High:* $180 *Low:* $180 *Average:* $180 *Median:* $180
Percent of Experts Having a Minimum Charge for Deps: 0% **Cancellation Fee for Deps or Trial:** 0%
Deposition Payment in Advance: 0% **Markup of Out-of-Pocket Expenses:** 0%

Up-front Retainer: 0% **Retainer Amount:** *High:* N/A *Low:* N/A *Average:* N/A *Median:* N/A
Travel Billed Portal-to-Portal: 100% **1st-class Airfare Required:** 0%

Written Fee Agreement: 0% **Majority of Work:** *Plaintiffs:* 100% *Defendants:* 0% *Neither:* 0%
Retaining Counsel Failed to Pay Last 5 Years: 0% **Opposing Counsel Failed to Pay Last 5 Years:** 0%

Law, Family

Responding Experts: *1*

Hourly Fees: **In-court Testimony:** *High:* $200 *Low:* $200 *Average:* $200 *Median:* $200
File Review/Prep: *High:* $250 *Low:* $250 *Average:* $250 *Median:* $250
Depositions: *High:* $180 *Low:* $180 *Average:* $180 *Median:* $180
Percent of Experts Having a Minimum Charge for Deps: 100% **Cancellation Fee for Deps or Trial:** 100%
Deposition Payment in Advance: 100% **Markup of Out-of-Pocket Expenses:** 0%

Up-front Retainer: 100% **Retainer Amount:** *High:* N/A *Low:* N/A *Average:* N/A *Median:* N/A
Travel Billed Portal-to-Portal: N/A **1st-class Airfare Required:** 0%

Written Fee Agreement: 100% **Majority of Work:** *Plaintiffs:* 0% *Defendants:* 0% *Neither:* 100%
Retaining Counsel Failed to Pay Last 5 Years: 0% **Opposing Counsel Failed to Pay Last 5 Years:** 0%

Law, Horses

Responding Experts: *1*

Hourly Fees: **In-court Testimony:** *High:* $250 *Low:* $250 *Average:* $250 *Median:* $250
File Review/Prep: *High:* $250 *Low:* $250 *Average:* $250 *Median:* $250
Depositions: *High:* $250 *Low:* $250 *Average:* $250 *Median:* $250
Percent of Experts Having a Minimum Charge for Deps: 100% **Cancellation Fee for Deps or Trial:** 100%
Deposition Payment in Advance: 100% **Markup of Out-of-Pocket Expenses:** 0%

Up-front Retainer: 100% **Retainer Amount:** *High:* $500 *Low:* $500 *Average:* $500 *Median:* $500
Travel Billed Portal-to-Portal: 100% **1st-class Airfare Required:** 0%

Written Fee Agreement: 100% **Majority of Work:** *Plaintiffs:* 0% *Defendants:* 0% *Neither:* 100%
Retaining Counsel Failed to Pay Last 5 Years: 100% **Opposing Counsel Failed to Pay Last 5 Years:** 100%

Law, Intellectual Property

Responding Experts: *1*

Hourly Fees: **In-court Testimony:** *High:* $325 *Low:* $325 *Average:* $325 *Median:* $325
File Review/Prep: *High:* $325 *Low:* $325 *Average:* $325 *Median:* $325
Depositions: *High:* $325 *Low:* $325 *Average:* $325 *Median:* $325
Percent of Experts Having a Minimum Charge for Deps: 0% **Cancellation Fee for Deps or Trial:** 0%
Deposition Payment in Advance: 0% **Markup of Out-of-Pocket Expenses:** 0%

Up-front Retainer: 100% **Retainer Amount:** *High:* $1,000 *Low:* $1,000 *Average:* $1,000 *Median:* $1,000
Travel Billed Portal-to-Portal: 100% **1st-class Airfare Required:** 10%

Written Fee Agreement: 0% **Majority of Work:** *Plaintiffs:* 0% *Defendants:* 0% *Neither:* 100%
Retaining Counsel Failed to Pay Last 5 Years: 0% **Opposing Counsel Failed to Pay Last 5 Years:** 100%

Law, Legal Malpractice

Responding Experts: *2*

Hourly Fees: **In-court Testimony:** *High:* $400 *Low:* $350 *Average:* $375 *Median:* $375
File Review/Prep: *High:* $400 *Low:* $350 *Average:* $375 *Median:* $375
Depositions: *High:* $400 *Low:* $350 *Average:* $375 *Median:* $375
Percent of Experts Having a Minimum Charge for Deps: 0% **Cancellation Fee for Deps or Trial:** 0%
Deposition Payment in Advance: 0% **Markup of Out-of-Pocket Expenses:** 0%

Up-front Retainer: 100% **Retainer Amount:** *High:* $8,000 *Low:* $5,000 *Average:* $6,500 *Median:* $6,500
Travel Billed Portal-to-Portal: 100% **1st-class Airfare Required:** 0%

Written Fee Agreement: 50% **Majority of Work:** *Plaintiffs:* 0% *Defendants:* 0% *Neither:* 100%
Retaining Counsel Failed to Pay Last 5 Years: 0% **Opposing Counsel Failed to Pay Last 5 Years:** 0%

Law, Medical Malpractice

Responding Experts: *2*

Hourly Fees:

	High	*Low*	*Average*	*Median*
In-court Testimony:	$500	$200	$350	$350
File Review/Prep:	$400	$400	$400	$400
Depositions:	$500	$500	$500	$500

Percent of Experts Having a Minimum Charge for Deps: 50% **Cancellation Fee for Deps or Trial:** 100%
Deposition Payment in Advance: 100% **Markup of Out-of-Pocket Expenses:** 0%

Up-front Retainer: 100% **Retainer Amount:** *High:* $500 *Low:* $500 *Average:* $500 *Median:* $500
Travel Billed Portal-to-Portal: 50% **1st-class Airfare Required:** 0%

Written Fee Agreement: 50% **Majority of Work:** *Plaintiffs:* 50% *Defendants:* 0% *Neither:* 50%
Retaining Counsel Failed to Pay Last 5 Years: 100% **Opposing Counsel Failed to Pay Last 5 Years:** 50%

Law, Patents

Responding Experts: *2*

Hourly Fees:

	High	*Low*	*Average*	*Median*
In-court Testimony:	$2,000	$500	$1,250	$1,250
File Review/Prep:	$450	$450	$450	$450
Depositions:	$800	$800	$800	$800

Percent of Experts Having a Minimum Charge for Deps: 0% **Cancellation Fee for Deps or Trial:** 0%
Deposition Payment in Advance: 0% **Markup of Out-of-Pocket Expenses:** 0%

Up-front Retainer: 50% **Retainer Amount:** *High:* N/A *Low:* N/A *Average:* N/A *Median:* N/A
Travel Billed Portal-to-Portal: 100% **1st-class Airfare Required:** 0%

Written Fee Agreement: 0% **Majority of Work:** *Plaintiffs:* 0% *Defendants:* 0% *Neither:* 100%
Retaining Counsel Failed to Pay Last 5 Years: 50% **Opposing Counsel Failed to Pay Last 5 Years:** 0%

Life Care Planning

Responding Experts: *11*

Hourly Fees:

	High	*Low*	*Average*	*Median*
In-court Testimony:	$500	$150	$250	$200
File Review/Prep:	$330	$80	$188	$150
Depositions:	$600	$150	$255	$200

Percent of Experts Having a Minimum Charge for Deps: 36% **Cancellation Fee for Deps or Trial:** 73%
Deposition Payment in Advance: 60% **Markup of Out-of-Pocket Expenses:** 9%

Up-front Retainer: 100% **Retainer Amount:** *High:* $3,000 *Low:* $500 *Average:* $1,900 *Median:* $2,000
Travel Billed Portal-to-Portal: 100% **1st-class Airfare Required:** 9%

Written Fee Agreement: 90% **Majority of Work:** *Plaintiffs:* 27% *Defendants:* 0% *Neither:* 73%
Retaining Counsel Failed to Pay Last 5 Years: 45% **Opposing Counsel Failed to Pay Last 5 Years:** 27%

Lighting

Responding Experts: *1*

Hourly Fees:

	High	*Low*	*Average*	*Median*
In-court Testimony:	$350	$350	$350	$350
File Review/Prep:	$150	$150	$150	$150
Depositions:	$275	$275	$275	$275

Percent of Experts Having a Minimum Charge for Deps: 0% **Cancellation Fee for Deps or Trial:** 0%
Deposition Payment in Advance: 0% **Markup of Out-of-Pocket Expenses:** 0%

Up-front Retainer: 100% **Retainer Amount:** *High:* $500 *Low:* $500 *Average:* $500 *Median:* $500
Travel Billed Portal-to-Portal: 100% **1st-class Airfare Required:** 0%

Written Fee Agreement: 100% **Majority of Work:** *Plaintiffs:* 100% *Defendants:* 0% *Neither:* 0%
Retaining Counsel Failed to Pay Last 5 Years: 0% **Opposing Counsel Failed to Pay Last 5 Years:** 100%

Linguistics

Responding Experts: *1*

Hourly Fees: **In-court Testimony:** *High:* $350 *Low:* $350 *Average:* $350 *Median:* $350
File Review/Prep: *High:* $300 *Low:* $300 *Average:* $300 *Median:* $300
Depositions: *High:* $350 *Low:* $350 *Average:* $350 *Median:* $350
Percent of Experts Having a Minimum Charge for Deps: 0% **Cancellation Fee for Deps or Trial:** 100%
Deposition Payment in Advance: 100% **Markup of Out-of-Pocket Expenses:** 0%

Up-front Retainer: N/A **Retainer Amount:** *High:* N/A *Low:* N/A *Average:* N/A *Median:* N/A
Travel Billed Portal-to-Portal: 100% **1st-class Airfare Required:** 0%

Written Fee Agreement: 0% **Majority of Work:** *Plaintiffs:* 0% *Defendants:* 0% *Neither:* 100%
Retaining Counsel Failed to Pay Last 5 Years: 0% **Opposing Counsel Failed to Pay Last 5 Years:** 0%

Long Term Care

Responding Experts: *4*

Hourly Fees: **In-court Testimony:** *High:* $500 *Low:* $165 *Average:* $305 *Median:* $275
File Review/Prep: *High:* $250 *Low:* $100 *Average:* $175 *Median:* $175
Depositions: *High:* $450 *Low:* $150 *Average:* $265 *Median:* $225
Percent of Experts Having a Minimum Charge for Deps: 50% **Cancellation Fee for Deps or Trial:** 50%
Deposition Payment in Advance: 50% **Markup of Out-of-Pocket Expenses:** 25%

Up-front Retainer: 75% **Retainer Amount:** *High:* $1,200 *Low:* $750 *Average:* $985 *Median:* $1,000
Travel Billed Portal-to-Portal: 75% **1st-class Airfare Required:** 0%

Written Fee Agreement: 100% **Majority of Work:** *Plaintiffs:* 50% *Defendants:* 25% *Neither:* 25%
Retaining Counsel Failed to Pay Last 5 Years: 50% **Opposing Counsel Failed to Pay Last 5 Years:** 0%

Machinery, (All)

Responding Experts: *5*

Hourly Fees: **In-court Testimony:** *High:* $400 *Low:* $100 *Average:* $258 *Median:* $200
File Review/Prep: *High:* $250 *Low:* $100 *Average:* $167 *Median:* $135
Depositions: *High:* $400 *Low:* $100 *Average:* $245 *Median:* $200
Percent of Experts Having a Minimum Charge for Deps: 60% **Cancellation Fee for Deps or Trial:** 40%
Deposition Payment in Advance: 40% **Markup of Out-of-Pocket Expenses:** 60%

Up-front Retainer: 60% **Retainer Amount:** *High:* $2,500 *Low:* $350 *Average:* $1,785 *Median:* $2,500
Travel Billed Portal-to-Portal: 80% **1st-class Airfare Required:** 20%

Written Fee Agreement: 60% **Majority of Work:** *Plaintiffs:* 20% *Defendants:* 20% *Neither:* 60%
Retaining Counsel Failed to Pay Last 5 Years: 40% **Opposing Counsel Failed to Pay Last 5 Years:** 20%

Machinery, Industrial

Responding Experts: *1*

Hourly Fees: **In-court Testimony:** *High:* $400 *Low:* $400 *Average:* $400 *Median:* $400
File Review/Prep: *High:* $250 *Low:* $250 *Average:* $250 *Median:* $250
Depositions: *High:* $400 *Low:* $400 *Average:* $400 *Median:* $400
Percent of Experts Having a Minimum Charge for Deps: 100% **Cancellation Fee for Deps or Trial:** 100%
Deposition Payment in Advance: 100% **Markup of Out-of-Pocket Expenses:** 100%

Up-front Retainer: 100% **Retainer Amount:** *High:* $2,500 *Low:* $2,500 *Average:* $2,500 *Median:* $2,500
Travel Billed Portal-to-Portal: 100% **1st-class Airfare Required:** 0%

Written Fee Agreement: 100% **Majority of Work:** *Plaintiffs:* 0% *Defendants:* 0% *Neither:* 100%
Retaining Counsel Failed to Pay Last 5 Years: 0% **Opposing Counsel Failed to Pay Last 5 Years:** 0%

Managed Care

Responding Experts: *1*

Hourly Fees:

In-court Testimony:	*High:* $200	*Low:* $200	*Average:* $200	*Median:* $200
File Review/Prep:	*High:* $200	*Low:* $200	*Average:* $200	*Median:* $200
Depositions:	*High:* $200	*Low:* $200	*Average:* $200	*Median:* $200

Percent of Experts Having a Minimum Charge for Deps: 0% **Cancellation Fee for Deps or Trial:** 0%
Deposition Payment in Advance: 0% **Markup of Out-of-Pocket Expenses:** 0%

Up-front Retainer: 100% **Retainer Amount:** *High:* $2,000 *Low:* $2,000 *Average:* $2,000 *Median:* $2,000
Travel Billed Portal-to-Portal: 100% **1st-class Airfare Required:** 100%

Written Fee Agreement: 100% **Majority of Work:** *Plaintiffs:* 0% *Defendants:* 0% *Neither:* 100%
Retaining Counsel Failed to Pay Last 5 Years: 0% **Opposing Counsel Failed to Pay Last 5 Years:** 0%

Manufacturing

Responding Experts: *1*

Hourly Fees:

In-court Testimony:	*High:* $400	*Low:* $400	*Average:* $400	*Median:* $400
File Review/Prep:	*High:* $250	*Low:* $250	*Average:* $250	*Median:* $250
Depositions:	*High:* $400	*Low:* $400	*Average:* $400	*Median:* $400

Percent of Experts Having a Minimum Charge for Deps: 100% **Cancellation Fee for Deps or Trial:** 100%
Deposition Payment in Advance: 100% **Markup of Out-of-Pocket Expenses:** 100%

Up-front Retainer: 100% **Retainer Amount:** *High:* $2,500 *Low:* $2,500 *Average:* $2,500 *Median:* $2,500
Travel Billed Portal-to-Portal: 100% **1st-class Airfare Required:** 100%

Written Fee Agreement: 100% **Majority of Work:** *Plaintiffs:* 0% *Defendants:* 0% *Neither:* 100%
Retaining Counsel Failed to Pay Last 5 Years: 0% **Opposing Counsel Failed to Pay Last 5 Years:** 0%

Marine, (All)

Responding Experts: *13*

Hourly Fees:

In-court Testimony:	*High:* $285	*Low:* $125	*Average:* $190	*Median:* $175
File Review/Prep:	*High:* $285	*Low:* $75	*Average:* $140	*Median:* $125
Depositions:	*High:* $285	*Low:* $100	*Average:* $180	*Median:* $165

Percent of Experts Having a Minimum Charge for Deps: 46% **Cancellation Fee for Deps or Trial:** 46%
Deposition Payment in Advance: 62% **Markup of Out-of-Pocket Expenses:** 31%

Up-front Retainer: 92% **Retainer Amount:** *High:* $4,000 *Low:* $1,000 *Average:* $2,190 *Median:* $2,000
Travel Billed Portal-to-Portal: 100% **1st-class Airfare Required:** 17%

Written Fee Agreement: 92% **Majority of Work:** *Plaintiffs:* 16% *Defendants:* 0% *Neither:* 84%
Retaining Counsel Failed to Pay Last 5 Years: 46% **Opposing Counsel Failed to Pay Last 5 Years:** 25%

Marine, Boating

Responding Experts: *4*

Hourly Fees:

In-court Testimony:	*High:* $200	*Low:* $175	*Average:* $195	*Median:* $200
File Review/Prep:	*High:* $165	*Low:* $125	*Average:* $148	*Median:* $150
Depositions:	*High:* $200	*Low:* $165	*Average:* $185	*Median:* $200

Percent of Experts Having a Minimum Charge for Deps: 50% **Cancellation Fee for Deps or Trial:** 50%
Deposition Payment in Advance: 50% **Markup of Out-of-Pocket Expenses:** 25%

Up-front Retainer: 100% **Retainer Amount:** *High:* $4,000 *Low:* $3,000 *Average:* $3,333 *Median:* $3,000
Travel Billed Portal-to-Portal: 100% **1st-class Airfare Required:** 0%

Written Fee Agreement: 100% **Majority of Work:** *Plaintiffs:* 25% *Defendants:* 0% *Neither:* 75%
Retaining Counsel Failed to Pay Last 5 Years: 25% **Opposing Counsel Failed to Pay Last 5 Years:** 0%

Marine, Docks

Responding Experts: *1*

Hourly Fees:

	High	*Low*	*Average*	*Median*
In-court Testimony:	$250	$250	$250	$250
File Review/Prep:	$175	$175	$175	$175
Depositions:	$250	$250	$250	$250

Percent of Experts Having a Minimum Charge for Deps: 0% **Cancellation Fee for Deps or Trial:** 0%
Deposition Payment in Advance: 0% **Markup of Out-of-Pocket Expenses:** 100%

Up-front Retainer: 0% **Retainer Amount:** *High:* N/A *Low:* N/A *Average:* N/A *Median:* N/A
Travel Billed Portal-to-Portal: 100% **1st-class Airfare Required:** 100%

Written Fee Agreement: 100% **Majority of Work:** *Plaintiffs:* 0% *Defendants:* 0% *Neither:* 100%
Retaining Counsel Failed to Pay Last 5 Years: 100% **Opposing Counsel Failed to Pay Last 5 Years:** N/A

Marine, Surveying

Responding Experts: *2*

Hourly Fees:

	High	*Low*	*Average*	*Median*
In-court Testimony:	$285	$125	$205	$205
File Review/Prep:	$285	$100	$192	$205
Depositions:	$285	$125	$205	$205

Percent of Experts Having a Minimum Charge for Deps: 50% **Cancellation Fee for Deps or Trial:** 50%
Deposition Payment in Advance: 100% **Markup of Out-of-Pocket Expenses:** 0%

Up-front Retainer: 100% **Retainer Amount:** *High:* $2,000 *Low:* $1,000 *Average:* $1,500 *Median:* $1,500
Travel Billed Portal-to-Portal: 100% **1st-class Airfare Required:** 0%

Written Fee Agreement: 100% **Majority of Work:** *Plaintiffs:* 0% *Defendants:* 0% *Neither:* 100%
Retaining Counsel Failed to Pay Last 5 Years: 50% **Opposing Counsel Failed to Pay Last 5 Years:** 50%

Marketing

Responding Experts: *3*

Hourly Fees:

	High	*Low*	*Average*	*Median*
In-court Testimony:	$400	$350	$383	$383
File Review/Prep:	$400	$350	$383	$383
Depositions:	$400	$350	$383	$383

Percent of Experts Having a Minimum Charge for Deps: 0% **Cancellation Fee for Deps or Trial:** 0%
Deposition Payment in Advance: 0% **Markup of Out-of-Pocket Expenses:** 0%

Up-front Retainer: 33% **Retainer Amount:** *High:* $10,000 *Low:* $10,000 *Average:* $10,000 *Median:* $10,000
Travel Billed Portal-to-Portal: 50% **1st-class Airfare Required:** 0%

Written Fee Agreement: 33% **Majority of Work:** *Plaintiffs:* 0% *Defendants:* 33% *Neither:* 66%
Retaining Counsel Failed to Pay Last 5 Years: 33% **Opposing Counsel Failed to Pay Last 5 Years:** 0%

Materials, (All)

Responding Experts: *3*

Hourly Fees:

	High	*Low*	*Average*	*Median*
In-court Testimony:	$340	$225	$289	$300
File Review/Prep:	$270	$150	$215	$220
Depositions:	$340	$225	$290	$300

Percent of Experts Having a Minimum Charge for Deps: 33% **Cancellation Fee for Deps or Trial:** 33%
Deposition Payment in Advance: 0% **Markup of Out-of-Pocket Expenses:** 66%

Up-front Retainer: 66% **Retainer Amount:** *High:* $1,500 *Low:* $1,000 *Average:* $1,250 *Median:* $1,250
Travel Billed Portal-to-Portal: 100% **1st-class Airfare Required:** 0%

Written Fee Agreement: 100% **Majority of Work:** *Plaintiffs:* 33% *Defendants:* 0% *Neither:* 66%
Retaining Counsel Failed to Pay Last 5 Years: 100% **Opposing Counsel Failed to Pay Last 5 Years:** 33%

Materials Failures

Responding Experts: *1*

Hourly Fees: **In-court Testimony:** *High:* $300 *Low:* $300 *Average:* $300 *Median:* $300
File Review/Prep: *High:* $220 *Low:* $220 *Average:* $220 *Median:* $220
Depositions: *High:* $300 *Low:* $300 *Average:* $300 *Median:* $300
Percent of Experts Having a Minimum Charge for Deps: 0% **Cancellation Fee for Deps or Trial:** 0%
Deposition Payment in Advance: 0% **Markup of Out-of-Pocket Expenses:** 100%

Up-front Retainer: 0% **Retainer Amount:** *High:* N/A *Low:* N/A *Average:* N/A *Median:* N/A
Travel Billed Portal-to-Portal: N/A **1st-class Airfare Required:** N/A

Written Fee Agreement: 100% **Majority of Work:** *Plaintiffs:* 0% *Defendants:* 0% *Neither:* 100%
Retaining Counsel Failed to Pay Last 5 Years: 100% **Opposing Counsel Failed to Pay Last 5 Years:** 0%

Materials, Polymeric

Responding Experts: *1*

Hourly Fees: **In-court Testimony:** *High:* $340 *Low:* $340 *Average:* $340 *Median:* $340
File Review/Prep: *High:* $270 *Low:* $270 *Average:* $270 *Median:* $270
Depositions: *High:* $340 *Low:* $340 *Average:* $340 *Median:* $340
Percent of Experts Having a Minimum Charge for Deps: 0% **Cancellation Fee for Deps or Trial:** 0%
Deposition Payment in Advance: 0% **Markup of Out-of-Pocket Expenses:** 100%

Up-front Retainer: 100% **Retainer Amount:** *High:* $1,000 *Low:* $1,000 *Average:* $1,000 *Median:* $1,000
Travel Billed Portal-to-Portal: 100% **1st-class Airfare Required:** 0%

Written Fee Agreement: 100% **Majority of Work:** *Plaintiffs:* 0% *Defendants:* 0% *Neither:* 100%
Retaining Counsel Failed to Pay Last 5 Years: 100% **Opposing Counsel Failed to Pay Last 5 Years:** 100%

Mechanical Systems

Responding Experts: *1*

Hourly Fees: **In-court Testimony:** *High:* $125 *Low:* $125 *Average:* $125 *Median:* $125
File Review/Prep: *High:* $125 *Low:* $125 *Average:* $125 *Median:* $125
Depositions: *High:* $125 *Low:* $125 *Average:* $125 *Median:* $125
Percent of Experts Having a Minimum Charge for Deps: 100% **Cancellation Fee for Deps or Trial:** 0%
Deposition Payment in Advance: 0% **Markup of Out-of-Pocket Expenses:** 0%

Up-front Retainer: 100% **Retainer Amount:** *High:* $250 *Low:* $250 *Average:* $250 *Median:* $250
Travel Billed Portal-to-Portal: 100% **1st-class Airfare Required:** 0%

Written Fee Agreement: 100% **Majority of Work:** *Plaintiffs:* 0% *Defendants:* 0% *Neither:* 100%
Retaining Counsel Failed to Pay Last 5 Years: 0% **Opposing Counsel Failed to Pay Last 5 Years:** 0%

Medical Doctor

Responding Experts: *5*

Hourly Fees: **In-court Testimony:** *High:* $2,500 *Low:* $250 *Average:* $810 *Median:* $450
File Review/Prep: *High:* $400 *Low:* $250 *Average:* $280 *Median:* $250
Depositions: *High:* $750 *Low:* $250 *Average:* $420 *Median:* $400
Percent of Experts Having a Minimum Charge for Deps: 40% **Cancellation Fee for Deps or Trial:** 80%
Deposition Payment in Advance: 60% **Markup of Out-of-Pocket Expenses:** 40%

Up-front Retainer: 100% **Retainer Amount:** *High:* $5,000 *Low:* $250 *Average:* $2,510 *Median:* $1,800
Travel Billed Portal-to-Portal: 40% **1st-class Airfare Required:** 0%

Written Fee Agreement: 60% **Majority of Work:** *Plaintiffs:* 0% *Defendants:* 20% *Neither:* 80%
Retaining Counsel Failed to Pay Last 5 Years: 60% **Opposing Counsel Failed to Pay Last 5 Years:** 40%

Medicine, Nuclear

Responding Experts: *1*

Hourly Fees:					
	In-court Testimony:	*High:* $500	*Low:* $500	*Average:* $500	*Median:* $500
	File Review/Prep:	*High:* $500	*Low:* $500	*Average:* $500	*Median:* $500
	Depositions:	*High:* $500	*Low:* $500	*Average:* $500	*Median:* $500

Percent of Experts Having a Minimum Charge for Deps: 100% **Cancellation Fee for Deps or Trial:** 0%
Deposition Payment in Advance: 0% **Markup of Out-of-Pocket Expenses:** 0%

Up-front Retainer: 0% **Retainer Amount:** *High:* N/A *Low:* N/A *Average:* N/A *Median:* N/A
Travel Billed Portal-to-Portal: 100% **1st-class Airfare Required:** 0%

Written Fee Agreement: 0% **Majority of Work:** *Plaintiffs:* 0% *Defendants:* 100% *Neither:* 0%
Retaining Counsel Failed to Pay Last 5 Years: 0% **Opposing Counsel Failed to Pay Last 5 Years:** 0%

Mental Health

Responding Experts: *1*

Hourly Fees:					
	In-court Testimony:	*High:* $250	*Low:* $250	*Average:* $250	*Median:* $250
	File Review/Prep:	*High:* $125	*Low:* $125	*Average:* $125	*Median:* $125
	Depositions:	*High:* $250	*Low:* $250	*Average:* $250	*Median:* $250

Percent of Experts Having a Minimum Charge for Deps: 100% **Cancellation Fee for Deps or Trial:** 100%
Deposition Payment in Advance: 100% **Markup of Out-of-Pocket Expenses:** 0%

Up-front Retainer: 100% **Retainer Amount:** *High:* $1,000 *Low:* $1,000 *Average:* $1,000 *Median:* $1,000
Travel Billed Portal-to-Portal: 100% **1st-class Airfare Required:** 0%

Written Fee Agreement: 100% **Majority of Work:** *Plaintiffs:* 0% *Defendants:* 0% *Neither:* 100%
Retaining Counsel Failed to Pay Last 5 Years: 100% **Opposing Counsel Failed to Pay Last 5 Years:** 0%

Mental Retardation

Responding Experts: *1*

Hourly Fees:					
	In-court Testimony:	*High:* $200	*Low:* $200	*Average:* $200	*Median:* $200
	File Review/Prep:	*High:* $200	*Low:* $200	*Average:* $200	*Median:* $200
	Depositions:	*High:* $200	*Low:* $200	*Average:* $200	*Median:* $200

Percent of Experts Having a Minimum Charge for Deps: 0% **Cancellation Fee for Deps or Trial:** 0%
Deposition Payment in Advance: 0% **Markup of Out-of-Pocket Expenses:** 0%

Up-front Retainer: 0% **Retainer Amount:** *High:* N/A *Low:* N/A *Average:* N/A *Median:* N/A
Travel Billed Portal-to-Portal: 100% **1st-class Airfare Required:** 0%

Written Fee Agreement: 100% **Majority of Work:** *Plaintiffs:* 100% *Defendants:* 0% *Neither:* 0%
Retaining Counsel Failed to Pay Last 5 Years: 100% **Opposing Counsel Failed to Pay Last 5 Years:** 100%

Metallurgy

Responding Experts: *2*

Hourly Fees:					
	In-court Testimony:	*High:* $275	*Low:* $270	*Average:* $272	*Median:* $272
	File Review/Prep:	*High:* $225	*Low:* $210	*Average:* $218	*Median:* $218
	Depositions:	*High:* $275	*Low:* $270	*Average:* $272	*Median:* $272

Percent of Experts Having a Minimum Charge for Deps: 100% **Cancellation Fee for Deps or Trial:** 50%
Deposition Payment in Advance: 50% **Markup of Out-of-Pocket Expenses:** 50%

Up-front Retainer: 50% **Retainer Amount:** *High:* $1,000 *Low:* $1,000 *Average:* $1,000 *Median:* $1,000
Travel Billed Portal-to-Portal: 100% **1st-class Airfare Required:** 50%

Written Fee Agreement: 100% **Majority of Work:** *Plaintiffs:* 0% *Defendants:* 0% *Neither:* 100%
Retaining Counsel Failed to Pay Last 5 Years: 50% **Opposing Counsel Failed to Pay Last 5 Years:** 50%

Meteorology

Responding Experts: *4*

Hourly Fees:

	High	*Low*	*Average*	*Median*
In-court Testimony:	$300	$150	$203	$180
File Review/Prep:	$200	$125	$165	$168
Depositions:	$300	$150	$203	$180

Percent of Experts Having a Minimum Charge for Deps: 25% **Cancellation Fee for Deps or Trial:** 25%
Deposition Payment in Advance: 25% **Markup of Out-of-Pocket Expenses:** 25%

Up-front Retainer: 75% **Retainer Amount:** *High:* $400 *Low:* $400 *Average:* $400 *Median:* $400
Travel Billed Portal-to-Portal: 75% **1st-class Airfare Required:** 0%

Written Fee Agreement: 75% **Majority of Work:** *Plaintiffs:* 0% *Defendants:* 25% *Neither:* 75%
Retaining Counsel Failed to Pay Last 5 Years: 50% **Opposing Counsel Failed to Pay Last 5 Years:** 25%

Midwife

Responding Experts: *1*

Hourly Fees:

	High	*Low*	*Average*	*Median*
In-court Testimony:	$300	$300	$300	$300
File Review/Prep:	$300	$300	$300	$300
Depositions:	$300	$300	$300	$300

Percent of Experts Having a Minimum Charge for Deps: 0% **Cancellation Fee for Deps or Trial:** 100%
Deposition Payment in Advance: 0% **Markup of Out-of-Pocket Expenses:** 0%

Up-front Retainer: 0% **Retainer Amount:** *High:* N/A *Low:* N/A *Average:* N/A *Median:* N/A
Travel Billed Portal-to-Portal: 100% **1st-class Airfare Required:** 0%

Written Fee Agreement: 0% **Majority of Work:** *Plaintiffs:* 0% *Defendants:* 100% *Neither:* 0%
Retaining Counsel Failed to Pay Last 5 Years: 0% **Opposing Counsel Failed to Pay Last 5 Years:** N/A

Mold

Responding Experts: *3*

Hourly Fees:

	High	*Low*	*Average*	*Median*
In-court Testimony:	$300	$275	$292	$300
File Review/Prep:	$150	$125	$142	$150
Depositions:	$300	$225	$267	$275

Percent of Experts Having a Minimum Charge for Deps: 33% **Cancellation Fee for Deps or Trial:** 33%
Deposition Payment in Advance: 33% **Markup of Out-of-Pocket Expenses:** 66%

Up-front Retainer: 66% **Retainer Amount:** *High:* $2,500 *Low:* $2,500 *Average:* $2,500 *Median:* $2,500
Travel Billed Portal-to-Portal: 66% **1st-class Airfare Required:** 0%

Written Fee Agreement: 100% **Majority of Work:** *Plaintiffs:* 66% *Defendants:* 0% *Neither:* 33%
Retaining Counsel Failed to Pay Last 5 Years: 66% **Opposing Counsel Failed to Pay Last 5 Years:** 0%

Mortuary Science

Responding Experts: *1*

Hourly Fees:

	High	*Low*	*Average*	*Median*
In-court Testimony:	$175	$175	$175	$175
File Review/Prep:	$175	$175	$175	$175
Depositions:	$175	$175	$175	$175

Percent of Experts Having a Minimum Charge for Deps: 100% **Cancellation Fee for Deps or Trial:** 0%
Deposition Payment in Advance: 0% **Markup of Out-of-Pocket Expenses:** 0%

Up-front Retainer: 100% **Retainer Amount:** *High:* $350 *Low:* $350 *Average:* $350 *Median:* $350
Travel Billed Portal-to-Portal: 100% **1st-class Airfare Required:** 0%

Written Fee Agreement: 100% **Majority of Work:** *Plaintiffs:* 100% *Defendants:* 0% *Neither:* 0%
Retaining Counsel Failed to Pay Last 5 Years: 0% **Opposing Counsel Failed to Pay Last 5 Years:** 0%

Nephrology

Responding Experts: *3*

Hourly Fees: **In-court Testimony:** *High:* $500 *Low:* $500 *Average:* $500 *Median:* $500
File Review/Prep: *High:* $400 *Low:* $250 *Average:* $316 *Median:* $300
Depositions: *High:* $500 *Low:* $350 *Average:* $450 *Median:* $500

Percent of Experts Having a Minimum Charge for Deps: 66% **Cancellation Fee for Deps or Trial:** 0%
Deposition Payment in Advance: 0% **Markup of Out-of-Pocket Expenses:** 0%

Up-front Retainer: 66% **Retainer Amount:** *High:* $800 *Low:* $600 *Average:* $700 *Median:* $700
Travel Billed Portal-to-Portal: 66% **1st-class Airfare Required:** 0%

Written Fee Agreement: 66% **Majority of Work:** *Plaintiffs:* 0% *Defendants:* 0% *Neither:* 100%
Retaining Counsel Failed to Pay Last 5 Years: 66% **Opposing Counsel Failed to Pay Last 5 Years:** 0%

Neurology, (All)

Responding Experts: *18*

Hourly Fees: **In-court Testimony:** *High:* $1,250 *Low:* $200 *Average:* $575 *Median:* $500
File Review/Prep: *High:* $600 *Low:* $200 *Average:* $365 *Median:* $350
Depositions: *High:* $875 *Low:* $200 *Average:* $500 *Median:* $500

Percent of Experts Having a Minimum Charge for Deps: 89% **Cancellation Fee for Deps or Trial:** 89%
Deposition Payment in Advance: 78% **Markup of Out-of-Pocket Expenses:** 29%

Up-front Retainer: 67% **Retainer Amount:** *High:* $7,500 *Low:* $500 *Average:* $1,675 *Median:* $775
Travel Billed Portal-to-Portal: 88% **1st-class Airfare Required:** 13%

Written Fee Agreement: 89% **Majority of Work:** *Plaintiffs:* 11% *Defendants:* 45% *Neither:* 44%
Retaining Counsel Failed to Pay Last 5 Years: 44% **Opposing Counsel Failed to Pay Last 5 Years:** 33%

Neurology, Child

Responding Experts: *1*

Hourly Fees: **In-court Testimony:** *High:* $500 *Low:* $500 *Average:* $500 *Median:* $500
File Review/Prep: *High:* $300 *Low:* $300 *Average:* $300 *Median:* $300
Depositions: *High:* $500 *Low:* $500 *Average:* $500 *Median:* $500

Percent of Experts Having a Minimum Charge for Deps: 100% **Cancellation Fee for Deps or Trial:** 100%
Deposition Payment in Advance: 0% **Markup of Out-of-Pocket Expenses:** 0%

Up-front Retainer: 0% **Retainer Amount:** *High:* N/A *Low:* N/A *Average:* N/A *Median:* N/A
Travel Billed Portal-to-Portal: 100% **1st-class Airfare Required:** 0%

Written Fee Agreement: 100% **Majority of Work:** *Plaintiffs:* 0% *Defendants:* 0% *Neither:* 100%
Retaining Counsel Failed to Pay Last 5 Years: 100% **Opposing Counsel Failed to Pay Last 5 Years:** 0%

Neuropsychology

Responding Experts: *7*

Hourly Fees: **In-court Testimony:** *High:* $2,000 *Low:* $250 *Average:* $657 *Median:* $500
File Review/Prep: *High:* $400 *Low:* $150 *Average:* $280 *Median:* $250
Depositions: *High:* $600 *Low:* $250 *Average:* $420 *Median:* $500

Percent of Experts Having a Minimum Charge for Deps: 86% **Cancellation Fee for Deps or Trial:** 100%
Deposition Payment in Advance: 71% **Markup of Out-of-Pocket Expenses:** 83%

Up-front Retainer: 86% **Retainer Amount:** *High:* $5,000 *Low:* $2,000 *Average:* $3,000 *Median:* $2,500
Travel Billed Portal-to-Portal: 100% **1st-class Airfare Required:** 16%

Written Fee Agreement: 71% **Majority of Work:** *Plaintiffs:* 0% *Defendants:* 14% *Neither:* 86%
Retaining Counsel Failed to Pay Last 5 Years: 57% **Opposing Counsel Failed to Pay Last 5 Years:** 40%

Neuroradiology

Responding Experts: *2*

Hourly Fees: **In-court Testimony:** *High:* $700 *Low:* $400 *Average:* $550 *Median:* $550
File Review/Prep: *High:* $400 *Low:* $350 *Average:* $375 *Median:* $375
Depositions: *High:* $700 *Low:* $400 *Average:* $550 *Median:* $550
Percent of Experts Having a Minimum Charge for Deps: 100% **Cancellation Fee for Deps or Trial:** 50%
Deposition Payment in Advance: 50% **Markup of Out-of-Pocket Expenses:** 50%

Up-front Retainer: 50% **Retainer Amount:** *High:* $400 *Low:* $400 *Average:* $400 *Median:* $400
Travel Billed Portal-to-Portal: 100% **1st-class Airfare Required:** 0%

Written Fee Agreement: 50% **Majority of Work:** *Plaintiffs:* 50% *Defendants:* 0% *Neither:* 50%
Retaining Counsel Failed to Pay Last 5 Years: 50% **Opposing Counsel Failed to Pay Last 5 Years:** 0%

Nursing

Responding Experts: *12*

Hourly Fees: **In-court Testimony:** *High:* $500 *Low:* $100 *Average:* $212 *Median:* $188
File Review/Prep: *High:* $200 *Low:* $100 *Average:* $120 *Median:* $113
Depositions: *High:* $400 *Low:* $100 *Average:* $190 *Median:* $150
Percent of Experts Having a Minimum Charge for Deps: 8% **Cancellation Fee for Deps or Trial:** 33%
Deposition Payment in Advance: 16% **Markup of Out-of-Pocket Expenses:** 8%

Up-front Retainer: 92% **Retainer Amount:** *High:* $1,500 *Low:* $300 *Average:* $614 *Median:* $500
Travel Billed Portal-to-Portal: 92% **1st-class Airfare Required:** 8%

Written Fee Agreement: 83% **Majority of Work:** *Plaintiffs:* 25% *Defendants:* 25% *Neither:* 50%
Retaining Counsel Failed to Pay Last 5 Years: 66% **Opposing Counsel Failed to Pay Last 5 Years:** 27%

Nursing Homes

Responding Experts: *1*

Hourly Fees: **In-court Testimony:** *High:* $150 *Low:* $150 *Average:* $150 *Median:* $150
File Review/Prep: *High:* $125 *Low:* $125 *Average:* $125 *Median:* $125
Depositions: *High:* $150 *Low:* $150 *Average:* $150 *Median:* $150
Percent of Experts Having a Minimum Charge for Deps: 0% **Cancellation Fee for Deps or Trial:** 0%
Deposition Payment in Advance: 0% **Markup of Out-of-Pocket Expenses:** 0%

Up-front Retainer: 0% **Retainer Amount:** *High:* N/A *Low:* N/A *Average:* N/A *Median:* N/A
Travel Billed Portal-to-Portal: 0% **1st-class Airfare Required:** 0%

Written Fee Agreement: 0% **Majority of Work:** *Plaintiffs:* 0% *Defendants:* 0% *Neither:* 100%
Retaining Counsel Failed to Pay Last 5 Years: 0% **Opposing Counsel Failed to Pay Last 5 Years:** 0%

Obstetrics & Gynecology

Responding Experts: *26*

Hourly Fees: **In-court Testimony:** *High:* $1,250 *Low:* $250 *Average:* $500 *Median:* $500
File Review/Prep: *High:* $500 *Low:* $150 *Average:* $325 *Median:* $325
Depositions: *High:* $750 *Low:* $250 *Average:* $445 *Median:* $400
Percent of Experts Having a Minimum Charge for Deps: 59% **Cancellation Fee for Deps or Trial:** 50%
Deposition Payment in Advance: 46% **Markup of Out-of-Pocket Expenses:** 7%

Up-front Retainer: 50% **Retainer Amount:** *High:* $2,000 *Low:* $400 *Average:* $977 *Median:* $1,000
Travel Billed Portal-to-Portal: 92% **1st-class Airfare Required:** 24%

Written Fee Agreement: 50% **Majority of Work:** *Plaintiffs:* 20% *Defendants:* 48% *Neither:* 32%
Retaining Counsel Failed to Pay Last 5 Years: 38% **Opposing Counsel Failed to Pay Last 5 Years:** 8%

Occupational Medicine

Responding Experts: *16*

Hourly Fees: **In-court Testimony:** *High:* $1,000 *Low:* $125 *Average:* $465 *Median:* $500
File Review/Prep: *High:* $500 *Low:* $100 *Average:* $290 *Median:* $275
Depositions: *High:* $750 *Low:* $250 *Average:* $465 *Median:* $500

Percent of Experts Having a Minimum Charge for Deps: 69% **Cancellation Fee for Deps or Trial:** 80%
Deposition Payment in Advance: 63% **Markup of Out-of-Pocket Expenses:** 22%

Up-front Retainer: 50% **Retainer Amount:** *High:* $1,000 *Low:* $250 *Average:* $650 *Median:* $625
Travel Billed Portal-to-Portal: 94% **1st-class Airfare Required:** 0%

Written Fee Agreement: 50% **Majority of Work:** *Plaintiffs:* 6% *Defendants:* 26% *Neither:* 68%
Retaining Counsel Failed to Pay Last 5 Years: 38% **Opposing Counsel Failed to Pay Last 5 Years:** 20%

Oil & Gas

Responding Experts: *3*

Hourly Fees: **In-court Testimony:** *High:* $225 *Low:* $175 *Average:* $192 *Median:* $175
File Review/Prep: *High:* $225 *Low:* $175 *Average:* $192 *Median:* $175
Depositions: *High:* $225 *Low:* $175 *Average:* $192 *Median:* $175

Percent of Experts Having a Minimum Charge for Deps: 0% **Cancellation Fee for Deps or Trial:** 33%
Deposition Payment in Advance: 0% **Markup of Out-of-Pocket Expenses:** 0%

Up-front Retainer: 100% **Retainer Amount:** *High:* $5,000 *Low:* $2,000 *Average:* $3,000 *Median:* $2,000
Travel Billed Portal-to-Portal: 100% **1st-class Airfare Required:** 0%

Written Fee Agreement: 100% **Majority of Work:** *Plaintiffs:* 0% *Defendants:* 33% *Neither:* 66%
Retaining Counsel Failed to Pay Last 5 Years: 66% **Opposing Counsel Failed to Pay Last 5 Years:** 0%

Oncology, (All)

Responding Experts: *6*

Hourly Fees: **In-court Testimony:** *High:* $1,250 *Low:* $300 *Average:* $675 *Median:* $500
File Review/Prep: *High:* $475 *Low:* $250 *Average:* $388 *Median:* $400
Depositions: *High:* $1,250 *Low:* $400 *Average:* $615 *Median:* $475

Percent of Experts Having a Minimum Charge for Deps: 100% **Cancellation Fee for Deps or Trial:** 66%
Deposition Payment in Advance: 66% **Markup of Out-of-Pocket Expenses:** 16%

Up-front Retainer: 83% **Retainer Amount:** *High:* $5,000 *Low:* $500 *Average:* $1,800 *Median:* $1,200
Travel Billed Portal-to-Portal: 83% **1st-class Airfare Required:** 50%

Written Fee Agreement: 66% **Majority of Work:** *Plaintiffs:* 33% *Defendants:* 0% *Neither:* 67%
Retaining Counsel Failed to Pay Last 5 Years: 16% **Opposing Counsel Failed to Pay Last 5 Years:** 33%

Oncology, Gynecological

Responding Experts: *1*

Hourly Fees: **In-court Testimony:** *High:* $300 *Low:* $300 *Average:* $300 *Median:* $300
File Review/Prep: *High:* $250 *Low:* $250 *Average:* $250 *Median:* $250
Depositions: *High:* $450 *Low:* $450 *Average:* $450 *Median:* $450

Percent of Experts Having a Minimum Charge for Deps: 100% **Cancellation Fee for Deps or Trial:** 100%
Deposition Payment in Advance: 100% **Markup of Out-of-Pocket Expenses:** 0%

Up-front Retainer: 100% **Retainer Amount:** *High:* $500 *Low:* $500 *Average:* $500 *Median:* $500
Travel Billed Portal-to-Portal: 100% **1st-class Airfare Required:** 100%

Written Fee Agreement: 100% **Majority of Work:** *Plaintiffs:* 100% *Defendants:* 0% *Neither:* 0%
Retaining Counsel Failed to Pay Last 5 Years: 0% **Opposing Counsel Failed to Pay Last 5 Years:** 0%

Oncology, Radiation

Responding Experts: *1*

Hourly Fees:

In-court Testimony:	*High:* $500	*Low:* $500	*Average:* $500	*Median:* $500
File Review/Prep:	*High:* $400	*Low:* $400	*Average:* $400	*Median:* $400
Depositions:	*High:* $400	*Low:* $400	*Average:* $400	*Median:* $400

Percent of Experts Having a Minimum Charge for Deps: 100% **Cancellation Fee for Deps or Trial:** 100%
Deposition Payment in Advance: 100% **Markup of Out-of-Pocket Expenses:** 0%

Up-front Retainer: 100% **Retainer Amount:** *High:* $1,200 *Low:* $1,200 *Average:* $1,200 *Median:* $1,200
Travel Billed Portal-to-Portal: 100% **1st-class Airfare Required:** 0%

Written Fee Agreement: 0% **Majority of Work:** *Plaintiffs:* 100% *Defendants:* 0% *Neither:* 0%
Retaining Counsel Failed to Pay Last 5 Years: 0% **Opposing Counsel Failed to Pay Last 5 Years:** 0%

Ophthalmology

Responding Experts: *17*

Hourly Fees:

In-court Testimony:	*High:* $7,500	*Low:* $200	*Average:* $1,260	*Median:* $625
File Review/Prep:	*High:* $750	*Low:* $200	*Average:* $375	*Median:* $350
Depositions:	*High:* $1,000	*Low:* $200	*Average:* $570	*Median:* $500

Percent of Experts Having a Minimum Charge for Deps: 76% **Cancellation Fee for Deps or Trial:** 76%
Deposition Payment in Advance: 60% **Markup of Out-of-Pocket Expenses:** 25%

Up-front Retainer: 50% **Retainer Amount:** *High:* $10,000 *Low:* $750 *Average:* $2,990 *Median:* $1,200
Travel Billed Portal-to-Portal: 87% **1st-class Airfare Required:** 6%

Written Fee Agreement: 75% **Majority of Work:** *Plaintiffs:* 41% *Defendants:* 25% *Neither:* 34%
Retaining Counsel Failed to Pay Last 5 Years: 38% **Opposing Counsel Failed to Pay Last 5 Years:** 24%

Optometry

Responding Experts: *1*

Hourly Fees:

In-court Testimony:	*High:* $250	*Low:* $250	*Average:* $250	*Median:* $250
File Review/Prep:	*High:* $250	*Low:* $250	*Average:* $250	*Median:* $250
Depositions:	*High:* $250	*Low:* $250	*Average:* $250	*Median:* $250

Percent of Experts Having a Minimum Charge for Deps: 0% **Cancellation Fee for Deps or Trial:** 0%
Deposition Payment in Advance: 0% **Markup of Out-of-Pocket Expenses:** 100%

Up-front Retainer: 100% **Retainer Amount:** *High:* $1,000 *Low:* $1,000 *Average:* $1,000 *Median:* $1,000
Travel Billed Portal-to-Portal: 100% **1st-class Airfare Required:** 0%

Written Fee Agreement: 0% **Majority of Work:** *Plaintiffs:* 100% *Defendants:* 0% *Neither:* 0%
Retaining Counsel Failed to Pay Last 5 Years: 0% **Opposing Counsel Failed to Pay Last 5 Years:** 0%

Orthopedics

Responding Experts: *53*

Hourly Fees:

In-court Testimony:	*High:* $3,000	*Low:* $200	*Average:* $870	*Median:* $600
File Review/Prep:	*High:* $1,000	*Low:* $150	*Average:* $400	*Median:* $350
Depositions:	*High:* $2,000	*Low:* $200	*Average:* $700	*Median:* $600

Percent of Experts Having a Minimum Charge for Deps: 89% **Cancellation Fee for Deps or Trial:** 91%
Deposition Payment in Advance: 56% **Markup of Out-of-Pocket Expenses:** 16%

Up-front Retainer: 62% **Retainer Amount:** *High:* $3,500 *Low:* $200 *Average:* $1,325 *Median:* $1,000
Travel Billed Portal-to-Portal: 68% **1st-class Airfare Required:** 12%

Written Fee Agreement: 82% **Majority of Work:** *Plaintiffs:* 18% *Defendants:* 40% *Neither:* 42%
Retaining Counsel Failed to Pay Last 5 Years: 34% **Opposing Counsel Failed to Pay Last 5 Years:** 27%

Orthotics

Responding Experts: *1*

Hourly Fees: **In-court Testimony:** *High:* $500 *Low:* $500 *Average:* $500 *Median:* $500
File Review/Prep: *High:* $350 *Low:* $350 *Average:* $350 *Median:* $350
Depositions: *High:* $500 *Low:* $500 *Average:* $500 *Median:* $500
Percent of Experts Having a Minimum Charge for Deps: 100% **Cancellation Fee for Deps or Trial:** 0%
Deposition Payment in Advance: 0% **Markup of Out-of-Pocket Expenses:** 0%

Up-front Retainer: 0% **Retainer Amount:** *High:* N/A *Low:* N/A *Average:* N/A *Median:* N/A
Travel Billed Portal-to-Portal: 0% **1st-class Airfare Required:** 0%

Written Fee Agreement: 100% **Majority of Work:** *Plaintiffs:* 0% *Defendants:* 0% *Neither:* 100%
Retaining Counsel Failed to Pay Last 5 Years: 0% **Opposing Counsel Failed to Pay Last 5 Years:** 0%

Osteopathy

Responding Experts: *1*

Hourly Fees: **In-court Testimony:** *High:* N/A *Low:* N/A *Average:* N/A *Median:* N/A
File Review/Prep: *High:* $340 *Low:* $340 *Average:* $340 *Median:* $340
Depositions: *High:* $400 *Low:* $400 *Average:* $400 *Median:* $400
Percent of Experts Having a Minimum Charge for Deps: 100% **Cancellation Fee for Deps or Trial:** 100%
Deposition Payment in Advance: 100% **Markup of Out-of-Pocket Expenses:** 100%

Up-front Retainer: 100% **Retainer Amount:** *High:* N/A *Low:* N/A *Average:* N/A *Median:* N/A
Travel Billed Portal-to-Portal: 100% **1st-class Airfare Required:** 0%

Written Fee Agreement: 100% **Majority of Work:** *Plaintiffs:* 0% *Defendants:* 0% *Neither:* 100%
Retaining Counsel Failed to Pay Last 5 Years: 0% **Opposing Counsel Failed to Pay Last 5 Years:** 0%

Otolaryngology

Responding Experts: *5*

Hourly Fees: **In-court Testimony:** *High:* $625 *Low:* $250 *Average:* $425 *Median:* $400
File Review/Prep: *High:* $350 *Low:* $250 *Average:* $315 *Median:* $325
Depositions: *High:* $450 *Low:* $250 *Average:* $360 *Median:* $350
Percent of Experts Having a Minimum Charge for Deps: 60% **Cancellation Fee for Deps or Trial:** 60%
Deposition Payment in Advance: 40% **Markup of Out-of-Pocket Expenses:** 20%

Up-front Retainer: 20% **Retainer Amount:** *High:* $1,625 *Low:* $1,625 *Average:* $1,625 *Median:* $1,625
Travel Billed Portal-to-Portal: 100% **1st-class Airfare Required:** 0%

Written Fee Agreement: 80% **Majority of Work:** *Plaintiffs:* 20% *Defendants:* 40% *Neither:* 40%
Retaining Counsel Failed to Pay Last 5 Years: 60% **Opposing Counsel Failed to Pay Last 5 Years:** 40%

Pain Management/Medicine

Responding Experts: *18*

Hourly Fees: **In-court Testimony:** *High:* $2,500 *Low:* $100 *Average:* $695 *Median:* $500
File Review/Prep: *High:* $650 *Low:* $100 *Average:* $390 *Median:* $350
Depositions: *High:* $2,500 *Low:* $100 *Average:* $645 *Median:* $500
Percent of Experts Having a Minimum Charge for Deps: 89% **Cancellation Fee for Deps or Trial:** 79%
Deposition Payment in Advance: 89% **Markup of Out-of-Pocket Expenses:** 5%

Up-front Retainer: 63% **Retainer Amount:** *High:* $4,000 *Low:* $400 *Average:* $1,400 *Median:* $1,050
Travel Billed Portal-to-Portal: 68% **1st-class Airfare Required:** 0%

Written Fee Agreement: 70% **Majority of Work:** *Plaintiffs:* 42% *Defendants:* 17% *Neither:* 41%
Retaining Counsel Failed to Pay Last 5 Years: 42% **Opposing Counsel Failed to Pay Last 5 Years:** 21%

Palliative Medicine

Responding Experts: *1*

Hourly Fees:
In-court Testimony: *High:* $500 *Low:* $500 *Average:* $500 *Median:* $500
File Review/Prep: *High:* $500 *Low:* $500 *Average:* $500 *Median:* $500
Depositions: *High:* $500 *Low:* $500 *Average:* $500 *Median:* $500

Percent of Experts Having a Minimum Charge for Deps: 0% **Cancellation Fee for Deps or Trial:** 0%
Deposition Payment in Advance: 100% **Markup of Out-of-Pocket Expenses:** 0%

Up-front Retainer: 0% **Retainer Amount:** *High:* N/A *Low:* N/A *Average:* N/A *Median:* N/A
Travel Billed Portal-to-Portal: 100% **1st-class Airfare Required:** 0%

Written Fee Agreement: 100% **Majority of Work:** *Plaintiffs:* 0% *Defendants:* 100% *Neither:* 0%
Retaining Counsel Failed to Pay Last 5 Years: 0% **Opposing Counsel Failed to Pay Last 5 Years:** 0%

Pathology, (All)

Responding Experts: *6*

Hourly Fees:
In-court Testimony: *High:* $500 *Low:* $300 *Average:* $375 *Median:* $375
File Review/Prep: *High:* $500 *Low:* $150 *Average:* $335 *Median:* $325
Depositions: *High:* $500 *Low:* $300 *Average:* $375 *Median:* $375

Percent of Experts Having a Minimum Charge for Deps: 50% **Cancellation Fee for Deps or Trial:** 16%
Deposition Payment in Advance: 33% **Markup of Out-of-Pocket Expenses:** 16%

Up-front Retainer: 33% **Retainer Amount:** *High:* $1,000 *Low:* $1,000 *Average:* $1,000 *Median:* $1,000
Travel Billed Portal-to-Portal: 100% **1st-class Airfare Required:** 32%

Written Fee Agreement: 32% **Majority of Work:** *Plaintiffs:* 0% *Defendants:* 16% *Neither:* 84%
Retaining Counsel Failed to Pay Last 5 Years: 48% **Opposing Counsel Failed to Pay Last 5 Years:** 0%

Pathology, Pediatric

Responding Experts: *1*

Hourly Fees:
In-court Testimony: *High:* $500 *Low:* $500 *Average:* $500 *Median:* $500
File Review/Prep: *High:* $500 *Low:* $500 *Average:* $500 *Median:* $500
Depositions: *High:* $500 *Low:* $500 *Average:* $500 *Median:* $500

Percent of Experts Having a Minimum Charge for Deps: 0% **Cancellation Fee for Deps or Trial:** 0%
Deposition Payment in Advance: 0% **Markup of Out-of-Pocket Expenses:** 100%

Up-front Retainer: 0% **Retainer Amount:** *High:* N/A *Low:* N/A *Average:* N/A *Median:* N/A
Travel Billed Portal-to-Portal: 100% **1st-class Airfare Required:** 100%

Written Fee Agreement: 0% **Majority of Work:** *Plaintiffs:* 0% *Defendants:* 0% *Neither:* 100%
Retaining Counsel Failed to Pay Last 5 Years: 0% **Opposing Counsel Failed to Pay Last 5 Years:** 0%

Pediatrics

Responding Experts: *4*

Hourly Fees:
In-court Testimony: *High:* $650 *Low:* $375 *Average:* $510 *Median:* $500
File Review/Prep: *High:* $400 *Low:* $300 *Average:* $370 *Median:* $385
Depositions: *High:* $650 *Low:* $375 *Average:* $510 *Median:* $500

Percent of Experts Having a Minimum Charge for Deps: 75% **Cancellation Fee for Deps or Trial:** 75%
Deposition Payment in Advance: 75% **Markup of Out-of-Pocket Expenses:** 0%

Up-front Retainer: 75% **Retainer Amount:** *High:* $1,500 *Low:* $1,500 *Average:* $1,500 *Median:* $1,500
Travel Billed Portal-to-Portal: 100% **1st-class Airfare Required:** 0%

Written Fee Agreement: 75% **Majority of Work:** *Plaintiffs:* 33% *Defendants:* 0% *Neither:* 66%
Retaining Counsel Failed to Pay Last 5 Years: 25% **Opposing Counsel Failed to Pay Last 5 Years:** 25%

Periodontics

Responding Experts: *1*

Hourly Fees: **In-court Testimony:** *High:* $250 *Low:* $250 *Average:* $250 *Median:* $250
File Review/Prep: *High:* $150 *Low:* $150 *Average:* $150 *Median:* $150
Depositions: *High:* $250 *Low:* $250 *Average:* $250 *Median:* $250

Percent of Experts Having a Minimum Charge for Deps: 100% **Cancellation Fee for Deps or Trial:** 100%
Deposition Payment in Advance: 100% **Markup of Out-of-Pocket Expenses:** 0%

Up-front Retainer: 100% **Retainer Amount:** *High:* N/A *Low:* N/A *Average:* N/A *Median:* N/A
Travel Billed Portal-to-Portal: N/A **1st-class Airfare Required:** 0%

Written Fee Agreement: 100% **Majority of Work:** *Plaintiffs:* 0% *Defendants:* 0% *Neither:* 100%
Retaining Counsel Failed to Pay Last 5 Years: 0% **Opposing Counsel Failed to Pay Last 5 Years:** 0%

Personal Injury

Responding Experts: *2*

Hourly Fees: **In-court Testimony:** *High:* $350 *Low:* $95 *Average:* $223 *Median:* $223
File Review/Prep: *High:* $175 *Low:* $95 *Average:* $135 *Median:* $135
Depositions: *High:* $350 *Low:* $150 *Average:* $250 *Median:* $250

Percent of Experts Having a Minimum Charge for Deps: 50% **Cancellation Fee for Deps or Trial:** 0%
Deposition Payment in Advance: 0% **Markup of Out-of-Pocket Expenses:** 0%

Up-front Retainer: 100% **Retainer Amount:** *High:* $800 *Low:* $800 *Average:* $800 *Median:* $800
Travel Billed Portal-to-Portal: 100% **1st-class Airfare Required:** 0%

Written Fee Agreement: 50% **Majority of Work:** *Plaintiffs:* 50% *Defendants:* 0% *Neither:* 50%
Retaining Counsel Failed to Pay Last 5 Years: 50% **Opposing Counsel Failed to Pay Last 5 Years:** 0%

Pharmacology

Responding Experts: *3*

Hourly Fees: **In-court Testimony:** *High:* $425 *Low:* $125 *Average:* $285 *Median:* $300
File Review/Prep: *High:* $425 *Low:* $125 *Average:* $270 *Median:* $250
Depositions: *High:* $425 *Low:* $125 *Average:* $285 *Median:* $300

Percent of Experts Having a Minimum Charge for Deps: 66% **Cancellation Fee for Deps or Trial:** 66%
Deposition Payment in Advance: 66% **Markup of Out-of-Pocket Expenses:** 0%

Up-front Retainer: 100% **Retainer Amount:** *High:* $2,000 *Low:* $500 *Average:* $1,500 *Median:* $2,000
Travel Billed Portal-to-Portal: 66% **1st-class Airfare Required:** 0%

Written Fee Agreement: 100% **Majority of Work:** *Plaintiffs:* 66% *Defendants:* 0% *Neither:* 34%
Retaining Counsel Failed to Pay Last 5 Years: 66% **Opposing Counsel Failed to Pay Last 5 Years:** 33%

Physical Medicine & Rehabilitation

Responding Experts: *34*

Hourly Fees: **In-court Testimony:** *High:* $2,000 *Low:* $325 *Average:* $640 *Median:* $500
File Review/Prep: *High:* $900 *Low:* $125 *Average:* $385 *Median:* $350
Depositions: *High:* $1,200 *Low:* $100 *Average:* $510 *Median:* $500

Percent of Experts Having a Minimum Charge for Deps: 91% **Cancellation Fee for Deps or Trial:** 93%
Deposition Payment in Advance: 70% **Markup of Out-of-Pocket Expenses:** 15%

Up-front Retainer: 50% **Retainer Amount:** *High:* $8,000 *Low:* $850 *Average:* $1,780 *Median:* $1,000
Travel Billed Portal-to-Portal: 71% **1st-class Airfare Required:** 9%

Written Fee Agreement: 71% **Majority of Work:** *Plaintiffs:* 32% *Defendants:* 15% *Neither:* 53%
Retaining Counsel Failed to Pay Last 5 Years: 38% **Opposing Counsel Failed to Pay Last 5 Years:** 26%

Physical Therapy

Responding Experts: *1*

Hourly Fees: **In-court Testimony:** *High:* $275 *Low:* $275 *Average:* $275 *Median:* $275
File Review/Prep: *High:* $225 *Low:* $225 *Average:* $225 *Median:* $225
Depositions: *High:* $275 *Low:* $275 *Average:* $275 *Median:* $275
Percent of Experts Having a Minimum Charge for Deps: 100% **Cancellation Fee for Deps or Trial:** 100%
Deposition Payment in Advance: 0% **Markup of Out-of-Pocket Expenses:** 0%

Up-front Retainer: 100% **Retainer Amount:** *High:* $525 *Low:* $525 *Average:* $525 *Median:* $525
Travel Billed Portal-to-Portal: 100% **1st-class Airfare Required:** 0%

Written Fee Agreement: 100% **Majority of Work:** *Plaintiffs:* 0% *Defendants:* 0% *Neither:* 100%
Retaining Counsel Failed to Pay Last 5 Years: 100% **Opposing Counsel Failed to Pay Last 5 Years:** 100%

Physics

Responding Experts: *1*

Hourly Fees: **In-court Testimony:** *High:* $230 *Low:* $230 *Average:* $230 *Median:* $230
File Review/Prep: *High:* $230 *Low:* $230 *Average:* $230 *Median:* $230
Depositions: *High:* $230 *Low:* $230 *Average:* $230 *Median:* $230
Percent of Experts Having a Minimum Charge for Deps: 0% **Cancellation Fee for Deps or Trial:** 0%
Deposition Payment in Advance: 0% **Markup of Out-of-Pocket Expenses:** 0%

Up-front Retainer: 0% **Retainer Amount:** *High:* N/A *Low:* N/A *Average:* N/A *Median:* N/A
Travel Billed Portal-to-Portal: 100% **1st-class Airfare Required:** 0%

Written Fee Agreement: 0% **Majority of Work:** *Plaintiffs:* 0% *Defendants:* 100% *Neither:* 0%
Retaining Counsel Failed to Pay Last 5 Years: 0% **Opposing Counsel Failed to Pay Last 5 Years:** 0%

Plastics

Responding Experts: *3*

Hourly Fees: **In-court Testimony:** *High:* $300 *Low:* $250 *Average:* $270 *Median:* $250
File Review/Prep: *High:* $300 *Low:* $175 *Average:* $220 *Median:* $185
Depositions: *High:* $500 *Low:* $250 *Average:* $350 *Median:* $300
Percent of Experts Having a Minimum Charge for Deps: 33% **Cancellation Fee for Deps or Trial:** 33%
Deposition Payment in Advance: 0% **Markup of Out-of-Pocket Expenses:** 33%

Up-front Retainer: 66% **Retainer Amount:** *High:* $2,500 *Low:* $500 *Average:* $1,500 *Median:* $1,500
Travel Billed Portal-to-Portal: 60% **1st-class Airfare Required:** 33%

Written Fee Agreement: 66% **Majority of Work:** *Plaintiffs:* 0% *Defendants:* 0% *Neither:* 100%
Retaining Counsel Failed to Pay Last 5 Years: 66% **Opposing Counsel Failed to Pay Last 5 Years:** 33%

Plumbing

Responding Experts: *1*

Hourly Fees: **In-court Testimony:** *High:* $250 *Low:* $250 *Average:* $250 *Median:* $250
File Review/Prep: *High:* $150 *Low:* $150 *Average:* $150 *Median:* $150
Depositions: *High:* $250 *Low:* $250 *Average:* $250 *Median:* $250
Percent of Experts Having a Minimum Charge for Deps: 0% **Cancellation Fee for Deps or Trial:** 0%
Deposition Payment in Advance: 0% **Markup of Out-of-Pocket Expenses:** 0%

Up-front Retainer: 100% **Retainer Amount:** *High:* $1,500 *Low:* $1,500 *Average:* $1,500 *Median:* $1,500
Travel Billed Portal-to-Portal: 100% **1st-class Airfare Required:** 0%

Written Fee Agreement: 100% **Majority of Work:** *Plaintiffs:* 0% *Defendants:* 100% *Neither:* 0%
Retaining Counsel Failed to Pay Last 5 Years: 0% **Opposing Counsel Failed to Pay Last 5 Years:** 0%

Podiatry

Responding Experts: *5*

Hourly Fees:

In-court Testimony:	*High:* $1,500	*Low:* $200	*Average:* $615	*Median:* $400
File Review/Prep:	*High:* $375	*Low:* $125	*Average:* $220	*Median:* $200
Depositions:	*High:* $1,500	*Low:* $200	*Average:* $575	*Median:* $300

Percent of Experts Having a Minimum Charge for Deps: 60% **Cancellation Fee for Deps or Trial:** 20%
Deposition Payment in Advance: 40% **Markup of Out-of-Pocket Expenses:** 0%

Up-front Retainer: 60% **Retainer Amount:** *High:* $2,500 *Low:* $800 *Average:* $1,367 *Median:* $800
Travel Billed Portal-to-Portal: 100% **1st-class Airfare Required:** 0%

Written Fee Agreement: 60% **Majority of Work:** *Plaintiffs:* 40% *Defendants:* 20% *Neither:* 40%
Retaining Counsel Failed to Pay Last 5 Years: 100% **Opposing Counsel Failed to Pay Last 5 Years:** 40%

Premises Liability

Responding Experts: *4*

Hourly Fees:

In-court Testimony:	*High:* $350	*Low:* $150	*Average:* $220	*Median:* $185
File Review/Prep:	*High:* $250	*Low:* $125	*Average:* $180	*Median:* $175
Depositions:	*High:* $350	*Low:* $150	*Average:* $220	*Median:* $185

Percent of Experts Having a Minimum Charge for Deps: 75% **Cancellation Fee for Deps or Trial:** 0%
Deposition Payment in Advance: 75% **Markup of Out-of-Pocket Expenses:** 0%

Up-front Retainer: 75% **Retainer Amount:** *High:* $2,000 *Low:* $1,500 *Average:* $1,833 *Median:* $2,000
Travel Billed Portal-to-Portal: 75% **1st-class Airfare Required:** 0%

Written Fee Agreement: 100% **Majority of Work:** *Plaintiffs:* 50% *Defendants:* 0% *Neither:* 50%
Retaining Counsel Failed to Pay Last 5 Years: 75% **Opposing Counsel Failed to Pay Last 5 Years:** 25%

Pressure Vessels

Responding Experts: *1*

Hourly Fees:

In-court Testimony:	*High:* $150	*Low:* $150	*Average:* $150	*Median:* $150
File Review/Prep:	*High:* $150	*Low:* $150	*Average:* $150	*Median:* $150
Depositions:	*High:* $150	*Low:* $150	*Average:* $150	*Median:* $150

Percent of Experts Having a Minimum Charge for Deps: 0% **Cancellation Fee for Deps or Trial:** 0%
Deposition Payment in Advance: 0% **Markup of Out-of-Pocket Expenses:** 0%

Up-front Retainer: 0% **Retainer Amount:** *High:* N/A *Low:* N/A *Average:* N/A *Median:* N/A
Travel Billed Portal-to-Portal: 100% **1st-class Airfare Required:** 0%

Written Fee Agreement: 0% **Majority of Work:** *Plaintiffs:* 0% *Defendants:* 100% *Neither:* 0%
Retaining Counsel Failed to Pay Last 5 Years: 0% **Opposing Counsel Failed to Pay Last 5 Years:** 0%

Product Liability

Responding Experts: *6*

Hourly Fees:

In-court Testimony:	*High:* $300	*Low:* $150	*Average:* $210	*Median:* $205
File Review/Prep:	*High:* $300	*Low:* $150	*Average:* $205	*Median:* $195
Depositions:	*High:* $300	*Low:* $150	*Average:* $210	*Median:* $205

Percent of Experts Having a Minimum Charge for Deps: 66% **Cancellation Fee for Deps or Trial:** 32%
Deposition Payment in Advance: 66% **Markup of Out-of-Pocket Expenses:** 48%

Up-front Retainer: 83% **Retainer Amount:** *High:* $3,000 *Low:* $600 *Average:* $1,820 *Median:* $2,000
Travel Billed Portal-to-Portal: 100% **1st-class Airfare Required:** 16%

Written Fee Agreement: 83% **Majority of Work:** *Plaintiffs:* 84% *Defendants:* 0% *Neither:* 16%
Retaining Counsel Failed to Pay Last 5 Years: 100% **Opposing Counsel Failed to Pay Last 5 Years:** 32%

Prosthetics

Responding Experts: *1*

Hourly Fees: **In-court Testimony:** *High:* $500 *Low:* $500 *Average:* $500 *Median:* $500
File Review/Prep: *High:* $350 *Low:* $350 *Average:* $350 *Median:* $350
Depositions: *High:* $500 *Low:* $500 *Average:* $500 *Median:* $500
Percent of Experts Having a Minimum Charge for Deps: 100% **Cancellation Fee for Deps or Trial:** 0%
Deposition Payment in Advance: 0% **Markup of Out-of-Pocket Expenses:** 0%

Up-front Retainer: 0% **Retainer Amount:** *High:* N/A *Low:* N/A *Average:* N/A *Median:* N/A
Travel Billed Portal-to-Portal: 0% **1st-class Airfare Required:** 0%

Written Fee Agreement: 100% **Majority of Work:** *Plaintiffs:* 0% *Defendants:* 0% *Neither:* 100%
Retaining Counsel Failed to Pay Last 5 Years: 0% **Opposing Counsel Failed to Pay Last 5 Years:** 0%

Psychiatry, (All)

Responding Experts: *36*

Hourly Fees: **In-court Testimony:** *High:* $750 *Low:* $100 *Average:* $375 *Median:* $375
File Review/Prep: *High:* $500 *Low:* $140 *Average:* $305 *Median:* $300
Depositions: *High:* $750 *Low:* $100 *Average:* $360 *Median:* $350
Percent of Experts Having a Minimum Charge for Deps: 50% **Cancellation Fee for Deps or Trial:** 52%
Deposition Payment in Advance: 54% **Markup of Out-of-Pocket Expenses:** 6%

Up-front Retainer: 70% **Retainer Amount:** *High:* $4,000 *Low:* $600 *Average:* $1,870 *Median:* $1,500
Travel Billed Portal-to-Portal: 83% **1st-class Airfare Required:** 20%

Written Fee Agreement: 72% **Majority of Work:** *Plaintiffs:* 6% *Defendants:* 25% *Neither:* 69%
Retaining Counsel Failed to Pay Last 5 Years: 40% **Opposing Counsel Failed to Pay Last 5 Years:** 28%

Psychiatry, Child

Responding Experts: *1*

Hourly Fees: **In-court Testimony:** *High:* $625 *Low:* $625 *Average:* $625 *Median:* $625
File Review/Prep: *High:* $380 *Low:* $380 *Average:* $380 *Median:* $380
Depositions: *High:* $500 *Low:* $500 *Average:* $500 *Median:* $500
Percent of Experts Having a Minimum Charge for Deps: 100% **Cancellation Fee for Deps or Trial:** 100%
Deposition Payment in Advance: 0% **Markup of Out-of-Pocket Expenses:** 0%

Up-front Retainer: 100% **Retainer Amount:** *High:* $1,500 *Low:* $1,500 *Average:* $1,500 *Median:* $1,500
Travel Billed Portal-to-Portal: 100% **1st-class Airfare Required:** 0%

Written Fee Agreement: 100% **Majority of Work:** *Plaintiffs:* 0% *Defendants:* 0% *Neither:* 100%
Retaining Counsel Failed to Pay Last 5 Years: 0% **Opposing Counsel Failed to Pay Last 5 Years:** 0%

Psychology, (All)

Responding Experts: *23*

Hourly Fees: **In-court Testimony:** *High:* $700 *Low:* $110 *Average:* $285 *Median:* $250
File Review/Prep: *High:* $495 *Low:* $100 *Average:* $190 *Median:* $190
Depositions: *High:* $800 *Low:* $100 *Average:* $300 *Median:* $300
Percent of Experts Having a Minimum Charge for Deps: 91% **Cancellation Fee for Deps or Trial:** 90%
Deposition Payment in Advance: 88% **Markup of Out-of-Pocket Expenses:** 13%

Up-front Retainer: 96% **Retainer Amount:** *High:* $5,000 *Low:* $500 *Average:* $1,725 *Median:* $1,500
Travel Billed Portal-to-Portal: 91% **1st-class Airfare Required:** 13%

Written Fee Agreement: 61% **Majority of Work:** *Plaintiffs:* 18% *Defendants:* 9% *Neither:* 73%
Retaining Counsel Failed to Pay Last 5 Years: 30% **Opposing Counsel Failed to Pay Last 5 Years:** 15%

Psychology, Child

Responding Experts: *1*

Hourly Fees: **In-court Testimony:** *High:* $375 *Low:* $375 *Average:* $375 *Median:* $375
File Review/Prep: *High:* $225 *Low:* $225 *Average:* $225 *Median:* $225
Depositions: *High:* $375 *Low:* $375 *Average:* $375 *Median:* $375
Percent of Experts Having a Minimum Charge for Deps: 100% **Cancellation Fee for Deps or Trial:** 100%
Deposition Payment in Advance: 100% **Markup of Out-of-Pocket Expenses:** 0%

Up-front Retainer: 100% **Retainer Amount:** *High:* N/A *Low:* N/A *Average:* N/A *Median:* N/A
Travel Billed Portal-to-Portal: 0% **1st-class Airfare Required:** 0%

Written Fee Agreement: 100% **Majority of Work:** *Plaintiffs:* 0% *Defendants:* 0% *Neither:* 100%
Retaining Counsel Failed to Pay Last 5 Years: 0% **Opposing Counsel Failed to Pay Last 5 Years:** 100%

Pulmonology

Responding Experts: *5*

Hourly Fees: **In-court Testimony:** *High:* $600 *Low:* $400 *Average:* $520 *Median:* $500
File Review/Prep: *High:* $500 *Low:* $250 *Average:* $350 *Median:* $350
Depositions: *High:* $500 *Low:* $300 *Average:* $400 *Median:* $400
Percent of Experts Having a Minimum Charge for Deps: 60% **Cancellation Fee for Deps or Trial:** 60%
Deposition Payment in Advance: 0% **Markup of Out-of-Pocket Expenses:** 40%

Up-front Retainer: 40% **Retainer Amount:** *High:* $2,000 *Low:* $300 *Average:* $1,150 *Median:* $1,150
Travel Billed Portal-to-Portal: 100% **1st-class Airfare Required:** 50%

Written Fee Agreement: 60% **Majority of Work:** *Plaintiffs:* 40% *Defendants:* 20% *Neither:* 40%
Retaining Counsel Failed to Pay Last 5 Years: 20% **Opposing Counsel Failed to Pay Last 5 Years:** 20%

Radiology

Responding Experts: *2*

Hourly Fees: **In-court Testimony:** *High:* $750 *Low:* $500 *Average:* $625 *Median:* $625
File Review/Prep: *High:* $600 *Low:* $500 *Average:* $550 *Median:* $550
Depositions: *High:* $750 *Low:* $500 *Average:* $550 *Median:* $550
Percent of Experts Having a Minimum Charge for Deps: 100% **Cancellation Fee for Deps or Trial:** 50%
Deposition Payment in Advance: 50% **Markup of Out-of-Pocket Expenses:** 0%

Up-front Retainer: 50% **Retainer Amount:** *High:* $600 *Low:* $600 *Average:* $600 *Median:* $600
Travel Billed Portal-to-Portal: 100% **1st-class Airfare Required:** 50%

Written Fee Agreement: 0% **Majority of Work:** *Plaintiffs:* 0% *Defendants:* 100% *Neither:* 0%
Retaining Counsel Failed to Pay Last 5 Years: 50% **Opposing Counsel Failed to Pay Last 5 Years:** 50%

Railroads

Responding Experts: *3*

Hourly Fees: **In-court Testimony:** *High:* $250 *Low:* $125 *Average:* $185 *Median:* $175
File Review/Prep: *High:* $175 *Low:* $125 *Average:* $150 *Median:* $150
Depositions: *High:* $250 *Low:* $125 *Average:* $185 *Median:* $175
Percent of Experts Having a Minimum Charge for Deps: 66% **Cancellation Fee for Deps or Trial:** 0%
Deposition Payment in Advance: 33% **Markup of Out-of-Pocket Expenses:** 0%

Up-front Retainer: 33% **Retainer Amount:** *High:* $650 *Low:* $650 *Average:* $650 *Median:* $650
Travel Billed Portal-to-Portal: 33% **1st-class Airfare Required:** 0%

Written Fee Agreement: 66% **Majority of Work:** *Plaintiffs:* 100% *Defendants:* 0% *Neither:* 0%
Retaining Counsel Failed to Pay Last 5 Years: 66% **Opposing Counsel Failed to Pay Last 5 Years:** 33%

Real Estate

Responding Experts: *16*

Hourly Fees: **In-court Testimony:** *High:* $500 *Low:* $100 *Average:* $275 *Median:* $265
File Review/Prep: *High:* $400 *Low:* $100 *Average:* $215 *Median:* $185
Depositions: *High:* $500 *Low:* $100 *Average:* $275 *Median:* $265
Percent of Experts Having a Minimum Charge for Deps: 19% **Cancellation Fee for Deps or Trial:** 21%
Deposition Payment in Advance: 69% **Markup of Out-of-Pocket Expenses:** 16%

Up-front Retainer: 98% **Retainer Amount:** *High:* $7,500 *Low:* $1,000 *Average:* $2,620 *Median:* $2,000
Travel Billed Portal-to-Portal: 98% **1st-class Airfare Required:** 7%

Written Fee Agreement: 66% **Majority of Work:** *Plaintiffs:* 19% *Defendants:* 13% *Neither:* 68%
Retaining Counsel Failed to Pay Last 5 Years: 50% **Opposing Counsel Failed to Pay Last 5 Years:** 14%

Recreation, (All)

Responding Experts: *5*

Hourly Fees: **In-court Testimony:** *High:* $300 *Low:* $115 *Average:* $190 *Median:* $200
File Review/Prep: *High:* $200 *Low:* $125 *Average:* $155 *Median:* $150
Depositions: *High:* $300 *Low:* $115 *Average:* $190 *Median:* $200
Percent of Experts Having a Minimum Charge for Deps: 100% **Cancellation Fee for Deps or Trial:** 40%
Deposition Payment in Advance: 80% **Markup of Out-of-Pocket Expenses:** 20%

Up-front Retainer: 100% **Retainer Amount:** *High:* $2,500 *Low:* $750 *Average:* $1,325 *Median:* $1,025
Travel Billed Portal-to-Portal: 100% **1st-class Airfare Required:** 0%

Written Fee Agreement: 60% **Majority of Work:** *Plaintiffs:* 40% *Defendants:* 0% *Neither:* 60%
Retaining Counsel Failed to Pay Last 5 Years: 40% **Opposing Counsel Failed to Pay Last 5 Years:** 20%

Regulatory Proceedings

Responding Experts: *1*

Hourly Fees: **In-court Testimony:** *High:* $160 *Low:* $160 *Average:* $160 *Median:* $160
File Review/Prep: *High:* $160 *Low:* $160 *Average:* $160 *Median:* $160
Depositions: *High:* $160 *Low:* $160 *Average:* $160 *Median:* $160
Percent of Experts Having a Minimum Charge for Deps: 0% **Cancellation Fee for Deps or Trial:** 0%
Deposition Payment in Advance: 0% **Markup of Out-of-Pocket Expenses:** 0%

Up-front Retainer: 0% **Retainer Amount:** *High:* N/A *Low:* N/A *Average:* N/A *Median:* N/A
Travel Billed Portal-to-Portal: 0% **1st-class Airfare Required:** 100%

Written Fee Agreement: 0% **Majority of Work:** *Plaintiffs:* 0% *Defendants:* 0% *Neither:* 100%
Retaining Counsel Failed to Pay Last 5 Years: 0% **Opposing Counsel Failed to Pay Last 5 Years:** 0%

Retail

Responding Experts: *1*

Hourly Fees: **In-court Testimony:** *High:* $300 *Low:* $300 *Average:* $300 *Median:* $300
File Review/Prep: *High:* $275 *Low:* $275 *Average:* $275 *Median:* $275
Depositions: *High:* $300 *Low:* $300 *Average:* $300 *Median:* $300
Percent of Experts Having a Minimum Charge for Deps: 0% **Cancellation Fee for Deps or Trial:** 100%
Deposition Payment in Advance: 0% **Markup of Out-of-Pocket Expenses:** 100%

Up-front Retainer: 100% **Retainer Amount:** *High:* $5,000 *Low:* $5,000 *Average:* $5,000 *Median:* $5,000
Travel Billed Portal-to-Portal: 100% **1st-class Airfare Required:** 0%

Written Fee Agreement: 100% **Majority of Work:** *Plaintiffs:* 0% *Defendants:* 0% *Neither:* 100%
Retaining Counsel Failed to Pay Last 5 Years: 0% **Opposing Counsel Failed to Pay Last 5 Years:** 0%

Rheumatology

Responding Experts: *2*

Hourly Fees: **In-court Testimony:** *High:* $400 *Low:* $300 *Average:* $350 *Median:* $350
File Review/Prep: *High:* $300 *Low:* $285 *Average:* $293 *Median:* $293
Depositions: *High:* $300 *Low:* $300 *Average:* $300 *Median:* $300
Percent of Experts Having a Minimum Charge for Deps: 50% **Cancellation Fee for Deps or Trial:** 0%
Deposition Payment in Advance: 0% **Markup of Out-of-Pocket Expenses:** 0%

Up-front Retainer: 50% **Retainer Amount:** *High:* $1,000 *Low:* $1,000 *Average:* $1,000 *Median:* $1,000
Travel Billed Portal-to-Portal: 100% **1st-class Airfare Required:** 0%

Written Fee Agreement: 0% **Majority of Work:** *Plaintiffs:* 50% *Defendants:* 0% *Neither:* 50%
Retaining Counsel Failed to Pay Last 5 Years: 50% **Opposing Counsel Failed to Pay Last 5 Years:** 0%

Risk Management

Responding Experts: *2*

Hourly Fees: **In-court Testimony:** *High:* $165 *Low:* $150 *Average:* $158 *Median:* $158
File Review/Prep: *High:* $165 *Low:* $150 *Average:* $158 *Median:* $158
Depositions: *High:* $165 *Low:* $150 *Average:* $158 *Median:* $158
Percent of Experts Having a Minimum Charge for Deps: 50% **Cancellation Fee for Deps or Trial:** 0%
Deposition Payment in Advance: 50% **Markup of Out-of-Pocket Expenses:** 0%

Up-front Retainer: 100% **Retainer Amount:** *High:* $2,000 *Low:* $1,500 *Average:* $1,750 *Median:* $1,750
Travel Billed Portal-to-Portal: 100% **1st-class Airfare Required:** 0%

Written Fee Agreement: 50% **Majority of Work:** *Plaintiffs:* 0% *Defendants:* 0% *Neither:* 100%
Retaining Counsel Failed to Pay Last 5 Years: 50% **Opposing Counsel Failed to Pay Last 5 Years:** 0%

Roofing

Responding Experts: *1*

Hourly Fees: **In-court Testimony:** *High:* $125 *Low:* $125 *Average:* $125 *Median:* $125
File Review/Prep: *High:* $100 *Low:* $100 *Average:* $100 *Median:* $100
Depositions: *High:* $125 *Low:* $125 *Average:* $125 *Median:* $125
Percent of Experts Having a Minimum Charge for Deps: 100% **Cancellation Fee for Deps or Trial:** 100%
Deposition Payment in Advance: 0% **Markup of Out-of-Pocket Expenses:** 100%

Up-front Retainer: 0% **Retainer Amount:** *High:* N/A *Low:* N/A *Average:* N/A *Median:* N/A
Travel Billed Portal-to-Portal: 100% **1st-class Airfare Required:** 0%

Written Fee Agreement: 100% **Majority of Work:** *Plaintiffs:* 0% *Defendants:* 0% *Neither:* 100%
Retaining Counsel Failed to Pay Last 5 Years: 0% **Opposing Counsel Failed to Pay Last 5 Years:** 0%

Safety, (All)

Responding Experts: *26*

Hourly Fees: **In-court Testimony:** *High:* $400 *Low:* $150 *Average:* $220 *Median:* $200
File Review/Prep: *High:* $360 *Low:* $85 *Average:* $188 *Median:* $175
Depositions: *High:* $360 *Low:* $150 *Average:* $220 *Median:* $200
Percent of Experts Having a Minimum Charge for Deps: 58% **Cancellation Fee for Deps or Trial:** 35%
Deposition Payment in Advance: 46% **Markup of Out-of-Pocket Expenses:** 12%

Up-front Retainer: 100% **Retainer Amount:** *High:* $5,000 *Low:* $600 *Average:* $2,800 *Median:* $800
Travel Billed Portal-to-Portal: 73% **1st-class Airfare Required:** 4%

Written Fee Agreement: 73% **Majority of Work:** *Plaintiffs:* 33% *Defendants:* 15% *Neither:* 52%
Retaining Counsel Failed to Pay Last 5 Years: 57% **Opposing Counsel Failed to Pay Last 5 Years:** 25%

Safety, Automotive

Responding Experts: *1*

Hourly Fees:
In-court Testimony: *High:* \$360 *Low:* \$360 *Average:* \$360 *Median:* \$360
File Review/Prep: *High:* \$360 *Low:* \$360 *Average:* \$360 *Median:* \$360
Depositions: *High:* \$360 *Low:* \$360 *Average:* \$360 *Median:* \$360

Percent of Experts Having a Minimum Charge for Deps: 0% **Cancellation Fee for Deps or Trial:** 0%
Deposition Payment in Advance: 0% **Markup of Out-of-Pocket Expenses:** 0%

Up-front Retainer: 100% **Retainer Amount:** *High:* \$5,000 *Low:* \$5,000 *Average:* \$5,000 *Median:* \$5,000
Travel Billed Portal-to-Portal: 100% **1st-class Airfare Required:** 0%

Written Fee Agreement: 0% **Majority of Work:** *Plaintiffs:* 100% *Defendants:* 0% *Neither:* 0%
Retaining Counsel Failed to Pay Last 5 Years: 100% **Opposing Counsel Failed to Pay Last 5 Years:** 0%

Safety, Chemical Plant

Responding Experts: *1*

Hourly Fees:
In-court Testimony: *High:* \$150 *Low:* \$150 *Average:* \$150 *Median:* \$150
File Review/Prep: *High:* \$150 *Low:* \$150 *Average:* \$150 *Median:* \$150
Depositions: *High:* \$150 *Low:* \$150 *Average:* \$150 *Median:* \$150

Percent of Experts Having a Minimum Charge for Deps: 0% **Cancellation Fee for Deps or Trial:** 0%
Deposition Payment in Advance: 0% **Markup of Out-of-Pocket Expenses:** 0%

Up-front Retainer: 100% **Retainer Amount:** *High:* \$900 *Low:* \$900 *Average:* \$900 *Median:* \$900
Travel Billed Portal-to-Portal: 100% **1st-class Airfare Required:** 0%

Written Fee Agreement: 0% **Majority of Work:** *Plaintiffs:* 100% *Defendants:* 0% *Neither:* 0%
Retaining Counsel Failed to Pay Last 5 Years: 0% **Opposing Counsel Failed to Pay Last 5 Years:** 0%

Safety, Chemical Process

Responding Experts: *1*

Hourly Fees:
In-court Testimony: *High:* \$400 *Low:* \$400 *Average:* \$400 *Median:* \$400
File Review/Prep: *High:* \$200 *Low:* \$200 *Average:* \$200 *Median:* \$200
Depositions: *High:* \$200 *Low:* \$200 *Average:* \$200 *Median:* \$200

Percent of Experts Having a Minimum Charge for Deps: 0% **Cancellation Fee for Deps or Trial:** 0%
Deposition Payment in Advance: 0% **Markup of Out-of-Pocket Expenses:** 0%

Up-front Retainer: 100% **Retainer Amount:** *High:* N/A *Low:* N/A *Average:* N/A *Median:* N/A
Travel Billed Portal-to-Portal: 0% **1st-class Airfare Required:** 0%

Written Fee Agreement: 0% **Majority of Work:** *Plaintiffs:* 0% *Defendants:* 100% *Neither:* 0%
Retaining Counsel Failed to Pay Last 5 Years: 0% **Opposing Counsel Failed to Pay Last 5 Years:** 0%

Safety, Construction

Responding Experts: *1*

Hourly Fees:
In-court Testimony: *High:* \$150 *Low:* \$150 *Average:* \$150 *Median:* \$150
File Review/Prep: *High:* \$150 *Low:* \$150 *Average:* \$150 *Median:* \$150
Depositions: *High:* \$150 *Low:* \$150 *Average:* \$150 *Median:* \$150

Percent of Experts Having a Minimum Charge for Deps: 0% **Cancellation Fee for Deps or Trial:** 100%
Deposition Payment in Advance: 0% **Markup of Out-of-Pocket Expenses:** 0%

Up-front Retainer: 0% **Retainer Amount:** *High:* N/A *Low:* N/A *Average:* N/A *Median:* N/A
Travel Billed Portal-to-Portal: 100% **1st-class Airfare Required:** 0%

Written Fee Agreement: 0% **Majority of Work:** *Plaintiffs:* 0% *Defendants:* 0% *Neither:* 100%
Retaining Counsel Failed to Pay Last 5 Years: 0% **Opposing Counsel Failed to Pay Last 5 Years:** 0%

Safety, Highway

Responding Experts: *1*

Hourly Fees: **In-court Testimony:** *High:* $300 *Low:* $300 *Average:* $300 *Median:* $300
File Review/Prep: *High:* $250 *Low:* $250 *Average:* $250 *Median:* $250
Depositions: *High:* $300 *Low:* $300 *Average:* $300 *Median:* $300
Percent of Experts Having a Minimum Charge for Deps: 100% **Cancellation Fee for Deps or Trial:** 0%
Deposition Payment in Advance: 0% **Markup of Out-of-Pocket Expenses:** 0%

Up-front Retainer: 100% **Retainer Amount:** *High:* $1,500 *Low:* $1,500 *Average:* $1,500 *Median:* $1,500
Travel Billed Portal-to-Portal: 0% **1st-class Airfare Required:** 0%

Written Fee Agreement: 100% **Majority of Work:** *Plaintiffs:* 100% *Defendants:* 0% *Neither:* 0%
Retaining Counsel Failed to Pay Last 5 Years: 0% **Opposing Counsel Failed to Pay Last 5 Years:** 100%

Safety, Industrial

Responding Experts: *1*

Hourly Fees: **In-court Testimony:** *High:* $200 *Low:* $200 *Average:* $200 *Median:* $200
File Review/Prep: *High:* $200 *Low:* $200 *Average:* $200 *Median:* $200
Depositions: *High:* $200 *Low:* $200 *Average:* $200 *Median:* $200
Percent of Experts Having a Minimum Charge for Deps: 100% **Cancellation Fee for Deps or Trial:** 0%
Deposition Payment in Advance: 0% **Markup of Out-of-Pocket Expenses:** 0%

Up-front Retainer: 100% **Retainer Amount:** *High:* $750 *Low:* $750 *Average:* $750 *Median:* $750
Travel Billed Portal-to-Portal: 0% **1st-class Airfare Required:** 100%

Written Fee Agreement: 100% **Majority of Work:** *Plaintiffs:* 0% *Defendants:* 0% *Neither:* 100%
Retaining Counsel Failed to Pay Last 5 Years: 100% **Opposing Counsel Failed to Pay Last 5 Years:** 0%

Safety, Machine

Responding Experts: *1*

Hourly Fees: **In-court Testimony:** *High:* $150 *Low:* $150 *Average:* $150 *Median:* $150
File Review/Prep: *High:* $150 *Low:* $150 *Average:* $150 *Median:* $150
Depositions: *High:* $150 *Low:* $150 *Average:* $150 *Median:* $150
Percent of Experts Having a Minimum Charge for Deps: 100% **Cancellation Fee for Deps or Trial:** 100%
Deposition Payment in Advance: 100% **Markup of Out-of-Pocket Expenses:** 0%

Up-front Retainer: 100% **Retainer Amount:** *High:* $600 *Low:* $600 *Average:* $600 *Median:* $600
Travel Billed Portal-to-Portal: 100% **1st-class Airfare Required:** 0%

Written Fee Agreement: 100% **Majority of Work:** *Plaintiffs:* 100% *Defendants:* 0% *Neither:* 0%
Retaining Counsel Failed to Pay Last 5 Years: 100% **Opposing Counsel Failed to Pay Last 5 Years:** 0%

Safety, Particle Acceleratory

Responding Experts: *1*

Hourly Fees: **In-court Testimony:** *High:* $200 *Low:* $200 *Average:* $200 *Median:* $200
File Review/Prep: *High:* $150 *Low:* $150 *Average:* $150 *Median:* $150
Depositions: *High:* $200 *Low:* $200 *Average:* $200 *Median:* $200
Percent of Experts Having a Minimum Charge for Deps: 0% **Cancellation Fee for Deps or Trial:** 0%
Deposition Payment in Advance: 100% **Markup of Out-of-Pocket Expenses:** 0%

Up-front Retainer: 100% **Retainer Amount:** *High:* $2,000 *Low:* $2,000 *Average:* $2,000 *Median:* $2,000
Travel Billed Portal-to-Portal: 0% **1st-class Airfare Required:** 0%

Written Fee Agreement: 0% **Majority of Work:** *Plaintiffs:* 0% *Defendants:* 0% *Neither:* 100%
Retaining Counsel Failed to Pay Last 5 Years: 0% **Opposing Counsel Failed to Pay Last 5 Years:** 0%

Safety, Pipeline

Responding Experts: *1*

Hourly Fees: **In-court Testimony:** *High:* $200 *Low:* $200 *Average:* $200 *Median:* $200
File Review/Prep: *High:* $175 *Low:* $175 *Average:* $175 *Median:* $175
Depositions: *High:* $200 *Low:* $200 *Average:* $200 *Median:* $200
Percent of Experts Having a Minimum Charge for Deps: 0% **Cancellation Fee for Deps or Trial:** 0%
Deposition Payment in Advance: 0% **Markup of Out-of-Pocket Expenses:** 0%

Up-front Retainer: 100% **Retainer Amount:** *High:* $5,000 *Low:* $5,000 *Average:* $5,000 *Median:* $5,000
Travel Billed Portal-to-Portal: 0% **1st-class Airfare Required:** 0%

Written Fee Agreement: 0% **Majority of Work:** *Plaintiffs:* 0% *Defendants:* 100% *Neither:* 0%
Retaining Counsel Failed to Pay Last 5 Years: 100% **Opposing Counsel Failed to Pay Last 5 Years:** 0%

Safety, Radiation

Responding Experts: *1*

Hourly Fees: **In-court Testimony:** *High:* $200 *Low:* $200 *Average:* $200 *Median:* $200
File Review/Prep: *High:* $150 *Low:* $150 *Average:* $150 *Median:* $150
Depositions: *High:* $200 *Low:* $200 *Average:* $200 *Median:* $200
Percent of Experts Having a Minimum Charge for Deps: 0% **Cancellation Fee for Deps or Trial:** 0%
Deposition Payment in Advance: 100% **Markup of Out-of-Pocket Expenses:** 0%

Up-front Retainer: 100% **Retainer Amount:** *High:* $2,000 *Low:* $2,000 *Average:* $2,000 *Median:* $2,000
Travel Billed Portal-to-Portal: 0% **1st-class Airfare Required:** 0%

Written Fee Agreement: 0% **Majority of Work:** *Plaintiffs:* 0% *Defendants:* 0% *Neither:* 100%
Retaining Counsel Failed to Pay Last 5 Years: 0% **Opposing Counsel Failed to Pay Last 5 Years:** 0%

Safety, Transportation

Responding Experts: *3*

Hourly Fees: **In-court Testimony:** *High:* $250 *Low:* $200 *Average:* $225 *Median:* $225
File Review/Prep: *High:* $200 *Low:* $175 *Average:* $190 *Median:* $195
Depositions: *High:* $250 *Low:* $200 *Average:* $225 *Median:* $225
Percent of Experts Having a Minimum Charge for Deps: 100% **Cancellation Fee for Deps or Trial:** 66%
Deposition Payment in Advance: 33% **Markup of Out-of-Pocket Expenses:** 0%

Up-front Retainer: 100% **Retainer Amount:** *High:* $4,000 *Low:* $1,000 *Average:* $2,170 *Median:* $1,500
Travel Billed Portal-to-Portal: 100% **1st-class Airfare Required:** 0%

Written Fee Agreement: 66% **Majority of Work:** *Plaintiffs:* 0% *Defendants:* 0% *Neither:* 100%
Retaining Counsel Failed to Pay Last 5 Years: 100% **Opposing Counsel Failed to Pay Last 5 Years:** 33%

Sales

Responding Experts: *1*

Hourly Fees: **In-court Testimony:** *High:* $400 *Low:* $400 *Average:* $400 *Median:* $400
File Review/Prep: *High:* $400 *Low:* $400 *Average:* $400 *Median:* $400
Depositions: *High:* $400 *Low:* $400 *Average:* $400 *Median:* $400
Percent of Experts Having a Minimum Charge for Deps: 0% **Cancellation Fee for Deps or Trial:** 0%
Deposition Payment in Advance: 0% **Markup of Out-of-Pocket Expenses:** 0%

Up-front Retainer: 0% **Retainer Amount:** *High:* N/A *Low:* N/A *Average:* N/A *Median:* N/A
Travel Billed Portal-to-Portal: 100% **1st-class Airfare Required:** 0%

Written Fee Agreement: 100% **Majority of Work:** *Plaintiffs:* 0% *Defendants:* 100% *Neither:* 0%
Retaining Counsel Failed to Pay Last 5 Years: 0% **Opposing Counsel Failed to Pay Last 5 Years:** 0%

Science

Responding Experts: *1*

Hourly Fees:

In-court Testimony:	*High:* $125	*Low:* $125	*Average:* $125	*Median:* $125
File Review/Prep:	*High:* $125	*Low:* $125	*Average:* $125	*Median:* $125
Depositions:	*High:* $125	*Low:* $125	*Average:* $125	*Median:* $125

Percent of Experts Having a Minimum Charge for Deps: 100% **Cancellation Fee for Deps or Trial:** 0%
Deposition Payment in Advance: 0% **Markup of Out-of-Pocket Expenses:** 0%

Up-front Retainer: 100% **Retainer Amount:** *High:* $750 *Low:* $750 *Average:* $750 *Median:* $750
Travel Billed Portal-to-Portal: 100% **1st-class Airfare Required:** 0%

Written Fee Agreement: 100% **Majority of Work:** *Plaintiffs:* 0% *Defendants:* 0% *Neither:* 100%
Retaining Counsel Failed to Pay Last 5 Years: 100% **Opposing Counsel Failed to Pay Last 5 Years:** 0%

Security

Responding Experts: *14*

Hourly Fees:

In-court Testimony:	*High:* $350	*Low:* $100	*Average:* $215	*Median:* $240
File Review/Prep:	*High:* $250	*Low:* $100	*Average:* $195	*Median:* $195
Depositions:	*High:* $350	*Low:* $100	*Average:* $225	*Median:* $250

Percent of Experts Having a Minimum Charge for Deps: 64% **Cancellation Fee for Deps or Trial:** 21%
Deposition Payment in Advance: 64% **Markup of Out-of-Pocket Expenses:** 7%

Up-front Retainer: 93% **Retainer Amount:** *High:* $3,000 *Low:* $1,000 *Average:* $1,980 *Median:* $2,000
Travel Billed Portal-to-Portal: 93% **1st-class Airfare Required:** 23%

Written Fee Agreement: 93% **Majority of Work:** *Plaintiffs:* 7% *Defendants:* 21% *Neither:* 72%
Retaining Counsel Failed to Pay Last 5 Years: 57% **Opposing Counsel Failed to Pay Last 5 Years:** 7%

Slip, Trip & Fall

Responding Experts: *6*

Hourly Fees:

In-court Testimony:	*High:* $400	*Low:* $150	*Average:* $270	*Median:* $275
File Review/Prep:	*High:* $200	*Low:* $100	*Average:* $175	*Median:* $195
Depositions:	*High:* $400	*Low:* $100	*Average:* $245	*Median:* $225

Percent of Experts Having a Minimum Charge for Deps: 50% **Cancellation Fee for Deps or Trial:** 0%
Deposition Payment in Advance: 33% **Markup of Out-of-Pocket Expenses:** 33%

Up-front Retainer: 66% **Retainer Amount:** *High:* $2,000 *Low:* $750 *Average:* $1,250 *Median:* $1,000
Travel Billed Portal-to-Portal: 83% **1st-class Airfare Required:** 0%

Written Fee Agreement: 100% **Majority of Work:** *Plaintiffs:* 16% *Defendants:* 16% *Neither:* 68%
Retaining Counsel Failed to Pay Last 5 Years: 66% **Opposing Counsel Failed to Pay Last 5 Years:** 0%

Snow & Ice

Responding Experts: *1*

Hourly Fees:

In-court Testimony:	*High:* $95	*Low:* $95	*Average:* $95	*Median:* $95
File Review/Prep:	*High:* $75	*Low:* $75	*Average:* $75	*Median:* $75
Depositions:	*High:* $95	*Low:* $95	*Average:* $95	*Median:* $95

Percent of Experts Having a Minimum Charge for Deps: 100% **Cancellation Fee for Deps or Trial:** 0%
Deposition Payment in Advance: 0% **Markup of Out-of-Pocket Expenses:** 100%

Up-front Retainer: 0% **Retainer Amount:** *High:* N/A *Low:* N/A *Average:* N/A *Median:* N/A
Travel Billed Portal-to-Portal: 100% **1st-class Airfare Required:** 0%

Written Fee Agreement: 100% **Majority of Work:** *Plaintiffs:* 100% *Defendants:* 0% *Neither:* 0%
Retaining Counsel Failed to Pay Last 5 Years: 0% **Opposing Counsel Failed to Pay Last 5 Years:** 100%

Social Work

Responding Experts: *2*

Hourly Fees:					
	In-court Testimony:	*High:* $250	*Low:* $180	*Average:* $215	*Median:* $215
	File Review/Prep:	*High:* $180	*Low:* $150	*Average:* $165	*Median:* $165
	Depositions:	*High:* $180	*Low:* $150	*Average:* $165	*Median:* $165

Percent of Experts Having a Minimum Charge for Deps: 100% **Cancellation Fee for Deps or Trial:** 50%
Deposition Payment in Advance: 100% **Markup of Out-of-Pocket Expenses:** 100%

Up-front Retainer: 100% **Retainer Amount:** *High:* $1,000 *Low:* $1,000 *Average:* $1,000 *Median:* $1,000
Travel Billed Portal-to-Portal: 100% **1st-class Airfare Required:** 0%

Written Fee Agreement: 0% **Majority of Work:** *Plaintiffs:* 50% *Defendants:* 0% *Neither:* 50%
Retaining Counsel Failed to Pay Last 5 Years: 50% **Opposing Counsel Failed to Pay Last 5 Years:** 50%

Soil

Responding Experts: *1*

Hourly Fees:					
	In-court Testimony:	*High:* $115	*Low:* $115	*Average:* $115	*Median:* $115
	File Review/Prep:	*High:* $115	*Low:* $115	*Average:* $115	*Median:* $115
	Depositions:	*High:* $115	*Low:* $115	*Average:* $115	*Median:* $115

Percent of Experts Having a Minimum Charge for Deps: 0% **Cancellation Fee for Deps or Trial:** 0%
Deposition Payment in Advance: 0% **Markup of Out-of-Pocket Expenses:** 100%

Up-front Retainer: 0% **Retainer Amount:** *High:* N/A *Low:* N/A *Average:* N/A *Median:* N/A
Travel Billed Portal-to-Portal: 100% **1st-class Airfare Required:** 0%

Written Fee Agreement: 0% **Majority of Work:** *Plaintiffs:* 100% *Defendants:* 0% *Neither:* 0%
Retaining Counsel Failed to Pay Last 5 Years: 0% **Opposing Counsel Failed to Pay Last 5 Years:** 0%

Statistics, (All)

Responding Experts: *2*

Hourly Fees:					
	In-court Testimony:	*High:* $350	*Low:* $200	*Average:* $275	*Median:* $275
	File Review/Prep:	*High:* $350	*Low:* $150	*Average:* $250	*Median:* $250
	Depositions:	*High:* $350	*Low:* $200	*Average:* $275	*Median:* $275

Percent of Experts Having a Minimum Charge for Deps: 50% **Cancellation Fee for Deps or Trial:** 0%
Deposition Payment in Advance: 50% **Markup of Out-of-Pocket Expenses:** 0%

Up-front Retainer: 50% **Retainer Amount:** *High:* $1,500 *Low:* $1,500 *Average:* $1,500 *Median:* $1,500
Travel Billed Portal-to-Portal: 100% **1st-class Airfare Required:** 0%

Written Fee Agreement: 100% **Majority of Work:** *Plaintiffs:* 50% *Defendants:* 0% *Neither:* 50%
Retaining Counsel Failed to Pay Last 5 Years: 50% **Opposing Counsel Failed to Pay Last 5 Years:** 0%

Statistics, Sampling

Responding Experts: *1*

Hourly Fees:					
	In-court Testimony:	*High:* $200	*Low:* $200	*Average:* $200	*Median:* $200
	File Review/Prep:	*High:* $150	*Low:* $150	*Average:* $150	*Median:* $150
	Depositions:	*High:* $200	*Low:* $200	*Average:* $200	*Median:* $200

Percent of Experts Having a Minimum Charge for Deps: 100% **Cancellation Fee for Deps or Trial:** 0%
Deposition Payment in Advance: 100% **Markup of Out-of-Pocket Expenses:** 0%

Up-front Retainer: 100% **Retainer Amount:** *High:* $1,500 *Low:* $1,500 *Average:* $1,500 *Median:* $1,500
Travel Billed Portal-to-Portal: 100% **1st-class Airfare Required:** 0%

Written Fee Agreement: 100% **Majority of Work:** *Plaintiffs:* 100% *Defendants:* 0% *Neither:* 0%
Retaining Counsel Failed to Pay Last 5 Years: 100% **Opposing Counsel Failed to Pay Last 5 Years:** 0%

Surgery, (All)

Responding Experts: *40*

Hourly Fees:

	High	Low	Average	Median
In-court Testimony:	$1,500	$250	$675	$650
File Review/Prep:	$1,000	$150	$385	$350
Depositions:	$3,000	$250	$625	$500

Percent of Experts Having a Minimum Charge for Deps: 78% **Cancellation Fee for Deps or Trial:** 73%
Deposition Payment in Advance: 45% **Markup of Out-of-Pocket Expenses:** 10%

Up-front Retainer: 60% **Retainer Amount:** *High:* $4,000 *Low:* $550 *Average:* $1,294 *Median:* $1,000
Travel Billed Portal-to-Portal: 75% **1st-class Airfare Required:** 15%

Written Fee Agreement: 78% **Majority of Work:** *Plaintiffs:* 23% *Defendants:* 33% *Neither:* 44%
Retaining Counsel Failed to Pay Last 5 Years: 33% **Opposing Counsel Failed to Pay Last 5 Years:** 10%

Surgery, Cardiothoracic

Responding Experts: *2*

Hourly Fees:

	High	Low	Average	Median
In-court Testimony:	$600	$500	$550	$550
File Review/Prep:	$450	$350	$400	$400
Depositions:	$500	$450	$475	$475

Percent of Experts Having a Minimum Charge for Deps: 50% **Cancellation Fee for Deps or Trial:** 0%
Deposition Payment in Advance: 0% **Markup of Out-of-Pocket Expenses:** 0%

Up-front Retainer: 100% **Retainer Amount:** *High:* $900 *Low:* $900 *Average:* $900 *Median:* $900
Travel Billed Portal-to-Portal: 100% **1st-class Airfare Required:** 0%

Written Fee Agreement: 50% **Majority of Work:** *Plaintiffs:* 0% *Defendants:* 50% *Neither:* 50%
Retaining Counsel Failed to Pay Last 5 Years: 0% **Opposing Counsel Failed to Pay Last 5 Years:** 0%

Surgery, Cardiovascular

Responding Experts: *2*

Hourly Fees:

	High	Low	Average	Median
In-court Testimony:	$1,000	$500	$750	$750
File Review/Prep:	$350	$300	$325	$325
Depositions:	$500	$500	$500	$500

Percent of Experts Having a Minimum Charge for Deps: 100% **Cancellation Fee for Deps or Trial:** 50%
Deposition Payment in Advance: 50% **Markup of Out-of-Pocket Expenses:** 0%

Up-front Retainer: 100% **Retainer Amount:** *High:* $900 *Low:* $700 *Average:* $800 *Median:* $800
Travel Billed Portal-to-Portal: 0% **1st-class Airfare Required:** 0%

Written Fee Agreement: 100% **Majority of Work:** *Plaintiffs:* 100% *Defendants:* 0% *Neither:* 0%
Retaining Counsel Failed to Pay Last 5 Years: 50% **Opposing Counsel Failed to Pay Last 5 Years:** 0%

Surgery, Colon & Rectal

Responding Experts: *2*

Hourly Fees:

	High	Low	Average	Median
In-court Testimony:	$750	$600	$675	$675
File Review/Prep:	$400	$300	$350	$350
Depositions:	$500	$500	$500	$500

Percent of Experts Having a Minimum Charge for Deps: 50% **Cancellation Fee for Deps or Trial:** 50%
Deposition Payment in Advance: 0% **Markup of Out-of-Pocket Expenses:** 0%

Up-front Retainer: 50% **Retainer Amount:** *High:* $1,000 *Low:* $1,000 *Average:* $1,000 *Median:* $1,000
Travel Billed Portal-to-Portal: 100% **1st-class Airfare Required:** 0%

Written Fee Agreement: 100% **Majority of Work:** *Plaintiffs:* 0% *Defendants:* 50% *Neither:* 50%
Retaining Counsel Failed to Pay Last 5 Years: 50% **Opposing Counsel Failed to Pay Last 5 Years:** 0%

Surgery, Cosmetic

Responding Experts: *1*

Hourly Fees: **In-court Testimony:** *High:* $500 *Low:* $500 *Average:* $500 *Median:* $500
File Review/Prep: *High:* $300 *Low:* $300 *Average:* $300 *Median:* $300
Depositions: *High:* $300 *Low:* $300 *Average:* $300 *Median:* $300
Percent of Experts Having a Minimum Charge for Deps: 100% **Cancellation Fee for Deps or Trial:** 100%
Deposition Payment in Advance: 0% **Markup of Out-of-Pocket Expenses:** 100%

Up-front Retainer: 0% **Retainer Amount:** *High:* N/A *Low:* N/A *Average:* N/A *Median:* N/A
Travel Billed Portal-to-Portal: 100% **1st-class Airfare Required:** 0%

Written Fee Agreement: 0% **Majority of Work:** *Plaintiffs:* 0% *Defendants:* 0% *Neither:* 100%
Retaining Counsel Failed to Pay Last 5 Years: 0% **Opposing Counsel Failed to Pay Last 5 Years:** 0%

Surgery, General

Responding Experts: *11*

Hourly Fees: **In-court Testimony:** *High:* $700 *Low:* $250 *Average:* $440 *Median:* $400
File Review/Prep: *High:* $500 *Low:* $150 *Average:* $310 *Median:* $350
Depositions: *High:* $1,750 *Low:* $250 *Average:* $520 *Median:* $400
Percent of Experts Having a Minimum Charge for Deps: 58% **Cancellation Fee for Deps or Trial:** 67%
Deposition Payment in Advance: 33% **Markup of Out-of-Pocket Expenses:** 0%

Up-front Retainer: 33% **Retainer Amount:** *High:* $4,000 *Low:* $1,000 *Average:* $2,050 *Median:* $1,150
Travel Billed Portal-to-Portal: 86% **1st-class Airfare Required:** 14%

Written Fee Agreement: 58% **Majority of Work:** *Plaintiffs:* 25% *Defendants:* 50% *Neither:* 25%
Retaining Counsel Failed to Pay Last 5 Years: 25% **Opposing Counsel Failed to Pay Last 5 Years:** 8%

Surgery, Hand

Responding Experts: *3*

Hourly Fees: **In-court Testimony:** *High:* $1,300 *Low:* $600 *Average:* $1,050 *Median:* $1,250
File Review/Prep: *High:* $600 *Low:* $450 *Average:* $525 *Median:* $525
Depositions: *High:* $900 *Low:* $600 *Average:* $750 *Median:* $750
Percent of Experts Having a Minimum Charge for Deps: 100% **Cancellation Fee for Deps or Trial:** 100%
Deposition Payment in Advance: 100% **Markup of Out-of-Pocket Expenses:** 33%

Up-front Retainer: 66% **Retainer Amount:** *High:* $550 *Low:* $550 *Average:* $550 *Median:* $550
Travel Billed Portal-to-Portal: 100% **1st-class Airfare Required:** 33%

Written Fee Agreement: 100% **Majority of Work:** *Plaintiffs:* 33% *Defendants:* 0% *Neither:* 66%
Retaining Counsel Failed to Pay Last 5 Years: 33% **Opposing Counsel Failed to Pay Last 5 Years:** 66%

Surgery, Head & Neck

Responding Experts: *1*

Hourly Fees: **In-court Testimony:** *High:* $400 *Low:* $400 *Average:* $400 *Median:* $400
File Review/Prep: *High:* $300 *Low:* $300 *Average:* $300 *Median:* $300
Depositions: *High:* $400 *Low:* $400 *Average:* $400 *Median:* $400
Percent of Experts Having a Minimum Charge for Deps: 100% **Cancellation Fee for Deps or Trial:** 0%
Deposition Payment in Advance: 0% **Markup of Out-of-Pocket Expenses:** 0%

Up-front Retainer: 0% **Retainer Amount:** *High:* N/A *Low:* N/A *Average:* N/A *Median:* N/A
Travel Billed Portal-to-Portal: 100% **1st-class Airfare Required:** 0%

Written Fee Agreement: 100% **Majority of Work:** *Plaintiffs:* 0% *Defendants:* 0% *Neither:* 100%
Retaining Counsel Failed to Pay Last 5 Years: 100% **Opposing Counsel Failed to Pay Last 5 Years:** 0%

Surgery, Neurological

Responding Experts: *11*

Hourly Fees:					
	In-court Testimony:	*High:* $1,500	*Low:* $450	*Average:* $750	*Median:* $750
	File Review/Prep:	*High:* $800	*Low:* $250	*Average:* $480	*Median:* $450
	Depositions:	*High:* $3,000	*Low:* $350	*Average:* $855	*Median:* $500

Percent of Experts Having a Minimum Charge for Deps: 81% **Cancellation Fee for Deps or Trial:** 81%
Deposition Payment in Advance: 76% **Markup of Out-of-Pocket Expenses:** 9%

Up-front Retainer: 81% **Retainer Amount:** *High:* $2,000 *Low:* $700 *Average:* $1,420 *Median:* $1,500
Travel Billed Portal-to-Portal: 77% **1st-class Airfare Required:** 11%

Written Fee Agreement: 100% **Majority of Work:** *Plaintiffs:* 27% *Defendants:* 18% *Neither:* 55%
Retaining Counsel Failed to Pay Last 5 Years: 50% **Opposing Counsel Failed to Pay Last 5 Years:** 9%

Surgery, Plastic

Responding Experts: *3*

Hourly Fees:					
	In-court Testimony:	*High:* $1,000	*Low:* $400	*Average:* $800	*Median:* $1,000
	File Review/Prep:	*High:* $1,000	*Low:* $250	*Average:* $535	*Median:* $350
	Depositions:	*High:* $1,000	*Low:* $250	*Average:* $685	*Median:* $800

Percent of Experts Having a Minimum Charge for Deps: 100% **Cancellation Fee for Deps or Trial:** 100%
Deposition Payment in Advance: 100% **Markup of Out-of-Pocket Expenses:** 0%

Up-front Retainer: 100% **Retainer Amount:** *High:* $1,000 *Low:* $1,000 *Average:* $1,000 *Median:* $1,000
Travel Billed Portal-to-Portal: 100% **1st-class Airfare Required:** 33%

Written Fee Agreement: 66% **Majority of Work:** *Plaintiffs:* 0% *Defendants:* 66% *Neither:* 33%
Retaining Counsel Failed to Pay Last 5 Years: 0% **Opposing Counsel Failed to Pay Last 5 Years:** 0%

Surgery, Podiatric

Responding Experts: *1*

Hourly Fees:					
	In-court Testimony:	*High:* $500	*Low:* $500	*Average:* $500	*Median:* $500
	File Review/Prep:	*High:* $175	*Low:* $175	*Average:* $175	*Median:* $175
	Depositions:	*High:* $500	*Low:* $500	*Average:* $500	*Median:* $500

Percent of Experts Having a Minimum Charge for Deps: 100% **Cancellation Fee for Deps or Trial:** 100%
Deposition Payment in Advance: 100% **Markup of Out-of-Pocket Expenses:** 0%

Up-front Retainer: 0% **Retainer Amount:** *High:* N/A *Low:* N/A *Average:* N/A *Median:* N/A
Travel Billed Portal-to-Portal: 100% **1st-class Airfare Required:** 0%

Written Fee Agreement: 100% **Majority of Work:** *Plaintiffs:* 0% *Defendants:* 100% *Neither:* 0%
Retaining Counsel Failed to Pay Last 5 Years: 0% **Opposing Counsel Failed to Pay Last 5 Years:** 0%

Surgery, Thoracic

Responding Experts: *1*

Hourly Fees:					
	In-court Testimony:	*High:* $500	*Low:* $500	*Average:* $500	*Median:* $500
	File Review/Prep:	*High:* $200	*Low:* $200	*Average:* $200	*Median:* $200
	Depositions:	*High:* $400	*Low:* $400	*Average:* $400	*Median:* $400

Percent of Experts Having a Minimum Charge for Deps: 0% **Cancellation Fee for Deps or Trial:** 100%
Deposition Payment in Advance: 100% **Markup of Out-of-Pocket Expenses:** 100%

Up-front Retainer: 100% **Retainer Amount:** *High:* $1,000 *Low:* $1,000 *Average:* $1,000 *Median:* $1,000
Travel Billed Portal-to-Portal: 0% **1st-class Airfare Required:** 0%

Written Fee Agreement: 100% **Majority of Work:** *Plaintiffs:* 0% *Defendants:* 0% *Neither:* 100%
Retaining Counsel Failed to Pay Last 5 Years: 0% **Opposing Counsel Failed to Pay Last 5 Years:** 0%

Surgery, Trauma

Responding Experts: *1*

Hourly Fees: **In-court Testimony:** *High:* $1,250 *Low:* $1,250 *Average:* $1,250 *Median:* $1,250
File Review/Prep: *High:* $250 *Low:* $250 *Average:* $250 *Median:* $250
Depositions: *High:* $600 *Low:* $600 *Average:* $600 *Median:* $600
Percent of Experts Having a Minimum Charge for Deps: 100% **Cancellation Fee for Deps or Trial:** 100%
Deposition Payment in Advance: 0% **Markup of Out-of-Pocket Expenses:** 0%

Up-front Retainer: 0% **Retainer Amount:** *High:* N/A *Low:* N/A *Average:* N/A *Median:* N/A
Travel Billed Portal-to-Portal: 100% **1st-class Airfare Required:** 100%

Written Fee Agreement: 0% **Majority of Work:** *Plaintiffs:* 0% *Defendants:* 100% *Neither:* 0%
Retaining Counsel Failed to Pay Last 5 Years: 100% **Opposing Counsel Failed to Pay Last 5 Years:** 0%

Surgery, Vascular

Responding Experts: *1*

Hourly Fees: **In-court Testimony:** *High:* N/A *Low:* N/A *Average:* N/A *Median:* N/A
File Review/Prep: *High:* $350 *Low:* $350 *Average:* $350 *Median:* $350
Depositions: *High:* $450 *Low:* $450 *Average:* $450 *Median:* $450
Percent of Experts Having a Minimum Charge for Deps: 0% **Cancellation Fee for Deps or Trial:** 0%
Deposition Payment in Advance: 0% **Markup of Out-of-Pocket Expenses:** 0%

Up-front Retainer: 0% **Retainer Amount:** *High:* N/A *Low:* N/A *Average:* N/A *Median:* N/A
Travel Billed Portal-to-Portal: 0% **1st-class Airfare Required:** 0%

Written Fee Agreement: 100% **Majority of Work:** *Plaintiffs:* 100% *Defendants:* 0% *Neither:* 0%
Retaining Counsel Failed to Pay Last 5 Years: 100% **Opposing Counsel Failed to Pay Last 5 Years:** 0%

Tankage

Responding Experts: *1*

Hourly Fees: **In-court Testimony:** *High:* $150 *Low:* $150 *Average:* $150 *Median:* $150
File Review/Prep: *High:* $150 *Low:* $150 *Average:* $150 *Median:* $150
Depositions: *High:* $150 *Low:* $150 *Average:* $150 *Median:* $150
Percent of Experts Having a Minimum Charge for Deps: 0% **Cancellation Fee for Deps or Trial:** 0%
Deposition Payment in Advance: 0% **Markup of Out-of-Pocket Expenses:** 0%

Up-front Retainer: 0% **Retainer Amount:** *High:* N/A *Low:* N/A *Average:* N/A *Median:* N/A
Travel Billed Portal-to-Portal: 100% **1st-class Airfare Required:** 0%

Written Fee Agreement: 0% **Majority of Work:** *Plaintiffs:* 0% *Defendants:* 100% *Neither:* 0%
Retaining Counsel Failed to Pay Last 5 Years: 0% **Opposing Counsel Failed to Pay Last 5 Years:** 0%

Taxation

Responding Experts: *4*

Hourly Fees: **In-court Testimony:** *High:* $375 *Low:* $210 *Average:* $310 *Median:* $325
File Review/Prep: *High:* $325 *Low:* $210 *Average:* $275 *Median:* $275
Depositions: *High:* $375 *Low:* $210 *Average:* $310 *Median:* $325
Percent of Experts Having a Minimum Charge for Deps: 50% **Cancellation Fee for Deps or Trial:** 50%
Deposition Payment in Advance: 75% **Markup of Out-of-Pocket Expenses:** 0%

Up-front Retainer: 100% **Retainer Amount:** *High:* $3,000 *Low:* $850 *Average:* $2,120 *Median:* $2,500
Travel Billed Portal-to-Portal: 100% **1st-class Airfare Required:** 0%

Written Fee Agreement: 25% **Majority of Work:** *Plaintiffs:* 25% *Defendants:* 25% *Neither:* 50%
Retaining Counsel Failed to Pay Last 5 Years: 0% **Opposing Counsel Failed to Pay Last 5 Years:** 25%

Telecommunications

Responding Experts: *2*

Hourly Fees: **In-court Testimony:** *High:* $390 *Low:* $295 *Average:* $345 *Median:* $345
File Review/Prep: *High:* $350 *Low:* $295 *Average:* $325 *Median:* $325
Depositions: *High:* $390 *Low:* $295 *Average:* $345 *Median:* $345
Percent of Experts Having a Minimum Charge for Deps: 0% **Cancellation Fee for Deps or Trial:** 0%
Deposition Payment in Advance: 50% **Markup of Out-of-Pocket Expenses:** 0%

Up-front Retainer: 100% **Retainer Amount:** *High:* $10,000 *Low:* $4,000 *Average:* $7,000 *Median:* $7,000
Travel Billed Portal-to-Portal: 100% **1st-class Airfare Required:** 0%

Written Fee Agreement: 50% **Majority of Work:** *Plaintiffs:* 50% *Defendants:* 0% *Neither:* 50%
Retaining Counsel Failed to Pay Last 5 Years: 0% **Opposing Counsel Failed to Pay Last 5 Years:** 0%

Textiles

Responding Experts: *1*

Hourly Fees: **In-court Testimony:** *High:* $250 *Low:* $250 *Average:* $250 *Median:* $250
File Review/Prep: *High:* $125 *Low:* $125 *Average:* $125 *Median:* $125
Depositions: *High:* $250 *Low:* $250 *Average:* $250 *Median:* $250
Percent of Experts Having a Minimum Charge for Deps: 0% **Cancellation Fee for Deps or Trial:** 0%
Deposition Payment in Advance: 0% **Markup of Out-of-Pocket Expenses:** 0%

Up-front Retainer: 100% **Retainer Amount:** *High:* $1,200 *Low:* $1,200 *Average:* $1,200 *Median:* $1,200
Travel Billed Portal-to-Portal: 100% **1st-class Airfare Required:** 100%

Written Fee Agreement: 100% **Majority of Work:** *Plaintiffs:* 100% *Defendants:* 0% *Neither:* 0%
Retaining Counsel Failed to Pay Last 5 Years: 0% **Opposing Counsel Failed to Pay Last 5 Years:** 0%

TMJ

Responding Experts: *2*

Hourly Fees: **In-court Testimony:** *High:* $600 *Low:* $360 *Average:* $480 *Median:* $480
File Review/Prep: *High:* $360 *Low:* $100 *Average:* $230 *Median:* $230
Depositions: *High:* $500 *Low:* $360 *Average:* $430 *Median:* $430
Percent of Experts Having a Minimum Charge for Deps: 100% **Cancellation Fee for Deps or Trial:** 100%
Deposition Payment in Advance: 100% **Markup of Out-of-Pocket Expenses:** 50%

Up-front Retainer: 100% **Retainer Amount:** *High:* $2,000 *Low:* $2,000 *Average:* $2,000 *Median:* $2,000
Travel Billed Portal-to-Portal: 100% **1st-class Airfare Required:** 100%

Written Fee Agreement: 100% **Majority of Work:** *Plaintiffs:* 100% *Defendants:* 0% *Neither:* 0%
Retaining Counsel Failed to Pay Last 5 Years: 50% **Opposing Counsel Failed to Pay Last 5 Years:** 50%

Toxicology

Responding Experts: *7*

Hourly Fees: **In-court Testimony:** *High:* $975 *Low:* $150 *Average:* $345 *Median:* $250
File Review/Prep: *High:* $975 *Low:* $150 *Average:* $330 *Median:* $250
Depositions: *High:* $975 *Low:* $150 *Average:* $355 *Median:* $295
Percent of Experts Having a Minimum Charge for Deps: 71% **Cancellation Fee for Deps or Trial:** 28%
Deposition Payment in Advance: 57% **Markup of Out-of-Pocket Expenses:** 14%

Up-front Retainer: 71% **Retainer Amount:** *High:* $9,800 *Low:* $150 *Average:* $4,615 *Median:* $4,250
Travel Billed Portal-to-Portal: 85% **1st-class Airfare Required:** 28%

Written Fee Agreement: 83% **Majority of Work:** *Plaintiffs:* 14% *Defendants:* 28% *Neither:* 57%
Retaining Counsel Failed to Pay Last 5 Years: 71% **Opposing Counsel Failed to Pay Last 5 Years:** 28%

Traffic

Responding Experts: *1*

Hourly Fees: **In-court Testimony:** *High:* $100 *Low:* $100 *Average:* $100 *Median:* $100
File Review/Prep: *High:* $75 *Low:* $75 *Average:* $75 *Median:* $75
Depositions: *High:* $100 *Low:* $100 *Average:* $100 *Median:* $100
Percent of Experts Having a Minimum Charge for Deps: 0% **Cancellation Fee for Deps or Trial:** 100%
Deposition Payment in Advance: 0% **Markup of Out-of-Pocket Expenses:** 0%

Up-front Retainer: 0% **Retainer Amount:** *High:* N/A *Low:* N/A *Average:* N/A *Median:* N/A
Travel Billed Portal-to-Portal: 100% **1st-class Airfare Required:** 0%

Written Fee Agreement: 100% **Majority of Work:** *Plaintiffs:* 0% *Defendants:* 100% *Neither:* 0%
Retaining Counsel Failed to Pay Last 5 Years: 0% **Opposing Counsel Failed to Pay Last 5 Years:** 0%

Transportation

Responding Experts: *5*

Hourly Fees: **In-court Testimony:** *High:* $300 *Low:* $200 *Average:* $250 *Median:* $250
File Review/Prep: *High:* $225 *Low:* $175 *Average:* $197 *Median:* $200
Depositions: *High:* $300 *Low:* $200 *Average:* $250 *Median:* $250
Percent of Experts Having a Minimum Charge for Deps: 80% **Cancellation Fee for Deps or Trial:** 40%
Deposition Payment in Advance: 40% **Markup of Out-of-Pocket Expenses:** 0%

Up-front Retainer: 100% **Retainer Amount:** *High:* $3,000 *Low:* $500 *Average:* $1,900 *Median:* $2,000
Travel Billed Portal-to-Portal: 100% **1st-class Airfare Required:** 0%

Written Fee Agreement: 100% **Majority of Work:** *Plaintiffs:* 20% *Defendants:* 0% *Neither:* 80%
Retaining Counsel Failed to Pay Last 5 Years: 80% **Opposing Counsel Failed to Pay Last 5 Years:** 20%

Trucking

Responding Experts: *3*

Hourly Fees: **In-court Testimony:** *High:* $250 *Low:* $250 *Average:* $250 *Median:* $250
File Review/Prep: *High:* $225 *Low:* $175 *Average:* $195 *Median:* $185
Depositions: *High:* $250 *Low:* $250 *Average:* $250 *Median:* $250
Percent of Experts Having a Minimum Charge for Deps: 100% **Cancellation Fee for Deps or Trial:** 100%
Deposition Payment in Advance: 33% **Markup of Out-of-Pocket Expenses:** 0%

Up-front Retainer: 100% **Retainer Amount:** *High:* $3,000 *Low:* $1,500 *Average:* $2,335 *Median:* $2,500
Travel Billed Portal-to-Portal: 100% **1st-class Airfare Required:** 0%

Written Fee Agreement: 100% **Majority of Work:** *Plaintiffs:* 33% *Defendants:* 0% *Neither:* 66%
Retaining Counsel Failed to Pay Last 5 Years: 66% **Opposing Counsel Failed to Pay Last 5 Years:** 0%

Trusts & Estates

Responding Experts: *5*

Hourly Fees: **In-court Testimony:** *High:* $500 *Low:* $150 *Average:* $280 *Median:* $200
File Review/Prep: *High:* $250 *Low:* $100 *Average:* $190 *Median:* $200
Depositions: *High:* $350 *Low:* $150 *Average:* $250 *Median:* $200
Percent of Experts Having a Minimum Charge for Deps: 60% **Cancellation Fee for Deps or Trial:** 40%
Deposition Payment in Advance: 20% **Markup of Out-of-Pocket Expenses:** 0%

Up-front Retainer: 100% **Retainer Amount:** *High:* $3,000 *Low:* $1,600 *Average:* $2,275 *Median:* $2,250
Travel Billed Portal-to-Portal: 20% **1st-class Airfare Required:** 0%

Written Fee Agreement: 20% **Majority of Work:** *Plaintiffs:* 60% *Defendants:* 0% *Neither:* 40%
Retaining Counsel Failed to Pay Last 5 Years: 60% **Opposing Counsel Failed to Pay Last 5 Years:** 40%

Urology

Responding Experts: *7*

Hourly Fees: **In-court Testimony:** *High:* $625 *Low:* $300 *Average:* $415 *Median:* $400
File Review/Prep: *High:* $400 *Low:* $300 *Average:* $370 *Median:* $375
Depositions: *High:* $500 *Low:* $400 *Average:* $435 *Median:* $400

Percent of Experts Having a Minimum Charge for Deps: 85% **Cancellation Fee for Deps or Trial:** 71%
Deposition Payment in Advance: 57% **Markup of Out-of-Pocket Expenses:** 17%

Up-front Retainer: 71% **Retainer Amount:** *High:* $800 *Low:* $400 *Average:* $630 *Median:* $700
Travel Billed Portal-to-Portal: 71% **1st-class Airfare Required:** 28%

Written Fee Agreement: 100% **Majority of Work:** *Plaintiffs:* 14% *Defendants:* 29% *Neither:* 57%
Retaining Counsel Failed to Pay Last 5 Years: 29% **Opposing Counsel Failed to Pay Last 5 Years:** 14%

Utilities, Underground

Responding Experts: *1*

Hourly Fees: **In-court Testimony:** *High:* $225 *Low:* $225 *Average:* $225 *Median:* $225
File Review/Prep: *High:* $225 *Low:* $225 *Average:* $225 *Median:* $225
Depositions: *High:* $225 *Low:* $225 *Average:* $225 *Median:* $225

Percent of Experts Having a Minimum Charge for Deps: 0% **Cancellation Fee for Deps or Trial:** 0%
Deposition Payment in Advance: 0% **Markup of Out-of-Pocket Expenses:** 0%

Up-front Retainer: 100% **Retainer Amount:** *High:* $1,500 *Low:* $1,500 *Average:* $1,500 *Median:* $1,500
Travel Billed Portal-to-Portal: 100% **1st-class Airfare Required:** 0%

Written Fee Agreement: 0% **Majority of Work:** *Plaintiffs:* 0% *Defendants:* 0% *Neither:* 100%
Retaining Counsel Failed to Pay Last 5 Years: 0% **Opposing Counsel Failed to Pay Last 5 Years:** 0%

Valuation, (All)

Responding Experts: *23*

Hourly Fees: **In-court Testimony:** *High:* $400 *Low:* $100 *Average:* $270 *Median:* $250
File Review/Prep: *High:* $350 *Low:* $125 *Average:* $250 *Median:* $250
Depositions: *High:* $350 *Low:* $100 *Average:* $260 *Median:* $250

Percent of Experts Having a Minimum Charge for Deps: 25% **Cancellation Fee for Deps or Trial:** 29%
Deposition Payment in Advance: 32% **Markup of Out-of-Pocket Expenses:** 4%

Up-front Retainer: 96% **Retainer Amount:** *High:* $10,000 *Low:* $725 *Average:* $5,000 *Median:* $5,000
Travel Billed Portal-to-Portal: 75% **1st-class Airfare Required:** 5%

Written Fee Agreement: 39% **Majority of Work:** *Plaintiffs:* 9% *Defendants:* 0% *Neither:* 91%
Retaining Counsel Failed to Pay Last 5 Years: 35% **Opposing Counsel Failed to Pay Last 5 Years:** 17%

Valuation, Business

Responding Experts: *21*

Hourly Fees: **In-court Testimony:** *High:* $400 *Low:* $100 *Average:* $275 *Median:* $295
File Review/Prep: *High:* $350 *Low:* $125 *Average:* $250 *Median:* $250
Depositions: *High:* $350 *Low:* $100 *Average:* $260 *Median:* $250

Percent of Experts Having a Minimum Charge for Deps: 27% **Cancellation Fee for Deps or Trial:** 31%
Deposition Payment in Advance: 36% **Markup of Out-of-Pocket Expenses:** 5%

Up-front Retainer: 95% **Retainer Amount:** *High:* $10,000 *Low:* $725 *Average:* $5,000 *Median:* $5,000
Travel Billed Portal-to-Portal: 81% **1st-class Airfare Required:** 5%

Written Fee Agreement: 43% **Majority of Work:** *Plaintiffs:* 5% *Defendants:* 0% *Neither:* 95%
Retaining Counsel Failed to Pay Last 5 Years: 33% **Opposing Counsel Failed to Pay Last 5 Years:** 15%

Video

Responding Experts: *1*

Hourly Fees: **In-court Testimony:** *High:* $300 *Low:* $300 *Average:* $300 *Median:* $300
File Review/Prep: *High:* $250 *Low:* $250 *Average:* $250 *Median:* $250
Depositions: *High:* $300 *Low:* $300 *Average:* $300 *Median:* $300
Percent of Experts Having a Minimum Charge for Deps: 100% **Cancellation Fee for Deps or Trial:** 100%
Deposition Payment in Advance: 0% **Markup of Out-of-Pocket Expenses:** 0%

Up-front Retainer: 100% **Retainer Amount:** *High:* $750 *Low:* $750 *Average:* $750 *Median:* $750
Travel Billed Portal-to-Portal: 100% **1st-class Airfare Required:** 0%

Written Fee Agreement: 100% **Majority of Work:** *Plaintiffs:* 0% *Defendants:* 100% *Neither:* 0%
Retaining Counsel Failed to Pay Last 5 Years: 0% **Opposing Counsel Failed to Pay Last 5 Years:** 0%

Vocational, (All)

Responding Experts: *30*

Hourly Fees: **In-court Testimony:** *High:* $600 *Low:* $115 *Average:* $220 *Median:* $200
File Review/Prep: *High:* $330 *Low:* $75 *Average:* $165 *Median:* $150
Depositions: *High:* $600 *Low:* $100 *Average:* $220 *Median:* $200
Percent of Experts Having a Minimum Charge for Deps: 50% **Cancellation Fee for Deps or Trial:** 66%
Deposition Payment in Advance: 58% **Markup of Out-of-Pocket Expenses:** 7%

Up-front Retainer: 87% **Retainer Amount:** *High:* $2,500 *Low:* $250 *Average:* $1,240 *Median:* $1,375
Travel Billed Portal-to-Portal: 97% **1st-class Airfare Required:** 9%

Written Fee Agreement: 87% **Majority of Work:** *Plaintiffs:* 31% *Defendants:* 7% *Neither:* 62%
Retaining Counsel Failed to Pay Last 5 Years: 30% **Opposing Counsel Failed to Pay Last 5 Years:** 17%

Vocational Economics

Responding Experts: *1*

Hourly Fees: **In-court Testimony:** *High:* $190 *Low:* $190 *Average:* $190 *Median:* $190
File Review/Prep: *High:* $100 *Low:* $100 *Average:* $100 *Median:* $100
Depositions: *High:* $200 *Low:* $200 *Average:* $200 *Median:* $200
Percent of Experts Having a Minimum Charge for Deps: 100% **Cancellation Fee for Deps or Trial:** 100%
Deposition Payment in Advance: 100% **Markup of Out-of-Pocket Expenses:** 0%

Up-front Retainer: 100% **Retainer Amount:** *High:* N/A *Low:* N/A *Average:* N/A *Median:* N/A
Travel Billed Portal-to-Portal: 0% **1st-class Airfare Required:** 0%

Written Fee Agreement: 0% **Majority of Work:** *Plaintiffs:* 0% *Defendants:* 0% *Neither:* 100%
Retaining Counsel Failed to Pay Last 5 Years: 0% **Opposing Counsel Failed to Pay Last 5 Years:** 0%

Vocational Rehabilitation

Responding Experts: *23*

Hourly Fees: **In-court Testimony:** *High:* $600 *Low:* $125 *Average:* $230 *Median:* $200
File Review/Prep: *High:* $330 *Low:* $75 *Average:* $170 *Median:* $150
Depositions: *High:* $600 *Low:* $125 *Average:* $235 *Median:* $200
Percent of Experts Having a Minimum Charge for Deps: 58% **Cancellation Fee for Deps or Trial:** 60%
Deposition Payment in Advance: 48% **Markup of Out-of-Pocket Expenses:** 9%

Up-front Retainer: 83% **Retainer Amount:** *High:* $2,500 *Low:* $250 *Average:* $1,225 *Median:* $1,250
Travel Billed Portal-to-Portal: 100% **1st-class Airfare Required:** 9%

Written Fee Agreement: 87% **Majority of Work:** *Plaintiffs:* 35% *Defendants:* 9% *Neither:* 56%
Retaining Counsel Failed to Pay Last 5 Years: 39% **Opposing Counsel Failed to Pay Last 5 Years:** 22%

Workers' Compensation

Responding Experts: *1*

Hourly Fees:					
	In-court Testimony:	*High:* $95	*Low:* $95	*Average:* $95	*Median:* $95
	File Review/Prep:	*High:* $95	*Low:* $95	*Average:* $95	*Median:* $95
	Depositions:	*High:* $150	*Low:* $150	*Average:* $150	*Median:* $150

Percent of Experts Having a Minimum Charge for Deps: 0% **Cancellation Fee for Deps or Trial:** 0%
Deposition Payment in Advance: 0% **Markup of Out-of-Pocket Expenses:** 0%

Up-front Retainer: 100% **Retainer Amount:** *High:* $800 *Low:* $800 *Average:* $800 *Median:* $800
Travel Billed Portal-to-Portal: 100% **1st-class Airfare Required:** 0%

Written Fee Agreement: 100% **Majority of Work:** *Plaintiffs:* 100% *Defendants:* 0% *Neither:* 0%
Retaining Counsel Failed to Pay Last 5 Years: 100% **Opposing Counsel Failed to Pay Last 5 Years:** 0%

Wound Care

Responding Experts: *1*

Hourly Fees:					
	In-court Testimony:	*High:* $150	*Low:* $150	*Average:* $150	*Median:* $150
	File Review/Prep:	*High:* $100	*Low:* $100	*Average:* $100	*Median:* $100
	Depositions:	*High:* $150	*Low:* $150	*Average:* $150	*Median:* $150

Percent of Experts Having a Minimum Charge for Deps: 100% **Cancellation Fee for Deps or Trial:** 100%
Deposition Payment in Advance: 100% **Markup of Out-of-Pocket Expenses:** 0%

Up-front Retainer: 100% **Retainer Amount:** *High:* $500 *Low:* $500 *Average:* $500 *Median:* $500
Travel Billed Portal-to-Portal: 100% **1st-class Airfare Required:** 0%

Written Fee Agreement: 100% **Majority of Work:** *Plaintiffs:* 0% *Defendants:* 0% *Neither:* 100%
Retaining Counsel Failed to Pay Last 5 Years: 100% **Opposing Counsel Failed to Pay Last 5 Years:** 0%

Chapter 5 Individual Expert Fees and Billing Procedures

Alabama

Engineering/Construction/Safety
Court: $200 **Review/Prep:** $180 **Deps:** $200
Majority: Plaintiff
Written Fee Schedule: Yes
Min Charge for Deps: Yes **Hours:** 2
Min Charge for Trial: Yes **Hours:** 2
Cancellation Charge for Deps/Trial: Yes
Retainer Required: Yes, Depends on case (Refundable, One Time)
Expenses Marked Up: Yes
Expenses Billed For: Photocopies, Telephone Calls, Lab/Testing, Photographs, Demonstrative Aids
Portal-to-Portal: Yes **1st-class Airfare:** No
Written Retainer Agreement: Yes
Terms: Lawyer is responsible for fee, not lawyer's client, Interest for delinquent accounts, Out-of-pocket expense policies, In-court testimony minimums, Retaining counsel pays all deposition charges, Fee schedules, Portal-to-portal travel time, Deposition minimum fee, Payment for preparation time
Failure to Pay Bill Last 5 Years; Retaining Counsel: Yes

Life Care Planning
Court: $150 **Review/Prep:** $150 **Deps:** $175
Years Testifying: 20
Written Fee Schedule: Yes
Min Charge for Deps: No
Min Charge for Trial: No
Cancellation Charge for Deps/Trial: No
Retainer Required: Yes (Refundable, One Time)
Expenses Marked Up: No
Expenses Billed For: Mileage, Airline Tickets, Photocopies, Telephone Calls, Lab/Testing, Photographs, Demonstrative Aids
Portal-to-Portal: Yes **1st-class Airfare:** No
Written Retainer Agreement: Yes
Terms: Lawyer is responsible for fee, not lawyer's client, Out-of-pocket expense policies, In-court testimony minimums, Retaining counsel pays all deposition charges, Fee schedules, Portal-to-portal travel time, Attorney's fees if forced to sue for collection
Failure to Pay Bill Last 5 Years; Retaining Counsel: Yes **Opposing(Deps):** Yes

Physical Medicine & Rehabilitation
Court: $500 **Review/Prep:** $300 **Deps:** $500
Years Testifying: 8 **Majority:** Defendant
Written Fee Schedule: No
Min Charge for Deps: Yes **Hours:** 4
Min Charge for Trial: Yes **Hours:** 4
Cancellation Charge for Deps/Trial: Yes
Procedure When Dep Exceeds Paid Time: Proceed without immediate payment
Expenses Marked Up: No
Portal-to-Portal: No **1st-class Airfare:** No
Written Retainer Agreement: No
Failure to Pay Bill Last 5 Years; Retaining Counsel: No **Opposing Counsel (Deps):** No

Podiatry
Court: $350 **Review/Prep:** $125 **Deps:** $250
Years Testifying: 15
Written Fee Schedule: Yes
Min Charge for Deps: No
Min Charge for Trial: No
Cancellation Charge for Deps/Trial: No
Retainer Required: No
Expenses Marked Up: No
Expenses Billed For: Mileage, Airline Tickets, Photocopies, Telephone Calls, Lab/Testing, Photographs, Demonstrative Aids
Portal-to-Portal: Yes **1st-class Airfare:** No
Written Retainer Agreement: No
Failure to Pay Bill Last 5 Years; Retaining Counsel: Yes **Opposing Counsel (Deps):** No

Psychology
Court: $250 **Review/Prep:** $150 **Deps:** $250
Years Testifying: 30
Min Charge for Deps: Yes **Hours:** 1
Min Charge for Trial: Yes **Hours:** 1
Cancellation Charge for Deps/Trial: No
Retainer Required: No
Expenses Marked Up: No
Expenses Billed For: Airline Tickets, Telephone Calls
Portal-to-Portal: Yes
Written Retainer Agreement: No
Failure to Pay Bill Last 5 Years; Retaining Counsel: Yes **Opposing Counsel (Deps):** No

Safety, Transportation
Court: $250 **Review/Prep:** $195 **Deps:** $250
Years Testifying: 13
Written Fee Schedule: Yes
Min Charge for Deps: Yes
Min Charge for Trial: No
Cancellation Charge for Deps/Trial: Yes
Retainer Required: Yes, $1,000 (Non-Refundable, One Time)
Expenses Marked Up: No
Expenses Billed For: Mileage, Airline Tickets, Photocopies, Photographs
Portal-to-Portal: Yes **1st-class Airfare:** No
Written Retainer Agreement: Yes
Terms: Lawyer is responsible for fee, not lawyer's client, Interest for delinquent accounts, Out-of-pocket expense policies, In-court testimony minimums, Retaining counsel pays all deposition charges, Fee schedules, Portal-to-portal travel time, Attorney's fees if forced to sue for collection, Deposition minimum fee
Failure to Pay Bill Last 5 Years; Retaining Counsel: Yes **Opposing (Deps):** Yes

Soils/Engineering
Court: $115 **Review/Prep:** $115 **Deps:** $115
Years Testifying: 15 **Majority:** Plaintiff
Written Fee Schedule: No
Min Charge for Deps: No
Min Charge for Trial: No
Cancellation Charge for Deps/Trial: No
Retainer Required: No
Expenses Marked Up: Yes
Expenses Billed For: Mileage, Photocopies, Telephone Calls, Photographs
Portal-to-Portal: Yes **1st-class Airfare:** No
Written Retainer Agreement: No
Failure to Pay Bill Last 5 Years; Retaining Counsel: No **Opposing Counsel (Deps):** No

Textiles
Court: $250 **Review/Prep:** $125 **Deps:** $250
Years Testifying: 30 **Majority:** Plaintiff
Written Fee Schedule: Yes
Min Charge for Deps: No
Min Charge for Trial: No
Cancellation Charge for Deps/Trial: No
Retainer Required: Yes, $1,200 (Non-Refundable, One Time)
Expenses Marked Up: No
Expenses Billed For: Mileage, Airline Tickets, Photocopies, Telephone Calls, Lab/Testing, Photographs, Demonstrative Aids
Portal-to-Portal: Yes **1st-class Airfare:** Yes
Written Retainer Agreement: No
Failure to Pay Bill Last 5 Years; Retaining Counsel: No **Opposing Counsel (Deps):** No

Alaska

Emergency Medicine
Court: $350 **Review/Prep:** $350 **Deps:** $350
Years Testifying: 10
Written Fee Schedule: Yes
Min Charge for Deps: No
Min Charge for Trial: No
Cancellation Charge for Deps/Trial: No
Retainer Required: Yes, $5,000 (Refundable, One Time)
Procedure When Dep Exceeds Paid Time: Proceed without immediate payment

Expenses Marked Up: No
Expenses Billed For: Airline Tickets
Portal-to-Portal: Yes **1st-class Airfare:** No
Written Retainer Agreement: No
Failure to Pay Bill Last 5 Years; Retaining Counsel: No **Opposing Counsel (Deps):** No

Valuation, Business
Court: $295 **Review/Prep:** $295 **Deps:** $295
Years Testifying: 25
Written Fee Schedule: Yes
Min Charge for Deps: No
Min Charge for Trial: No
Cancellation Charge for Deps/Trial: No
Retainer Required: Yes, $2,500 (Refundable, Replenishable)
Expenses Marked Up: No
Expenses Billed For: Airline Tickets, Demonstrative Aids
Portal-to-Portal: Yes **1st-class Airfare:** No
Written Retainer Agreement: Yes
Terms: Interest for delinquent accounts, Out-of-pocket expense policies, Retaining counsel pays all deposition charges, Attorney's fees if forced to sue for collection
Failure to Pay Bill Last 5 Years; Retaining Counsel: Yes **Opposing Counsel (Deps):** No

Arizona

Biomechanics
Court: $250 **Review/Prep:** $250 **Deps:** $250
Years Testifying: 10
Written Fee Schedule: Yes
Min Charge for Deps: Yes **Hours:** 2
Min Charge for Trial: Yes **Hours:** 2
Cancellation Charge for Deps/Trial: Yes
Retainer Required: Yes, $3,000 (Refundable, One Time)
Procedure When Dep Exceeds Paid Time: Proceed without immediate payment
Expenses Marked Up: Yes
Expenses Billed For: Mileage, Airline Tickets, Photocopies, Lab/Testing, Photographs
Portal-to-Portal: Yes **1st-class Airfare:** No
Written Retainer Agreement: Yes
Terms: Lawyer is responsible for fee, not lawyer's client, Interest for delinquent accounts, In-court testimony minimums, Retaining counsel pays all deposition charges, Fee schedules, Attorney's fees if forced to sue for collection, Deposition minimum fee
Failure to Pay Bill Last 5 Years; Retaining Counsel: Yes **Opposing Counsel (Deps):** No

Engineering, Traffic
Court: $180 **Review/Prep:** $180 **Deps:** $180
Years Testifying: 30
Written Fee Schedule: Yes
Min Charge for Deps: No
Min Charge for Trial: No
Cancellation Charge for Deps/Trial: No
Retainer Required: Yes, Total est. fee (Refundable, Replenishable)
Procedure When Dep Exceeds Paid Time: Proceed without immediate payment
Expenses Marked Up: No
Expenses Billed For: Mileage, Airline Tickets, Telephone Calls, Lab/Testing, Photographs, Demonstrative Aids
Portal-to-Portal: Yes **1st-class Airfare:** No
Written Retainer Agreement: No
Failure to Pay Bill Last 5 Years; Retaining Counsel: Yes **Opposing (Deps):** Yes

Fire
Court: $300 **Review/Prep:** $125 **Deps:** $300
Years Testifying: 24 **Majority:** Plaintiff
Written Fee Schedule: Yes
Min Charge for Deps: Yes **Hours:** 4
Min Charge for Trial: Yes **Hours:** 4
Cancellation Charge for Deps/Trial: No
Retainer Required: Yes, $2,500 (Refundable, One Time)
Expenses Marked Up: Yes
Expenses Billed For: Mileage, Airline Tickets, Photocopies, Telephone Calls, Lab/Testing, Photographs, Demonstrative Aids
Portal-to-Portal: Yes **1st-class Airfare:** No
Written Retainer Agreement: Yes
Terms: Lawyer is responsible for fee, not lawyer's client, Interest for delinquent accounts, Out-of-pocket expense policies, In-court testimony minimums, Retaining counsel pays all deposition charges, Fee schedules, Portal-to-portal travel time, Deposition minimum fee, Payment for preparation time
Failure to Pay Bill Last 5 Years; Retaining Counsel: No **Opposing Counsel (Deps):** No

Fire Protection
Court: $200 **Review/Prep:** $135 **Deps:** $200
Years Testifying: 19
Written Fee Schedule: Yes
Min Charge for Deps: Yes
Min Charge for Trial: No
Cancellation Charge for Deps/Trial: Yes
Retainer Required: Yes, Depends on case (Refundable, One Time)
Procedure When Dep Exceeds Paid Time: Get payment before proceeding further
Expenses Marked Up: Yes
Expenses Billed For: Mileage, Airline Tickets, Lab/Testing, Demonstrative Aids
Portal-to-Portal: Yes **1st-class Airfare:** No
Written Retainer Agreement: Yes
Terms: Lawyer is responsible for fee, not lawyer's client, Interest for delinquent accounts, Out-of-pocket expense policies, In-court testimony minimums, Retaining counsel pays all deposition charges, Fee schedules, Portal-to-portal travel time, Attorney's fees if forced to sue for collection, Deposition minimum fee, Payment for preparation time
Failure to Pay Bill Last 5 Years; Retaining Counsel: No **Opposing Counsel (Deps):** No

Human Factors/Ergonomics/Safety
Court: $275 **Review/Prep:** $210 **Deps:** $275
Years Testifying: 25
Written Fee Schedule: Yes
Min Charge for Deps: No
Min Charge for Trial: No
Cancellation Charge for Deps/Trial: No
Retainer Required: Yes, $1,250 (Non-Refundable, One Time)
Procedure When Dep Exceeds Paid Time: Proceed without immediate payment
Expenses Marked Up: No
Expenses Billed For: Airline Tickets, Photocopies, Lab/Testing, Photographs, Demonstrative Aids
Portal-to-Portal: Yes **1st-class Airfare:** No
Written Retainer Agreement: Yes
Terms: Lawyer is responsible for fee, not lawyer's client, Interest for delinquent accounts, Out-of-pocket expense policies, In-court testimony minimums, Retaining counsel pays all deposition charges, Fee schedules, Deposition minimum fee, Payment for preparation time, No guaranteed results-No bias given, Cooperation by counsel is necessary
Failure to Pay Bill Last 5 Years; Retaining Counsel: Yes **Opposing (Deps):** Yes

Law, Horses
Court: $2,000 **Review/Prep:** $250 **Deps:** $800
Years Testifying: 11
Written Fee Schedule: Yes
Min Charge for Deps: Yes **Hours:** 4
Min Charge for Trial: Yes **Hours:** 4
Cancellation Charge for Deps/Trial: Yes
Retainer Required: Yes, $1,000 (Non-Refundable, One Time)
Procedure When Dep Exceeds Paid Time: Proceed without immediate payment
Expenses Marked Up: No
Expenses Billed For: Mileage, Airline Tickets, Photocopies, Telephone Calls, Photographs, Demonstrative Aids
Portal-to-Portal: Yes **1st-class Airfare:** No
Written Retainer Agreement: Yes
Terms: Lawyer is responsible for fee, not lawyer's client, Out-of-pocket expense policies, Indemnification
Failure to Pay Bill Last 5 Years; Retaining Counsel: Yes **Opposing (Deps):** Yes

Nephrology/Internal Medicine
Court: $500 **Review/Prep:** $250 **Deps:** $350
Years Testifying: 6
Written Fee Schedule: No
Min Charge for Deps: No **Hours:** 8
Min Charge for Trial: Yes **Hours:** 8
Cancellation Charge for Deps/Trial: No
Retainer Required: No
Expenses Marked Up: No
Expenses Billed For: Mileage, Airline Tickets
Portal-to-Portal: Yes **1st-class Airfare:** No
Written Retainer Agreement: No
Failure to Pay Bill Last 5 Years; Retaining Counsel: No **Opposing Counsel (Deps):** No

Orthopedics
Court: $625 **Review/Prep:** $400 **Deps:** $1,000
Years Testifying: 11 **Majority:** Defendant
Written Fee Schedule: Yes
Min Charge for Deps: Yes **Hours:** 8
Min Charge for Trial: Yes **Hours:** 8
Cancellation Charge for Deps/Trial: Yes
Retainer Required: Yes, $500 (Non-Refundable, One Time)
Procedure When Dep Exceeds Paid Time: Proceed without immediate payment
Expenses Marked Up: No
Expenses Billed For: Mileage, Airline Tickets
Portal-to-Portal: Yes **1st-class Airfare:** No
Written Retainer Agreement: Yes
Terms: Lawyer is responsible for fee, not lawyer's client, Interest for delinquent accounts, Out-of-pocket expense policies, In-court testimony minimums, Retaining counsel pays all deposition charges, Fee schedules, Attorney's fees if forced to sue for collection
Failure to Pay Bill Last 5 Years; Retaining Counsel: No **Opposing Counsel (Deps):** Yes

Roofing
Court: $125 **Review/Prep:** $100 **Deps:** $125
Years Testifying: 18
Written Fee Schedule: Yes
Min Charge for Deps: Yes **Hours:** 4
Min Charge for Trial: Yes **Hours:** 4
Cancellation Charge for Deps/Trial: Yes
Retainer Required: No
Expenses Marked Up: Yes
Expenses Billed For: Mileage, Airline Tickets, Photocopies, Telephone Calls, Lab/Testing, Photographs, Demonstrative Aids
Portal-to-Portal: Yes **1st-class Airfare:** No
Written Retainer Agreement: No
Failure to Pay Bill Last 5 Years; Retaining Counsel: No **Opposing Counsel (Deps):** No

Taxation
Court: $300 **Review/Prep:** $300 **Deps:** $300
Years Testifying: 40
Written Fee Schedule: No
Min Charge for Deps: No
Min Charge for Trial: No
Cancellation Charge for Deps/Trial: No
Retainer Required: Yes, $3,000 (Non-Refundable, One Time)
Expenses Marked Up: No
Expenses Billed For: Airline Tickets, Demonstrative Aids
Portal-to-Portal: Yes **1st-class Airfare:** No
Written Retainer Agreement: Yes
Terms: Lawyer is responsible for fee, not lawyer's client, Out-of-pocket expense policies, Retaining counsel pays all deposition charges, Portal-to-portal travel time, Payment for preparation time
Failure to Pay Bill Last 5 Years; Retaining Counsel: No **Opposing Counsel (Deps):** No

Arkansas

Accident Reconstruction
Court: $75 **Review/Prep:** $75 **Deps:** $75
Years Testifying: 28 **Majority:** Plaintiff
Written Fee Schedule: Yes
Min Charge for Deps: Yes **Hours:** 4
Min Charge for Trial: Yes **Hours:** 4
Cancellation Charge for Deps/Trial: No
Retainer Required: Yes, $1,000 (Non-Refundable, One Time)
Expenses Marked Up: No
Expenses Billed For: Mileage, Airline Tickets, Photocopies, Telephone Calls, Photographs
Portal-to-Portal: Yes **1st-class Airfare:** No
Written Retainer Agreement: No
Failure to Pay Bill Last 5 Years; Retaining Counsel: No **Opposing Counsel (Deps):** No

Damages, Business
Court: $200 **Review/Prep:** $200 **Deps:** $200
Years Testifying: 23 **Majority:** Plaintiff
Written Fee Schedule: No
Min Charge for Deps: No
Min Charge for Trial: No
Cancellation Charge for Deps/Trial: No
Retainer Required: Yes, $800 (Refundable, One Time)
Expenses Marked Up: No
Expenses Billed For: Mileage, Airline Tickets, Photocopies
Portal-to-Portal: Yes **1st-class Airfare:** No
Written Retainer Agreement: Yes
Terms: Fee schedules, Attorney's fees if forced to sue for collection
Failure to Pay Bill Last 5 Years; Retaining Counsel: Yes **Opposing (Deps):** Yes

Dentistry
Court: $500 **Review/Prep:** $200 **Deps:** $400
Years Testifying: 10
Written Fee Schedule: Yes
Min Charge for Deps: Yes **Hours:** 4
Min Charge for Trial: Yes **Hours:** 4
Cancellation Charge for Deps/Trial: No
Retainer Required: No
Expenses Marked Up: No
Expenses Billed For: Airline Tickets, Lab/Testing
Portal-to-Portal: No **1st-class Airfare:** No
Written Retainer Agreement: Yes
Terms: Lawyer is responsible for fee, not lawyer's client, Out-of-pocket expense policies, In-court testimony minimums, Fee schedules, Deposition minimum fee, Payment for preparation time
Failure to Pay Bill Last 5 Years; Retaining Counsel: Yes **Opposing Counsel (Deps):** No

Engineering, Civil
Court: $135 **Review/Prep:** $90 **Deps:** $135
Years Testifying: 20
Written Fee Schedule: Yes
Min Charge for Deps: No
Min Charge for Trial: No
Cancellation Charge for Deps/Trial: No
Retainer Required: No
Expenses Marked Up: Yes
Expenses Billed For: Mileage, Airline Tickets, Photocopies, Lab/Testing, Photographs
Portal-to-Portal: Yes **1st-class Airfare:** No
Written Retainer Agreement: Yes
Terms: Interest for delinquent accounts, Out-of-pocket expense policies, In-court testimony minimums, Fee schedules, Portal-to-portal travel time, Attorney's fees if forced to sue for collection, Payment for preparation time
Failure to Pay Bill Last 5 Years; Retaining Counsel: Yes **Opposing Counsel (Deps):** No

Engineering, Mechanical
Court: $250 **Review/Prep:** $175 **Deps:** $250
Years Testifying: 2 **Majority:** Plaintiff
Written Fee Schedule: Yes
Min Charge for Deps: Yes **Hours:** 4
Min Charge for Trial: Yes **Hours:** 4
Cancellation Charge for Deps/Trial: Yes
Retainer Required: Yes, $1,500 (Non-Refundable, One Time)
Procedure When Dep Exceeds Paid Time: Proceed without immediate payment
Expenses Marked Up: Yes
Expenses Billed For: Mileage, Airline Tickets, Lab/Testing, Photographs, Demonstrative Aids
Portal-to-Portal: No **1st-class Airfare:** No
Written Retainer Agreement: Yes
Terms: Lawyer is responsible for fee, not

lawyer's client, Out-of-pocket expense policies, In-court testimony minimums, Retaining counsel pays all deposition charges, Fee schedules, Deposition minimum fee, Payment for preparation time
Failure to Pay Bill Last 5 Years; Retaining Counsel: No **Opposing Counsel (Deps):** No

Engineering, Structural
Court: $160 **Review/Prep:** $120 **Deps:** $160
Years Testifying: 31 **Majority:** Defendant
Written Fee Schedule: No
Min Charge for Deps: No
Min Charge for Trial: No
Cancellation Charge for Deps/Trial: No
Retainer Required: No
Expenses Marked Up: No
Expenses Billed For: Mileage, Airline Tickets, Lab/Testing, Photographs, Demonstrative Aids
Portal-to-Portal: Yes **1st-class Airfare:** No
Written Retainer Agreement: No
Failure to Pay Bill Last 5 Years; Retaining Counsel: No **Opposing Counsel (Deps):** No

Orthopedics/Physical Medicine & Rehabilitation
Court: $325 **Review/Prep:** $300 **Deps:** $325
Years Testifying: 2 **Majority:** Plaintiff
Written Fee Schedule: Yes
Min Charge for Deps: Yes **Hours:** 4
Min Charge for Trial: Yes **Hours:** 4
Cancellation Charge for Deps/Trial: Yes
Retainer Required: Yes, $2,500 (Partially Refundable, Replenishable)
Procedure When Dep Exceeds Paid Time: Proceed without immediate payment
Expenses Marked Up: No
Expenses Billed For: Mileage, Airline Tickets
Portal-to-Portal: Yes **1st-class Airfare:** No
Written Retainer Agreement: No
Failure to Pay Bill Last 5 Years; Retaining Counsel: No **Opposing Counsel (Deps):** No

California

Accident Reconstruction/Fire
Court: $300 **Review/Prep:** $215 **Deps:** $300
Years Testifying: 15
Written Fee Schedule: Yes
Min Charge for Deps: Yes **Hours:** 2
Min Charge for Trial: Yes **Hours:** 2
Retainer Required: Yes, $1,500 (Refundable, Replenishable)
Procedure When Dep Exceeds Paid Time: Proceed without immediate payment
Expenses Marked Up: Yes
Expenses Billed For: Mileage, Airline Tickets, Telephone Calls, Lab/Testing, Photographs, Demonstrative Aids
Portal-to-Portal: Yes **1st-class Airfare:** No
Written Retainer Agreement: No
Failure to Pay Bill Last 5 Years; Retaining Counsel: Yes **Opposing (Deps):** Yes

Accident Reconstruction
Court: $300 **Review/Prep:** $250 **Deps:** $300
Years Testifying: 30
Written Fee Schedule: Yes
Min Charge for Deps: Yes **Hours:** 2
Min Charge for Trial: Yes **Hours:** 2
Cancellation Charge for Deps/Trial: No
Retainer Required: Yes, Depends on case (Refundable, Replenishable)
Procedure When Dep Exceeds Paid Time: Proceed without immediate payment
Expenses Marked Up: No
Expenses Billed For: Mileage, Airline Tickets, Photocopies, Telephone Calls, Lab/Testing, Photographs, Demonstrative Aids
Portal-to-Portal: Yes **1st-class Airfare:** No
Written Retainer Agreement: Yes
Terms: Lawyer is responsible for fee, not lawyer's client, Out-of-pocket expense policies, In-court testimony minimums, Retaining counsel pays all deposition charges, Fee schedules, Portal-to-portal travel time, Attorney's fees if forced to sue for collection, Deposition minimum fee
Failure to Pay Bill Last 5 Years; Retaining Counsel: Yes **Opposing (Deps):** Yes

Accident Reconstruction
Court: $220 **Review/Prep:** $220 **Deps:** $220
Years Testifying: 34
Written Fee Schedule: Yes
Min Charge for Deps: Yes **Hours:** 4
Min Charge for Trial: Yes **Hours:** 4
Cancellation Charge for Deps/Trial: No
Retainer Required: Yes, $1,500 (Refundable, Replenishable)
Procedure When Dep Exceeds Paid Time: Proceed without immediate payment
Expenses Marked Up: No
Expenses Billed For: Mileage, Airline Tickets, Telephone Calls, Lab/Testing, Photographs, Demonstrative Aids
Portal-to-Portal: Yes **1st-class Airfare:** No
Written Retainer Agreement: No
Failure to Pay Bill Last 5 Years; Retaining Counsel: Yes **Opposing Counsel (Deps):** No

Accident Reconstruction
Court: $250 **Review/Prep:** $250 **Deps:** $250
Years Testifying: 21
Written Fee Schedule: Yes
Min Charge for Deps: No
Min Charge for Trial: No
Cancellation Charge for Deps/Trial: No
Retainer Required: Yes, $1,500 (Refundable, One Time)
Expenses Marked Up: Yes
Expenses Billed For: Mileage, Airline Tickets, Photocopies, Lab/Testing, Photographs, Demonstrative Aids
Portal-to-Portal: Yes **1st-class Airfare:** No
Written Retainer Agreement: Yes
Terms: Lawyer is responsible for fee, not lawyer's client, Interest for delinquent accounts, Out-of-pocket expense policies, Retaining counsel pays all deposition charges, Fee schedules, Attorney's fees if forced to sue for collection, Payment for preparation time
Failure to Pay Bill Last 5 Years; Retaining Counsel: Yes **Opposing Counsel (Deps):** No

Accidents, Industrial
Court: $300 **Review/Prep:** $300 **Deps:** $300
Years Testifying: 3 **Majority:** Plaintiff
Written Fee Schedule: No
Min Charge for Deps: No
Min Charge for Trial: No
Cancellation Charge for Deps/Trial: No
Retainer Required: Yes, $1,000 (Non-Refundable)
Expenses Marked Up: No
Expenses Billed For: Mileage, Airline Tickets, Photocopies, Telephone Calls, Lab/Testing, Photographs, Demonstrative Aids
Portal-to-Portal: Yes **1st-class Airfare:** Yes
Written Retainer Agreement: No
Failure to Pay Bill Last 5 Years; Retaining Counsel: No **Opposing Counsel (Deps):** No

Accounting
Court: $370 **Review/Prep:** $370 **Deps:** $370
Years Testifying: 10 **Majority:** Plaintiff
Written Fee Schedule: No
Min Charge for Deps: No
Min Charge for Trial: No
Cancellation Charge for Deps/Trial: No
Retainer Required: Yes, 40% est. fee (Refundable, One Time)
Expenses Marked Up: Yes
Expenses Billed For: Airline Tickets, Lab/Testing, Photographs, Demonstrative Aids
Portal-to-Portal: Yes **1st-class Airfare:** No
Written Retainer Agreement: Yes
Terms: Interest for delinquent accounts, Out-of-pocket expense policies, Retaining counsel pays all deposition charges, Attorney's fees if forced to sue for collection
Failure to Pay Bill Last 5 Years; Retaining Counsel: Yes **Opposing Counsel (Deps):** No

Accounting
Court: $300 **Review/Prep:** $300 **Deps:** $300
Years Testifying: 20
Written Fee Schedule: No
Min Charge for Deps: No
Min Charge for Trial: No

Cancellation Charge for Deps/Trial: No
Retainer Required: Yes, Depends on case (Non-Refundable, One Time)
Expenses Marked Up: No
Expenses Billed For: Mileage, Airline Tickets, Telephone Calls
Portal-to-Portal: Yes **1st-class Airfare:** No
Written Retainer Agreement: Yes
Terms: Out-of-pocket expense policies, Retaining counsel pays all deposition charges, Fee schedules
Failure to Pay Bill Last 5 Years; Retaining Counsel: Yes **Opposing Counsel (Deps):** No

Appraisal, Gem & Jewelry
Court: $400 **Review/Prep:** $250 **Deps:** $350
Years Testifying: 14
Min Charge for Deps: No **Hours:** 4
Min Charge for Trial: Yes **Hours:** 4
Cancellation Charge for Deps/Trial: No
Retainer Required: Yes, $1,500 (Non-Refundable, One Time)
Expenses Marked Up: No
Expenses Billed For: Mileage, Airline Tickets, Telephone Calls, Lab/Testing, Photographs, Demonstrative Aids
Portal-to-Portal: Yes **1st-class Airfare:** No
Written Retainer Agreement: No
Failure to Pay Bill Last 5 Years; Retaining Counsel: No **Opposing Counsel (Deps):** No

Appraisal, Real Estate
Court: $250 **Review/Prep:** $200 **Deps:** $250
Years Testifying: 20 **Majority:** Defendant
Written Fee Schedule: No
Min Charge for Deps: Yes **Hours:** 4
Min Charge for Trial: Yes **Hours:** 4
Cancellation Charge for Deps/Trial: No
Retainer Required: Yes, 50% of est. fee (Refundable, Replenishable)
Expenses Marked Up: No
Portal-to-Portal: Yes
Written Retainer Agreement: Yes
Terms: Lawyer is responsible for fee, not lawyer's client, Retaining counsel pays all deposition charges, Fee schedules, Deposition minimum fee, Payment for preparation time
Failure to Pay Bill Last 5 Years; Retaining Counsel: No **Opposing Counsel (Deps):** No

Architecture
Court: $300 **Review/Prep:** $150 **Deps:** $300
Years Testifying: 10 **Majority:** Defendant
Written Fee Schedule: Yes
Min Charge for Deps: No
Min Charge for Trial: No
Cancellation Charge for Deps/Trial: No
Retainer Required: No
Expenses Marked Up: No
Expenses Billed For: Mileage, Airline Tickets, Photographs, Demonstrative Aids
Portal-to-Portal: Yes **1st-class Airfare:** No
Written Retainer Agreement: Yes
Terms: Out-of-pocket expense policies, In-court testimony minimums, Fee schedules, Portal-to-portal travel time
Failure to Pay Bill Last 5 Years; Retaining Counsel: Yes **Opposing Counsel (Deps):** No

Architecture
Court: $250 **Review/Prep:** $175 **Deps:** $250
Years Testifying: 13 **Majority:** Defendant
Written Fee Schedule: Yes
Min Charge for Deps: Yes
Min Charge for Trial: No
Cancellation Charge for Deps/Trial: No
Retainer Required: Yes, $500 (Refundable, One Time)
Expenses Marked Up: No
Expenses Billed For: Airline Tickets, Photocopies, Lab/Testing
Portal-to-Portal: Yes **1st-class Airfare:** No
Written Retainer Agreement: No
Failure to Pay Bill Last 5 Years; Retaining Counsel: Yes **Opposing Counsel (Deps):** No

Architecture/Construction
Court: $500 **Review/Prep:** $250 **Deps:** $500
Years Testifying: 20
Written Fee Schedule: Yes
Min Charge for Deps: No
Min Charge for Trial: No
Cancellation Charge for Deps/Trial: No
Retainer Required: Yes, Depends on case (Non-Refundable, One Time)
Procedure When Dep Exceeds Paid Time: Proceed without immediate payment
Expenses Marked Up: No
Expenses Billed For: Mileage, Airline Tickets, Photocopies, Telephone Calls, Lab/Testing, Photographs, Demonstrative Aids
Portal-to-Portal: Yes **1st-class Airfare:** No
Written Retainer Agreement: No
Failure to Pay Bill Last 5 Years; Retaining Counsel: No **Opposing Counsel (Deps):** No

Architecture/Construction
Court: $353 **Review/Prep:** $235 **Deps:** $353
Years Testifying: 20 **Majority:** Plaintiff
Written Fee Schedule: Yes
Min Charge for Deps: No
Min Charge for Trial: No
Cancellation Charge for Deps/Trial: No
Retainer Required: Yes, $3,000 (Refundable, One Time)
Expenses Marked Up: Yes
Expenses Billed For: Mileage, Airline Tickets, Photocopies, Telephone Calls, Lab/Testing, Photographs, Demonstrative Aids
Portal-to-Portal: Yes **1st-class Airfare:** No
Written Retainer Agreement: Yes
Terms: Interest for delinquent accounts, Out-of-pocket expense policies, Retaining counsel pays all deposition charges, Fee schedules, Portal-to-portal travel time, Attorney's fees if forced to sue for collection, Payment for preparation time
Failure to Pay Bill Last 5 Years; Retaining Counsel: Yes **Opposing (Deps):** Yes

Banking
Court: $300 **Review/Prep:** $225 **Deps:** $300
Years Testifying: 13 **Majority:** Plaintiff
Written Fee Schedule: Yes
Min Charge for Deps: Yes **Hours:** 4
Min Charge for Trial: Yes **Hours:** 4
Cancellation Charge for Deps/Trial: No
Retainer Required: Yes, $2,500 (Non-Refundable, Replenishable)
Expenses Marked Up: No
Expenses Billed For: Mileage, Airline Tickets, Photocopies, Telephone Calls, Lab/Testing, Photographs, Demonstrative Aids
Portal-to-Portal: Yes **1st-class Airfare:** No
Written Retainer Agreement: Yes
Terms: Interest for delinquent accounts, Out-of-pocket expense policies, In-court testimony minimums, Retaining counsel pays all deposition charges, Fee schedules, Portal-to-portal travel time, Deposition minimum fee, Payment for preparation time
Failure to Pay Bill Last 5 Years; Retaining Counsel: Yes **Opposing Counsel (Deps):** No

Biomedical, Biotechnology
Court: $350 **Review/Prep:** $250 **Deps:** $350
Years Testifying: 15 **Majority:** Defendant
Written Fee Schedule: Yes
Min Charge for Deps: No
Min Charge for Trial: No
Cancellation Charge for Deps/Trial: No
Retainer Required: Yes, $2,000 (Non-Refundable, One Time)
Procedure When Dep Exceeds Paid Time: Proceed without immediate payment
Expenses Marked Up: No
Expenses Billed For: Lab/Testing, Photographs, Demonstrative Aids
Portal-to-Portal: No **1st-class Airfare:** No
Written Retainer Agreement: Yes
Terms: Lawyer is responsible for fee, not lawyer's client, Out-of-pocket expense policies, Retaining counsel pays all deposition charges, Fee schedules, Portal-to-portal travel time, Payment for preparation time
Failure to Pay Bill Last 5 Years; Retaining Counsel: Yes **Opposing Counsel (Deps):** No

Cardiology
Court: $500 **Review/Prep:** $350 **Deps:** $500
Years Testifying: 12
Written Fee Schedule: Yes
Min Charge for Deps: Yes **Hours:** 4
Min Charge for Trial: Yes **Hours:** 4
Cancellation Charge for Deps/Trial: Yes
Retainer Required: Yes, $1,500 (Refundable, One Time)
Expenses Marked Up: No
Expenses Billed For: Mileage, Airline Tickets
Portal-to-Portal: Yes **1st-class Airfare:** No
Written Retainer Agreement: No
Failure to Pay Bill Last 5 Years; Retaining Counsel: Yes **Opposing Counsel (Deps):** No

Chiropractic
Court: $350 **Review/Prep:** $300 **Deps:** $450
Written Fee Schedule: Yes
Min Charge for Deps: Yes
Min Charge for Trial: No
Cancellation Charge for Deps/Trial: Yes
Retainer Required: Yes, $700 (Refundable, One Time)
Procedure When Dep Exceeds Paid Time: Get payment before proceeding further
Expenses Billed For:
Portal-to-Portal: Yes **1st-class Airfare:** Yes
Written Retainer Agreement: Yes
Failure to Pay Bill Last 5 Years; Retaining Counsel: No **Opposing Counsel (Deps):** No

Chiropractic
Court: $250 **Review/Prep:** $0 **Deps:** $250
Years Testifying: 5 **Majority:** Plaintiff
Written Fee Schedule: Yes
Min Charge for Deps: Yes **Hours:** 1
Min Charge for Trial: Yes **Hours:** 1
Cancellation Charge for Deps/Trial: Yes
Retainer Required: Yes, $250 (Non-Refundable, One Time)
Expenses Marked Up: No
Expenses Billed For:
Failure to Pay Bill Last 5 Years; Retaining Counsel: No **Opposing Counsel (Deps):** No

Chiropractic
Court: $250 **Review/Prep:** $150 **Deps:** $150
Years Testifying: 10 **Majority:** Defendant
Written Fee Schedule: Yes
Min Charge for Deps: No **Hours:** 3
Min Charge for Trial: Yes **Hours:** 3
Cancellation Charge for Deps/Trial: Yes
Retainer Required: Yes, $500 (Non-Refundable)
Expenses Marked Up: No
Expenses Billed For: Mileage, Airline Tickets
Portal-to-Portal: Yes **1st-class Airfare:** No
Written Retainer Agreement: Yes
Terms: In-court testimony minimums, Retaining counsel pays all deposition charges, Fee schedules
Failure to Pay Bill Last 5 Years; Retaining Counsel: Yes **Opposing (Deps):** Yes

Chiropractic
Court: $250 **Review/Prep:** $150 **Deps:** $250
Years Testifying: 6
Written Fee Schedule: Yes
Min Charge for Deps: Yes **Hours:** 4
Min Charge for Trial: Yes **Hours:** 4
Cancellation Charge for Deps/Trial: Yes
Retainer Required: Yes, $150 (Non-Refundable, One Time)
Procedure When Dep Exceeds Paid Time: Get payment before proceeding further
Expenses Marked Up: No
Expenses Billed For: Mileage, Airline Tickets, Demonstrative Aids
Portal-to-Portal: Yes **1st-class Airfare:** No
Written Retainer Agreement: No
Failure to Pay Bill Last 5 Years; Retaining Counsel: No **Opposing Counsel (Deps):** No

Coins
Court: $300 **Review/Prep:** $250 **Deps:** $250
Years Testifying: 1
Written Fee Schedule: Yes
Min Charge for Deps: Yes **Hours:** 4
Min Charge for Trial: Yes **Hours:** 4
Cancellation Charge for Deps/Trial: Yes
Retainer Required: Yes, $500 (Non-Refundable, Replenishable)
Procedure When Dep Exceeds Paid Time: Get payment before proceeding further
Expenses Marked Up: No
Expenses Billed For: Mileage, Airline Tickets, Photocopies, Telephone Calls, Lab/Testing, Photographs, Demonstrative Aids
Portal-to-Portal: Yes **1st-class Airfare:** No
Written Retainer Agreement: Yes
Terms: Interest for delinquent accounts, Out-of-pocket expense policies, In-court testimony minimums, Retaining counsel pays all deposition charges, Portal-to-portal travel time, Deposition minimum fee, Payment for preparation time
Failure to Pay Bill Last 5 Years; Retaining Counsel: No **Opposing Counsel (Deps):** No

Computers
Court: $400 **Review/Prep:** $350 **Deps:** $500
Years Testifying: 4
Written Fee Schedule: Yes
Min Charge for Deps: Yes **Hours:** 8
Min Charge for Trial: Yes **Hours:** 8
Cancellation Charge for Deps/Trial: No
Retainer Required: Yes, $10,000 (Non-Refundable, One Time)
Expenses Marked Up: No
Expenses Billed For: Lab/Testing
Portal-to-Portal: Yes **1st-class Airfare:** Yes
Written Retainer Agreement: Yes
Terms: In-court testimony minimums, Retaining counsel pays all deposition charges, Fee schedules, Portal-to-portal travel time, Attorney's fees if forced to sue for collection, Payment for preparation time, First class air travel
Failure to Pay Bill Last 5 Years; Retaining Counsel: Yes **Opposing Counsel (Deps):** No

Computers
Court: $200 **Review/Prep:** $200 **Deps:** $200
Years Testifying: 5
Written Fee Schedule: No
Min Charge for Deps: No
Min Charge for Trial: No
Cancellation Charge for Deps/Trial: No
Retainer Required: No
Expenses Marked Up: No
Expenses Billed For: Airline Tickets, Photographs, Demonstrative Aids
Portal-to-Portal: Yes **1st-class Airfare:** No
Written Retainer Agreement: Yes
Terms: Lawyer is responsible for fee, not lawyer's client, Out-of-pocket expense policies, Fee schedules, Portal-to-portal travel time, Payment for preparation time
Failure to Pay Bill Last 5 Years; Retaining Counsel: No **Opposing Counsel (Deps):** No

Computers, Software
Court: $220 **Review/Prep:** $170 **Deps:** $220
Years Testifying: 5
Written Fee Schedule: Yes
Min Charge for Deps: Yes
Min Charge for Trial: No
Cancellation Charge for Deps/Trial: No
Retainer Required: Yes, $5,000 (Refundable, One Time)
Procedure When Dep Exceeds Paid Time: Proceed without immediate payment
Expenses Marked Up: No
Expenses Billed For: Airline Tickets, Photocopies, Demonstrative Aids
Portal-to-Portal: Yes **1st-class Airfare:** No
Written Retainer Agreement: Yes
Terms: Interest for delinquent accounts, Out-of-pocket expense policies, Retaining counsel pays all deposition charges, Fee schedules, Portal-to-portal travel time, Attorney's fees if forced to sue for collection, Payment for preparation time, Venue clause for collection action
Failure to Pay Bill Last 5 Years; Retaining Counsel: Yes **Opposing (Deps):** Yes

Computers, Software
Court: $350 **Review/Prep:** $350 **Deps:** $350
Years Testifying: 3 **Majority:** Defendant
Written Fee Schedule: Yes
Min Charge for Deps: No
Min Charge for Trial: No
Cancellation Charge for Deps/Trial: No
Retainer Required: Yes (Refundable, Replenishable)
Procedure When Dep Exceeds Paid Time: Get payment before proceeding further
Expenses Marked Up: No
Expenses Billed For: Airline Tickets, Photocopies, Telephone Calls, Lab/Testing, Photographs, Demonstrative Aids
Portal-to-Portal: Yes **1st-class Airfare:** No
Written Retainer Agreement: Yes
Terms: Lawyer is responsible for fee, not lawyer's client, Out-of-pocket expense policies, Retaining counsel pays all deposition charges, Fee schedules, Portal-to-portal travel time, Attorney's fees if forced to sue for collection, Payment for preparation time
Failure to Pay Bill Last 5 Years; Retaining Counsel: Yes **Opposing Counsel (Deps):** No

Construction
Court: $185 **Review/Prep:** $185 **Deps:** $185
Years Testifying: 10
Written Fee Schedule: Yes
Min Charge for Deps: No
Min Charge for Trial: No
Cancellation Charge for Deps/Trial: No
Retainer Required: Yes, $5,000 (Refundable, Replenishable)
Procedure When Dep Exceeds Paid Time: Proceed without immediate payment
Expenses Marked Up: No
Expenses Billed For: Mileage, Airline Tickets, Photocopies, Telephone Calls, Lab/Testing, Photographs, Demonstrative Aids
Portal-to-Portal: Yes **1st-class Airfare:** No
Written Retainer Agreement: Yes
Terms: Interest for delinquent accounts, Out-of-pocket expense policies, Retaining counsel pays all deposition charges, Fee schedules, Portal-to-portal travel time, Attorney's fees if forced to sue for collection, Payment for preparation time
Failure to Pay Bill Last 5 Years; Retaining Counsel: Yes **Opposing Counsel (Deps):** No

Construction
Court: $250 **Review/Prep:** $125 **Deps:** $250
Years Testifying: 10
Written Fee Schedule: Yes
Min Charge for Deps: Yes **Hours:** 4
Min Charge for Trial: Yes **Hours:** 4
Cancellation Charge for Deps/Trial: Yes
Retainer Required: Yes, $1,000 (Refundable, Replenishable)
Procedure When Dep Exceeds Paid Time: Proceed without immediate payment
Expenses Marked Up: No
Expenses Billed For: Mileage, Airline Tickets, Photocopies, Telephone Calls, Lab/Testing, Photographs, Demonstrative Aids
Portal-to-Portal: Yes **1st-class Airfare:** No
Written Retainer Agreement: Yes
Terms: Lawyer is responsible for fee, not lawyer's client, Interest for delinquent accounts, Out-of-pocket expense policies, In-court testimony minimums, Retaining counsel pays all deposition charges, Fee schedules, Portal-to-portal travel time, Attorney's fees if forced to sue for collection, Payment for preparation time, Hold harmless clause
Failure to Pay Bill Last 5 Years; Retaining Counsel: No **Opposing Counsel (Deps):** No

Construction
Court: $350 **Review/Prep:** $250 **Deps:** $350
Years Testifying: 20 **Majority:** Plaintiff
Written Fee Schedule: Yes
Min Charge for Deps: No
Min Charge for Trial: No
Cancellation Charge for Deps/Trial: No
Retainer Required: Yes, $1,000 (Refundable, Replenishable)
Procedure When Dep Exceeds Paid Time: Proceed without immediate payment
Expenses Marked Up: No
Expenses Billed For: Mileage, Airline Tickets, Lab/Testing, Demonstrative Aids
Portal-to-Portal: Yes **1st-class Airfare:** No
Written Retainer Agreement: Yes
Terms: Lawyer is responsible for fee, not lawyer's client, Interest for delinquent accounts, Out-of-pocket expense policies, In-court testimony minimums, Retaining counsel pays all deposition charges, Fee schedules, Attorney's fees if forced to sue for collection, Payment for preparation time
Failure to Pay Bill Last 5 Years; Retaining Counsel: Yes **Opposing Counsel (Deps):** No

Construction/Architecture
Court: $300 **Review/Prep:** $150 **Deps:** $300
Years Testifying: 10
Written Fee Schedule: Yes
Min Charge for Deps: No
Min Charge for Trial: No
Cancellation Charge for Deps/Trial: No
Retainer Required: Yes (Non-Refundable, Replenishable)
Expenses Marked Up: Yes
Expenses Billed For: Mileage, Airline Tickets, Photocopies, Telephone Calls, Lab/Testing, Photographs, Demonstrative Aids
Portal-to-Portal: Yes **1st-class Airfare:** No
Written Retainer Agreement: Yes
Terms: Interest for delinquent accounts, Out-of-pocket expense policies, Retaining counsel pays all deposition charges, Fee schedules, Portal-to-portal travel time, Attorney's fees if forced to sue for collection, Fees charged on hourly basis, basic terms and conditions
Failure to Pay Bill Last 5 Years; Retaining Counsel: Yes **Opposing (Deps):** Yes

Construction
Court: $350 **Deps:** $150
Years Testifying: 20
Written Fee Schedule: Yes
Min Charge for Deps: No
Min Charge for Trial: No
Cancellation Charge for Deps/Trial: No
Retainer Required: No
Expenses Marked Up: No
Expenses Billed For: Mileage, Airline Tickets, Photocopies, Lab/Testing, Photographs, Demonstrative Aids
Portal-to-Portal: Yes **1st-class Airfare:** No
Written Retainer Agreement: Yes
Terms: Lawyer is responsible for fee, not lawyer's client, Interest for delinquent accounts, Out-of-pocket expense policies, Fee schedules, Portal-to-portal travel time, Payment for preparation time
Failure to Pay Bill Last 5 Years; Retaining Counsel: Yes **Opposing Counsel (Deps):** No

Construction
Court: $150 **Review/Prep:** $125 **Deps:** $150
Years Testifying: 30
Written Fee Schedule: Yes
Min Charge for Deps: No
Min Charge for Trial: No
Cancellation Charge for Deps/Trial: No
Retainer Required: No
Procedure When Dep Exceeds Paid Time: Proceed without immediate payment
Expenses Marked Up: No
Expenses Billed For: Airline Tickets, Photocopies, Telephone Calls, Lab/Testing, Photographs, Demonstrative Aids
Portal-to-Portal: Yes **1st-class Airfare:** No
Written Retainer Agreement: No
Failure to Pay Bill Last 5 Years; Retaining Counsel: No **Opposing Counsel (Deps):** No

Construction
Court: $300 **Review/Prep:** $300 **Deps:** $300
Years Testifying: 12
Written Fee Schedule: Yes
Min Charge for Deps: No
Min Charge for Trial: No
Cancellation Charge for Deps/Trial: No
Retainer Required: Yes, $2,500 (Non-Refundable, Replenishable)

Expenses Marked Up: No
Expenses Billed For: Mileage, Airline Tickets, Lab/Testing, Demonstrative Aids
Portal-to-Portal: Yes **1st-class Airfare:** No
Written Retainer Agreement: No
Failure to Pay Bill Last 5 Years; Retaining Counsel: No **Opposing Counsel (Deps):** No

Construction
Court: $240 **Review/Prep:** $150 **Deps:** $240
Years Testifying: 12 **Majority:** Defendant
Written Fee Schedule: Yes
Min Charge for Deps: Yes **Hours:** 4
Min Charge for Trial: Yes **Hours:** 4
Cancellation Charge for Deps/Trial: No
Retainer Required: Yes, $2,000 (Refundable, Replenishable)
Expenses Marked Up: Yes
Expenses Billed For: Airline Tickets, Lab/Testing, Photographs, Demonstrative Aids
Portal-to-Portal: Yes
Written Retainer Agreement: Yes
Terms: Lawyer is responsible for fee, not lawyer's client, Interest for delinquent accounts, In-court testimony minimums, Retaining counsel pays all deposition charges, Fee schedules, Attorney's fees if forced to sue for collection, Deposition minimum fee, Payment for preparation time
Failure to Pay Bill Last 5 Years; Retaining Counsel: Yes **Opposing Counsel (Deps):** No

Construction/Architecture
Court: $375 **Review/Prep:** $240
Years Testifying: 20
Written Fee Schedule: Yes
Min Charge for Deps: Yes **Hours:** 4
Min Charge for Trial: Yes **Hours:** 4
Cancellation Charge for Deps/Trial: No
Retainer Required: Yes, $750 (Refundable, One Time)
Expenses Marked Up: Yes
Expenses Billed For: Airline Tickets, Photocopies, Telephone Calls, Lab/Testing, Photographs
Portal-to-Portal: Yes
Written Retainer Agreement: Yes
Terms: Interest for delinquent accounts, Out-of-pocket expense policies, In-court testimony minimums, Retaining counsel pays all deposition charges, Fee schedules, Attorney's fees if forced to sue for collection, Deposition minimum fee, Payment for preparation time, First class air travel
Failure to Pay Bill Last 5 Years; Retaining Counsel: Yes **Opposing (Deps):** Yes

Construction
Court: $250 **Review/Prep:** $250 **Deps:** $250
Years Testifying: 3
Written Fee Schedule: Yes
Min Charge for Deps: Yes **Hours:** 8
Min Charge for Trial: Yes **Hours:** 8
Cancellation Charge for Deps/Trial: No
Retainer Required: Yes, $5,000 (Non-Refundable, Replenishable)
Expenses Marked Up: Yes
Expenses Billed For: Mileage, Airline Tickets, Photocopies, Lab/Testing, Photographs, Demonstrative Aids
Portal-to-Portal: Yes **1st-class Airfare:** No
Written Retainer Agreement: Yes
Terms: Lawyer is responsible for fee, not lawyer's client, Interest for delinquent accounts, Out-of-pocket expense policies, In-court testimony minimums, Retaining counsel pays all deposition charges, Fee schedules, Portal-to-portal travel time, Attorney's fees if forced to sue for collection, Deposition minimum fee, Payment for preparation time, First class air travel
Failure to Pay Bill Last 5 Years; Retaining Counsel: No **Opposing Counsel (Deps):** No

Damages, Business/ Accounting/Economics
Court: $450 **Review/Prep:** $450 **Deps:** $450
Years Testifying: 15
Written Fee Schedule: Yes
Min Charge for Deps: No
Min Charge for Trial: No
Cancellation Charge for Deps/Trial: No
Retainer Required: Yes, $10,000 (Refundable, Replenishable)
Expenses Marked Up: No
Expenses Billed For: Mileage, Airline Tickets, Photocopies, Demonstrative Aids
Portal-to-Portal: Yes **1st-class Airfare:** No
Written Retainer Agreement: Yes
Terms: Interest for delinquent accounts, Out-of-pocket expense policies, Retaining counsel pays all deposition charges, Fee schedules, Attorney's fees if forced to sue for collection, Payment for preparation time
Failure to Pay Bill Last 5 Years; Retaining Counsel: No **Opposing Counsel (Deps):** No

Damages, Economic
Court: $295 **Review/Prep:** $295 **Deps:** $295
Years Testifying: 20
Written Fee Schedule: Yes
Min Charge for Deps: Yes **Hours:** 4
Min Charge for Trial: Yes **Hours:** 4
Cancellation Charge for Deps/Trial: No
Retainer Required: Yes, $15,000 (Refundable, Replenishable)
Procedure When Dep Exceeds Paid Time: Proceed without immediate payment
Expenses Marked Up: No
Expenses Billed For:
Portal-to-Portal: Yes **1st-class Airfare:** No
Written Retainer Agreement: Yes
Terms: In-court testimony minimums, Retaining counsel pays all deposition charges, Fee schedules, Attorney's fees if forced to sue for collection, Deposition minimum fee, Payment for preparation time
Failure to Pay Bill Last 5 Years; Retaining Counsel: Yes **Opposing Counsel (Deps):** No

Damages, Economic
Court: $275 **Review/Prep:** $250 **Deps:** $275
Years Testifying: 22 **Majority:** Defendant
Written Fee Schedule: Yes
Min Charge for Deps: No
Min Charge for Trial: No
Cancellation Charge for Deps/Trial: No
Retainer Required: Depends, Depends on case
Expenses Marked Up: No
Expenses Billed For: Mileage, Airline Tickets, Photocopies
Portal-to-Portal: Yes **1st-class Airfare:** No
Written Retainer Agreement: Yes
Terms: Lawyer is responsible for fee, not lawyer's client, Out-of-pocket expense policies, Retaining counsel pays all deposition charges, Fee schedules
Failure to Pay Bill Last 5 Years; Retaining Counsel: No **Opposing Counsel (Deps):** No

Dermatology
Court: $750 **Review/Prep:** $250 **Deps:** $300
Years Testifying: 7
Written Fee Schedule: Yes
Min Charge for Deps: No **Hours:** 3
Min Charge for Trial: Yes **Hours:** 3
Cancellation Charge for Deps/Trial: Yes
Retainer Required: Yes, 50% of est. fee (Refundable, One Time)
Procedure When Dep Exceeds Paid Time: Get payment before proceeding further
Expenses Marked Up: No
Expenses Billed For: Mileage, Airline Tickets, Lab/Testing, Photographs, Demonstrative Aids
Portal-to-Portal: Yes **1st-class Airfare:** No
Written Retainer Agreement: No
Failure to Pay Bill Last 5 Years; Retaining Counsel: No **Opposing Counsel (Deps):** No

Document Examiner
Court: $225 **Review/Prep:** $225 **Deps:** $600
Years Testifying: 20
Written Fee Schedule: Yes
Min Charge for Deps: Yes **Hours:** 2
Min Charge for Trial: Yes **Hours:** 2
Cancellation Charge for Deps/Trial: No
Retainer Required: Yes, $700 (Non-Refundable, One Time)
Procedure When Dep Exceeds Paid Time: Proceed without immediate payment

Expenses Billed For: Airline Tickets, Telephone Calls
Portal-to-Portal: No **1st-class Airfare:** No
Written Retainer Agreement: Yes
Terms: Lawyer is responsible for fee, not lawyer's client, Interest for delinquent accounts, Out-of-pocket expense policies, In-court testimony minimums, Retaining counsel pays all deposition charges, Fee schedules, Attorney's fees if forced to sue for collection, Deposition minimum fee, Payment for preparation time, First class air travel, Retaining counsel pays transit to & from depo., Board prep-exhibits
Failure to Pay Bill Last 5 Years; Retaining Counsel: Yes **Opposing Counsel (Deps):** No

Document Examiner
Court: $250 **Review/Prep:** $150 **Deps:** $250
Years Testifying: 12
Written Fee Schedule: Yes
Min Charge for Deps: No
Min Charge for Trial: No
Cancellation Charge for Deps/Trial: No
Retainer Required: Yes, $500 (Non-Refundable, One Time)
Procedure When Dep Exceeds Paid Time: Proceed without immediate payment
Expenses Marked Up: No
Expenses Billed For: Mileage, Airline Tickets, Photocopies, Lab/Testing, Photographs, Demonstrative Aids
Portal-to-Portal: Yes **1st-class Airfare:** No
Written Retainer Agreement: No
Failure to Pay Bill Last 5 Years; Retaining Counsel: Yes **Opposing Counsel (Deps):** No

Document Examiner
Court: $150 **Review/Prep:** $150 **Deps:** $150
Years Testifying: 18
Written Fee Schedule: Yes
Min Charge for Deps: No
Min Charge for Trial: No
Cancellation Charge for Deps/Trial: Yes
Retainer Required: Yes, $300 (Non-Refundable)
Expenses Marked Up: No
Expenses Billed For: Mileage, Airline Tickets, Photocopies, Telephone Calls, Lab/Testing, Photographs, Demonstrative Aids
Portal-to-Portal: Yes **1st-class Airfare:** No
Written Retainer Agreement: No
Failure to Pay Bill Last 5 Years; Retaining Counsel: Yes **Opposing Counsel (Deps):** No

Electrical
Court: $275 **Review/Prep:** $225 **Deps:** $275
Years Testifying: 20
Written Fee Schedule: Yes
Min Charge for Deps: No **Hours:** 4
Min Charge for Trial: Yes **Hours:** 4
Cancellation Charge for Deps/Trial: No
Retainer Required: Yes, $2,500 (Refundable)
Expenses Marked Up: Yes
Expenses Billed For: Mileage, Airline Tickets, Lab/Testing, Photographs, Demonstrative Aids
Portal-to-Portal: Yes **1st-class Airfare:** No
Written Retainer Agreement: Yes
Terms: Lawyer is responsible for fee, not lawyer's client, Out-of-pocket expense policies, In-court testimony minimums, Retaining counsel pays all deposition charges, Fee schedules, Portal-to-portal travel time, Attorney's fees if forced to sue for collection, Deposition minimum fee, Payment for preparation time
Failure to Pay Bill Last 5 Years; Retaining Counsel: Yes **Opposing Counsel (Deps):** No

Emergency Medicine
Court: $600 **Review/Prep:** $480 **Deps:** $600
Years Testifying: 30 **Majority:** Defendant
Written Fee Schedule: Yes
Min Charge for Deps: Yes **Hours:** 2
Min Charge for Trial: Yes **Hours:** 2
Cancellation Charge for Deps/Trial: Yes
Retainer Required: Yes, $1,500 (Refundable, One Time)
Procedure When Dep Exceeds Paid Time: Proceed without immediate payment
Expenses Marked Up: No
Expenses Billed For: Airline Tickets
Portal-to-Portal: Yes **1st-class Airfare:** No
Written Retainer Agreement: No
Failure to Pay Bill Last 5 Years; Retaining Counsel: No **Opposing Counsel (Deps):** No

Emergency Medicine
Court: $500 **Review/Prep:** $500 **Deps:** $500
Years Testifying: 5
Written Fee Schedule: No
Min Charge for Deps: Yes **Hours:** 2
Min Charge for Trial: Yes **Hours:** 2
Cancellation Charge for Deps/Trial: Yes
Retainer Required: No
Expenses Marked Up: No
Expenses Billed For: Mileage, Airline Tickets, Photocopies, Lab/Testing, Photographs, Demonstrative Aids
Portal-to-Portal: Yes **1st-class Airfare:** No
Written Retainer Agreement: No
Failure to Pay Bill Last 5 Years; Retaining Counsel: No **Opposing Counsel (Deps):** No

Emergency Medicine
Court: $600 **Review/Prep:** $400 **Deps:** $400
Years Testifying: 9 **Majority:** Plaintiff
Written Fee Schedule: Yes
Min Charge for Deps: No **Hours:** 4
Min Charge for Trial: Yes **Hours:** 4
Cancellation Charge for Deps/Trial: Yes
Retainer Required: Yes, $1,600 (Non-Refundable, One Time)
Procedure When Dep Exceeds Paid Time: Proceed without immediate payment
Expenses Marked Up: No
Portal-to-Portal: Yes **1st-class Airfare:** No
Written Retainer Agreement: Yes
Terms: In-court testimony minimums, Retaining counsel pays all deposition charges, Fee schedules, Portal-to-portal travel time, Payment for preparation time, Tail-end retainer
Failure to Pay Bill Last 5 Years; Retaining Counsel: Yes **Opposing Counsel (Deps):** No

Employment
Court: $220 **Review/Prep:** $185 **Deps:** $220
Years Testifying: 10 **Majority:** Plaintiff
Written Fee Schedule: Yes
Min Charge for Deps: No
Min Charge for Trial: No
Cancellation Charge for Deps/Trial: No
Retainer Required: Yes, $1,500 (Refundable, One Time)
Expenses Marked Up: No
Expenses Billed For: Mileage, Airline Tickets
Portal-to-Portal: Yes **1st-class Airfare:** No
Written Retainer Agreement: Yes
Terms: Lawyer is responsible for fee, not lawyer's client, Interest for delinquent accounts, Out-of-pocket expense policies, Retaining counsel pays all deposition charges, Fee schedules, Portal-to-portal travel time, Attorney's fees if forced to sue for collection
Failure to Pay Bill Last 5 Years; Retaining Counsel: Yes **Opposing Counsel (Deps):** No

Employment
Court: $295 **Review/Prep:** $195 **Deps:** $295
Years Testifying: 13
Written Fee Schedule: Yes
Min Charge for Deps: No
Min Charge for Trial: No
Cancellation Charge for Deps/Trial: Yes
Retainer Required: Yes, $2,000 (Refundable, One Time)
Expenses Marked Up: No
Expenses Billed For: Airline Tickets
Portal-to-Portal: Yes **1st-class Airfare:** No
Written Retainer Agreement: Yes
Terms: Lawyer is responsible for fee, not lawyer's client, Interest for delinquent accounts, Retaining counsel pays all deposition charges, Fee schedules
Failure to Pay Bill Last 5 Years; Retaining Counsel: Yes **Opposing Counsel (Deps):** No

Engineering
Court: $220 **Review/Prep:** $180 **Deps:** $220
Years Testifying: 30 **Majority:** Defendant
Written Fee Schedule: Yes
Min Charge for Deps: Yes **Hours:** 4
Min Charge for Trial: Yes **Hours:** 4
Cancellation Charge for Deps/Trial: No
Retainer Required: No
Procedure When Dep Exceeds Paid Time: Proceed without immediate payment
Expenses Marked Up: Yes
Expenses Billed For: Mileage, Airline Tickets, Lab/Testing, Photographs, Demonstrative Aids
Portal-to-Portal: Yes **1st-class Airfare:** No
Written Retainer Agreement: No
Failure to Pay Bill Last 5 Years; Retaining Counsel: Yes **Opposing Counsel (Deps):** No

Engineering, Civil/Engineering, Structural
Court: $150 **Review/Prep:** $150 **Deps:** $150
Years Testifying: 20
Written Fee Schedule: No
Min Charge for Deps: No
Min Charge for Trial: No
Cancellation Charge for Deps/Trial: No
Retainer Required: Depends, Depends on case
Expenses Marked Up: No
Expenses Billed For: Mileage, Airline Tickets, Lab/Testing
Portal-to-Portal: Yes **1st-class Airfare:** No
Written Retainer Agreement: Yes
Terms: Fee schedules
Failure to Pay Bill Last 5 Years; Retaining Counsel: No **Opposing Counsel (Deps):** No

Engineering, Civil/Hydrology
Court: $250 **Review/Prep:** $150 **Deps:** $250
Years Testifying: 14
Written Fee Schedule: Yes
Min Charge for Deps: Yes **Hours:** 4
Min Charge for Trial: Yes **Hours:** 4
Cancellation Charge for Deps/Trial: No
Retainer Required: Yes, $2,000 (Refundable, One Time)
Procedure When Dep Exceeds Paid Time: Proceed without immediate payment
Expenses Marked Up: Yes
Expenses Billed For: Airline Tickets, Demonstrative Aids
Portal-to-Portal: Yes **1st-class Airfare:** No
Written Retainer Agreement: Yes
Terms: Interest for delinquent accounts, Out-of-pocket expense policies, In-court testimony minimums, Retaining counsel pays all deposition charges, Fee schedules, Portal-to-portal travel time, Attorney's fees if forced to sue for collection, Deposition minimum fee
Failure to Pay Bill Last 5 Years; Retaining Counsel: Yes **Opposing Counsel (Deps):** No

Engineering, Civil
Court: $200 **Review/Prep:** $150 **Deps:** $200
Years Testifying: 20 **Majority:** Defendant
Written Fee Schedule: Yes
Min Charge for Deps: Yes **Hours:** 4
Min Charge for Trial: Yes **Hours:** 4
Cancellation Charge for Deps/Trial: No
Retainer Required: No
Expenses Marked Up: No
Expenses Billed For: Mileage, Airline Tickets, Lab/Testing, Photographs, Demonstrative Aids
Portal-to-Portal: Yes **1st-class Airfare:** No
Written Retainer Agreement: Yes
Terms: Interest for delinquent accounts, In-court testimony minimums, Deposition minimum fee
Failure to Pay Bill Last 5 Years; Retaining Counsel: No **Opposing Counsel (Deps):** No

Engineering, Electrical
Court: $200 **Review/Prep:** $200 **Deps:** $200
Years Testifying: 10
Written Fee Schedule: Yes
Min Charge for Deps: Yes **Hours:** 4
Min Charge for Trial: Yes **Hours:** 4
Cancellation Charge for Deps/Trial: No
Retainer Required: Yes, $3,200 (Refundable, Replenishable)
Expenses Marked Up: No
Expenses Billed For: Airline Tickets
Portal-to-Portal: Yes **1st-class Airfare:** No
Written Retainer Agreement: Yes
Terms: Lawyer is responsible for fee, not lawyer's client, Out-of-pocket expense policies, In-court testimony minimums, Retaining counsel pays all deposition charges, Fee schedules, Portal-to-portal travel time, Attorney's fees if forced to sue for collection, Deposition minimum fee, Payment for preparation time
Failure to Pay Bill Last 5 Years; Retaining Counsel: Yes **Opposing Counsel (Deps):** No

Engineering, Electrical
Court: $250 **Review/Prep:** $200 **Deps:** $250
Years Testifying: 25
Written Fee Schedule: Yes
Min Charge for Deps: Yes **Hours:** 4
Min Charge for Trial: Yes **Hours:** 4
Cancellation Charge for Deps/Trial: Yes
Retainer Required: Yes, $2,000 (Non-Refundable, One Time)
Procedure When Dep Exceeds Paid Time: Get payment before proceeding further
Expenses Marked Up: No
Expenses Billed For: Airline Tickets, Photographs, Demonstrative Aids
Portal-to-Portal: No **1st-class Airfare:** Yes
Written Retainer Agreement: Yes
Terms: Lawyer is responsible for fee, not lawyer's client, Interest for delinquent accounts, In-court testimony minimums, Retaining counsel pays all deposition charges, Fee schedules, Attorney's fees if forced to sue for collection, Deposition minimum fee, Payment for preparation time, First class air travel
Failure to Pay Bill Last 5 Years; Retaining Counsel: No **Opposing Counsel (Deps):** No

Engineering, Geotechnical/Geology
Court: $300 **Review/Prep:** $185 **Deps:** $300
Years Testifying: 18
Written Fee Schedule: Yes
Min Charge for Deps: Yes **Hours:** 4
Min Charge for Trial: Yes **Hours:** 4
Cancellation Charge for Deps/Trial: No
Retainer Required: Yes, $1,000 (Non-Refundable, One Time)
Expenses Marked Up: Yes
Expenses Billed For: Mileage, Airline Tickets, Lab/Testing, Photographs, Demonstrative Aids
Portal-to-Portal: Yes **1st-class Airfare:** No
Written Retainer Agreement: Yes
Terms: Interest for delinquent accounts, Out-of-pocket expense policies, In-court testimony minimums, Retaining counsel pays all deposition charges, Fee schedules, Portal-to-portal travel time, Attorney's fees if forced to sue for collection, Deposition minimum fee, Payment for preparation time
Failure to Pay Bill Last 5 Years; Retaining Counsel: No **Opposing Counsel (Deps):** No

Engineering, Mechanical/Law, Patents
Court: $350 **Review/Prep:** $350 **Deps:** $350
Years Testifying: 13
Written Fee Schedule: No
Min Charge for Deps: No
Min Charge for Trial: No
Cancellation Charge for Deps/Trial: No
Retainer Required: Yes, Depends on case (Non-Refundable, Replenishable)
Expenses Marked Up: No
Expenses Billed For: Mileage, Airline Tickets, Lab/Testing, Photographs, Demonstrative Aids
Portal-to-Portal: Yes **1st-class Airfare:** No
Written Retainer Agreement: Yes
Terms: Lawyer is responsible for fee, not lawyer's client, Interest for delinquent accounts, Out-of-pocket expense policies, Retaining counsel pays all deposition charges, Fee schedules, Portal-to-portal travel time, Attorney's fees if forced to sue for collection, Payment for preparation time

Failure to Pay Bill Last 5 Years; Retaining Counsel: No **Opposing Counsel (Deps):** No

Engineering, Mechanical
Court: $380 **Review/Prep:** $200 **Deps:** $380
Years Testifying: 10 **Majority:** Plaintiff
Written Fee Schedule: Yes
Min Charge for Deps: No
Min Charge for Trial: No
Cancellation Charge for Deps/Trial: No
Retainer Required: Yes, $2,000 (Refundable, One Time)
Expenses Marked Up: No
Expenses Billed For: Mileage, Airline Tickets, Lab/Testing, Photographs, Demonstrative Aids
Portal-to-Portal: No **1st-class Airfare:** No
Written Retainer Agreement: Yes
Terms: Interest for delinquent accounts, Out-of-pocket expense policies, Retaining counsel pays all deposition charges, Fee schedules, Portal-to-portal travel time, Attorney's fees if forced to sue for collection, Deposition minimum fee, Payment for preparation time, Arbitration, Upfront payment in court & account balance prior to appearance.
Failure to Pay Bill Last 5 Years; Retaining Counsel: No **Opposing Counsel (Deps):** No

Engineering, Mechanical/Electrical
Court: $360 **Review/Prep:** $250 **Deps:** $360
Years Testifying: 15 **Majority:** Defendant
Written Fee Schedule: Yes
Min Charge for Deps: No **Hours:** 4
Min Charge for Trial: Yes **Hours:** 4
Cancellation Charge for Deps/Trial: No
Retainer Required: Yes, $2,500 (Refundable, Replenishable)
Expenses Marked Up: Yes
Expenses Billed For: Mileage, Airline Tickets, Photocopies, Lab/Testing, Photographs
Portal-to-Portal: Yes **1st-class Airfare:** No
Written Retainer Agreement: Yes
Terms: Lawyer is responsible for fee, not lawyer's client, Interest for delinquent accounts, Out-of-pocket expense policies, Retaining counsel pays all deposition charges, Fee schedules, Attorney's fees if forced to sue for collection
Failure to Pay Bill Last 5 Years; Retaining Counsel: Yes **Opposing Counsel (Deps):** No

Engineering, Mechanical
Court: $330 **Review/Prep:** $220 **Deps:** $330
Years Testifying: 10
Written Fee Schedule: Yes
Min Charge for Deps: No
Min Charge for Trial: No
Cancellation Charge for Deps/Trial: No
Retainer Required: Yes, $2,000 (Refundable, One Time)
Procedure When Dep Exceeds Paid Time: Proceed without immediate payment
Expenses Marked Up: No
Expenses Billed For: Mileage, Airline Tickets, Photographs
Portal-to-Portal: Yes **1st-class Airfare:** No
Written Retainer Agreement: Yes
Terms: Lawyer is responsible for fee, not lawyer's client, Interest for delinquent accounts, Attorney's fees if forced to sue for collection
Failure to Pay Bill Last 5 Years; Retaining Counsel: Yes **Opposing (Deps):** Yes

Engineering, Mechanical
Court: $215 **Review/Prep:** $215 **Deps:** $215
Years Testifying: 16
Written Fee Schedule: Yes
Min Charge for Deps: No
Min Charge for Trial: No
Cancellation Charge for Deps/Trial: No
Retainer Required: Yes, Depends on case (Refundable, Replenishable)
Expenses Marked Up: No
Expenses Billed For: Mileage, Airline Tickets, Lab/Testing, Photographs
Portal-to-Portal: Yes **1st-class Airfare:** No
Written Retainer Agreement: Yes
Terms: Lawyer is responsible for fee, not lawyer's client, Retaining counsel pays all deposition charges, Fee schedules, Portal-to-portal travel time, Attorney's fees if forced to sue for collection
Failure to Pay Bill Last 5 Years; Retaining Counsel: No **Opposing Counsel (Deps):** No

Engineering, Structural
Court: $225 **Review/Prep:** $150 **Deps:** $225
Years Testifying: 10
Written Fee Schedule: Yes
Min Charge for Deps: Yes **Hours:** 4
Min Charge for Trial: Yes **Hours:** 4
Cancellation Charge for Deps/Trial: No
Retainer Required: No
Expenses Marked Up: Yes
Expenses Billed For: Lab/Testing, Demonstrative Aids
Portal-to-Portal: Yes **1st-class Airfare:** No
Written Retainer Agreement: Yes
Terms: Out-of-pocket expense policies, In-court testimony minimums, Fee schedules, Portal-to-portal travel time, Deposition minimum fee, Payment for preparation time
Failure to Pay Bill Last 5 Years; Retaining Counsel: Yes **Opposing Counsel (Deps):** No

Engineering, Structural
Court: $375 **Review/Prep:** $260 **Deps:** $375
Years Testifying: 30
Written Fee Schedule: Yes
Min Charge for Deps: Yes **Hours:** 4
Min Charge for Trial: Yes **Hours:** 4
Cancellation Charge for Deps/Trial: No
Retainer Required: Yes, $1,500 (Refundable, One Time)
Expenses Marked Up: No
Expenses Billed For: Airline Tickets, Photocopies, Lab/Testing, Demonstrative Aids
Portal-to-Portal: Yes **1st-class Airfare:** No
Written Retainer Agreement: Yes
Terms: Interest for delinquent accounts, Out-of-pocket expense policies, In-court testimony minimums, Retaining counsel pays all deposition charges, Fee schedules, Portal-to-portal travel time, Attorney's fees if forced to sue for collection, Deposition minimum fee, Payment for preparation time
Failure to Pay Bill Last 5 Years; Retaining Counsel: Yes **Opposing (Deps):** Yes

Engineering, Structural
Court: $350 **Review/Prep:** $250 **Deps:** $350
Years Testifying: 12
Written Fee Schedule: Yes
Min Charge for Deps: Yes **Hours:** 4
Min Charge for Trial: Yes **Hours:** 4
Cancellation Charge for Deps/Trial: Yes
Retainer Required: Yes, $4,000 (Refundable, Replenishable)
Procedure When Dep Exceeds Paid Time: Get payment before proceeding further
Expenses Marked Up: Yes
Expenses Billed For: Mileage, Airline Tickets, Lab/Testing, Photographs, Demonstrative Aids
Portal-to-Portal: Yes **1st-class Airfare:** No
Written Retainer Agreement: No
Failure to Pay Bill Last 5 Years; Retaining Counsel: Yes **Opposing Counsel (Deps):** No

Engineering, Structural/ Earthquakes
Court: $220 **Review/Prep:** $220 **Deps:** $220
Years Testifying: 10
Written Fee Schedule: Yes
Min Charge for Deps: No
Min Charge for Trial: No
Cancellation Charge for Deps/Trial: No
Retainer Required: No
Expenses Marked Up: Yes
Expenses Billed For: Mileage, Airline Tickets, Demonstrative Aids
Portal-to-Portal: Yes **1st-class Airfare:** No
Written Retainer Agreement: No
Failure to Pay Bill Last 5 Years; Retaining Counsel: No **Opposing Counsel (Deps):** No

Engineering, Traffic
Court: $210 **Review/Prep:** $100 **Deps:** $210
Years Testifying: 5 **Majority:** Plaintiff

Written Fee Schedule: Yes
Min Charge for Deps: No
Min Charge for Trial: No
Cancellation Charge for Deps/Trial: No
Retainer Required: Yes, 10% est. fee (Refundable, Replenishable)
Procedure When Dep Exceeds Paid Time: Proceed without immediate payment
Expenses Marked Up: Yes
Expenses Billed For: Mileage, Airline Tickets, Photocopies, Lab/Testing, Demonstrative Aids
Portal-to-Portal: Yes **1st-class Airfare:** No
Written Retainer Agreement: Yes
Terms: Lawyer is responsible for fee, not lawyer's client, Interest for delinquent accounts, Out-of-pocket expense policies, Retaining counsel pays all deposition charges, Fee schedules, Attorney's fees if forced to sue for collection, Deposition minimum fee, Payment for preparation time
Failure to Pay Bill Last 5 Years; Retaining Counsel: Yes **Opposing Counsel (Deps):** No

Environmental, Air Pollution
Court: $225 **Review/Prep:** $225 **Deps:** $225
Years Testifying: 28 **Majority:** Plaintiff
Written Fee Schedule: Yes
Min Charge for Deps: No
Min Charge for Trial: No
Cancellation Charge for Deps/Trial: No
Retainer Required: Yes, $4,000 (Non-Refundable, One Time)
Expenses Marked Up: No
Expenses Billed For: Mileage, Airline Tickets, Lab/Testing, Photographs, Demonstrative Aids
Portal-to-Portal: Yes **1st-class Airfare:** No
Written Retainer Agreement: No
Failure to Pay Bill Last 5 Years; Retaining Counsel: Yes **Opposing Counsel (Deps):** No

Failure Analysis
Court: $400 **Review/Prep:** $250 **Deps:** $400
Years Testifying: 15
Written Fee Schedule: Yes
Min Charge for Deps: No
Min Charge for Trial: No
Cancellation Charge for Deps/Trial: No
Retainer Required: Yes, $2,000 (Refundable, One Time)
Expenses Marked Up: No
Expenses Billed For: Airline Tickets, Lab/Testing
Portal-to-Portal: Yes **1st-class Airfare:** Yes
Written Retainer Agreement: No
Failure to Pay Bill Last 5 Years; Retaining Counsel: Yes **Opposing Counsel (Deps):** No

Fingerprints/Document Examiner
Court: $125 **Review/Prep:** $125 **Deps:** $125
Years Testifying: 27 **Majority:** Defendant
Written Fee Schedule: Yes
Min Charge for Deps: Yes **Hours:** 3
Min Charge for Trial: Yes **Hours:** 3
Cancellation Charge for Deps/Trial: No
Retainer Required: Yes, $500 (Refundable, One Time)
Procedure When Dep Exceeds Paid Time: Proceed without immediate payment
Expenses Marked Up: No
Expenses Billed For: Mileage, Airline Tickets, Lab/Testing, Photographs, Demonstrative Aids
Portal-to-Portal: Yes **1st-class Airfare:** No
Written Retainer Agreement: No
Failure to Pay Bill Last 5 Years; Retaining Counsel: Yes **Opposing Counsel (Deps):** No

Fire
Court: $225 **Review/Prep:** $95 **Deps:** $225
Years Testifying: 30 **Majority:** Defendant
Written Fee Schedule: Yes
Min Charge for Deps: No
Min Charge for Trial: No
Cancellation Charge for Deps/Trial: No
Retainer Required: No
Expenses Marked Up: No
Expenses Billed For: Mileage, Airline Tickets, Photocopies, Telephone Calls, Lab/Testing, Photographs, Demonstrative Aids
Portal-to-Portal: Yes **1st-class Airfare:** No
Written Retainer Agreement: No
Failure to Pay Bill Last 5 Years; Retaining Counsel: No **Opposing Counsel (Deps):** No

Gastroenterology
Court: $550 **Review/Prep:** $550 **Deps:** $550
Years Testifying: 25
Written Fee Schedule: Yes
Min Charge for Deps: Yes **Hours:** 8
Min Charge for Trial: Yes **Hours:** 8
Cancellation Charge for Deps/Trial: Yes
Retainer Required: Yes, $1,650 (Refundable, Replenishable)
Procedure When Dep Exceeds Paid Time: Get payment before proceeding further
Expenses Marked Up: Yes
Expenses Billed For: Mileage, Airline Tickets, Photocopies, Telephone Calls, Lab/Testing, Photographs, Demonstrative Aids
Portal-to-Portal: Yes **1st-class Airfare:** Yes
Written Retainer Agreement: Yes
Terms: Lawyer is responsible for fee, not lawyer's client, Interest for delinquent accounts, Out-of-pocket expense policies, In-court testimony minimums, Retaining counsel pays all deposition charges, Fee schedules, Portal-to-portal travel time, Attorney's fees if forced to sue for collection, Deposition minimum fee, Payment for preparation time, First class air travel
Failure to Pay Bill Last 5 Years; Retaining Counsel: Yes **Opposing (Deps):** Yes

Geology
Court: $290 **Review/Prep:** $145 **Deps:** $290
Years Testifying: 28
Written Fee Schedule: Yes
Min Charge for Deps: No
Min Charge for Trial: No
Cancellation Charge for Deps/Trial: No
Retainer Required: No
Expenses Marked Up: Yes
Expenses Billed For: Mileage, Airline Tickets, Photocopies, Telephone Calls, Lab/Testing, Photographs, Demonstrative Aids
Portal-to-Portal: Yes **1st-class Airfare:** No
Written Retainer Agreement: No
Failure to Pay Bill Last 5 Years; Retaining Counsel: No **Opposing Counsel (Deps):** No

Geology
Court: $240 **Review/Prep:** $120 **Deps:** $120
Years Testifying: 4
Written Fee Schedule: Yes
Min Charge for Deps: Yes **Hours:** 4
Min Charge for Trial: Yes **Hours:** 4
Cancellation Charge for Deps/Trial: No
Retainer Required: Yes, 50% est. fee (Refundable, One Time)
Expenses Marked Up: Yes
Expenses Billed For: Mileage, Airline Tickets, Photocopies, Telephone Calls, Lab/Testing, Photographs, Demonstrative Aids
Portal-to-Portal: Yes **1st-class Airfare:** No
Written Retainer Agreement: Yes
Terms: Lawyer is responsible for fee, not lawyer's client, Interest for delinquent accounts, Out-of-pocket expense policies, In-court testimony minimums, Retaining counsel pays all deposition charges, Fee schedules, Portal-to-portal travel time, Attorney's fees if forced to sue for collection, Deposition minimum fee, Payment for preparation time
Failure to Pay Bill Last 5 Years; Retaining Counsel: No **Opposing Counsel (Deps):** No

Geriatrics/Long Term Care
Court: $500 **Review/Prep:** $250 **Deps:** $450
Years Testifying: 8
Written Fee Schedule: Yes
Min Charge for Deps: Yes **Hours:** 2
Min Charge for Trial: Yes **Hours:** 2
Cancellation Charge for Deps/Trial: Yes
Retainer Required: Yes, $750 (Non-Refundable, One Time)

Expenses Marked Up: No
Expenses Billed For: Mileage, Airline Tickets
Portal-to-Portal: No **1st-class Airfare:** No
Written Retainer Agreement: No
Failure to Pay Bill Last 5 Years; Retaining Counsel: Yes **Opposing Counsel (Deps):** No

Horses
Court: $250 **Review/Prep:** $125 **Deps:** $250
Years Testifying: 20
Written Fee Schedule: Yes
Min Charge for Deps: No
Min Charge for Trial: No
Cancellation Charge for Deps/Trial: No
Retainer Required: Yes, $1,000 (Non-Refundable, One Time)
Expenses Marked Up: No
Expenses Billed For: Airline Tickets
Portal-to-Portal: Yes **1st-class Airfare:** No
Written Retainer Agreement: Yes
Terms: Lawyer is responsible for fee, not lawyer's client, Interest for delinquent accounts, Out-of-pocket expense policies, In-court testimony minimums, Retaining counsel pays all deposition charges, Fee schedules, Portal-to-portal travel time, Attorney's fees if forced to sue for collection, Payment for preparation time
Failure to Pay Bill Last 5 Years; Retaining Counsel: No **Opposing Counsel (Deps):** No

Hospitality
Court: $415 **Review/Prep:** $415 **Deps:** $425
Years Testifying: 25 **Majority:** Plaintiff
Written Fee Schedule: Yes
Min Charge for Deps: No
Min Charge for Trial: No
Cancellation Charge for Deps/Trial: No
Retainer Required: Yes, Depends on case (Replenishable)
Procedure When Dep Exceeds Paid Time: Proceed without immediate payment
Expenses Marked Up: No
Expenses Billed For: Mileage, Airline Tickets
Portal-to-Portal: Yes **1st-class Airfare:** No
Written Retainer Agreement: Yes
Terms: Out-of-pocket expense policies, Retaining counsel pays all deposition charges, Fee schedules
Failure to Pay Bill Last 5 Years; Retaining Counsel: Yes **Opposing Counsel (Deps):** No

Hospitality, Hotels
Court: $275 **Review/Prep:** $275 **Deps:** $275
Years Testifying: 10 **Majority:** Plaintiff
Written Fee Schedule: Yes
Min Charge for Deps: No **Hours:** 8
Min Charge for Trial: Yes **Hours:** 8
Cancellation Charge for Deps/Trial: Yes
Retainer Required: Yes, (Refundable, One Time)
Expenses Marked Up: No
Expenses Billed For: Mileage, Airline Tickets, Photocopies, Telephone Calls, Lab/Testing, Photographs, Demonstrative Aids
Portal-to-Portal: Yes **1st-class Airfare:** No
Written Retainer Agreement: No
Failure to Pay Bill Last 5 Years; Retaining Counsel: No **Opposing Counsel (Deps):** No

Human Factors
Court: $250 **Review/Prep:** $110 **Deps:** $250
Years Testifying: 12 **Majority:** Plaintiff
Written Fee Schedule: Yes
Min Charge for Deps: No
Min Charge for Trial: No
Cancellation Charge for Deps/Trial: No
Retainer Required: Yes, $350 (Non-Refundable, One Time)
Procedure When Dep Exceeds Paid Time: Proceed without immediate payment
Expenses Marked Up: No
Expenses Billed For: Mileage, Airline Tickets, Photocopies, Telephone Calls, Lab/Testing, Photographs, Demonstrative Aids
Portal-to-Portal: Yes **1st-class Airfare:** No
Written Retainer Agreement: No
Failure to Pay Bill Last 5 Years; Retaining Counsel: Yes **Opposing Counsel (Deps):** No

Human Resources
Court: $300 **Review/Prep:** $275 **Deps:** $300
Years Testifying: 8
Written Fee Schedule: Yes
Min Charge for Deps: Yes **Hours:** 4
Min Charge for Trial: Yes **Hours:** 4
Cancellation Charge for Deps/Trial: No
Retainer Required: Yes, $2,500 (Non-Refundable, One Time)
Expenses Marked Up: No
Expenses Billed For: Mileage, Airline Tickets, Photocopies
Portal-to-Portal: Yes **1st-class Airfare:** No
Written Retainer Agreement: Yes
Terms: Out-of-pocket expense policies, In-court testimony minimums, Retaining counsel pays all deposition charges, Portal-to-portal travel time, Deposition minimum fee
Failure to Pay Bill Last 5 Years; Retaining Counsel: Yes **Opposing (Deps):** Yes

Human Resources
Court: $250 **Review/Prep:** $150 **Deps:** $250
Years Testifying: 5
Written Fee Schedule: Yes
Min Charge for Deps: No
Min Charge for Trial: No
Cancellation Charge for Deps/Trial: No
Retainer Required: Yes, $650 (Non-Refundable, One Time)
Expenses Marked Up: No
Expenses Billed For: Mileage, Airline Tickets
Portal-to-Portal: Yes **1st-class Airfare:** No
Written Retainer Agreement: Yes
Terms: Out-of-pocket expense policies, In-court testimony minimums, Retaining counsel pays all deposition charges, Fee schedules, Portal-to-portal travel time, Attorney's fees if forced to sue for collection
Failure to Pay Bill Last 5 Years; Retaining Counsel: Yes **Opposing Counsel (Deps):** No

Infectious Diseases
Court: $750 **Review/Prep:** $500 **Deps:** $650
Written Fee Schedule: Yes
Min Charge for Deps: No **Hours:** 4
Min Charge for Trial: Yes **Hours:** 4
Cancellation Charge for Deps/Trial: Yes
Retainer Required: Yes, $1,500 (Non-Refundable, One Time)
Expenses Marked Up: No
Expenses Billed For: Mileage, Airline Tickets
Portal-to-Portal: Yes **1st-class Airfare:** No
Written Retainer Agreement: No
Failure to Pay Bill Last 5 Years; Retaining Counsel: Yes **Opposing (Deps):** Yes

Insurance
Court: $250 **Review/Prep:** $220 **Deps:** $250
Years Testifying: 20 **Majority:** Plaintiff
Min Charge for Deps: No
Min Charge for Trial: No
Cancellation Charge for Deps/Trial: No
Retainer Required: Yes, $2,800 (Refundable)
Procedure When Dep Exceeds Paid Time: Proceed without immediate payment
Expenses Marked Up: No
Expenses Billed For: Mileage, Airline Tickets
Portal-to-Portal: Yes **1st-class Airfare:** No
Written Retainer Agreement: Yes
Terms: Lawyer is responsible for fee, not lawyer's client, Interest for delinquent accounts, Out-of-pocket expense policies, Retaining counsel pays all deposition charges, Portal-to-portal travel time, Attorney's fees if forced to sue for collection, Payment for preparation time
Failure to Pay Bill Last 5 Years; Retaining Counsel: Yes **Opposing Counsel (Deps):** No

Insurance
Court: $250 **Review/Prep:** $200 **Deps:** $250
Years Testifying: 5
Written Fee Schedule: No
Min Charge for Deps: No

Min Charge for Trial: No
Cancellation Charge for Deps/Trial: No
Retainer Required: Yes, $2,500 (Refundable, One Time)
Expenses Marked Up: No
Expenses Billed For: Mileage, Airline Tickets, Photocopies, Photographs
Portal-to-Portal: Yes **1st-class Airfare:** No
Written Retainer Agreement: Yes
Terms: Out-of-pocket expense policies, In-court testimony minimums, Retaining counsel pays all deposition charges, Fee schedules, Portal-to-portal travel time, Deposition minimum fee, Payment for preparation time
Failure to Pay Bill Last 5 Years; Retaining Counsel: Yes **Opposing Counsel (Deps):** No

Insurance
Court: $250 **Review/Prep:** $250 **Deps:** $250
Years Testifying: 20
Written Fee Schedule: No
Min Charge for Deps: No
Min Charge for Trial: No
Cancellation Charge for Deps/Trial: No
Retainer Required: Yes, $10,000 (Refundable, One Time)
Expenses Marked Up: No
Expenses Billed For: Mileage, Airline Tickets, Photocopies, Telephone Calls, Demonstrative Aids
Portal-to-Portal: Yes **1st-class Airfare:** No
Written Retainer Agreement: No
Failure to Pay Bill Last 5 Years; Retaining Counsel: No **Opposing Counsel (Deps):** No

Insurance, Property & Casualty
Court: $300 **Review/Prep:** $300 **Deps:** $300
Years Testifying: 20
Written Fee Schedule: No
Min Charge for Deps: Yes
Min Charge for Trial: No
Cancellation Charge for Deps/Trial: No
Retainer Required: Yes, $500 (Non-Refundable, One Time)
Expenses Marked Up: No
Expenses Billed For: Mileage, Airline Tickets, Photocopies, Telephone Calls
Portal-to-Portal: Yes **1st-class Airfare:** No
Written Retainer Agreement: No
Failure to Pay Bill Last 5 Years; Retaining Counsel: Yes **Opposing Counsel (Deps):** No

Internal Medicine
Court: $400 **Review/Prep:** $300 **Deps:** $400
Years Testifying: 15
Written Fee Schedule: Yes
Min Charge for Deps: Yes **Hours:** 4
Min Charge for Trial: Yes **Hours:** 4
Cancellation Charge for Deps/Trial: Yes
Retainer Required: Yes, $1,500 (Refundable, One Time)
Procedure When Dep Exceeds Paid Time: Proceed without immediate payment
Expenses Marked Up: No
Expenses Billed For: Airline Tickets, Photocopies, Telephone Calls, Lab/Testing
Portal-to-Portal: Yes **1st-class Airfare:** Yes
Written Retainer Agreement: No
Failure to Pay Bill Last 5 Years; Retaining Counsel: No **Opposing Counsel (Deps):** No

Internal Medicine
Court: $800 **Review/Prep:** $350 **Deps:** $500
Years Testifying: 7 **Majority:** Defendant
Written Fee Schedule: Yes
Min Charge for Deps: Yes **Hours:** 4
Min Charge for Trial: Yes **Hours:** 4
Cancellation Charge for Deps/Trial: Yes
Retainer Required: Yes, $2,000 (Refundable, Replenishable)
Expenses Marked Up: No
Portal-to-Portal: Yes **1st-class Airfare:** Yes
Written Retainer Agreement: Yes
Terms: Lawyer is responsible for fee, not lawyer's client, In-court testimony minimums, Retaining counsel pays all deposition charges, Fee schedules, Portal-to-portal travel time, Payment for preparation time
Failure to Pay Bill Last 5 Years; Retaining Counsel: Yes **Opposing (Deps):** Yes

Law, Legal Malpractice
Court: $500 **Review/Prep:** $400 **Deps:** $500
Years Testifying: 22
Written Fee Schedule: Yes
Min Charge for Deps: No
Min Charge for Trial: No
Cancellation Charge for Deps/Trial: No
Retainer Required: Yes, Depends on case (Refundable, Replenishable)
Expenses Marked Up: No
Expenses Billed For: Airline Tickets
Portal-to-Portal: Yes **1st-class Airfare:** No
Written Retainer Agreement: Yes
Terms: Lawyer is responsible for fee, not lawyer's client, Interest for delinquent accounts, Out-of-pocket expense policies, Retaining counsel pays all deposition charges, Fee schedules, Portal-to-portal travel time, Attorney's fees if forced to sue for collection
Failure to Pay Bill Last 5 Years; Retaining Counsel: Yes **Opposing (Deps):** Yes

Life Care Planning
Court: $160 **Review/Prep:** $80 **Deps:** $160
Years Testifying: 12
Written Fee Schedule: Yes
Min Charge for Deps: Yes **Hours:** 2
Min Charge for Trial: Yes **Hours:** 2
Cancellation Charge for Deps/Trial: No
Retainer Required: Yes, $2,500 (Refundable, Replenishable)
Expenses Marked Up: No
Expenses Billed For: Mileage, Airline Tickets
Portal-to-Portal: Yes **1st-class Airfare:** No
Written Retainer Agreement: No
Failure to Pay Bill Last 5 Years; Retaining Counsel: No **Opposing Counsel (Deps):** No

Marine
Court: $250 **Review/Prep:** $200 **Deps:** $250
Years Testifying: 23 **Majority:** Plaintiff
Written Fee Schedule: Yes
Min Charge for Deps: Yes **Hours:** 4
Min Charge for Trial: Yes **Hours:** 4
Cancellation Charge for Deps/Trial: Yes
Expenses Marked Up: Yes
Expenses Billed For:
Portal-to-Portal: Yes **1st-class Airfare:** No
Written Retainer Agreement: Yes
Terms: Lawyer is responsible for fee, not lawyer's client, Interest for delinquent accounts, Out-of-pocket expense policies, In-court testimony minimums, Retaining counsel pays all deposition charges, Fee schedules, Portal-to-portal travel time, Attorney's fees if forced to sue for collection, Deposition minimum fee, Payment for preparation time
Failure to Pay Bill Last 5 Years; Retaining Counsel: No **Opposing Counsel (Deps):** No

Marine
Court: $275 **Review/Prep:** $175 **Deps:** $275
Years Testifying: 3
Written Fee Schedule: No
Min Charge for Deps: No
Min Charge for Trial: No
Cancellation Charge for Deps/Trial: No
Retainer Required: Yes, $1,000 (Refundable)
Expenses Marked Up: No
Expenses Billed For: Mileage, Airline Tickets, Lab/Testing, Photographs, Demonstrative Aids
Portal-to-Portal: Yes **1st-class Airfare:** No
Written Retainer Agreement: No
Failure to Pay Bill Last 5 Years; Retaining Counsel: No **Opposing Counsel (Deps):** No

Marine, Boating
Court: $150 **Review/Prep:** $90 **Deps:** $100
Years Testifying: 10
Written Fee Schedule: Yes
Min Charge for Deps: Yes **Hours:** 3
Min Charge for Trial: Yes **Hours:** 3
Cancellation Charge for Deps/Trial: Yes
Retainer Required: Yes, 50% (Refundable, Replenishable)
Procedure When Dep Exceeds Paid Time: Proceed without immediate payment
Expenses Marked Up: Yes
Expenses Billed For: Mileage, Airline

Tickets, Photocopies, Telephone Calls, Lab/Testing, Photographs, Demonstrative Aids
Portal-to-Portal: Yes **1st-class Airfare:** No
Written Retainer Agreement: Yes
Terms: Interest for delinquent accounts, Out-of-pocket expense policies, Retaining counsel pays all deposition charges, Limit liability
Failure to Pay Bill Last 5 Years; Retaining Counsel: No **Opposing Counsel (Deps):** No

Marine, Boating
Court: $200 **Review/Prep:** $100 **Deps:** $200
Years Testifying: 20
Written Fee Schedule: Yes
Min Charge for Deps: No
Min Charge for Trial: No
Cancellation Charge for Deps/Trial: No
Retainer Required: Yes, $3,000 (Non-Refundable, One Time)
Expenses Marked Up: No
Expenses Billed For: Mileage, Airline Tickets, Lab/Testing, Photographs, Demonstrative Aids
Portal-to-Portal: Yes **1st-class Airfare:** No
Written Retainer Agreement: No
Failure to Pay Bill Last 5 Years; Retaining Counsel: No **Opposing Counsel (Deps):** No

Mold
Court: $300 **Review/Prep:** $125 **Deps:** $225
Years Testifying: 4 **Majority:** Plaintiff
Written Fee Schedule: Yes
Min Charge for Deps: No **Hours:** 2
Min Charge for Trial: Yes **Hours:** 2
Cancellation Charge for Deps/Trial: No
Retainer Required: Yes, $2,500 (Refundable, Replenishable)
Expenses Marked Up: Yes
Expenses Billed For: Mileage, Airline Tickets, Lab/Testing, Photographs, Demonstrative Aids
Portal-to-Portal: No **1st-class Airfare:** No
Written Retainer Agreement: Yes
Terms: Lawyer is responsible for fee, not lawyer's client, Out-of-pocket expense policies, In-court testimony minimums, Retaining counsel pays all deposition charges, Fee schedules, Attorney's fees if forced to sue for collection, Payment for preparation time
Failure to Pay Bill Last 5 Years; Retaining Counsel: Yes **Opposing Counsel (Deps):** No

Nephrology
Court: $500 **Review/Prep:** $300 **Deps:** $500
Years Testifying: 10
Written Fee Schedule: Yes
Min Charge for Deps: Yes
Min Charge for Trial: No
Cancellation Charge for Deps/Trial: No
Retainer Required: Yes, $600 (Non-Refundable, Replenishable)
Expenses Marked Up: No
Expenses Billed For: Mileage, Airline Tickets
Portal-to-Portal: Yes **1st-class Airfare:** No
Written Retainer Agreement: No
Failure to Pay Bill Last 5 Years; Retaining Counsel: Yes **Opposing Counsel (Deps):** No

Neurology
Court: $625 **Review/Prep:** $450 **Deps:** $600
Years Testifying: 10 **Majority:** Defendant
Written Fee Schedule: Yes
Min Charge for Deps: Yes **Hours:** 4
Min Charge for Trial: Yes **Hours:** 4
Cancellation Charge for Deps/Trial: Yes
Retainer Required: Yes, Depends on case (Non-Refundable, One Time)
Procedure When Dep Exceeds Paid Time: Proceed without immediate payment
Expenses Marked Up: Yes
Expenses Billed For: Airline Tickets, Photocopies, Telephone Calls
Portal-to-Portal: Yes **1st-class Airfare:** Yes
Written Retainer Agreement: Yes
Terms: Lawyer is responsible for fee, not lawyer's client, Interest for delinquent accounts, Out-of-pocket expense policies, In-court testimony minimums, Retaining counsel pays all deposition charges, Attorney's fees if forced to sue for collection, Payment for preparation time
Failure to Pay Bill Last 5 Years; Retaining Counsel: Yes **Opposing Counsel (Deps):** No

Neuroradiology
Court: $400 **Review/Prep:** $400 **Deps:** $400
Years Testifying: 15 **Majority:** Plaintiff
Written Fee Schedule: Yes
Min Charge for Deps: Yes **Hours:** 1
Min Charge for Trial: Yes **Hours:** 1
Cancellation Charge for Deps/Trial: Yes
Retainer Required: Yes, $400 (Non-Refundable)
Procedure When Dep Exceeds Paid Time: Proceed without immediate payment
Expenses Marked Up: Yes
Expenses Billed For: Mileage, Airline Tickets, Photocopies, Telephone Calls, Lab/Testing, Photographs, Demonstrative Aids
Portal-to-Portal: Yes **1st-class Airfare:** No
Written Retainer Agreement: No
Failure to Pay Bill Last 5 Years; Retaining Counsel: No **Opposing Counsel (Deps):** No

Nursing
Court: $250 **Review/Prep:** $100 **Deps:** $150
Years Testifying: 4
Written Fee Schedule: Yes
Min Charge for Deps: No
Min Charge for Trial: No
Cancellation Charge for Deps/Trial: Yes
Retainer Required: Yes, $1,000 (Refundable, Replenishable)
Procedure When Dep Exceeds Paid Time: Proceed without immediate payment
Expenses Marked Up: No
Expenses Billed For: Mileage, Airline Tickets, Photocopies, Telephone Calls, Lab/Testing, Photographs, Demonstrative Aids
Portal-to-Portal: Yes **1st-class Airfare:** No
Written Retainer Agreement: Yes
Terms: Lawyer is responsible for fee, not lawyer's client, Interest for delinquent accounts, Retaining counsel pays all deposition charges, Fee schedules, Portal-to-portal travel time
Failure to Pay Bill Last 5 Years; Retaining Counsel: Yes **Opposing Counsel (Deps):** No

Nursing
Court: $250 **Review/Prep:** $125 **Deps:** $250
Years Testifying: 3 **Majority:** Defendant
Written Fee Schedule: Yes
Min Charge for Deps: No
Min Charge for Trial: No
Cancellation Charge for Deps/Trial: Yes
Retainer Required: Yes, $750 (Refundable, Replenishable)
Procedure When Dep Exceeds Paid Time: Proceed without immediate payment
Expenses Marked Up: Yes
Expenses Billed For: Mileage, Airline Tickets, Photocopies, Telephone Calls, Lab/Testing, Photographs, Demonstrative Aids
Portal-to-Portal: Yes **1st-class Airfare:** No
Failure to Pay Bill Last 5 Years; Retaining Counsel: Yes **Opposing (Deps):** Yes

Obstetrics & Gynecology
Court: $650 **Review/Prep:** $500 **Deps:** $650
Years Testifying: 25
Written Fee Schedule: Yes
Min Charge for Deps: No **Hours:** 4
Min Charge for Trial: Yes **Hours:** 4
Cancellation Charge for Deps/Trial: No
Retainer Required: Yes, $1,000 (Refundable, One Time)
Expenses Marked Up: No
Expenses Billed For: Mileage, Airline Tickets
Portal-to-Portal: Yes **1st-class Airfare:** No
Written Retainer Agreement: No
Failure to Pay Bill Last 5 Years; Retaining Counsel: Yes **Opposing Counsel (Deps):** No

Obstetrics & Gynecology
Court: $625 **Review/Prep:** $300 **Deps:** $600
Years Testifying: 15 **Majority:** Defendant

Written Fee Schedule: Yes
Min Charge for Deps: Yes **Hours:** 4
Min Charge for Trial: Yes **Hours:** 4
Cancellation Charge for Deps/Trial: No
Retainer Required: No
Expenses Marked Up: No
Portal-to-Portal: Yes **1st-class Airfare:** No
Written Retainer Agreement: No
Failure to Pay Bill Last 5 Years; Retaining Counsel: Yes **Opposing Counsel (Deps):** No

Obstetrics & Gynecology
Court: $400 **Review/Prep:** $300 **Deps:** $400
Years Testifying: 3 **Majority:** Plaintiff
Written Fee Schedule: Yes
Min Charge for Deps: No **Hours:** 4
Min Charge for Trial: Yes **Hours:** 4
Cancellation Charge for Deps/Trial: Yes
Retainer Required: Yes, $600 (Non-Refundable, One Time)
Expenses Marked Up: No
Expenses Billed For: Mileage, Airline Tickets
Portal-to-Portal: Yes **1st-class Airfare:** No
Written Retainer Agreement: Yes
Terms: Lawyer is responsible for fee, not lawyer's client, Interest for delinquent accounts, Out-of-pocket expense policies, In-court testimony minimums, Fee schedules, Portal-to-portal travel time, Attorney's fees if forced to sue for collection, Deposition minimum fee
Failure to Pay Bill Last 5 Years; Retaining Counsel: Yes **Opposing Counsel (Deps):** No

Oncology
Court: $500 **Review/Prep:** $400 **Deps:** $450
Years Testifying: 30
Written Fee Schedule: Yes
Min Charge for Deps: Yes
Min Charge for Trial: No
Cancellation Charge for Deps/Trial: Yes
Retainer Required: Yes, $800 (Non-Refundable, One Time)
Procedure When Dep Exceeds Paid Time: Proceed without immediate payment
Expenses Marked Up: Yes
Expenses Billed For: Airline Tickets
Portal-to-Portal: Yes **1st-class Airfare:** No
Written Retainer Agreement: No
Failure to Pay Bill Last 5 Years; Retaining Counsel: No **Opposing Counsel (Deps):** Yes

Oncology
Court: $500 **Review/Prep:** $400 **Deps:** $500
Years Testifying: 20
Written Fee Schedule: Yes
Min Charge for Deps: Yes **Hours:** 4
Min Charge for Trial: Yes **Hours:** 4
Cancellation Charge for Deps/Trial: No
Retainer Required: Yes, $5,000 (Partially Refundable, One Time)
Expenses Marked Up: No
Expenses Billed For: Mileage, Airline Tickets
Portal-to-Portal: Yes **1st-class Airfare:** Yes
Written Retainer Agreement: Yes
Terms: Lawyer is responsible for fee, not lawyer's client, Interest for delinquent accounts, Out-of-pocket expense policies, In-court testimony minimums, Retaining counsel pays all deposition charges, Fee schedules, Portal-to-portal travel time, Attorney's fees if forced to sue for collection, Deposition minimum fee, Payment for preparation time, First class air travel, Jurisdiction if dispute, Copy to me of all legal docs with my opinion
Failure to Pay Bill Last 5 Years; Retaining Counsel: Yes **Opposing (Deps):** Yes

Ophthalmology
Court: $625 **Review/Prep:** $500 **Deps:** $500
Years Testifying: 25 **Majority:** Plaintiff
Written Fee Schedule: Yes
Min Charge for Deps: Yes **Hours:** 4
Min Charge for Trial: Yes **Hours:** 4
Cancellation Charge for Deps/Trial: Yes
Retainer Required: Yes, Depends on case (Partially Refundable, One Time)
Procedure When Dep Exceeds Paid Time: Proceed without immediate payment
Expenses Marked Up: No
Expenses Billed For: Mileage, Airline Tickets, Photocopies, Telephone Calls, Photographs, Demonstrative Aids
Portal-to-Portal: Yes **1st-class Airfare:** Yes
Written Retainer Agreement: Yes
Terms: Lawyer is responsible for fee, not lawyer's client, Interest for delinquent accounts, In-court testimony minimums, Retaining counsel pays all deposition charges, Fee schedules, Portal-to-portal travel time, Deposition minimum fee, Payment for preparation time, First class air travel
Failure to Pay Bill Last 5 Years; Retaining Counsel: Yes **Opposing Counsel (Deps):** No

Optometry
Court: $250 **Review/Prep:** $250 **Deps:** $250
Years Testifying: 10 **Majority:** Plaintiff
Written Fee Schedule: No
Min Charge for Deps: No
Min Charge for Trial: No
Cancellation Charge for Deps/Trial: No
Retainer Required: Yes, $1,000 (Non-Refundable, One Time)
Expenses Marked Up: Yes
Expenses Billed For: Mileage, Airline Tickets, Photocopies, Telephone Calls
Portal-to-Portal: Yes **1st-class Airfare:** No
Written Retainer Agreement: No
Failure to Pay Bill Last 5 Years; Retaining Counsel: No **Opposing Counsel (Deps):** No

Orthopedics
Court: $500 **Review/Prep:** $300 **Deps:** $500
Years Testifying: 20 **Majority:** Defendant
Written Fee Schedule: Yes
Min Charge for Deps: Yes **Hours:** 4
Min Charge for Trial: Yes **Hours:** 4
Cancellation Charge for Deps/Trial: Yes
Retainer Required: No
Procedure When Dep Exceeds Paid Time: Get payment before proceeding further
Expenses Marked Up: No
Expenses Billed For: Mileage, Airline Tickets, Telephone Calls
Portal-to-Portal: Yes **1st-class Airfare:** Yes
Written Retainer Agreement: No
Failure to Pay Bill Last 5 Years; Retaining Counsel: No **Opposing Counsel (Deps):** No

Orthopedics
Court: $600 **Review/Prep:** $250 **Deps:** $350
Years Testifying: 10 **Majority:** Defendant
Written Fee Schedule: Yes
Min Charge for Deps: Yes **Hours:** 4
Min Charge for Trial: Yes **Hours:** 4
Cancellation Charge for Deps/Trial: Yes
Retainer Required: No
Expenses Marked Up: No
Expenses Billed For: Airline Tickets
Portal-to-Portal: Yes **1st-class Airfare:** No
Written Retainer Agreement: Yes
Terms: Lawyer is responsible for fee, not lawyer's client, Interest for delinquent accounts, In-court testimony minimums, Fee schedules, Portal-to-portal travel time, Deposition minimum fee, Payment for preparation time
Failure to Pay Bill Last 5 Years; Retaining Counsel: Yes **Opposing Counsel (Deps):** No

Orthopedics
Court: $800 **Review/Prep:** $300 **Deps:** $400
Years Testifying: 48
Written Fee Schedule: Yes
Min Charge for Deps: Yes **Hours:** 3
Min Charge for Trial: Yes **Hours:** 3
Cancellation Charge for Deps/Trial: Yes
Retainer Required: No
Expenses Marked Up: No
Portal-to-Portal: Yes **1st-class Airfare:** No
Written Retainer Agreement: No
Failure to Pay Bill Last 5 Years; Retaining Counsel: No **Opposing Counsel (Deps):** No

Orthopedics
Court: $500 **Review/Prep:** $450 **Deps:** $450
Years Testifying: 15 **Majority:** Plaintiff
Written Fee Schedule: Yes
Min Charge for Deps: Yes **Hours:** 2
Min Charge for Trial: Yes **Hours:** 2

Cancellation Charge for Deps/Trial: Yes
Retainer Required: Yes, $600 (Non-Refundable)
Procedure When Dep Exceeds Paid Time: Proceed without immediate payment
Expenses Marked Up: Yes
Expenses Billed For: Mileage, Airline Tickets, Photocopies, Telephone Calls, Demonstrative Aids
Portal-to-Portal: Yes **1st-class Airfare:** Yes
Written Retainer Agreement: Yes
Terms: Lawyer is responsible for fee, not lawyer's client, Interest for delinquent accounts, Out-of-pocket expense policies, In-court testimony minimums, Retaining counsel pays all deposition charges, Fee schedules, Portal-to-portal travel time, Attorney's fees if forced to sue for collection, Deposition minimum fee, Payment for preparation time, First class air travel
Failure to Pay Bill Last 5 Years; Retaining Counsel: No **Opposing Counsel (Deps):** No

Orthopedics
Court: $2,000 **Review/Prep:** $300 **Deps:** $500
Years Testifying: 25
Written Fee Schedule: Yes
Min Charge for Deps: Yes **Hours:** 1
Min Charge for Trial: Yes **Hours:** 1
Cancellation Charge for Deps/Trial: Yes
Retainer Required: Yes, $3,500 (Refundable)
Procedure When Dep Exceeds Paid Time: Proceed without immediate payment
Expenses Marked Up: No
Portal-to-Portal: No **1st-class Airfare:** No
Written Retainer Agreement: Yes
Terms: Lawyer is responsible for fee, not lawyer's client, In-court testimony minimums, Retaining counsel pays all deposition charges, Fee schedules, Attorney's fees if forced to sue for collection, Deposition minimum fee
Failure to Pay Bill Last 5 Years; Retaining Counsel: Yes **Opposing (Deps):** Yes

Orthopedics
Court: $750 **Review/Prep:** $300 **Deps:** $750
Years Testifying: 25
Written Fee Schedule: Yes
Min Charge for Deps: Yes
Min Charge for Trial: No
Cancellation Charge for Deps/Trial: No
Retainer Required: No
Procedure When Dep Exceeds Paid Time: Proceed without immediate payment
Expenses Marked Up: No
Expenses Billed For: Telephone Calls, Lab/Testing, Photographs, Demonstrative Aids
Portal-to-Portal: Yes **1st-class Airfare:** No
Written Retainer Agreement: No
Failure to Pay Bill Last 5 Years; Retaining Counsel: No **Opposing Counsel (Deps):** No

Orthopedics
Court: $500 **Review/Prep:** $500 **Deps:** $500
Years Testifying: 3 **Majority:** Defendant
Written Fee Schedule: Yes
Min Charge for Deps: Yes **Hours:** 4
Min Charge for Trial: Yes **Hours:** 4
Cancellation Charge for Deps/Trial: Yes
Retainer Required: No
Expenses Marked Up: No
Expenses Billed For:
Portal-to-Portal: Yes **1st-class Airfare:** No
Written Retainer Agreement: No
Failure to Pay Bill Last 5 Years; Retaining Counsel: Yes **Opposing Counsel (Deps):** No

Orthopedics
Court: $750 **Deps:** $400
Years Testifying: 15
Written Fee Schedule: Yes
Min Charge for Deps: Yes **Hours:** 1
Min Charge for Trial: Yes **Hours:** 1
Cancellation Charge for Deps/Trial: Yes
Retainer Required: No
Procedure When Dep Exceeds Paid Time: Get payment before proceeding further
Expenses Marked Up: No
Expenses Billed For: Mileage, Airline Tickets
Portal-to-Portal: No **1st-class Airfare:** No
Written Retainer Agreement: No
Failure to Pay Bill Last 5 Years; Retaining Counsel: Yes **Opposing (Deps):** Yes

Orthopedics
Court: $350 **Review/Prep:** $350 **Deps:** $350
Years Testifying: 4 **Majority:** Plaintiff
Written Fee Schedule: Yes
Min Charge for Deps: Yes **Hours:** 4
Min Charge for Trial: Yes **Hours:** 4
Cancellation Charge for Deps/Trial: Yes
Retainer Required: Yes, $700 (Refundable, One Time)
Expenses Marked Up: Yes
Expenses Billed For: Mileage, Airline Tickets, Photocopies, Telephone Calls, Lab/Testing, Photographs, Demonstrative Aids
Portal-to-Portal: Yes **1st-class Airfare:** No
Written Retainer Agreement: No
Failure to Pay Bill Last 5 Years; Retaining Counsel: Yes **Opposing Counsel (Deps):** No

Pain Management/Medicine
Court: $500 **Review/Prep:** $250 **Deps:** $400
Years Testifying: 5
Written Fee Schedule: No
Min Charge for Deps: Yes **Hours:** 2
Min Charge for Trial: Yes **Hours:** 2
Cancellation Charge for Deps/Trial: No
Retainer Required: No
Procedure When Dep Exceeds Paid Time: Proceed without immediate payment
Expenses Marked Up: No
Portal-to-Portal: No **1st-class Airfare:** No
Written Retainer Agreement: No
Failure to Pay Bill Last 5 Years; Retaining Counsel: Yes **Opposing (Deps):** Yes

Pathology
Court: $350 **Review/Prep:** $350 **Deps:** $350
Years Testifying: 35
Written Fee Schedule: No
Min Charge for Deps: Yes
Min Charge for Trial: No
Cancellation Charge for Deps/Trial: No
Retainer Required: No
Expenses Marked Up: No
Expenses Billed For: Mileage, Airline Tickets
Portal-to-Portal: Yes **1st-class Airfare:** No
Written Retainer Agreement: No
Failure to Pay Bill Last 5 Years; Retaining Counsel: Yes **Opposing Counsel (Deps):** No

Physical Medicine & Rehabilitation
Court: $600 **Review/Prep:** $600 **Deps:** $600
Years Testifying: 6 **Majority:** Plaintiff
Written Fee Schedule: Yes
Min Charge for Deps: Yes **Hours:** 4
Min Charge for Trial: Yes **Hours:** 4
Cancellation Charge for Deps/Trial: Yes
Retainer Required: No
Expenses Marked Up: Yes
Expenses Billed For: Mileage, Airline Tickets, Photocopies, Telephone Calls
Portal-to-Portal: Yes **1st-class Airfare:** No
Written Retainer Agreement: No
Failure to Pay Bill Last 5 Years; Retaining Counsel: No **Opposing Counsel (Deps):** No

Physical Medicine & Rehabilitation
Court: $500 **Review/Prep:** $500 **Deps:** $500
Years Testifying: 20
Written Fee Schedule: Yes
Min Charge for Deps: Yes **Hours:** 8
Min Charge for Trial: Yes **Hours:** 8
Cancellation Charge for Deps/Trial: Yes
Retainer Required: Yes, Total est. fee (Non-Refundable)
Procedure When Dep Exceeds Paid Time: Get payment before proceeding further
Expenses Marked Up: Yes
Expenses Billed For: Mileage, Airline Tickets, Photocopies, Telephone Calls, Lab/Testing
Portal-to-Portal: Yes **1st-class Airfare:** Yes
Written Retainer Agreement: Yes
Terms: Interest for delinquent accounts,

Out-of-pocket expense policies, In-court testimony minimums, Retaining counsel pays all deposition charges, Fee schedules, Portal-to-portal travel time, Attorney's fees if forced to sue for collection, Payment for preparation time, First class air travel
Failure to Pay Bill Last 5 Years; Retaining Counsel: Yes **Opposing Counsel (Deps):** No

Plastics
Court: $250 **Review/Prep:** $185 **Deps:** $500
Years Testifying: 15
Written Fee Schedule: Yes
Min Charge for Deps: Yes **Hours:** 4
Min Charge for Trial: Yes **Hours:** 4
Cancellation Charge for Deps/Trial: Yes
Retainer Required: Yes, $500 (Refundable, One Time)
Expenses Marked Up: No
Expenses Billed For: Mileage, Airline Tickets, Lab/Testing, Photographs, Demonstrative Aids
Portal-to-Portal: Yes **1st-class Airfare:** Yes
Written Retainer Agreement: No
Failure to Pay Bill Last 5 Years; Retaining Counsel: Yes **Opposing Counsel (Deps):** No

Plumbing/HVAC
Court: $250 **Review/Prep:** $150 **Deps:** $250
Years Testifying: 10 **Majority:** Defendant
Written Fee Schedule: Yes
Min Charge for Deps: No
Min Charge for Trial: No
Cancellation Charge for Deps/Trial: No
Retainer Required: Yes, $1,500 (Refundable, Replenishable)
Expenses Marked Up: No
Expenses Billed For: Airline Tickets, Lab/Testing
Portal-to-Portal: Yes **1st-class Airfare:** No
Written Retainer Agreement: No
Failure to Pay Bill Last 5 Years; Retaining Counsel: No **Opposing Counsel (Deps):** No

Psychiatry
Court: $450 **Review/Prep:** $225 **Deps:** $450
Years Testifying: 4 **Majority:** Defendant
Written Fee Schedule: Yes
Min Charge for Deps: No
Min Charge for Trial: No
Cancellation Charge for Deps/Trial: No
Retainer Required: Yes, (Refundable, Replenishable)
Expenses Marked Up: No
Expenses Billed For: Mileage, Airline Tickets, Photocopies, Telephone Calls, Lab/Testing, Photographs, Demonstrative Aids
Portal-to-Portal: No **1st-class Airfare:** No
Written Retainer Agreement: No
Failure to Pay Bill Last 5 Years; Retaining Counsel: No **Opposing Counsel (Deps):** No

Psychiatry
Court: $300 **Review/Prep:** $300 **Deps:** $300
Years Testifying: 8
Written Fee Schedule: Yes
Min Charge for Deps: Yes **Hours:** 4
Min Charge for Trial: Yes **Hours:** 4
Cancellation Charge for Deps/Trial: Yes
Retainer Required: Yes, $3,000 (Non-Refundable, One Time)
Procedure When Dep Exceeds Paid Time: Get payment before proceeding further
Expenses Marked Up: No
Expenses Billed For: Airline Tickets
Portal-to-Portal: No **1st-class Airfare:** No
Written Retainer Agreement: Yes
Terms: Lawyer is responsible for fee, not lawyer's client, Interest for delinquent accounts, Out-of-pocket expense policies, Retaining counsel pays all deposition charges
Failure to Pay Bill Last 5 Years; Retaining Counsel: No **Opposing Counsel (Deps):** No

Psychology
Court: $700 **Review/Prep:** $495 **Deps:** $700
Years Testifying: 30
Written Fee Schedule: No
Min Charge for Deps: Yes **Hours:** 4
Min Charge for Trial: Yes **Hours:** 4
Cancellation Charge for Deps/Trial: Yes
Retainer Required: Yes, $5,000 (Refundable, Replenishable)
Procedure When Dep Exceeds Paid Time: Proceed without immediate payment
Expenses Marked Up: No
Expenses Billed For: Mileage, Airline Tickets, Photocopies, Telephone Calls, Lab/Testing, Photographs, Demonstrative Aids
Portal-to-Portal: Yes **1st-class Airfare:** No
Written Retainer Agreement: Yes
Terms: Lawyer is responsible for fee, not lawyer's client, Interest for delinquent accounts, Out-of-pocket expense policies, In-court testimony minimums, Retaining counsel pays all deposition charges, Fee schedules, Portal-to-portal travel time, Attorney's fees if forced to sue for collection, Deposition minimum fee, Payment for preparation time, All expenses
Failure to Pay Bill Last 5 Years; Retaining Counsel: Yes **Opposing Counsel (Deps):** No

Psychology/Neuropsychology
Court: $450 **Review/Prep:** $150 **Deps:** $350
Years Testifying: 10
Written Fee Schedule: No
Min Charge for Deps: Yes **Hours:** 3
Min Charge for Trial: Yes **Hours:** 3
Cancellation Charge for Deps/Trial: Yes
Retainer Required: Yes, (Refundable, One Time)
Procedure When Dep Exceeds Paid Time: Get payment before proceeding further
Expenses Marked Up: No
Expenses Billed For: Mileage
Portal-to-Portal: Yes **1st-class Airfare:** No
Written Retainer Agreement: No
Failure to Pay Bill Last 5 Years; Retaining Counsel: No **Opposing Counsel (Deps):** No

Psychology
Court: $250 **Review/Prep:** $175 **Deps:** $250
Years Testifying: 16 **Majority:** Defendant
Written Fee Schedule: Yes
Min Charge for Deps: Yes **Hours:** 3
Min Charge for Trial: Yes **Hours:** 3
Cancellation Charge for Deps/Trial: Yes
Retainer Required: Yes, $2,000 (Refundable, Replenishable)
Procedure When Dep Exceeds Paid Time: Get payment before proceeding further
Expenses Marked Up: No
Expenses Billed For: Airline Tickets, Photocopies
Portal-to-Portal: Yes **1st-class Airfare:** No
Written Retainer Agreement: Yes
Terms: Interest for delinquent accounts, In-court testimony minimums, Retaining counsel pays all deposition charges, Fee schedules, Portal-to-portal travel time, Attorney's fees if forced to sue for collection, Deposition minimum fee, Payment for preparation time
Failure to Pay Bill Last 5 Years; Retaining Counsel: No **Opposing Counsel (Deps):** No

Psychology
Court: $500 **Review/Prep:** $150 **Deps:** $500
Years Testifying: 20 **Majority:** Plaintiff
Written Fee Schedule: Yes
Min Charge for Deps: Yes **Hours:** 2
Min Charge for Trial: Yes **Hours:** 2
Cancellation Charge for Deps/Trial: No
Retainer Required: Yes, (Refundable)
Procedure When Dep Exceeds Paid Time: Proceed without immediate payment
Expenses Marked Up: Yes
Expenses Billed For: Mileage, Airline Tickets, Photocopies, Telephone Calls
Portal-to-Portal: Yes **1st-class Airfare:** Yes
Failure to Pay Bill Last 5 Years; Retaining Counsel: Yes **Opposing Counsel (Deps):** No

Psychology
Court: $150 **Review/Prep:** $150 **Deps:** $300
Years Testifying: 12
Written Fee Schedule: Yes
Min Charge for Deps: No **Hours:** 5
Min Charge for Trial: Yes **Hours:** 5
Cancellation Charge for Deps/Trial: Yes

Retainer Required: Yes, Total est. fee (Refundable, Replenishable)
Procedure When Dep Exceeds Paid Time: Get payment before proceeding further
Expenses Marked Up: No
Expenses Billed For: Mileage, Airline Tickets
Portal-to-Portal: No **1st-class Airfare:** No
Written Retainer Agreement: No
Failure to Pay Bill Last 5 Years; Retaining Counsel: No **Opposing Counsel (Deps):** No

Pulmonology/Internal Medicine
Court: $600 **Review/Prep:** $250 **Deps:** $300
Years Testifying: 30 **Majority:** Plaintiff
Written Fee Schedule: Yes
Min Charge for Deps: Yes **Hours:** 5
Min Charge for Trial: Yes **Hours:** 5
Cancellation Charge for Deps/Trial: Yes
Retainer Required: Yes, $2,000 (Non-Refundable, Replenishable)
Expenses Marked Up: No
Portal-to-Portal: Yes **1st-class Airfare:** Yes
Written Retainer Agreement: Yes
Terms: Lawyer is responsible for fee, not lawyer's client, Interest for delinquent accounts, Out-of-pocket expense policies, In-court testimony minimums, Retaining counsel pays all deposition charges, Fee schedules, Portal-to-portal travel time, Attorney's fees if forced to sue for collection, Deposition minimum fee, Payment for preparation time, First class air travel
Failure to Pay Bill Last 5 Years; Retaining Counsel: No **Opposing Counsel (Deps):** No

Real Estate
Court: $300 **Review/Prep:** $240 **Deps:** $300
Years Testifying: 14
Written Fee Schedule: Yes
Min Charge for Deps: No
Min Charge for Trial: No
Cancellation Charge for Deps/Trial: Yes
Retainer Required: Yes, $1,500 (Non-Refundable, One Time)
Procedure When Dep Exceeds Paid Time: Proceed without immediate payment
Expenses Marked Up: No
Expenses Billed For: Airline Tickets, Photographs
Portal-to-Portal: Yes **1st-class Airfare:** No
Written Retainer Agreement: Yes
Terms: Lawyer is responsible for fee, not lawyer's client, Out-of-pocket expense policies, In-court testimony minimums, Retaining counsel pays all deposition charges, Fee schedules, Portal-to-portal travel time, Payment for preparation time
Failure to Pay Bill Last 5 Years; Retaining Counsel: Yes **Opposing (Deps):** Yes

Real Estate
Court: $250 **Review/Prep:** $250 **Deps:** $250
Years Testifying: 17 **Majority:** Defendant
Min Charge for Deps: No
Min Charge for Trial: No
Cancellation Charge for Deps/Trial: No
Retainer Required: Yes, $2,000 (Non-Refundable, One Time)
Expenses Marked Up: No
Expenses Billed For: Mileage, Airline Tickets, Telephone Calls
Portal-to-Portal: Yes **1st-class Airfare:** No
Written Retainer Agreement: No
Failure to Pay Bill Last 5 Years; Retaining Counsel: Yes **Opposing Counsel (Deps):** No

Real Estate
Court: $350 **Review/Prep:** $250 **Deps:** $350
Years Testifying: 15
Written Fee Schedule: Yes
Min Charge for Deps: No
Min Charge for Trial: No
Cancellation Charge for Deps/Trial: No
Retainer Required: Yes, $2,000 (Non-Refundable, Replenishable)
Procedure When Dep Exceeds Paid Time: Get payment before proceeding further
Expenses Marked Up: No
Expenses Billed For: Airline Tickets, Photocopies
Portal-to-Portal: Yes **1st-class Airfare:** No
Written Retainer Agreement: Yes
Terms: Lawyer is responsible for fee, not lawyer's client, Interest for delinquent accounts, Out-of-pocket expense policies, In-court testimony minimums, Retaining counsel pays all deposition charges, Fee schedules, Portal to portal travel time, Deposition minimum fee, Payment for preparation time
Failure to Pay Bill Last 5 Years; Retaining Counsel: Yes **Opposing Counsel (Deps):** No

Real Estate/Hospitality, Hotels
Court: $400 **Review/Prep:** $400 **Deps:** $400
Years Testifying: 17
Written Fee Schedule: Yes
Min Charge for Deps: No
Min Charge for Trial: No
Cancellation Charge for Deps/Trial: No
Retainer Required: Yes, $5,000 (Refundable, Replenishable)
Expenses Marked Up: No
Expenses Billed For: Mileage, Airline Tickets, Photographs, Demonstrative Aids
Portal-to-Portal: Yes **1st-class Airfare:** No
Written Retainer Agreement: Yes
Terms: Out-of-pocket expense policies, Retaining counsel pays all deposition charges, Fee schedules, If sued, damages limited to fee
Failure to Pay Bill Last 5 Years; Retaining Counsel: No **Opposing Counsel (Deps):** No

Real Estate
Court: $250 **Review/Prep:** $175 **Deps:** $250
Years Testifying: 5
Written Fee Schedule: Yes
Min Charge for Deps: Yes **Hours:** 4
Min Charge for Trial: Yes **Hours:** 4
Cancellation Charge for Deps/Trial: Yes
Retainer Required: Yes, $1,500 (Non-Refundable, Replenishable)
Procedure When Dep Exceeds Paid Time: Proceed without immediate payment
Expenses Marked Up: No
Expenses Billed For: Photocopies, Photographs
Portal-to-Portal: Yes **1st-class Airfare:** No
Written Retainer Agreement: Yes
Terms: Lawyer is responsible for fee, not lawyer's client, Interest for delinquent accounts, Out-of-pocket expense policies, In-court testimony minimums, Retaining counsel pays all deposition charges, Fee schedules, Portal-to-portal travel time, Attorney's fees if forced to sue for collection, Deposition minimum fee, Payment for preparation time
Failure to Pay Bill Last 5 Years; Retaining Counsel: No **Opposing Counsel (Deps):** No

Real Estate
Court: $350 **Review/Prep:** $250 **Deps:** $350
Years Testifying: 16
Written Fee Schedule: Yes
Min Charge for Deps: No
Min Charge for Trial: No
Cancellation Charge for Deps/Trial: No
Retainer Required: Yes, $1,500 (Non-Refundable)
Expenses Marked Up: Yes
Portal-to-Portal: Yes
Written Retainer Agreement: Yes
Terms: Lawyer is responsible for fee, not lawyer's client, Out-of-pocket expense policies, Retaining counsel pays all deposition charges, Fee schedules, Portal-to-portal travel time, Attorney's fees if forced to sue for collection
Failure to Pay Bill Last 5 Years; Retaining Counsel: No **Opposing Counsel (Deps):** No

Real Estate
Court: $300 **Review/Prep:** $250 **Deps:** $300
Years Testifying: 7
Written Fee Schedule: Yes
Min Charge for Deps: No **Hours:** 3
Min Charge for Trial: Yes **Hours:** 3
Cancellation Charge for Deps/Trial: Yes
Retainer Required: Yes, $1,200 (Non-Refundable, One Time)
Procedure When Dep Exceeds Paid Time: Proceed without immediate payment
Expenses Marked Up: No
Expenses Billed For: Mileage, Airline

Tickets, Photocopies, Telephone Calls, Photographs, Demonstrative Aids
Portal-to-Portal: Yes **1st-class Airfare:** No
Written Retainer Agreement: Yes
Terms: Lawyer is responsible for fee, not lawyer's client, Out-of-pocket expense policies, Retaining counsel pays all deposition charges, Fee schedules, Portal-to-portal travel time, Deposition minimum fee, Payment for preparation time
Failure to Pay Bill Last 5 Years; Retaining Counsel: Yes **Opposing Counsel (Deps):** No

Recreation, Aquatic
Court: $200 **Review/Prep:** $150 **Deps:** $200
Years Testifying: 16
Written Fee Schedule: No
Min Charge for Deps: Yes
Min Charge for Trial: No
Cancellation Charge for Deps/Trial: No
Retainer Required: Yes, $1,050 (Non-Refundable, One Time)
Procedure When Dep Exceeds Paid Time: Varies depending on case
Expenses Marked Up: No
Expenses Billed For: Mileage, Airline Tickets, Photocopies, Telephone Calls, Photographs, Demonstrative Aids
Portal-to-Portal: Yes **1st-class Airfare:** No
Written Retainer Agreement: Yes
Terms: Lawyer is responsible for fee, not lawyer's client, Interest for delinquent accounts, Out-of-pocket expense policies, Retaining counsel pays all deposition charges, Fee schedules, Portal-to-portal travel time, Deposition minimum fee, Payment for preparation time, Discovery request expenses, Fees not contingent
Failure to Pay Bill Last 5 Years; Retaining Counsel: Yes **Opposing Counsel (Deps):** No

Safety/Construction
Court: $300 **Review/Prep:** $150 **Deps:** $300
Years Testifying: 8 **Majority:** Defendant
Written Fee Schedule: Yes
Min Charge for Deps: Yes **Hours:** 2
Min Charge for Trial: Yes **Hours:** 2
Cancellation Charge for Deps/Trial: No
Retainer Required: Yes, $1,500 (Refundable, One Time)
Procedure When Dep Exceeds Paid Time: Proceed without immediate payment
Expenses Marked Up: Yes
Expenses Billed For: Lab/Testing, Demonstrative Aids
Portal-to-Portal: Yes **1st-class Airfare:** No
Written Retainer Agreement: No
Failure to Pay Bill Last 5 Years; Retaining Counsel: Yes **Opposing Counsel (Deps):** No

Safety/Construction
Court: $290 **Review/Prep:** $290 **Deps:** $290
Years Testifying: 5 **Majority:** Defendant
Written Fee Schedule: Yes
Min Charge for Deps: No **Hours:** 8
Min Charge for Trial: Yes **Hours:** 8
Cancellation Charge for Deps/Trial: Yes
Retainer Required: Yes, $1,160 (Refundable, One Time)
Expenses Marked Up: Yes
Expenses Billed For: Mileage, Airline Tickets, Lab/Testing, Photographs, Demonstrative Aids
Portal-to-Portal: Yes **1st-class Airfare:** No
Written Retainer Agreement: No
Failure to Pay Bill Last 5 Years; Retaining Counsel: Yes **Opposing Counsel (Deps):** No

Sales/Marketing
Court: $400 **Review/Prep:** $400 **Deps:** $400
Years Testifying: 3 **Majority:** Defendant
Written Fee Schedule: Yes
Min Charge for Deps: No
Min Charge for Trial: No
Cancellation Charge for Deps/Trial: No
Retainer Required: No
Expenses Marked Up: No
Expenses Billed For: Mileage, Airline Tickets
Portal-to-Portal: Yes **1st-class Airfare:** No
Written Retainer Agreement: No
Failure to Pay Bill Last 5 Years; Retaining Counsel: No **Opposing Counsel (Deps):** No

Security/Law Enforcement
Court: $250 **Review/Prep:** $250 **Deps:** $250
Years Testifying: 49
Written Fee Schedule: Yes
Min Charge for Deps: Yes **Hours:** 4
Min Charge for Trial: Yes **Hours:** 4
Cancellation Charge for Deps/Trial: No
Retainer Required: Yes, $1,250 (Non-Refundable, One Time)
Procedure When Dep Exceeds Paid Time: Other
Expenses Marked Up: No
Expenses Billed For: Airline Tickets, Lab/Testing, Photographs, Demonstrative Aids
Portal-to-Portal: Yes **1st-class Airfare:** Yes
Written Retainer Agreement: Yes
Terms: Lawyer is responsible for fee, not lawyer's client, Interest for delinquent accounts, Out-of-pocket expense policies, In-court testimony minimums, Retaining counsel pays all deposition charges, Fee schedules, Portal-to-portal travel time, Attorney's fees if forced to sue for collection, Deposition minimum fee, Payment for preparation time, First class air travel
Failure to Pay Bill Last 5 Years; Retaining Counsel: Yes **Opposing Counsel (Deps):** No

Security
Court: $350 **Review/Prep:** $250 **Deps:** $350
Years Testifying: 14 **Majority:** Defendant
Written Fee Schedule: Yes
Min Charge for Deps: No
Min Charge for Trial: No
Cancellation Charge for Deps/Trial: Yes
Retainer Required: Yes, $3,000 (Non-Refundable, Replenishable)
Procedure When Dep Exceeds Paid Time: Get payment before proceeding further
Expenses Marked Up: No
Expenses Billed For: Mileage, Airline Tickets, Photographs
Portal-to-Portal: Yes **1st-class Airfare:** No
Written Retainer Agreement: Yes
Terms: Lawyer is responsible for fee, not lawyer's client, Interest for delinquent accounts, Out-of-pocket expense policies, Retaining counsel pays all deposition charges, Fee schedules, Attorney's fees if forced to sue for collection
Failure to Pay Bill Last 5 Years; Retaining Counsel: No **Opposing Counsel (Deps):** No

Slip, Trip & Fall
Court: $300 **Review/Prep:** $185 **Deps:** $300
Years Testifying: 10 **Majority:** Plaintiff
Written Fee Schedule: Yes
Min Charge for Deps: No
Min Charge for Trial: No
Cancellation Charge for Deps/Trial: No
Retainer Required: Yes, $750 (Refundable, One Time)
Expenses Marked Up: No
Expenses Billed For: Mileage, Airline Tickets, Photographs, Demonstrative Aids
Portal-to-Portal: Yes **1st-class Airfare:** No
Written Retainer Agreement: No
Failure to Pay Bill Last 5 Years; Retaining Counsel: Yes **Opposing Counsel (Deps):** No

Slip, Trip & Fall/Fire
Court: $250 **Review/Prep:** $200 **Deps:** $250
Years Testifying: 31
Written Fee Schedule: Yes
Min Charge for Deps: No
Min Charge for Trial: No
Cancellation Charge for Deps/Trial: No
Retainer Required: Depends,
Expenses Marked Up: No
Expenses Billed For: Mileage, Airline Tickets, Lab/Testing, Photographs, Demonstrative Aids
Portal-to-Portal: Yes **1st-class Airfare:** No
Written Retainer Agreement: No
Failure to Pay Bill Last 5 Years; Retaining Counsel: Yes **Opposing Counsel (Deps):** No

Slip, Trip & Fall
Court: $400 **Review/Prep:** $200 **Deps:** $400
Years Testifying: 20
Written Fee Schedule: Yes
Min Charge for Deps: Yes **Hours:** 2
Min Charge for Trial: Yes **Hours:** 2
Cancellation Charge for Deps/Trial: No
Retainer Required: Yes, $1,000 (Partially Refundable, One Time)
Procedure When Dep Exceeds Paid Time: Proceed without immediate payment
Expenses Marked Up: No
Expenses Billed For: Photocopies, Lab/Testing, Photographs, Demonstrative Aids
Portal-to-Portal: Yes **1st-class Airfare:** No
Written Retainer Agreement: Yes
Terms: Lawyer is responsible for fee, not lawyer's client, Interest for delinquent accounts, Out-of-pocket expense policies, In-court testimony minimums, Retaining counsel pays all deposition charges, Fee schedules, Portal-to-portal travel time, Attorney's fees if forced to sue for collection, Deposition minimum fee, Payment for preparation time
Failure to Pay Bill Last 5 Years; Retaining Counsel: Yes **Opposing Counsel (Deps):** No

Social Work
Court: $250 **Review/Prep:** $150 **Deps:** $150
Years Testifying: 20 **Majority:** Plaintiff
Written Fee Schedule: No
Min Charge for Deps: Yes **Hours:** 4
Min Charge for Trial: Yes **Hours:** 4
Cancellation Charge for Deps/Trial: No
Retainer Required: Yes, Depends on case (Refundable, Replenishable)
Procedure When Dep Exceeds Paid Time: Get payment before proceeding further
Expenses Marked Up: Yes
Expenses Billed For: Mileage, Airline Tickets, Photocopies, Telephone Calls
Portal-to-Portal: Yes **1st-class Airfare:** No
Written Retainer Agreement: Yes
Terms: Lawyer is responsible for fee, not lawyer's client, Interest for delinquent accounts, Out-of-pocket expense policies, In-court testimony minimums, Retaining counsel pays all deposition charges, Portal-to-portal travel time, Deposition minimum fee, Payment for preparation time
Failure to Pay Bill Last 5 Years; Retaining Counsel: No **Opposing Counsel (Deps):** Yes

Surgery, Cardiovascular
Court: $500 **Review/Prep:** $300 **Deps:** $500
Years Testifying: 6 **Majority:** Plaintiff
Written Fee Schedule: Yes
Min Charge for Deps: Yes **Hours:** 5
Min Charge for Trial: Yes **Hours:** 5
Cancellation Charge for Deps/Trial: No
Retainer Required: Yes, $900 (Non-Refundable, One Time)
Procedure When Dep Exceeds Paid Time: Proceed without immediate payment
Expenses Marked Up: No
Expenses Billed For: Airline Tickets
Portal-to-Portal: No **1st-class Airfare:** No
Written Retainer Agreement: Yes
Terms: Interest for delinquent accounts, Out-of-pocket expense policies, In-court testimony minimums, Retaining counsel pays all deposition charges, Fee schedules, Deposition minimum fee, Payment for preparation time
Failure to Pay Bill Last 5 Years; Retaining Counsel: Yes **Opposing Counsel (Deps):** No

Surgery, Neurological
Court: $450 **Review/Prep:** $350 **Deps:** $450
Years Testifying: 20
Written Fee Schedule: Yes
Min Charge for Deps: Yes **Hours:** 4
Min Charge for Trial: Yes **Hours:** 4
Cancellation Charge for Deps/Trial: No
Retainer Required: Yes, $700 (Non-Refundable, One Time)
Procedure When Dep Exceeds Paid Time: Proceed without immediate payment
Expenses Marked Up: Yes
Expenses Billed For: Mileage, Airline Tickets, Photocopies, Telephone Calls
Portal-to-Portal: Yes **1st-class Airfare:** No
Written Retainer Agreement: Yes
Terms: Lawyer is responsible for fee, not lawyer's client, Out-of-pocket expense policies
Failure to Pay Bill Last 5 Years; Retaining Counsel: Yes **Opposing Counsel (Deps):** No

Surgery, Neurological
Court: $750 **Review/Prep:** $400 **Deps:** $700
Years Testifying: 30
Written Fee Schedule: Yes
Min Charge for Deps: Yes **Hours:** 4
Min Charge for Trial: Yes **Hours:** 4
Cancellation Charge for Deps/Trial: Yes
Retainer Required: Yes, $2,000 (Refundable)
Procedure When Dep Exceeds Paid Time: Proceed without immediate payment
Expenses Marked Up: No
Portal-to-Portal: No **1st-class Airfare:** No
Written Retainer Agreement: No
Failure to Pay Bill Last 5 Years; Retaining Counsel: No **Opposing Counsel (Deps):** No

Taxation
Court: $375 **Review/Prep:** $325 **Deps:** $375
Years Testifying: 28
Written Fee Schedule: No
Min Charge for Deps: Yes **Hours:** 4
Min Charge for Trial: Yes **Hours:** 4
Cancellation Charge for Deps/Trial: No
Retainer Required: Yes, Depends on case (Refundable, Replenishable)
Procedure When Dep Exceeds Paid Time: Get payment before proceeding further
Expenses Marked Up: No
Expenses Billed For: Mileage, Airline Tickets, Lab/Testing, Photographs, Demonstrative Aids
Portal-to-Portal: Yes **1st-class Airfare:** No
Written Retainer Agreement: Yes
Terms: Lawyer is responsible for fee, not lawyer's client, Interest for delinquent accounts, Out-of-pocket expense policies, In-court testimony minimums, Retaining counsel pays all deposition charges, Deposition minimum fee
Failure to Pay Bill Last 5 Years; Retaining Counsel: No **Opposing Counsel (Deps):** No

Toxicology
Court: $975 **Review/Prep:** $975 **Deps:** $975
Years Testifying: 25
Written Fee Schedule: Yes
Min Charge for Deps: Yes **Hours:** 8
Min Charge for Trial: Yes **Hours:** 8
Cancellation Charge for Deps/Trial: Yes
Retainer Required: Yes, $9,800 (Non-Refundable, Replenishable)
Procedure When Dep Exceeds Paid Time: Proceed without immediate payment
Expenses Marked Up: No
Expenses Billed For: Mileage, Airline Tickets, Photocopies, Telephone Calls, Lab/Testing, Photographs, Demonstrative Aids
Portal-to-Portal: Yes **1st-class Airfare:** Yes
Written Retainer Agreement: No
Failure to Pay Bill Last 5 Years; Retaining Counsel: Yes **Opposing (Deps):** Yes

Toxicology
Court: $300 **Review/Prep:** $250 **Deps:** $300
Years Testifying: 18 **Majority:** Plaintiff
Written Fee Schedule: Yes
Min Charge for Deps: Yes **Hours:** 4
Min Charge for Trial: Yes **Hours:** 4
Cancellation Charge for Deps/Trial: No
Retainer Required: No
Expenses Marked Up: No
Expenses Billed For: Mileage, Airline Tickets, Photocopies, Telephone Calls, Lab/Testing, Photographs, Demonstrative Aids
Portal-to-Portal: Yes **1st-class Airfare:** No
Written Retainer Agreement: No
Failure to Pay Bill Last 5 Years; Retaining Counsel: Yes **Opposing Counsel (Deps):** No

Toxicology
Court: $295 **Review/Prep:** $195 **Deps:** $295
Years Testifying: 20
Written Fee Schedule: Yes
Min Charge for Deps: Yes
Min Charge for Trial: No
Cancellation Charge for Deps/Trial: No
Retainer Required: Yes, (Refundable, One Time)
Procedure When Dep Exceeds Paid Time: Proceed without immediate payment
Expenses Marked Up: Yes
Expenses Billed For: Mileage, Airline Tickets, Lab/Testing, Photographs
Portal-to-Portal: Yes **1st-class Airfare:** No
Written Retainer Agreement: No
Failure to Pay Bill Last 5 Years; Retaining Counsel: Yes **Opposing Counsel (Deps):** No

Urology
Court: $300 **Review/Prep:** $300 **Deps:** $400
Years Testifying: 14 **Majority:** Defendant
Written Fee Schedule: Yes
Min Charge for Deps: Yes **Hours:** 8
Min Charge for Trial: Yes **Hours:** 8
Cancellation Charge for Deps/Trial: No
Retainer Required: No
Expenses Marked Up: No
Portal-to-Portal: Yes **1st-class Airfare:** No
Written Retainer Agreement: No
Failure to Pay Bill Last 5 Years; Retaining Counsel: No **Opposing Counsel (Deps):** No

Urology
Court: $320 **Review/Prep:** $350 **Deps:** $500
Years Testifying: 30
Written Fee Schedule: Yes
Min Charge for Deps: Yes **Hours:** 4
Min Charge for Trial: Yes **Hours:** 4
Cancellation Charge for Deps/Trial: Yes
Retainer Required: Yes, $700 (Refundable, Replenishable)
Procedure When Dep Exceeds Paid Time: Proceed without immediate payment
Expenses Marked Up: No
Expenses Billed For: Mileage, Airline Tickets
Portal-to-Portal: Yes **1st-class Airfare:** No
Written Retainer Agreement: No
Failure to Pay Bill Last 5 Years; Retaining Counsel: Yes **Opposing Counsel (Deps):** No

Video
Court: $300 **Review/Prep:** $250 **Deps:** $300
Years Testifying: 10 **Majority:** Defendant
Written Fee Schedule: Yes
Min Charge for Deps: Yes **Hours:** 3
Min Charge for Trial: Yes **Hours:** 3
Cancellation Charge for Deps/Trial: Yes
Retainer Required: Yes, $750 (Non-Refundable, One Time)
Expenses Marked Up: No
Expenses Billed For: Mileage, Airline Tickets, Photocopies, Telephone Calls, Photographs
Portal-to-Portal: Yes **1st-class Airfare:** No
Written Retainer Agreement: No
Failure to Pay Bill Last 5 Years; Retaining Counsel: No **Opposing Counsel (Deps):** No

Vocational Rehabilitation
Court: $200 **Review/Prep:** $200 **Deps:** $200
Years Testifying: 13 **Majority:** Plaintiff
Written Fee Schedule: Yes
Min Charge for Deps: Yes **Hours:** 4
Min Charge for Trial: Yes **Hours:** 4
Cancellation Charge for Deps/Trial: Yes
Retainer Required: Yes, $1,500 (Refundable, One Time)
Expenses Marked Up: No
Expenses Billed For: Airline Tickets
Portal-to-Portal: Yes **1st-class Airfare:** Yes
Written Retainer Agreement: Yes
Failure to Pay Bill Last 5 Years; Retaining Counsel: No **Opposing Counsel (Deps):** No

Vocational Rehabilitation
Court: $175 **Review/Prep:** $175 **Deps:** $175
Years Testifying: 15 **Majority:** Plaintiff
Written Fee Schedule: No
Min Charge for Deps: Yes **Hours:** 4
Min Charge for Trial: Yes **Hours:** 4
Cancellation Charge for Deps/Trial: No
Retainer Required: Yes, $1,500 (Refundable, Replenishable)
Expenses Marked Up: No
Portal-to-Portal: Yes **1st-class Airfare:** No
Written Retainer Agreement: No
Failure to Pay Bill Last 5 Years; Retaining Counsel: No **Opposing Counsel (Deps):** No

Vocational Rehabilitation
Court: $300 **Review/Prep:** $200 **Deps:** $300
Years Testifying: 8 **Majority:** Plaintiff
Written Fee Schedule: Yes
Min Charge for Deps: Yes
Min Charge for Trial: No
Cancellation Charge for Deps/Trial: Yes
Retainer Required: Yes, $1,500 (Refundable, One Time)
Expenses Marked Up: No
Expenses Billed For: Mileage, Airline Tickets, Telephone Calls
Portal-to-Portal: Yes **1st-class Airfare:** No
Written Retainer Agreement: No
Failure to Pay Bill Last 5 Years; Retaining Counsel: Yes **Opposing Counsel (Deps):** No

Vocational Rehabilitation
Court: $300 **Review/Prep:** $200 **Deps:** $300
Years Testifying: 11
Written Fee Schedule: Yes
Min Charge for Deps: Yes **Hours:** 3
Min Charge for Trial: Yes **Hours:** 3
Cancellation Charge for Deps/Trial: Yes
Retainer Required: Yes, $500 (Non-Refundable, Replenishable)
Procedure When Dep Exceeds Paid Time: Get payment before proceeding further
Expenses Marked Up: No
Expenses Billed For: Mileage
Portal-to-Portal: Yes **1st-class Airfare:** No
Written Retainer Agreement: Yes
Terms: Lawyer is responsible for fee, not lawyer's client, Interest for delinquent accounts, In-court testimony minimums, Retaining counsel pays all deposition charges, Fee schedules, Attorney's fees if forced to sue for collection
Failure to Pay Bill Last 5 Years; Retaining Counsel: No **Opposing Counsel (Deps):** No

Colorado

Actuary
Court: $415 **Review/Prep:** $415 **Deps:** $425
Years Testifying: 13
Written Fee Schedule: No
Min Charge for Deps: No
Min Charge for Trial: No
Cancellation Charge for Deps/Trial: No
Retainer Required: Depends
Expenses Marked Up: No
Expenses Billed For: Mileage, Airline Tickets, Demonstrative Aids
Portal-to-Portal: No **1st-class Airfare:** No
Written Retainer Agreement: No
Failure to Pay Bill Last 5 Years; Retaining Counsel: No **Opposing Counsel (Deps):** No

Architecture/Construction
Court: $245 **Review/Prep:** $245 **Deps:** $245
Years Testifying: 21 **Majority:** Defendant
Written Fee Schedule: Yes
Min Charge for Deps: No
Min Charge for Trial: No
Cancellation Charge for Deps/Trial: No
Retainer Required: Yes, $2,000 (Refundable, One Time)
Expenses Marked Up: No
Expenses Billed For: Mileage, Airline Tickets, Photocopies, Telephone Calls, Lab/Testing, Photographs, Demonstrative Aids
Portal-to-Portal: Yes **1st-class Airfare:** No
Written Retainer Agreement: Yes
Terms: Interest for delinquent accounts, Out-of-pocket expense policies, Retaining counsel pays all deposition charges, Fee schedules, Portal-to-portal travel time, Payment for preparation time
Failure to Pay Bill Last 5 Years; Retaining Counsel: No **Opposing Counsel (Deps):** No

Biomedical, Biotechnology
Court: $300 **Review/Prep:** $250 **Deps:** $300
Years Testifying: 3 **Majority:** Defendant
Written Fee Schedule: Yes
Min Charge for Deps: Yes **Hours:** 4
Min Charge for Trial: Yes **Hours:** 4
Cancellation Charge for Deps/Trial: No
Retainer Required: Yes, $500 (Refundable, One Time)
Procedure When Dep Exceeds Paid Time: Proceed without immediate payment
Expenses Marked Up: No
Expenses Billed For: Mileage, Airline Tickets, Lab/Testing, Photographs, Demonstrative Aids
Portal-to-Portal: Yes **1st-class Airfare:** No
Written Retainer Agreement: No
Failure to Pay Bill Last 5 Years; Retaining Counsel: Yes **Opposing Counsel (Deps):** No

Engineering/Accident Reconstruction
Court: $275 **Review/Prep:** $275 **Deps:** $275
Years Testifying: 28
Written Fee Schedule: No
Min Charge for Deps: No
Min Charge for Trial: No
Cancellation Charge for Deps/Trial: No
Retainer Required: Yes, $3,000 (Refundable, One Time)
Expenses Marked Up: No
Expenses Billed For: Mileage, Airline Tickets, Photocopies, Telephone Calls, Lab/Testing, Photographs, Demonstrative Aids
Portal-to-Portal: Yes **1st-class Airfare:** No
Written Retainer Agreement: Yes
Terms: Lawyer is responsible for fee, not lawyer's client, Interest for delinquent accounts, Out-of-pocket expense policies, Retaining counsel pays all deposition charges, Portal-to-portal travel time, Attorney's fees if forced to sue for collection
Failure to Pay Bill Last 5 Years; Retaining Counsel: Yes **Opposing (Deps):** Yes

Engineering, Aeronautical
Court: $290 **Review/Prep:** $290 **Deps:** $290
Years Testifying: 30 **Majority:** Defendant
Written Fee Schedule: Yes
Min Charge for Deps: Yes **Hours:** 4
Min Charge for Trial: Yes **Hours:** 4
Cancellation Charge for Deps/Trial: No
Retainer Required: No
Expenses Marked Up: No
Expenses Billed For: Mileage, Airline Tickets, Telephone Calls, Lab/Testing, Photographs, Demonstrative Aids
Portal-to-Portal: Yes **1st-class Airfare:** No
Written Retainer Agreement: Yes
Terms: Interest for delinquent accounts, Out-of-pocket expense policies, Fee schedules
Failure to Pay Bill Last 5 Years; Retaining Counsel: Yes **Opposing Counsel (Deps):** No

Engineering, Electrical
Court: $195 **Review/Prep:** $195 **Deps:** $195
Years Testifying: 15
Written Fee Schedule: Yes
Min Charge for Deps: No
Min Charge for Trial: No
Cancellation Charge for Deps/Trial: No
Retainer Required: No
Expenses Marked Up: No
Expenses Billed For: Mileage, Airline Tickets, Photocopies, Telephone Calls, Lab/Testing, Photographs, Demonstrative Aids
Portal-to-Portal: Yes **1st-class Airfare:** No
Written Retainer Agreement: No
Failure to Pay Bill Last 5 Years; Retaining Counsel: No **Opposing Counsel (Deps):** Yes

Engineering, Geotechnical
Court: $175 **Review/Prep:** $175 **Deps:** $175
Years Testifying: 11 **Majority:** Plaintiff
Written Fee Schedule: Yes
Min Charge for Deps: No
Min Charge for Trial: No
Cancellation Charge for Deps/Trial: No
Retainer Required: No
Expenses Marked Up: Yes
Expenses Billed For: Lab/Testing, Photographs
Portal-to-Portal: Yes **1st-class Airfare:** No
Written Retainer Agreement: Yes
Terms: Lawyer is responsible for fee, not lawyer's client, Interest for delinquent accounts, Out-of-pocket expense policies, Fee schedules, Portal-to-portal travel time, Payment for preparation time
Failure to Pay Bill Last 5 Years; Retaining Counsel: No **Opposing Counsel (Deps):** No

Engineering, Residential
Court: $250 **Review/Prep:** $165 **Deps:** $200
Years Testifying: 10 **Majority:** Plaintiff
Written Fee Schedule: Yes
Min Charge for Deps: No
Min Charge for Trial: No
Cancellation Charge for Deps/Trial: Yes
Retainer Required: Yes, Depends on case (Refundable, Replenishable)
Procedure When Dep Exceeds Paid Time: Proceed after deposing counsel agrees to paymt on record.
Expenses Marked Up: No
Expenses Billed For: Mileage, Airline Tickets, Photocopies, Lab/Testing, Photographs, Demonstrative Aids
Portal-to-Portal: Yes **1st-class Airfare:** No
Written Retainer Agreement: No
Failure to Pay Bill Last 5 Years; Retaining Counsel: No **Opposing Counsel (Deps):** No

Engineering, Structural/Failure Analysis
Court: $250 **Review/Prep:** $200 **Deps:** $250
Years Testifying: 34
Written Fee Schedule: Yes
Min Charge for Deps: No
Min Charge for Trial: No
Cancellation Charge for Deps/Trial: No
Retainer Required: Yes, 40% (Non-Refundable, One Time)
Expenses Marked Up: Yes
Expenses Billed For: Mileage, Airline Tickets, Lab/Testing, Photographs, Demonstrative Aids
Portal-to-Portal: Yes **1st-class Airfare:** Yes
Written Retainer Agreement: Yes
Terms: Lawyer is responsible for fee, not lawyer's client, Interest for delinquent accounts, Out-of-pocket expense policies, Retaining counsel pays all deposition charges, Fee schedules, Portal-to-portal travel time, Attorney's fees if forced to sue for collection, Payment for preparation time, First class air travel
Failure to Pay Bill Last 5 Years; Retaining Counsel: No **Opposing Counsel (Deps):** No

Engineering, Wind
Court: $200 **Review/Prep:** $100 **Deps:** $200
Years Testifying: 2
Written Fee Schedule: Yes
Min Charge for Deps: No
Min Charge for Trial: No
Cancellation Charge for Deps/Trial: No
Retainer Required: No
Expenses Marked Up: No
Expenses Billed For: Airline Tickets
Portal-to-Portal: No **1st-class Airfare:** No
Written Retainer Agreement: Yes
Terms: Interest for delinquent accounts, Fee schedules, Attorney's fees if forced to sue for collection, Portal-to-portal travel time, Attorney's fees if forced to sue for collection
Failure to Pay Bill Last 5 Years; Retaining Counsel: No **Opposing Counsel (Deps):** No

Healthcare, Correctional
Court: $315 **Review/Prep:** $315 **Deps:** $315
Years Testifying: 10
Written Fee Schedule: Yes
Min Charge for Deps: Yes **Hours:** 8
Min Charge for Trial: Yes **Hours:** 8
Cancellation Charge for Deps/Trial: No
Retainer Required: Yes, $3,000 (Refundable, One Time)
Expenses Marked Up: No
Expenses Billed For: Mileage, Airline Tickets

Portal-to-Portal: Yes **1st-class Airfare:** No
Written Retainer Agreement: No
Failure to Pay Bill Last 5 Years; Retaining Counsel: No **Opposing Counsel (Deps):** No

Human Factors/Engineering
Court: $160 **Review/Prep:** $160 **Deps:** $160
Years Testifying: 14 **Majority:** Plaintiff
Written Fee Schedule: Yes
Min Charge for Deps: No
Min Charge for Trial: No
Cancellation Charge for Deps/Trial: No
Retainer Required: Yes, $160 (Refundable, Replenishable)
Expenses Marked Up: No
Expenses Billed For: Airline Tickets, Photographs, Demonstrative Aids
Portal-to-Portal: Yes **1st-class Airfare:** No
Written Retainer Agreement: No
Failure to Pay Bill Last 5 Years; Retaining Counsel: Yes **Opposing (Deps):** Yes

Insurance
Court: $400 **Review/Prep:** $400 **Deps:** $400
Years Testifying: 5 **Majority:** Plaintiff
Min Charge for Deps: No
Min Charge for Trial: No
Cancellation Charge for Deps/Trial: Yes
Retainer Required: Yes, $5,000 (One Time)
Expenses Marked Up: No
Expenses Billed For: Mileage, Airline Tickets, Telephone Calls
Portal-to-Portal: No **1st-class Airfare:** No
Written Retainer Agreement: Yes
Terms: Out-of-pocket expense policies, Retaining counsel pays all deposition charges, Fee schedules, Payment for preparation time
Failure to Pay Bill Last 5 Years; Retaining Counsel: No **Opposing Counsel (Deps):** No

Insurance
Court: $200 **Review/Prep:** $200 **Deps:** $200
Years Testifying: 5
Min Charge for Deps: No
Min Charge for Trial: No
Cancellation Charge for Deps/Trial: No
Retainer Required: No
Expenses Marked Up: No
Expenses Billed For: Airline Tickets
Portal-to-Portal: Yes **1st-class Airfare:** No
Written Retainer Agreement: Yes
Terms: Out-of-pocket expense policies, Fee schedules, Portal-to-portal travel time, Payment for preparation time
Failure to Pay Bill Last 5 Years; Retaining Counsel: No **Opposing Counsel (Deps):** No

Materials, Polymeric
Court: $340 **Review/Prep:** $270 **Deps:** $340
Years Testifying: 41
Written Fee Schedule: Yes
Min Charge for Deps: No
Min Charge for Trial: No
Cancellation Charge for Deps/Trial: No
Retainer Required: Yes, $1,000 (Non-Refundable, One Time)
Expenses Marked Up: Yes
Expenses Billed For: Mileage, Airline Tickets, Photocopies, Lab/Testing, Photographs, Demonstrative Aids
Portal-to-Portal: Yes **1st-class Airfare:** No
Written Retainer Agreement: No
Failure to Pay Bill Last 5 Years; Retaining Counsel: Yes **Opposing (Deps):** Yes

Meteorology/Air Quality
Court: $150 **Review/Prep:** $125 **Deps:** $150
Years Testifying: 25 **Majority:** Defendant
Written Fee Schedule: Yes
Min Charge for Deps: No
Min Charge for Trial: No
Cancellation Charge for Deps/Trial: No
Retainer Required: No
Expenses Marked Up: Yes
Expenses Billed For: Airline Tickets, Photocopies, Lab/Testing, Photographs, Demonstrative Aids
Portal-to-Portal: Yes **1st-class Airfare:** No
Written Retainer Agreement: Yes
Terms: Out-of-pocket expense policies, Fee schedules, Payment for preparation time
Failure to Pay Bill Last 5 Years; Retaining Counsel: No **Opposing Counsel (Deps):** No

Obstetrics & Gynecology
Court: $400 **Review/Prep:** $350 **Deps:** $400
Years Testifying: 10 **Majority:** Plaintiff
Written Fee Schedule: No
Min Charge for Deps: Yes **Hours:** 4
Min Charge for Trial: Yes **Hours:** 4
Cancellation Charge for Deps/Trial: No
Retainer Required: Yes, $600 (Non-Refundable, One Time)
Expenses Marked Up: No
Written Retainer Agreement: No
Failure to Pay Bill Last 5 Years; Retaining Counsel: Yes **Opposing Counsel (Deps):** No

Physical Medicine & Rehabilitation
Court: $500 **Review/Prep:** $350 **Deps:** $400
Written Fee Schedule: Yes
Min Charge for Deps: Yes **Hours:** 4
Min Charge for Trial: Yes **Hours:** 4
Cancellation Charge for Deps/Trial: Yes
Retainer Required: Yes, Total est. fee (Refundable, One Time)
Expenses Marked Up: No
Expenses Billed For: Airline Tickets
Portal-to-Portal: Yes **1st-class Airfare:** No
Written Retainer Agreement: No
Failure to Pay Bill Last 5 Years; Retaining Counsel: Yes **Opposing (Deps):** Yes

Premises Liability
Court: $150 **Review/Prep:** $125 **Deps:** $150
Years Testifying: 8 **Majority:** Plaintiff
Written Fee Schedule: Yes
Min Charge for Deps: Yes **Hours:** 4
Min Charge for Trial: Yes **Hours:** 4
Cancellation Charge for Deps/Trial: No
Retainer Required: Yes, $1,500 (Non-Refundable, Replenishable)
Procedure When Dep Exceeds Paid Time: Proceed without immediate payment
Expenses Marked Up: No
Expenses Billed For: Mileage, Airline Tickets, Photocopies, Photographs
Portal-to-Portal: No **1st-class Airfare:** No
Written Retainer Agreement: Yes
Terms: Lawyer is responsible for fee, not lawyer's client, Interest for delinquent accounts, Out-of-pocket expense policies, In-court testimony minimums, Retaining counsel pays all deposition charges, Fee schedules, Attorney's fees if forced to sue for collection, Deposition minimum fee, Payment for preparation time
Failure to Pay Bill Last 5 Years; Retaining Counsel: No **Opposing Counsel (Deps):** No

Psychiatry
Court: $250 **Review/Prep:** $250 **Deps:** $250
Years Testifying: 9 **Majority:** Defendant
Written Fee Schedule: Yes
Min Charge for Deps: No
Min Charge for Trial: No
Cancellation Charge for Deps/Trial: No
Retainer Required: Yes, $1,000
Procedure When Dep Exceeds Paid Time: Proceed without immediate payment
Expenses Marked Up: No
Expenses Billed For: Lab/Testing
Portal-to-Portal: Yes **1st-class Airfare:** No
Written Retainer Agreement: Yes
Terms: Fee schedules, Payment for preparation time
Failure to Pay Bill Last 5 Years; Retaining Counsel: No **Opposing Counsel (Deps):** No

Safety, Construction
Court: $150 **Review/Prep:** $150 **Deps:** $150
Years Testifying: 8
Written Fee Schedule: Yes
Min Charge for Deps: No **Hours:** 5
Min Charge for Trial: Yes **Hours:** 5
Cancellation Charge for Deps/Trial: Yes
Retainer Required: Depends, Depends on case
Expenses Marked Up: No
Expenses Billed For: Mileage, Airline Tickets, Lab/Testing, Photographs, Demonstrative Aids
Portal-to-Portal: Yes **1st-class Airfare:** No
Written Retainer Agreement: Yes

Terms: Lawyer is responsible for fee, not lawyer's client, Interest for delinquent accounts, Out-of-pocket expense policies, In-court testimony minimums, Retaining counsel pays all deposition charges, Fee schedules, Portal-to-portal travel time
Failure to Pay Bill Last 5 Years; Retaining Counsel: No **Opposing Counsel (Deps):** No

Vocational/Life Care Planning
Court: $200 **Review/Prep:** $150 **Deps:** $250
Years Testifying: 25
Written Fee Schedule: Yes
Min Charge for Deps: Yes **Hours:** 2
Min Charge for Trial: Yes **Hours:** 2
Cancellation Charge for Deps/Trial: Yes
Retainer Required: Yes, $1,500 (Refundable, One Time)
Procedure When Dep Exceeds Paid Time: Get payment before proceeding further
Expenses Marked Up: No
Expenses Billed For: Mileage, Airline Tickets, Photocopies, Telephone Calls, Lab/Testing, Demonstrative Aids
Portal-to-Portal: Yes **1st-class Airfare:** No
Written Retainer Agreement: No
Failure to Pay Bill Last 5 Years; Retaining Counsel: Yes **Opposing Counsel (Deps):** No

Connecticut

Accident Reconstruction
Court: $200 **Review/Prep:** $100 **Deps:** $200
Years Testifying: 3 **Majority:** Defendant
Written Fee Schedule: No
Min Charge for Deps: No
Min Charge for Trial: No
Cancellation Charge for Deps/Trial: No
Retainer Required: No
Expenses Marked Up: No
Expenses Billed For: Mileage, Airline Tickets, Lab/Testing, Photographs, Demonstrative Aids
Portal-to-Portal: No **1st-class Airfare:** No
Written Retainer Agreement: No
Failure to Pay Bill Last 5 Years; Retaining Counsel: No **Opposing Counsel (Deps):** No

Accounting
Court: $200 **Review/Prep:** $175 **Deps:** $200
Years Testifying: 4
Written Fee Schedule: Yes
Min Charge for Deps: No
Min Charge for Trial: No
Cancellation Charge for Deps/Trial: No
Retainer Required: Yes, 80% est. fee (Refundable, Replenishable)
Expenses Marked Up: No
Expenses Billed For: Airline Tickets, Demonstrative Aids
Portal-to-Portal: Yes **1st-class Airfare:** No
Written Retainer Agreement: Yes
Terms: Out-of-pocket expense policies, Retaining counsel pays all deposition charges, Fee schedules, Attorney's fees if forced to sue for collection
Failure to Pay Bill Last 5 Years; Retaining Counsel: Yes **Opposing Counsel (Deps):** No

Air Quality
Court: $300 **Review/Prep:** $300 **Deps:** $300
Years Testifying: 30 **Majority:** Defendant
Written Fee Schedule: Yes
Min Charge for Deps: No
Min Charge for Trial: No
Cancellation Charge for Deps/Trial: No
Retainer Required: No
Expenses Marked Up: Yes
Expenses Billed For: Mileage, Airline Tickets, Photocopies, Telephone Calls, Lab/Testing, Photographs, Demonstrative Aids
Portal-to-Portal: No **1st-class Airfare:** No
Written Retainer Agreement: Yes
Terms: Lawyer is responsible for fee, not lawyer's client, Interest for delinquent accounts, Out-of-pocket expense policies, Fee schedules, Payment for preparation time
Failure to Pay Bill Last 5 Years; Retaining Counsel: Yes **Opposing (Deps):** Yes

Anesthesiology
Court: $300 **Review/Prep:** $300 **Deps:** $300
Years Testifying: 75 **Majority:** Plaintiff
Written Fee Schedule: Yes
Min Charge for Deps: Yes **Hours:** 4
Min Charge for Trial: Yes **Hours:** 4
Cancellation Charge for Deps/Trial: Yes
Retainer Required: Yes, $1,200 (Non Refundable)
Procedure When Dep Exceeds Paid Time: Proceed without immediate payment
Expenses Marked Up: No
Expenses Billed For: Mileage, Airline Tickets
Portal-to-Portal: Yes **1st-class Airfare:** No
Written Retainer Agreement: Yes
Terms: In-court testimony minimums, Retaining counsel pays all deposition charges, Fee schedules, Portal-to-portal travel time, Deposition minimum fee, Payment for preparation time
Failure to Pay Bill Last 5 Years; Retaining Counsel: No **Opposing Counsel (Deps):** No

Chiropractic
Court: $300 **Deps:** $250
Years Testifying: 45 **Majority:** Plaintiff
Written Fee Schedule: Yes
Min Charge for Deps: Yes **Hours:** 1
Min Charge for Trial: Yes **Hours:** 1
Cancellation Charge for Deps/Trial: Yes
Retainer Required: No
Expenses Marked Up: No
Portal-to-Portal: Yes **1st-class Airfare:** No
Written Retainer Agreement: Yes
Terms: Lawyer is responsible for fee, not lawyer's client, In-court testimony minimums, Fee schedules, Portal-to-portal travel time, Deposition minimum fee
Failure to Pay Bill Last 5 Years; Retaining Counsel: No **Opposing Counsel (Deps):** No

Damages, Business
Court: $300 **Review/Prep:** $250 **Deps:** $300
Years Testifying: 20 **Majority:** Plaintiff
Written Fee Schedule: Yes
Min Charge for Deps: No
Min Charge for Trial: No
Retainer Required: Yes, $2,000 (Refundable, One Time)
Procedure When Dep Exceeds Paid Time: Proceed without immediate payment
Expenses Marked Up: No
Expenses Billed For: Mileage, Airline Tickets, Photocopies, Telephone Calls
Portal-to-Portal: Yes **1st-class Airfare:** No
Written Retainer Agreement: Yes
Terms: Lawyer is responsible for fee, not lawyer's client, Interest for delinquent accounts, Retaining counsel pays all deposition charges, Fee schedules
Failure to Pay Bill Last 5 Years; Retaining Counsel: Yes **Opposing Counsel (Deps):** No

Damages, Economic
Court: $225 **Review/Prep:** $225 **Deps:** $225
Years Testifying: 7 **Majority:** Plaintiff
Written Fee Schedule: No
Min Charge for Deps: Yes **Hours:** 4
Min Charge for Trial: Yes **Hours:** 4
Cancellation Charge for Deps/Trial: Yes
Retainer Required: Yes, $900 (Non-Refundable, One Time)
Procedure When Dep Exceeds Paid Time: Proceed without immediate payment
Expenses Marked Up: Yes
Expenses Billed For: Airline Tickets, Photocopies
Portal-to-Portal: Yes **1st-class Airfare:** No
Written Retainer Agreement: Yes
Terms: Lawyer is responsible for fee, not lawyer's client, Interest for delinquent accounts, In-court testimony minimums, Retaining counsel pays all deposition charges, Fee schedules, Portal-to-portal travel time, Attorney's fees if forced to sue for collection, Deposition minimum fee, Payment for preparation time
Failure to Pay Bill Last 5 Years; Retaining Counsel: Yes **Opposing Counsel (Deps):** No

Document Examiner
Court: $1,000 **Deps:** $800
Years Testifying: 15
Written Fee Schedule: No
Min Charge for Deps: Yes **Hours:** 1
Min Charge for Trial: Yes **Hours:** 1
Cancellation Charge for Deps/Trial: No
Retainer Required: Yes, Depends on case (Non-Refundable, One Time)
Procedure When Dep Exceeds Paid Time: Proceed without immediate payment
Expenses Marked Up: No
Expenses Billed For: Mileage, Airline Tickets
Portal-to-Portal: Yes **1st-class Airfare:** No
Written Retainer Agreement: No
Failure to Pay Bill Last 5 Years; Retaining Counsel: No **Opposing Counsel (Deps):** No

Economics
Court: $250 **Review/Prep:** $200 **Deps:** $250
Years Testifying: 14 **Majority:** Plaintiff
Written Fee Schedule: Yes
Min Charge for Deps: No
Min Charge for Trial: No
Cancellation Charge for Deps/Trial: No
Retainer Required: Yes, $1,000 (Refundable, One Time)
Procedure When Dep Exceeds Paid Time: Proceed without immediate payment
Expenses Marked Up: Yes
Expenses Billed For: Airline Tickets, Demonstrative Aids
Portal-to-Portal: Yes **1st-class Airfare:** No
Written Retainer Agreement: Yes
Terms: Out-of-pocket expense policies, Retaining counsel pays all deposition charges, Fee schedules, Portal-to-portal travel time, Payment for preparation time
Failure to Pay Bill Last 5 Years; Retaining Counsel: Yes **Opposing Counsel (Deps):** No

Emergency Medicine
Court: $600 **Review/Prep:** $465 **Deps:** $600
Years Testifying: 1 **Majority:** Defendant
Written Fee Schedule: Yes
Min Charge for Deps: Yes **Hours:** 8
Min Charge for Trial: Yes **Hours:** 8
Cancellation Charge for Deps/Trial: No
Retainer Required: No
Expenses Marked Up: No
Expenses Billed For: Mileage, Airline Tickets, Photocopies, Telephone Calls, Lab/Testing, Photographs, Demonstrative Aids
Portal-to-Portal: Yes **1st-class Airfare:** No
Written Retainer Agreement: Yes
Terms: Lawyer is responsible for fee, not lawyer's client, Interest for delinquent accounts, Out-of-pocket expense policies, In-court testimony minimums, Fee schedules, Portal-to-portal travel time, Attorney's fees if forced to sue for collection, Deposition minimum fee, Payment for preparation time
Failure to Pay Bill Last 5 Years; Retaining Counsel: No **Opposing Counsel (Deps):** No

Engineering, Biomedical
Court: $400 **Review/Prep:** $250 **Deps:** $400
Years Testifying: 4
Written Fee Schedule: Yes
Min Charge for Deps: Yes
Min Charge for Trial: No
Cancellation Charge for Deps/Trial: No
Retainer Required: Yes, $2,500 (Refundable, One Time)
Expenses Marked Up: No
Expenses Billed For: Mileage, Airline Tickets, Photocopies, Lab/Testing, Photographs, Demonstrative Aids
Portal-to-Portal: No **1st-class Airfare:** No
Written Retainer Agreement: No
Failure to Pay Bill Last 5 Years; Retaining Counsel: No **Opposing Counsel (Deps):** No

Engineering, Electrical
Court: $250 **Review/Prep:** $180 **Deps:** $250
Years Testifying: 10
Written Fee Schedule: Yes
Min Charge for Deps: No
Min Charge for Trial: No
Cancellation Charge for Deps/Trial: No
Retainer Required: No
Expenses Marked Up: Yes
Expenses Billed For: Airline Tickets, Photocopies, Lab/Testing, Photographs, Demonstrative Aids
Portal-to-Portal: Yes **1st-class Airfare:** No
Written Retainer Agreement: No
Failure to Pay Bill Last 5 Years; Retaining Counsel: No **Opposing Counsel (Deps):** No

Engineering, Safety
Court: $150 **Review/Prep:** $125 **Deps:** $150
Years Testifying: 8 **Majority:** Plaintiff
Written Fee Schedule: Yes
Min Charge for Deps: Yes **Hours:** 2
Min Charge for Trial: Yes **Hours:** 2
Cancellation Charge for Deps/Trial: No
Retainer Required: Yes, $500 (Refundable, One Time)
Procedure When Dep Exceeds Paid Time: Proceed without immediate payment
Expenses Marked Up: Yes
Expenses Billed For: Lab/Testing
Portal-to-Portal: Yes **1st-class Airfare:** No
Written Retainer Agreement: Yes
Terms: Out-of-pocket expense policies, In-court testimony minimums, Retaining counsel pays all deposition charges, Fee schedules, Deposition minimum fee, Payment for preparation time
Failure to Pay Bill Last 5 Years; Retaining Counsel: Yes **Opposing (Deps):** Yes

Environmental Health
Court: $400 **Review/Prep:** $225 **Deps:** $400
Years Testifying: 31
Written Fee Schedule: Yes
Min Charge for Deps: No
Min Charge for Trial: No
Cancellation Charge for Deps/Trial: No
Retainer Required: No
Expenses Marked Up: Yes
Expenses Billed For: Mileage, Airline Tickets, Photocopies, Telephone Calls, Lab/Testing, Photographs, Demonstrative Aids
Portal-to-Portal: Yes **1st-class Airfare:** No
Written Retainer Agreement: No
Failure to Pay Bill Last 5 Years; Retaining Counsel: Yes **Opposing Counsel (Deps):** No

Horticulture
Court: $150 **Review/Prep:** $150 **Deps:** $150
Years Testifying: 20
Written Fee Schedule: Yes
Min Charge for Deps: Yes **Hours:** 4
Min Charge for Trial: Yes **Hours:** 4
Cancellation Charge for Deps/Trial: No
Retainer Required: Yes, $1,000 (Refundable, Replenishable)
Expenses Marked Up: No
Expenses Billed For: Lab/Testing
Portal-to-Portal: Yes **1st-class Airfare:** No
Written Retainer Agreement: Yes
Terms: Lawyer is responsible for fee, not lawyer's client, Out-of-pocket expense policies, In-court testimony minimums, Fee schedules, Portal-to-portal travel time, Deposition minimum fee
Failure to Pay Bill Last 5 Years; Retaining Counsel: No **Opposing Counsel (Deps):** No

Internal Medicine
Court: $450 **Review/Prep:** $450 **Deps:** $450
Years Testifying: 9 **Majority:** Defendant
Written Fee Schedule: No
Min Charge for Deps: No
Min Charge for Trial: No
Cancellation Charge for Deps/Trial: No
Retainer Required: No
Expenses Marked Up: No
Portal-to-Portal: Yes **1st-class Airfare:** No
Written Retainer Agreement: No
Failure to Pay Bill Last 5 Years; Retaining Counsel: No **Opposing Counsel (Deps):** No

Medicine/Genetics
Court: $300 **Review/Prep:** $300 **Deps:** $300
Years Testifying: 20
Written Fee Schedule: No
Min Charge for Deps: No

Min Charge for Trial: No
Cancellation Charge for Deps/Trial: No
Retainer Required: No
Expenses Marked Up: No
Expenses Billed For: Mileage, Airline Tickets, Lab/Testing
Portal-to-Portal: Yes **1st-class Airfare:** No
Written Retainer Agreement: No
Failure to Pay Bill Last 5 Years; Retaining Counsel: No **Opposing Counsel (Deps):** No

Neurology
Court: $500 **Review/Prep:** $350 **Deps:** $350
Years Testifying: 10 **Majority:** Defendant
Written Fee Schedule: Yes
Min Charge for Deps: Yes **Hours:** 4
Min Charge for Trial: Yes **Hours:** 4
Cancellation Charge for Deps/Trial: Yes
Retainer Required: Yes, (Refundable)
Procedure When Dep Exceeds Paid Time: Proceed without immediate payment
Portal-to-Portal: Yes
Written Retainer Agreement: Yes
Terms: In-court testimony minimums, Retaining counsel pays all deposition charges, Fee schedules, Portal-to-portal travel time, Deposition minimum fee
Failure to Pay Bill Last 5 Years; Retaining Counsel: No **Opposing Counsel (Deps):** No

Neuropsychology
Court: $600 **Review/Prep:** $250 **Deps:** $600
Years Testifying: 22 **Majority:** Defendant
Written Fee Schedule: Yes
Min Charge for Deps: No
Min Charge for Trial: No
Cancellation Charge for Deps/Trial: Yes
Retainer Required: Yes, $2,000 (Refundable, One Time)
Expenses Marked Up: Yes
Expenses Billed For: Airline Tickets, Photocopies, Demonstrative Aids
Portal-to-Portal: Yes **1st-class Airfare:** No
Written Retainer Agreement: Yes
Terms: Lawyer is responsible for fee, not lawyer's client, Retaining counsel pays all deposition charges, Fee schedules, Portal-to-portal travel time, Payment for preparation time
Failure to Pay Bill Last 5 Years; Retaining Counsel: Yes

Obstetrics & Gynecology
Court: $400 **Review/Prep:** $250 **Deps:** $350
Years Testifying: 20
Written Fee Schedule: Yes
Min Charge for Deps: Yes **Hours:** 3
Min Charge for Trial: Yes **Hours:** 3
Cancellation Charge for Deps/Trial: No
Retainer Required: Yes, $1,200 (Refundable, One Time)
Expenses Marked Up: No
Expenses Billed For: Mileage, Airline Tickets, Lab/Testing, Photographs
Portal-to-Portal: Yes **1st-class Airfare:** Yes
Written Retainer Agreement: Yes
Terms: Lawyer is responsible for fee, not lawyer's client, Out-of-pocket expense policies, In-court testimony minimums, Retaining counsel pays all deposition charges, Fee schedules, Portal-to-portal travel time, Attorney's fees if forced to sue for collection, Deposition minimum fee, Payment for preparation time, First class air travel
Failure to Pay Bill Last 5 Years; Retaining Counsel: Yes **Opposing Counsel (Deps):** No

Orthopedics
Court: $500 **Review/Prep:** $300 **Deps:** $500
Years Testifying: 25 **Majority:** Plaintiff
Written Fee Schedule: Yes
Min Charge for Deps: Yes **Hours:** 5
Min Charge for Trial: Yes **Hours:** 5
Cancellation Charge for Deps/Trial: Yes
Retainer Required: Yes, (Non-Refundable, One Time)
Procedure When Dep Exceeds Paid Time: Proceed without immediate payment
Expenses Marked Up: Yes
Expenses Billed For: Mileage, Airline Tickets, Lab/Testing, Photographs, Demonstrative Aids
Portal-to-Portal: Yes **1st-class Airfare:** Yes
Written Retainer Agreement: Yes
Terms: Lawyer is responsible for fee, not lawyer's client, Interest for delinquent accounts, Out-of-pocket expense policies, In-court testimony minimums, Retaining counsel pays all deposition charges, Fee schedules, Portal-to-portal travel time, Attorney's fees if forced to sue for collection, Deposition minimum fee
Failure to Pay Bill Last 5 Years; Retaining Counsel: Yes **Opposing (Deps):** Yes

Psychiatry
Court: $750 **Review/Prep:** $400 **Deps:** $750
Years Testifying: 21
Written Fee Schedule: No
Min Charge for Deps: Yes **Hours:** 4
Min Charge for Trial: Yes **Hours:** 4
Cancellation Charge for Deps/Trial: Yes
Retainer Required: Yes, Total est. fee (Refundable, One Time)
Procedure When Dep Exceeds Paid Time: Get payment before proceeding further
Expenses Marked Up: No
Portal-to-Portal: Yes **1st-class Airfare:** No
Written Retainer Agreement: No
Failure to Pay Bill Last 5 Years; Retaining Counsel: No **Opposing Counsel (Deps):** No

Recreation, Playgrounds/Education, Physical
Court: $112 **Review/Prep:** $150 **Deps:** $112
Years Testifying: 10 **Majority:** Plaintiff
Written Fee Schedule: Yes
Min Charge for Deps: Yes **Hours:** 8
Min Charge for Trial: Yes **Hours:** 8
Cancellation Charge for Deps/Trial: Yes
Retainer Required: Yes, $750 (Refundable, One Time)
Expenses Marked Up: No
Expenses Billed For: Mileage
Portal-to-Portal: Yes **1st-class Airfare:** No
Written Retainer Agreement: No
Failure to Pay Bill Last 5 Years; Retaining Counsel: No **Opposing Counsel (Deps):** No

Rheumatology
Court: $400 **Review/Prep:** $285 **Deps:** $300
Years Testifying: 5
Written Fee Schedule: No
Min Charge for Deps: No
Min Charge for Trial: No
Cancellation Charge for Deps/Trial: No
Retainer Required: No
Expenses Marked Up: No
Portal-to-Portal: Yes **1st-class Airfare:** No
Written Retainer Agreement: No
Failure to Pay Bill Last 5 Years; Retaining Counsel: Yes **Opposing Counsel (Deps):** No

Toxicology
Court: $195 **Review/Prep:** $195 **Deps:** $195
Years Testifying: 30 **Majority:** Defendant
Min Charge for Deps: No
Min Charge for Trial: No
Cancellation Charge for Deps/Trial: No
Retainer Required: No
Expenses Marked Up: No
Expenses Billed For:
Portal-to-Portal: Yes **1st-class Airfare:** No
Written Retainer Agreement: No
Failure to Pay Bill Last 5 Years; Retaining Counsel: Yes **Opposing Counsel (Deps):** No

Transportation/Hazardous Materials
Court: $250 **Review/Prep:** $200 **Deps:** $250
Years Testifying: 6
Written Fee Schedule: Yes
Min Charge for Deps: Yes **Hours:** 4
Min Charge for Trial: Yes **Hours:** 4
Cancellation Charge for Deps/Trial: No
Retainer Required: Yes, $2,500 (Refundable, One Time)
Procedure When Dep Exceeds Paid Time: Proceed without immediate payment
Expenses Marked Up: No
Expenses Billed For: Mileage, Airline Tickets, Photocopies, Telephone Calls
Portal-to-Portal: Yes **1st-class Airfare:** No
Written Retainer Agreement: Yes

Terms: Lawyer is responsible for fee, not lawyer's client, Out-of-pocket expense policies, In-court testimony minimums, Retaining counsel pays all deposition charges, Fee schedules, Portal-to-portal travel time, Deposition minimum fee, Payment for preparation time
Failure to Pay Bill Last 5 Years; Retaining Counsel: Yes **Opposing Counsel (Deps):** No

Valuation, Business/Damages, Business
Court: $250 **Review/Prep:** $250 **Deps:** $250
Years Testifying: 12
Written Fee Schedule: Yes
Min Charge for Deps: Yes **Hours:** 8
Min Charge for Trial: Yes **Hours:** 8
Cancellation Charge for Deps/Trial: No
Retainer Required: Yes, $4,000 (Refundable, One Time)
Expenses Marked Up: No
Expenses Billed For: Mileage, Airline Tickets
Portal-to-Portal: Yes **1st-class Airfare:** No
Written Retainer Agreement: Yes
Failure to Pay Bill Last 5 Years; Retaining Counsel: Yes **Opposing (Deps):** Yes

Valuation, Business
Court: $200 **Review/Prep:** $200 **Deps:** $200
Years Testifying: 15
Written Fee Schedule: No
Min Charge for Deps: No
Min Charge for Trial: No
Cancellation Charge for Deps/Trial: Yes
Retainer Required: Yes, (Non-Refundable, Replenishable)
Procedure When Dep Exceeds Paid Time: Get payment before proceeding further
Expenses Marked Up: No
Expenses Billed For: Airline Tickets
Portal-to-Portal: No **1st-class Airfare:** No
Written Retainer Agreement: Yes
Terms: Interest for delinquent accounts, Out-of-pocket expense policies, Retaining counsel pays all deposition charges, Attorney's fees if forced to sue for collection, Payment for preparation time
Failure to Pay Bill Last 5 Years; Retaining Counsel: No **Opposing Counsel (Deps):** No

Delaware

Corrosion/Metallurgy
Court: $275 **Review/Prep:** $225 **Deps:** $275
Years Testifying: 15
Written Fee Schedule: Yes
Min Charge for Deps: Yes **Hours:** 4
Min Charge for Trial: Yes **Hours:** 4
Cancellation Charge for Deps/Trial: Yes
Retainer Required: Yes, $1,000 (Refundable, One Time)
Procedure When Dep Exceeds Paid Time: Get payment before proceeding further
Expenses Marked Up: No
Expenses Billed For: Mileage, Airline Tickets, Lab/Testing, Photographs, Demonstrative Aids
Portal-to-Portal: Yes **1st-class Airfare:** Yes
Written Retainer Agreement: Yes
Terms: Lawyer is responsible for fee, not lawyer's client, Interest for delinquent accounts, Out-of-pocket expense policies, In-court testimony minimums, Retaining counsel pays all deposition charges, Fee schedules, Deposition minimum fee, Payment for preparation time
Failure to Pay Bill Last 5 Years; Retaining Counsel: No **Opposing Counsel (Deps):** No

Orthopedics
Court: $660 **Review/Prep:** $395 **Deps:** $1,000
Years Testifying: 5
Written Fee Schedule: Yes
Min Charge for Deps: Yes **Hours:** 4
Min Charge for Trial: Yes **Hours:** 4
Cancellation Charge for Deps/Trial: Yes
Retainer Required: Yes, $800 (Non-Refundable)
Procedure When Dep Exceeds Paid Time: Proceed without immediate payment
Expenses Marked Up: No
Expenses Billed For: Mileage, Airline Tickets
Portal-to-Portal: Yes **1st-class Airfare:** No
Written Retainer Agreement: No
Failure to Pay Bill Last 5 Years; Retaining Counsel: Yes **Opposing (Deps):** Yes

District of Columbia

Obstetrics & Gynecology
Court: $350 **Review/Prep:** $350 **Deps:** $350
Years Testifying: 10 **Majority:** Defendant
Written Fee Schedule: No
Min Charge for Deps: No **Hours:** 4
Min Charge for Trial: Yes **Hours:** 4
Cancellation Charge for Deps/Trial: Yes
Retainer Required: No
Expenses Marked Up: No
Expenses Billed For: Airline Tickets, Telephone Calls, Lab/Testing, Photographs
Portal-to-Portal: Yes **1st-class Airfare:** No
Written Retainer Agreement: No
Failure to Pay Bill Last 5 Years; Retaining Counsel: No **Opposing Counsel (Deps):** Yes

Pain Management/ Medicine/Anesthesiology
Court: $400 **Review/Prep:** $350 **Deps:** $400
Years Testifying: 5
Written Fee Schedule: Yes
Min Charge for Deps: Yes **Hours:** 4
Min Charge for Trial: Yes **Hours:** 4
Cancellation Charge for Deps/Trial: Yes
Retainer Required: Yes, $1,500 (Non-Refundable, Replenishable)
Procedure When Dep Exceeds Paid Time: Get payment before proceeding further
Expenses Marked Up: No
Expenses Billed For: Mileage, Airline Tickets
Portal-to-Portal: No **1st-class Airfare:** No
Written Retainer Agreement: No
Failure to Pay Bill Last 5 Years; Retaining Counsel: No **Opposing Counsel (Deps):** No

Psychiatry
Court: $450 **Review/Prep:** $450 **Deps:** $450
Years Testifying: 40 **Majority:** Defendant
Written Fee Schedule: Yes
Min Charge for Deps: No
Min Charge for Trial: No
Cancellation Charge for Deps/Trial: Yes
Retainer Required: Yes, Depends on case (Non-Refundable, One Time)
Procedure When Dep Exceeds Paid Time: Get payment before proceeding further
Expenses Marked Up: No
Expenses Billed For: Mileage, Airline Tickets
Portal-to-Portal: Yes **1st-class Airfare:** Yes
Written Retainer Agreement: Yes
Terms: Lawyer is responsible for fee, not lawyer's client, Interest for delinquent accounts, Out-of-pocket expense policies, Retaining counsel pays all deposition charges, Fee schedules, Portal-to-portal travel time, First class air travel
Failure to Pay Bill Last 5 Years; Retaining Counsel: Yes **Opposing (Deps):** Yes

Florida

Accident Reconstruction
Court: $150 **Review/Prep:** $500 **Deps:** $150
Years Testifying: 6
Written Fee Schedule: No
Min Charge for Deps: Yes **Hours:** 2
Min Charge for Trial: Yes **Hours:** 2
Cancellation Charge for Deps/Trial: No
Retainer Required: Yes, $1,000 (Non-Refundable, Replenishable)
Expenses Marked Up: No
Expenses Billed For: Airline Tickets, Photographs, Demonstrative Aids
Portal-to-Portal: Yes **1st-class Airfare:** No
Written Retainer Agreement: No
Failure to Pay Bill Last 5 Years; Retaining Counsel: No **Opposing Counsel (Deps):** No

Accident Reconstruction
Court: $250 **Review/Prep:** $250 **Deps:** $250
Years Testifying: 22
Written Fee Schedule: Yes
Min Charge for Deps: Yes
Min Charge for Trial: No
Cancellation Charge for Deps/Trial: No
Retainer Required: Yes, $1,500 (Non-Refundable, One Time)
Procedure When Dep Exceeds Paid Time: Proceed without immediate payment
Expenses Marked Up: Yes
Expenses Billed For: Mileage, Airline Tickets, Photocopies, Telephone Calls, Lab/Testing, Photographs, Demonstrative Aids
Portal-to-Portal: Yes **1st-class Airfare:** No
Written Retainer Agreement: Yes
Terms: Lawyer is responsible for fee, not lawyer's client, Interest for delinquent accounts, Out-of-pocket expense policies, In-court testimony minimums, Retaining counsel pays all deposition charges, Fee schedules, Portal-to-portal travel time, Attorney's fees if forced to sue for collection, Payment for preparation time
Failure to Pay Bill Last 5 Years; Retaining Counsel: Yes **Opposing (Deps):** Yes

Accident Reconstruction
Court: $175 **Review/Prep:** $150 **Deps:** $175
Years Testifying: 20 **Majority:** Plaintiff
Written Fee Schedule: Yes
Min Charge for Deps: Yes **Hours:** 3
Min Charge for Trial: Yes **Hours:** 3
Retainer Required: Yes, $2,500 (Non-Refundable, One Time)
Procedure When Dep Exceeds Paid Time: Proceed without immediate payment
Expenses Marked Up: No
Expenses Billed For: Airline Tickets, Lab/Testing, Photographs, Demonstrative Aids
Portal-to-Portal: Yes **1st-class Airfare:** No
Written Retainer Agreement: Yes
Terms: Lawyer is responsible for fee, not lawyer's client, Interest for delinquent accounts, Out-of-pocket expense policies, In-court testimony minimums, Retaining counsel pays all deposition charges, Fee schedules, Portal-to-portal travel time, Attorney's fees if forced to sue for collection, Deposition minimum fee
Failure to Pay Bill Last 5 Years; Retaining Counsel: Yes **Opposing (Deps):** Yes

Anesthesiology
Court: $1,000 **Review/Prep:** $500 **Deps:** $500
Years Testifying: 5
Written Fee Schedule: Yes
Min Charge for Deps: No
Min Charge for Trial: No
Cancellation Charge for Deps/Trial: No
Retainer Required: No
Procedure When Dep Exceeds Paid Time: Proceed without immediate payment
Expenses Billed For: Airline Tickets
Portal-to-Portal: Yes **1st-class Airfare:** No
Written Retainer Agreement: No
Failure to Pay Bill Last 5 Years; Retaining Counsel: No **Opposing Counsel (Deps):** No

Anesthesiology
Court: $300 **Review/Prep:** $300 **Deps:** $300
Years Testifying: 3 **Majority:** Defendant
Written Fee Schedule: Yes
Min Charge for Deps: No
Min Charge for Trial: No
Cancellation Charge for Deps/Trial: No
Retainer Required: No
Expenses Marked Up: No
Expenses Billed For: Mileage, Airline Tickets
Portal-to-Portal: Yes **1st-class Airfare:** No
Written Retainer Agreement: Yes
Terms: Lawyer is responsible for fee, not lawyer's client, Interest for delinquent accounts, Portal-to-portal travel time, Payment for preparation time
Failure to Pay Bill Last 5 Years; Retaining Counsel: No **Opposing Counsel (Deps):** No

Automotive
Court: $300 **Review/Prep:** $250 **Deps:** $300
Years Testifying: 22
Written Fee Schedule: No
Min Charge for Deps: No
Min Charge for Trial: No
Cancellation Charge for Deps/Trial: No
Retainer Required: Yes, $5,000 (Refundable, One Time)
Expenses Marked Up: No
Expenses Billed For: Airline Tickets
Portal-to-Portal: No **1st-class Airfare:** No
Failure to Pay Bill Last 5 Years; Retaining Counsel: No **Opposing Counsel (Deps):** No

Automotive, Collisions
Court: $150 **Review/Prep:** $150 **Deps:** $150
Years Testifying: 10 **Majority:** Plaintiff
Written Fee Schedule: Yes
Min Charge for Deps: Yes **Hours:** 8
Min Charge for Trial: Yes **Hours:** 8
Cancellation Charge for Deps/Trial: No
Retainer Required: Yes, $750 (Non-Refundable, One Time)
Expenses Marked Up: Yes
Expenses Billed For: Photographs, Demonstrative Aids
Portal-to-Portal: Yes **1st-class Airfare:** No
Written Retainer Agreement: Yes
Terms: Out-of-pocket expense policies, In-court testimony minimums, Retaining counsel pays all deposition charges, Fee schedules, Payment for preparation time
Failure to Pay Bill Last 5 Years; Retaining Counsel: Yes **Opposing (Deps):** Yes

Automotive, Tires
Court: $450 **Review/Prep:** $450 **Deps:** $450
Years Testifying: 4 **Majority:** Defendant
Written Fee Schedule: No
Min Charge for Deps: No
Min Charge for Trial: No
Cancellation Charge for Deps/Trial: No
Retainer Required: Yes, $5,000 (Non-Refundable, One Time)
Expenses Marked Up: No
Expenses Billed For: Mileage, Airline Tickets, Photocopies, Telephone Calls, Lab/Testing, Photographs, Demonstrative Aids
Portal-to-Portal: Yes **1st-class Airfare:** Yes
Written Retainer Agreement: Yes
Terms: Lawyer is responsible for fee, not lawyer's client, Interest for delinquent accounts, Out-of-pocket expense policies, Retaining counsel pays all deposition charges, Portal-to-portal travel time, Attorney's fees if forced to sue for collection, Payment for preparation time, First class air travel
Failure to Pay Bill Last 5 Years; Retaining Counsel: No **Opposing Counsel (Deps):** No

Cardiology
Court: $400 **Review/Prep:** $275 **Deps:** $400
Years Testifying: 3 **Majority:** Plaintiff
Written Fee Schedule: Yes
Min Charge for Deps: Yes **Hours:** 6
Min Charge for Trial: Yes **Hours:** 6
Cancellation Charge for Deps/Trial: Yes
Retainer Required: No
Expenses Marked Up: No
Expenses Billed For: Mileage, Airline Tickets
Portal-to-Portal: No **1st-class Airfare:** No
Written Retainer Agreement: No
Failure to Pay Bill Last 5 Years; Retaining Counsel: No **Opposing Counsel (Deps):** No

Chiropractic/Orthopedics
Court: $400 **Review/Prep:** $175 **Deps:** $400
Years Testifying: 10
Written Fee Schedule: Yes
Min Charge for Deps: Yes **Hours:** 1
Min Charge for Trial: Yes **Hours:** 1
Cancellation Charge for Deps/Trial: Yes
Retainer Required: Yes, $400 (Non-Refundable, One Time)
Procedure When Dep Exceeds Paid Time: Proceed without immediate payment
Expenses Marked Up: No

Expenses Billed For: Mileage, Airline Tickets, Photocopies
Portal-to-Portal: Yes **1st-class Airfare:** Yes
Written Retainer Agreement: No
Failure to Pay Bill Last 5 Years; Retaining Counsel: No **Opposing Counsel (Deps):** No

Chiropractic
Court: $500 **Review/Prep:** $300 **Deps:** $300
Years Testifying: 22 **Majority:** Plaintiff
Written Fee Schedule: Yes
Min Charge for Deps: Yes **Hours:** 1
Min Charge for Trial: Yes **Hours:** 1
Cancellation Charge for Deps/Trial: Yes
Retainer Required: Yes, $500 (Refundable, One Time)
Procedure When Dep Exceeds Paid Time: Proceed without immediate payment
Expenses Marked Up: Yes
Expenses Billed For: Mileage, Airline Tickets, Photocopies, Telephone Calls, Photographs, Demonstrative Aids
Portal-to-Portal: Yes **1st-class Airfare:** No
Written Retainer Agreement: No
Failure to Pay Bill Last 5 Years; Retaining Counsel: No **Opposing Counsel (Deps):** No

Chiropractic
Court: $350 **Review/Prep:** $350 **Deps:** $350
Years Testifying: 10 **Majority:** Defendant
Written Fee Schedule: No
Min Charge for Deps: Yes **Hours:** 3
Min Charge for Trial: Yes **Hours:** 3
Cancellation Charge for Deps/Trial: Yes
Retainer Required: Yes, $700 (Refundable, Replenishable)
Procedure When Dep Exceeds Paid Time: Get payment before proceeding further
Expenses Marked Up: No
Expenses Billed For: Photocopies, Telephone Calls
Portal-to-Portal: Yes **1st-class Airfare:** No
Written Retainer Agreement: Yes
Failure to Pay Bill Last 5 Years; Retaining Counsel: Yes **Opposing Counsel (Deps):** No

Chiropractic
Court: $400 **Review/Prep:** $200 **Deps:** $400
Years Testifying: 40
Written Fee Schedule: Yes
Min Charge for Deps: Yes **Hours:** 1
Min Charge for Trial: Yes **Hours:** 1
Cancellation Charge for Deps/Trial: Yes
Retainer Required: No
Expenses Marked Up: No
Expenses Billed For: Mileage, Airline Tickets, Photocopies, Telephone Calls, Lab/Testing
Portal-to-Portal: Yes **1st-class Airfare:** No
Written Retainer Agreement: Yes
Terms: Lawyer is responsible for fee, not lawyer's client, Fee schedules
Failure to Pay Bill Last 5 Years; Retaining Counsel: No **Opposing Counsel (Deps):** No

Chiropractic
Court: $500 **Review/Prep:** $200 **Deps:** $500
Years Testifying: 13
Written Fee Schedule: No
Min Charge for Deps: Yes **Hours:** 2
Min Charge for Trial: Yes **Hours:** 2
Cancellation Charge for Deps/Trial: Yes
Retainer Required: Yes, $500 (Refundable, One Time)
Procedure When Dep Exceeds Paid Time: Proceed without immediate payment
Expenses Marked Up: No
Portal-to-Portal: Yes **1st-class Airfare:** No
Written Retainer Agreement: No
Failure to Pay Bill Last 5 Years; Retaining Counsel: No **Opposing Counsel (Deps):** No

Chiropractic
Court: $350 **Review/Prep:** $350 **Deps:** $350
Years Testifying: 20
Written Fee Schedule: No
Min Charge for Deps: Yes **Hours:** 3
Min Charge for Trial: Yes **Hours:** 3
Cancellation Charge for Deps/Trial: Yes
Retainer Required: Yes, $350 (Refundable, One Time)
Expenses Marked Up: No
Expenses Billed For: Mileage, Airline Tickets, Photocopies, Telephone Calls, Demonstrative Aids
Portal-to-Portal: Yes **1st-class Airfare:** No
Written Retainer Agreement: Yes
Terms: Lawyer is responsible for fee, not lawyer's client, Out-of-pocket expense policies, In-court testimony minimums, Retaining counsel pays all deposition charges, Fee schedules, Portal-to-portal travel time, Attorney's fees if forced to sue for collection, Deposition minimum fee, Payment for preparation time
Failure to Pay Bill Last 5 Years; Retaining Counsel: No **Opposing Counsel (Deps):** No

Chiropractic
Court: $500 **Review/Prep:** $400 **Deps:** $450
Years Testifying: 23
Written Fee Schedule: Yes
Min Charge for Deps: Yes **Hours:** 1
Min Charge for Trial: Yes **Hours:** 1
Cancellation Charge for Deps/Trial: Yes
Retainer Required: Yes, $500 (Refundable, Replenishable)
Procedure When Dep Exceeds Paid Time: Get payment before proceeding further
Expenses Marked Up: Yes
Expenses Billed For: Mileage, Airline Tickets, Photocopies, Telephone Calls, Lab/Testing, Photographs, Demonstrative Aids
Portal-to-Portal: Yes **1st-class Airfare:** No
Written Retainer Agreement: Yes
Terms: Lawyer is responsible for fee, not lawyer's client, Interest for delinquent accounts, Out-of-pocket expense policies, In-court testimony minimums, Retaining counsel pays all deposition charges, Fee schedules, Portal-to-portal travel time, Attorney's fees if forced to sue for collection, Deposition minimum fee, Payment for preparation time
Failure to Pay Bill Last 5 Years; Retaining Counsel: No **Opposing Counsel (Deps):** No

Chiropractic
Court: $350 **Review/Prep:** $100 **Deps:** $350
Years Testifying: 15 **Majority:** Plaintiff
Written Fee Schedule: Yes
Min Charge for Deps: Yes **Hours:** 1
Min Charge for Trial: Yes **Hours:** 1
Cancellation Charge for Deps/Trial: Yes
Retainer Required: Yes, $350 (Refundable, One Time)
Procedure When Dep Exceeds Paid Time: Get payment before proceeding further
Expenses Billed For: Mileage, Airline Tickets, Photocopies
Portal-to-Portal: Yes **1st-class Airfare:** No
Written Retainer Agreement: Yes
Terms: Lawyer is responsible for fee, not lawyer's client, In-court testimony minimums, Retaining counsel pays all deposition charges, Fee schedules, Portal-to-portal travel time, Deposition minimum fee
Failure to Pay Bill Last 5 Years; Retaining Counsel: Yes **Opposing Counsel (Deps):** No

Coatings/Cement
Court: $175 **Review/Prep:** $150 **Deps:** $175
Years Testifying: 8
Written Fee Schedule: Yes
Min Charge for Deps: Yes **Hours:** 4
Min Charge for Trial: Yes **Hours:** 4
Cancellation Charge for Deps/Trial: No
Retainer Required: Yes, 25% (Refundable, Replenishable)
Expenses Marked Up: Yes
Expenses Billed For: Mileage, Airline Tickets, Photocopies, Telephone Calls, Lab/Testing, Photographs, Demonstrative Aids
Portal-to-Portal: Yes **1st-class Airfare:** No
Written Retainer Agreement: No
Failure to Pay Bill Last 5 Years; Retaining Counsel: Yes **Opposing (Deps):** Yes

Construction/Mold
Court: $275 **Review/Prep:** $150 **Deps:** $275
Years Testifying: 18
Written Fee Schedule: Yes

Min Charge for Deps: Yes **Hours:** 4
Min Charge for Trial: Yes **Hours:** 4
Cancellation Charge for Deps/Trial: Yes
Retainer Required: Yes, Depends on case (Non-Refundable, One Time)
Procedure When Dep Exceeds Paid Time: Proceed without immediate payment
Expenses Marked Up: Yes
Expenses Billed For: Airline Tickets, Lab/Testing, Photographs
Portal-to-Portal: Yes **1st-class Airfare:** No
Written Retainer Agreement: No
Failure to Pay Bill Last 5 Years; Retaining Counsel: No **Opposing Counsel (Deps):** No

Construction

Court: $200 **Review/Prep:** $100 **Deps:** $200
Years Testifying: 50
Written Fee Schedule: Yes
Min Charge for Deps: No
Min Charge for Trial: No
Cancellation Charge for Deps/Trial: No
Retainer Required: Depends
Expenses Marked Up: No
Expenses Billed For: Mileage, Airline Tickets, Photocopies, Telephone Calls, Lab/Testing, Photographs, Demonstrative Aids
Portal-to-Portal: Yes **1st-class Airfare:** No
Written Retainer Agreement: Yes
Terms: Retaining counsel pays all deposition charges, Fee schedules, Portal-to-portal travel time, Payment for preparation time
Failure to Pay Bill Last 5 Years; Retaining Counsel: No **Opposing Counsel (Deps):** No

Critical Care Medicine/Compliance

Court: $240 **Review/Prep:** $120 **Deps:** $240
Years Testifying: 1 **Majority:** Plaintiff
Written Fee Schedule: Yes
Min Charge for Deps: No
Min Charge for Trial: No
Cancellation Charge for Deps/Trial: Yes
Retainer Required: Yes, $1,000 (Non-Refundable, One Time)
Procedure When Dep Exceeds Paid Time: Proceed without immediate payment
Expenses Marked Up: No
Expenses Billed For: Airline Tickets, Photocopies, Telephone Calls
Portal-to-Portal: No **1st-class Airfare:** No
Written Retainer Agreement: Yes
Terms: In-court testimony minimums, Retaining counsel pays all deposition charges, Fee schedules, Deposition minimum fee, Payment for preparation time
Failure to Pay Bill Last 5 Years; Retaining Counsel: No **Opposing Counsel (Deps):** No

Damages, Business/Taxation

Court: $210 **Review/Prep:** $210 **Deps:** $210
Years Testifying: 10 **Majority:** Defendant
Written Fee Schedule: Yes
Min Charge for Deps: No
Min Charge for Trial: No
Cancellation Charge for Deps/Trial: Yes
Retainer Required: Yes, $850 (Refundable, One Time)
Procedure When Dep Exceeds Paid Time: Get payment before proceeding further
Expenses Marked Up: No
Expenses Billed For: Mileage, Airline Tickets, Photocopies, Telephone Calls
Portal-to-Portal: Yes **1st-class Airfare:** No
Written Retainer Agreement: Yes
Terms: Interest for delinquent accounts, Out-of-pocket expense policies, Retaining counsel pays all deposition charges, Fee schedules, Portal-to-portal travel time, Attorney's fees if forced to sue for collection
Failure to Pay Bill Last 5 Years; Retaining Counsel: No **Opposing Counsel (Deps):** Yes

Damages, Business

Court: $225 **Review/Prep:** $225 **Deps:** $225
Years Testifying: 15
Written Fee Schedule: Yes
Min Charge for Deps: No
Min Charge for Trial: No
Cancellation Charge for Deps/Trial: No
Retainer Required: Yes, $7,500 (Refundable, Replenishable)
Expenses Marked Up: No
Expenses Billed For: Mileage, Airline Tickets, Photocopies, Telephone Calls, Lab/Testing, Photographs, Demonstrative Aids
Portal-to-Portal: Yes **1st-class Airfare:** No
Written Retainer Agreement: Yes
Terms: Interest for delinquent accounts, Out-of-pocket expense policies, Retaining counsel pays all deposition charges, Fee schedules, Attorney's fees if forced to sue for collection, Arbitration Clause, Indemnification Clause
Failure to Pay Bill Last 5 Years; Retaining Counsel: No **Opposing Counsel (Deps):** No

Document Examiner

Court: $350
Years Testifying: 20
Written Fee Schedule: No
Min Charge for Deps: Yes **Hours:** 1
Min Charge for Trial: Yes **Hours:** 1
Cancellation Charge for Deps/Trial: No
Retainer Required: Yes, $2,250 (Non-Refundable, One Time)
Expenses Marked Up: No
Expenses Billed For: Mileage, Airline Tickets, Photocopies, Lab/Testing, Photographs, Demonstrative Aids
Portal-to-Portal: Yes **1st-class Airfare:** No
Written Retainer Agreement: Yes
Terms: Interest for delinquent accounts, Out-of-pocket expense policies, In-court testimony minimums, Retaining counsel pays all deposition charges, Portal-to-portal travel time, Attorney's fees if forced to sue for collection, Deposition minimum fee, Payment for preparation time
Failure to Pay Bill Last 5 Years; Retaining Counsel: No **Opposing Counsel (Deps):** No

Economics

Court: $290 **Review/Prep:** $150 **Deps:** $290
Majority: Plaintiff
Written Fee Schedule: Yes
Min Charge for Deps: No
Min Charge for Trial: No
Cancellation Charge for Deps/Trial: No
Retainer Required: Yes, $1,000 (Refundable, Replenishable)
Procedure When Dep Exceeds Paid Time: Send payment within week, get opposing counsel to agree.
Expenses Marked Up: No
Expenses Billed For: Airline Tickets, Photocopies, Telephone Calls
Portal-to-Portal: Yes **1st-class Airfare:** No
Written Retainer Agreement: Yes
Terms: Lawyer is responsible for fee, not lawyer's client, Interest for delinquent accounts, Out-of-pocket expense policies, In-court testimony minimums, Retaining counsel pays all deposition charges, Fee schedules, Portal-to-portal travel time, Attorney's fees if forced to sue for collection, Payment for preparation time, Indemnity clause
Failure to Pay Bill Last 5 Years; Retaining Counsel: Yes **Opposing Counsel (Deps):** No

Economics

Court: $350 **Review/Prep:** $315 **Deps:** $350
Years Testifying: 35
Written Fee Schedule: Yes
Min Charge for Deps: Yes **Hours:** 2
Min Charge for Trial: Yes **Hours:** 2
Cancellation Charge for Deps/Trial: Yes
Retainer Required: Yes, $2,500 (Non-Refundable, One Time)
Procedure When Dep Exceeds Paid Time: Proceed without immediate payment
Expenses Marked Up: Yes
Expenses Billed For: Mileage, Airline Tickets, Photocopies, Telephone Calls, Photographs, Demonstrative Aids
Portal-to-Portal: Yes **1st-class Airfare:** No
Written Retainer Agreement: Yes
Terms: Lawyer is responsible for fee, not lawyer's client, Interest for delinquent accounts, Out-of-pocket expense policies, In-court testimony minimums, Retaining counsel

pays all deposition charges, Fee schedules, Portal-to-portal travel time, Attorney's fees if forced to sue for collection, Deposition minimum fee, Payment for preparation time
Failure to Pay Bill Last 5 Years; Retaining Counsel: Yes **Opposing (Deps):** Yes

Economics
Court: $250 **Review/Prep:** $250 **Deps:** $250
Years Testifying: 18 **Majority:** Plaintiff
Written Fee Schedule: Yes
Min Charge for Deps: No
Min Charge for Trial: No
Cancellation Charge for Deps/Trial: No
Retainer Required: Yes, $4,000 (Refundable, One Time)
Expenses Marked Up: No
Expenses Billed For: Mileage, Airline Tickets, Photocopies, Demonstrative Aids
Portal-to-Portal: Yes
Written Retainer Agreement: Yes
Terms: Interest for delinquent accounts, Out-of-pocket expense policies, Retaining counsel pays all deposition charges, Fee schedules
Failure to Pay Bill Last 5 Years; Retaining Counsel: No **Opposing Counsel (Deps):** No

Economics/Employment
Court: $350 **Review/Prep:** $350 **Deps:** $350
Years Testifying: 15 **Majority:** Defendant
Written Fee Schedule: Yes
Min Charge for Deps: No
Min Charge for Trial: No
Cancellation Charge for Deps/Trial: No
Retainer Required: No
Expenses Marked Up: No
Expenses Billed For: Mileage, Airline Tickets, Telephone Calls
Portal-to-Portal: No **1st-class Airfare:** No
Written Retainer Agreement: Yes
Terms: Out-of-pocket expense policies, Fee schedules, Payment for preparation time
Failure to Pay Bill Last 5 Years; Retaining Counsel: Yes **Opposing (Deps):** Yes

Emergency Medicine
Court: $500 **Review/Prep:** $250 **Deps:** $350
Years Testifying: 17
Written Fee Schedule: Yes
Min Charge for Deps: Yes **Hours:** 1
Min Charge for Trial: Yes **Hours:** 1
Cancellation Charge for Deps/Trial: No
Retainer Required: Yes, $250 (Non-Refundable, One Time)
Expenses Marked Up: No
Expenses Billed For: Airline Tickets
Portal-to-Portal: Yes **1st-class Airfare:** No
Written Retainer Agreement: No
Failure to Pay Bill Last 5 Years; Retaining Counsel: Yes **Opposing (Deps):** Yes

Engineering/Accident Reconstruction
Court: $250 **Review/Prep:** $175 **Deps:** $250
Years Testifying: 5
Written Fee Schedule: Yes
Min Charge for Deps: No
Min Charge for Trial: No
Cancellation Charge for Deps/Trial: No
Retainer Required: Yes, $1,500 (Refundable, One Time)
Expenses Marked Up: Yes
Expenses Billed For: Mileage, Airline Tickets, Photocopies, Photographs, Demonstrative Aids
Portal-to-Portal: Yes **1st-class Airfare:** No
Written Retainer Agreement: Yes
Terms: Lawyer is responsible for fee, not lawyer's client, Interest for delinquent accounts, Out-of-pocket expense policies, Retaining counsel pays all deposition charges, Fee schedules, Portal-to-portal travel time, Attorney's fees if forced to sue for collection, Payment for preparation time
Failure to Pay Bill Last 5 Years; Retaining Counsel: No **Opposing Counsel (Deps):** No

Engineering
Court: $250 **Review/Prep:** $175 **Deps:** $250
Years Testifying: 30 **Majority:** Plaintiff
Written Fee Schedule: Yes
Min Charge for Deps: Yes **Hours:** 4
Min Charge for Trial: Yes **Hours:** 4
Cancellation Charge for Deps/Trial: No
Retainer Required: Yes, $1,500 (Refundable, One Time)
Expenses Marked Up: No
Expenses Billed For: Airline Tickets, Photographs, Demonstrative Aids
Portal-to-Portal: Yes **1st-class Airfare:** No
Written Retainer Agreement: No
Failure to Pay Bill Last 5 Years; Retaining Counsel: No **Opposing Counsel (Deps):** No

Engineering, Civil
Court: $250 **Review/Prep:** $200 **Deps:** $250
Years Testifying: 30
Written Fee Schedule: Yes
Min Charge for Deps: Yes **Hours:** 2
Min Charge for Trial: Yes **Hours:** 2
Cancellation Charge for Deps/Trial: No
Retainer Required: Yes, $2,000 (Non-Refundable, One Time)
Procedure When Dep Exceeds Paid Time: Proceed without immediate payment
Expenses Marked Up: No
Expenses Billed For: Mileage, Airline Tickets, Photocopies, Telephone Calls, Lab/Testing, Photographs, Demonstrative Aids
Portal-to-Portal: Yes **1st-class Airfare:** No
Written Retainer Agreement: Yes
Terms: Lawyer is responsible for fee, not lawyer's client, In-court testimony minimums, Retaining counsel pays all deposition charges, Fee schedules, Deposition minimum fee
Failure to Pay Bill Last 5 Years; Retaining Counsel: No **Opposing Counsel (Deps):** No

Engineering, Environmental
Court: $200 **Review/Prep:** $200 **Deps:** $200
Years Testifying: 15 **Majority:** Defendant
Written Fee Schedule: No
Min Charge for Deps: No
Min Charge for Trial: No
Cancellation Charge for Deps/Trial: No
Retainer Required: No
Expenses Marked Up: Yes
Expenses Billed For: Mileage, Airline Tickets, Photocopies, Telephone Calls, Lab/Testing, Photographs, Demonstrative Aids
Portal-to-Portal: Yes **1st-class Airfare:** No
Written Retainer Agreement: Yes
Terms: Lawyer is responsible for fee, not lawyer's client, Interest for delinquent accounts, Out-of-pocket expense policies, Fee schedules, Portal-to-portal travel time, Payment for preparation time
Failure to Pay Bill Last 5 Years; Retaining Counsel: No **Opposing Counsel (Deps):** No

Engineering, Forensic
Court: $195 **Review/Prep:** $195 **Deps:** $195
Years Testifying: 7
Written Fee Schedule: Yes
Min Charge for Deps: Yes
Min Charge for Trial: No
Cancellation Charge for Deps/Trial: No
Retainer Required: Yes, $2,500 (Refundable, Replenishable)
Procedure When Dep Exceeds Paid Time: Proceed without immediate payment
Expenses Marked Up: Yes
Expenses Billed For: Mileage, Airline Tickets, Photocopies, Lab/Testing, Photographs, Demonstrative Aids
Portal-to-Portal: Yes **1st-class Airfare:** No
Written Retainer Agreement: Yes
Terms: Lawyer is responsible for fee, not lawyer's client, Interest for delinquent accounts, Out-of-pocket expense policies, Retaining counsel pays all deposition charges, Fee schedules, Portal-to-portal travel time, Attorney's fees if forced to sue for collection, Deposition minimum fee, Payment for preparation time
Failure to Pay Bill Last 5 Years; Retaining Counsel: Yes **Opposing (Deps):** Yes

Engineering, Metallurgical
Court: $125 **Review/Prep:** $80 **Deps:** $115
Years Testifying: 2 **Majority:** Defendant
Written Fee Schedule: No
Min Charge for Deps: No
Min Charge for Trial: No
Cancellation Charge for Deps/Trial: No
Retainer Required: No
Expenses Marked Up: No
Expenses Billed For: Mileage, Airline Tickets, Photocopies, Telephone Calls, Lab/Testing, Photographs, Demonstrative Aids
Portal-to-Portal: Yes **1st-class Airfare:** No
Written Retainer Agreement: No
Failure to Pay Bill Last 5 Years; Retaining Counsel: No **Opposing Counsel (Deps):** No

Engineering, Structural
Court: $350 **Review/Prep:** $350 **Deps:** $350
Years Testifying: 25
Written Fee Schedule: No
Min Charge for Deps: No
Min Charge for Trial: No
Cancellation Charge for Deps/Trial: No
Retainer Required: Yes, $2,500 (One Time)
Procedure When Dep Exceeds Paid Time: Proceed without immediate payment
Expenses Marked Up: No
Expenses Billed For: Mileage, Airline Tickets, Photocopies, Telephone Calls, Lab/Testing, Photographs, Demonstrative Aids
Portal-to-Portal: Yes **1st-class Airfare:** No
Written Retainer Agreement: No
Failure to Pay Bill Last 5 Years; Retaining Counsel: No **Opposing Counsel (Deps):** No

Family Practice
Court: $850 **Review/Prep:** $300 **Deps:** $600
Years Testifying: 10 **Majority:** Plaintiff
Written Fee Schedule: Yes
Min Charge for Deps: Yes **Hours:** 2
Min Charge for Trial: Yes **Hours:** 2
Cancellation Charge for Deps/Trial: Yes
Retainer Required: Yes, $1,000 (Partially Refundable, One Time)
Procedure When Dep Exceeds Paid Time: Proceed without immediate payment
Expenses Marked Up: No
Portal-to-Portal: Yes **1st-class Airfare:** No
Written Retainer Agreement: No
Failure to Pay Bill Last 5 Years; Retaining Counsel: No **Opposing Counsel (Deps):** No

Infectious Diseases
Court: $500 **Review/Prep:** $500 **Deps:** $500
Years Testifying: 15
Written Fee Schedule: Yes
Min Charge for Deps: Yes **Hours:** 3
Min Charge for Trial: Yes **Hours:** 3
Cancellation Charge for Deps/Trial: Yes
Retainer Required: Yes, $500 (Non-Refundable, One Time)
Procedure When Dep Exceeds Paid Time: Proceed without immediate payment
Expenses Marked Up: No
Expenses Billed For: Mileage, Airline Tickets, Lab/Testing
Portal-to-Portal: Yes **1st-class Airfare:** No
Written Retainer Agreement: No
Failure to Pay Bill Last 5 Years; Retaining Counsel: Yes **Opposing (Deps):** Yes

Insurance
Court: $300 **Review/Prep:** $260 **Deps:** $300
Years Testifying: 20 **Majority:** Plaintiff
Written Fee Schedule: Yes
Min Charge for Deps: No
Min Charge for Trial: No
Cancellation Charge for Deps/Trial: No
Retainer Required: Yes, $1,750 (Refundable, Replenishable)
Expenses Marked Up: No
Expenses Billed For: Airline Tickets, Demonstrative Aids
Portal-to-Portal: Yes **1st-class Airfare:** No
Written Retainer Agreement: Yes
Terms: Lawyer is responsible for fee, not lawyer's client, Interest for delinquent accounts, Out-of-pocket expense policies, Retaining counsel pays all deposition charges, Fee schedules, Portal-to-portal travel time, Attorney's fees if forced to sue for collection, Payment for preparation time, Disclaimers
Failure to Pay Bill Last 5 Years; Retaining Counsel: No **Opposing Counsel (Deps):** No

Insurance
Court: $250 **Review/Prep:** $250 **Deps:** $250
Years Testifying: 30
Written Fee Schedule: No
Min Charge for Deps: Yes **Hours:** 2
Min Charge for Trial: Yes **Hours:** 2
Cancellation Charge for Deps/Trial: No
Retainer Required: Yes, $2,500 (Refundable, One Time)
Procedure When Dep Exceeds Paid Time: Proceed without immediate payment
Expenses Marked Up: No
Expenses Billed For: Mileage, Airline Tickets, Telephone Calls
Portal-to-Portal: Yes **1st-class Airfare:** Yes
Written Retainer Agreement: No
Failure to Pay Bill Last 5 Years; Retaining Counsel: Yes **Opposing Counsel (Deps):** No

Insurance
Court: $250 **Review/Prep:** $250 **Deps:** $250
Years Testifying: 7
Written Fee Schedule: Yes
Min Charge for Deps: No
Min Charge for Trial: No
Cancellation Charge for Deps/Trial: No
Retainer Required: Yes, $2,500 (Refundable, One Time)
Procedure When Dep Exceeds Paid Time: Proceed without immediate payment
Expenses Marked Up: No
Expenses Billed For: Mileage, Airline Tickets, Photocopies, Telephone Calls
Portal-to-Portal: Yes **1st-class Airfare:** No
Written Retainer Agreement: Yes
Terms: Lawyer is responsible for fee, not lawyer's client, Interest for delinquent accounts, Out-of-pocket expense policies, Retaining counsel pays all deposition charges, Fee schedules, Portal-to-portal travel time, Attorney's fees if forced to sue for collection, Payment for preparation time
Failure to Pay Bill Last 5 Years; Retaining Counsel: Yes **Opposing Counsel (Deps):** No

Internal Medicine/Gastroenterology
Court: $600 **Review/Prep:** $375 **Deps:** $600
Years Testifying: 15
Written Fee Schedule: Yes
Min Charge for Deps: Yes **Hours:** 8
Min Charge for Trial: Yes **Hours:** 8
Cancellation Charge for Deps/Trial: Yes
Retainer Required: Yes, $1,500 (Non-Refundable, One Time)
Procedure When Dep Exceeds Paid Time: Get payment before proceeding further
Expenses Marked Up: No
Expenses Billed For: Mileage, Airline Tickets, Photocopies, Telephone Calls, Lab/Testing, Photographs, Demonstrative Aids
Portal-to-Portal: Yes **1st-class Airfare:** Yes
Written Retainer Agreement: Yes
Terms: Lawyer is responsible for fee, not lawyer's client, Out-of-pocket expense policies, In-court testimony minimums, Retaining counsel pays all deposition charges, Fee schedules, Portal-to-portal travel time, Deposition minimum fee, Payment for preparation time, First class air travel
Failure to Pay Bill Last 5 Years; Retaining Counsel: Yes **Opposing Counsel (Deps):** No

Internal Medicine/Geriatrics
Court: $500 **Review/Prep:** $350 **Deps:** $500
Years Testifying: 3 **Majority:** Plaintiff
Written Fee Schedule: No
Min Charge for Deps: No
Min Charge for Trial: No
Cancellation Charge for Deps/Trial: No
Retainer Required: Yes, $1,500 (Refundable)
Expenses Marked Up: No
Expenses Billed For: Airline Tickets
Portal-to-Portal: Yes **1st-class Airfare:** No

Written Retainer Agreement: No
Failure to Pay Bill Last 5 Years; Retaining Counsel: No **Opposing Counsel (Deps):** Yes

Internal Medicine
Court: $300 **Review/Prep:** $300 **Deps:** $300
Years Testifying: 20
Written Fee Schedule: No
Min Charge for Deps: Yes **Hours:** 1
Min Charge for Trial: Yes **Hours:** 1
Cancellation Charge for Deps/Trial: Yes
Retainer Required: Yes, $600 (Non-Refundable, Replenishable)
Procedure When Dep Exceeds Paid Time: Proceed without immediate payment
Expenses Marked Up: No
Expenses Billed For: Airline Tickets
Portal-to-Portal: Yes **1st-class Airfare:** No
Written Retainer Agreement: Yes
Terms: Lawyer is responsible for fee, not lawyer's client, Interest for delinquent accounts, Out-of-pocket expense policies, In-court testimony minimums, Retaining counsel pays all deposition charges, Attorney's fees if forced to sue for collection
Failure to Pay Bill Last 5 Years; Retaining Counsel: Yes **Opposing (Deps):** Yes

Lighting
Court: $350 **Review/Prep:** $150 **Deps:** $275
Years Testifying: 6 **Majority:** Plaintiff
Written Fee Schedule: Yes
Min Charge for Deps: No **Hours:** 4
Min Charge for Trial: Yes **Hours:** 4
Cancellation Charge for Deps/Trial: No
Retainer Required: Yes, $500 (Refundable, One Time)
Expenses Marked Up: No
Expenses Billed For: Airline Tickets, Demonstrative Aids
Portal-to-Portal: Yes **1st-class Airfare:** No
Written Retainer Agreement: Yes
Terms: Lawyer is responsible for fee, not lawyer's client, Out-of-pocket expense policies, In-court testimony minimums, Retaining counsel pays all deposition charges, Portal-to-portal travel time, Payment for preparation time
Failure to Pay Bill Last 5 Years; Retaining Counsel: No **Opposing Counsel (Deps):** Yes

Marine
Court: $150 **Review/Prep:** $95 **Deps:** $125
Years Testifying: 10
Written Fee Schedule: Yes
Min Charge for Deps: Yes **Hours:** 4
Min Charge for Trial: Yes **Hours:** 4
Cancellation Charge for Deps/Trial: Yes
Retainer Required: Yes, Depends on case (Refundable, Replenishable)
Expenses Marked Up: Yes
Expenses Billed For: Mileage, Airline Tickets, Telephone Calls, Lab/Testing, Photographs, Demonstrative Aids
Portal-to-Portal: Yes **1st-class Airfare:** No
Written Retainer Agreement: Yes
Terms: Lawyer is responsible for fee, not lawyer's client, Interest for delinquent accounts, Retaining counsel pays all deposition charges, Fee schedules, Attorney's fees if forced to sue for collection
Failure to Pay Bill Last 5 Years; Retaining Counsel: Yes **Opposing (Deps):** Yes

Marine
Court: $200 **Review/Prep:** $75 **Deps:** $150
Years Testifying: 3
Written Fee Schedule: Yes
Min Charge for Deps: Yes **Hours:** 2
Min Charge for Trial: Yes **Hours:** 2
Cancellation Charge for Deps/Trial: No
Retainer Required: Yes, $2,000 (Refundable, One Time)
Procedure When Dep Exceeds Paid Time: Proceed without immediate payment
Expenses Marked Up: No
Expenses Billed For: Mileage, Airline Tickets, Photocopies, Telephone Calls, Lab/Testing, Photographs, Demonstrative Aids
Portal-to-Portal: Yes **1st-class Airfare:** Yes
Written Retainer Agreement: Yes
Terms: Lawyer is responsible for fee, not lawyer's client, Interest for delinquent accounts, Out-of-pocket expense policies, In-court testimony minimums, Retaining counsel pays all deposition charges, Fee schedules, Portal-to-portal travel time, Attorney's fees if forced to sue for collection, Deposition minimum fee, Payment for preparation time, First class air travel
Failure to Pay Bill Last 5 Years; Retaining Counsel: No **Opposing Counsel (Deps):** No

Medical Doctor
Court: $450 **Review/Prep:** $250 **Deps:** $450
Years Testifying: 15 **Majority:** Defendant
Written Fee Schedule: No
Min Charge for Deps: No **Hours:** 2
Min Charge for Trial: Yes **Hours:** 2
Cancellation Charge for Deps/Trial: Yes
Retainer Required: Yes, $4,500 (Refundable, Replenishable)
Procedure When Dep Exceeds Paid Time: Get payment before proceeding further
Expenses Marked Up: No
Expenses Billed For: Mileage, Airline Tickets, Lab/Testing, Photographs, Demonstrative Aids
Portal-to-Portal: No **1st-class Airfare:** No
Written Retainer Agreement: No
Failure to Pay Bill Last 5 Years; Retaining Counsel: Yes **Opposing Counsel (Deps):** No

Meteorology
Court: $185 **Review/Prep:** $185 **Deps:** $185
Years Testifying: 10
Written Fee Schedule: Yes
Min Charge for Deps: No
Min Charge for Trial: No
Cancellation Charge for Deps/Trial: No
Retainer Required: Yes, (Refundable, One Time)
Procedure When Dep Exceeds Paid Time: Proceed without immediate payment
Expenses Marked Up: No
Expenses Billed For: Mileage, Airline Tickets, Photocopies, Demonstrative Aids
Portal-to-Portal: Yes **1st-class Airfare:** No
Written Retainer Agreement: No
Failure to Pay Bill Last 5 Years; Retaining Counsel: Yes **Opposing (Deps):** Yes

Neurology
Court: $750 **Deps:** $875
Years Testifying: 10 **Majority:** Defendant
Written Fee Schedule: Yes
Min Charge for Deps: Yes **Hours:** 2
Min Charge for Trial: Yes **Hours:** 2
Cancellation Charge for Deps/Trial: Yes
Retainer Required: Yes, $500 (Refundable)
Procedure When Dep Exceeds Paid Time: Proceed without immediate payment
Expenses Marked Up: No
Expenses Billed For: Airline Tickets
Portal-to-Portal: Yes **1st-class Airfare:** No
Written Retainer Agreement: No
Failure to Pay Bill Last 5 Years; Retaining Counsel: Yes **Opposing (Deps):** Yes

Neurology
Court: $400 **Review/Prep:** $400 **Deps:** $400
Years Testifying: 5 **Majority:** Defendant
Written Fee Schedule: Yes
Min Charge for Deps: Yes **Hours:** 3
Min Charge for Trial: Yes **Hours:** 3
Cancellation Charge for Deps/Trial: Yes
Retainer Required: Yes, $1,200 (Refundable, One Time)
Expenses Marked Up: No
Expenses Billed For: Airline Tickets
Portal-to-Portal: Yes **1st-class Airfare:** No
Written Retainer Agreement: No
Failure to Pay Bill Last 5 Years; Retaining Counsel: Yes **Opposing Counsel (Deps):** No

Neurology
Court: $400 **Review/Prep:** $400 **Deps:** $400
Years Testifying: 8 **Majority:** Defendant
Written Fee Schedule: Yes
Min Charge for Deps: Yes **Hours:** 4
Min Charge for Trial: Yes **Hours:** 4

Cancellation Charge for Deps/Trial: Yes
Retainer Required: Depends, $800
Procedure When Dep Exceeds Paid Time: Proceed without immediate payment
Expenses Marked Up: No
Expenses Billed For: Airline Tickets
Portal-to-Portal: Yes **1st-class Airfare:** No
Written Retainer Agreement: No
Failure to Pay Bill Last 5 Years; Retaining Counsel: Yes **Opposing (Deps):** Yes

Nursing
Court: $175 **Review/Prep:** $100 **Deps:** $150
Years Testifying: 20 **Majority:** Plaintiff
Written Fee Schedule: Yes
Min Charge for Deps: Yes **Hours:** 4
Min Charge for Trial: Yes **Hours:** 4
Cancellation Charge for Deps/Trial: Yes
Retainer Required: Yes, $300 (Non-Refundable, Replenishable)
Expenses Marked Up: No
Expenses Billed For: Mileage, Airline Tickets, Photocopies, Lab/Testing, Photographs, Demonstrative Aids
Portal-to-Portal: Yes **1st-class Airfare:** Yes
Written Retainer Agreement: Yes
Terms: Lawyer is responsible for fee, not lawyer's client, Out-of-pocket expense policies, Retaining counsel pays all deposition charges, Fee schedules
Failure to Pay Bill Last 5 Years; Retaining Counsel: No **Opposing Counsel (Deps):** Yes

Obstetrics & Gynecology
Court: $700 **Review/Prep:** $450 **Deps:** $600
Years Testifying: 7 **Majority:** Defendant
Written Fee Schedule: Yes
Min Charge for Deps: Yes
Min Charge for Trial: No
Cancellation Charge for Deps/Trial: Yes
Retainer Required: No
Procedure When Dep Exceeds Paid Time: Proceed without immediate payment
Expenses Marked Up: No
Expenses Billed For: Mileage, Airline Tickets
Portal-to-Portal: Yes **1st-class Airfare:** No
Written Retainer Agreement: No
Failure to Pay Bill Last 5 Years; Retaining Counsel: No **Opposing Counsel (Deps):** No

Obstetrics & Gynecology
Court: $500 **Review/Prep:** $350 **Deps:** $400
Years Testifying: 5
Written Fee Schedule: Yes
Min Charge for Deps: Yes **Hours:** 8
Min Charge for Trial: Yes **Hours:** 8
Cancellation Charge for Deps/Trial: No
Retainer Required: Yes, $500 (Non-Refundable, One Time)
Procedure When Dep Exceeds Paid Time: Proceed without immediate payment
Expenses Marked Up: No
Expenses Billed For: Airline Tickets
Portal-to-Portal: No **1st-class Airfare:** No
Written Retainer Agreement: No
Failure to Pay Bill Last 5 Years; Retaining Counsel: No **Opposing Counsel (Deps):** No

Occupational Medicine
Review/Prep: $150 **Deps:** $500
Years Testifying: 20
Written Fee Schedule: Yes
Min Charge for Deps: No
Min Charge for Trial: No
Cancellation Charge for Deps/Trial: Yes
Retainer Required: No
Procedure When Dep Exceeds Paid Time: Proceed without immediate payment
Expenses Marked Up: No
Expenses Billed For: Mileage, Airline Tickets, Photocopies, Telephone Calls, Lab/Testing, Photographs, Demonstrative Aids
Portal-to-Portal: Yes **1st-class Airfare:** No
Written Retainer Agreement: No
Failure to Pay Bill Last 5 Years; Retaining Counsel: No **Opposing Counsel (Deps):** No

Oncology, Radiation
Court: $500 **Review/Prep:** $400 **Deps:** $400
Years Testifying: 8 **Majority:** Plaintiff
Written Fee Schedule: No
Min Charge for Deps: Yes **Hours:** 4
Min Charge for Trial: Yes **Hours:** 4
Cancellation Charge for Deps/Trial: Yes
Retainer Required: Yes, $1,200 (Non-Refundable, One Time)
Procedure When Dep Exceeds Paid Time: Proceed without immediate payment
Expenses Marked Up: No
Expenses Billed For: Mileage, Airline Tickets, Photocopies, Telephone Calls, Lab/Testing, Photographs, Demonstrative Aids
Portal-to-Portal: Yes **1st-class Airfare:** No
Written Retainer Agreement: No
Failure to Pay Bill Last 5 Years; Retaining Counsel: No **Opposing Counsel (Deps):** No

Ophthalmology
Court: $625 **Review/Prep:** $350 **Deps:** $1,000
Years Testifying: 2
Written Fee Schedule: No
Min Charge for Deps: Yes **Hours:** 8
Min Charge for Trial: Yes **Hours:** 8
Cancellation Charge for Deps/Trial: Yes
Retainer Required: Yes, $2,000 (Non-Refundable, One Time)
Procedure When Dep Exceeds Paid Time: Proceed without immediate payment
Expenses Marked Up: No
Expenses Billed For: Airline Tickets
Portal-to-Portal: No **1st-class Airfare:** No
Written Retainer Agreement: No
Failure to Pay Bill Last 5 Years; Retaining Counsel: Yes **Opposing Counsel (Deps):** No

Orthopedics
Court: $1,400 **Review/Prep:** $350 **Deps:** $1,400
Written Fee Schedule: Yes
Min Charge for Deps: Yes **Hours:** 4
Min Charge for Trial: Yes **Hours:** 4
Retainer Required: Yes, $750 (Non-Refundable)
Procedure When Dep Exceeds Paid Time: Proceed without immediate payment
Expenses Marked Up: No
Expenses Billed For: Airline Tickets, Telephone Calls
Portal-to-Portal: Yes **1st-class Airfare:** No
Failure to Pay Bill Last 5 Years; Retaining Counsel: No **Opposing Counsel (Deps):** No

Orthopedics
Court: $1,500 **Review/Prep:** $1,000 **Deps:** $1,000
Written Fee Schedule: No
Min Charge for Deps: Yes **Hours:** 1
Min Charge for Trial: Yes **Hours:** 1
Cancellation Charge for Deps/Trial: Yes
Retainer Required: Yes, $1,000 (Refundable)
Procedure When Dep Exceeds Paid Time: Proceed without immediate payment
Expenses Marked Up: No
Expenses Billed For: Mileage, Airline Tickets
Portal-to-Portal: Yes **1st-class Airfare:** No
Written Retainer Agreement: No
Failure to Pay Bill Last 5 Years; Retaining Counsel: No **Opposing Counsel (Deps):** No

Otolaryngology
Court: $500 **Review/Prep:** $350 **Deps:** $350
Years Testifying: 20 **Majority:** Defendant
Written Fee Schedule: Yes
Min Charge for Deps: Yes
Min Charge for Trial: No
Cancellation Charge for Deps/Trial: Yes
Retainer Required: No
Procedure When Dep Exceeds Paid Time: Proceed without immediate payment
Expenses Marked Up: Yes
Expenses Billed For: Mileage, Airline Tickets, Photocopies, Telephone Calls, Photographs
Portal-to-Portal: Yes **1st-class Airfare:** No
Written Retainer Agreement: No
Failure to Pay Bill Last 5 Years; Retaining Counsel: Yes **Opposing (Deps):** Yes

Pain Management/Medicine

Court: $1,000 **Review/Prep:** $350 **Deps:** $600
Years Testifying: 10 **Majority:** Defendant
Written Fee Schedule: Yes
Min Charge for Deps: Yes **Hours:** 4
Min Charge for Trial: Yes **Hours:** 4
Cancellation Charge for Deps/Trial: Yes
Retainer Required: Yes, $600 (Refundable)
Procedure When Dep Exceeds Paid Time: Proceed without immediate payment
Expenses Marked Up: No
Expenses Billed For: Mileage, Airline Tickets, Photocopies, Telephone Calls, Lab/Testing, Photographs, Demonstrative Aids
Portal-to-Portal: Yes **1st-class Airfare:** No
Written Retainer Agreement: No
Failure to Pay Bill Last 5 Years; Retaining Counsel: Yes **Opposing Counsel (Deps):** No

Pain Management/Medicine

Court: $500 **Deps:** $400
Years Testifying: 4 **Majority:** Plaintiff
Written Fee Schedule: No
Min Charge for Deps: Yes **Hours:** 2
Min Charge for Trial: Yes **Hours:** 2
Cancellation Charge for Deps/Trial: Yes
Retainer Required: Yes, $400 (Non-Refundable, Replenishable)
Procedure When Dep Exceeds Paid Time: Proceed without immediate payment
Expenses Marked Up: No
Expenses Billed For: Mileage, Airline Tickets, Photocopies, Telephone Calls, Lab/Testing
Portal-to-Portal: Yes **1st-class Airfare:** No
Written Retainer Agreement: No
Failure to Pay Bill Last 5 Years; Retaining Counsel: No **Opposing Counsel (Deps):** No

Pain Management/ Medicine/Palliative Medicine

Court: $500 **Review/Prep:** $500 **Deps:** $500
Years Testifying: 4 **Majority:** Defendant
Written Fee Schedule: Yes
Min Charge for Deps: No
Min Charge for Trial: No
Cancellation Charge for Deps/Trial: No
Retainer Required: No
Procedure When Dep Exceeds Paid Time: Proceed without immediate payment
Expenses Marked Up: No
Expenses Billed For: Mileage, Airline Tickets
Portal-to-Portal: Yes **1st-class Airfare:** No
Written Retainer Agreement: No
Failure to Pay Bill Last 5 Years; Retaining Counsel: No **Opposing Counsel (Deps):** No

Pain Management/Medicine

Court: $1,100 **Review/Prep:** $250 **Deps:** $1,100
Written Fee Schedule: Yes
Min Charge for Deps: Yes **Hours:** 1
Min Charge for Trial: Yes **Hours:** 1
Cancellation Charge for Deps/Trial: Yes
Retainer Required: Yes, $1,000 (Non-Refundable, Replenishable)
Procedure When Dep Exceeds Paid Time: Proceed without immediate payment
Expenses Marked Up: No
Expenses Billed For: Mileage, Airline Tickets, Photocopies, Telephone Calls, Lab/Testing
Portal-to-Portal: Yes **1st-class Airfare:** No
Written Retainer Agreement: Yes
Terms: Lawyer is responsible for fee, not lawyer's client, Interest for delinquent accounts, Out-of-pocket expense policies, In-court testimony minimums, Retaining counsel pays all deposition charges, Fee schedules, Portal-to-portal travel time, Attorney's fees if forced to sue for collection, Deposition minimum fee, Payment for preparation time
Failure to Pay Bill Last 5 Years; Retaining Counsel: No **Opposing Counsel (Deps):** No

Physical Medicine & Rehabilitation/ Acupuncture

Court: $500 **Review/Prep:** $250 **Deps:** $800
Years Testifying: 10
Written Fee Schedule: Yes
Min Charge for Deps: Yes **Hours:** 2
Min Charge for Trial: Yes **Hours:** 2
Cancellation Charge for Deps/Trial: Yes
Retainer Required: Yes, Depends on case (Non-Refundable, One Time)
Expenses Marked Up: No
Expenses Billed For: Photocopies
Portal-to-Portal: Yes **1st-class Airfare:** No
Written Retainer Agreement: No
Failure to Pay Bill Last 5 Years; Retaining Counsel: No **Opposing Counsel (Deps):** No

Physical Medicine & Rehabilitation/Pain Management/Medicine

Court: $950 **Review/Prep:** $650 **Deps:** $650
Years Testifying: 15
Written Fee Schedule: Yes
Min Charge for Deps: Yes **Hours:** 2
Min Charge for Trial: Yes **Hours:** 2
Cancellation Charge for Deps/Trial: Yes
Retainer Required: Yes, $1,500 (Non-Refundable, One Time)
Procedure When Dep Exceeds Paid Time: Proceed without immediate payment
Expenses Marked Up: Yes
Expenses Billed For: Mileage, Airline Tickets, Photocopies, Telephone Calls, Lab/Testing, Photographs, Demonstrative Aids
Portal-to-Portal: Yes **1st-class Airfare:** No
Written Retainer Agreement: Yes
Terms: Lawyer is responsible for fee, not lawyer's client, Interest for delinquent accounts, Out-of-pocket expense policies, In-court testimony minimums, Retaining counsel pays all deposition charges, Fee schedules, Portal-to-portal travel time, Attorney's fees if forced to sue for collection, Deposition minimum fee, Payment for preparation time
Failure to Pay Bill Last 5 Years; Retaining Counsel: Yes **Opposing (Deps):** Yes

Physical Medicine & Rehabilitation

Court: $500 **Review/Prep:** $350 **Deps:** $350
Years Testifying: 23
Written Fee Schedule: Yes
Min Charge for Deps: Yes **Hours:** 4
Min Charge for Trial: Yes **Hours:** 4
Cancellation Charge for Deps/Trial: Yes
Retainer Required: Yes, $1,750 (Refundable, One Time)
Procedure When Dep Exceeds Paid Time: Proceed without immediate payment
Expenses Marked Up: No
Expenses Billed For: Airline Tickets, Photographs
Portal-to-Portal: No **1st-class Airfare:** No
Written Retainer Agreement: Yes
Terms: In-court testimony minimums, Retaining counsel pays all deposition charges, Fee schedules, Portal-to-portal travel time, Attorney's fees if forced to sue for collection, Deposition minimum fee, Payment for preparation time
Failure to Pay Bill Last 5 Years; Retaining Counsel: Yes **Opposing (Deps):** Yes

Product Liability

Court: $200 **Review/Prep:** $175 **Deps:** $200
Years Testifying: 30 **Majority:** Plaintiff
Written Fee Schedule: Yes
Min Charge for Deps: Yes
Min Charge for Trial: No
Cancellation Charge for Deps/Trial: No
Retainer Required: Yes, $1,000 (Partially Refundable, One Time)
Procedure When Dep Exceeds Paid Time: Proceed without immediate payment
Expenses Marked Up: Yes
Expenses Billed For: Mileage, Airline Tickets, Photocopies, Telephone Calls, Lab/Testing, Photographs, Demonstrative Aids
Portal-to-Portal: Yes **1st-class Airfare:** Yes
Written Retainer Agreement: No
Failure to Pay Bill Last 5 Years; Retaining Counsel: Yes **Opposing Counsel (Deps):** No

Psychiatry
Court: $300 **Review/Prep:** $300 **Deps:** $300
Years Testifying: 3
Written Fee Schedule: Yes
Min Charge for Deps: Yes **Hours:** 4
Min Charge for Trial: Yes **Hours:** 4
Cancellation Charge for Deps/Trial: Yes
Retainer Required: Yes, $1,200 (Refundable, One Time)
Procedure When Dep Exceeds Paid Time: Get payment before proceeding further
Expenses Marked Up: No
Expenses Billed For: Mileage, Airline Tickets
Portal-to-Portal: Yes **1st-class Airfare:** No
Written Retainer Agreement: Yes
Terms: Lawyer is responsible for fee, not lawyer's client, Out-of-pocket expense policies, In-court testimony minimums, Retaining counsel pays all deposition charges, Fee schedules, Payment for preparation time
Failure to Pay Bill Last 5 Years; Retaining Counsel: Yes **Opposing Counsel (Deps):** No

Psychiatry
Court: $350 **Review/Prep:** $350 **Deps:** $350
Years Testifying: 16
Written Fee Schedule: Yes
Min Charge for Deps: Yes **Hours:** 1
Min Charge for Trial: Yes **Hours:** 1
Cancellation Charge for Deps/Trial: Yes
Retainer Required: Yes, Depends on case (Refundable, One Time)
Procedure When Dep Exceeds Paid Time: Proceed without immediate payment
Expenses Marked Up: No
Portal-to-Portal: Yes **1st-class Airfare:** No
Written Retainer Agreement: No
Failure to Pay Bill Last 5 Years; Retaining Counsel: No **Opposing Counsel (Deps):** Yes

Psychology
Court: $250 **Review/Prep:** $150 **Deps:** $250
Years Testifying: 10
Written Fee Schedule: No
Min Charge for Deps: Yes **Hours:** 4
Min Charge for Trial: Yes **Hours:** 4
Cancellation Charge for Deps/Trial: Yes
Retainer Required: Yes, Depends on case (Refundable, One Time)
Procedure When Dep Exceeds Paid Time: Get payment before proceeding further
Expenses Marked Up: No
Expenses Billed For: Mileage, Airline Tickets, Photocopies, Telephone Calls, Lab/Testing, Photographs, Demonstrative Aids
Portal-to-Portal: Yes **1st-class Airfare:** No
Written Retainer Agreement: Yes
Terms: Lawyer is responsible for fee, not lawyer's client, Interest for delinquent accounts, Out-of-pocket expense policies, In-court testimony minimums, Retaining counsel pays all deposition charges, Portal-to-portal travel time, Attorney's fees if forced to sue for collection, Deposition minimum fee, Payment for preparation time
Failure to Pay Bill Last 5 Years; Retaining Counsel: No **Opposing Counsel (Deps):** No

Psychology
Court: $300 **Review/Prep:** $200 **Deps:** $300
Years Testifying: 20
Written Fee Schedule: Yes
Min Charge for Deps: Yes
Min Charge for Trial: No
Cancellation Charge for Deps/Trial: Yes
Retainer Required: Yes, $1,000 (Non-Refundable, One Time)
Procedure When Dep Exceeds Paid Time: Get payment before proceeding further
Expenses Marked Up: Yes
Expenses Billed For: Airline Tickets, Photocopies
Portal-to-Portal: Yes **1st-class Airfare:** No
Written Retainer Agreement: Yes
Terms: Lawyer is responsible for fee, not lawyer's client, Interest for delinquent accounts, Out-of-pocket expense policies, Retaining counsel pays all deposition charges, Fee schedules, Portal-to-portal travel time, Attorney's fees if forced to sue for collection, Deposition minimum fee, Payment for preparation time
Failure to Pay Bill Last 5 Years; Retaining Counsel: No **Opposing Counsel (Deps):** No

Pulmonology
Court: $500 **Review/Prep:** $350 **Deps:** $400
Years Testifying: 14
Written Fee Schedule: No
Min Charge for Deps: No **Hours:** 8
Min Charge for Trial: Yes **Hours:** 8
Cancellation Charge for Deps/Trial: Yes
Retainer Required: Yes, $300 (Refundable, One Time)
Procedure When Dep Exceeds Paid Time: Proceed without immediate payment
Expenses Marked Up: No
Expenses Billed For: Mileage, Airline Tickets, Photocopies, Telephone Calls, Lab/Testing, Photographs, Demonstrative Aids
Portal-to-Portal: Yes **1st-class Airfare:** No
Written Retainer Agreement: No
Failure to Pay Bill Last 5 Years; Retaining Counsel: Yes **Opposing (Deps):** Yes

Pulmonology
Court: $400 **Review/Prep:** $350 **Deps:** $400
Years Testifying: 1 **Majority:** Plaintiff
Written Fee Schedule: Yes
Min Charge for Deps: Yes **Hours:** 2
Min Charge for Trial: Yes **Hours:** 2
Cancellation Charge for Deps/Trial: No
Retainer Required: No
Procedure When Dep Exceeds Paid Time: Proceed without immediate payment
Expenses Marked Up: No
Expenses Billed For: Mileage, Airline Tickets
Portal-to-Portal: Yes **1st-class Airfare:** No
Written Retainer Agreement: No
Failure to Pay Bill Last 5 Years; Retaining Counsel: No **Opposing Counsel (Deps):** No

Radiology
Court: $750 **Review/Prep:** $600 **Deps:** $750
Years Testifying: 15 **Majority:** Defendant
Written Fee Schedule: No
Min Charge for Deps: Yes **Hours:** 1
Min Charge for Trial: Yes **Hours:** 1
Cancellation Charge for Deps/Trial: Yes
Retainer Required: Yes, $600 (Refundable, One Time)
Expenses Marked Up: No
Expenses Billed For: Airline Tickets
Portal-to-Portal: Yes **1st-class Airfare:** Yes
Written Retainer Agreement: No
Failure to Pay Bill Last 5 Years; Retaining Counsel: Yes **Opposing (Deps):** Yes

Real Estate
Court: $225 **Review/Prep:** $175 **Deps:** $225
Years Testifying: 4 **Majority:** Plaintiff
Written Fee Schedule: Yes
Min Charge for Deps: No
Min Charge for Trial: No
Cancellation Charge for Deps/Trial: No
Retainer Required: Yes, $2,000 (Refundable, One Time)
Procedure When Dep Exceeds Paid Time: Proceed without immediate payment
Expenses Marked Up: Yes
Expenses Billed For: Mileage, Airline Tickets, Demonstrative Aids
Portal-to-Portal: Yes **1st-class Airfare:** No
Written Retainer Agreement: No
Failure to Pay Bill Last 5 Years; Retaining Counsel: No **Opposing Counsel (Deps):** No

Safety/Security
Court: $180 **Review/Prep:** $180 **Deps:** $250
Years Testifying: 30 **Majority:** Plaintiff
Written Fee Schedule: Yes
Min Charge for Deps: Yes **Hours:** 8
Min Charge for Trial: Yes **Hours:** 8
Cancellation Charge for Deps/Trial: No
Retainer Required: Yes, $1,000 (Non-Refundable, One Time)
Procedure When Dep Exceeds Paid Time: Proceed without immediate payment
Expenses Marked Up: No

Expenses Billed For: Mileage, Airline Tickets, Photocopies, Telephone Calls, Lab/Testing, Photographs, Demonstrative Aids
Portal-to-Portal: No **1st-class Airfare:** No
Written Retainer Agreement: Yes
Terms: In-court testimony minimums, Retaining counsel pays all deposition charges, Fee schedules, Deposition minimum fee
Failure to Pay Bill Last 5 Years; Retaining Counsel: No **Opposing Counsel (Deps):** No

Safety, Transportation
Court: $200 **Review/Prep:** $200 **Deps:** $200
Years Testifying: 22
Written Fee Schedule: No
Min Charge for Deps: Yes **Hours:** 8
Min Charge for Trial: Yes **Hours:** 8
Cancellation Charge for Deps/Trial: No
Retainer Required: Yes, $4,000 (Non-Refundable, Replenishable)
Procedure When Dep Exceeds Paid Time: Proceed without immediate payment
Expenses Marked Up: No
Expenses Billed For: Mileage, Airline Tickets, Telephone Calls, Photographs, Demonstrative Aids
Portal-to-Portal: Yes **1st-class Airfare:** No
Written Retainer Agreement: No
Failure to Pay Bill Last 5 Years; Retaining Counsel: Yes **Opposing Counsel (Deps):** No

Securities/Trusts & Estates/ Investments
Court: $200 **Review/Prep:** $200 **Deps:** $200
Years Testifying: 7 **Majority:** Plaintiff
Written Fee Schedule: No
Min Charge for Deps: No
Min Charge for Trial: No
Cancellation Charge for Deps/Trial: No
Retainer Required: Yes, $2,000 (Refundable, One Time)
Expenses Marked Up: No
Expenses Billed For: Airline Tickets, Demonstrative Aids
Portal-to-Portal: No **1st-class Airfare:** No
Written Retainer Agreement: No
Failure to Pay Bill Last 5 Years; Retaining Counsel: Yes **Opposing Counsel (Deps):** No

Security
Court: $280 **Review/Prep:** $240 **Deps:** $280
Years Testifying: 12
Written Fee Schedule: Yes
Min Charge for Deps: Yes
Min Charge for Trial: No
Cancellation Charge for Deps/Trial: No
Retainer Required: Yes, $1,000 (Non-Refundable)
Procedure When Dep Exceeds Paid Time: Proceed without immediate payment
Expenses Marked Up: No
Expenses Billed For: Mileage, Airline Tickets, Photocopies, Photographs
Portal-to-Portal: Yes **1st-class Airfare:** Yes
Written Retainer Agreement: No
Failure to Pay Bill Last 5 Years; Retaining Counsel: No **Opposing Counsel (Deps):** No

Surgery, General
Court: $300 **Review/Prep:** $150 **Deps:** $300
Years Testifying: 20
Written Fee Schedule: No
Min Charge for Deps: Yes **Hours:** 1
Min Charge for Trial: Yes **Hours:** 1
Cancellation Charge for Deps/Trial: No
Retainer Required: No
Expenses Marked Up: No
Portal-to-Portal: No **1st-class Airfare:** No
Written Retainer Agreement: No
Failure to Pay Bill Last 5 Years; Retaining Counsel: No **Opposing Counsel (Deps):** No

Surgery, General/Healthcare, Medical Staff Issues
Court: $600 **Review/Prep:** $350 **Deps:** $550
Years Testifying: 13 **Majority:** Plaintiff
Written Fee Schedule: Yes
Min Charge for Deps: Yes
Cancellation Charge for Deps/Trial: Yes
Retainer Required: Yes, $1,150 (Non-Refundable, One Time)
Procedure When Dep Exceeds Paid Time: Proceed without immediate payment
Expenses Marked Up: No
Expenses Billed For: Airline Tickets, Photocopies
Portal-to-Portal: Yes **1st-class Airfare:** No
Written Retainer Agreement: Yes
Terms: In-court testimony minimums, Retaining counsel pays all deposition charges, Fee schedules, Portal-to-portal travel time, Deposition minimum fee
Failure to Pay Bill Last 5 Years; Retaining Counsel: Yes **Opposing (Deps):** Yes

Surgery, Hand
Court: $1,250 **Review/Prep:** $600 **Deps:** $750
Years Testifying: 24
Written Fee Schedule: Yes
Min Charge for Deps: Yes **Hours:** 4
Min Charge for Trial: Yes **Hours:** 4
Cancellation Charge for Deps/Trial: Yes
Retainer Required: Yes, Depends on case (Refundable, One Time)
Procedure When Dep Exceeds Paid Time: Proceed without immediate payment
Expenses Marked Up: No
Expenses Billed For: Photocopies, Telephone Calls, Photographs
Portal-to-Portal: Yes **1st-class Airfare:** Yes
Written Retainer Agreement: Yes
Terms: Lawyer is responsible for fee, not lawyer's client, Out-of-pocket expense policies, In-court testimony minimums, Retaining counsel pays all deposition charges, Portal-to-portal travel time, Deposition minimum fee
Failure to Pay Bill Last 5 Years; Retaining Counsel: No **Opposing Counsel (Deps):** No

Transportation/Trucking
Court: $250 **Review/Prep:** $225 **Deps:** $250
Years Testifying: 14
Written Fee Schedule: Yes
Min Charge for Deps: Yes **Hours:** 4
Min Charge for Trial: Yes **Hours:** 4
Cancellation Charge for Deps/Trial: Yes
Retainer Required: Yes, $1,500 (Non-Refundable, Replenishable)
Procedure When Dep Exceeds Paid Time: Proceed without immediate payment
Expenses Marked Up: No
Expenses Billed For: Mileage, Airline Tickets, Photographs, Demonstrative Aids
Portal-to-Portal: Yes **1st-class Airfare:** No
Written Retainer Agreement: Yes
Terms: Lawyer is responsible for fee, not lawyer's client, Interest for delinquent accounts, Out-of-pocket expense policies, In-court testimony minimums, Retaining counsel pays all deposition charges, Fee schedules, Portal-to-portal travel time, Attorney's fees if forced to sue for collection, Deposition minimum fee, Payment for preparation time
Failure to Pay Bill Last 5 Years; Retaining Counsel: No **Opposing Counsel (Deps):** No

Trucking/Transportation
Court: $250 **Review/Prep:** $185 **Deps:** $250
Years Testifying: 15
Written Fee Schedule: Yes
Min Charge for Deps: Yes **Hours:** 8
Min Charge for Trial: Yes **Hours:** 8
Cancellation Charge for Deps/Trial: Yes
Retainer Required: Yes, $3,000 (Non-Refundable, Replenishable)
Expenses Marked Up: No
Expenses Billed For: Mileage, Airline Tickets, Photocopies, Telephone Calls, Photographs, Demonstrative Aids
Portal-to-Portal: Yes **1st-class Airfare:** No
Written Retainer Agreement: Yes
Terms: Lawyer is responsible for fee, not lawyer's client, Out-of-pocket expense policies, In-court testimony minimums, Retaining counsel pays all deposition charges, Fee schedules, Portal-to-portal travel time, Deposition minimum fee, Payment for preparation time
Failure to Pay Bill Last 5 Years; Retaining Counsel: Yes **Opposing Counsel (Deps):** No

Valuation, Business/ Damages, Business
Court: $200 **Review/Prep:** $200 **Deps:** $200
Years Testifying: 12
Written Fee Schedule: No
Min Charge for Deps: No
Min Charge for Trial: No
Cancellation Charge for Deps/Trial: No
Retainer Required: Yes, $5,000 (Refundable, Replenishable)
Expenses Marked Up: No
Expenses Billed For: Mileage, Airline Tickets, Photographs, Demonstrative Aids
Portal-to-Portal: Yes **1st-class Airfare:** No
Written Retainer Agreement: Yes
Terms: Interest for delinquent accounts, Out-of-pocket expense policies, Retaining counsel pays all deposition charges, Portal-to-portal travel time, Attorney's fees if forced to sue for collection, Payment for preparation time
Failure to Pay Bill Last 5 Years; Retaining Counsel: No **Opposing Counsel (Deps):** No

Valuation, Business
Court: $400 **Review/Prep:** $275 **Deps:** $275
Years Testifying: 15
Written Fee Schedule: Yes
Min Charge for Deps: Yes **Hours:** 4
Min Charge for Trial: Yes **Hours:** 4
Cancellation Charge for Deps/Trial: Yes
Retainer Required: Yes, 50% est. fee (Refundable, Replenishable)
Procedure When Dep Exceeds Paid Time: Proceed without immediate payment
Expenses Marked Up: Yes
Expenses Billed For: Airline Tickets, Lab/Testing, Photographs, Demonstrative Aids
Portal-to-Portal: Yes **1st-class Airfare:** No
Written Retainer Agreement: No
Failure to Pay Bill Last 5 Years; Retaining Counsel: No **Opposing Counsel (Deps):** No

Vocational/Life Care Planning
Court: $200 **Review/Prep:** $200 **Deps:** $200
Years Testifying: 20 **Majority:** Plaintiff
Written Fee Schedule: No
Min Charge for Deps: No
Min Charge for Trial: No
Cancellation Charge for Deps/Trial: Yes
Retainer Required: Yes, $2,000 (Non-Refundable, One Time)
Procedure When Dep Exceeds Paid Time: Get payment before proceeding further
Expenses Marked Up: No
Expenses Billed For: Mileage, Airline Tickets
Portal-to-Portal: Yes **1st-class Airfare:** No
Written Retainer Agreement: Yes
Terms: Lawyer is responsible for fee, not lawyer's client, Interest for delinquent accounts, Out-of-pocket expense policies, In-court testimony minimums, Retaining counsel pays all deposition charges, Portal-to-portal travel time
Failure to Pay Bill Last 5 Years; Retaining Counsel: No **Opposing Counsel (Deps):** No

Vocational Evaluation
Court: $125 **Review/Prep:** $75 **Deps:** $125
Years Testifying: 25
Written Fee Schedule: Yes
Min Charge for Deps: Yes **Hours:** 2
Min Charge for Trial: Yes **Hours:** 2
Cancellation Charge for Deps/Trial: Yes
Retainer Required: Yes, $1,750 (Refundable, One Time)
Expenses Marked Up: Yes
Expenses Billed For: Mileage, Airline Tickets, Photocopies, Telephone Calls, Lab/Testing, Photographs, Demonstrative Aids
Portal-to-Portal: Yes **1st-class Airfare:** No
Written Retainer Agreement: No
Failure to Pay Bill Last 5 Years; Retaining Counsel: No **Opposing Counsel (Deps):** No

Vocational Rehabilitation/Life Care Planning
Court: $330 **Review/Prep:** $330 **Deps:** $330
Years Testifying: 20
Written Fee Schedule: Yes
Min Charge for Deps: Yes
Min Charge for Trial: No
Cancellation Charge for Deps/Trial: Yes
Retainer Required: Yes, $2,500 (Non-Refundable, One Time)
Procedure When Dep Exceeds Paid Time: Proceed without immediate payment
Expenses Marked Up: No
Expenses Billed For: Mileage, Airline Tickets, Photocopies, Telephone Calls, Demonstrative Aids
Portal-to-Portal: Yes **1st-class Airfare:** Yes
Written Retainer Agreement: Yes
Terms: Lawyer is responsible for fee, not lawyer's client, Out-of-pocket expense policies, Retaining counsel pays all deposition charges, Fee schedules
Failure to Pay Bill Last 5 Years; Retaining Counsel: Yes **Opposing (Deps):** Yes

Wound Care
Court: $150 **Review/Prep:** $100 **Deps:** $150
Years Testifying: 1
Written Fee Schedule: Yes
Min Charge for Deps: Yes **Hours:** 4
Min Charge for Trial: Yes **Hours:** 4
Cancellation Charge for Deps/Trial: Yes
Retainer Required: Yes, $500 (Non-Refundable, One Time)
Expenses Marked Up: No
Expenses Billed For: Mileage, Airline Tickets, Photocopies, Lab/Testing, Photographs, Demonstrative Aids
Portal-to-Portal: Yes **1st-class Airfare:** No
Written Retainer Agreement: Yes
Terms: Interest for delinquent accounts, In-court testimony minimums, Retaining counsel pays all deposition charges, Fee schedules, Portal-to-portal travel time, Deposition minimum fee
Failure to Pay Bill Last 5 Years; Retaining Counsel: Yes **Opposing Counsel (Deps):** No

Georgia

Accident Reconstruction
Court: $125 **Review/Prep:** $125 **Deps:** $125
Years Testifying: 25 **Majority:** Defendant
Written Fee Schedule: Yes
Min Charge for Deps: No
Min Charge for Trial: No
Cancellation Charge for Deps/Trial: No
Retainer Required: No
Expenses Marked Up: No
Expenses Billed For: Mileage, Airline Tickets, Photographs, Demonstrative Aids
Portal-to-Portal: Yes **1st-class Airfare:** No
Written Retainer Agreement: No
Failure to Pay Bill Last 5 Years; Retaining Counsel: No **Opposing Counsel (Deps):** No

Accidents, Chemical/Explosions
Court: $250 **Review/Prep:** $100 **Deps:** $150
Years Testifying: 5
Written Fee Schedule: No
Min Charge for Deps: No
Min Charge for Trial: No
Cancellation Charge for Deps/Trial: No
Retainer Required: No
Procedure When Dep Exceeds Paid Time: Get payment before proceeding further
Expenses Marked Up: No
Expenses Billed For: Mileage, Airline Tickets, Photocopies, Telephone Calls, Lab/Testing, Photographs, Demonstrative Aids
Portal-to-Portal: Yes **1st-class Airfare:** No
Written Retainer Agreement: Yes
Terms: Lawyer is responsible for fee, not lawyer's client, Interest for delinquent accounts, Out-of-pocket expense policies, In-court testimony minimums, Retaining counsel pays all deposition charges, Fee schedules, Portal-to-portal travel time, Attorney's fees if forced to sue for collection, Deposition minimum fee, Payment for preparation time
Failure to Pay Bill Last 5 Years; Retaining Counsel: No **Opposing Counsel (Deps):** No

Accounting
Court: $415 **Review/Prep:** $415 **Deps:** $425
Years Testifying: 25
Written Fee Schedule: No
Min Charge for Deps: No
Min Charge for Trial: No
Cancellation Charge for Deps/Trial: No
Retainer Required: Yes, (Refundable, One Time)
Expenses Marked Up: No
Portal-to-Portal: Yes **1st-class Airfare:** No
Written Retainer Agreement: Yes
Terms: Interest for delinquent accounts, Out-of-pocket expense policies, Retaining counsel pays all deposition charges, Attorney's fees if forced to sue for collection
Failure to Pay Bill Last 5 Years; Retaining Counsel: No **Opposing Counsel (Deps):** No

Advertising/Law, Intellectual Property
Court: $400 **Review/Prep:** $400 **Deps:** $400
Years Testifying: 10
Written Fee Schedule: No
Min Charge for Deps: No
Min Charge for Trial: No
Cancellation Charge for Deps/Trial: No
Retainer Required: Yes, $8,000 (Non-Refundable, One Time)
Expenses Marked Up: No
Expenses Billed For: Mileage, Airline Tickets, Photocopies, Lab/Testing, Photographs, Demonstrative Aids
Portal-to-Portal: Yes **1st-class Airfare:** Yes
Written Retainer Agreement: Yes
Terms: Lawyer is responsible for fee, not lawyer's client, Out-of-pocket expense policies, Retaining counsel pays all deposition charges, Portal-to-portal travel time, Attorney's fees if forced to sue for collection
Failure to Pay Bill Last 5 Years; Retaining Counsel: No **Opposing Counsel (Deps):** Yes

Appraisal, Real Estate
Court: $175 **Deps:** $175
Years Testifying: 30
Written Fee Schedule: Yes
Min Charge for Deps: Yes **Hours:** 3
Min Charge for Trial: Yes **Hours:** 3
Cancellation Charge for Deps/Trial: No
Retainer Required: Yes, $500 (Non-Refundable, One Time)
Expenses Marked Up: No
Expenses Billed For: Airline Tickets, Demonstrative Aids
1st-class Airfare: No
Written Retainer Agreement: Yes
Failure to Pay Bill Last 5 Years; Retaining Counsel: No **Opposing Counsel (Deps):** No

Automotive/Industrial
Court: $500 **Review/Prep:** $250 **Deps:** $500
Majority: Plaintiff
Written Fee Schedule: Yes
Min Charge for Deps: Yes **Hours:** 1
Min Charge for Trial: Yes **Hours:** 1
Cancellation Charge for Deps/Trial: Yes
Retainer Required: Yes, $750 (Non-Refundable, Replenishable)
Expenses Marked Up: Yes
Expenses Billed For: Mileage, Airline Tickets, Photocopies, Telephone Calls, Lab/Testing, Photographs, Demonstrative Aids
Portal-to-Portal: Yes **1st-class Airfare:** Yes
Written Retainer Agreement: Yes
Terms: Lawyer is responsible for fee, not lawyer's client, Out-of-pocket expense policies, In-court testimony minimums, Retaining counsel pays all deposition charges, Fee schedules, Portal-to-portal travel time, Attorney's fees if forced to sue for collection, Deposition minimum fee, Payment for preparation time, First class air travel
Failure to Pay Bill Last 5 Years; Retaining Counsel: Yes **Opposing (Deps):** Yes

Automotive/Retail/Franchises
Court: $300 **Review/Prep:** $275 **Deps:** $300
Years Testifying: 18
Written Fee Schedule: Yes
Min Charge for Deps: No
Min Charge for Trial: No
Cancellation Charge for Deps/Trial: Yes
Retainer Required: Yes, $5,000 (Refundable, One Time)
Expenses Marked Up: Yes
Expenses Billed For: Mileage, Airline Tickets, Photocopies, Telephone Calls, Photographs, Demonstrative Aids
Portal-to-Portal: Yes **1st-class Airfare:** No
Written Retainer Agreement: Yes
Terms: Interest for delinquent accounts, Out-of-pocket expense policies, In-court testimony minimums, Retaining counsel pays all deposition charges, Fee schedules, Portal-to-portal travel time, Attorney's fees if forced to sue for collection, Deposition minimum fee, Payment for preparation time
Failure to Pay Bill Last 5 Years; Retaining Counsel: No **Opposing Counsel (Deps):** No

Construction
Court: $300 **Review/Prep:** $150 **Deps:** $300
Years Testifying: 25
Written Fee Schedule: Yes
Min Charge for Deps: Yes
Min Charge for Trial: No
Cancellation Charge for Deps/Trial: No
Retainer Required: Yes, $2,500 (Refundable, Replenishable)
Procedure When Dep Exceeds Paid Time: Get payment before proceeding further
Expenses Marked Up: Yes
Expenses Billed For: Mileage, Airline Tickets, Photocopies, Telephone Calls, Lab/Testing, Photographs, Demonstrative Aids
Portal-to-Portal: Yes **1st-class Airfare:** Yes
Written Retainer Agreement: Yes
Terms: Lawyer is responsible for fee, not lawyer's client, Interest for delinquent accounts, Out-of-pocket expense policies, In-court testimony minimums, Retaining counsel pays all deposition charges, Fee schedules, Portal-to-portal travel time, Attorney's fees if forced to sue for collection, Deposition minimum fee, Payment for preparation time, First class air travel
Failure to Pay Bill Last 5 Years; Retaining Counsel: Yes **Opposing Counsel (Deps):** No

Construction
Court: $175 **Review/Prep:** $165 **Deps:** $155
Years Testifying: 8
Written Fee Schedule: Yes
Min Charge for Deps: Yes **Hours:** 6
Min Charge for Trial: Yes **Hours:** 6
Cancellation Charge for Deps/Trial: Yes
Retainer Required: Yes, 50% est. fee (Non-Refundable, One Time)
Expenses Marked Up: Yes
Expenses Billed For: Mileage, Airline Tickets, Photocopies, Telephone Calls, Demonstrative Aids
Portal-to-Portal: Yes **1st-class Airfare:** No
Written Retainer Agreement: Yes
Terms: Lawyer is responsible for fee, not lawyer's client, Interest for delinquent accounts, Out-of-pocket expense policies, In-court testimony minimums, Retaining counsel pays all deposition charges, Payment for preparation time
Failure to Pay Bill Last 5 Years; Retaining Counsel: No **Opposing Counsel (Deps):** No

Engineering, Mechanical/ Engineering, Electrical
Court: $225 **Review/Prep:** $175 **Deps:** $225
Years Testifying: 15
Written Fee Schedule: Yes
Min Charge for Deps: No
Min Charge for Trial: No
Cancellation Charge for Deps/Trial: No
Retainer Required: Yes, Depends on case (Refundable, One Time)
Expenses Marked Up: No
Expenses Billed For: Mileage, Airline Tickets, Photocopies, Lab/Testing, Photographs
Portal-to-Portal: Yes **1st-class Airfare:** No
Written Retainer Agreement: No

Failure to Pay Bill Last 5 Years; Retaining Counsel: Yes **Opposing (Deps):** Yes

Law Enforcement
Court: $300 **Review/Prep:** $200 **Deps:** $300
Years Testifying: 9 **Majority:** Plaintiff
Written Fee Schedule: Yes
Min Charge for Deps: Yes **Hours:** 8
Min Charge for Trial: Yes **Hours:** 8
Cancellation Charge for Deps/Trial: No
Retainer Required: Yes, $5,000 (Non-Refundable, One Time)
Procedure When Dep Exceeds Paid Time: Proceed without immediate payment
Expenses Marked Up: No
Expenses Billed For: Mileage, Airline Tickets, Lab/Testing, Photographs
Portal-to-Portal: Yes **1st-class Airfare:** No
Written Retainer Agreement: Yes
Terms: Lawyer is responsible for fee, not lawyer's client, Interest for delinquent accounts, Out-of-pocket expense policies, In-court testimony minimums, Retaining counsel pays all deposition charges, Fee schedules, Deposition minimum fee, Venue clause, Per diem
Failure to Pay Bill Last 5 Years; Retaining Counsel: Yes **Opposing (Deps):** Yes

Nursing
Court: $175 **Review/Prep:** $100 **Deps:** $150
Years Testifying: 6 **Majority:** Plaintiff
Written Fee Schedule: Yes
Min Charge for Deps: No
Min Charge for Trial: No
Cancellation Charge for Deps/Trial: No
Retainer Required: Yes, $400 (Non-Refundable, Replenishable)
Expenses Marked Up: No
Expenses Billed For: Mileage, Airline Tickets, Photocopies
Portal-to-Portal: Yes **1st-class Airfare:** No
Written Retainer Agreement: Yes
Terms: Lawyer is responsible for fee, not lawyer's client, Retaining counsel pays all deposition charges, Fee schedules, Portal-to-portal travel time, Work product expectations
Failure to Pay Bill Last 5 Years; Retaining Counsel: Yes **Opposing Counsel (Deps):** No

Nursing
Court: $175 **Review/Prep:** $100 **Deps:** $150
Years Testifying: 3 **Majority:** Defendant
Written Fee Schedule: Yes
Min Charge for Deps: No
Min Charge for Trial: No
Cancellation Charge for Deps/Trial: No
Retainer Required: Yes, $400 (Refundable)
Expenses Marked Up: No
Expenses Billed For: Mileage, Airline Tickets, Photocopies, Lab/Testing, Photographs
Portal-to-Portal: Yes **1st-class Airfare:** No
Written Retainer Agreement: Yes
Failure to Pay Bill Last 5 Years; Retaining Counsel: Yes **Opposing Counsel (Deps):** No

Orthopedics
Court: $850 **Review/Prep:** $375 **Deps:** $700
Years Testifying: 13
Written Fee Schedule: Yes
Min Charge for Deps: Yes **Hours:** 5
Min Charge for Trial: Yes **Hours:** 5
Cancellation Charge for Deps/Trial: Yes
Retainer Required: Yes, $1,000 (Non-Refundable, One Time)
Procedure When Dep Exceeds Paid Time: Get payment before proceeding further
Expenses Marked Up: No
Portal-to-Portal: Yes **1st-class Airfare:** No
Written Retainer Agreement: No
Failure to Pay Bill Last 5 Years; Retaining Counsel: No **Opposing Counsel (Deps):** No

Orthopedics
Court: $500 **Review/Prep:** $500 **Deps:** $500
Years Testifying: 15 **Majority:** Defendant
Written Fee Schedule: Yes
Min Charge for Deps: Yes **Hours:** 5
Min Charge for Trial: Yes **Hours:** 5
Cancellation Charge for Deps/Trial: No
Retainer Required: No
Expenses Marked Up: No
Expenses Billed For: Mileage
Portal-to-Portal: Yes **1st-class Airfare:** No
Written Retainer Agreement: No
Failure to Pay Bill Last 5 Years; Retaining Counsel: No **Opposing Counsel (Deps):** No

Pain Management/Medicine
Court: $500 **Review/Prep:** $300 **Deps:** $500
Years Testifying: 8 **Majority:** Plaintiff
Written Fee Schedule: No
Min Charge for Deps: Yes **Hours:** 5
Min Charge for Trial: Yes **Hours:** 5
Cancellation Charge for Deps/Trial: Yes
Retainer Required: No
Procedure When Dep Exceeds Paid Time: Proceed without immediate payment
Expenses Marked Up: No
Expenses Billed For: Mileage, Photocopies, Demonstrative Aids
Portal-to-Portal: No **1st-class Airfare:** No
Written Retainer Agreement: No
Failure to Pay Bill Last 5 Years; Retaining Counsel: Yes

Physical Medicine & Rehabilitation/Pain Management/Medicine
Review/Prep: $300 **Deps:** $600
Years Testifying: 13 **Majority:** Plaintiff
Written Fee Schedule: No
Min Charge for Deps: Yes
Min Charge for Trial: Yes
Cancellation Charge for Deps/Trial: Yes
Retainer Required: Yes, $600 (Refundable)
Procedure When Dep Exceeds Paid Time: Proceed without immediate payment
Expenses Marked Up: No
Expenses Billed For:
Portal-to-Portal: Yes
Written Retainer Agreement: No
Failure to Pay Bill Last 5 Years; Retaining Counsel: No **Opposing Counsel (Deps):** No

Psychiatry
Court: $500 **Review/Prep:** $450 **Deps:** $500
Years Testifying: 30
Written Fee Schedule: Yes
Min Charge for Deps: Yes **Hours:** 4
Min Charge for Trial: Yes **Hours:** 4
Cancellation Charge for Deps/Trial: Yes
Retainer Required: Yes, $1,500 (Non-Refundable, Replenishable)
Procedure When Dep Exceeds Paid Time: Get payment before proceeding further
Expenses Marked Up: No
Expenses Billed For: Mileage, Airline Tickets, Photocopies, Telephone Calls, Lab/Testing, Photographs, Demonstrative Aids
Portal-to-Portal: Yes **1st-class Airfare:** No
Written Retainer Agreement: Yes
Terms: Lawyer is responsible for fee, not lawyer's client, Interest for delinquent accounts, Out-of-pocket expense policies, In-court testimony minimums, Retaining counsel pays all deposition charges, Fee schedules, Portal-to-portal travel time, Deposition minimum fee, Payment for preparation time
Failure to Pay Bill Last 5 Years; Retaining Counsel: Yes **Opposing (Deps):** Yes

Psychology
Court: $300 **Review/Prep:** $200 **Deps:** $300
Years Testifying: 10
Written Fee Schedule: Yes
Min Charge for Deps: Yes **Hours:** 2
Min Charge for Trial: Yes **Hours:** 2
Cancellation Charge for Deps/Trial: Yes
Retainer Required: Yes, $2,000 (Non-Refundable, Replenishable)
Procedure When Dep Exceeds Paid Time: Get payment before proceeding further
Expenses Marked Up: No
Expenses Billed For: Mileage, Airline Tickets, Photocopies, Telephone Calls

Portal-to-Portal: Yes **1st-class Airfare:** No
Written Retainer Agreement: Yes
Terms: Lawyer is responsible for fee, not lawyer's client, Interest for delinquent accounts, Out-of-pocket expense policies, In-court testimony minimums, Retaining counsel pays all deposition charges, Fee schedules, Portal-to-portal travel time, Attorney's fees if forced to sue for collection, Payment for preparation time
Failure to Pay Bill Last 5 Years; Retaining Counsel: No **Opposing Counsel (Deps):** No

Psychology
Review/Prep: $250 **Deps:** $800
Years Testifying: 25
Written Fee Schedule: No
Min Charge for Deps: Yes
Cancellation Charge for Deps/Trial: Yes
Retainer Required: Yes, $1,100 (Non-Refundable, One Time)
Procedure When Dep Exceeds Paid Time: Proceed without immediate payment
Expenses Billed For:
Written Retainer Agreement: No
Failure to Pay Bill Last 5 Years; Retaining Counsel: No **Opposing Counsel (Deps):** No

Regulatory Proceedings
Court: $160 **Review/Prep:** $160 **Deps:** $160
Years Testifying: 15
Written Fee Schedule: No
Min Charge for Deps: No
Min Charge for Trial: No
Cancellation Charge for Deps/Trial: No
Retainer Required: No
Expenses Marked Up: No
Expenses Billed For: Airline Tickets, Photocopies
Portal-to-Portal: No **1st-class Airfare:** Yes
Written Retainer Agreement: No
Failure to Pay Bill Last 5 Years; Retaining Counsel: No **Opposing Counsel (Deps):** No

Security
Court: $100 **Review/Prep:** $100 **Deps:** $100
Years Testifying: 10
Written Fee Schedule: No
Min Charge for Deps: Yes **Hours:** 8
Min Charge for Trial: Yes **Hours:** 8
Cancellation Charge for Deps/Trial: No
Retainer Required: Yes, $1,500 (Non-Refundable, One Time)
Procedure When Dep Exceeds Paid Time: Proceed without immediate payment
Expenses Marked Up: No
Expenses Billed For: Airline Tickets, Photocopies, Telephone Calls, Photographs, Demonstrative Aids
Portal-to-Portal: Yes **1st-class Airfare:** No
Written Retainer Agreement: No
Failure to Pay Bill Last 5 Years; Retaining Counsel: No **Opposing Counsel (Deps):** No

Security
Court: $125 **Review/Prep:** $125 **Deps:** $125
Years Testifying: 15 **Majority:** Defendant
Written Fee Schedule: Yes
Min Charge for Deps: Yes **Hours:** 4
Min Charge for Trial: Yes **Hours:** 4
Cancellation Charge for Deps/Trial: No
Retainer Required: Yes, Depends on case (Refundable, Replenishable)
Expenses Marked Up: No
Expenses Billed For: Mileage, Airline Tickets, Photocopies, Telephone Calls, Photographs, Demonstrative Aids
Portal-to-Portal: Yes **1st-class Airfare:** No
Written Retainer Agreement: No
Failure to Pay Bill Last 5 Years; Retaining Counsel: No **Opposing Counsel (Deps):** No

Surgery, General
Court: $300 **Review/Prep:** $200 **Deps:** $300
Years Testifying: 30 **Majority:** Defendant
Written Fee Schedule: No
Min Charge for Deps: Yes **Hours:** 2
Min Charge for Trial: Yes **Hours:** 2
Cancellation Charge for Deps/Trial: No
Retainer Required: No
Expenses Marked Up: No
Expenses Billed For: Mileage, Airline Tickets
Portal-to-Portal: Yes **1st-class Airfare:** Yes
Written Retainer Agreement: No
Failure to Pay Bill Last 5 Years; Retaining Counsel: No **Opposing Counsel (Deps):** No

Hawaii

Accident Reconstruction
Court: $185 **Review/Prep:** $135 **Deps:** $185
Years Testifying: 18
Written Fee Schedule: Yes
Min Charge for Deps: Yes **Hours:** 4
Min Charge for Trial: Yes **Hours:** 4
Cancellation Charge for Deps/Trial: No
Retainer Required: Yes, $1,000 (Refundable, One Time)
Expenses Marked Up: No
Expenses Billed For: Photocopies, Telephone Calls, Lab/Testing, Photographs, Demonstrative Aids
Portal-to-Portal: Yes **1st-class Airfare:** Yes
Written Retainer Agreement: No
Failure to Pay Bill Last 5 Years; Retaining Counsel: Yes **Opposing Counsel (Deps):** No

Construction
Court: $400 **Review/Prep:** $225 **Deps:** $400
Years Testifying: 28
Written Fee Schedule: Yes
Min Charge for Deps: No
Min Charge for Trial: No
Cancellation Charge for Deps/Trial: No
Retainer Required: Yes, Depends on case (Refundable, Replenishable)
Expenses Marked Up: Yes
Expenses Billed For: Mileage, Airline Tickets, Photocopies, Telephone Calls, Lab/Testing, Photographs, Demonstrative Aids
Portal-to-Portal: Yes **1st-class Airfare:** No
Written Retainer Agreement: No
Failure to Pay Bill Last 5 Years; Retaining Counsel: No **Opposing Counsel (Deps):** No

Document Examiner
Court: $125 **Review/Prep:** $90 **Deps:** $100
Years Testifying: 23
Written Fee Schedule: No
Min Charge for Deps: No **Hours:** 1
Min Charge for Trial: Yes **Hours:** 1
Cancellation Charge for Deps/Trial: No
Retainer Required: Yes, $180 (Non-Refundable, One Time)
Expenses Marked Up: No
Expenses Billed For: Airline Tickets
Portal-to-Portal: Yes **1st-class Airfare:** No
Written Retainer Agreement: No
Failure to Pay Bill Last 5 Years; Retaining Counsel: No **Opposing Counsel (Deps):** No

Valuation, Business
Court: $250 **Review/Prep:** $250 **Deps:** $250
Years Testifying: 10
Written Fee Schedule: No
Min Charge for Deps: No
Min Charge for Trial: No
Cancellation Charge for Deps/Trial: No
Retainer Required: Yes, $4,000 (Refundable, Replenishable)
Expenses Marked Up: No
Expenses Billed For: Airline Tickets, Photocopies
Portal-to-Portal: Yes **1st-class Airfare:** No
Written Retainer Agreement: Yes
Terms: Out-of-pocket expense policies, Retaining counsel pays all deposition charges, Fee schedules, Payment for preparation time
Failure to Pay Bill Last 5 Years; Retaining Counsel: Yes **Opposing Counsel (Deps):** No

Idaho

Accident Reconstruction
Court: $135 **Review/Prep:** $150 **Deps:** $135
Years Testifying: 6 **Majority:** Defendant
Written Fee Schedule: Yes
Min Charge for Deps: Yes
Min Charge for Trial: No
Cancellation Charge for Deps/Trial: No

Retainer Required: Yes, $500 (Refundable, Replenishable)
Expenses Marked Up: No
Expenses Billed For: Mileage, Photocopies, Telephone Calls, Photographs
Portal-to-Portal: Yes **1st-class Airfare:** No
Written Retainer Agreement: No
Failure to Pay Bill Last 5 Years; Retaining Counsel: Yes **Opposing Counsel (Deps):** No

Illinois

Accident Reconstruction
Court: $150 **Review/Prep:** $100 **Deps:** $150
Years Testifying: 11
Written Fee Schedule: Yes
Min Charge for Deps: Yes **Hours:** 4
Min Charge for Trial: Yes **Hours:** 4
Cancellation Charge for Deps/Trial: No
Retainer Required: Yes, $1,000 (Non-Refundable, Replenishable)
Procedure When Dep Exceeds Paid Time: Proceed without immediate payment
Expenses Marked Up: No
Expenses Billed For: Mileage, Airline Tickets, Photocopies, Telephone Calls, Lab/Testing, Photographs, Demonstrative Aids
Portal-to-Portal: Yes **1st-class Airfare:** No
Written Retainer Agreement: Yes
Terms: Lawyer is responsible for fee, not lawyer's client, Interest for delinquent accounts, Out-of-pocket expense policies, In-court testimony minimums, Retaining counsel pays all deposition charges, Fee schedules, Portal-to-portal travel time, Attorney's fees if forced to sue for collection, Deposition minimum fee, Payment for preparation time
Failure to Pay Bill Last 5 Years; Retaining Counsel: No **Opposing Counsel (Deps):** No

Accident Reconstruction
Court: $100 **Review/Prep:** $75 **Deps:** $100
Years Testifying: 22
Written Fee Schedule: Yes
Min Charge for Deps: Yes **Hours:** 2
Min Charge for Trial: Yes **Hours:** 2
Cancellation Charge for Deps/Trial: No
Retainer Required: Yes, $300 (Refundable, One Time)
Expenses Billed For: Mileage, Airline Tickets, Lab/Testing, Photographs, Demonstrative Aids
Portal-to-Portal: Yes **1st-class Airfare:** No
Written Retainer Agreement: Yes
Terms: Lawyer is responsible for fee, not lawyer's client, Out-of-pocket expense policies, In-court testimony minimums, Retaining counsel pays all deposition charges, Fee schedules, Portal-to-portal travel time, Deposition minimum fee
Failure to Pay Bill Last 5 Years; Retaining Counsel: Yes **Opposing Counsel (Deps):** No

Accident Reconstruction/Automotive
Court: $400 **Review/Prep:** $300 **Deps:** $400
Years Testifying: 33 **Majority:** Defendant
Written Fee Schedule: Yes
Min Charge for Deps: Yes **Hours:** 6
Min Charge for Trial: Yes **Hours:** 6
Cancellation Charge for Deps/Trial: No
Retainer Required: Yes, $3,000 (Non-Refundable, One Time)
Expenses Marked Up: Yes
Expenses Billed For: Mileage, Airline Tickets
Portal-to-Portal: Yes **1st-class Airfare:** Yes
Written Retainer Agreement: Yes
Terms: Lawyer is responsible for fee, not lawyer's client, Interest for delinquent accounts, Out-of-pocket expense policies, In-court testimony minimums, Retaining counsel pays all deposition charges, Fee schedules
Failure to Pay Bill Last 5 Years; Retaining Counsel: Yes **Opposing (Deps):** Yes

Accounting
Court: $250 **Review/Prep:** $250 **Deps:** $250
Years Testifying: 4 **Majority:** Defendant
Written Fee Schedule: Yes
Min Charge for Deps: No
Min Charge for Trial: No
Cancellation Charge for Deps/Trial: No
Retainer Required: Yes, $7,500 (Refundable, Replenishable)
Expenses Billed For: Mileage, Airline Tickets, Photocopies, Telephone Calls, Lab/Testing, Photographs, Demonstrative Aids
Portal-to-Portal: Yes **1st-class Airfare:** No
Written Retainer Agreement: Yes
Terms: Lawyer is responsible for fee, not lawyer's client, Out-of-pocket expense policies, Fee schedules, Attorney's fees if forced to sue for collection
Failure to Pay Bill Last 5 Years; Retaining Counsel: No **Opposing Counsel (Deps):** No

Appraisals
Court: $285 **Review/Prep:** $285 **Deps:** $285
Written Fee Schedule: Yes
Min Charge for Deps: Yes **Hours:** 4
Min Charge for Trial: Yes **Hours:** 4
Cancellation Charge for Deps/Trial: Yes
Retainer Required: Yes, $1,875 (Non-Refundable, Replenishable)
Procedure When Dep Exceeds Paid Time: Get payment before proceeding further
Expenses Marked Up: Yes
Expenses Billed For: Mileage, Airline Tickets, Photocopies, Telephone Calls, Photographs
Portal-to-Portal: Yes **1st-class Airfare:** No
Written Retainer Agreement: Yes
Terms: Out-of-pocket expense policies, In-court testimony minimums, Retaining counsel pays all deposition charges, Fee schedules, Portal-to-portal travel time, Deposition minimum fee, Payment for preparation time, First class air travel
Failure to Pay Bill Last 5 Years; Retaining Counsel: No **Opposing Counsel (Deps):** No

Cardiology
Court: $400 **Review/Prep:** $400 **Deps:** $400
Years Testifying: 20
Written Fee Schedule: Yes
Min Charge for Deps: No **Hours:** 10
Min Charge for Trial: Yes **Hours:** 10
Cancellation Charge for Deps/Trial: No
Retainer Required: No
Expenses Marked Up: No
Expenses Billed For: Mileage, Airline Tickets
Portal-to-Portal: Yes **1st-class Airfare:** No
Written Retainer Agreement: No
Failure to Pay Bill Last 5 Years; Retaining Counsel: No **Opposing Counsel (Deps):** No

Chemicals/Hazardous Materials
Court: $375 **Review/Prep:** $275 **Deps:** $375
Years Testifying: 9
Written Fee Schedule: Yes
Min Charge for Deps: Yes
Min Charge for Trial: No
Cancellation Charge for Deps/Trial: No
Retainer Required: Yes, $3,000 (Refundable, Replenishable)
Procedure When Dep Exceeds Paid Time: Proceed without immediate payment
Expenses Marked Up: Yes
Expenses Billed For: Mileage, Airline Tickets, Lab/Testing, Photographs
Portal-to-Portal: Yes **1st-class Airfare:** No
Written Retainer Agreement: No
Failure to Pay Bill Last 5 Years; Retaining Counsel: Yes **Opposing (Deps):** Yes

Concrete
Court: $190 **Review/Prep:** $190 **Deps:** $190
Years Testifying: 30
Written Fee Schedule: Yes
Min Charge for Deps: No
Min Charge for Trial: No
Cancellation Charge for Deps/Trial: No
Retainer Required: No
Expenses Marked Up: Yes
Expenses Billed For: Mileage, Airline Tickets, Lab/Testing, Photographs
Portal-to-Portal: Yes **1st-class Airfare:** No
Written Retainer Agreement: No
Failure to Pay Bill Last 5 Years; Retaining Counsel: No **Opposing Counsel (Deps):** No

Concrete/Materials Failures
Court: $300 **Review/Prep:** $220 **Deps:** $300
Years Testifying: 22
Written Fee Schedule: Yes
Min Charge for Deps: No
Min Charge for Trial: No
Cancellation Charge for Deps/Trial: No
Retainer Required: No
Expenses Marked Up: Yes
Expenses Billed For: Mileage, Airline Tickets, Photocopies, Lab/Testing, Photographs, Demonstrative Aids
Written Retainer Agreement: No
Failure to Pay Bill Last 5 Years; Retaining Counsel: Yes **Opposing Counsel (Deps):** No

Engineering, Marine
Court: $200 **Review/Prep:** $150 **Deps:** $150
Years Testifying: 10 **Majority:** Defendant
Written Fee Schedule: No
Min Charge for Deps: Yes **Hours:** 4
Min Charge for Trial: Yes **Hours:** 4
Cancellation Charge for Deps/Trial: Yes
Retainer Required: No
Procedure When Dep Exceeds Paid Time: Proceed without immediate payment
Expenses Marked Up: No
Expenses Billed For: Mileage, Telephone Calls, Lab/Testing
1st-class Airfare: Yes
Written Retainer Agreement: No
Failure to Pay Bill Last 5 Years; Retaining Counsel: No **Opposing Counsel (Deps):** No

Engineering, Structural
Court: $180 **Review/Prep:** $175 **Deps:** $178
Years Testifying: 10
Written Fee Schedule: Yes
Min Charge for Deps: No
Min Charge for Trial: No
Cancellation Charge for Deps/Trial: No
Retainer Required: No
Expenses Marked Up: Yes
Expenses Billed For: Mileage, Airline Tickets, Photocopies, Telephone Calls, Lab/Testing, Photographs, Demonstrative Aids
Portal-to-Portal: Yes **1st-class Airfare:** No
Written Retainer Agreement: Yes
Terms: Lawyer is responsible for fee, not lawyer's client, Interest for delinquent accounts, Out-of-pocket expense policies, Fee schedules, Portal-to-portal travel time, Attorney's fees if forced to sue for collection, Payment for preparation time
Failure to Pay Bill Last 5 Years; Retaining Counsel: Yes **Opposing (Deps):** Yes

Fire Investigation
Court: $150 **Review/Prep:** $125 **Deps:** $150
Years Testifying: 12
Written Fee Schedule: Yes
Min Charge for Deps: No
Min Charge for Trial: No
Cancellation Charge for Deps/Trial: No
Retainer Required: Yes, $5,000 (Refundable, Replenishable)
Procedure When Dep Exceeds Paid Time: Proceed without immediate payment
Expenses Marked Up: No
Expenses Billed For: Mileage, Airline Tickets, Photocopies, Telephone Calls, Lab/Testing, Photographs, Demonstrative Aids
Portal-to-Portal: Yes **1st-class Airfare:** No
Written Retainer Agreement: No
Failure to Pay Bill Last 5 Years; Retaining Counsel: No **Opposing Counsel (Deps):** No

Fraud, Securities
Court: $300 **Review/Prep:** $300 **Deps:** $300
Years Testifying: 20
Written Fee Schedule: Yes
Min Charge for Deps: No
Min Charge for Trial: No
Cancellation Charge for Deps/Trial: Yes
Retainer Required: Yes, $3,000 (Non-Refundable)
Expenses Marked Up: No
Expenses Billed For: Mileage, Airline Tickets, Demonstrative Aids
Portal-to-Portal: Yes **1st-class Airfare:** No
Written Retainer Agreement: Yes
Terms: Lawyer is responsible for fee, not lawyer's client, Out-of-pocket expense policies, In-court testimony minimums, Retaining counsel pays all deposition charges, Fee schedules, Portal-to-portal travel time, Payment for preparation time
Failure to Pay Bill Last 5 Years; Retaining Counsel: Yes **Opposing Counsel (Deps):** No

Geriatrics/Long Term Care
Court: $165 **Review/Prep:** $100 **Deps:** $150
Years Testifying: 6 **Majority:** Plaintiff
Written Fee Schedule: Yes
Min Charge for Deps: No
Min Charge for Trial: No
Cancellation Charge for Deps/Trial: No
Retainer Required: No
Expenses Marked Up: No
Expenses Billed For: Mileage, Airline Tickets, Photocopies, Telephone Calls, Lab/Testing, Photographs, Demonstrative Aids
Portal-to-Portal: Yes **1st-class Airfare:** No
Written Retainer Agreement: No
Failure to Pay Bill Last 5 Years; Retaining Counsel: Yes **Opposing Counsel (Deps):** No

Human Factors
Court: $350 **Review/Prep:** $350 **Deps:** $350
Years Testifying: 30
Written Fee Schedule: Yes
Min Charge for Deps: Yes **Hours:** 2
Min Charge for Trial: Yes **Hours:** 2
Cancellation Charge for Deps/Trial: No
Retainer Required: Yes, $2,500 (Non-Refundable, One Time)
Expenses Marked Up: No
Expenses Billed For: Mileage, Airline Tickets, Photocopies, Lab/Testing, Photographs, Demonstrative Aids
Portal-to-Portal: Yes **1st-class Airfare:** No
Written Retainer Agreement: Yes
Terms: Lawyer is responsible for fee, not lawyer's client, Interest for delinquent accounts, Out-of-pocket expense policies, In-court testimony minimums, Retaining counsel pays all deposition charges, Fee schedules, Portal-to-portal travel time, Attorney's fees if forced to sue for collection, Deposition minimum fee, Payment for preparation time
Failure to Pay Bill Last 5 Years; Retaining Counsel: Yes **Opposing (Deps):** Yes

Ladders
Court: $225 **Review/Prep:** $185 **Deps:** $225
Years Testifying: 14 **Majority:** Plaintiff
Written Fee Schedule: Yes
Min Charge for Deps: Yes
Min Charge for Trial: No
Cancellation Charge for Deps/Trial: No
Retainer Required: Yes, (Refundable, Replenishable)
Procedure When Dep Exceeds Paid Time: Proceed without immediate payment
Expenses Marked Up: No
Expenses Billed For: Mileage, Airline Tickets, Lab/Testing, Photographs, Demonstrative Aids
Portal-to-Portal: No **1st-class Airfare:** No
Written Retainer Agreement: No
Failure to Pay Bill Last 5 Years; Retaining Counsel: Yes **Opposing Counsel (Deps):** No

Law Enforcement
Court: $150 **Review/Prep:** $150 **Deps:** $150
Years Testifying: 15
Written Fee Schedule: Yes
Min Charge for Deps: Yes **Hours:** 8
Min Charge for Trial: Yes **Hours:** 8
Cancellation Charge for Deps/Trial: No
Retainer Required: Yes, $1,500 (Refundable, One Time)
Procedure When Dep Exceeds Paid Time: Proceed without immediate payment

Expenses Marked Up: No
Expenses Billed For: Airline Tickets
Portal-to-Portal: Yes **1st-class Airfare:** No
Written Retainer Agreement: No
Failure to Pay Bill Last 5 Years; Retaining Counsel: No **Opposing Counsel (Deps):** No

Law Enforcement
Court: $185 **Review/Prep:** $100 **Deps:** $185
Years Testifying: 21
Written Fee Schedule: Yes
Min Charge for Deps: Yes **Hours:** 4
Min Charge for Trial: Yes **Hours:** 4
Cancellation Charge for Deps/Trial: Yes
Retainer Required: Yes, (Refundable, Replenishable)
Procedure When Dep Exceeds Paid Time: Proceed without immediate payment
Expenses Marked Up: Yes
Expenses Billed For: Telephone Calls, Demonstrative Aids
Portal-to-Portal: Yes **1st-class Airfare:** No
Written Retainer Agreement: No
Failure to Pay Bill Last 5 Years; Retaining Counsel: Yes **Opposing Counsel (Deps):** No

Law, Patents
Court: $250 **Review/Prep:** $250 **Deps:** $250
Years Testifying: 25
Written Fee Schedule: No
Min Charge for Deps: No
Min Charge for Trial: No
Cancellation Charge for Deps/Trial: No
Retainer Required: No
Expenses Marked Up: No
Expenses Billed For: Mileage, Airline Tickets, Photocopies, Telephone Calls, Photographs, Demonstrative Aids
Portal-to-Portal: Yes **1st-class Airfare:** No
Written Retainer Agreement: No
Failure to Pay Bill Last 5 Years; Retaining Counsel: Yes **Opposing Counsel (Deps):** No

Linguistics
Court: $350 **Review/Prep:** $300 **Deps:** $350
Written Fee Schedule: No
Cancellation Charge for Deps/Trial: Yes
Retainer Required: Depends, Depends on case
Procedure When Dep Exceeds Paid Time: Get payment before proceeding further
Expenses Marked Up: No
Expenses Billed For: Mileage, Airline Tickets, Photocopies, Telephone Calls, Demonstrative Aids
Portal-to-Portal: Yes **1st-class Airfare:** No
Written Retainer Agreement: Yes
Terms: Lawyer is responsible for fee, not lawyer's client, Out-of-pocket expense policies, In-court testimony minimums, Retaining counsel pays all deposition charges, Fee schedules, Portal-to-portal travel time, Attorney's fees if forced to sue for collection, Deposition minimum fee, Payment for preparation time, Payment for Analysis & Report Writing
Failure to Pay Bill Last 5 Years; Retaining Counsel: No **Opposing Counsel (Deps):** No

Neurology
Court: $500 **Review/Prep:** $350 **Deps:** $350
Years Testifying: 15
Written Fee Schedule: No
Min Charge for Deps: Yes **Hours:** 4
Min Charge for Trial: Yes **Hours:** 4
Cancellation Charge for Deps/Trial: Yes
Retainer Required: Yes, (Refundable, Replenishable)
Procedure When Dep Exceeds Paid Time: Proceed without immediate payment
Expenses Marked Up: No
Expenses Billed For: Airline Tickets, Demonstrative Aids
Portal-to-Portal: Yes **1st-class Airfare:** No
Written Retainer Agreement: No
Failure to Pay Bill Last 5 Years; Retaining Counsel: Yes **Opposing Counsel (Deps):** No

Obstetrics & Gynecology
Court: $400 **Review/Prep:** $150 **Deps:** $250
Written Fee Schedule: Yes
Min Charge for Deps: Yes **Hours:** 1
Min Charge for Trial: Yes **Hours:** 1
Cancellation Charge for Deps/Trial: Yes
Retainer Required: Yes, $400 (Refundable, Replenishable)
Procedure When Dep Exceeds Paid Time: Get payment before proceeding further
Expenses Marked Up: Yes
Expenses Billed For: Mileage, Airline Tickets, Photocopies, Telephone Calls, Lab/Testing, Photographs, Demonstrative Aids
Portal-to-Portal: Yes **1st-class Airfare:** No
Written Retainer Agreement: Yes
Terms: Lawyer is responsible for fee, not lawyer's client, Interest for delinquent accounts, Out-of-pocket expense policies, In-court testimony minimums, Retaining counsel pays all deposition charges, Fee schedules, Portal-to-portal travel time, Attorney's fees if forced to sue for collection, Deposition minimum fee, Payment for preparation time, First class air travel
Failure to Pay Bill Last 5 Years; Retaining Counsel: No **Opposing Counsel (Deps):** No

Obstetrics & Gynecology
Court: $500 **Review/Prep:** $250 **Deps:** $350
Years Testifying: 5 **Majority:** Defendant
Written Fee Schedule: Yes
Min Charge for Deps: No
Min Charge for Trial: No
Cancellation Charge for Deps/Trial: Yes
Retainer Required: No
Expenses Marked Up: No
Portal-to-Portal: Yes **1st-class Airfare:** No
Written Retainer Agreement: No
Failure to Pay Bill Last 5 Years; Retaining Counsel: No **Opposing Counsel (Deps):** No

Occupational Medicine
Court: $500 **Review/Prep:** $500 **Deps:** $500
Years Testifying: 2 **Majority:** Plaintiff
Written Fee Schedule: Yes
Min Charge for Deps: Yes **Hours:** 2
Min Charge for Trial: Yes **Hours:** 2
Cancellation Charge for Deps/Trial: Yes
Retainer Required: No
Procedure When Dep Exceeds Paid Time: Proceed without immediate payment
Expenses Billed For: Mileage, Airline Tickets, Photographs
Portal-to-Portal: Yes **1st-class Airfare:** No
Written Retainer Agreement: No
Failure to Pay Bill Last 5 Years; Retaining Counsel: Yes **Opposing Counsel (Deps):** No

Oncology, Gynecological
Court: $300 **Review/Prep:** $250 **Deps:** $450
Years Testifying: 20 **Majority:** Plaintiff
Written Fee Schedule: Yes
Min Charge for Deps: Yes **Hours:** 10
Min Charge for Trial: Yes **Hours:** 10
Cancellation Charge for Deps/Trial: Yes
Retainer Required: Yes, $500 (Non-Refundable, One Time)
Procedure When Dep Exceeds Paid Time: Proceed without immediate payment
Expenses Marked Up: No
Expenses Billed For: Telephone Calls
Portal-to-Portal: Yes **1st-class Airfare:** Yes
Written Retainer Agreement: No
Failure to Pay Bill Last 5 Years; Retaining Counsel: No **Opposing Counsel (Deps):** No

Ophthalmology
Court: $2,750 **Review/Prep:** $350 **Deps:** $1,000
Years Testifying: 30 **Majority:** Plaintiff
Written Fee Schedule: Yes
Min Charge for Deps: Yes
Min Charge for Trial: No
Cancellation Charge for Deps/Trial: Yes
Retainer Required: No
Expenses Marked Up: Yes
Expenses Billed For: Mileage
1st-class Airfare: No
Written Retainer Agreement: No
Failure to Pay Bill Last 5 Years; Retaining Counsel: No **Opposing Counsel (Deps):** No

Orthopedics
Court: $600 **Review/Prep:** $450 **Deps:** $600
Years Testifying: 5
Written Fee Schedule: Yes
Min Charge for Deps: Yes **Hours:** 2
Min Charge for Trial: Yes **Hours:** 2
Cancellation Charge for Deps/Trial: Yes
Retainer Required: No
Expenses Billed For: Airline Tickets, Photocopies, Photographs, Demonstrative Aids
Portal-to-Portal: No **1st-class Airfare:** No
Written Retainer Agreement: No
Failure to Pay Bill Last 5 Years; Retaining Counsel: No **Opposing Counsel (Deps):** No

Orthopedics
Court: $375 **Review/Prep:** $300 **Deps:** $600
Years Testifying: 25
Written Fee Schedule: Yes
Min Charge for Deps: Yes **Hours:** 8
Min Charge for Trial: Yes **Hours:** 8
Cancellation Charge for Deps/Trial: No
Retainer Required: Yes, $900 (Non-Refundable, One Time)
Procedure When Dep Exceeds Paid Time: Proceed without immediate payment
Expenses Marked Up: No
Expenses Billed For: Mileage, Airline Tickets
Portal-to-Portal: No **1st-class Airfare:** No
Written Retainer Agreement: No
Failure to Pay Bill Last 5 Years; Retaining Counsel: No **Opposing Counsel (Deps):** No

Orthopedics
Court: $500 **Review/Prep:** $500 **Deps:** $500
Years Testifying: 25 **Majority:** Defendant
Written Fee Schedule: Yes
Min Charge for Deps: Yes
Min Charge for Trial: No
Cancellation Charge for Deps/Trial: Yes
Retainer Required: Yes, Total est. fee (Non-Refundable, Replenishable)
Procedure When Dep Exceeds Paid Time: Proceed without immediate payment
Expenses Billed For: Mileage, Airline Tickets, Photocopies, Telephone Calls
Portal-to-Portal: Yes **1st-class Airfare:** No
Written Retainer Agreement: No
Failure to Pay Bill Last 5 Years; Retaining Counsel: No **Opposing Counsel (Deps):** No

Orthopedics
Court: $750 **Review/Prep:** $325 **Deps:** $650
Years Testifying: 18 **Majority:** Defendant
Written Fee Schedule: Yes
Min Charge for Deps: No
Min Charge for Trial: No
Cancellation Charge for Deps/Trial: Yes
Retainer Required: No
Procedure When Dep Exceeds Paid Time: Proceed without immediate payment
Expenses Marked Up: No
Expenses Billed For: Mileage, Airline Tickets, Telephone Calls
Portal-to-Portal: Yes **1st-class Airfare:** No
Written Retainer Agreement: Yes
Terms: Fee schedules
Failure to Pay Bill Last 5 Years; Retaining Counsel: Yes **Opposing (Deps):** Yes

Osteopathy/Disability/Acupuncture
Review/Prep: $340 **Deps:** $400
Years Testifying: 22
Written Fee Schedule: Yes
Min Charge for Deps: Yes **Hours:** 4
Min Charge for Trial: Yes **Hours:** 4
Cancellation Charge for Deps/Trial: Yes
Retainer Required: Yes, Depends on case (Non-Refundable)
Procedure When Dep Exceeds Paid Time: Get payment before proceeding further
Expenses Marked Up: Yes
Expenses Billed For: Mileage, Airline Tickets
Portal-to-Portal: Yes
Written Retainer Agreement: Yes
Terms: In-court testimony minimums, Retaining counsel pays all deposition charges, Fee schedules, Portal-to-portal travel time, Deposition minimum fee
Failure to Pay Bill Last 5 Years; Retaining Counsel: No

Pharmacology/Pharmacy
Court: $425 **Review/Prep:** $425 **Deps:** $425
Years Testifying: 25
Written Fee Schedule: Yes
Min Charge for Deps: Yes **Hours:** 8
Min Charge for Trial: Yes **Hours:** 8
Cancellation Charge for Deps/Trial: Yes
Retainer Required: Yes, $2,000 (Refundable, Replenishable)
Procedure When Dep Exceeds Paid Time: Proceed without immediate payment
Expenses Marked Up: No
Expenses Billed For: Airline Tickets, Photocopies, Lab/Testing, Demonstrative Aids
Portal-to-Portal: Yes **1st-class Airfare:** No
Written Retainer Agreement: No
Failure to Pay Bill Last 5 Years; Retaining Counsel: Yes **Opposing (Deps):** Yes

Physical Medicine & Rehabilitation
Court: $500 **Review/Prep:** $300 **Deps:** $500
Years Testifying: 15 **Majority:** Plaintiff
Written Fee Schedule: No
Min Charge for Deps: Yes **Hours:** 4
Min Charge for Trial: Yes **Hours:** 4
Cancellation Charge for Deps/Trial: Yes
Retainer Required: No
Procedure When Dep Exceeds Paid Time: Proceed without immediate payment
Expenses Marked Up: No
Expenses Billed For: Mileage, Airline Tickets, Telephone Calls
Portal-to-Portal: Yes **1st-class Airfare:** No
Written Retainer Agreement: No
Failure to Pay Bill Last 5 Years; Retaining Counsel: No **Opposing Counsel (Deps):** No

Physical Medicine & Rehabilitation/ Pain Management/Medicine
Court: $400 **Review/Prep:** $400 **Deps:** $400
Written Fee Schedule: Yes
Min Charge for Deps: Yes **Hours:** 2
Min Charge for Trial: Yes **Hours:** 2
Cancellation Charge for Deps/Trial: Yes
Retainer Required: Yes, $800 (Non-Refundable, One Time)
Procedure When Dep Exceeds Paid Time: Proceed without immediate payment
Expenses Marked Up: No
Expenses Billed For: Mileage, Airline Tickets, Telephone Calls, Demonstrative Aids
Portal-to-Portal: Yes **1st-class Airfare:** No
Written Retainer Agreement: No
Failure to Pay Bill Last 5 Years; Retaining Counsel: No **Opposing Counsel (Deps):** No

Plastics
Court: $300 **Review/Prep:** $300 **Deps:** $300
Years Testifying: 7
Written Fee Schedule: Yes
Min Charge for Deps: No
Min Charge for Trial: No
Cancellation Charge for Deps/Trial: No
Retainer Required: Yes, $2,500 (Refundable, One Time)
Expenses Marked Up: Yes
Expenses Billed For: Mileage, Airline Tickets, Photocopies, Photographs, Demonstrative Aids
Portal-to-Portal: Yes **1st-class Airfare:** No
Written Retainer Agreement: Yes
Terms: Interest for delinquent accounts, Out-of-pocket expense policies, Retaining counsel pays all deposition charges, Fee schedules, Portal-to-portal travel time
Failure to Pay Bill Last 5 Years; Retaining Counsel: Yes **Opposing (Deps):** Yes

Psychiatry
Court: $400 **Review/Prep:** $400 **Deps:** $400
Years Testifying: 25
Written Fee Schedule: No
Min Charge for Deps: Yes **Hours:** 3
Min Charge for Trial: Yes **Hours:** 3
Cancellation Charge for Deps/Trial: Yes
Retainer Required: Yes, Total est. fee (Refundable, Replenishable)

Procedure When Dep Exceeds Paid Time: Varies depending on case
Expenses Marked Up: Yes
Expenses Billed For: Mileage, Airline Tickets, Photocopies, Telephone Calls, Demonstrative Aids
Portal-to-Portal: Yes **1st-class Airfare:** No
Written Retainer Agreement: Yes
Terms: Out-of-pocket expense policies, Retaining counsel pays all deposition charges, Fee schedules, Portal-to-portal travel time, Attorney's fees if forced to sue for collection, Payment for preparation time
Failure to Pay Bill Last 5 Years; Retaining Counsel: Yes **Opposing (Deps):** Yes

Psychology, Child

Court: $375 **Review/Prep:** $225 **Deps:** $375
Years Testifying: 10
Written Fee Schedule: Yes
Min Charge for Deps: Yes **Hours:** 4
Min Charge for Trial: Yes **Hours:** 4
Cancellation Charge for Deps/Trial: Yes
Retainer Required: Yes, Depends on case (Refundable, One Time)
Expenses Marked Up: No
Expenses Billed For: Mileage, Airline Tickets, Photocopies, Telephone Calls, Lab/Testing
Portal-to-Portal: No **1st-class Airfare:** No
Written Retainer Agreement: No
Failure to Pay Bill Last 5 Years; Retaining Counsel: No **Opposing Counsel (Deps):** Yes

Safety

Court: $175 **Review/Prep:** $175 **Deps:** $175
Years Testifying: 14 **Majority:** Plaintiff
Written Fee Schedule: Yes
Min Charge for Deps: Yes **Hours:** 4
Min Charge for Trial: Yes **Hours:** 4
Cancellation Charge for Deps/Trial: No
Retainer Required: Yes, $1,400 (Non-Refundable, One Time)
Expenses Marked Up: No
Expenses Billed For: Mileage, Airline Tickets, Photographs, Demonstrative Aids
Portal-to-Portal: Yes **1st-class Airfare:** No
Written Retainer Agreement: Yes
Terms: Lawyer is responsible for fee, not lawyer's client, Interest for delinquent accounts, Out-of-pocket expense policies, In-court testimony minimums, Retaining counsel pays all deposition charges, Fee schedules, Portal-to-portal travel time, Attorney's fees if forced to sue for collection, Deposition minimum fee, First class air travel
Failure to Pay Bill Last 5 Years; Retaining Counsel: Yes **Opposing (Deps):** Yes

Safety

Court: $175 **Review/Prep:** $175 **Deps:** $175
Years Testifying: 13 **Majority:** Plaintiff
Written Fee Schedule: Yes
Min Charge for Deps: Yes **Hours:** 4
Min Charge for Trial: Yes **Hours:** 4
Cancellation Charge for Deps/Trial: No
Retainer Required: Yes, $1,400 (Non-Refundable, One Time)
Expenses Marked Up: No
Expenses Billed For: Mileage, Airline Tickets, Photographs
Portal-to-Portal: Yes **1st-class Airfare:** No
Written Retainer Agreement: Yes
Terms: Lawyer is responsible for fee, not lawyer's client, Interest for delinquent accounts, Out-of-pocket expense policies, Retaining counsel pays all deposition charges, Fee schedules, Portal-to-portal travel time, Attorney's fees if forced to sue for collection, Deposition minimum fee
Failure to Pay Bill Last 5 Years; Retaining Counsel: Yes **Opposing Counsel (Deps):** No

Safety, Chemical Plant

Court: $150 **Review/Prep:** $150 **Deps:** $150
Years Testifying: 4 **Majority:** Plaintiff
Written Fee Schedule: Yes
Min Charge for Deps: No
Min Charge for Trial: No
Cancellation Charge for Deps/Trial: No
Retainer Required: Yes, $900 (Non-Refundable)
Procedure When Dep Exceeds Paid Time: Proceed without immediate payment
Expenses Marked Up: No
Expenses Billed For: Airline Tickets
Portal-to-Portal: Yes **1st-class Airfare:** No
Written Retainer Agreement: No
Failure to Pay Bill Last 5 Years; Retaining Counsel: No **Opposing Counsel (Deps):** No

Security

Court: $225 **Review/Prep:** $190 **Deps:** $225
Years Testifying: 6 **Majority:** Defendant
Written Fee Schedule: Yes
Min Charge for Deps: Yes **Hours:** 4
Min Charge for Trial: Yes **Hours:** 4
Cancellation Charge for Deps/Trial: No
Retainer Required: Yes, $1,500 (Non-Refundable, One Time)
Expenses Marked Up: No
Expenses Billed For: Mileage, Airline Tickets
Portal-to-Portal: Yes **1st-class Airfare:** No
Written Retainer Agreement: No
Failure to Pay Bill Last 5 Years; Retaining Counsel: No **Opposing Counsel (Deps):** No

Surgery, Colon & Rectal

Court: $600 **Review/Prep:** $400 **Deps:** $500
Years Testifying: 25
Written Fee Schedule: Yes
Min Charge for Deps: No
Min Charge for Trial: No
Cancellation Charge for Deps/Trial: No
Retainer Required: Yes, $1,000 (Non-Refundable, One Time)
Expenses Marked Up: No
Expenses Billed For: Mileage, Airline Tickets, Photocopies, Telephone Calls, Lab/Testing, Photographs, Demonstrative Aids
Portal-to-Portal: Yes **1st-class Airfare:** No
Written Retainer Agreement: No
Failure to Pay Bill Last 5 Years; Retaining Counsel: Yes **Opposing Counsel (Deps):** No

Surgery, Hand/Orthopedics

Court: $600 **Review/Prep:** $450 **Deps:** $600
Years Testifying: 1
Written Fee Schedule: Yes
Min Charge for Deps: Yes **Hours:** 2
Min Charge for Trial: Yes **Hours:** 2
Cancellation Charge for Deps/Trial: Yes
Retainer Required: No
Procedure When Dep Exceeds Paid Time: Proceed without immediate payment
Expenses Marked Up: No
Expenses Billed For: Mileage, Airline Tickets, Photocopies, Telephone Calls, Photographs, Demonstrative Aids
Portal-to-Portal: Yes **1st-class Airfare:** No
Written Retainer Agreement: No
Failure to Pay Bill Last 5 Years; Retaining Counsel: No **Opposing Counsel (Deps):** Yes

Valuation, Business

Court: $250 **Review/Prep:** $300 **Deps:** $250
Years Testifying: 7
Written Fee Schedule: No
Min Charge for Deps: Yes **Hours:** 4
Min Charge for Trial: Yes **Hours:** 4
Cancellation Charge for Deps/Trial: Yes
Retainer Required: Yes, 50% est. fee (Partially Refundable, One Time)
Procedure When Dep Exceeds Paid Time: Get payment before proceeding further
Expenses Marked Up: No
Expenses Billed For: Airline Tickets, Lab/Testing
Portal-to-Portal: No **1st-class Airfare:** No
Written Retainer Agreement: Yes
Terms: Retaining counsel pays all deposition charges, Deposition minimum fee
Failure to Pay Bill Last 5 Years; Retaining Counsel: No **Opposing Counsel (Deps):** No

Vocational Rehabilitation

Court: $200 **Review/Prep:** $180 **Deps:** $200
Years Testifying: 24
Written Fee Schedule: Yes
Min Charge for Deps: No
Min Charge for Trial: No
Cancellation Charge for Deps/Trial: No
Retainer Required: Yes, $1,000 (Refundable, One Time)
Expenses Marked Up: No
Expenses Billed For: Mileage, Airline Tickets, Photocopies, Telephone Calls
Portal-to-Portal: Yes **1st-class Airfare:** No
Written Retainer Agreement: Yes
Terms: Lawyer is responsible for fee, not lawyer's client, Out-of-pocket expense policies, Retaining counsel pays all deposition charges, Portal-to-portal travel time
Failure to Pay Bill Last 5 Years; Retaining Counsel: Yes **Opposing (Deps):** Yes

Indiana

Engineering, Highway/Highways

Court: $180 **Review/Prep:** $180 **Deps:** $180
Years Testifying: 25 **Majority:** Plaintiff
Written Fee Schedule: Yes
Min Charge for Deps: No
Min Charge for Trial: No
Cancellation Charge for Deps/Trial: No
Retainer Required: No
Expenses Marked Up: No
Expenses Billed For: Mileage, Airline Tickets, Lab/Testing, Demonstrative Aids
Portal-to-Portal: No **1st-class Airfare:** No
Written Retainer Agreement: No
Failure to Pay Bill Last 5 Years; Retaining Counsel: No **Opposing Counsel (Deps):** No

Machinery/Construction

Court: $190 **Review/Prep:** $135 **Deps:** $125
Years Testifying: 21
Written Fee Schedule: Yes
Min Charge for Deps: Yes **Hours:** 8
Min Charge for Trial: Yes **Hours:** 8
Cancellation Charge for Deps/Trial: No
Retainer Required: No
Expenses Marked Up: No
Expenses Billed For: Mileage, Airline Tickets, Photocopies, Lab/Testing, Photographs, Demonstrative Aids
Portal-to-Portal: Yes **1st-class Airfare:** No
Written Retainer Agreement: No
Failure to Pay Bill Last 5 Years; Retaining Counsel: Yes **Opposing (Deps):** Yes

Mortuary Science

Court: $175 **Review/Prep:** $175 **Deps:** $175
Years Testifying: 9 **Majority:** Plaintiff
Written Fee Schedule: Yes
Min Charge for Deps: Yes **Hours:** 4
Min Charge for Trial: Yes **Hours:** 4
Cancellation Charge for Deps/Trial: No
Retainer Required: Yes, $350 (Non-Refundable, One Time)
Expenses Marked Up: No
Expenses Billed For: Mileage, Airline Tickets, Photocopies, Telephone Calls, Photographs, Demonstrative Aids
Portal-to-Portal: Yes **1st-class Airfare:** No
Written Retainer Agreement: No
Failure to Pay Bill Last 5 Years; Retaining Counsel: No **Opposing Counsel (Deps):** No

Nursing

Court: $100 **Review/Prep:** $100 **Deps:** $100
Years Testifying: 1
Written Fee Schedule: No
Min Charge for Deps: No
Min Charge for Trial: No
Cancellation Charge for Deps/Trial: No
Retainer Required: Yes, $500 (Non-Refundable, One Time)
Expenses Marked Up: No
Expenses Billed For: Mileage, Airline Tickets, Photocopies, Telephone Calls, Demonstrative Aids
Portal-to-Portal: Yes **1st-class Airfare:** No
Written Retainer Agreement: No
Failure to Pay Bill Last 5 Years; Retaining Counsel: No **Opposing Counsel (Deps):** Yes

Obstetrics & Gynecology

Court: $500 **Review/Prep:** $250 **Deps:** $500
Years Testifying: 10 **Majority:** Defendant
Written Fee Schedule: No
Min Charge for Deps: Yes **Hours:** 2
Min Charge for Trial: Yes **Hours:** 2
Cancellation Charge for Deps/Trial: No
Retainer Required: Yes, $1,000 (Refundable, One Time)
Procedure When Dep Exceeds Paid Time: Proceed without immediate payment
Expenses Marked Up: No
Expenses Billed For: Mileage, Airline Tickets
Portal-to-Portal: Yes **1st-class Airfare:** No
Written Retainer Agreement: No
Failure to Pay Bill Last 5 Years; Retaining Counsel: No **Opposing Counsel (Deps):** No

Orthopedics

Court: $450 **Review/Prep:** $450 **Deps:** $450
Years Testifying: 30
Written Fee Schedule: No
Min Charge for Deps: Yes **Hours:** 8
Min Charge for Trial: Yes **Hours:** 8
Cancellation Charge for Deps/Trial: Yes
Retainer Required: Yes, $450 (Refundable, Replenishable)
Procedure When Dep Exceeds Paid Time: Proceed without immediate payment
Expenses Marked Up: Yes
Expenses Billed For: Mileage, Airline Tickets, Photocopies, Telephone Calls, Photographs, Demonstrative Aids
Portal-to-Portal: No **1st-class Airfare:** No
Written Retainer Agreement: No
Failure to Pay Bill Last 5 Years; Retaining Counsel: Yes **Opposing Counsel (Deps):** No

Orthopedics

Court: $750 **Review/Prep:** $500 **Deps:** $850
Years Testifying: 10
Written Fee Schedule: Yes
Min Charge for Deps: Yes
Min Charge for Trial: No
Cancellation Charge for Deps/Trial: Yes
Retainer Required: Yes, (Non-Refundable, Replenishable)
Procedure When Dep Exceeds Paid Time: Proceed without immediate payment
Expenses Marked Up: No
Expenses Billed For: Mileage, Airline Tickets, Photocopies, Telephone Calls, Lab/Testing, Photographs, Demonstrative Aids
Portal-to-Portal: Yes **1st-class Airfare:** No
Written Retainer Agreement: No
Failure to Pay Bill Last 5 Years; Retaining Counsel: No **Opposing Counsel (Deps):** No

Physical Medicine & Rehabilitation

Court: $1,000 **Review/Prep:** $350 **Deps:** $500
Years Testifying: 5
Written Fee Schedule: Yes
Min Charge for Deps: Yes **Hours:** 1
Min Charge for Trial: Yes **Hours:** 1
Cancellation Charge for Deps/Trial: Yes
Retainer Required: Yes, $1,000 (Non-Refundable, One Time)
Procedure When Dep Exceeds Paid Time: Proceed without immediate payment
Expenses Marked Up: Yes
Expenses Billed For: Mileage, Airline Tickets, Photocopies
Portal-to-Portal: Yes **1st-class Airfare:** No
Written Retainer Agreement: No
Failure to Pay Bill Last 5 Years; Retaining Counsel: No **Opposing Counsel (Deps):** No

Physical Medicine & Rehabilitation/ Neurology

Court: $500 **Review/Prep:** $500 **Deps:** $500
Years Testifying: 30 **Majority:** Plaintiff
Written Fee Schedule: No
Min Charge for Deps: Yes **Hours:** 2
Min Charge for Trial: Yes **Hours:** 2
Cancellation Charge for Deps/Trial: Yes
Retainer Required: Yes, $1,000 (Refundable, One Time)

Procedure When Dep Exceeds Paid Time: Proceed without immediate payment
Expenses Marked Up: No
Expenses Billed For: Mileage, Airline Tickets
Portal-to-Portal: Yes **1st-class Airfare:** No
Written Retainer Agreement: Yes
Terms: Lawyer is responsible for fee, not lawyer's client, Out-of-pocket expense policies, In-court testimony minimums, Retaining counsel pays all deposition charges, Deposition minimum fee, Payment for preparation time
Failure to Pay Bill Last 5 Years; Retaining Counsel: Yes **Opposing (Deps):** Yes

Physical Medicine & Rehabilitation

Court: $500 **Review/Prep:** $200 **Deps:** $500
Years Testifying: 15 **Majority:** Plaintiff
Written Fee Schedule: Yes
Min Charge for Deps: Yes **Hours:** 1
Min Charge for Trial: Yes **Hours:** 1
Cancellation Charge for Deps/Trial: Yes
Retainer Required: No
Expenses Marked Up: No
Expenses Billed For: Mileage, Airline Tickets
Portal-to-Portal: Yes **1st-class Airfare:** No
Written Retainer Agreement: Yes
Terms: Lawyer is responsible for fee, not lawyer's client, In-court testimony minimums, Fee schedules
Failure to Pay Bill Last 5 Years; Retaining Counsel: Yes **Opposing (Deps):** Yes

Physical Medicine & Rehabilitation

Court: $1,700 **Review/Prep:** $900 **Deps:** $1,200
Years Testifying: 10
Written Fee Schedule: Yes
Min Charge for Deps: Yes **Hours:** 3
Min Charge for Trial: Yes **Hours:** 3
Cancellation Charge for Deps/Trial: Yes
Retainer Required: Yes, $850 (Non-Refundable, One Time)
Procedure When Dep Exceeds Paid Time: Proceed without immediate payment
Expenses Marked Up: No
Portal-to-Portal: Yes **1st-class Airfare:** No
Written Retainer Agreement: No
Failure to Pay Bill Last 5 Years; Retaining Counsel: No **Opposing Counsel (Deps):** No

Physical Medicine & Rehabilitation/ Pain Management/Medicine

Court: $625 **Review/Prep:** $600 **Deps:** $600
Majority: Plaintiff
Written Fee Schedule: Yes
Min Charge for Deps: Yes **Hours:** 4
Min Charge for Trial: Yes **Hours:** 4
Cancellation Charge for Deps/Trial: Yes
Retainer Required: Yes, Depends on case
Procedure When Dep Exceeds Paid Time: Proceed without immediate payment
Expenses Marked Up: No
Expenses Billed For: Mileage, Airline Tickets, Photocopies, Telephone Calls
Portal-to-Portal: No **1st-class Airfare:** No
Written Retainer Agreement: Yes
Terms: In-court testimony minimums, Retaining counsel pays all deposition charges, Fee schedules, Deposition minimum fee
Failure to Pay Bill Last 5 Years; Retaining Counsel: Yes **Opposing (Deps):** Yes

Psychiatry

Court: $100 **Review/Prep:** $150 **Deps:** $100
Years Testifying: 7
Written Fee Schedule: Yes
Min Charge for Deps: Yes **Hours:** 3
Min Charge for Trial: Yes **Hours:** 3
Retainer Required: Yes, $750 (Replenishable)
Expenses Marked Up: Yes
Expenses Billed For: Mileage, Airline Tickets, Photocopies, Telephone Calls
Portal-to-Portal: Yes **1st-class Airfare:** No
Written Retainer Agreement: Yes
Terms: Lawyer is responsible for fee, not lawyer's client, Interest for delinquent accounts, Out-of-pocket expense policies, In-court testimony minimums, Retaining counsel pays all deposition charges, Fee schedules, Portal-to-portal travel time, Attorney's fees if forced to sue for collection, Deposition minimum fee, Payment for preparation time
Failure to Pay Bill Last 5 Years; Retaining Counsel: No **Opposing Counsel (Deps):** No

Safety, Transportation

Court: $225 **Review/Prep:** $175 **Deps:** $225
Years Testifying: 7
Written Fee Schedule: Yes
Min Charge for Deps: Yes **Hours:** 6
Min Charge for Trial: Yes **Hours:** 6
Cancellation Charge for Deps/Trial: Yes
Retainer Required: Yes, $1,500 (Non-Refundable, One Time)
Expenses Billed For: Mileage, Airline Tickets, Photocopies, Telephone Calls, Photographs
Portal-to-Portal: Yes **1st-class Airfare:** No
Written Retainer Agreement: Yes
Terms: Lawyer is responsible for fee, not lawyer's client, Interest for delinquent accounts, Out-of-pocket expense policies, In-court testimony minimums, Retaining counsel pays all deposition charges, Fee schedules, Portal-to-portal travel time, Attorney's fees if forced to sue for collection, Deposition minimum fee, Payment for preparation time
Failure to Pay Bill Last 5 Years; Retaining Counsel: Yes **Opposing Counsel (Deps):** No

Surgery, Cardiothoracic

Court: $500 **Review/Prep:** $350 **Deps:** $500
Years Testifying: 4
Written Fee Schedule: Yes
Min Charge for Deps: Yes **Hours:** 4
Min Charge for Trial: Yes **Hours:** 4
Cancellation Charge for Deps/Trial: No
Retainer Required: Yes, Depends on case (Refundable, One Time)
Expenses Marked Up: No
Expenses Billed For: Mileage, Airline Tickets
Portal-to-Portal: Yes **1st-class Airfare:** No
Written Retainer Agreement: No
Failure to Pay Bill Last 5 Years; Retaining Counsel: No **Opposing Counsel (Deps):** No

Surgery, Neurological/ Pain Management/Medicine

Court: $500 **Review/Prep:** $500 **Deps:** $500
Majority: Plaintiff
Written Fee Schedule: Yes
Min Charge for Deps: Yes
Min Charge for Trial: No
Cancellation Charge for Deps/Trial: Yes
Retainer Required: No
Procedure When Dep Exceeds Paid Time: Get payment before proceeding further
Expenses Marked Up: No
Portal-to-Portal: Yes **1st-class Airfare:** No
Written Retainer Agreement: No
Failure to Pay Bill Last 5 Years; Retaining Counsel: Yes **Opposing Counsel (Deps):** No

Vocational Rehabilitation

Court: $600 **Review/Prep:** $150 **Deps:** $350
Years Testifying: 28 **Majority:** Plaintiff
Written Fee Schedule: Yes
Min Charge for Deps: Yes **Hours:** 4
Min Charge for Trial: Yes **Hours:** 4
Cancellation Charge for Deps/Trial: Yes
Retainer Required: No
Procedure When Dep Exceeds Paid Time: Proceed without immediate payment
Expenses Marked Up: No
Expenses Billed For: Mileage, Airline Tickets, Photocopies
Portal-to-Portal: Yes **1st-class Airfare:** No
Written Retainer Agreement: No
Failure to Pay Bill Last 5 Years; Retaining Counsel: Yes **Opposing Counsel (Deps):** No

Iowa

Accident Reconstruction
Court: $440 **Review/Prep:** $350 **Deps:** $350
Years Testifying: 39 **Majority:** Defendant
Written Fee Schedule: Yes
Min Charge for Deps: Yes
Min Charge for Trial: No
Cancellation Charge for Deps/Trial: No
Retainer Required: Yes, $2,000 (Refundable, One Time)
Procedure When Dep Exceeds Paid Time: Proceed without immediate payment
Expenses Marked Up: Yes
Expenses Billed For: Mileage, Airline Tickets, Demonstrative Aids
Portal-to-Portal: Yes **1st-class Airfare:** Yes
Written Retainer Agreement: Yes
Terms: Lawyer is responsible for fee, not lawyer's client, Interest for delinquent accounts, Out-of-pocket expense policies, Retaining counsel pays all deposition charges, Fee schedules, Portal-to-portal travel time, Attorney's fees if forced to sue for collection, Deposition minimum fee, Payment for preparation time, First class air travel
Failure to Pay Bill Last 5 Years; Retaining Counsel: Yes **Opposing Counsel (Deps):** Yes

Chiropractic
Court: $400 **Review/Prep:** $85 **Deps:** $85
Years Testifying: 20 **Majority:** Plaintiff
Written Fee Schedule: No
Min Charge for Deps: Yes
Min Charge for Trial: No
Cancellation Charge for Deps/Trial: No
Retainer Required: No
Procedure When Dep Exceeds Paid Time: Proceed without immediate payment
Expenses Marked Up: Yes
Expenses Billed For: Photocopies, Telephone Calls
Portal-to-Portal: Yes **1st-class Airfare:** No
Written Retainer Agreement: No
Failure to Pay Bill Last 5 Years; Retaining Counsel: No **Opposing Counsel (Deps):** No

Physical Medicine & Rehabilitation
Court: $1,000 **Review/Prep:** $300 **Deps:** $500
Years Testifying: 9 **Majority:** Plaintiff
Written Fee Schedule: Yes
Min Charge for Deps: Yes **Hours:** 1
Min Charge for Trial: Yes **Hours:** 1
Cancellation Charge for Deps/Trial: Yes
Retainer Required: Yes, Total est. fee (Refundable)
Procedure When Dep Exceeds Paid Time: Proceed without immediate payment
Expenses Marked Up: No
Portal-to-Portal: Yes
Written Retainer Agreement: No
Failure to Pay Bill Last 5 Years; Retaining Counsel: No **Opposing Counsel (Deps):** No

Physical Medicine & Rehabilitation
Court: $2,000 **Review/Prep:** $600 **Deps:** $800
Years Testifying: 3
Written Fee Schedule: Yes
Min Charge for Deps: Yes **Hours:** 4
Min Charge for Trial: Yes **Hours:** 4
Cancellation Charge for Deps/Trial: Yes
Retainer Required: Yes, $8,000 (Refundable)
Procedure When Dep Exceeds Paid Time: Proceed without immediate payment
Expenses Marked Up: No
Portal-to-Portal: Yes **1st-class Airfare:** No
Written Retainer Agreement: Yes
Terms: Lawyer is responsible for fee, not lawyer's client, Interest for delinquent accounts, Out-of-pocket expense policies, In-court testimony minimums, Retaining counsel pays all deposition charges, Fee schedules, Portal-to-portal travel time, Attorney's fees if forced to sue for collection, Deposition minimum fee, Payment for preparation time
Failure to Pay Bill Last 5 Years; Retaining Counsel: No **Opposing Counsel (Deps):** Yes

Physical Medicine & Rehabilitation
Court: $500 **Review/Prep:** $200 **Deps:** $500
Years Testifying: 4 **Majority:** Defendant
Written Fee Schedule: No
Min Charge for Deps: Yes **Hours:** 5
Min Charge for Trial: Yes **Hours:** 5
Cancellation Charge for Deps/Trial: No
Retainer Required: No
Procedure When Dep Exceeds Paid Time: Get payment before proceeding further
Expenses Marked Up: No
Expenses Billed For: Mileage, Airline Tickets, Photocopies, Telephone Calls, Demonstrative Aids
Portal-to-Portal: Yes **1st-class Airfare:** No
Written Retainer Agreement: No
Failure to Pay Bill Last 5 Years; Retaining Counsel: No **Opposing Counsel (Deps):** No

Snow & Ice/Slip, Trip & Fall
Court: $95 **Review/Prep:** $75 **Deps:** $95
Majority: Plaintiff
Written Fee Schedule: Yes
Min Charge for Deps: Yes **Hours:** 4
Min Charge for Trial: Yes **Hours:** 4
Cancellation Charge for Deps/Trial: No
Retainer Required: No
Expenses Marked Up: Yes
Expenses Billed For: Mileage, Airline Tickets, Photocopies, Telephone Calls, Photographs
Portal-to-Portal: Yes **1st-class Airfare:** No
Written Retainer Agreement: Yes
Terms: Lawyer is responsible for fee, not lawyer's client, Out-of-pocket expense policies, In-court testimony minimums, Fee schedules, Portal-to-portal travel time, Deposition minimum fee, Payment for preparation time
Failure to Pay Bill Last 5 Years; Retaining Counsel: No **Opposing Counsel (Deps):** Yes

Vocational Rehabilitation
Court: $240 **Review/Prep:** $120 **Deps:** $240
Years Testifying: 3
Written Fee Schedule: No
Min Charge for Deps: No
Min Charge for Trial: No
Cancellation Charge for Deps/Trial: No
Retainer Required: Yes, $1,000 (Refundable, One Time)
Procedure When Dep Exceeds Paid Time: Proceed without immediate payment
Expenses Marked Up: No
Expenses Billed For: Airline Tickets, Photocopies, Lab/Testing, Photographs, Demonstrative Aids
Portal-to-Portal: Yes **1st-class Airfare:** No
Written Retainer Agreement: Yes
Terms: Interest for delinquent accounts, Retaining counsel pays all deposition charges, Fee schedules, Portal-to-portal travel time, Deposition minimum fee
Failure to Pay Bill Last 5 Years; Retaining Counsel: No **Opposing Counsel (Deps):** No

Kansas

Chiropractic
Court: $350 **Review/Prep:** $200 **Deps:** $250
Years Testifying: 3 **Majority:** Plaintiff
Written Fee Schedule: No
Min Charge for Deps: Yes **Hours:** 2
Min Charge for Trial: Yes **Hours:** 2
Cancellation Charge for Deps/Trial: Yes
Retainer Required: No
Expenses Marked Up: Yes
Expenses Billed For: Mileage, Photocopies, Telephone Calls
Portal-to-Portal: Yes **1st-class Airfare:** No
Written Retainer Agreement: No
Failure to Pay Bill Last 5 Years; Retaining Counsel: No **Opposing Counsel (Deps):** No

Highways
Court: $200 **Review/Prep:** $100 **Deps:** $200
Years Testifying: 4 **Majority:** Defendant
Written Fee Schedule: No
Min Charge for Deps: Yes **Hours:** 2
Min Charge for Trial: Yes **Hours:** 2
Cancellation Charge for Deps/Trial: No

Retainer Required: No
Expenses Marked Up: No
Expenses Billed For: Mileage, Airline Tickets, Photocopies, Lab/Testing, Photographs, Demonstrative Aids
Portal-to-Portal: Yes **1st-class Airfare:** No
Written Retainer Agreement: No
Failure to Pay Bill Last 5 Years; Retaining Counsel: Yes **Opposing Counsel (Deps):** No

Internal Medicine/Occupational Medicine
Court: $500 **Review/Prep:** $300 **Deps:** $500
Majority: Defendant
Written Fee Schedule: Yes
Min Charge for Deps: No
Min Charge for Trial: No
Cancellation Charge for Deps/Trial: Yes
Retainer Required: No
Expenses Marked Up: No
Portal-to-Portal: No **1st-class Airfare:** No
Written Retainer Agreement: No
Failure to Pay Bill Last 5 Years; Retaining Counsel: Yes **Opposing (Deps):** Yes

Mental Retardation
Court: $200 **Review/Prep:** $200 **Deps:** $200
Years Testifying: 10 **Majority:** Plaintiff
Written Fee Schedule: Yes
Min Charge for Deps: No
Min Charge for Trial: No
Cancellation Charge for Deps/Trial: No
Retainer Required: No
Expenses Marked Up: No
Expenses Billed For: Mileage, Airline Tickets
Portal-to-Portal: Yes
Written Retainer Agreement: No
Failure to Pay Bill Last 5 Years; Retaining Counsel: Yes **Opposing (Deps):** Yes

Personal Injury
Court: $350 **Review/Prep:** $175 **Deps:** $350
Years Testifying: 23
Written Fee Schedule: No
Min Charge for Deps: Yes **Hours:** 2
Min Charge for Trial: Yes **Hours:** 2
Cancellation Charge for Deps/Trial: No
Retainer Required: No
Expenses Marked Up: No
Portal-to-Portal: Yes **1st-class Airfare:** No
Written Retainer Agreement: No
Failure to Pay Bill Last 5 Years; Retaining Counsel: No **Opposing Counsel (Deps):** No

Surgery, Cardiovascular
Court: $1,000 **Review/Prep:** $350 **Deps:** $500
Years Testifying: 8 **Majority:** Plaintiff
Written Fee Schedule: Yes
Min Charge for Deps: Yes **Hours:** 5
Min Charge for Trial: Yes **Hours:** 5
Cancellation Charge for Deps/Trial: Yes
Retainer Required: Yes, $700 (Refundable, Replenishable)
Expenses Marked Up: No
Expenses Billed For: Mileage, Airline Tickets, Photocopies, Telephone Calls
Portal-to-Portal: No **1st-class Airfare:** No
Written Retainer Agreement: No
Failure to Pay Bill Last 5 Years; Retaining Counsel: No **Opposing Counsel (Deps):** No

Kentucky

Banking/Damages, Commercial
Court: $170 **Review/Prep:** $170 **Deps:** $170
Years Testifying: 20
Written Fee Schedule: Yes
Min Charge for Deps: No
Min Charge for Trial: No
Cancellation Charge for Deps/Trial: No
Retainer Required: Yes, Depends on case (Refundable)
Expenses Marked Up: No
Expenses Billed For: Mileage, Airline Tickets, Photocopies, Telephone Calls, Photographs, Demonstrative Aids
Portal-to-Portal: Yes **1st-class Airfare:** No
Written Retainer Agreement: Yes
Terms: Lawyer is responsible for fee, not lawyer's client, Out-of-pocket expense policies, Retaining counsel pays all deposition charges, Fee schedules, Payment for preparation time
Failure to Pay Bill Last 5 Years; Retaining Counsel: No **Opposing Counsel (Deps):** No

Electrical
Court: $175 **Review/Prep:** $175 **Deps:** $175
Years Testifying: 25
Written Fee Schedule: Yes
Min Charge for Deps: Yes **Hours:** 8
Min Charge for Trial: Yes **Hours:** 8
Cancellation Charge for Deps/Trial: No
Retainer Required: No
Expenses Marked Up: Yes
Expenses Billed For: Mileage, Airline Tickets, Lab/Testing, Photographs, Demonstrative Aids
Portal-to-Portal: Yes **1st-class Airfare:** No
Written Retainer Agreement: Yes
Terms: Lawyer is responsible for fee, not lawyer's client, Interest for delinquent accounts, Out-of-pocket expense policies, In-court testimony minimums, Fee schedules, Portal-to-portal travel time, Attorney's fees if forced to sue for collection, Deposition minimum fee, Payment for preparation time
Failure to Pay Bill Last 5 Years; Retaining Counsel: No **Opposing Counsel (Deps):** No

Physical Medicine & Rehabilitation/ Pain Management/Medicine
Court: $500 **Review/Prep:** $600 **Deps:** $650
Years Testifying: 4 **Majority:** Plaintiff
Written Fee Schedule: Yes
Min Charge for Deps: Yes **Hours:** 4
Min Charge for Trial: Yes **Hours:** 4
Cancellation Charge for Deps/Trial: Yes
Retainer Required: No
Expenses Marked Up: No
Portal-to-Portal: Yes **1st-class Airfare:** No
Written Retainer Agreement: No
Failure to Pay Bill Last 5 Years; Retaining Counsel: No **Opposing Counsel (Deps):** No

Trusts & Estates
Court: $150 **Review/Prep:** $100 **Deps:** $150
Years Testifying: 10 **Majority:** Plaintiff
Written Fee Schedule: No
Min Charge for Deps: Yes **Hours:** 2
Min Charge for Trial: Yes **Hours:** 2
Cancellation Charge for Deps/Trial: No
Expenses Marked Up: No
Portal-to-Portal: No **1st-class Airfare:** No
Written Retainer Agreement: Yes
Failure to Pay Bill Last 5 Years; Retaining Counsel: Yes **Opposing (Deps):** Yes

Louisiana

Accident Reconstruction
Court: $200 **Review/Prep:** $160 **Deps:** $160
Years Testifying: 15
Written Fee Schedule: Yes
Min Charge for Deps: Yes **Hours:** 8
Min Charge for Trial: Yes **Hours:** 8
Cancellation Charge for Deps/Trial: Yes
Retainer Required: Yes, $3,500 (Non-Refundable, One Time)
Procedure When Dep Exceeds Paid Time: Get payment before proceeding further
Expenses Marked Up: No
Expenses Billed For: Mileage, Airline Tickets, Telephone Calls, Lab/Testing, Photographs, Demonstrative Aids
Portal-to-Portal: Yes **1st-class Airfare:** No
Written Retainer Agreement: Yes
Terms: Lawyer is responsible for fee, not lawyer's client, Out-of-pocket expense policies, In-court testimony minimums, Retaining counsel pays all deposition charges, Fee schedules, Portal-to-portal travel time, Deposition minimum fee, Payment for preparation time
Failure to Pay Bill Last 5 Years; Retaining Counsel: No **Opposing Counsel (Deps):** No

Damages, Business
Court: $250 **Review/Prep:** $225 **Deps:** $250
Years Testifying: 20
Written Fee Schedule: No
Min Charge for Deps: Yes **Hours:** 4
Min Charge for Trial: Yes **Hours:** 4
Cancellation Charge for Deps/Trial: No
Retainer Required: Yes, $5,000 (Refundable, One Time)
Expenses Marked Up: No
Expenses Billed For: Mileage, Airline Tickets, Photocopies, Telephone Calls, Demonstrative Aids
Portal-to-Portal: No **1st-class Airfare:** No
Written Retainer Agreement: Yes
Terms: Out-of-pocket expense policies, In-court testimony minimums, Retaining counsel pays all deposition charges, Fee schedules, Deposition minimum fee, Payment for preparation time
Failure to Pay Bill Last 5 Years; Retaining Counsel: No **Opposing Counsel (Deps):** No

Economics/Employment, Earning Capacity
Court: $205 **Review/Prep:** $205 **Deps:** $500
Years Testifying: 10
Written Fee Schedule: Yes
Min Charge for Trial: No
Cancellation Charge for Deps/Trial: No
Retainer Required: No
Procedure When Dep Exceeds Paid Time: Proceed without immediate payment
Expenses Marked Up: No
Expenses Billed For: Airline Tickets, Demonstrative Aids
Portal-to-Portal: Yes **1st-class Airfare:** No
Written Retainer Agreement: No
Failure to Pay Bill Last 5 Years; Retaining Counsel: Yes **Opposing Counsel (Deps):** Yes

Engineering, Agricultural
Court: $200 **Review/Prep:** $200 **Deps:** $200
Years Testifying: 15
Written Fee Schedule: Yes
Min Charge for Deps: No
Min Charge for Trial: No
Cancellation Charge for Deps/Trial: No
Retainer Required: Yes, $1,000 (Non-Refundable, One Time)
Expenses Marked Up: No
Expenses Billed For: Mileage, Airline Tickets, Photocopies, Lab/Testing, Photographs, Demonstrative Aids
Portal-to-Portal: Yes **1st-class Airfare:** No
Written Retainer Agreement: Yes
Terms: Lawyer is responsible for fee, not lawyer's client, Interest for delinquent accounts, Out-of-pocket expense policies, Retaining counsel pays all deposition charges, Fee schedules, Portal-to-portal travel time, Attorney's fees if forced to sue for collection
Failure to Pay Bill Last 5 Years; Retaining Counsel: No **Opposing Counsel (Deps):** No

Engineering, Petroleum
Court: $195 **Review/Prep:** $195 **Deps:** $195
Years Testifying: 16
Written Fee Schedule: Yes
Min Charge for Deps: No
Min Charge for Trial: No
Cancellation Charge for Deps/Trial: No
Retainer Required: Yes, Depends on case
Expenses Marked Up: No
Expenses Billed For: Mileage, Airline Tickets, Demonstrative Aids
Portal-to-Portal: Yes **1st-class Airfare:** No
Written Retainer Agreement: No
Failure to Pay Bill Last 5 Years; Retaining Counsel: No **Opposing Counsel (Deps):** No

Engineering, Structural/Marine, Docks
Court: $150 **Review/Prep:** $125 **Deps:** $150
Years Testifying: 23
Written Fee Schedule: Yes
Min Charge for Deps: No
Min Charge for Trial: No
Cancellation Charge for Deps/Trial: No
Retainer Required: No
Expenses Marked Up: Yes
Expenses Billed For: Mileage, Airline Tickets, Photographs, Demonstrative Aids
Portal-to-Portal: Yes **1st-class Airfare:** Yes
Written Retainer Agreement: No
Failure to Pay Bill Last 5 Years; Retaining Counsel: Yes

Insurance
Court: $250 **Review/Prep:** $125 **Deps:** $125
Years Testifying: 38 **Majority:** Defendant
Written Fee Schedule: Yes
Min Charge for Deps: Yes **Hours:** 2
Min Charge for Trial: Yes **Hours:** 2
Cancellation Charge for Deps/Trial: No
Retainer Required: No
Expenses Marked Up: Yes
Expenses Billed For: Airline Tickets, Lab/Testing
1st-class Airfare: No
Written Retainer Agreement: No
Failure to Pay Bill Last 5 Years; Retaining Counsel: No **Opposing Counsel (Deps):** No

Orthopedics/Surgery, Hand
Court: $1,300 **Deps:** $900
Years Testifying: 20 **Majority:** Plaintiff
Written Fee Schedule: Yes
Min Charge for Deps: Yes **Hours:** 1
Min Charge for Trial: Yes **Hours:** 1
Cancellation Charge for Deps/Trial: Yes
Retainer Required: Yes, $550 (Refundable, Replenishable)
Procedure When Dep Exceeds Paid Time: Proceed without immediate payment
Expenses Marked Up: Yes
Expenses Billed For: Lab/Testing, Photographs
Portal-to-Portal: Yes **1st-class Airfare:** No
Written Retainer Agreement: No
Failure to Pay Bill Last 5 Years; Retaining Counsel: Yes **Opposing (Deps):** Yes

Pain Management/ Medicine/Psychiatry
Court: $500 **Review/Prep:** $350 **Deps:** $500
Years Testifying: 15
Written Fee Schedule: No
Min Charge for Deps: Yes **Hours:** 8
Min Charge for Trial: Yes **Hours:** 8
Cancellation Charge for Deps/Trial: Yes
Retainer Required: Yes, $4,000 (Refundable, Replenishable)
Expenses Marked Up: No
Expenses Billed For: Mileage, Airline Tickets
Portal-to-Portal: No **1st-class Airfare:** No
Written Retainer Agreement: No
Failure to Pay Bill Last 5 Years; Retaining Counsel: No **Opposing Counsel (Deps):** Yes

Pathology
Court: $300 **Review/Prep:** $150 **Deps:** $300
Years Testifying: 22
Written Fee Schedule: No
Min Charge for Deps: No
Min Charge for Trial: No
Cancellation Charge for Deps/Trial: No
Retainer Required: No
Procedure When Dep Exceeds Paid Time: Proceed without immediate payment
Expenses Marked Up: No
Expenses Billed For: Mileage, Airline Tickets, Photocopies, Telephone Calls, Lab/Testing, Photographs, Demonstrative Aids
Portal-to-Portal: Yes **1st-class Airfare:** Yes
Written Retainer Agreement: No
Failure to Pay Bill Last 5 Years; Retaining Counsel: No **Opposing Counsel (Deps):** No

Psychiatry
Court: $400 **Review/Prep:** $140 **Deps:** $350
Years Testifying: 33
Written Fee Schedule: Yes
Min Charge for Deps: No
Min Charge for Trial: No
Cancellation Charge for Deps/Trial: No
Retainer Required: No
Expenses Marked Up: No
Expenses Billed For: Photocopies, Telephone Calls

Portal-to-Portal: Yes **1st-class Airfare:** Yes
Written Retainer Agreement: No
Failure to Pay Bill Last 5 Years; Retaining Counsel: No **Opposing Counsel (Deps):** No

Real Estate
Court: $275 **Review/Prep:** $175 **Deps:** $275
Years Testifying: 9
Written Fee Schedule: No
Min Charge for Deps: No
Min Charge for Trial: No
Cancellation Charge for Deps/Trial: Yes
Retainer Required: Yes, $1,500 (Refundable, One Time)
Procedure When Dep Exceeds Paid Time: Proceed without immediate payment
Expenses Marked Up: No
Expenses Billed For: Mileage, Airline Tickets
Portal-to-Portal: Yes **1st-class Airfare:** No
Written Retainer Agreement: Yes
Terms: Lawyer is responsible for fee, not lawyer's client, Out-of-pocket expense policies, In-court testimony minimums, Retaining counsel pays all deposition charges, Portal-to-portal travel time, Deposition minimum fee, Payment for preparation time, Overnight lodging & meals as required
Failure to Pay Bill Last 5 Years; Retaining Counsel: No **Opposing Counsel (Deps):** No

Safety, Chemical Process
Court: $400 **Review/Prep:** $200 **Deps:** $200
Years Testifying: 11 **Majority:** Defendant
Written Fee Schedule: No
Min Charge for Deps: No
Min Charge for Trial: No
Cancellation Charge for Deps/Trial: No
Retainer Required: Yes, Depends on case (Refundable, Replenishable)
Expenses Marked Up: No
Expenses Billed For: Mileage, Airline Tickets, Lab/Testing, Photographs, Demonstrative Aids
Portal-to-Portal: No **1st-class Airfare:** No
Written Retainer Agreement: Yes
Terms: Out-of-pocket expense policies, Retaining counsel pays all deposition charges, Fee schedules, Payment for preparation time, Travel or actual
Failure to Pay Bill Last 5 Years; Retaining Counsel: No **Opposing Counsel (Deps):** No

Security/Premises Liability
Court: $175 **Review/Prep:** $150 **Deps:** $175
Years Testifying: 23
Written Fee Schedule: Yes
Min Charge for Deps: No
Min Charge for Trial: No
Cancellation Charge for Deps/Trial: No
Retainer Required: No
Expenses Marked Up: No
Expenses Billed For: Mileage, Airline Tickets, Telephone Calls, Lab/Testing, Photographs, Demonstrative Aids
Portal-to-Portal: Yes **1st-class Airfare:** No
Written Retainer Agreement: Yes
Terms: Lawyer is responsible for fee, not lawyer's client, Interest for delinquent accounts, Fee schedules, Attorney's fees if forced to sue for collection
Failure to Pay Bill Last 5 Years; Retaining Counsel: Yes **Opposing Counsel (Deps):** No

Social Work
Court: $180 **Review/Prep:** $180 **Deps:** $180
Years Testifying: 9
Written Fee Schedule: No
Min Charge for Deps: Yes **Hours:** 4
Min Charge for Trial: Yes **Hours:** 4
Cancellation Charge for Deps/Trial: Yes
Retainer Required: Yes, $1,000 (Non-Refundable, Replenishable)
Procedure When Dep Exceeds Paid Time: Get payment before proceeding further
Expenses Marked Up: Yes
Expenses Billed For: Photocopies, Telephone Calls
Portal-to-Portal: Yes **1st-class Airfare:** No
Written Retainer Agreement: Yes
Terms: Lawyer is responsible for fee, not lawyer's client, Interest for delinquent accounts, Out-of-pocket expense policies, In-court testimony minimums, Retaining counsel pays all deposition charges, Fee schedules, Portal-to-portal travel time, Attorney's fees if forced to sue for collection, Deposition minimum fee, Payment for preparation time
Failure to Pay Bill Last 5 Years; Retaining Counsel: Yes **Opposing Counsel (Deps):** No

Vocational Rehabilitation
Court: $160 **Review/Prep:** $160 **Deps:** $600
Years Testifying: 21 **Majority:** Defendant
Written Fee Schedule: Yes
Min Charge for Deps: Yes
Cancellation Charge for Deps/Trial: No
Retainer Required: Depends, $1,000
Procedure When Dep Exceeds Paid Time: Proceed without immediate payment
Expenses Marked Up: No
Expenses Billed For: Mileage, Airline Tickets, Photocopies, Photographs, Demonstrative Aids
Portal-to-Portal: Yes **1st-class Airfare:** No
Written Retainer Agreement: Yes
Terms: Lawyer is responsible for fee, not lawyer's client, Out-of-pocket expense policies, Retaining counsel pays all deposition charges, Fee schedules, Portal-to-portal travel time, Attorney's fees if forced to sue for collection, Deposition minimum fee, Payment for preparation time
Failure to Pay Bill Last 5 Years; Retaining Counsel: Yes **Opposing Counsel (Deps):** No

Maine

Psychiatry
Court: $300 **Review/Prep:** $300 **Deps:** $300
Years Testifying: 25
Min Charge for Deps: Yes
Min Charge for Trial: No
Cancellation Charge for Deps/Trial: Yes
Retainer Required: Yes, $3,000 (Refundable, Replenishable)
Procedure When Dep Exceeds Paid Time: Extra payment at time of depo
Expenses Marked Up: No
Expenses Billed For: Mileage, Airline Tickets, Telephone Calls
Portal-to-Portal: Yes **1st-class Airfare:** No
Written Retainer Agreement: Yes
Terms: Lawyer is responsible for fee, not lawyer's client, Out-of-pocket expense policies, In-court testimony minimums, Retaining counsel pays all deposition charges, Portal-to-portal travel time, Payment for preparation time
Failure to Pay Bill Last 5 Years; Retaining Counsel: No **Opposing Counsel (Deps):** No

Real Estate/Investments
Court: $200 **Review/Prep:** $150 **Deps:** $200
Years Testifying: 25
Written Fee Schedule: Yes
Min Charge for Deps: No
Min Charge for Trial: No
Cancellation Charge for Deps/Trial: No
Retainer Required: Yes, $7,500 (Non-Refundable, One Time)
Procedure When Dep Exceeds Paid Time: Proceed without immediate payment
Expenses Marked Up: No
Expenses Billed For: Mileage, Airline Tickets, Photocopies, Telephone Calls, Lab/Testing, Photographs, Demonstrative Aids
Portal-to-Portal: Yes **1st-class Airfare:** No
Written Retainer Agreement: Yes
Terms: Out-of-pocket expense policies, In-court testimony minimums, Retaining counsel pays all deposition charges, Fee schedules
Failure to Pay Bill Last 5 Years; Retaining Counsel: No **Opposing Counsel (Deps):** No

Maryland

Accident Reconstruction
Court: $150 **Review/Prep:** $150 **Deps:** $150
Years Testifying: 17
Written Fee Schedule: Yes

Min Charge for Deps: Yes **Hours:** 8
Min Charge for Trial: Yes **Hours:** 8
Cancellation Charge for Deps/Trial: No
Retainer Required: Yes, $1,000 (Refundable, One Time)
Procedure When Dep Exceeds Paid Time: Proceed without immediate payment
Expenses Marked Up: No
Expenses Billed For: Mileage, Airline Tickets, Photocopies, Telephone Calls, Lab/Testing, Photographs, Demonstrative Aids
Portal-to-Portal: Yes **1st-class Airfare:** Yes
Written Retainer Agreement: Yes
Terms: Lawyer is responsible for fee, not lawyer's client, Interest for delinquent accounts, Out-of-pocket expense policies, In-court testimony minimums, Retaining counsel pays all deposition charges, Fee schedules, Portal-to-portal travel time, Attorney's fees if forced to sue for collection, Deposition minimum fee, Payment for preparation time, First class air travel
Failure to Pay Bill Last 5 Years; Retaining Counsel: No **Opposing Counsel (Deps):** No

Anesthesiology/Critical Care Medicine
Court: $900 **Review/Prep:** $375 **Deps:** $600
Years Testifying: 25 **Majority:** Defendant
Written Fee Schedule: Yes
Min Charge for Deps: No **Hours:** 5
Min Charge for Trial: Yes **Hours:** 5
Cancellation Charge for Deps/Trial: Yes
Retainer Required: Yes, $3,500 (Refundable, Replenishable)
Expenses Marked Up: No
Portal-to-Portal: Yes **1st-class Airfare:** No
Written Retainer Agreement: No
Failure to Pay Bill Last 5 Years; Retaining Counsel: No **Opposing Counsel (Deps):** No

Appraisal, Gem & Jewelry
Court: $200 **Review/Prep:** $150 **Deps:** $200
Written Fee Schedule: No
Min Charge for Deps: Yes **Hours:** 3
Min Charge for Trial: Yes **Hours:** 3
Cancellation Charge for Deps/Trial: Yes
Retainer Required: Yes, 50% est. fee (Non-Refundable, Replenishable)
Procedure When Dep Exceeds Paid Time: Proceed without immediate payment
Expenses Marked Up: No
Expenses Billed For: Mileage, Airline Tickets, Photocopies, Telephone Calls, Lab/Testing, Photographs, Demonstrative Aids
Portal-to-Portal: Yes **1st-class Airfare:** No
Written Retainer Agreement: Yes
Terms: Lawyer is responsible for fee, not lawyer's client, Interest for delinquent accounts, Out-of-pocket expense policies, In-court testimony minimums, Retaining counsel pays all deposition charges, Fee schedules, Portal-to-portal travel time, Attorney's fees if forced to sue for collection, Deposition minimum fee, Payment for preparation time, First class air travel
Failure to Pay Bill Last 5 Years; Retaining Counsel: No **Opposing Counsel (Deps):** No

Cardiology
Court: $450 **Review/Prep:** $300 **Deps:** $450
Years Testifying: 4
Written Fee Schedule: Yes
Min Charge for Deps: Yes **Hours:** 2
Min Charge for Trial: Yes **Hours:** 2
Cancellation Charge for Deps/Trial: No
Retainer Required: Yes, $900 (Refundable, One Time)
Expenses Marked Up: No
Expenses Billed For: Photocopies, Lab/Testing, Photographs, Demonstrative Aids
Portal-to-Portal: Yes **1st-class Airfare:** No
Written Retainer Agreement: No
Failure to Pay Bill Last 5 Years; Retaining Counsel: No **Opposing Counsel (Deps):** No

Emergency Medicine/Geriatrics
Court: $300 **Review/Prep:** $300 **Deps:** $300
Years Testifying: 20
Written Fee Schedule: Yes
Min Charge for Deps: Yes **Hours:** 4
Min Charge for Trial: Yes **Hours:** 4
Cancellation Charge for Deps/Trial: Yes
Retainer Required: Yes, $750 (Non-Refundable, One Time)
Expenses Marked Up: No
Expenses Billed For: Mileage, Airline Tickets, Photocopies, Telephone Calls, Photographs, Demonstrative Aids
Portal-to-Portal: No **1st-class Airfare:** No
Written Retainer Agreement: Yes
Terms: Lawyer is responsible for fee, not lawyer's client, Interest for delinquent accounts, Out-of-pocket expense policies, In-court testimony minimums, Retaining counsel pays all deposition charges, Fee schedules, Portal-to-portal travel time, Attorney's fees if forced to sue for collection, Deposition minimum fee, Payment for preparation time
Failure to Pay Bill Last 5 Years; Retaining Counsel: No **Opposing Counsel (Deps):** No

Employment, Wrongful Discharge
Court: $450 **Review/Prep:** $300 **Deps:** $450
Years Testifying: 20 **Majority:** Plaintiff
Written Fee Schedule: Yes
Min Charge for Deps: Yes **Hours:** 5
Min Charge for Trial: Yes **Hours:** 5
Cancellation Charge for Deps/Trial: Yes
Retainer Required: Yes, $2,500 (Non-Refundable, Replenishable)
Procedure When Dep Exceeds Paid Time: Proceed without immediate payment
Expenses Marked Up: No
Expenses Billed For: Mileage, Airline Tickets, Photocopies, Telephone Calls, Demonstrative Aids
Portal-to-Portal: Yes **1st-class Airfare:** No
Written Retainer Agreement: Yes
Terms: Interest for delinquent accounts, In-court testimony minimums, Retaining counsel pays all deposition charges, Fee schedules, Portal-to-portal travel time, Deposition minimum fee, Payment for preparation time
Failure to Pay Bill Last 5 Years; Retaining Counsel: Yes **Opposing (Deps):** Yes

Engineering, Mechanical
Court: $300 **Review/Prep:** $250 **Deps:** $300
Years Testifying: 20 **Majority:** Plaintiff
Written Fee Schedule: Yes
Min Charge for Deps: Yes **Hours:** 4
Min Charge for Trial: Yes **Hours:** 4
Cancellation Charge for Deps/Trial: No
Retainer Required: Yes, $1,000 (Refundable, One Time)
Expenses Marked Up: No
Expenses Billed For: Mileage, Airline Tickets, Photographs
Portal-to-Portal: Yes **1st-class Airfare:** No
Written Retainer Agreement: No
Failure to Pay Bill Last 5 Years; Retaining Counsel: Yes **Opposing (Deps):** Yes

Family Practice
Court: $300 **Review/Prep:** $300 **Deps:** $300
Years Testifying: 20
Written Fee Schedule: Yes
Min Charge for Deps: Yes **Hours:** 8
Min Charge for Trial: Yes **Hours:** 8
Cancellation Charge for Deps/Trial: Yes
Retainer Required: Yes, $700 (Non-Refundable, One Time)
Expenses Marked Up: No
Expenses Billed For: Mileage, Airline Tickets, Photocopies, Telephone Calls, Lab/Testing, Photographs, Demonstrative Aids
Portal-to-Portal: Yes **1st-class Airfare:** No
Written Retainer Agreement: Yes
Terms: Lawyer is responsible for fee, not lawyer's client, Interest for delinquent accounts, Out-of-pocket expense policies, In-court testimony minimums, Retaining counsel pays all deposition charges, Fee schedules, Portal-to-portal travel time, Attorney's fees if forced to sue for collection, Deposition minimum fee, Payment for preparation time
Failure to Pay Bill Last 5 Years; Retaining Counsel: No **Opposing Counsel (Deps):** No

Gastroenterology
Court: $500 **Review/Prep:** $400 **Deps:** $500
Years Testifying: 5 **Majority:** Defendant
Written Fee Schedule: No
Min Charge for Deps: No
Min Charge for Trial: No
Cancellation Charge for Deps/Trial: No
Retainer Required: No
Expenses Marked Up: No
Portal-to-Portal: Yes **1st-class Airfare:** No
Written Retainer Agreement: No
Failure to Pay Bill Last 5 Years; Retaining Counsel: No **Opposing Counsel (Deps):** No

Geology, Hydro
Court: $150 **Review/Prep:** $150 **Deps:** $150
Years Testifying: 10
Written Fee Schedule: Yes
Min Charge for Deps: No
Min Charge for Trial: No
Cancellation Charge for Deps/Trial: No
Retainer Required: No
Expenses Marked Up: Yes
Expenses Billed For: Mileage, Airline Tickets, Photocopies, Telephone Calls, Lab/Testing, Photographs, Demonstrative Aids
Portal-to-Portal: Yes **1st-class Airfare:** No
Written Retainer Agreement: Yes
Terms: Lawyer is responsible for fee, not lawyer's client, Interest for delinquent accounts, Out-of-pocket expense policies, Retaining counsel pays all deposition charges, Fee schedules, Attorney's fees if forced to sue for collection, Payment for preparation time
Failure to Pay Bill Last 5 Years; Retaining Counsel: No **Opposing Counsel (Deps):** No

Human Factors
Court: $600 **Review/Prep:** $600 **Deps:** $600
Years Testifying: 25 **Majority:** Plaintiff
Written Fee Schedule: Yes
Min Charge for Deps: No
Min Charge for Trial: No
Cancellation Charge for Deps/Trial: Yes
Retainer Required: Yes, $6,000 (Non-Refundable, One Time)
Expenses Marked Up: No
Expenses Billed For: Mileage, Airline Tickets, Photocopies, Lab/Testing, Photographs, Demonstrative Aids
Portal-to-Portal: Yes **1st-class Airfare:** Yes
Written Retainer Agreement: Yes
Terms: Lawyer is responsible for fee, not lawyer's client, Interest for delinquent accounts, Out-of-pocket expense policies, Retaining counsel pays all deposition charges, Fee schedules, Attorney's fees if forced to sue for collection
Failure to Pay Bill Last 5 Years; Retaining Counsel: Yes **Opposing Counsel (Deps):** No

Obstetrics & Gynecology
Court: $350 **Review/Prep:** $350 **Deps:** $350
Years Testifying: 3 **Majority:** Defendant
Written Fee Schedule: No
Min Charge for Deps: Yes **Hours:** 4
Min Charge for Trial: Yes **Hours:** 4
Cancellation Charge for Deps/Trial: No
Retainer Required: No
Expenses Marked Up: No
Expenses Billed For: Mileage, Airline Tickets, Lab/Testing, Photographs, Demonstrative Aids
Portal-to-Portal: Yes **1st-class Airfare:** No
Written Retainer Agreement: No
Failure to Pay Bill Last 5 Years; Retaining Counsel: No **Opposing Counsel (Deps):** No

Orthopedics
Court: $500 **Review/Prep:** $150 **Deps:** $500
Years Testifying: 15
Written Fee Schedule: Yes
Min Charge for Deps: No
Min Charge for Trial: No
Cancellation Charge for Deps/Trial: Yes
Retainer Required: No
Expenses Marked Up: No
Expenses Billed For: Mileage, Airline Tickets
1st-class Airfare: No
Written Retainer Agreement: No
Failure to Pay Bill Last 5 Years; Retaining Counsel: No **Opposing Counsel (Deps):** No

Otolaryngology/Allergy
Court: $350 **Review/Prep:** $350 **Deps:** $350
Years Testifying: 20
Written Fee Schedule: Yes
Min Charge for Deps: No
Min Charge for Trial: No
Cancellation Charge for Deps/Trial: Yes
Retainer Required: No
Expenses Marked Up: No
Expenses Billed For: Airline Tickets
Portal-to-Portal: Yes **1st-class Airfare:** No
Written Retainer Agreement: No
Failure to Pay Bill Last 5 Years; Retaining Counsel: Yes **Opposing (Deps):** Yes

Physical Medicine & Rehabilitation
Court: $375 **Review/Prep:** $375 **Deps:** $375
Years Testifying: 20 **Majority:** Plaintiff
Written Fee Schedule: Yes
Min Charge for Deps: Yes **Hours:** 5
Min Charge for Trial: Yes **Hours:** 5
Cancellation Charge for Deps/Trial: Yes
Retainer Required: Yes, $1,500 (Non-Refundable, One Time)
Procedure When Dep Exceeds Paid Time: Get payment before proceeding further
Expenses Marked Up: No
Portal-to-Portal: Yes **1st-class Airfare:** No
Written Retainer Agreement: Yes
Terms: Lawyer is responsible for fee, not lawyer's client, In-court testimony minimums, Retaining counsel pays all deposition charges, Fee schedules, Portal-to-portal travel time, Deposition minimum fee, Payment for preparation time
Failure to Pay Bill Last 5 Years; Retaining Counsel: Yes **Opposing (Deps):** Yes

Psychiatry
Court: $250 **Review/Prep:** $250 **Deps:** $250
Years Testifying: 30
Written Fee Schedule: No
Min Charge for Deps: Yes **Hours:** 4
Min Charge for Trial: Yes **Hours:** 4
Cancellation Charge for Deps/Trial: Yes
Retainer Required: Yes, Total est. fee (Refundable, One Time)
Expenses Marked Up: No
Expenses Billed For: Telephone Calls
Portal-to-Portal: Yes **1st-class Airfare:** No
Written Retainer Agreement: No
Failure to Pay Bill Last 5 Years; Retaining Counsel: Yes **Opposing Counsel (Deps):** No

Psychiatry
Court: $300 **Review/Prep:** $300 **Deps:** $300
Years Testifying: 20
Written Fee Schedule: No
Min Charge for Deps: No
Min Charge for Trial: No
Cancellation Charge for Deps/Trial: Yes
Retainer Required: Yes, $600 (Refundable)
Expenses Marked Up: No
Expenses Billed For: Airline Tickets
Portal-to-Portal: Yes **1st-class Airfare:** No
Written Retainer Agreement: No
Failure to Pay Bill Last 5 Years; Retaining Counsel: Yes **Opposing (Deps):** Yes

Safety, Automotive
Court: $360 **Review/Prep:** $360 **Deps:** $360
Years Testifying: 3 **Majority:** Plaintiff
Written Fee Schedule: No
Min Charge for Deps: No
Min Charge for Trial: No
Cancellation Charge for Deps/Trial: No
Retainer Required: New Client
Expenses Marked Up: No
Expenses Billed For: Mileage, Airline Tickets
Portal-to-Portal: Yes **1st-class Airfare:** No
Written Retainer Agreement: No
Failure to Pay Bill Last 5 Years; Retaining Counsel: Yes **Opposing Counsel (Deps):** No

Valuation, Business
Court: $350 **Review/Prep:** $350 **Deps:** $350
Years Testifying: 20
Written Fee Schedule: No

Min Charge for Deps: Yes **Hours:** 2
Min Charge for Trial: Yes **Hours:** 2
Cancellation Charge for Deps/Trial: No
Retainer Required: Yes, $10,000 (Refundable, Replenishable)
Procedure When Dep Exceeds Paid Time: Proceed without immediate payment
Expenses Marked Up: No
Expenses Billed For: Mileage, Airline Tickets
Portal-to-Portal: Yes **1st-class Airfare:** No
Written Retainer Agreement: Yes
Terms: Lawyer is responsible for fee, not lawyer's client, Interest for delinquent accounts, Out-of-pocket expense policies, In-court testimony minimums, Retaining counsel pays all deposition charges
Failure to Pay Bill Last 5 Years; Retaining Counsel: No **Opposing Counsel (Deps):** No

Valuation, Business

Court: $250 **Review/Prep:** $250 **Deps:** $250
Years Testifying: 20
Written Fee Schedule: Yes
Min Charge for Deps: No
Min Charge for Trial: No
Cancellation Charge for Deps/Trial: No
Retainer Required: Yes, $7,000 (Refundable)
Expenses Marked Up: No
Expenses Billed For: Airline Tickets, Photocopies, Demonstrative Aids
Portal-to-Portal: Yes **1st-class Airfare:** No
Written Retainer Agreement: Yes
Terms: Interest for delinquent accounts, Out-of-pocket expense policies, Retaining counsel pays all deposition charges, Fee schedules, Attorney's fees if forced to sue for collection
Failure to Pay Bill Last 5 Years; Retaining Counsel: No **Opposing Counsel (Deps):** No

Massachusetts

Accident Reconstruction

Court: $170 **Review/Prep:** $120 **Deps:** $170
Years Testifying: 16 **Majority:** Plaintiff
Written Fee Schedule: Yes
Min Charge for Deps: Yes **Hours:** 2
Min Charge for Trial: Yes **Hours:** 2
Cancellation Charge for Deps/Trial: Yes
Retainer Required: Depends, $2,000
Procedure When Dep Exceeds Paid Time: Proceed without immediate payment
Expenses Marked Up: No
Expenses Billed For: Photocopies, Telephone Calls, Photographs
Portal-to-Portal: Yes **1st-class Airfare:** No
Written Retainer Agreement: No
Failure to Pay Bill Last 5 Years; Retaining Counsel: No **Opposing Counsel (Deps):** No

Accident Reconstruction

Court: $180 **Review/Prep:** $180 **Deps:** $180
Years Testifying: 20
Written Fee Schedule: Yes
Min Charge for Deps: Yes **Hours:** 4
Min Charge for Trial: Yes **Hours:** 4
Retainer Required: Yes, $1,500 (Refundable, One Time)
Procedure When Dep Exceeds Paid Time: Proceed without immediate payment
Expenses Marked Up: No
Expenses Billed For: Airline Tickets, Photographs, Demonstrative Aids
Portal-to-Portal: Yes **1st-class Airfare:** No
Written Retainer Agreement: Yes
Terms: Lawyer is responsible for fee, not lawyer's client, Out-of-pocket expense policies, In-court testimony minimums, Retaining counsel pays all deposition charges, Fee schedules, Portal-to-portal travel time, Deposition minimum fee, Payment for preparation time
Failure to Pay Bill Last 5 Years; Retaining Counsel: Yes **Opposing Counsel (Deps):** No

Accounting

Court: $350 **Review/Prep:** $350 **Deps:** $350
Years Testifying: 17
Written Fee Schedule: No
Min Charge for Deps: Yes **Hours:** 8
Min Charge for Trial: Yes **Hours:** 8
Cancellation Charge for Deps/Trial: No
Retainer Required: Yes, $6,000 (Refundable, One Time)
Expenses Marked Up: No
Expenses Billed For: Mileage, Airline Tickets, Demonstrative Aids
Portal-to-Portal: Yes **1st-class Airfare:** No
Written Retainer Agreement: Yes
Terms: Out-of-pocket expense policies, Retaining counsel pays all deposition charges, Portal-to-portal travel time
Failure to Pay Bill Last 5 Years; Retaining Counsel: Yes **Opposing Counsel (Deps):** No

Allergy/Asthma

Court: $500 **Review/Prep:** $300 **Deps:** $500
Years Testifying: 8 **Majority:** Defendant
Written Fee Schedule: Yes
Min Charge for Deps: No **Hours:** 3
Min Charge for Trial: Yes **Hours:** 3
Cancellation Charge for Deps/Trial: Yes
Retainer Required: Yes, $1,000 (Refundable, Replenishable)
Procedure When Dep Exceeds Paid Time: Proceed without immediate payment
Expenses Marked Up: No
Expenses Billed For: Mileage, Airline Tickets
Portal-to-Portal: Yes **1st-class Airfare:** No
Written Retainer Agreement: No
Failure to Pay Bill Last 5 Years; Retaining Counsel: No **Opposing Counsel (Deps):** No

Appraisal, Industrial

Court: $150 **Review/Prep:** $150 **Deps:** $150
Years Testifying: 40
Written Fee Schedule: No
Min Charge for Deps: Yes **Hours:** 4
Min Charge for Trial: Yes **Hours:** 4
Cancellation Charge for Deps/Trial: Yes
Retainer Required: Yes, $500 (Non-Refundable, One Time)
Procedure When Dep Exceeds Paid Time: Get payment before proceeding further
Expenses Marked Up: Yes
Expenses Billed For: Mileage, Airline Tickets
Portal-to-Portal: Yes **1st-class Airfare:** No
Written Retainer Agreement: No
Failure to Pay Bill Last 5 Years; Retaining Counsel: No **Opposing Counsel (Deps):** No

Appraisal, Machinery & Equipment

Court: $300 **Review/Prep:** $200 **Deps:** $300
Years Testifying: 48 **Majority:** Defendant
Written Fee Schedule: No
Min Charge for Deps: No
Min Charge for Trial: No
Cancellation Charge for Deps/Trial: No
Retainer Required: No
Expenses Marked Up: No
Expenses Billed For: Mileage, Airline Tickets, Photocopies, Lab/Testing, Photographs, Demonstrative Aids
Portal-to-Portal: No **1st-class Airfare:** No
Written Retainer Agreement: No
Failure to Pay Bill Last 5 Years; Retaining Counsel: Yes **Opposing (Deps):** Yes

Appraisal, Marine/ Marine, Surveying

Court: $125 **Review/Prep:** $100 **Deps:** $125
Years Testifying: 20
Written Fee Schedule: Yes
Min Charge for Deps: No
Min Charge for Trial: No
Cancellation Charge for Deps/Trial: No
Retainer Required: Yes, $1,000 (Refundable, One Time)
Expenses Marked Up: No
Expenses Billed For: Mileage, Airline Tickets, Lab/Testing, Photographs
Portal-to-Portal: Yes **1st-class Airfare:** No
Written Retainer Agreement: Yes
Terms: Lawyer is responsible for fee, not lawyer's client, Interest for delinquent accounts, Out-of-pocket expense policies, In-court testimony minimums, Retaining counsel pays all deposition charges, Fee schedules, Portal-to-portal travel time, Attorney's fees if forced to sue for collection, Deposition

minimum fee, Payment for preparation time
Failure to Pay Bill Last 5 Years; Retaining Counsel: No **Opposing Counsel (Deps):** No

Appraisals
Court: $155 **Review/Prep:** $155 **Deps:** $155
Years Testifying: 15
Written Fee Schedule: Yes
Min Charge for Deps: Yes **Hours:** 8
Min Charge for Trial: Yes **Hours:** 8
Retainer Required: Depends, $2,000
Expenses Marked Up: No
Expenses Billed For: Airline Tickets, Telephone Calls
Portal-to-Portal: Yes **1st-class Airfare:** No
Written Retainer Agreement: Yes
Terms: Lawyer is responsible for fee, not lawyer's client, In-court testimony minimums, Retaining counsel pays all deposition charges, Fee schedules, Portal-to-portal travel time, Deposition minimum fee, Payment for preparation time
Failure to Pay Bill Last 5 Years; Retaining Counsel: Yes **Opposing Counsel (Deps):** No

Biomedical
Court: $350 **Review/Prep:** $350 **Deps:** $350
Years Testifying: 3
Written Fee Schedule: Yes
Min Charge for Deps: Yes
Min Charge for Trial: No
Cancellation Charge for Deps/Trial: Yes
Retainer Required: No
Expenses Marked Up: No
Expenses Billed For: Mileage, Airline Tickets, Photocopies, Telephone Calls, Lab/Testing, Photographs, Demonstrative Aids
Portal-to-Portal: Yes **1st-class Airfare:** No
Written Retainer Agreement: Yes
Terms: Lawyer is responsible for fee, not lawyer's client, Out-of-pocket expense policies, In-court testimony minimums, Fee schedules, Portal-to-portal travel time, Deposition minimum fee, Payment for preparation time
Failure to Pay Bill Last 5 Years; Retaining Counsel: No **Opposing Counsel (Deps):** No

Biomedical, Biotechnology
Court: $300 **Review/Prep:** $200 **Deps:** $200
Years Testifying: 20
Written Fee Schedule: No
Min Charge for Deps: Yes **Hours:** 2
Min Charge for Trial: Yes **Hours:** 2
Cancellation Charge for Deps/Trial: No
Retainer Required: Yes, 20% est. fee (Refundable, One Time)
Expenses Marked Up: Yes
Expenses Billed For: Mileage, Airline Tickets, Photocopies, Telephone Calls, Lab/Testing, Photographs, Demonstrative Aids
Portal-to-Portal: Yes **1st-class Airfare:** No
Written Retainer Agreement: Yes
Terms: Lawyer is responsible for fee, not lawyer's client, Out-of-pocket expense policies, Retaining counsel pays all deposition charges, Portal-to-portal travel time, Attorney's fees if forced to sue for collection, Deposition minimum fee, Payment for preparation time
Failure to Pay Bill Last 5 Years; Retaining Counsel: No **Opposing Counsel (Deps):** No

Electronics
Court: $250 **Review/Prep:** $250 **Deps:** $250
Years Testifying: 10
Written Fee Schedule: Yes
Min Charge for Deps: No
Min Charge for Trial: No
Cancellation Charge for Deps/Trial: No
Retainer Required: Yes, $5,000 (Refundable)
Expenses Billed For: Mileage, Airline Tickets, Photocopies, Telephone Calls, Lab/Testing, Photographs, Demonstrative Aids
Portal-to-Portal: Yes **1st-class Airfare:** No
Written Retainer Agreement: Yes
Terms: Lawyer is responsible for fee, not lawyer's client, Interest for delinquent accounts, Out-of-pocket expense policies, Retaining counsel pays all deposition charges, Fee schedules, Portal-to-portal travel time, Attorney's fees if forced to sue for collection, Payment for preparation time
Failure to Pay Bill Last 5 Years; Retaining Counsel: Yes **Opposing Counsel (Deps):** No

Engineering
Court: $175 **Review/Prep:** $115 **Deps:** $175
Years Testifying: 5
Written Fee Schedule: Yes
Min Charge for Deps: No
Min Charge for Trial: No
Cancellation Charge for Deps/Trial: No
Retainer Required: Yes, $2,000 (Refundable, Replenishable)
Procedure When Dep Exceeds Paid Time: Proceed without immediate payment
Expenses Marked Up: No
Expenses Billed For: Mileage, Photocopies, Lab/Testing, Photographs
Portal-to-Portal: Yes **1st-class Airfare:** No
Written Retainer Agreement: No
Failure to Pay Bill Last 5 Years; Retaining Counsel: Yes **Opposing (Deps):** Yes

Engineering, Biomechanical
Court: $200 **Review/Prep:** $125 **Deps:** $200
Written Fee Schedule: Yes
Min Charge for Deps: Yes **Hours:** 2
Min Charge for Trial: Yes **Hours:** 2
Cancellation Charge for Deps/Trial: No
Retainer Required: No
Expenses Marked Up: No
Expenses Billed For: Mileage, Airline Tickets, Photographs, Demonstrative Aids
Portal-to-Portal: Yes **1st-class Airfare:** No
Written Retainer Agreement: No
Failure to Pay Bill Last 5 Years; Retaining Counsel: No **Opposing Counsel (Deps):** No

Engineering, Electrical
Court: $225 **Review/Prep:** $175 **Deps:** $225
Years Testifying: 20
Min Charge for Deps: Yes **Hours:** 4
Min Charge for Trial: Yes **Hours:** 4
Cancellation Charge for Deps/Trial: No
Retainer Required: Yes, $1,500 (Non-Refundable, One Time)
Procedure When Dep Exceeds Paid Time: Proceed without immediate payment
Expenses Marked Up: No
Expenses Billed For: Mileage, Airline Tickets, Lab/Testing, Photographs, Demonstrative Aids
Portal-to-Portal: Yes **1st-class Airfare:** No
Written Retainer Agreement: No
Failure to Pay Bill Last 5 Years; Retaining Counsel: No **Opposing Counsel (Deps):** No

Fire
Court: $225 **Review/Prep:** $150 **Deps:** $225
Years Testifying: 15 **Majority:** Defendant
Written Fee Schedule: Yes
Min Charge for Deps: No
Min Charge for Trial: No
Cancellation Charge for Deps/Trial: No
Retainer Required: Yes, Depends on case (Refundable, One Time)
Procedure When Dep Exceeds Paid Time: Proceed without immediate payment
Expenses Marked Up: No
Expenses Billed For: Mileage, Airline Tickets, Photocopies, Telephone Calls, Lab/Testing, Photographs, Demonstrative Aids
Portal-to-Portal: Yes **1st-class Airfare:** No
Written Retainer Agreement: Yes
Terms: Interest for delinquent accounts, Out-of-pocket expense policies, In-court testimony minimums, Retaining counsel pays all deposition charges, Fee schedules, Portal-to-portal travel time, Deposition minimum fee, Payment for preparation time, Cost of outside professionals productions fees, Collection costs

Failure to Pay Bill Last 5 Years; Retaining Counsel: Yes **Opposing Counsel (Deps):** No

Floors, Wood
Court: $115 **Review/Prep:** $115 **Deps:** $115
Years Testifying: 25
Written Fee Schedule: No
Min Charge for Deps: No
Min Charge for Trial: No
Cancellation Charge for Deps/Trial: No
Retainer Required: No
Expenses Marked Up: No
Expenses Billed For: Mileage, Airline Tickets, Telephone Calls, Lab/Testing
Portal-to-Portal: Yes **1st-class Airfare:** No
Written Retainer Agreement: No
Failure to Pay Bill Last 5 Years; Retaining Counsel: No **Opposing Counsel (Deps):** Yes

Fraud
Court: $280 **Review/Prep:** $280 **Deps:** $280
Years Testifying: 30
Written Fee Schedule: No
Min Charge for Deps: Yes **Hours:** 4
Min Charge for Trial: Yes **Hours:** 4
Cancellation Charge for Deps/Trial: No
Retainer Required: Yes, $2,500 (Refundable, Replenishable)
Procedure When Dep Exceeds Paid Time: Get payment before proceeding further
Expenses Marked Up: No
Expenses Billed For: Mileage, Airline Tickets, Photocopies, Telephone Calls, Lab/Testing, Photographs, Demonstrative Aids
Portal-to-Portal: No **1st-class Airfare:** No
Written Retainer Agreement: No
Failure to Pay Bill Last 5 Years; Retaining Counsel: No **Opposing Counsel (Deps):** No

Insurance
Court: $150 **Review/Prep:** $125 **Deps:** $150
Years Testifying: 5
Written Fee Schedule: No
Min Charge for Deps: Yes **Hours:** 8
Min Charge for Trial: Yes **Hours:** 8
Cancellation Charge for Deps/Trial: No
Retainer Required: No
Expenses Marked Up: No
Expenses Billed For: Mileage, Airline Tickets, Photocopies, Telephone Calls, Lab/Testing, Photographs
Portal-to-Portal: Yes **1st-class Airfare:** Yes
Written Retainer Agreement: No
Failure to Pay Bill Last 5 Years; Retaining Counsel: No **Opposing Counsel (Deps):** No

Law, Medical Malpractice
Court: $200 **Deps:** $100
Years Testifying: 5
Written Fee Schedule: No
Min Charge for Deps: No
Min Charge for Trial: No
Cancellation Charge for Deps/Trial: Yes
Retainer Required: Yes, Depends on case (Refundable, Replenishable)
Procedure When Dep Exceeds Paid Time: Get payment before proceeding further
Expenses Marked Up: No
Expenses Billed For: Mileage, Airline Tickets, Photocopies, Telephone Calls, Lab/Testing, Photographs, Demonstrative Aids
Portal-to-Portal: No **1st-class Airfare:** No
Written Retainer Agreement: Yes
Terms: Lawyer is responsible for fee, not lawyer's client, Interest for delinquent accounts, Out-of-pocket expense policies, In-court testimony minimums, Retaining counsel pays all deposition charges, Attorney's fees if forced to sue for collection, Deposition minimum fee, Payment for preparation time
Failure to Pay Bill Last 5 Years; Retaining Counsel: Yes **Opposing (Deps):** Yes

Life Care Planning
Court: $500 **Review/Prep:** $300 **Deps:** $600
Years Testifying: 10
Written Fee Schedule: Yes
Min Charge for Deps: No
Min Charge for Trial: No
Cancellation Charge for Deps/Trial: No
Retainer Required: Yes, $1,500 (Non-Refundable, One Time)
Expenses Marked Up: No
Expenses Billed For: Mileage, Airline Tickets, Photocopies, Demonstrative Aids
Portal-to-Portal: Yes **1st-class Airfare:** No
Written Retainer Agreement: No
Failure to Pay Bill Last 5 Years; Retaining Counsel: No **Opposing Counsel (Deps):** No

Marine, Surveying
Court: $285 **Review/Prep:** $285 **Deps:** $285
Years Testifying: 11
Written Fee Schedule: Yes
Min Charge for Deps: Yes
Min Charge for Trial: Yes
Cancellation Charge for Deps/Trial: Yes
Retainer Required: Yes, $2,000 (Non-Refundable, Replenishable)
Procedure When Dep Exceeds Paid Time: Get payment before proceeding further
Expenses Marked Up: No
Expenses Billed For: Airline Tickets, Photocopies, Telephone Calls, Lab/Testing, Demonstrative Aids
Portal-to-Portal: Yes
Written Retainer Agreement: Yes
Terms: Retaining counsel pays all deposition charges, Fee schedules, Portal-to-portal travel time, Deposition minimum fee
Failure to Pay Bill Last 5 Years; Retaining Counsel: Yes **Opposing (Deps):** Yes

Marketing
Court: $400 **Review/Prep:** $400 **Deps:** $400
Years Testifying: 4
Written Fee Schedule: Yes
Min Charge for Deps: No
Min Charge for Trial: No
Cancellation Charge for Deps/Trial: No
Retainer Required: Yes, $10,000 (Refundable, One Time)
Expenses Marked Up: No
Expenses Billed For: Mileage, Airline Tickets, Lab/Testing, Photographs, Demonstrative Aids
1st-class Airfare: No
Written Retainer Agreement: Yes
Terms: Lawyer is responsible for fee, not lawyer's client, Interest for delinquent accounts, Out-of-pocket expense policies, Retaining counsel pays all deposition charges, Fee schedules, Payment for preparation time
Failure to Pay Bill Last 5 Years; Retaining Counsel: Yes **Opposing Counsel (Deps):** No

Neuropsychology
Court: $2,000 **Review/Prep:** $250 **Deps:** $500
Years Testifying: 7
Written Fee Schedule: No
Min Charge for Deps: Yes **Hours:** 4
Min Charge for Trial: Yes **Hours:** 4
Cancellation Charge for Deps/Trial: Yes
Retainer Required: Yes, $5,000 (Non-Refundable, One Time)
Procedure When Dep Exceeds Paid Time: Get payment before proceeding further
Expenses Billed For: Mileage, Airline Tickets, Photocopies, Telephone Calls, Demonstrative Aids
Portal-to-Portal: Yes **1st-class Airfare:** Yes
Written Retainer Agreement: Yes
Terms: Lawyer is responsible for fee, not lawyer's client, Interest for delinquent accounts, Out-of-pocket expense policies, In-court testimony minimums, Retaining counsel pays all deposition charges, Fee schedules, Portal-to-portal travel time, Attorney's fees if forced to sue for collection, Deposition minimum fee, Payment for preparation time, First class air travel, Minimum hours policy
Failure to Pay Bill Last 5 Years; Retaining Counsel: Yes **Opposing Counsel (Deps):** No

Obstetrics & Gynecology
Court: $250 **Review/Prep:** $350 **Deps:** $500
Years Testifying: 5
Written Fee Schedule: Yes
Min Charge for Deps: Yes **Hours:** 8
Min Charge for Trial: Yes **Hours:** 8

Cancellation Charge for Deps/Trial: Yes
Retainer Required: Yes, $1,750 (Non-Refundable, One Time)
Procedure When Dep Exceeds Paid Time: Proceed without immediate payment
Expenses Marked Up: Yes
Expenses Billed For: Mileage, Airline Tickets, Telephone Calls
Portal-to-Portal: Yes **1st-class Airfare:** Yes
Written Retainer Agreement: Yes
Terms: Lawyer is responsible for fee, not lawyer's client, Interest for delinquent accounts, Out-of-pocket expense policies, In-court testimony minimums, Retaining counsel pays all deposition charges, Fee schedules, Portal-to-portal travel time, Attorney's fees if forced to sue for collection, Deposition minimum fee, Payment for preparation time, First class air travel
Failure to Pay Bill Last 5 Years; Retaining Counsel: Yes **Opposing Counsel (Deps):** No

Occupational Medicine
Court: $500 **Review/Prep:** $350 **Deps:** $500
Years Testifying: 12
Written Fee Schedule: No
Min Charge for Deps: Yes **Hours:** 4
Min Charge for Trial: Yes **Hours:** 4
Cancellation Charge for Deps/Trial: No
Retainer Required: No
Expenses Marked Up: No
Expenses Billed For: Airline Tickets
Portal-to-Portal: Yes **1st-class Airfare:** No
Written Retainer Agreement: No
Failure to Pay Bill Last 5 Years; Retaining Counsel: No **Opposing Counsel (Deps):** No

Ophthalmology
Court: $400 **Review/Prep:** $350 **Deps:** $400
Years Testifying: 20 **Majority:** Defendant
Written Fee Schedule: Yes
Min Charge for Deps: No
Min Charge for Trial: No
Cancellation Charge for Deps/Trial: No
Retainer Required: Yes, $1,000 (Non-Refundable, One Time)
Expenses Marked Up: No
Expenses Billed For: Airline Tickets
Portal-to-Portal: Yes **1st-class Airfare:** No
Written Retainer Agreement: Yes
Terms: Lawyer is responsible for fee, not lawyer's client, In-court testimony minimums, Retaining counsel pays all deposition charges, Fee schedules, Portal-to-portal travel time, Payment for preparation time
Failure to Pay Bill Last 5 Years; Retaining Counsel: No **Opposing Counsel (Deps):** No

Otolaryngology/Surgery, Head & Neck
Court: $400 **Review/Prep:** $300 **Deps:** $400
Years Testifying: 10
Written Fee Schedule: Yes
Min Charge for Deps: Yes **Hours:** 2
Min Charge for Trial: Yes **Hours:** 2
Cancellation Charge for Deps/Trial: No
Retainer Required: No
Expenses Marked Up: No
Expenses Billed For: Mileage, Airline Tickets, Photocopies, Lab/Testing, Photographs, Demonstrative Aids
Portal-to-Portal: Yes **1st-class Airfare:** No
Written Retainer Agreement: No
Failure to Pay Bill Last 5 Years; Retaining Counsel: Yes **Opposing Counsel (Deps):** No

Physical Medicine & Rehabilitation
Court: $400 **Review/Prep:** $350 **Deps:** $400
Written Fee Schedule: No
Min Charge for Deps: Yes **Hours:** 4
Min Charge for Trial: Yes **Hours:** 4
Retainer Required: Yes, Depends on case (Non-Refundable, Replenishable)
Procedure When Dep Exceeds Paid Time: Get payment before proceeding further
Expenses Marked Up: No
Expenses Billed For: Airline Tickets
Portal-to-Portal: Yes **1st-class Airfare:** No
Written Retainer Agreement: No
Failure to Pay Bill Last 5 Years; Retaining Counsel: Yes **Opposing Counsel (Deps):** No

Psychiatry
Court: $400 **Review/Prep:** $400 **Deps:** $400
Years Testifying: 30
Written Fee Schedule: Yes
Min Charge for Deps: Yes
Min Charge for Trial: No
Cancellation Charge for Deps/Trial: Yes
Retainer Required: Yes, $4,000 (Non-Refundable, Replenishable)
Procedure When Dep Exceeds Paid Time: Proceed without immediate payment
Expenses Marked Up: No
Expenses Billed For: Airline Tickets, Telephone Calls, Lab/Testing
Portal-to-Portal: Yes **1st-class Airfare:** Yes
Written Retainer Agreement: Yes
Failure to Pay Bill Last 5 Years; Retaining Counsel: Yes **Opposing (Deps):** Yes

Psychology
Court: $250 **Review/Prep:** $250 **Deps:** $250
Years Testifying: 20 **Majority:** Defendant
Written Fee Schedule: Yes
Min Charge for Deps: No
Min Charge for Trial: No
Cancellation Charge for Deps/Trial: Yes
Retainer Required: Yes, $2,500 (Refundable, Replenishable)
Procedure When Dep Exceeds Paid Time: Proceed without immediate payment
Expenses Marked Up: No
Expenses Billed For: Airline Tickets, Telephone Calls
Portal-to-Portal: Yes **1st-class Airfare:** No
Written Retainer Agreement: No
Failure to Pay Bill Last 5 Years; Retaining Counsel: Yes **Opposing (Deps):** Yes

Pulmonology
Court: $500 **Review/Prep:** $300 **Deps:** $400
Years Testifying: 10
Written Fee Schedule: Yes
Min Charge for Deps: Yes **Hours:** 1
Min Charge for Trial: Yes **Hours:** 1
Cancellation Charge for Deps/Trial: No
Retainer Required: No
Expenses Marked Up: No
Expenses Billed For: Mileage, Airline Tickets
Portal-to-Portal: Yes **1st-class Airfare:** No
Written Retainer Agreement: No
Failure to Pay Bill Last 5 Years; Retaining Counsel: No **Opposing Counsel (Deps):** No

Securities/Trusts & Estates/Banking
Court: $500 **Review/Prep:** $200 **Deps:** $350
Years Testifying: 5
Written Fee Schedule: No
Min Charge for Deps: No
Min Charge for Trial: No
Cancellation Charge for Deps/Trial: No
Retainer Required: Yes, $3,000 (Refundable, Replenishable)
Expenses Marked Up: No
Expenses Billed For: Photocopies, Telephone Calls, Photographs
Portal-to-Portal: No **1st-class Airfare:** No
Written Retainer Agreement: Yes
Terms: Lawyer is responsible for fee, not lawyer's client, Interest for delinquent accounts, Out-of-pocket expense policies, In-court testimony minimums, Retaining counsel pays all deposition charges, Fee schedules, Attorney's fees if forced to sue for collection, All out of pocket expenses
Failure to Pay Bill Last 5 Years; Retaining Counsel: Yes **Opposing (Deps):** Yes

Security/Premises Liability
Court: $195 **Review/Prep:** $195 **Deps:** $195
Years Testifying: 17
Written Fee Schedule: Yes
Min Charge for Deps: Yes **Hours:** 4
Min Charge for Trial: Yes **Hours:** 4
Cancellation Charge for Deps/Trial: No

Retainer Required: Yes, $2,000 (Non-Refundable, One Time)
Procedure When Dep Exceeds Paid Time: Proceed without immediate payment
Expenses Marked Up: No
Expenses Billed For: Airline Tickets, Photocopies, Photographs, Demonstrative Aids
Portal-to-Portal: Yes **1st-class Airfare:** No
Written Retainer Agreement: Yes
Terms: Lawyer is responsible for fee, not lawyer's client, Interest for delinquent accounts, Out-of-pocket expense policies, In-court testimony minimums, Retaining counsel pays all deposition charges, Fee schedules, Portal-to-portal travel time, Attorney's fees if forced to sue for collection, Deposition minimum fee, Payment for preparation time
Failure to Pay Bill Last 5 Years; Retaining Counsel: Yes **Opposing Counsel (Deps):** No

Slip, Trip & Fall
Court: $200 **Review/Prep:** $200 **Deps:** $200
Years Testifying: 40
Written Fee Schedule: Yes
Min Charge for Deps: Yes **Hours:** 8
Min Charge for Trial: Yes **Hours:** 8
Cancellation Charge for Deps/Trial: No
Retainer Required: Yes, $2,000 (Refundable, Replenishable)
Procedure When Dep Exceeds Paid Time: Get payment before proceeding further
Expenses Marked Up: Yes
Expenses Billed For: Airline Tickets, Photocopies, Telephone Calls, Lab/Testing, Photographs, Demonstrative Aids
Portal-to-Portal: Yes **1st-class Airfare:** No
Written Retainer Agreement: No
Failure to Pay Bill Last 5 Years; Retaining Counsel: Yes **Opposing Counsel (Deps):** No

Surgery, Neurological
Court: $500 **Review/Prep:** $300 **Deps:** $350
Years Testifying: 10 **Majority:** Defendant
Written Fee Schedule: Yes
Min Charge for Deps: Yes **Hours:** 1
Min Charge for Trial: Yes **Hours:** 1
Cancellation Charge for Deps/Trial: No
Retainer Required: No
Procedure When Dep Exceeds Paid Time: Proceed without immediate payment
Expenses Marked Up: No
Portal-to-Portal: No
Written Retainer Agreement: No
Failure to Pay Bill Last 5 Years; Retaining Counsel: No **Opposing Counsel (Deps):** No

Surgery, Neurological
Court: $900 **Review/Prep:** $800 **Deps:** $800
Majority: Plaintiff
Written Fee Schedule: Yes
Min Charge for Deps: Yes **Hours:** 4
Min Charge for Trial: Yes **Hours:** 4
Cancellation Charge for Deps/Trial: Yes
Retainer Required: Yes, (Refundable)
Procedure When Dep Exceeds Paid Time: Get payment before proceeding further
Expenses Marked Up: No
Written Retainer Agreement: No

Surgery, Plastic
Court: $400 **Review/Prep:** $250 **Deps:** $250
Written Fee Schedule: No
Min Charge for Deps: Yes **Hours:** 1
Min Charge for Trial: Yes **Hours:** 1
Cancellation Charge for Deps/Trial: Yes
Retainer Required: Yes, (Non-Refundable, Replenishable)
Procedure When Dep Exceeds Paid Time: Proceed without immediate payment
Expenses Marked Up: No
Expenses Billed For: Mileage, Airline Tickets, Photocopies, Photographs
Portal-to-Portal: Yes **1st-class Airfare:** No
Written Retainer Agreement: Yes
Terms: Lawyer is responsible for fee, not lawyer's client, Out-of-pocket expense policies, In-court testimony minimums, Retaining counsel pays all deposition charges, Fee schedules, Portal-to-portal travel time, Deposition minimum fee, Payment for preparation time
Failure to Pay Bill Last 5 Years; Retaining Counsel: No

Surgery, Vascular
Review/Prep: $350 **Deps:** $450
Years Testifying: 10 **Majority:** Plaintiff
Written Fee Schedule: Yes
Min Charge for Deps: No
Min Charge for Trial: No
Cancellation Charge for Deps/Trial: No
Retainer Required: No
Expenses Marked Up: No
Expenses Billed For: Mileage, Airline Tickets, Telephone Calls, Demonstrative Aids
Portal-to-Portal: No **1st-class Airfare:** No
Written Retainer Agreement: No
Failure to Pay Bill Last 5 Years; Retaining Counsel: Yes **Opposing Counsel (Deps):** No

TMJ
Court: $360 **Review/Prep:** $360 **Deps:** $360
Years Testifying: 15 **Majority:** Plaintiff
Written Fee Schedule: Yes
Min Charge for Deps: Yes **Hours:** 4
Min Charge for Trial: Yes **Hours:** 4
Cancellation Charge for Deps/Trial: Yes
Retainer Required: Yes, $2,000 (Non-Refundable)
Expenses Marked Up: No
Expenses Billed For: Telephone Calls, Lab/Testing, Photographs
Portal-to-Portal: Yes
Written Retainer Agreement: No
Failure to Pay Bill Last 5 Years; Retaining Counsel: No **Opposing Counsel (Deps):** No

Valuation, Business
Court: $300 **Review/Prep:** $225 **Deps:** $300
Years Testifying: 6
Written Fee Schedule: Yes
Min Charge for Deps: Yes **Hours:** 4
Min Charge for Trial: Yes **Hours:** 4
Cancellation Charge for Deps/Trial: Yes
Retainer Required: Yes, Total est. fee (Refundable)
Procedure When Dep Exceeds Paid Time: Proceed without immediate payment
Expenses Marked Up: No
Expenses Billed For: Mileage, Airline Tickets
Portal-to-Portal: Yes **1st-class Airfare:** No
Written Retainer Agreement: No
Failure to Pay Bill Last 5 Years; Retaining Counsel: No **Opposing Counsel (Deps):** No

Vocational/Employment
Court: $250 **Review/Prep:** $200 **Deps:** $200
Years Testifying: 20
Written Fee Schedule: No
Min Charge for Deps: No
Min Charge for Trial: No
Cancellation Charge for Deps/Trial: No
Retainer Required: Yes, $500 (Refundable, One Time)
Procedure When Dep Exceeds Paid Time: Proceed without immediate payment
Expenses Marked Up: No
Expenses Billed For: Mileage
Portal-to-Portal: Yes **1st-class Airfare:** No
Written Retainer Agreement: No
Failure to Pay Bill Last 5 Years; Retaining Counsel: No **Opposing Counsel (Deps):** No

Michigan

Accident Reconstruction/Disability, Handicapped Vehicles
Court: $150 **Review/Prep:** $150 **Deps:** $150
Years Testifying: 22 **Majority:** Defendant
Written Fee Schedule: Yes
Min Charge for Deps: No
Min Charge for Trial: No
Cancellation Charge for Deps/Trial: No
Retainer Required: Yes, $1,500 (Refundable, One Time)
Expenses Marked Up: No
Expenses Billed For: Mileage, Airline Tickets, Lab/Testing, Photographs, Demonstrative Aids
Portal-to-Portal: Yes **1st-class Airfare:** No
Written Retainer Agreement: No

Failure to Pay Bill Last 5 Years; Retaining Counsel: No **Opposing Counsel (Deps):** No

Accident Reconstruction
Court: $150 **Review/Prep:** $150 **Deps:** $150
Years Testifying: 30
Written Fee Schedule: Yes
Min Charge for Deps: Yes **Hours:** 4
Min Charge for Trial: Yes **Hours:** 4
Cancellation Charge for Deps/Trial: Yes
Retainer Required: Yes, $500 (Non-Refundable, One Time)
Expenses Marked Up: No
Portal-to-Portal: Yes **1st-class Airfare:** No
Written Retainer Agreement: No
Failure to Pay Bill Last 5 Years; Retaining Counsel: Yes **Opposing (Deps):** Yes

Appraisal, Coin/Appraisal, Gem & Jewelry
Court: $240 **Review/Prep:** $240 **Deps:** $240
Written Fee Schedule: Yes
Min Charge for Deps: Yes **Hours:** 4
Min Charge for Trial: Yes **Hours:** 4
Retainer Required: Yes, Depends on case (Refundable, Replenishable)
Procedure When Dep Exceeds Paid Time: Proceed without immediate payment
Expenses Marked Up: No
Expenses Billed For: Mileage, Airline Tickets, Lab/Testing
Portal-to-Portal: Yes **1st-class Airfare:** Yes
Written Retainer Agreement: Yes
Terms: Interest for delinquent accounts, In-court testimony minimums, Retaining counsel pays all deposition charges, Fee schedules, Portal-to-portal travel time, Deposition minimum fee, Payment for preparation time, First class air travel
Failure to Pay Bill Last 5 Years; Retaining Counsel: Yes **Opposing Counsel (Deps):** No

Emergency Medicine
Court: $250 **Review/Prep:** $250 **Deps:** $250
Years Testifying: 10 **Majority:** Defendant
Written Fee Schedule: Yes
Min Charge for Deps: No
Min Charge for Trial: No
Cancellation Charge for Deps/Trial: No
Retainer Required: No
Expenses Marked Up: No
Portal-to-Portal: No **1st-class Airfare:** No
Written Retainer Agreement: No
Failure to Pay Bill Last 5 Years; Retaining Counsel: No **Opposing Counsel (Deps):** No

Employment, Earning Capacity
Court: $135 **Review/Prep:** $130 **Deps:** $135
Years Testifying: 15
Written Fee Schedule: Yes
Min Charge for Deps: No
Min Charge for Trial: No
Cancellation Charge for Deps/Trial: No
Retainer Required: No
Expenses Marked Up: No
Expenses Billed For: Mileage, Airline Tickets, Telephone Calls
Portal-to-Portal: Yes **1st-class Airfare:** No
Written Retainer Agreement: No
Failure to Pay Bill Last 5 Years; Retaining Counsel: No **Opposing Counsel (Deps):** Yes

Engineering, Civil/Fire Investigation
Court: $240 **Review/Prep:** $150 **Deps:** $190
Years Testifying: 10
Written Fee Schedule: Yes
Min Charge for Deps: No
Min Charge for Trial: No
Cancellation Charge for Deps/Trial: No
Retainer Required: Yes, $1,000 (Refundable, One Time)
Procedure When Dep Exceeds Paid Time: Proceed without immediate payment
Expenses Marked Up: Yes
Expenses Billed For: Airline Tickets, Photographs, Demonstrative Aids
Portal-to-Portal: Yes **1st-class Airfare:** No
Written Retainer Agreement: No
Failure to Pay Bill Last 5 Years; Retaining Counsel: No **Opposing Counsel (Deps):** No

Family Practice
Court: $325 **Review/Prep:** $250 **Deps:** $300
Years Testifying: 10 **Majority:** Plaintiff
Written Fee Schedule: No
Min Charge for Deps: Yes **Hours:** 8
Min Charge for Trial: Yes **Hours:** 8
Cancellation Charge for Deps/Trial: No
Retainer Required: No
Procedure When Dep Exceeds Paid Time: Proceed without immediate payment
Expenses Marked Up: No
Portal-to-Portal: No **1st-class Airfare:** No
Written Retainer Agreement: No
Failure to Pay Bill Last 5 Years; Retaining Counsel: No **Opposing Counsel (Deps):** No

Fasteners/Attachments
Court: $175 **Review/Prep:** $175 **Deps:** $175
Years Testifying: 8
Written Fee Schedule: Yes
Min Charge for Deps: No
Min Charge for Trial: No
Cancellation Charge for Deps/Trial: Yes
Retainer Required: Yes, $850 (Non-Refundable, One Time)
Expenses Marked Up: Yes
Expenses Billed For: Telephone Calls
Portal-to-Portal: Yes **1st-class Airfare:** No
Written Retainer Agreement: Yes
Terms: Lawyer is responsible for fee, not lawyer's client, Interest for delinquent accounts, Out-of-pocket expense policies, Retaining counsel pays all deposition charges, Fee schedules, Portal-to-portal travel time, Payment for preparation time
Failure to Pay Bill Last 5 Years; Retaining Counsel: No **Opposing Counsel (Deps):** No

Life Care Planning
Court: $333 **Review/Prep:** $140 **Deps:** $333
Years Testifying: 23
Written Fee Schedule: Yes
Min Charge for Deps: Yes **Hours:** 3
Min Charge for Trial: Yes **Hours:** 3
Cancellation Charge for Deps/Trial: Yes
Retainer Required: Yes, $3,000 (Non-Refundable)
Procedure When Dep Exceeds Paid Time: Get payment before proceeding further
Expenses Marked Up: Yes
Expenses Billed For: Mileage, Airline Tickets, Photocopies, Telephone Calls, Lab/Testing, Demonstrative Aids
Portal-to-Portal: Yes **1st-class Airfare:** No
Written Retainer Agreement: Yes
Terms: Lawyer is responsible for fee, not lawyer's client, Interest for delinquent accounts, Out-of-pocket expense policies, In-court testimony minimums, Retaining counsel pays all deposition charges, Fee schedules, Portal-to-portal travel time, Attorney's fees if forced to sue for collection, Deposition minimum fee, Payment for preparation time
Failure to Pay Bill Last 5 Years; Retaining Counsel: No **Opposing Counsel (Deps):** No

Life Care Planning/Vocational Rehabilitation
Court: $150 **Review/Prep:** $150 **Deps:** $150
Years Testifying: 7
Written Fee Schedule: Yes
Min Charge for Deps: No
Min Charge for Trial: No
Cancellation Charge for Deps/Trial: Yes
Retainer Required: Yes, $500 (Non-Refundable, One Time)
Procedure When Dep Exceeds Paid Time: Proceed without immediate payment
Expenses Marked Up: No
Expenses Billed For: Mileage, Airline Tickets, Photocopies, Telephone Calls, Demonstrative Aids
Portal-to-Portal: Yes **1st-class Airfare:** No
Written Retainer Agreement: Yes
Terms: Lawyer is responsible for fee, not lawyer's client, Out-of-pocket expense policies, Retaining counsel pays all deposition charges, Fee schedules, Portal-to-portal travel time
Failure to Pay Bill Last 5 Years; Retaining Counsel: No **Opposing Counsel (Deps):** No

Machinery/Manufacturing

Court: $400 **Review/Prep:** $250 **Deps:** $400
Years Testifying: 4
Written Fee Schedule: Yes
Min Charge for Deps: Yes **Hours:** 10
Min Charge for Trial: Yes **Hours:** 10
Cancellation Charge for Deps/Trial: Yes
Retainer Required: Yes, $2,500 (Non-Refundable)
Procedure When Dep Exceeds Paid Time: Proceed without immediate payment
Expenses Marked Up: Yes
Expenses Billed For: Mileage, Airline Tickets, Photocopies, Telephone Calls, Lab/Testing, Photographs, Demonstrative Aids
Portal-to-Portal: Yes **1st-class Airfare:** Yes
Written Retainer Agreement: Yes
Terms: Lawyer is responsible for fee, not lawyer's client, Interest for delinquent accounts, Out-of-pocket expense policies, In-court testimony minimums, Retaining counsel pays all deposition charges, Fee schedules, Portal-to-portal travel time, Deposition minimum fee, Payment for preparation time, First class air travel
Failure to Pay Bill Last 5 Years; Retaining Counsel: No **Opposing Counsel (Deps):** No

Mechanical Systems

Court: $125 **Review/Prep:** $125 **Deps:** $125
Written Fee Schedule: Yes
Min Charge for Deps: Yes
Min Charge for Trial: Yes
Cancellation Charge for Deps/Trial: No
Retainer Required: Yes, $250 (Non-Refundable, One Time)
Expenses Marked Up: No
Expenses Billed For: Mileage, Airline Tickets, Photocopies, Telephone Calls, Lab/Testing, Photographs
Portal-to-Portal: Yes **1st-class Airfare:** No
Written Retainer Agreement: No
Failure to Pay Bill Last 5 Years; Retaining Counsel: No **Opposing Counsel (Deps):** No

Nephrology

Court: $500 **Review/Prep:** $400 **Deps:** $500
Years Testifying: 30
Written Fee Schedule: Yes
Min Charge for Deps: Yes **Hours:** 5
Min Charge for Trial: Yes **Hours:** 5
Cancellation Charge for Deps/Trial: No
Retainer Required: Yes, $800 (Refundable, One Time)
Expenses Marked Up: No
Expenses Billed For: Mileage, Airline Tickets, Demonstrative Aids
Portal-to-Portal: No **1st-class Airfare:** No
Written Retainer Agreement: No
Failure to Pay Bill Last 5 Years; Retaining Counsel: Yes **Opposing Counsel (Deps):** No

Neurology

Court: $500 **Review/Prep:** $200 **Deps:** $300
Years Testifying: 12 **Majority:** Defendant
Written Fee Schedule: Yes
Min Charge for Deps: Yes
Cancellation Charge for Deps/Trial: Yes
Retainer Required: No
Procedure When Dep Exceeds Paid Time: Proceed without immediate payment
Expenses Marked Up: Yes
Expenses Billed For: Photocopies, Telephone Calls
Written Retainer Agreement: No
Failure to Pay Bill Last 5 Years; Retaining Counsel: No **Opposing Counsel (Deps):** No

Neuropsychology

Court: $300 **Review/Prep:** $250 **Deps:** $250
Years Testifying: 6
Written Fee Schedule: Yes
Min Charge for Deps: Yes **Hours:** 5
Min Charge for Trial: Yes **Hours:** 5
Cancellation Charge for Deps/Trial: Yes
Retainer Required: No **Expenses Marked Up:** Yes
Portal-to-Portal: Yes **1st-class Airfare:** No
Written Retainer Agreement: No
Failure to Pay Bill Last 5 Years; Retaining Counsel: No **Opposing Counsel (Deps):** No

Occupational Medicine

Court: $500 **Review/Prep:** $350 **Deps:** $500
Years Testifying: 10
Written Fee Schedule: Yes
Min Charge for Deps: Yes **Hours:** 2
Min Charge for Trial: Yes **Hours:** 2
Cancellation Charge for Deps/Trial: Yes
Retainer Required: No
Expenses Marked Up: No
Expenses Billed For: Mileage, Airline Tickets, Photocopies, Telephone Calls, Lab/Testing, Photographs, Demonstrative Aids
Portal-to-Portal: Yes **1st-class Airfare:** No
Written Retainer Agreement: No
Failure to Pay Bill Last 5 Years; Retaining Counsel: No **Opposing Counsel (Deps):** No

Occupational Medicine

Court: $125 **Review/Prep:** $125 **Deps:** $750
Years Testifying: 2
Written Fee Schedule: No
Min Charge for Deps: Yes **Hours:** 6
Min Charge for Trial: Yes **Hours:** 6
Cancellation Charge for Deps/Trial: No
Retainer Required: Yes, $750 (Refundable, One Time)
Procedure When Dep Exceeds Paid Time: Proceed without immediate payment
Expenses Marked Up: Yes
Expenses Billed For: Mileage, Airline Tickets, Photocopies, Lab/Testing, Photographs, Demonstrative Aids
Portal-to-Portal: Yes **1st-class Airfare:** No
Written Retainer Agreement: No
Failure to Pay Bill Last 5 Years; Retaining Counsel: No **Opposing Counsel (Deps):** No

Orthotics/Prosthetics

Court: $500 **Review/Prep:** $350 **Deps:** $500
Years Testifying: 20
Written Fee Schedule: Yes
Min Charge for Deps: Yes **Hours:** 1
Min Charge for Trial: Yes **Hours:** 1
Cancellation Charge for Deps/Trial: No
Retainer Required: No
Procedure When Dep Exceeds Paid Time: Varies depending on case
Expenses Marked Up: No
Expenses Billed For: Mileage, Airline Tickets
Portal-to-Portal: No **1st-class Airfare:** No
Written Retainer Agreement: No

Physical Medicine & Rehabilitation

Court: $600 **Review/Prep:** $300 **Deps:** $100
Years Testifying: 3 **Majority:** Plaintiff
Written Fee Schedule: Yes
Min Charge for Deps: No **Hours:** 1
Min Charge for Trial: Yes **Hours:** 1
Cancellation Charge for Deps/Trial: Yes
Retainer Required: No
Procedure When Dep Exceeds Paid Time: Proceed without immediate payment
Expenses Marked Up: No
Portal-to-Portal: No
Written Retainer Agreement: No
Failure to Pay Bill Last 5 Years; Retaining Counsel: Yes **Opposing (Deps):** Yes

Psychiatry

Court: $300 **Review/Prep:** $300 **Deps:** $300
Years Testifying: 12 **Majority:** Defendant
Written Fee Schedule: Yes
Min Charge for Deps: Yes **Hours:** 2
Min Charge for Trial: Yes **Hours:** 2
Cancellation Charge for Deps/Trial: No
Retainer Required: Yes, 25% est. fee (Refundable, One Time)
Procedure When Dep Exceeds Paid Time: Proceed without immediate payment
Expenses Marked Up: No
Expenses Billed For: Mileage, Airline Tickets, Photocopies, Lab/Testing, Demonstrative Aids
Portal-to-Portal: Yes **1st-class Airfare:** No
Written Retainer Agreement: Yes

Terms: Lawyer is responsible for fee, not lawyer's client, Interest for delinquent accounts, Out-of-pocket expense policies, In-court testimony minimums, Retaining counsel pays all deposition charges, Fee schedules, Portal-to-portal travel time, Deposition minimum fee, Payment for preparation time
Failure to Pay Bill Last 5 Years; Retaining Counsel: No **Opposing Counsel (Deps):** No

TMJ
Court: $600 **Review/Prep:** $100 **Deps:** $500
Years Testifying: 15 **Majority:** Plaintiff
Written Fee Schedule: Yes
Min Charge for Deps: Yes **Hours:** 4
Min Charge for Trial: Yes **Hours:** 4
Cancellation Charge for Deps/Trial: Yes
Retainer Required: Yes, Total est. fee (Non-Refundable, One Time)
Procedure When Dep Exceeds Paid Time: Proceed without immediate payment
Expenses Marked Up: Yes
Expenses Billed For: Mileage, Airline Tickets, Photographs
Portal-to-Portal: Yes **1st-class Airfare:** Yes
Written Retainer Agreement: Yes
Terms: Lawyer is responsible for fee, not lawyer's client, In-court testimony minimums, Retaining counsel pays all deposition charges, Portal-to-portal travel time, Deposition minimum fee, Payment for preparation time, First class air travel
Failure to Pay Bill Last 5 Years; Retaining Counsel: Yes **Opposing (Deps):** Yes

Valuation, Business
Court: $335 **Review/Prep:** $335 **Deps:** $335
Years Testifying: 15
Written Fee Schedule: No
Min Charge for Deps: No
Min Charge for Trial: No
Cancellation Charge for Deps/Trial: No
Retainer Required: Yes, Depends on case (Refundable, One Time)
Expenses Marked Up: No
Expenses Billed For: Mileage, Airline Tickets, Demonstrative Aids
Portal-to-Portal: Yes **1st-class Airfare:** No
Written Retainer Agreement: Yes
Terms: Interest for delinquent accounts, Out-of-pocket expense policies, Retaining counsel pays all deposition charges, Fee schedules, Attorney's fees if forced to sue for collection
Failure to Pay Bill Last 5 Years; Retaining Counsel: Yes **Opposing Counsel (Deps):** No

Minnesota

Engineering/Failure Analysis
Court: $180 **Review/Prep:** $180 **Deps:** $180
Years Testifying: 20
Written Fee Schedule: Yes
Min Charge for Deps: No
Min Charge for Trial: No
Cancellation Charge for Deps/Trial: No
Retainer Required: No
Expenses Marked Up: Yes
Expenses Billed For: Mileage, Airline Tickets, Photocopies, Lab/Testing, Photographs, Demonstrative Aids
Portal-to-Portal: Yes **1st-class Airfare:** No
Written Retainer Agreement: No
Failure to Pay Bill Last 5 Years; Retaining Counsel: Yes **Opposing (Deps):** Yes

Engineering/Accident Reconstruction
Court: $150 **Review/Prep:** $150 **Deps:** $150
Years Testifying: 31 **Majority:** Plaintiff
Written Fee Schedule: Yes
Min Charge for Deps: Yes **Hours:** 8
Min Charge for Trial: Yes **Hours:** 8
Cancellation Charge for Deps/Trial: Yes
Retainer Required: Yes, $600 (Non-Refundable, One Time)
Procedure When Dep Exceeds Paid Time: Get payment before proceeding further
Expenses Marked Up: Yes
Expenses Billed For: Mileage, Airline Tickets, Photocopies, Lab/Testing, Photographs, Demonstrative Aids
Portal-to-Portal: Yes **1st-class Airfare:** No
Written Retainer Agreement: No
Failure to Pay Bill Last 5 Years; Retaining Counsel: Yes **Opposing (Deps):** Yes

Neurology
Court: $500 **Review/Prep:** $500 **Deps:** $500
Years Testifying: 8 **Majority:** Defendant
Written Fee Schedule: Yes
Min Charge for Deps: Yes **Hours:** 10
Min Charge for Trial: Yes **Hours:** 10
Cancellation Charge for Deps/Trial: Yes
Retainer Required: Yes, Total est. fee (Refundable, One Time)
Procedure When Dep Exceeds Paid Time: Proceed without immediate payment
Expenses Marked Up: No
Portal-to-Portal: No **1st-class Airfare:** No
Written Retainer Agreement: Yes
Terms: Lawyer is responsible for fee, not lawyer's client, Out-of-pocket expense policies, Retaining counsel pays all deposition charges, Fee schedules
Failure to Pay Bill Last 5 Years; Retaining Counsel: No **Opposing Counsel (Deps):** No

Utilities, Underground Damage
Court: $225 **Review/Prep:** $225 **Deps:** $225
Years Testifying: 6
Written Fee Schedule: Yes
Min Charge for Deps: No
Min Charge for Trial: No
Cancellation Charge for Deps/Trial: No
Retainer Required: Yes, $1,500 (Refundable, Replenishable)
Expenses Marked Up: No
Expenses Billed For: Mileage, Airline Tickets, Lab/Testing, Photographs, Demonstrative Aids
Portal-to-Portal: Yes **1st-class Airfare:** No
Written Retainer Agreement: Yes
Terms: Interest for delinquent accounts, Out-of-pocket expense policies, Retaining counsel pays all deposition charges, Fee schedules, Portal-to-portal travel time
Failure to Pay Bill Last 5 Years; Retaining Counsel: No **Opposing Counsel (Deps):** No

Valuation/Damages, Financial
Court: $240 **Review/Prep:** $240 **Deps:** $240
Years Testifying: 10 **Majority:** Plaintiff
Written Fee Schedule: No
Min Charge for Deps: No
Min Charge for Trial: No
Cancellation Charge for Deps/Trial: No
Retainer Required: Yes, $5,000 (Refundable, One Time)
Expenses Marked Up: No
Expenses Billed For: Mileage, Airline Tickets, Photocopies, Demonstrative Aids
Portal-to-Portal: Yes **1st-class Airfare:** No
Written Retainer Agreement: Yes
Terms: Interest for delinquent accounts, Out-of-pocket expense policies, Retaining counsel pays all deposition charges, Fee schedules, Attorney's fees if forced to sue for collection, Payment for preparation time
Failure to Pay Bill Last 5 Years; Retaining Counsel: No **Opposing Counsel (Deps):** No

Mississippi

Accident Reconstruction
Court: $75 **Review/Prep:** $90 **Deps:** $90
Years Testifying: 15 **Majority:** Defendant
Written Fee Schedule: No
Min Charge for Deps: No
Min Charge for Trial: No
Cancellation Charge for Deps/Trial: No
Retainer Required: No
Expenses Marked Up: No
Portal-to-Portal: Yes **1st-class Airfare:** No
Written Retainer Agreement: No
Failure to Pay Bill Last 5 Years; Retaining Counsel: No **Opposing Counsel (Deps):** No

Damages, Business
Court: $175 **Review/Prep:** $175 **Deps:** $175
Years Testifying: 10
Written Fee Schedule: Yes
Min Charge for Deps: No
Min Charge for Trial: No
Cancellation Charge for Deps/Trial: No
Retainer Required: Yes, Depends on case (Refundable, Replenishable)
Procedure When Dep Exceeds Paid Time: Proceed without immediate payment
Expenses Marked Up: No
Expenses Billed For: Mileage, Airline Tickets
Portal-to-Portal: Yes **1st-class Airfare:** No
Written Retainer Agreement: Yes
Terms: Lawyer is responsible for fee, not lawyer's client, Interest for delinquent accounts, Out-of-pocket expense policies, Retaining counsel pays all deposition charges, Fee schedules, Attorney's fees if forced to sue for collection, Payment for preparation time, Privacy policy
Failure to Pay Bill Last 5 Years; Retaining Counsel: No **Opposing Counsel (Deps):** No

Damages, Economic
Court: $100 **Review/Prep:** $100 **Deps:** $100
Years Testifying: 20
Written Fee Schedule: No
Min Charge for Deps: No
Min Charge for Trial: No
Cancellation Charge for Deps/Trial: No
Retainer Required: No
Expenses Marked Up: No
Expenses Billed For: Mileage, Airline Tickets, Telephone Calls
Portal-to-Portal: No
Written Retainer Agreement: No
Failure to Pay Bill Last 5 Years; Retaining Counsel: Yes **Opposing Counsel (Deps):** No

Engineering, Electrical
Court: $175 **Review/Prep:** $175 **Deps:** $175
Years Testifying: 14
Written Fee Schedule: Yes
Min Charge for Deps: No
Min Charge for Trial: No
Cancellation Charge for Deps/Trial: No
Retainer Required: No
Expenses Marked Up: No
Expenses Billed For: Mileage, Airline Tickets, Photocopies, Telephone Calls, Lab/Testing, Photographs, Demonstrative Aids
Portal-to-Portal: Yes **1st-class Airfare:** No
Written Retainer Agreement: No
Failure to Pay Bill Last 5 Years; Retaining Counsel: No **Opposing Counsel (Deps):** Yes

Engineering, Structural
Court: $100 **Review/Prep:** $100 **Deps:** $100
Written Fee Schedule: No
Min Charge for Deps: No
Min Charge for Trial: No
Cancellation Charge for Deps/Trial: No
Retainer Required: No
Procedure When Dep Exceeds Paid Time: Proceed without immediate payment
Expenses Marked Up: No
Expenses Billed For: Mileage, Airline Tickets, Lab/Testing, Photographs, Demonstrative Aids
Portal-to-Portal: Yes **1st-class Airfare:** No
Written Retainer Agreement: No
Failure to Pay Bill Last 5 Years; Retaining Counsel: No **Opposing Counsel (Deps):** No

Fire Investigation/Accident Reconstruction
Court: $125 **Review/Prep:** $25 **Deps:** $125
Years Testifying: 35
Written Fee Schedule: No
Min Charge for Deps: Yes **Hours:** 2
Min Charge for Trial: Yes **Hours:** 2
Cancellation Charge for Deps/Trial: No
Retainer Required: No
Expenses Marked Up: No
Expenses Billed For: Mileage, Airline Tickets, Lab/Testing, Photographs, Demonstrative Aids
Portal-to-Portal: No **1st-class Airfare:** No
Written Retainer Agreement: No
Failure to Pay Bill Last 5 Years; Retaining Counsel: Yes **Opposing (Deps):** Yes

Law Enforcement
Court: $125 **Review/Prep:** $125 **Deps:** $125
Years Testifying: 11 **Majority:** Defendant
Written Fee Schedule: Yes
Min Charge for Deps: Yes **Hours:** 8
Min Charge for Trial: Yes **Hours:** 8
Cancellation Charge for Deps/Trial: Yes
Retainer Required: Yes, $3,000 (Non-Refundable, One Time)
Expenses Marked Up: No
Expenses Billed For: Mileage, Airline Tickets, Photographs
Portal-to-Portal: No **1st-class Airfare:** No
Written Retainer Agreement: Yes
Terms: Lawyer is responsible for fee, not lawyer's client, In-court testimony minimums, Retaining counsel pays all deposition charges, Fee schedules, Cancellation issues
Failure to Pay Bill Last 5 Years; Retaining Counsel: No **Opposing Counsel (Deps):** No

Obstetrics & Gynecology
Court: $375 **Review/Prep:** $350 **Deps:** $250
Years Testifying: 15
Written Fee Schedule: Yes
Min Charge for Deps: Yes **Hours:** 8
Min Charge for Trial: Yes **Hours:** 8
Cancellation Charge for Deps/Trial: Yes
Retainer Required: Yes, $500 (Refundable, One Time)
Expenses Marked Up: No
Expenses Billed For: Mileage, Airline Tickets, Telephone Calls
Portal-to-Portal: Yes **1st-class Airfare:** Yes
Written Retainer Agreement: No
Failure to Pay Bill Last 5 Years; Retaining Counsel: No **Opposing Counsel (Deps):** No

Obstetrics & Gynecology
Court: $1,250 **Review/Prep:** $375 **Deps:** $750
Years Testifying: 4 **Majority:** Defendant
Written Fee Schedule: No
Min Charge for Deps: Yes **Hours:** 3
Min Charge for Trial: Yes **Hours:** 3
Cancellation Charge for Deps/Trial: Yes
Retainer Required: No
Expenses Marked Up: No
Expenses Billed For: Mileage, Airline Tickets, Demonstrative Aids
Portal-to-Portal: Yes **1st-class Airfare:** No
Written Retainer Agreement: No
Failure to Pay Bill Last 5 Years; Retaining Counsel: Yes **Opposing (Deps):** Yes

Pain Management/Medicine
Court: $100 **Review/Prep:** $100 **Deps:** $100
Years Testifying: 5
Written Fee Schedule: No
Min Charge for Deps: Yes
Min Charge for Trial: No
Cancellation Charge for Deps/Trial: No
Retainer Required: Yes, (Refundable)
Procedure When Dep Exceeds Paid Time: Proceed without immediate payment
Expenses Marked Up: No
Expenses Billed For: Mileage, Airline Tickets, Telephone Calls, Demonstrative Aids
Portal-to-Portal: Yes **1st-class Airfare:** No
Written Retainer Agreement: No
Failure to Pay Bill Last 5 Years; Retaining Counsel: No **Opposing Counsel (Deps):** No

Missouri

Aviation
Court: $150 **Review/Prep:** $150 **Deps:** $150
Years Testifying: 1 **Majority:** Defendant
Written Fee Schedule: Yes
Min Charge for Deps: No
Min Charge for Trial: No
Cancellation Charge for Deps/Trial: No
Retainer Required: No
Expenses Marked Up: No
Expenses Billed For: Mileage, Airline Tickets, Lab/Testing, Photographs,

Demonstrative Aids
Portal-to-Portal: Yes **1st-class Airfare:** No
Written Retainer Agreement: No
Failure to Pay Bill Last 5 Years; Retaining Counsel: No **Opposing Counsel (Deps):** No

Document Examiner
Court: $125 **Review/Prep:** $125 **Deps:** $125
Years Testifying: 10
Written Fee Schedule: Yes
Min Charge for Deps: Yes **Hours:** 4
Min Charge for Trial: Yes **Hours:** 4
Cancellation Charge for Deps/Trial: Yes
Retainer Required: Yes, $375 (Refundable, Replenishable)
Procedure When Dep Exceeds Paid Time: Get payment before proceeding further
Expenses Marked Up: No
Expenses Billed For: Mileage, Airline Tickets, Photographs, Demonstrative Aids
Portal-to-Portal: Yes **1st-class Airfare:** No
Written Retainer Agreement: No
Failure to Pay Bill Last 5 Years; Retaining Counsel: Yes **Opposing Counsel (Deps):** No

Engineering, Electrical
Court: $235 **Review/Prep:** $210 **Deps:** $235
Years Testifying: 24
Written Fee Schedule: No
Min Charge for Deps: Yes **Hours:** 4
Min Charge for Trial: Yes **Hours:** 4
Cancellation Charge for Deps/Trial: No
Retainer Required: Yes, $1,000 (Non-Refundable, One Time)
Expenses Marked Up: Yes
Expenses Billed For: Mileage, Airline Tickets, Photocopies, Telephone Calls, Lab/Testing, Photographs, Demonstrative Aids
Portal-to-Portal: Yes **1st-class Airfare:** No
Written Retainer Agreement: Yes
Terms: Lawyer is responsible for fee, not lawyer's client, Interest for delinquent accounts, Out-of-pocket expense policies, In-court testimony minimums, Retaining counsel pays all deposition charges, Portal-to-portal travel time, Attorney's fees if forced to sue for collection, Deposition minimum fee, Payment for preparation time
Failure to Pay Bill Last 5 Years; Retaining Counsel: No **Opposing Counsel (Deps):** No

Engineering, Mechanical
Court: $275 **Review/Prep:** $225 **Deps:** $275
Years Testifying: 27 **Majority:** Plaintiff
Written Fee Schedule: Yes
Min Charge for Deps: No
Min Charge for Trial: No
Cancellation Charge for Deps/Trial: No
Retainer Required: Yes, $2,500 (Refundable, Replenishable)
Expenses Marked Up: Yes
Expenses Billed For: Mileage, Airline Tickets, Photocopies, Telephone Calls, Lab/Testing, Photographs, Demonstrative Aids
Portal-to-Portal: Yes **1st-class Airfare:** Yes
Written Retainer Agreement: Yes
Terms: Lawyer is responsible for fee, not lawyer's client, Interest for delinquent accounts, Out-of-pocket expense policies, Retaining counsel pays all deposition charges, Fee schedules, Portal-to-portal travel time, Attorney's fees if forced to sue for collection
Failure to Pay Bill Last 5 Years; Retaining Counsel: Yes **Opposing Counsel (Deps):** No

Engineering, Mechanical
Court: $230 **Review/Prep:** $230 **Deps:** $230
Years Testifying: 15
Written Fee Schedule: No
Min Charge for Deps: No
Min Charge for Trial: No
Cancellation Charge for Deps/Trial: Yes
Retainer Required: Yes, $920 (Non-Refundable, One Time)
Expenses Marked Up: Yes
Expenses Billed For: Mileage, Airline Tickets, Photocopies, Lab/Testing, Demonstrative Aids
Portal-to-Portal: Yes **1st-class Airfare:** No
Written Retainer Agreement: Yes
Terms: Lawyer is responsible for fee, not lawyer's client, Interest for delinquent accounts, Retaining counsel pays all deposition charges, Portal-to-portal travel time, Attorney's fees if forced to sue for collection, Payment for preparation time
Failure to Pay Bill Last 5 Years; Retaining Counsel: Yes **Opposing (Deps):** Yes

Engineering, Mechanical
Court: $180 **Review/Prep:** $180 **Deps:** $180
Years Testifying: 7 **Majority:** Defendant
Written Fee Schedule: No
Min Charge for Deps: No
Min Charge for Trial: No
Cancellation Charge for Deps/Trial: No
Retainer Required: No
Expenses Marked Up: No
Expenses Billed For: Mileage, Airline Tickets, Lab/Testing, Photographs, Demonstrative Aids
Portal-to-Portal: Yes **1st-class Airfare:** No
Written Retainer Agreement: No
Failure to Pay Bill Last 5 Years; Retaining Counsel: Yes **Opposing Counsel (Deps):** No

Environmental
Court: $400 **Review/Prep:** $200 **Deps:** $400
Majority: Defendant
Written Fee Schedule: Yes
Min Charge for Deps: No
Min Charge for Trial: No
Cancellation Charge for Deps/Trial: No
Retainer Required: No
Expenses Marked Up: Yes
Expenses Billed For: Mileage, Airline Tickets, Photocopies, Telephone Calls, Lab/Testing, Photographs, Demonstrative Aids
Portal-to-Portal: Yes **1st-class Airfare:** No
Written Retainer Agreement: Yes
Terms: Interest for delinquent accounts, Out-of-pocket expense policies, Fee schedules, Portal-to-portal travel time, Payment for preparation time
Failure to Pay Bill Last 5 Years; Retaining Counsel: Yes **Opposing Counsel (Deps):** No

Geriatrics
Court: $150 **Review/Prep:** $75 **Deps:** $125
Written Fee Schedule: Yes
Min Charge for Deps: Yes **Hours:** 3
Min Charge for Trial: Yes **Hours:** 3
Retainer Required: Yes, $500 (Non-Refundable, One Time)
Procedure When Dep Exceeds Paid Time: Get payment before proceeding further
Expenses Marked Up: No
Expenses Billed For: Mileage, Airline Tickets, Lab/Testing, Demonstrative Aids
Portal-to-Portal: Yes **1st-class Airfare:** Yes
Written Retainer Agreement: Yes
Terms: Lawyer is responsible for fee, not lawyer's client, Interest for delinquent accounts, Out-of-pocket expense policies, In-court testimony minimums, Retaining counsel pays all deposition charges, Fee schedules, Portal-to-portal travel time, Attorney's fees if forced to sue for collection, Deposition minimum fee, Payment for preparation time, First class air travel

Metallurgy/Engineering, Materials
Court: $270 **Review/Prep:** $210 **Deps:** $270
Written Fee Schedule: Yes
Min Charge for Deps: Yes **Hours:** 4
Min Charge for Trial: Yes **Hours:** 4
Cancellation Charge for Deps/Trial: No
Retainer Required: No
Expenses Marked Up: Yes
Expenses Billed For: Mileage, Airline Tickets, Lab/Testing, Photographs, Demonstrative Aids
Portal-to-Portal: Yes **1st-class Airfare:** No
Written Retainer Agreement: Yes
Failure to Pay Bill Last 5 Years; Retaining Counsel: Yes **Opposing (Deps):** Yes

Neurology, Child
Court: $500 **Review/Prep:** $300 **Deps:** $500
Years Testifying: 12
Written Fee Schedule: Yes
Min Charge for Deps: Yes **Hours:** 8
Min Charge for Trial: Yes **Hours:** 8
Cancellation Charge for Deps/Trial: Yes
Retainer Required: No
Expenses Marked Up: No
Expenses Billed For: Mileage, Airline Tickets
Portal-to-Portal: Yes **1st-class Airfare:** No
Written Retainer Agreement: No
Failure to Pay Bill Last 5 Years; Retaining Counsel: No **Opposing Counsel (Deps):** Yes

Ophthalmology
Court: $1,500 **Review/Prep:** $350 **Deps:** $500
Years Testifying: 20 **Majority:** Defendant
Written Fee Schedule: Yes
Min Charge for Deps: Yes **Hours:** 2
Min Charge for Trial: Yes **Hours:** 2
Cancellation Charge for Deps/Trial: Yes
Retainer Required: No
Procedure When Dep Exceeds Paid Time: Proceed without immediate payment
Expenses Marked Up: No
Expenses Billed For: Mileage, Airline Tickets, Photocopies, Telephone Calls
Portal-to-Portal: Yes **1st-class Airfare:** No
Written Retainer Agreement: No
Failure to Pay Bill Last 5 Years; Retaining Counsel: No **Opposing Counsel (Deps):** No

Pathology, Pediatric
Court: $500 **Review/Prep:** $500 **Deps:** $500
Years Testifying: 10
Written Fee Schedule: No
Min Charge for Deps: No **Hours:** 4
Min Charge for Trial: Yes **Hours:** 4
Cancellation Charge for Deps/Trial: No
Retainer Required: No
Expenses Marked Up: Yes
Expenses Billed For: Mileage, Airline Tickets, Telephone Calls, Photographs, Demonstrative Aids
Portal-to-Portal: Yes **1st-class Airfare:** Yes
Written Retainer Agreement: No
Failure to Pay Bill Last 5 Years; Retaining Counsel: No **Opposing Counsel (Deps):** No

Physical Medicine & Rehabilitation
Court: $1,000 **Review/Prep:** $300 **Deps:** $750
Years Testifying: 4 **Majority:** Defendant
Written Fee Schedule: Yes
Min Charge for Deps: Yes **Hours:** 2
Min Charge for Trial: Yes **Hours:** 2
Cancellation Charge for Deps/Trial: Yes
Retainer Required: No
Procedure When Dep Exceeds Paid Time: Proceed without immediate payment
Expenses Marked Up: No
Expenses Billed For: Mileage, Airline Tickets
Portal-to-Portal: No **1st-class Airfare:** No
Written Retainer Agreement: No
Failure to Pay Bill Last 5 Years; Retaining Counsel: No **Opposing Counsel (Deps):** No

Psychiatry
Court: $300 **Review/Prep:** $200 **Deps:** $200
Years Testifying: 20
Written Fee Schedule: Yes
Min Charge for Deps: No **Hours:** 4
Min Charge for Trial: Yes **Hours:** 4
Cancellation Charge for Deps/Trial: Yes
Procedure When Dep Exceeds Paid Time: Proceed without immediate payment
Expenses Marked Up: No
Portal-to-Portal: No **1st-class Airfare:** No
Written Retainer Agreement: Yes
Terms: Lawyer is responsible for fee, not lawyer's client, In-court testimony minimums, Retaining counsel pays all deposition charges, Fee schedules, Deposition minimum fee, Payment for preparation time
Failure to Pay Bill Last 5 Years; Retaining Counsel: No **Opposing Counsel (Deps):** No

Psychiatry
Court: $250 **Review/Prep:** $250 **Deps:** $250
Years Testifying: 20
Written Fee Schedule: Yes
Min Charge for Deps: Yes **Hours:** 4
Min Charge for Trial: Yes **Hours:** 4
Cancellation Charge for Deps/Trial: Yes
Retainer Required: Yes, $1,000 (Refundable, One Time)
Procedure When Dep Exceeds Paid Time: Proceed without immediate payment
Expenses Marked Up: No
Portal-to-Portal: Yes **1st-class Airfare:** No
Written Retainer Agreement: Yes
Terms: Lawyer is responsible for fee, not lawyer's client, Interest for delinquent accounts, Retaining counsel pays all deposition charges, Fee schedules, Portal-to-portal travel time, Payment for preparation time
Failure to Pay Bill Last 5 Years; Retaining Counsel: No **Opposing Counsel (Deps):** No

Real Estate
Court: $200 **Review/Prep:** $175 **Deps:** $200
Years Testifying: 35
Written Fee Schedule: No
Min Charge for Deps: Yes **Hours:** 1
Min Charge for Trial: Yes **Hours:** 1
Cancellation Charge for Deps/Trial: Yes
Retainer Required: Yes, Depends on case (Non-Refundable, Replenishable)
Procedure When Dep Exceeds Paid Time: Get payment before proceeding further
Expenses Marked Up: No
Expenses Billed For: Mileage, Airline Tickets, Lab/Testing, Demonstrative Aids
Portal-to-Portal: Yes **1st-class Airfare:** Yes
Written Retainer Agreement: No
Failure to Pay Bill Last 5 Years; Retaining Counsel: No **Opposing Counsel (Deps):** No

Trusts & Estates
Court: $200 **Review/Prep:** $200 **Deps:** $200
Years Testifying: 20
Written Fee Schedule: Yes
Min Charge for Deps: Yes **Hours:** 8
Min Charge for Trial: Yes **Hours:** 8
Cancellation Charge for Deps/Trial: Yes
Retainer Required: Yes, $1,600 (Non-Refundable, One Time)
Expenses Marked Up: No
Expenses Billed For: Photocopies, Telephone Calls, Demonstrative Aids
Portal-to-Portal: No **1st-class Airfare:** No
Written Retainer Agreement: Yes
Terms: Lawyer is responsible for fee, not lawyer's client, Interest for delinquent accounts, Out-of-pocket expense policies, In-court testimony minimums, Retaining counsel pays all deposition charges, Attorney's fees if forced to sue for collection, Deposition minimum fee, Payment for preparation time
Failure to Pay Bill Last 5 Years; Retaining Counsel: No **Opposing Counsel (Deps):** No

Valuation
Court: $225 **Review/Prep:** $225 **Deps:** $225
Years Testifying: 20
Written Fee Schedule: No
Min Charge for Deps: No
Min Charge for Trial: No
Cancellation Charge for Deps/Trial: No
Retainer Required: Yes, Depends on case (Refundable, One Time)
Expenses Marked Up: No
Expenses Billed For: Mileage, Airline Tickets, Photocopies, Telephone Calls
Portal-to-Portal: No **1st-class Airfare:** No
Written Retainer Agreement: No
Failure to Pay Bill Last 5 Years; Retaining Counsel: Yes **Opposing (Deps):** Yes

Valuation, Business
Court: $100 **Review/Prep:** $150 **Deps:** $100
Years Testifying: 35
Written Fee Schedule: No
Min Charge for Deps: No **Hours:** 4
Min Charge for Trial: Yes **Hours:** 4
Cancellation Charge for Deps/Trial: Yes
Retainer Required: No
Expenses Marked Up: No

Expenses Billed For: Mileage, Airline Tickets, Photocopies, Telephone Calls, Lab/Testing, Photographs, Demonstrative Aids
Portal-to-Portal: Yes **1st-class Airfare:** No
Written Retainer Agreement: Yes
Terms: Out-of-pocket expense policies, In-court testimony minimums, Retaining counsel pays all deposition charges, Fee schedules, Portal-to-portal travel time, Deposition minimum fee, Payment for preparation time
Failure to Pay Bill Last 5 Years; Retaining Counsel: Yes **Opposing Counsel (Deps):** No

Montana

Accident Reconstruction
Court: $360 **Review/Prep:** $240 **Deps:** $360
Years Testifying: 25 **Majority:** Plaintiff
Written Fee Schedule: Yes
Min Charge for Deps: No
Min Charge for Trial: No
Cancellation Charge for Deps/Trial: Yes
Retainer Required: Yes, $6,000 (Refundable, One Time)
Expenses Marked Up: No
Expenses Billed For: Mileage, Airline Tickets, Photocopies, Lab/Testing, Photographs, Demonstrative Aids
Portal-to-Portal: Yes **1st-class Airfare:** No
Written Retainer Agreement: Yes
Terms: Lawyer is responsible for fee, not lawyer's client, Interest for delinquent accounts, Out-of-pocket expense policies, In-court testimony minimums, Retaining counsel pays all deposition charges, Fee schedules, Portal-to-portal travel time, Attorney's fees if forced to sue for collection, Deposition minimum fee, Payment for preparation time, First class air travel
Failure to Pay Bill Last 5 Years; Retaining Counsel: Yes **Opposing Counsel (Deps):** No

Damages, Business
Court: $200 **Review/Prep:** $160 **Deps:** $160
Years Testifying: 7
Written Fee Schedule: No
Min Charge for Deps: No
Min Charge for Trial: No
Cancellation Charge for Deps/Trial: No
Retainer Required: Yes, $3,500 (Refundable, One Time)
Expenses Marked Up: No
Expenses Billed For: Mileage, Airline Tickets
Portal-to-Portal: Yes **1st-class Airfare:** No
Written Retainer Agreement: Yes
Terms: Retaining counsel pays all deposition charges
Failure to Pay Bill Last 5 Years; Retaining Counsel: No **Opposing Counsel (Deps):** No

Pediatrics
Court: $500 **Review/Prep:** $300
Years Testifying: 5
Written Fee Schedule: No
Min Charge for Deps: No
Min Charge for Trial: No
Cancellation Charge for Deps/Trial: No
Retainer Required: No
Expenses Marked Up: No
Expenses Billed For: Mileage, Airline Tickets, Lab/Testing
Portal-to-Portal: Yes **1st-class Airfare:** No
Written Retainer Agreement: No
Failure to Pay Bill Last 5 Years; Retaining Counsel: No **Opposing Counsel (Deps):** No

Psychiatry
Court: $500 **Review/Prep:** $250 **Deps:** $500
Years Testifying: 30
Written Fee Schedule: Yes
Min Charge for Deps: No
Min Charge for Trial: No
Cancellation Charge for Deps/Trial: Yes
Retainer Required: No
Expenses Marked Up: No
Expenses Billed For: Mileage, Airline Tickets, Photocopies, Telephone Calls
Portal-to-Portal: Yes **1st-class Airfare:** No
Written Retainer Agreement: Yes
Terms: Lawyer is responsible for fee, not lawyer's client, Interest for delinquent accounts, Out-of-pocket expense policies, In-court testimony minimums, Retaining counsel pays all deposition charges, Fee schedules
Failure to Pay Bill Last 5 Years; Retaining Counsel: No **Opposing Counsel (Deps):** No

Psychology
Court: $110 **Review/Prep:** $100 **Deps:** $100
Years Testifying: 20
Written Fee Schedule: Yes
Min Charge for Deps: Yes **Hours:** 4
Min Charge for Trial: Yes **Hours:** 4
Cancellation Charge for Deps/Trial: No
Retainer Required: Yes, $500 (Non-Refundable, One Time)
Expenses Marked Up: No
Expenses Billed For: Mileage, Airline Tickets, Telephone Calls
Portal-to-Portal: Yes **1st-class Airfare:** No
Written Retainer Agreement: No
Failure to Pay Bill Last 5 Years; Retaining Counsel: No **Opposing Counsel (Deps):** No

Nebraska

Genetics
Court: $250 **Review/Prep:** $250 **Deps:** $250
Years Testifying: 13 **Majority:** Defendant
Written Fee Schedule: Yes
Min Charge for Deps: No
Min Charge for Trial: No
Cancellation Charge for Deps/Trial: No
Retainer Required: No
Expenses Marked Up: No
Expenses Billed For: Mileage, Airline Tickets, Telephone Calls
Portal-to-Portal: Yes **1st-class Airfare:** No
Written Retainer Agreement: Yes
Terms: Lawyer is responsible for fee, not lawyer's client, Out-of-pocket expense policies, Fee schedules, Portal-to-portal travel time, Payment for preparation time
Failure to Pay Bill Last 5 Years; Retaining Counsel: No **Opposing Counsel (Deps):** No

Occupational Medicine
Court: $350 **Review/Prep:** $175 **Deps:** $350
Years Testifying: 30 **Majority:** Defendant
Written Fee Schedule: Yes
Min Charge for Deps: Yes **Hours:** 4
Min Charge for Trial: Yes **Hours:** 4
Cancellation Charge for Deps/Trial: Yes
Retainer Required: Yes, $900 (One Time)
Procedure When Dep Exceeds Paid Time: Proceed without immediate payment
Expenses Billed For: Mileage, Airline Tickets, Photocopies, Telephone Calls, Lab/Testing
Portal-to-Portal: Yes **1st-class Airfare:** No
Written Retainer Agreement: No
Failure to Pay Bill Last 5 Years; Retaining Counsel: Yes **Opposing (Deps):** Yes

Nevada

Anesthesiology
Court: $700 **Review/Prep:** $400 **Deps:** $700
Years Testifying: 4
Written Fee Schedule: Yes
Min Charge for Deps: No
Min Charge for Trial: No
Cancellation Charge for Deps/Trial: Yes
Retainer Required: Yes, $750 (Non-Refundable, One Time)
Procedure When Dep Exceeds Paid Time: Proceed without immediate payment
Expenses Billed For: Mileage, Airline Tickets
Portal-to-Portal: Yes **1st-class Airfare:** No
Written Retainer Agreement: No

Appraisal, Real Estate
Court: $165 **Review/Prep:** $140 **Deps:** $165
Years Testifying: 10
Written Fee Schedule: Yes
Min Charge for Deps: No
Min Charge for Trial: No
Cancellation Charge for Deps/Trial: No
Retainer Required: Yes, 80% est fee, 100% est. expense (Refundable, One Time)
Expenses Marked Up: No

Expenses Billed For: Mileage, Airline Tickets, Photocopies, Lab/Testing, Photographs, Demonstrative Aids
Portal-to-Portal: Yes **1st-class Airfare:** No
Written Retainer Agreement: Yes
Terms: Interest for delinquent accounts, Out-of-pocket expense policies, Retaining counsel pays all deposition charges, Attorney's fees if forced to sue for collection
Failure to Pay Bill Last 5 Years; Retaining Counsel: Yes **Opposing (Deps):** Yes

Chiropractic

Court: $500 **Review/Prep:** $250 **Deps:** $250
Years Testifying: 2
Written Fee Schedule: Yes
Min Charge for Deps: Yes **Hours:** 1
Min Charge for Trial: Yes **Hours:** 1
Cancellation Charge for Deps/Trial: Yes
Retainer Required: Yes, $500 (Refundable)
Procedure When Dep Exceeds Paid Time: Get payment before proceeding further
Expenses Marked Up: No
Expenses Billed For: Mileage, Airline Tickets, Photocopies, Telephone Calls, Lab/Testing, Photographs, Demonstrative Aids
Portal-to-Portal: Yes **1st-class Airfare:** No
Written Retainer Agreement: No
Failure to Pay Bill Last 5 Years; Retaining Counsel: No **Opposing Counsel (Deps):** No

Insurance, Disability

Court: $300 **Review/Prep:** $225 **Deps:** $300
Years Testifying: 5
Written Fee Schedule: Yes
Min Charge for Deps: Yes **Hours:** 4
Min Charge for Trial: Yes **Hours:** 4
Cancellation Charge for Deps/Trial: No
Retainer Required: Yes, $2,500 (Refundable, One Time)
Expenses Marked Up: No
Expenses Billed For: Airline Tickets, Photocopies, Telephone Calls
Portal-to-Portal: No **1st-class Airfare:** No
Written Retainer Agreement: Yes
Terms: Lawyer is responsible for fee, not lawyer's client, Out-of-pocket expense policies, In-court testimony minimums, Retaining counsel pays all deposition charges, Fee schedules, Deposition minimum fee, Payment for preparation time
Failure to Pay Bill Last 5 Years; Retaining Counsel: Yes **Opposing Counsel (Deps):** No

Orthopedics

Court: $450 **Review/Prep:** $500 **Deps:** $500
Years Testifying: 9 **Majority:** Defendant
Written Fee Schedule: Yes
Min Charge for Deps: Yes **Hours:** 1
Min Charge for Trial: Yes **Hours:** 1
Cancellation Charge for Deps/Trial: Yes
Retainer Required: Yes, $1,000 (Non-Refundable, One Time)
Procedure When Dep Exceeds Paid Time: Proceed without immediate payment
Expenses Marked Up: Yes
Expenses Billed For: Mileage, Airline Tickets, Photocopies, Telephone Calls
Portal-to-Portal: Yes **1st-class Airfare:** Yes
Written Retainer Agreement: No
Failure to Pay Bill Last 5 Years; Retaining Counsel: Yes **Opposing (Deps):** Yes

Pain Management/Medicine

Court: $600 **Review/Prep:** $300 **Deps:** $750
Years Testifying: 5
Written Fee Schedule: Yes
Min Charge for Deps: Yes **Hours:** 4
Min Charge for Trial: Yes **Hours:** 4
Cancellation Charge for Deps/Trial: Yes
Retainer Required: No
Procedure When Dep Exceeds Paid Time: Proceed without immediate payment
Expenses Marked Up: No
Expenses Billed For: Mileage, Airline Tickets, Telephone Calls, Lab/Testing
Portal-to-Portal: Yes **1st-class Airfare:** No
Written Retainer Agreement: Yes
Terms: Lawyer is responsible for fee, not lawyer's client, Out-of-pocket expense policies, In-court testimony minimums, Retaining counsel pays all deposition charges, Fee schedules, Deposition minimum fee, Payment for preparation time
Failure to Pay Bill Last 5 Years; Retaining Counsel: Yes **Opposing Counsel (Deps):** No

Security

Court: $250 **Review/Prep:** $250 **Deps:** $250
Years Testifying: 30
Written Fee Schedule: Yes
Min Charge for Deps: No
Min Charge for Trial: No
Cancellation Charge for Deps/Trial: No
Retainer Required: Yes, $2,000 (Non-Refundable, One Time)
Expenses Marked Up: No
Expenses Billed For: Mileage, Airline Tickets
Portal-to-Portal: Yes **1st-class Airfare:** No
Written Retainer Agreement: No
Failure to Pay Bill Last 5 Years; Retaining Counsel: Yes **Opposing Counsel (Deps):** No

Surgery, General

Court: $400 **Review/Prep:** $350 **Deps:** $400
Years Testifying: 10 **Majority:** Defendant
Written Fee Schedule: Yes
Min Charge for Deps: No **Hours:** 4
Min Charge for Trial: Yes **Hours:** 4
Cancellation Charge for Deps/Trial: No
Retainer Required: No
Expenses Marked Up: No
Portal-to-Portal: Yes **1st-class Airfare:** No
Written Retainer Agreement: No
Failure to Pay Bill Last 5 Years; Retaining Counsel: Yes **Opposing Counsel (Deps):** No

Transportation

Court: $300 **Review/Prep:** $175 **Deps:** $300
Years Testifying: 20
Written Fee Schedule: Yes
Min Charge for Deps: Yes **Hours:** 4
Min Charge for Trial: Yes **Hours:** 4
Cancellation Charge for Deps/Trial: No
Retainer Required: Yes, $2,000 (Non-Refundable, One Time)
Expenses Marked Up: No
Expenses Billed For: Mileage, Airline Tickets, Photocopies, Lab/Testing, Photographs, Demonstrative Aids
Portal-to-Portal: Yes **1st-class Airfare:** No
Written Retainer Agreement: No
Failure to Pay Bill Last 5 Years; Retaining Counsel: Yes **Opposing Counsel (Deps):** No

New Hampshire

Construction

Court: $100 **Review/Prep:** $75 **Deps:** $100
Years Testifying: 10 **Majority:** Plaintiff
Written Fee Schedule: Yes
Min Charge for Deps: Yes **Hours:** 4
Min Charge for Trial: Yes **Hours:** 4
Cancellation Charge for Deps/Trial: Yes
Retainer Required: Yes, $750 (Non-Refundable, Replenishable)
Expenses Marked Up: No
Expenses Billed For: Mileage, Airline Tickets, Photocopies, Telephone Calls, Lab/Testing, Photographs, Demonstrative Aids
Portal-to-Portal: Yes **1st-class Airfare:** No
Written Retainer Agreement: Yes
Terms: Lawyer is responsible for fee, not lawyer's client, Out-of-pocket expense policies, In-court testimony minimums, Retaining counsel pays all deposition charges, Fee schedules, Portal-to-portal travel time, Deposition minimum fee, Payment for preparation time
Failure to Pay Bill Last 5 Years; Retaining Counsel: Yes **Opposing Counsel (Deps):** No

Engineering, Mechanical/Product Liability

Court: $210 **Review/Prep:** $210 **Deps:** $210
Years Testifying: 12 **Majority:** Plaintiff
Written Fee Schedule: Yes
Min Charge for Deps: No
Min Charge for Trial: No
Cancellation Charge for Deps/Trial: No

Retainer Required: Yes, $3,000 (Refundable, One Time)
Procedure When Dep Exceeds Paid Time: Proceed without immediate payment
Expenses Marked Up: No
Expenses Billed For: Mileage, Airline Tickets, Lab/Testing, Photographs, Demonstrative Aids
Portal-to-Portal: Yes **1st-class Airfare:** No
Written Retainer Agreement: Yes
Terms: Out-of-pocket expense policies, Retaining counsel pays all deposition charges, Fee schedules, Portal-to-portal travel time
Failure to Pay Bill Last 5 Years; Retaining Counsel: Yes **Opposing Counsel (Deps):** No

Engineering, Mechanical

Court: $200 **Review/Prep:** $200 **Deps:** $200
Years Testifying: 30 **Majority:** Defendant
Min Charge for Deps: Yes **Hours:** 4
Min Charge for Trial: Yes **Hours:** 4
Cancellation Charge for Deps/Trial: No
Retainer Required: New Client
Procedure When Dep Exceeds Paid Time:
Expenses Billed For: Mileage, Airline Tickets, Photocopies, Lab/Testing, Photographs, Demonstrative Aids
Portal-to-Portal: Yes **1st-class Airfare:** No
Written Retainer Agreement: No
Failure to Pay Bill Last 5 Years; Retaining Counsel: No **Opposing Counsel (Deps):** No

Medical Doctor

Court: $250 **Review/Prep:** $250 **Deps:** $250
Years Testifying: 11
Written Fee Schedule: Yes
Min Charge for Deps: No
Min Charge for Trial: No
Cancellation Charge for Deps/Trial: No
Retainer Required: Yes, $250 (Non-Refundable, One Time)
Expenses Marked Up: Yes
Expenses Billed For: Mileage, Airline Tickets, Photocopies, Lab/Testing, Photographs
Portal-to-Portal: No **1st-class Airfare:** No
Written Retainer Agreement: No
Failure to Pay Bill Last 5 Years; Retaining Counsel: No **Opposing Counsel (Deps):** No

Occupational Medicine/Emergency Medicine

Court: $300 **Review/Prep:** $250 **Deps:** $300
Years Testifying: 5
Written Fee Schedule: No
Min Charge for Deps: Yes **Hours:** 8
Min Charge for Trial: Yes **Hours:** 8
Cancellation Charge for Deps/Trial: Yes
Retainer Required: Yes, $250 (Non-Refundable, Replenishable)
Procedure When Dep Exceeds Paid Time: Proceed without immediate payment
Expenses Marked Up: No
Portal-to-Portal: Yes
Written Retainer Agreement: No
Failure to Pay Bill Last 5 Years; Retaining Counsel: Yes **Opposing Counsel (Deps):** No

Surgery, Podiatric

Court: $500 **Review/Prep:** $175 **Deps:** $500
Years Testifying: 15 **Majority:** Defendant
Written Fee Schedule: No
Min Charge for Deps: Yes **Hours:** 3
Min Charge for Trial: Yes **Hours:** 3
Cancellation Charge for Deps/Trial: Yes
Retainer Required: No
Procedure When Dep Exceeds Paid Time: Get payment before proceeding further
Expenses Marked Up: No
Expenses Billed For: Mileage, Airline Tickets, Telephone Calls, Lab/Testing, Photographs, Demonstrative Aids
Portal-to-Portal: Yes **1st-class Airfare:** No
Written Retainer Agreement: No
Failure to Pay Bill Last 5 Years; Retaining Counsel: No **Opposing Counsel (Deps):** No

Vocational Rehabilitation

Court: $175 **Review/Prep:** $175 **Deps:** $175
Years Testifying: 15 **Majority:** Plaintiff
Written Fee Schedule: Yes
Cancellation Charge for Deps/Trial: Yes
Retainer Required: Yes, $2,000 (Refundable, One Time)
Procedure When Dep Exceeds Paid Time: Proceed without immediate payment
Expenses Marked Up: No
Portal-to-Portal: Yes **1st-class Airfare:** No
Written Retainer Agreement: Yes
Terms: Retaining counsel pays all deposition charges, Fee schedules, Portal-to-portal travel time, Attorney's fees if forced to sue for collection, Payment for preparation time
Failure to Pay Bill Last 5 Years; Retaining Counsel: Yes **Opposing Counsel (Deps):** No

New Jersey

Accident Reconstruction/ Engineering

Court: $250 **Review/Prep:** $170 **Deps:** $250
Years Testifying: 35
Written Fee Schedule: No
Min Charge for Deps: Yes **Hours:** 4
Min Charge for Trial: Yes **Hours:** 4
Cancellation Charge for Deps/Trial: Yes
Retainer Required: Yes, $1,000 (Non-Refundable, One Time)
Procedure When Dep Exceeds Paid Time: Proceed without immediate payment
Expenses Marked Up: No
Expenses Billed For: Airline Tickets, Lab/Testing, Demonstrative Aids
Portal-to-Portal: Yes **1st-class Airfare:** No
Written Retainer Agreement: Yes
Terms: Lawyer is responsible for fee, not lawyer's client, Interest for delinquent accounts, In-court testimony minimums, Retaining counsel pays all deposition charges, Portal-to-portal travel time, Deposition minimum fee, Payment for preparation time
Failure to Pay Bill Last 5 Years; Retaining Counsel: Yes **Opposing (Deps):** Yes

Biomechanics/Accident Reconstruction

Court: $400 **Review/Prep:** $400 **Deps:** $400
Years Testifying: 35
Written Fee Schedule: Yes
Min Charge for Deps: Yes **Hours:** 4
Min Charge for Trial: Yes **Hours:** 4
Cancellation Charge for Deps/Trial: Yes
Retainer Required: Yes, $3,500 (Non-Refundable, Replenishable)
Procedure When Dep Exceeds Paid Time: Proceed without immediate payment
Expenses Marked Up: No
Expenses Billed For: Mileage, Airline Tickets, Photocopies, Lab/Testing, Photographs, Demonstrative Aids
Portal-to-Portal: Yes **1st-class Airfare:** No
Written Retainer Agreement: Yes
Terms: Lawyer is responsible for fee, not lawyer's client, Interest for delinquent accounts, Out-of-pocket expense policies, In-court testimony minimums, Retaining counsel pays all deposition charges, Fee schedules, Portal-to-portal travel time, Deposition minimum fee, Payment for preparation time, All invoices must be paid prior to depo or trial
Failure to Pay Bill Last 5 Years; Retaining Counsel: Yes **Opposing (Deps):** Yes

Cardiology, Pediatric

Court: $400 **Review/Prep:** $375 **Deps:** $400
Years Testifying: 13 **Majority:** Plaintiff
Written Fee Schedule: No
Min Charge for Deps: No **Hours:** 6
Min Charge for Trial: Yes **Hours:** 6
Cancellation Charge for Deps/Trial: Yes
Retainer Required: Yes, 50% est. fee (Non-Refundable)
Procedure When Dep Exceeds Paid Time: Get payment before proceeding further
Expenses Marked Up: No
Expenses Billed For: Mileage, Airline Tickets, Photocopies
Portal-to-Portal: Yes **1st-class Airfare:** No
Written Retainer Agreement: No
Failure to Pay Bill Last 5 Years; Retaining Counsel: No **Opposing Counsel (Deps):** No

Chiropractic
Court: $150 **Review/Prep:** $100 **Deps:** $150
Years Testifying: 17
Written Fee Schedule: Yes
Min Charge for Deps: Yes **Hours:** 4
Min Charge for Trial: Yes **Hours:** 4
Cancellation Charge for Deps/Trial: No
Retainer Required: Yes, $150 (Non-Refundable, One Time)
Procedure When Dep Exceeds Paid Time: Proceed without immediate payment
Expenses Marked Up: No
Expenses Billed For: Photocopies
Portal-to-Portal: Yes **1st-class Airfare:** No
Written Retainer Agreement: No
Failure to Pay Bill Last 5 Years; Retaining Counsel: Yes **Opposing Counsel (Deps):** No

Computers
Court: $250 **Deps:** $250
Years Testifying: 15
Written Fee Schedule: No
Min Charge for Deps: No
Cancellation Charge for Deps/Trial: No
Retainer Required: No
Expenses Marked Up: No
Expenses Billed For: Photocopies, Telephone Calls, Demonstrative Aids
Portal-to-Portal: No **1st-class Airfare:** No
Written Retainer Agreement: No
Failure to Pay Bill Last 5 Years; Retaining Counsel: No **Opposing Counsel (Deps):** No

Document Examiner
Court: $300 **Review/Prep:** $300 **Deps:** $300
Years Testifying: 10
Written Fee Schedule: Yes
Min Charge for Deps: Yes **Hours:** 3
Min Charge for Trial: Yes **Hours:** 3
Cancellation Charge for Deps/Trial: Yes
Retainer Required: Yes, $1,800 for court (Non-Refundable, One Time)
Procedure When Dep Exceeds Paid Time: Proceed without immediate payment
Expenses Marked Up: No
Expenses Billed For: Airline Tickets, Lab/Testing
Portal-to-Portal: No **1st-class Airfare:** No
Written Retainer Agreement: No
Failure to Pay Bill Last 5 Years; Retaining Counsel: No **Opposing Counsel (Deps):** No

Education/Education, Schools
Court: $475 **Review/Prep:** $350 **Deps:** $475
Years Testifying: 10
Written Fee Schedule: Yes
Min Charge for Deps: No **Hours:** 8
Min Charge for Trial: Yes **Hours:** 8
Cancellation Charge for Deps/Trial: Yes
Retainer Required: Yes, $6,500 (Non-Refundable, Replenishable)
Procedure When Dep Exceeds Paid Time: Get payment before proceeding further
Expenses Marked Up: No
Expenses Billed For: Mileage, Airline Tickets, Photocopies, Telephone Calls, Photographs
Portal-to-Portal: Yes **1st-class Airfare:** No
Written Retainer Agreement: Yes
Terms: Lawyer is responsible for fee, not lawyer's client, Interest for delinquent accounts, Out-of-pocket expense policies, In-court testimony minimums, Retaining counsel pays all deposition charges, Portal-to-portal travel time, Payment for preparation time
Failure to Pay Bill Last 5 Years; Retaining Counsel: Yes **Opposing Counsel (Deps):** No

Emergency Medicine
Court: $425 **Review/Prep:** $325 **Deps:** $425
Years Testifying: 4
Written Fee Schedule: Yes
Min Charge for Deps: Yes **Hours:** 4
Min Charge for Trial: Yes **Hours:** 4
Cancellation Charge for Deps/Trial: Yes
Retainer Required: Yes, $1,000 (Non-Refundable, One Time)
Procedure When Dep Exceeds Paid Time: Get payment before proceeding further
Expenses Marked Up: No
Portal-to-Portal: Yes **1st-class Airfare:** No
Written Retainer Agreement: No
Failure to Pay Bill Last 5 Years; Retaining Counsel: No **Opposing Counsel (Deps):** Yes

Engineering/Construction
Court: $250 **Review/Prep:** $185 **Deps:** $200
Years Testifying: 10 **Majority:** Plaintiff
Written Fee Schedule: Yes
Min Charge for Deps: Yes **Hours:** 4
Min Charge for Trial: Yes **Hours:** 4
Cancellation Charge for Deps/Trial: Yes
Retainer Required: Yes, $2,000 (Refundable, One Time)
Procedure When Dep Exceeds Paid Time: Proceed without immediate payment
Expenses Marked Up: No
Expenses Billed For: Mileage, Airline Tickets, Photocopies, Lab/Testing, Photographs, Demonstrative Aids
Portal-to-Portal: Yes **1st-class Airfare:** Yes
Written Retainer Agreement: Yes
Terms: Lawyer is responsible for fee, not lawyer's client, Interest for delinquent accounts, Out-of-pocket expense policies, In-court testimony minimums, Retaining counsel pays all deposition charges, Fee schedules, Portal-to-portal travel time, Attorney's fees if forced to sue for collection, Deposition minimum fee
Failure to Pay Bill Last 5 Years; Retaining Counsel: No **Opposing Counsel (Deps):** No

Engineering/Accident Reconstruction
Court: $300 **Review/Prep:** $150 **Deps:** $300
Years Testifying: 29
Written Fee Schedule: No
Min Charge for Deps: Yes **Hours:** 4
Min Charge for Trial: Yes **Hours:** 4
Cancellation Charge for Deps/Trial: Yes
Retainer Required: Yes, $750 (Refundable, Replenishable)
Procedure When Dep Exceeds Paid Time: Get payment before proceeding further
Expenses Marked Up: No
Expenses Billed For: Airline Tickets, Lab/Testing, Photographs, Demonstrative Aids
Portal-to-Portal: Yes **1st-class Airfare:** No
Written Retainer Agreement: No
Failure to Pay Bill Last 5 Years; Retaining Counsel: No **Opposing Counsel (Deps):** Yes

Engineering, Civil/Land Surveying
Court: $275 **Review/Prep:** $225 **Deps:** $275
Years Testifying: 30 **Majority:** Defendant
Written Fee Schedule: Yes
Min Charge for Deps: Yes **Hours:** 4
Min Charge for Trial: Yes **Hours:** 4
Cancellation Charge for Deps/Trial: No
Retainer Required: Yes, $1,000 (Non-Refundable, One Time)
Expenses Marked Up: No
Expenses Billed For: Airline Tickets
Portal-to-Portal: Yes **1st-class Airfare:** No
Written Retainer Agreement: No
Failure to Pay Bill Last 5 Years; Retaining Counsel: No **Opposing Counsel (Deps):** No

Engineering, Civil
Court: $175 **Review/Prep:** $175 **Deps:** $175
Years Testifying: 10 **Majority:** Defendant
Written Fee Schedule: Yes
Min Charge for Deps: No
Min Charge for Trial: No
Cancellation Charge for Deps/Trial: No
Retainer Required: No
Expenses Marked Up: No
Expenses Billed For: Mileage, Airline Tickets, Lab/Testing
Portal-to-Portal: Yes **1st-class Airfare:** No
Written Retainer Agreement: Yes
Terms: Fee schedules, Payment for preparation time
Failure to Pay Bill Last 5 Years; Retaining Counsel: Yes **Opposing Counsel (Deps):** No

Engineering, Civil/Construction
Court: $250 **Review/Prep:** $205 **Deps:** $250
Years Testifying: 25
Written Fee Schedule: Yes
Min Charge for Deps: No
Min Charge for Trial: No

Cancellation Charge for Deps/Trial: Yes
Retainer Required: Yes, $2,000 (Refundable, Replenishable)
Expenses Marked Up: Yes
Expenses Billed For: Airline Tickets, Lab/Testing, Photographs, Demonstrative Aids
Portal-to-Portal: Yes **1st-class Airfare:** No
Written Retainer Agreement: Yes
Terms: Lawyer is responsible for fee, not lawyer's client, Interest for delinquent accounts, Out-of-pocket expense policies, In-court testimony minimums, Retaining counsel pays all deposition charges, Fee schedules, Portal-to-portal travel time
Failure to Pay Bill Last 5 Years; Retaining Counsel: Yes **Opposing Counsel (Deps):** No

Epidemiology
Court: $1,000 **Review/Prep:** $650 **Deps:** $650
Years Testifying: 15
Written Fee Schedule: Yes
Min Charge for Deps: Yes **Hours:** 5
Min Charge for Trial: Yes **Hours:** 5
Cancellation Charge for Deps/Trial: Yes
Retainer Required: No
Expenses Marked Up: No
Expenses Billed For: Mileage, Airline Tickets, Photocopies, Telephone Calls
Portal-to-Portal: Yes **1st-class Airfare:** No
Written Retainer Agreement: No
Failure to Pay Bill Last 5 Years; Retaining Counsel: Yes **Opposing (Deps):** Yes

Fraud
Court: $300 **Review/Prep:** $300 **Deps:** $300
Years Testifying: 13
Written Fee Schedule: Yes
Min Charge for Deps: No
Min Charge for Trial: No
Cancellation Charge for Deps/Trial: No
Retainer Required: Depends, 25-50% est. fee
Expenses Marked Up: No
Expenses Billed For: Mileage, Airline Tickets, Photocopies, Telephone Calls, Photographs, Demonstrative Aids
Portal-to-Portal: Yes **1st-class Airfare:** No
Written Retainer Agreement: Yes
Terms: Out-of-pocket expense policies, Retaining counsel pays all deposition charges, Fee schedules
Failure to Pay Bill Last 5 Years; Retaining Counsel: No **Opposing Counsel (Deps):** No

Law Enforcement
Court: $200 **Review/Prep:** $200 **Deps:** $200
Years Testifying: 30
Written Fee Schedule: Yes
Min Charge for Deps: No **Hours:** 8
Min Charge for Trial: Yes **Hours:** 8
Cancellation Charge for Deps/Trial: No
Retainer Required: Yes, $1,600 (Non-Refundable, Replenishable)
Expenses Marked Up: No
Expenses Billed For: Mileage, Airline Tickets, Photocopies, Telephone Calls, Lab/Testing, Photographs
1st-class Airfare: Yes
Written Retainer Agreement: Yes
Terms: Lawyer is responsible for fee, not lawyer's client, Out-of-pocket expense policies, In-court testimony minimums, Fee schedules, Deposition minimum fee, Payment for preparation time, First class air travel
Failure to Pay Bill Last 5 Years; Retaining Counsel: No **Opposing Counsel (Deps):** No

Machinery
Court: $100 **Review/Prep:** $100 **Deps:** $100
Years Testifying: 30 **Majority:** Defendant
Written Fee Schedule: No
Min Charge for Deps: No
Min Charge for Trial: No
Cancellation Charge for Deps/Trial: No
Retainer Required: No
Expenses Marked Up: No
Expenses Billed For: Airline Tickets
Portal-to-Portal: No **1st-class Airfare:** No
Written Retainer Agreement: Yes
Failure to Pay Bill Last 5 Years; Retaining Counsel: Yes **Opposing Counsel (Deps):** No

Marine
Court: $165 **Review/Prep:** $165 **Deps:** $165
Years Testifying: 5
Written Fee Schedule: Yes
Min Charge for Deps: No
Min Charge for Trial: No
Cancellation Charge for Deps/Trial: No
Retainer Required: Yes, $4,000 (Refundable)
Expenses Marked Up: No
Expenses Billed For: Airline Tickets, Photocopies, Telephone Calls, Lab/Testing, Photographs, Demonstrative Aids
Portal-to-Portal: Yes **1st-class Airfare:** No
Written Retainer Agreement: Yes
Terms: Lawyer is responsible for fee, not lawyer's client, Interest for delinquent accounts, Out-of-pocket expense policies, Retaining counsel pays all deposition charges, Fee schedules
Failure to Pay Bill Last 5 Years; Retaining Counsel: Yes **Opposing (Deps):** Yes

Marine, Boating
Court: $150 **Review/Prep:** $150 **Deps:** $150
Years Testifying: 28 **Majority:** Plaintiff
Written Fee Schedule: Yes
Min Charge for Deps: Yes **Hours:** 10
Min Charge for Trial: Yes **Hours:** 10
Cancellation Charge for Deps/Trial: Yes
Retainer Required: Yes, $1,200 (Non-Refundable, One Time)
Procedure When Dep Exceeds Paid Time: Proceed without immediate payment
Expenses Marked Up: No
Portal-to-Portal: Yes **1st-class Airfare:** No
Written Retainer Agreement: No
Failure to Pay Bill Last 5 Years; Retaining Counsel: Yes **Opposing Counsel (Deps):** No

Ophthalmology
Court: $2,000 **Review/Prep:** $350 **Deps:** $1,000
Years Testifying: 18
Written Fee Schedule: Yes
Min Charge for Deps: Yes **Hours:** 4
Min Charge for Trial: Yes **Hours:** 4
Cancellation Charge for Deps/Trial: Yes
Retainer Required: Yes, Depends on case (Non-Refundable, One Time)
Procedure When Dep Exceeds Paid Time: Varies depending on case
Expenses Marked Up: No
Expenses Billed For:
Portal-to-Portal: Yes **1st-class Airfare:** No
Written Retainer Agreement: Yes
Terms: In-court testimony minimums, Retaining counsel pays all deposition charges, Deposition minimum fee, Payment for preparation time
Failure to Pay Bill Last 5 Years; Retaining Counsel: No **Opposing Counsel (Deps):** No

Orthopedics
Court: $725 **Review/Prep:** $300 **Deps:** $450
Years Testifying: 20 **Majority:** Plaintiff
Written Fee Schedule: Yes
Min Charge for Deps: Yes **Hours:** 4
Min Charge for Trial: Yes **Hours:** 4
Cancellation Charge for Deps/Trial: Yes
Retainer Required: Yes, Depends on case (Refundable, Replenishable)
Procedure When Dep Exceeds Paid Time: Proceed without immediate payment
Expenses Marked Up: No
Expenses Billed For: Airline Tickets, Photocopies, Telephone Calls, Lab/Testing, Photographs, Demonstrative Aids
Portal-to-Portal: Yes **1st-class Airfare:** No
Written Retainer Agreement: Yes
Terms: Lawyer is responsible for fee, not lawyer's client, Out-of-pocket expense policies, In-court testimony minimums, Retaining counsel pays all deposition charges, Fee schedules, Portal-to-portal travel time, Attorney's fees if forced to sue for collection
Failure to Pay Bill Last 5 Years; Retaining Counsel: Yes **Opposing (Deps):** Yes

Orthopedics

Court: $600 **Review/Prep:** $600 **Deps:** $600
Written Fee Schedule: Yes
Min Charge for Deps: No
Min Charge for Trial: No
Cancellation Charge for Deps/Trial: Yes
Retainer Required: Yes, $2,000 (Refundable, Replenishable)
Procedure When Dep Exceeds Paid Time: Proceed without immediate payment
Expenses Marked Up: No
Portal-to-Portal: Yes **1st-class Airfare:** No
Written Retainer Agreement: Yes
Terms: Lawyer is responsible for fee, not lawyer's client, Interest for delinquent accounts, In-court testimony minimums, Retaining counsel pays all deposition charges, Fee schedules, Portal-to-portal travel time, Attorney's fees if forced to sue for collection, Deposition minimum fee, Payment for preparation time
Failure to Pay Bill Last 5 Years; Retaining Counsel: No **Opposing Counsel (Deps):** No

Orthopedics

Court: $3,000 **Review/Prep:** $1,000 **Deps:** $2,000
Years Testifying: 10 **Majority:** Plaintiff
Written Fee Schedule: Yes
Min Charge for Deps: Yes **Hours:** 1
Min Charge for Trial: Yes **Hours:** 1
Cancellation Charge for Deps/Trial: Yes
Retainer Required: Yes, $1,000 (Non-Refundable, One Time)
Procedure When Dep Exceeds Paid Time: Proceed without immediate payment
Expenses Marked Up: No
Expenses Billed For: Mileage
Portal-to-Portal: Yes **1st-class Airfare:** No
Written Retainer Agreement: No
Failure to Pay Bill Last 5 Years; Retaining Counsel: No **Opposing Counsel (Deps):** No

Physical Medicine & Rehabilitation

Court: $500 **Review/Prep:** $200 **Deps:** $500
Years Testifying: 5
Written Fee Schedule: Yes
Min Charge for Deps: No **Hours:** 5
Min Charge for Trial: Yes **Hours:** 5
Cancellation Charge for Deps/Trial: Yes
Retainer Required: No
Expenses Marked Up: No
Portal-to-Portal: No **1st-class Airfare:** No
Written Retainer Agreement: No
Failure to Pay Bill Last 5 Years; Retaining Counsel: Yes **Opposing Counsel (Deps):** No

Podiatry

Court: $200 **Review/Prep:** $200 **Deps:** $200
Years Testifying: 5
Written Fee Schedule: No
Min Charge for Deps: No
Min Charge for Trial: No
Cancellation Charge for Deps/Trial: No
Retainer Required: No
Expenses Marked Up: No
Expenses Billed For: Mileage, Airline Tickets, Photographs
Portal-to-Portal: Yes **1st-class Airfare:** No
Written Retainer Agreement: No
Failure to Pay Bill Last 5 Years; Retaining Counsel: Yes **Opposing Counsel (Deps):** No

Psychiatry

Court: $600 **Review/Prep:** $500 **Deps:** $500
Years Testifying: 10
Written Fee Schedule: Yes
Min Charge for Deps: Yes **Hours:** 3
Min Charge for Trial: Yes **Hours:** 3
Cancellation Charge for Deps/Trial: Yes
Retainer Required: Yes, $2,500 (Refundable, Replenishable)
Procedure When Dep Exceeds Paid Time: Proceed without immediate payment
Expenses Marked Up: No
Expenses Billed For: Mileage, Airline Tickets, Photocopies, Telephone Calls
Portal-to-Portal: Yes **1st-class Airfare:** Yes
Written Retainer Agreement: Yes
Terms: Lawyer is responsible for fee, not lawyer's client, Interest for delinquent accounts, Out-of-pocket expense policies, In-court testimony minimums, Retaining counsel pays all deposition charges, Fee schedules, Portal-to-portal travel time, Attorney's fees if forced to sue for collection, Deposition minimum fee, Payment for preparation time, First class air travel
Failure to Pay Bill Last 5 Years; Retaining Counsel: Yes **Opposing Counsel (Deps):** No

Psychiatry

Court: $500 **Review/Prep:** $500 **Deps:** $500
Years Testifying: 28 **Majority:** Plaintiff
Written Fee Schedule: No
Min Charge for Deps: No
Min Charge for Trial: No
Cancellation Charge for Deps/Trial: No
Retainer Required: No
Expenses Marked Up: No
Expenses Billed For: Airline Tickets
Portal-to-Portal: Yes **1st-class Airfare:** No
Written Retainer Agreement: No
Failure to Pay Bill Last 5 Years; Retaining Counsel: Yes **Opposing Counsel (Deps):** No

Psychiatry

Court: $500 **Review/Prep:** $350 **Deps:** $350
Years Testifying: 20
Written Fee Schedule: No
Min Charge for Deps: No **Hours:** 5
Min Charge for Trial: Yes **Hours:** 5
Cancellation Charge for Deps/Trial: No
Retainer Required: Yes, $2,750 (Refundable, One Time)
Expenses Marked Up: No
Expenses Billed For: Mileage, Airline Tickets, Telephone Calls, Lab/Testing
Portal-to-Portal: Yes **1st-class Airfare:** No
Written Retainer Agreement: No
Failure to Pay Bill Last 5 Years; Retaining Counsel: Yes **Opposing Counsel (Deps):** No

Psychiatry/Addiction Medicine

Court: $300 **Review/Prep:** $300 **Deps:** $300
Years Testifying: 30 **Majority:** Defendant
Written Fee Schedule: No
Min Charge for Deps: No
Min Charge for Trial: No
Cancellation Charge for Deps/Trial: Yes
Retainer Required: Yes, $2,000 (Non-Refundable, One Time)
Procedure When Dep Exceeds Paid Time: Proceed without immediate payment
Expenses Marked Up: No
Portal-to-Portal: Yes **1st-class Airfare:** No
Written Retainer Agreement: No
Failure to Pay Bill Last 5 Years; Retaining Counsel: Yes **Opposing Counsel (Deps):** No

Psychiatry, Child

Court: $625 **Review/Prep:** $380 **Deps:** $500
Years Testifying: 30
Written Fee Schedule: Yes
Min Charge for Deps: Yes **Hours:** 4
Min Charge for Trial: Yes **Hours:** 4
Cancellation Charge for Deps/Trial: Yes
Retainer Required: Yes, $1,500 (Refundable, Replenishable)
Expenses Marked Up: No
Expenses Billed For: Mileage, Airline Tickets, Telephone Calls
Portal-to-Portal: Yes **1st-class Airfare:** No
Written Retainer Agreement: Yes
Terms: In-court testimony minimums, Fee schedules, Deposition minimum fee
Failure to Pay Bill Last 5 Years; Retaining Counsel: No **Opposing Counsel (Deps):** No

Real Estate

Court: $200 **Review/Prep:** $100 **Deps:** $150
Years Testifying: 20 **Majority:** Defendant
Written Fee Schedule: No
Min Charge for Deps: Yes **Hours:** 1
Min Charge for Trial: Yes **Hours:** 1
Cancellation Charge for Deps/Trial: No
Retainer Required: Yes, $1,000 (Refundable, One Time)
Procedure When Dep Exceeds Paid Time: Get payment before proceeding further
Expenses Marked Up: No
Expenses Billed For: Photographs, Demonstrative Aids

Portal-to-Portal: No
Written Retainer Agreement: No
Failure to Pay Bill Last 5 Years; Retaining Counsel: Yes **Opposing (Deps):** Yes

Recreation
Court: $300 **Review/Prep:** $150 **Deps:** $300
Years Testifying: 40 **Majority:** Plaintiff
Written Fee Schedule: No
Min Charge for Deps: Yes **Hours:** 8
Min Charge for Trial: Yes **Hours:** 8
Retainer Required: Yes, $1,000 (Partially Refundable, One Time)
Expenses Marked Up: No
Expenses Billed For: Mileage, Photocopies, Telephone Calls, Lab/Testing, Photographs, Demonstrative Aids
1st-class Airfare: No
Written Retainer Agreement: No
Failure to Pay Bill Last 5 Years; Retaining Counsel: Yes **Opposing (Deps):** Yes

Safety
Court: $150 **Review/Prep:** $150 **Deps:** $150
Years Testifying: 15 **Majority:** Plaintiff
Written Fee Schedule: Yes
Min Charge for Deps: Yes
Min Charge for Trial: No
Cancellation Charge for Deps/Trial: No
Retainer Required: Yes, $1,500 (Refundable, Replenishable)
Procedure When Dep Exceeds Paid Time: Proceed without immediate payment
Expenses Marked Up: No
Expenses Billed For: Mileage, Airline Tickets, Photographs
Portal-to-Portal: Yes **1st-class Airfare:** No
Written Retainer Agreement: Yes
Terms: Lawyer is responsible for fee, not lawyer's client, Interest for delinquent accounts, Out-of-pocket expense policies, Retaining counsel pays all deposition charges, Fee schedules, Portal-to-portal travel time, Attorney's fees if forced to sue for collection, Deposition minimum fee, Payment for preparation time
Failure to Pay Bill Last 5 Years; Retaining Counsel: No **Opposing Counsel (Deps):** No

Surgery, General
Court: $700 **Review/Prep:** $350 **Deps:** $550
Years Testifying: 4 **Majority:** Plaintiff
Written Fee Schedule: Yes
Min Charge for Deps: Yes **Hours:** 4
Min Charge for Trial: Yes **Hours:** 4
Cancellation Charge for Deps/Trial: Yes
Retainer Required: Yes, $1,000 (Refundable, Replenishable)
Procedure When Dep Exceeds Paid Time: Proceed without immediate payment
Expenses Marked Up: No
Expenses Billed For: Airline Tickets, Photocopies, Telephone Calls, Photographs, Demonstrative Aids
Portal-to-Portal: Yes **1st-class Airfare:** No
Written Retainer Agreement: No
Failure to Pay Bill Last 5 Years; Retaining Counsel: No **Opposing Counsel (Deps):** No

Urology
Court: $625 **Review/Prep:** $400 **Deps:** $400
Years Testifying: 15 **Majority:** Plaintiff
Written Fee Schedule: Yes
Min Charge for Deps: No **Hours:** 4
Min Charge for Trial: Yes **Hours:** 4
Cancellation Charge for Deps/Trial: Yes
Retainer Required: No
Expenses Marked Up: No
Expenses Billed For: Airline Tickets, Lab/Testing
Portal-to-Portal: No **1st-class Airfare:** Yes
Written Retainer Agreement: No
Failure to Pay Bill Last 5 Years; Retaining Counsel: No **Opposing Counsel (Deps):** No

Urology
Court: $400 **Review/Prep:** $350 **Deps:** $500
Years Testifying: 10
Written Fee Schedule: Yes
Min Charge for Deps: Yes **Hours:** 4
Min Charge for Trial: Yes **Hours:** 4
Cancellation Charge for Deps/Trial: Yes
Retainer Required: Yes, $750 (Non-Refundable, One Time)
Expenses Marked Up: No
Expenses Billed For: Airline Tickets
Portal-to-Portal: No **1st-class Airfare:** No
Written Retainer Agreement: No
Failure to Pay Bill Last 5 Years; Retaining Counsel: No **Opposing Counsel (Deps):** Yes

Valuation, Business
Court: $300 **Review/Prep:** $300 **Deps:** $300
Years Testifying: 20
Written Fee Schedule: Yes
Min Charge for Deps: No
Min Charge for Trial: No
Cancellation Charge for Deps/Trial: No
Retainer Required: Yes, $5,000 (Refundable, One Time)
Expenses Marked Up: No
Expenses Billed For: Airline Tickets, Lab/Testing, Photographs, Demonstrative Aids
Portal-to-Portal: Yes **1st-class Airfare:** No
Written Retainer Agreement: Yes
Terms: Interest for delinquent accounts, Out-of-pocket expense policies, Retaining counsel pays all deposition charges, Fee schedules, Portal-to-portal travel time, Attorney's fees if forced to sue for collection, Payment for preparation time
Failure to Pay Bill Last 5 Years; Retaining Counsel: No **Opposing Counsel (Deps):** No

Valuation, Business
Court: $350 **Review/Prep:** $350 **Deps:** $350
Years Testifying: 25
Written Fee Schedule: Yes
Min Charge for Deps: No
Min Charge for Trial: No
Cancellation Charge for Deps/Trial: No
Retainer Required: Yes, 50% est. fee (Refundable, One Time)
Expenses Marked Up: No
Expenses Billed For: Mileage, Airline Tickets, Photocopies, Telephone Calls
Portal-to-Portal: Yes **1st-class Airfare:** No
Written Retainer Agreement: Yes
Terms: Interest for delinquent accounts, Out-of-pocket expense policies, In-court testimony minimums, Retaining counsel pays all deposition charges, Fee schedules, Attorney's fees if forced to sue for collection, Payment for preparation time, Indemnification
Failure to Pay Bill Last 5 Years; Retaining Counsel: Yes **Opposing (Deps):** Yes

New Mexico

Appraisal, Art
Court: $350 **Review/Prep:** $240 **Deps:** $350
Years Testifying: 20
Written Fee Schedule: Yes
Min Charge for Deps: Yes **Hours:** 2
Min Charge for Trial: Yes **Hours:** 2
Cancellation Charge for Deps/Trial: Yes
Retainer Required: Yes, $3,000 (Partially Refundable, Replenishable)
Procedure When Dep Exceeds Paid Time: Proceed without immediate payment
Expenses Marked Up: No
Expenses Billed For: Mileage, Airline Tickets, Telephone Calls, Lab/Testing, Demonstrative Aids
Portal-to-Portal: Yes **1st-class Airfare:** Yes
Written Retainer Agreement: Yes
Terms: Lawyer is responsible for fee, not lawyer's client, Out-of-pocket expense policies, In-court testimony minimums, Retaining counsel pays all deposition charges, Fee schedules, Portal-to-portal travel time, Deposition minimum fee, Payment for preparation time, First class air travel
Failure to Pay Bill Last 5 Years; Retaining Counsel: Yes **Opposing Counsel (Deps):** No

Chemicals/Hydrology
Court: $225 **Review/Prep:** $150 **Deps:** $225
Years Testifying: 10 **Majority:** Plaintiff
Written Fee Schedule: Yes
Min Charge for Deps: No
Min Charge for Trial: No

Cancellation Charge for Deps/Trial: No
Retainer Required: No
Expenses Marked Up: No
Expenses Billed For: Photocopies, Telephone Calls, Lab/Testing
Portal-to-Portal: Yes **1st-class Airfare:** No
Written Retainer Agreement: No
Failure to Pay Bill Last 5 Years; Retaining Counsel: Yes **Opposing Counsel (Deps):** No

Chiropractic
Court: $400 **Review/Prep:** $180 **Deps:** $400
Years Testifying: 14
Written Fee Schedule: Yes
Min Charge for Deps: Yes **Hours:** 1
Min Charge for Trial: Yes **Hours:** 1
Cancellation Charge for Deps/Trial: Yes
Retainer Required: No
Expenses Marked Up: No
Expenses Billed For: Mileage, Airline Tickets
Portal-to-Portal: Yes **1st-class Airfare:** No
Written Retainer Agreement: No
Failure to Pay Bill Last 5 Years; Retaining Counsel: No **Opposing Counsel (Deps):** No

Law, Medical Malpractice
Court: $500 **Review/Prep:** $400 **Deps:** $500
Years Testifying: 20 **Majority:** Plaintiff
Written Fee Schedule: Yes
Min Charge for Deps: Yes **Hours:** 4
Min Charge for Trial: Yes **Hours:** 4
Cancellation Charge for Deps/Trial: Yes
Retainer Required: Yes, $500 (Non-Refundable, One Time)
Procedure When Dep Exceeds Paid Time: Get payment before proceeding further
Expenses Marked Up: No
Expenses Billed For: Mileage, Airline Tickets, Demonstrative Aids
Portal-to-Portal: Yes **1st-class Airfare:** No
Written Retainer Agreement: Yes
Terms: Lawyer is responsible for fee, not lawyer's client, Interest for delinquent accounts, Out-of-pocket expense policies, In-court testimony minimums, Retaining counsel pays all deposition charges, Fee schedules, Portal-to-portal travel time, Attorney's fees if forced to sue for collection, Deposition minimum fee, Payment for preparation time
Failure to Pay Bill Last 5 Years; Retaining Counsel: Yes **Opposing Counsel (Deps):** No

Nursing
Court: $250 **Review/Prep:** $125 **Deps:** $250
Years Testifying: 15 **Majority:** Plaintiff
Written Fee Schedule: Yes
Min Charge for Deps: No
Min Charge for Trial: No
Cancellation Charge for Deps/Trial: No
Retainer Required: No
Expenses Marked Up: No
Expenses Billed For: Mileage, Airline Tickets, Photocopies, Telephone Calls, Demonstrative Aids
Portal-to-Portal: Yes **1st-class Airfare:** No
Written Retainer Agreement: No
Failure to Pay Bill Last 5 Years; Retaining Counsel: Yes **Opposing Counsel (Deps):** No

Recreation, Snow Sports
Court: $200 **Review/Prep:** $200 **Deps:** $200
Years Testifying: 23
Written Fee Schedule: Yes
Min Charge for Deps: Yes **Hours:** 4
Min Charge for Trial: Yes **Hours:** 4
Retainer Required: Yes, $2,500 (Non-Refundable)
Expenses Marked Up: Yes
Expenses Billed For: Mileage, Airline Tickets, Photocopies, Telephone Calls, Lab/Testing, Photographs, Demonstrative Aids
Portal-to-Portal: Yes **1st-class Airfare:** No
Written Retainer Agreement: No
Failure to Pay Bill Last 5 Years; Retaining Counsel: No **Opposing Counsel (Deps):** No

New York

Accident Reconstruction
Court: $200 **Review/Prep:** $150 **Deps:** $150
Years Testifying: 12 **Majority:** Defendant
Written Fee Schedule: Yes
Min Charge for Deps: No
Min Charge for Trial: No
Cancellation Charge for Deps/Trial: No
Retainer Required: No
Expenses Marked Up: Yes
Expenses Billed For: Mileage, Airline Tickets, Photocopies, Lab/Testing, Photographs, Demonstrative Aids
Portal-to-Portal: Yes **1st-class Airfare:** No
Written Retainer Agreement: Yes
Terms: Lawyer is responsible for fee, not lawyer's client, Interest for delinquent accounts, Out-of-pocket expense policies, Fee schedules, Portal-to-portal travel time, Attorney's fees if forced to sue for collection, Payment for preparation time
Failure to Pay Bill Last 5 Years; Retaining Counsel: No **Opposing Counsel (Deps):** No

Accident Reconstruction/ Engineering, Mechanical
Court: $300 **Review/Prep:** $200 **Deps:** $300
Years Testifying: 10
Written Fee Schedule: Yes
Min Charge for Deps: Yes **Hours:** 4
Min Charge for Trial: Yes **Hours:** 4
Cancellation Charge for Deps/Trial: No
Retainer Required: Yes, $1,400 (Refundable, Replenishable)
Procedure When Dep Exceeds Paid Time: Varies depending on case
Expenses Marked Up: Yes
Expenses Billed For: Mileage, Airline Tickets, Photocopies, Lab/Testing, Photographs, Demonstrative Aids
Portal-to-Portal: Yes **1st-class Airfare:** No
Written Retainer Agreement: No
Failure to Pay Bill Last 5 Years; Retaining Counsel: Yes **Opposing Counsel (Deps):** No

Accident Reconstruction/Product Liability
Court: $175 **Review/Prep:** $175 **Deps:** $175
Years Testifying: 20
Written Fee Schedule: No
Min Charge for Deps: No
Min Charge for Trial: No
Cancellation Charge for Deps/Trial: No
Retainer Required: No
Expenses Marked Up: No
Expenses Billed For: Mileage, Airline Tickets, Lab/Testing, Photographs, Demonstrative Aids
Portal-to-Portal: Yes **1st-class Airfare:** No
Written Retainer Agreement: No
Failure to Pay Bill Last 5 Years; Retaining Counsel: Yes **Opposing (Deps):** Yes

Accident Reconstruction
Court: $150 **Review/Prep:** $100
Years Testifying: 12 **Majority:** Plaintiff
Written Fee Schedule: Yes
Hours: 4
Min Charge for Trial: Yes **Hours:** 4
Cancellation Charge for Deps/Trial: No
Retainer Required: Yes, $1,000 (Refundable, One Time)
Expenses Marked Up: Yes
Expenses Billed For: Mileage, Airline Tickets, Photocopies, Telephone Calls, Lab/Testing, Photographs, Demonstrative Aids
Portal-to-Portal: Yes
Written Retainer Agreement: Yes
Terms: Lawyer is responsible for fee, not lawyer's client, Interest for delinquent accounts, Out-of-pocket expense policies, In-court testimony minimums, Retaining counsel pays all deposition charges, Fee schedules, Portal-to-portal travel time
Failure to Pay Bill Last 5 Years; Retaining Counsel: Yes

Accounting
Court: $675 **Review/Prep:** $675 **Deps:** $675
Years Testifying: 15 **Majority:** Plaintiff
Written Fee Schedule: No
Min Charge for Deps: No
Min Charge for Trial: No

Cancellation Charge for Deps/Trial: No
Retainer Required: No
Expenses Marked Up: No
Expenses Billed For: Mileage, Airline Tickets, Photocopies, Telephone Calls
Portal-to-Portal: No **1st-class Airfare:** No
Written Retainer Agreement: Yes
Terms: Lawyer is responsible for fee, not lawyer's client, Out-of-pocket expense policies, Retaining counsel pays all deposition charges, Fee Disputes-Arbitration
Failure to Pay Bill Last 5 Years; Retaining Counsel: Yes

Alcoholism
Court: $350 **Review/Prep:** $150 **Deps:** $175
Years Testifying: 20
Written Fee Schedule: Yes
Min Charge for Deps: Yes **Hours:** 8
Min Charge for Trial: Yes **Hours:** 8
Cancellation Charge for Deps/Trial: Yes
Retainer Required: Yes, $3,000 (Non-Refundable, One Time)
Expenses Marked Up: Yes
Expenses Billed For: Mileage, Airline Tickets, Photocopies
Portal-to-Portal: Yes **1st-class Airfare:** No
Written Retainer Agreement: No
Failure to Pay Bill Last 5 Years; Retaining Counsel: No **Opposing Counsel (Deps):** Yes

Anesthesiology
Court: $300 **Review/Prep:** $300 **Deps:** $400
Years Testifying: 20
Written Fee Schedule: Yes
Min Charge for Deps: Yes **Hours:** 8
Min Charge for Trial: Yes **Hours:** 8
Cancellation Charge for Deps/Trial: No
Retainer Required: Yes, $1,000 (Non-Refundable, Replenishable)
Expenses Marked Up: No
Expenses Billed For: Airline Tickets
Portal-to-Portal: No **1st-class Airfare:** No
Written Retainer Agreement: No
Failure to Pay Bill Last 5 Years; Retaining Counsel: Yes **Opposing (Deps):** Yes

Appraisal, Art
Court: $300 **Review/Prep:** $250 **Deps:** $275
Years Testifying: 15
Written Fee Schedule: Yes
Min Charge for Deps: Yes **Hours:** 8
Min Charge for Trial: Yes **Hours:** 8
Cancellation Charge for Deps/Trial: Yes
Retainer Required: Yes, $1,000 (Replenishable)
Procedure When Dep Exceeds Paid Time: Get payment before proceeding further
Expenses Marked Up: No
Expenses Billed For: Airline Tickets, Lab/Testing, Photographs, Demonstrative Aids
Portal-to-Portal: Yes **1st-class Airfare:** No
Written Retainer Agreement: Yes
Terms: Interest for delinquent accounts, Out-of-pocket expense policies, In-court testimony minimums, Retaining counsel pays all deposition charges, Fee schedules, Portal-to-portal travel time, Attorney's fees if forced to sue for collection, Deposition minimum fee, Payment for preparation time
Failure to Pay Bill Last 5 Years; Retaining Counsel: Yes **Opposing Counsel (Deps):** No

Appraisal, Real Estate
Court: $500 **Review/Prep:** $300 **Deps:** $300
Years Testifying: 40
Written Fee Schedule: Yes
Min Charge for Deps: Yes **Hours:** 4
Min Charge for Trial: Yes **Hours:** 4
Cancellation Charge for Deps/Trial: Yes
Retainer Required: No
Expenses Marked Up: No
Expenses Billed For: Mileage, Airline Tickets, Telephone Calls
Portal-to-Portal: Yes **1st-class Airfare:** No
Written Retainer Agreement: Yes
Terms: Interest for delinquent accounts, Out-of-pocket expense policies, In-court testimony minimums, Retaining counsel pays all deposition charges, Fee schedules, Portal-to-portal travel time, Deposition minimum fee, Payment for preparation time
Failure to Pay Bill Last 5 Years; Retaining Counsel: No **Opposing Counsel (Deps):** No

Appraisal, Real Estate
Court: $200 **Review/Prep:** $200 **Deps:** $200
Years Testifying: 35 **Majority:** Plaintiff
Written Fee Schedule: Yes
Min Charge for Deps: No **Hours:** 1
Min Charge for Trial: Yes **Hours:** 1
Cancellation Charge for Deps/Trial: No
Retainer Required: Yes, 50% est. fee (Refundable, One Time)
Procedure When Dep Exceeds Paid Time: Get payment before proceeding further
Expenses Marked Up: No
Expenses Billed For: Mileage, Airline Tickets, Photocopies, Telephone Calls, Lab/Testing, Photographs, Demonstrative Aids
Portal-to-Portal: Yes **1st-class Airfare:** No
Written Retainer Agreement: Yes
Terms: Lawyer is responsible for fee, not lawyer's client, Interest for delinquent accounts, Out-of-pocket expense policies, Retaining counsel pays all deposition charges, Portal-to-portal travel time, Attorney's fees if forced to sue for collection, Deposition minimum fee, Payment for preparation time
Failure to Pay Bill Last 5 Years; Retaining Counsel: Yes **Opposing Counsel (Deps):** No

Cardiology/Internal Medicine
Court: $400 **Review/Prep:** $325 **Deps:** $400
Years Testifying: 15
Written Fee Schedule: Yes
Min Charge for Deps: No **Hours:** 8
Min Charge for Trial: Yes **Hours:** 8
Cancellation Charge for Deps/Trial: Yes
Retainer Required: Yes, $1,000 (Refundable, One Time)
Expenses Marked Up: Yes
Expenses Billed For: Airline Tickets
Portal-to-Portal: No **1st-class Airfare:** No
Written Retainer Agreement: No
Failure to Pay Bill Last 5 Years; Retaining Counsel: Yes **Opposing Counsel (Deps):** No

Chemicals
Court: $300 **Review/Prep:** $300 **Deps:** $350
Years Testifying: 39
Written Fee Schedule: Yes
Min Charge for Deps: Yes **Hours:** 10
Min Charge for Trial: Yes **Hours:** 10
Cancellation Charge for Deps/Trial: No
Retainer Required: Yes, $2,500
Expenses Marked Up: No
Expenses Billed For: Mileage, Airline Tickets, Photocopies, Telephone Calls, Lab/Testing, Photographs, Demonstrative Aids
Portal-to-Portal: Yes **1st-class Airfare:** No
Written Retainer Agreement: No
Failure to Pay Bill Last 5 Years; Retaining Counsel: No **Opposing Counsel (Deps):** No

Chiropractic/Acupuncture
Court: $300 **Deps:** $300
Years Testifying: 20 **Majority:** Defendant
Written Fee Schedule: No
Min Charge for Deps: Yes **Hours:** 4
Min Charge for Trial: Yes **Hours:** 4
Cancellation Charge for Deps/Trial: Yes
Retainer Required: No
Procedure When Dep Exceeds Paid Time: Proceed without immediate payment
Expenses Marked Up: No
Portal-to-Portal: No
Written Retainer Agreement: No
Failure to Pay Bill Last 5 Years; Retaining Counsel: No **Opposing Counsel (Deps):** No

Dentistry
Court: $750 **Review/Prep:** $250 **Deps:** $500
Years Testifying: 20
Written Fee Schedule: Yes
Min Charge for Deps: Yes **Hours:** 4
Min Charge for Trial: Yes **Hours:** 4
Cancellation Charge for Deps/Trial: Yes

Retainer Required: Yes, $1,000 (Refundable)
Procedure When Dep Exceeds Paid Time: Proceed without immediate payment
Expenses Marked Up: No
Expenses Billed For: Mileage, Airline Tickets, Lab/Testing, Photographs, Demonstrative Aids
Portal-to-Portal: Yes **1st-class Airfare:** No
Written Retainer Agreement: Yes
Terms: Lawyer is responsible for fee, not lawyer's client, In-court testimony minimums, Retaining counsel pays all deposition charges, Fee schedules, Portal-to-portal travel time, Deposition minimum fee, Payment for preparation time
Failure to Pay Bill Last 5 Years; Retaining Counsel: No **Opposing Counsel (Deps):** No

Economics
Court: $125 **Deps:** $125
Years Testifying: 33 **Majority:** Plaintiff
Written Fee Schedule: No
Min Charge for Deps: No
Min Charge for Trial: No
Cancellation Charge for Deps/Trial: Yes
Retainer Required: Yes, $1,000 (Non-Refundable, One Time)
Expenses Marked Up: No
Portal-to-Portal: Yes **1st-class Airfare:** No
Written Retainer Agreement: No
Failure to Pay Bill Last 5 Years; Retaining Counsel: No **Opposing Counsel (Deps):** No

Elevators & Escalators
Court: $275 **Review/Prep:** $275 **Deps:** $275
Years Testifying: 4
Written Fee Schedule: Yes
Min Charge for Deps: No
Min Charge for Trial: No
Cancellation Charge for Deps/Trial: No
Retainer Required: Yes, $2,000 (Non-Refundable, One Time)
Expenses Marked Up: No
Expenses Billed For: Mileage, Airline Tickets, Photographs
Portal-to-Portal: Yes **1st-class Airfare:** No
Written Retainer Agreement: Yes
Terms: Lawyer is responsible for fee, not lawyer's client, Interest for delinquent accounts, Out-of-pocket expense policies, Retaining counsel pays all deposition charges, Fee schedules, Portal-to-portal travel time
Failure to Pay Bill Last 5 Years; Retaining Counsel: Yes **Opposing Counsel (Deps):** No

Emergency Medicine
Review/Prep: $300 **Deps:** $500
Years Testifying: 5 **Majority:** Plaintiff
Written Fee Schedule: No
Min Charge for Deps: Yes
Min Charge for Trial: No
Cancellation Charge for Deps/Trial: Yes
Retainer Required: Yes, $500 (Non-Refundable)
Expenses Marked Up: No
Expenses Billed For: Mileage, Airline Tickets
Portal-to-Portal: No **1st-class Airfare:** No
Written Retainer Agreement: No
Failure to Pay Bill Last 5 Years; Retaining Counsel: No **Opposing Counsel (Deps):** No

Emergency Medicine
Court: $500 **Review/Prep:** $250 **Deps:** $250
Years Testifying: 3 **Majority:** Plaintiff
Written Fee Schedule: No
Min Charge for Trial: Yes **Hours:** 4
Cancellation Charge for Deps/Trial: Yes
Retainer Required: No
Expenses Marked Up: No
Expenses Billed For: Mileage
Portal-to-Portal: Yes **1st-class Airfare:** No
Written Retainer Agreement: No
Failure to Pay Bill Last 5 Years; Retaining Counsel: No **Opposing Counsel (Deps):** No

Emergency Medicine
Court: $350 **Review/Prep:** $300 **Deps:** $300
Years Testifying: 7
Written Fee Schedule: Yes
Min Charge for Deps: Yes **Hours:** 1
Min Charge for Trial: Yes **Hours:** 1
Cancellation Charge for Deps/Trial: No
Retainer Required: Yes, $300 (Non-Refundable, One Time)
Expenses Marked Up: No
Expenses Billed For: Mileage, Airline Tickets
Portal-to-Portal: Yes **1st-class Airfare:** No
Written Retainer Agreement: No
Failure to Pay Bill Last 5 Years; Retaining Counsel: Yes **Opposing Counsel (Deps):** No

Engineering/Biomedical
Court: $300 **Review/Prep:** $250 **Deps:** $250
Years Testifying: 20
Written Fee Schedule: Yes
Min Charge for Deps: Yes **Hours:** 8
Min Charge for Trial: Yes **Hours:** 8
Cancellation Charge for Deps/Trial: No
Retainer Required: Yes, $2,500 (Non-Refundable)
Expenses Marked Up: No
Expenses Billed For: Mileage, Airline Tickets, Lab/Testing, Photographs, Demonstrative Aids
Portal-to-Portal: Yes **1st-class Airfare:** No
Written Retainer Agreement: Yes
Terms: Out-of-pocket expense policies, In-court testimony minimums, Retaining counsel pays all deposition charges, Fee schedules, Portal-to-portal travel time
Failure to Pay Bill Last 5 Years; Retaining Counsel: No **Opposing Counsel (Deps):** No

Engineering
Court: $175 **Review/Prep:** $175 **Deps:** $175
Years Testifying: 14 **Majority:** Defendant
Written Fee Schedule: Yes
Min Charge for Deps: No
Min Charge for Trial: No
Cancellation Charge for Deps/Trial: No
Retainer Required: No
Procedure When Dep Exceeds Paid Time: Proceed without immediate payment
Expenses Marked Up: Yes
Expenses Billed For: Airline Tickets, Photocopies, Lab/Testing, Photographs, Demonstrative Aids
Portal-to-Portal: Yes **1st-class Airfare:** No
Written Retainer Agreement: No
Failure to Pay Bill Last 5 Years; Retaining Counsel: Yes **Opposing Counsel (Deps):** No

Engineering
Court: $150 **Review/Prep:** $150 **Deps:** $150
Years Testifying: 10
Written Fee Schedule: No
Min Charge for Deps: No
Min Charge for Trial: No
Cancellation Charge for Deps/Trial: No
Retainer Required: Yes, $2,500 (Refundable, One Time)
Expenses Marked Up: No
Expenses Billed For: Mileage, Airline Tickets
Portal-to-Portal: Yes **1st-class Airfare:** No
Written Retainer Agreement: No
Failure to Pay Bill Last 5 Years; Retaining Counsel: Yes **Opposing Counsel (Deps):** No

Engineering, Biomedical
Court: $300 **Review/Prep:** $300 **Deps:** $300
Years Testifying: 23
Written Fee Schedule: Yes
Min Charge for Deps: No
Min Charge for Trial: No
Cancellation Charge for Deps/Trial: No
Retainer Required: Yes, $3,000 (Non-Refundable, Replenishable)
Expenses Marked Up: No
Expenses Billed For: Mileage, Airline Tickets, Lab/Testing, Photographs, Demonstrative Aids
Portal-to-Portal: Yes **1st-class Airfare:** No
Written Retainer Agreement: No
Failure to Pay Bill Last 5 Years; Retaining Counsel: No **Opposing Counsel (Deps):** No

Engineering, Mechanical/Accident Reconstruction
Court: $300 **Review/Prep:** $200 **Deps:** $300
Years Testifying: 10
Written Fee Schedule: Yes
Min Charge for Deps: Yes **Hours:** 4
Min Charge for Trial: Yes **Hours:** 4
Cancellation Charge for Deps/Trial: No
Retainer Required: Yes, $2,000 (Refundable, Replenishable)
Procedure When Dep Exceeds Paid Time: Proceed without immediate payment
Expenses Marked Up: No
Expenses Billed For: Mileage, Airline Tickets, Lab/Testing, Photographs, Demonstrative Aids
Portal-to-Portal: Yes **1st-class Airfare:** No
Written Retainer Agreement: No
Failure to Pay Bill Last 5 Years; Retaining Counsel: Yes **Opposing Counsel (Deps):** No

Fire Investigation
Court: $125 **Review/Prep:** $125 **Deps:** $125
Years Testifying: 8
Written Fee Schedule: Yes
Min Charge for Deps: No
Min Charge for Trial: No
Cancellation Charge for Deps/Trial: No
Retainer Required: Yes, $1,500 (Refundable, One Time)
Expenses Marked Up: No
Expenses Billed For: Mileage, Airline Tickets, Lab/Testing, Photographs, Demonstrative Aids
Portal-to-Portal: Yes **1st-class Airfare:** No
Written Retainer Agreement: Yes
Terms: Lawyer is responsible for fee, not lawyer's client, Interest for delinquent accounts, Out-of-pocket expense policies, Retaining counsel pays all deposition charges, Fee schedules, Portal-to-portal travel time, Deposition minimum fee, Payment for preparation time
Failure to Pay Bill Last 5 Years; Retaining Counsel: Yes **Opposing Counsel (Deps):** No

Fires, Electrical
Court: $195 **Review/Prep:** $195 **Deps:** $195
Years Testifying: 20 **Majority:** Defendant
Written Fee Schedule: Yes
Min Charge for Deps: No
Min Charge for Trial: No
Cancellation Charge for Deps/Trial: No
Retainer Required: No
Expenses Billed For: Mileage, Lab/Testing, Photographs, Demonstrative Aids
Portal-to-Portal: Yes **1st-class Airfare:** Yes
Failure to Pay Bill Last 5 Years; Retaining Counsel: Yes **Opposing Counsel (Deps):** No

Geology, Hydro/Groundwater
Court: $350 **Review/Prep:** $250 **Deps:** $250
Years Testifying: 20
Written Fee Schedule: Yes
Min Charge for Deps: Yes
Min Charge for Trial: No
Cancellation Charge for Deps/Trial: No
Retainer Required: No
Procedure When Dep Exceeds Paid Time: Proceed without immediate payment
Expenses Marked Up: Yes
Expenses Billed For: Mileage, Airline Tickets, Photocopies, Telephone Calls, Lab/Testing, Photographs, Demonstrative Aids
Portal-to-Portal: Yes **1st-class Airfare:** No
Written Retainer Agreement: Yes
Terms: Interest for delinquent accounts, Out-of-pocket expense policies, In-court testimony minimums, Retaining counsel pays all deposition charges, Fee schedules, Portal-to-portal travel time, Attorney's fees if forced to sue for collection, Deposition minimum fee, Payment for preparation time, Scope of work
Failure to Pay Bill Last 5 Years; Retaining Counsel: No **Opposing Counsel (Deps):** No

Insurance
Court: $140 **Review/Prep:** $140 **Deps:** $140
Years Testifying: 5 **Majority:** Plaintiff
Written Fee Schedule: No
Min Charge for Deps: No
Min Charge for Trial: No
Cancellation Charge for Deps/Trial: No
Retainer Required: Yes, $1,000 (Non-Refundable, One Time)
Expenses Marked Up: No
Expenses Billed For: Mileage, Airline Tickets, Photocopies, Telephone Calls
Portal-to-Portal: Yes **1st-class Airfare:** No
Written Retainer Agreement: Yes
Terms: Lawyer is responsible for fee, not lawyer's client, Out-of-pocket expense policies, Retaining counsel pays all deposition charges, Portal-to-portal travel time, Deposition minimum fee, Payment for preparation time
Failure to Pay Bill Last 5 Years; Retaining Counsel: Yes **Opposing Counsel (Deps):** No

Internal Medicine
Court: $400 **Review/Prep:** $200 **Deps:** $300
Years Testifying: 2 **Majority:** Plaintiff
Written Fee Schedule: No
Min Charge for Deps: Yes **Hours:** 3
Min Charge for Trial: Yes **Hours:** 3
Cancellation Charge for Deps/Trial: No
Retainer Required: No
Expenses Marked Up: No
Expenses Billed For:
Portal-to-Portal: No **1st-class Airfare:** No
Written Retainer Agreement: No
Failure to Pay Bill Last 5 Years; Retaining Counsel: No

Internal Medicine/Endocrinology
Court: $400 **Review/Prep:** $360 **Deps:** $400
Years Testifying: 4 **Majority:** Plaintiff
Written Fee Schedule: Yes
Min Charge for Deps: Yes **Hours:** 4
Min Charge for Trial: Yes **Hours:** 4
Cancellation Charge for Deps/Trial: Yes
Retainer Required: Yes, (Refundable, One Time)
Procedure When Dep Exceeds Paid Time: Proceed without immediate payment
Expenses Billed For: Airline Tickets
Portal-to-Portal: Yes **1st-class Airfare:** Yes
Written Retainer Agreement: No
Failure to Pay Bill Last 5 Years; Retaining Counsel: Yes **Opposing Counsel (Deps):** No

Medicine, Nuclear/Radiology
Court: $500 **Review/Prep:** $500 **Deps:** $500
Years Testifying: 20 **Majority:** Defendant
Written Fee Schedule: No
Min Charge for Deps: Yes **Hours:** 2
Min Charge for Trial: Yes **Hours:** 2
Cancellation Charge for Deps/Trial: No
Retainer Required: No
Expenses Marked Up: No
Expenses Billed For: Mileage, Airline Tickets, Telephone Calls, Demonstrative Aids
Portal-to-Portal: Yes **1st-class Airfare:** No
Written Retainer Agreement: No
Failure to Pay Bill Last 5 Years; Retaining Counsel: No **Opposing Counsel (Deps):** No

Meteorology
Court: $175 **Review/Prep:** $150 **Deps:** $175
Years Testifying: 25
Written Fee Schedule: Yes
Min Charge for Deps: No
Min Charge for Trial: No
Cancellation Charge for Deps/Trial: No
Retainer Required: Yes, Depends on case (One Time)
Expenses Marked Up: No
Expenses Billed For: Mileage, Airline Tickets, Photographs, Demonstrative Aids
Portal-to-Portal: Yes **1st-class Airfare:** No
Written Retainer Agreement: No
Failure to Pay Bill Last 5 Years; Retaining Counsel: Yes **Opposing Counsel (Deps):** No

Meteorology
Court: $300 **Review/Prep:** $200 **Deps:** $300
Years Testifying: 16
Written Fee Schedule: No
Min Charge for Deps: Yes **Hours:** 5
Min Charge for Trial: Yes **Hours:** 5
Cancellation Charge for Deps/Trial: Yes

Retainer Required: Yes, $400 (Non-Refundable, One Time)
Procedure When Dep Exceeds Paid Time: Proceed without immediate payment
Expenses Marked Up: No
Expenses Billed For: Mileage, Airline Tickets, Photographs, Demonstrative Aids
Portal-to-Portal: No **1st-class Airfare:** No
Written Retainer Agreement: No
Failure to Pay Bill Last 5 Years; Retaining Counsel: No **Opposing Counsel (Deps):** No

Midwife/Obstetrics & Gynecology
Court: $300 **Review/Prep:** $300 **Deps:** $300
Years Testifying: 1 **Majority:** Defendant
Written Fee Schedule: No
Min Charge for Deps: No **Hours:** 10
Min Charge for Trial: Yes **Hours:** 10
Cancellation Charge for Deps/Trial: Yes
Retainer Required: No
Expenses Marked Up: No
Expenses Billed For: Airline Tickets
Portal-to-Portal: Yes **1st-class Airfare:** No
Written Retainer Agreement: Yes
Terms: Lawyer is responsible for fee, not lawyer's client, Fee schedules, Payment for preparation time
Failure to Pay Bill Last 5 Years; Retaining Counsel: No

Neurology
Court: $700 **Review/Prep:** $200 **Deps:** $700
Years Testifying: 5 **Majority:** Defendant
Written Fee Schedule: Yes
Min Charge for Deps: Yes **Hours:** 5
Min Charge for Trial: Yes **Hours:** 5
Cancellation Charge for Deps/Trial: Yes
Retainer Required: Yes, $1,500 (Non-Refundable, One Time)
Procedure When Dep Exceeds Paid Time: Proceed without immediate payment
Expenses Marked Up: No
Expenses Billed For: Mileage, Airline Tickets
1st-class Airfare: Yes
Written Retainer Agreement: Yes
Terms: Lawyer is responsible for fee, not lawyer's client, Retaining counsel pays all deposition charges, Fee schedules, Payment for preparation time
Failure to Pay Bill Last 5 Years; Retaining Counsel: Yes **Opposing Counsel (Deps):** No

Neurology/Pain Management/ Medicine
Court: $550 **Review/Prep:** $550 **Deps:** $550
Years Testifying: 10 **Majority:** Defendant
Written Fee Schedule: Yes
Min Charge for Deps: No **Hours:** 6
Min Charge for Trial: Yes **Hours:** 6
Cancellation Charge for Deps/Trial: Yes
Retainer Required: No
Expenses Marked Up: No
Expenses Billed For: Mileage, Airline Tickets, Photocopies, Telephone Calls, Lab/Testing, Photographs, Demonstrative Aids
Portal-to-Portal: Yes **1st-class Airfare:** No
Written Retainer Agreement: No
Failure to Pay Bill Last 5 Years; Retaining Counsel: No **Opposing Counsel (Deps):** No

Obstetrics & Gynecology
Court: $1,000 **Review/Prep:** $400 **Deps:** $750
Years Testifying: 14 **Majority:** Plaintiff
Written Fee Schedule: Yes
Min Charge for Deps: Yes **Hours:** 8
Min Charge for Trial: Yes **Hours:** 8
Cancellation Charge for Deps/Trial: Yes
Retainer Required: Yes, $1,500 (Non-Refundable, One Time)
Procedure When Dep Exceeds Paid Time: Proceed without immediate payment
Expenses Marked Up: No
Expenses Billed For: Mileage, Airline Tickets, Photographs, Demonstrative Aids
Portal-to-Portal: Yes **1st-class Airfare:** No
Written Retainer Agreement: Yes
Terms: Out-of-pocket expense policies, In-court testimony minimums, Fee schedules, Deposition minimum fee, Payment for preparation time, Cancellation policy
Failure to Pay Bill Last 5 Years; Retaining Counsel: No **Opposing Counsel (Deps):** No

Obstetrics & Gynecology
Court: $500 **Review/Prep:** $350 **Deps:** $400
Years Testifying: 15 **Majority:** Defendant
Written Fee Schedule: No
Min Charge for Deps: No
Min Charge for Trial: No
Cancellation Charge for Deps/Trial: No
Retainer Required: Yes, $1,000 (Refundable, One Time)
Procedure When Dep Exceeds Paid Time: Proceed without immediate payment
Expenses Marked Up: No
Expenses Billed For: Mileage, Airline Tickets, Photocopies, Photographs, Demonstrative Aids
Portal-to-Portal: Yes **1st-class Airfare:** Yes
Written Retainer Agreement: No
Failure to Pay Bill Last 5 Years; Retaining Counsel: No **Opposing Counsel (Deps):** No

Oncology
Court: $1,000 **Review/Prep:** $400 **Deps:** $625
Years Testifying: 10
Written Fee Schedule: Yes
Min Charge for Deps: Yes **Hours:** 8
Min Charge for Trial: Yes **Hours:** 8
Cancellation Charge for Deps/Trial: Yes
Retainer Required: Yes, $1,500 (Non-Refundable, One Time)
Procedure When Dep Exceeds Paid Time: Proceed without immediate payment
Expenses Marked Up: No
Expenses Billed For: Airline Tickets, Demonstrative Aids
Portal-to-Portal: Yes **1st-class Airfare:** No
Written Retainer Agreement: Yes
Terms: Out-of-pocket expense policies, In-court testimony minimums, Fee schedules, Deposition minimum fee, Payment for preparation time, Cancellation Policy
Failure to Pay Bill Last 5 Years; Retaining Counsel: No **Opposing Counsel (Deps):** No

Oncology
Court: $1,250 **Review/Prep:** $475 **Deps:** $1,250
Years Testifying: 5
Written Fee Schedule: No
Min Charge for Deps: Yes
Min Charge for Trial: No
Cancellation Charge for Deps/Trial: No
Retainer Required: No
Expenses Marked Up: No
Portal-to-Portal: No **1st-class Airfare:** Yes
Written Retainer Agreement: No
Failure to Pay Bill Last 5 Years; Retaining Counsel: No **Opposing Counsel (Deps):** No

Ophthalmology
Court: $625 **Review/Prep:** $300 **Deps:** $300
Years Testifying: 25
Written Fee Schedule: Yes
Min Charge for Deps: Yes **Hours:** 8
Min Charge for Trial: Yes **Hours:** 8
Cancellation Charge for Deps/Trial: Yes
Retainer Required: Yes, $1,200 (Non-Refundable, One Time)
Procedure When Dep Exceeds Paid Time: Proceed without immediate payment
Expenses Marked Up: No
Expenses Billed For: Mileage, Airline Tickets, Lab/Testing, Photographs, Demonstrative Aids
Portal-to-Portal: Yes **1st-class Airfare:** No
Written Retainer Agreement: No
Failure to Pay Bill Last 5 Years; Retaining Counsel: No **Opposing Counsel (Deps):** No

Ophthalmology
Court: $200 **Review/Prep:** $200 **Deps:** $200
Years Testifying: 30
Written Fee Schedule: Yes
Min Charge for Deps: Yes **Hours:** 1
Min Charge for Trial: Yes **Hours:** 1
Cancellation Charge for Deps/Trial: Yes
Retainer Required: No

Expenses Marked Up: No
Expenses Billed For: Mileage, Airline Tickets, Lab/Testing, Photographs
Portal-to-Portal: Yes **1st-class Airfare:** No
Written Retainer Agreement: No
Failure to Pay Bill Last 5 Years; Retaining Counsel: No **Opposing Counsel (Deps):** No

Ophthalmology
Court: $750 **Review/Prep:** $500 **Deps:** $750
Years Testifying: 3
Written Fee Schedule: No
Min Charge for Deps: Yes **Hours:** 20
Min Charge for Trial: Yes **Hours:** 20
Cancellation Charge for Deps/Trial: Yes
Retainer Required: Yes, $10,000 (Non-Refundable, Replenishable)
Procedure When Dep Exceeds Paid Time: Get payment before proceeding further
Expenses Marked Up: Yes
Expenses Billed For: Mileage, Photocopies, Telephone Calls, Demonstrative Aids
Portal-to-Portal: Yes **1st-class Airfare:** No
Written Retainer Agreement: Yes
Terms: Lawyer is responsible for fee, not lawyer's client, Interest for delinquent accounts, Out-of-pocket expense policies, In-court testimony minimums, Retaining counsel pays all deposition charges, Portal-to-portal travel time, Attorney's fees if forced to sue for collection, Deposition minimum fee
Failure to Pay Bill Last 5 Years; Retaining Counsel: No **Opposing Counsel (Deps):** Yes

Ophthalmology
Court: $500 **Review/Prep:** $400 **Deps:** $500
Years Testifying: 25 **Majority:** Plaintiff
Written Fee Schedule: No
Min Charge for Deps: No **Hours:** 10
Min Charge for Trial: Yes **Hours:** 10
Cancellation Charge for Deps/Trial: No
Retainer Required: Court-if new attorney
Expenses Marked Up: No
Expenses Billed For: Mileage, Airline Tickets, Photographs
Portal-to-Portal: Yes **1st-class Airfare:** No
Written Retainer Agreement: No
Failure to Pay Bill Last 5 Years; Retaining Counsel: Yes **Opposing (Deps):** Yes

Ophthalmology
Court: $500 **Review/Prep:** $295 **Deps:** $295
Years Testifying: 7 **Majority:** Plaintiff
Written Fee Schedule: Yes
Min Charge for Deps: Yes **Hours:** 4
Min Charge for Trial: Yes **Hours:** 4
Cancellation Charge for Deps/Trial: No
Retainer Required: No
Expenses Marked Up: No
Expenses Billed For: Mileage, Airline Tickets
Portal-to-Portal: Yes **1st-class Airfare:** No
Written Retainer Agreement: No
Failure to Pay Bill Last 5 Years; Retaining Counsel: No **Opposing Counsel (Deps):** Yes

Orthopedics
Court: $1,500 **Review/Prep:** $850 **Deps:** $1,500
Years Testifying: 28
Written Fee Schedule: Yes
Min Charge for Deps: Yes **Hours:** 3
Min Charge for Trial: Yes **Hours:** 3
Cancellation Charge for Deps/Trial: Yes
Retainer Required: Yes, $2,000 (Non-Refundable, One Time)
Procedure When Dep Exceeds Paid Time: Proceed without immediate payment
Expenses Marked Up: No
Expenses Billed For: Telephone Calls
Portal-to-Portal: Yes
Written Retainer Agreement: No
Failure to Pay Bill Last 5 Years; Retaining Counsel: No **Opposing Counsel (Deps):** No

Orthopedics
Court: $1,125 **Deps:** $600
Years Testifying: 30 **Majority:** Defendant
Written Fee Schedule: Yes
Min Charge for Deps: Yes **Hours:** 4
Min Charge for Trial: Yes **Hours:** 4
Cancellation Charge for Deps/Trial: Yes
Retainer Required: Yes, Total est. fee (Partially Refundable, One Time)
Procedure When Dep Exceeds Paid Time: Proceed without immediate payment
Expenses Marked Up: No
Expenses Billed For: Airline Tickets
Portal-to-Portal: No **1st-class Airfare:** No
Written Retainer Agreement: No
Failure to Pay Bill Last 5 Years; Retaining Counsel: No **Opposing Counsel (Deps):** No

Orthopedics
Court: $1,500 **Review/Prep:** $300 **Deps:** $750
Years Testifying: 16 **Majority:** Plaintiff
Min Charge for Deps: Yes **Hours:** 4
Min Charge for Trial: Yes **Hours:** 4
Cancellation Charge for Deps/Trial: Yes
Retainer Required: Yes, $1,000 (Non-Refundable)
Procedure When Dep Exceeds Paid Time: Proceed without immediate payment
Expenses Marked Up: No
Expenses Billed For: Mileage, Airline Tickets
Portal-to-Portal: Yes **1st-class Airfare:** No
Written Retainer Agreement: No
Failure to Pay Bill Last 5 Years; Retaining Counsel: Yes **Opposing Counsel (Deps):** No

Orthopedics
Court: $1,500 **Review/Prep:** $650 **Deps:** $1,500
Years Testifying: 7 **Majority:** Defendant
Written Fee Schedule: Yes
Min Charge for Deps: No
Min Charge for Trial: No
Cancellation Charge for Deps/Trial: Yes
Retainer Required: Yes, $1,500 (Refundable, One Time)
Procedure When Dep Exceeds Paid Time: Proceed without immediate payment
Expenses Marked Up: No
Portal-to-Portal: No **1st-class Airfare:** No
Written Retainer Agreement: No
Failure to Pay Bill Last 5 Years; Retaining Counsel: No **Opposing Counsel (Deps):** No

Orthopedics
Court: $200 **Review/Prep:** $200 **Deps:** $200
Years Testifying: 7
Written Fee Schedule: No
Min Charge for Deps: Yes **Hours:** 8
Min Charge for Trial: Yes **Hours:** 8
Cancellation Charge for Deps/Trial: Yes
Retainer Required: Yes, $1,000 (Non-Refundable, One Time)
Procedure When Dep Exceeds Paid Time: Get payment before proceeding further
Expenses Marked Up: Yes
Expenses Billed For:
Portal-to-Portal: No **1st-class Airfare:** No
Written Retainer Agreement: No
Failure to Pay Bill Last 5 Years; Retaining Counsel: No **Opposing Counsel (Deps):** No

Orthopedics
Court: $1,250 **Review/Prep:** $400 **Deps:** $1,250
Years Testifying: 17 **Majority:** Defendant
Written Fee Schedule: Yes
Min Charge for Deps: Yes **Hours:** 1
Min Charge for Trial: Yes **Hours:** 1
Cancellation Charge for Deps/Trial: Yes
Retainer Required: Yes, $1,000 (Non-Refundable)
Expenses Marked Up: No
Expenses Billed For: Airline Tickets
Portal-to-Portal: No **1st-class Airfare:** No
Written Retainer Agreement: No
Failure to Pay Bill Last 5 Years; Retaining Counsel: Yes **Opposing Counsel (Deps):** No

Otolaryngology
Court: $625 **Review/Prep:** $325 **Deps:** $450
Years Testifying: 10 **Majority:** Plaintiff
Written Fee Schedule: Yes
Min Charge for Deps: Yes **Hours:** 8
Min Charge for Trial: Yes **Hours:** 8
Cancellation Charge for Deps/Trial: Yes
Retainer Required: Yes, $1,625

(Refundable, Replenishable)
Expenses Marked Up: No
Expenses Billed For:
Portal-to-Portal: Yes **1st-class Airfare:** No
Written Retainer Agreement: No
Failure to Pay Bill Last 5 Years; Retaining Counsel: No **Opposing Counsel (Deps):** No

Pathology
Court: $400 **Review/Prep:** $300 **Deps:** $400
Years Testifying: 30
Written Fee Schedule: Yes
Min Charge for Deps: Yes **Hours:** 1
Min Charge for Trial: Yes **Hours:** 1
Cancellation Charge for Deps/Trial: No
Retainer Required: Yes, $1,000 (Non-Refundable, One Time)
Expenses Marked Up: No
Expenses Billed For: Mileage, Airline Tickets
Portal-to-Portal: Yes **1st-class Airfare:** No
Written Retainer Agreement: No
Failure to Pay Bill Last 5 Years; Retaining Counsel: Yes **Opposing Counsel (Deps):** No

Pediatrics
Court: $375 **Review/Prep:** $375 **Deps:** $375
Years Testifying: 5 **Majority:** Plaintiff
Written Fee Schedule: Yes
Min Charge for Deps: Yes **Hours:** 10
Min Charge for Trial: Yes **Hours:** 10
Cancellation Charge for Deps/Trial: Yes
Retainer Required: Yes, $1,500 (Refundable, One Time)
Procedure When Dep Exceeds Paid Time: Proceed without immediate payment
Expenses Marked Up: No
Expenses Billed For: Mileage, Airline Tickets, Photocopies, Telephone Calls
Portal-to-Portal: Yes **1st-class Airfare:** No
Written Retainer Agreement: No
Failure to Pay Bill Last 5 Years; Retaining Counsel: No **Opposing Counsel (Deps):** No

Pediatrics
Court: $500 **Review/Prep:** $400 **Deps:** $500
Years Testifying: 17
Written Fee Schedule: Yes
Min Charge for Deps: Yes **Hours:** 8
Min Charge for Trial: Yes **Hours:** 8
Cancellation Charge for Deps/Trial: Yes
Retainer Required: Yes, $1,500 (Non-Refundable, One Time)
Procedure When Dep Exceeds Paid Time: Proceed without immediate payment
Expenses Marked Up: No
Expenses Billed For: Airline Tickets
Portal-to-Portal: Yes **1st-class Airfare:** No
Written Retainer Agreement: No
Failure to Pay Bill Last 5 Years; Retaining Counsel: No **Opposing Counsel (Deps):** No

Periodontics
Court: $250 **Review/Prep:** $150 **Deps:** $250
Years Testifying: 1
Written Fee Schedule: Yes
Min Charge for Deps: Yes **Hours:** 10
Min Charge for Trial: Yes **Hours:** 10
Cancellation Charge for Deps/Trial: Yes
Retainer Required: Yes
Procedure When Dep Exceeds Paid Time: Proceed without immediate payment
Expenses Marked Up: No
Expenses Billed For: Mileage, Airline Tickets, Photocopies, Telephone Calls
1st-class Airfare: No
Written Retainer Agreement: Yes
Terms: Out-of-pocket expense policies, In-court testimony minimums, Retaining counsel pays all deposition charges, Fee schedules, Deposition minimum fee, Payment for preparation time
Failure to Pay Bill Last 5 Years; Retaining Counsel: No **Opposing Counsel (Deps):** No

Personal Injury/Workers' Compensation
Court: $95 **Review/Prep:** $95 **Deps:** $150
Years Testifying: 12 **Majority:** Plaintiff
Written Fee Schedule: Yes
Min Charge for Deps: No
Min Charge for Trial: No
Cancellation Charge for Deps/Trial: No
Retainer Required: Yes, $800 (Refundable, One Time)
Expenses Marked Up: No
Expenses Billed For: Mileage, Airline Tickets, Telephone Calls, Demonstrative Aids
Portal-to-Portal: Yes **1st-class Airfare:** No
Written Retainer Agreement: No
Failure to Pay Bill Last 5 Years; Retaining Counsel: Yes **Opposing Counsel (Deps):** No

Physical Medicine & Rehabilitation
Court: $375 **Deps:** $375
Years Testifying: 6 **Majority:** Defendant
Written Fee Schedule: Yes
Min Charge for Deps: Yes **Hours:** 4
Min Charge for Trial: Yes **Hours:** 4
Retainer Required: No
Expenses Marked Up: No
Portal-to-Portal: No **1st-class Airfare:** No
Written Retainer Agreement: No
Failure to Pay Bill Last 5 Years; Retaining Counsel: No **Opposing Counsel (Deps):** No

Physical Medicine & Rehabilitation
Court: $500 **Review/Prep:** $500 **Deps:** $500
Years Testifying: 10
Written Fee Schedule: Yes
Min Charge for Deps: Yes **Hours:** 4
Min Charge for Trial: Yes **Hours:** 4
Cancellation Charge for Deps/Trial: Yes
Retainer Required: Yes, $2,000 (Refundable, One Time)
Expenses Marked Up: No
Expenses Billed For: Airline Tickets
Portal-to-Portal: Yes **1st-class Airfare:** Yes
Failure to Pay Bill Last 5 Years; Retaining Counsel: No **Opposing Counsel (Deps):** No

Podiatry
Court: $625 **Review/Prep:** $200 **Deps:** $625
Years Testifying: 20 **Majority:** Plaintiff
Written Fee Schedule: Yes
Min Charge for Deps: Yes **Hours:** 4
Min Charge for Trial: Yes **Hours:** 4
Cancellation Charge for Deps/Trial: No
Retainer Required: Yes, $800 (Non-Refundable, One Time)
Procedure When Dep Exceeds Paid Time: Proceed without immediate payment
Expenses Marked Up: No
Expenses Billed For: Mileage, Airline Tickets, Telephone Calls
Portal-to-Portal: Yes **1st-class Airfare:** No
Written Retainer Agreement: Yes
Terms: Lawyer is responsible for fee, not lawyer's client, Out-of-pocket expense policies, In-court testimony minimums, Retaining counsel pays all deposition charges, Fee schedules, Deposition minimum fee
Failure to Pay Bill Last 5 Years; Retaining Counsel: Yes **Opposing (Deps):** Yes

Psychiatry
Court: $250 **Review/Prep:** $250 **Deps:** $250
Years Testifying: 17 **Majority:** Defendant
Written Fee Schedule: No
Min Charge for Deps: Yes **Hours:** 4
Min Charge for Trial: Yes **Hours:** 4
Cancellation Charge for Deps/Trial: Yes
Retainer Required: Yes, Depends on case (Refundable, Replenishable)
Expenses Marked Up: No
Expenses Billed For: Airline Tickets, Lab/Testing
Portal-to-Portal: Yes **1st-class Airfare:** No
Written Retainer Agreement: No
Failure to Pay Bill Last 5 Years; Retaining Counsel: No **Opposing Counsel (Deps):** No

Psychology
Court: $250 **Review/Prep:** $175 **Deps:** $200
Years Testifying: 25
Written Fee Schedule: No
Min Charge for Deps: No **Hours:** 4
Min Charge for Trial: Yes **Hours:** 4
Cancellation Charge for Deps/Trial: Yes
Retainer Required: Yes, Depends on case (Refundable, Replenishable)
Expenses Marked Up: No
Expenses Billed For: Mileage, Airline Tickets, Photocopies, Telephone Calls,

Lab/Testing, Demonstrative Aids
Portal-to-Portal: Yes **1st-class Airfare:** No
Written Retainer Agreement: No
Failure to Pay Bill Last 5 Years; Retaining Counsel: No **Opposing Counsel (Deps):** No

Recreation, Sports
Court: $125 **Review/Prep:** $125 **Deps:** $125
Years Testifying: 18
Written Fee Schedule: Yes
Min Charge for Deps: Yes **Hours:** 4
Min Charge for Trial: Yes **Hours:** 4
Cancellation Charge for Deps/Trial: Yes
Retainer Required: Yes, 25% of est. fee (Refundable, Replenishable)
Procedure When Dep Exceeds Paid Time: Proceed without immediate payment
Expenses Marked Up: No
Expenses Billed For: Airline Tickets, Lab/Testing, Demonstrative Aids
Portal-to-Portal: Yes **1st-class Airfare:** No
Written Retainer Agreement: Yes
Terms: Lawyer is responsible for fee, not lawyer's client, Out-of-pocket expense policies, In-court testimony minimums, Retaining counsel pays all deposition charges, Portal-to-portal travel time, Attorney's fees if forced to sue for collection, Deposition minimum fee, Payment for preparation time
Failure to Pay Bill Last 5 Years; Retaining Counsel: No **Opposing Counsel (Deps):** No

Rheumatology
Court: $300 **Review/Prep:** $300 **Deps:** $300
Years Testifying: 8 **Majority:** Plaintiff
Written Fee Schedule: No
Min Charge for Deps: Yes **Hours:** 8
Min Charge for Trial: Yes **Hours:** 8
Cancellation Charge for Deps/Trial: No
Retainer Required: Yes, $1,000 (Non-Refundable, One Time)
Expenses Marked Up: No
Expenses Billed For: Mileage, Airline Tickets
Portal-to-Portal: Yes **1st-class Airfare:** No
Written Retainer Agreement: No
Failure to Pay Bill Last 5 Years; Retaining Counsel: No **Opposing Counsel (Deps):** No

Safety
Court: $220 **Review/Prep:** $250 **Deps:** $350
Written Fee Schedule: Yes
Min Charge for Deps: Yes **Hours:** 10
Min Charge for Trial: Yes **Hours:** 10
Cancellation Charge for Deps/Trial: Yes
Retainer Required: Yes, $1,000 (Refundable, One Time)
Procedure When Dep Exceeds Paid Time: Proceed without immediate payment
Expenses Marked Up: No
Expenses Billed For: Mileage, Airline Tickets, Lab/Testing, Photographs, Demonstrative Aids
Portal-to-Portal: Yes **1st-class Airfare:** No
Written Retainer Agreement: No
Failure to Pay Bill Last 5 Years; Retaining Counsel: Yes **Opposing Counsel (Deps):** No

Safety, Industrial
Court: $200 **Review/Prep:** $200 **Deps:** $200
Years Testifying: 10
Written Fee Schedule: Yes
Min Charge for Deps: Yes **Hours:** 8
Min Charge for Trial: Yes **Hours:** 8
Cancellation Charge for Deps/Trial: No
Retainer Required: Yes, $750 (Non-Refundable)
Expenses Marked Up: No
Expenses Billed For: Airline Tickets, Lab/Testing
Portal-to-Portal: No **1st-class Airfare:** Yes
Written Retainer Agreement: No
Failure to Pay Bill Last 5 Years; Retaining Counsel: Yes **Opposing Counsel (Deps):** No

Surgery, Trauma
Court: $1,250 **Review/Prep:** $250 **Deps:** $600
Years Testifying: 15 **Majority:** Defendant
Written Fee Schedule: No
Min Charge for Deps: Yes **Hours:** 4
Min Charge for Trial: Yes **Hours:** 4
Cancellation Charge for Deps/Trial: Yes
Retainer Required: No
Expenses Marked Up: No
Expenses Billed For: Mileage, Airline Tickets
Portal-to-Portal: Yes **1st-class Airfare:** Yes
Written Retainer Agreement: No
Failure to Pay Bill Last 5 Years; Retaining Counsel: Yes **Opposing Counsel (Deps):** No

Telecommunications
Court: $390 **Review/Prep:** $350 **Deps:** $390
Years Testifying: 7
Written Fee Schedule: Yes
Min Charge for Deps: No
Min Charge for Trial: No
Cancellation Charge for Deps/Trial: No
Retainer Required: Yes, $10,000 (Refundable, One Time)
Procedure When Dep Exceeds Paid Time: Get payment before proceeding further
Expenses Marked Up: No
Expenses Billed For: Mileage, Airline Tickets, Photocopies, Telephone Calls, Demonstrative Aids
Portal-to-Portal: Yes **1st-class Airfare:** No
Written Retainer Agreement: No
Failure to Pay Bill Last 5 Years; Retaining Counsel: No **Opposing Counsel (Deps):** No

Telecommunications
Court: $295 **Review/Prep:** $295 **Deps:** $295
Years Testifying: 7 **Majority:** Plaintiff
Written Fee Schedule: No
Min Charge for Deps: No
Min Charge for Trial: No
Cancellation Charge for Deps/Trial: No
Retainer Required: Yes, $4,000 (Refundable, Replenishable)
Expenses Marked Up: No
Expenses Billed For: Airline Tickets, Photographs, Demonstrative Aids
Portal-to-Portal: Yes **1st-class Airfare:** No
Written Retainer Agreement: Yes
Terms: Out-of-pocket expense policies, Retaining counsel pays all deposition charges, Fee schedules, Portal-to-portal travel time, Payment for preparation time
Failure to Pay Bill Last 5 Years; Retaining Counsel: Yes **Opposing Counsel (Deps):** No

Toxicology
Court: $150 **Review/Prep:** $150 **Deps:** $150
Years Testifying: 3
Written Fee Schedule: No
Min Charge for Deps: Yes **Hours:** 1
Min Charge for Trial: Yes **Hours:** 1
Cancellation Charge for Deps/Trial: No
Retainer Required: Yes, $150 (Non-Refundable, Replenishable)
Procedure When Dep Exceeds Paid Time: Get payment before proceeding further
Expenses Marked Up: No
Expenses Billed For: Mileage, Lab/Testing
Portal-to-Portal: Yes **1st-class Airfare:** No
Written Retainer Agreement: No
Failure to Pay Bill Last 5 Years; Retaining Counsel: Yes **Opposing Counsel (Deps):** No

Valuation, Business
Court: $300 **Review/Prep:** $300 **Deps:** $300
Years Testifying: 20 **Majority:** Plaintiff
Written Fee Schedule: Yes
Min Charge for Deps: No
Min Charge for Trial: No
Cancellation Charge for Deps/Trial: No
Retainer Required: Yes, $5,000 (Refundable, One Time)
Expenses Marked Up: No
Expenses Billed For: Airline Tickets, Photocopies, Photographs, Demonstrative Aids
Portal-to-Portal: No **1st-class Airfare:** No
Written Retainer Agreement: Yes
Terms: Out-of-pocket expense policies, Retaining counsel pays all deposition charges, Fee schedules, Attorney's fees if forced to sue for collection, Payment for preparation time
Failure to Pay Bill Last 5 Years; Retaining Counsel: No

Valuation, Business
Court: $250 **Review/Prep:** $250 **Deps:** $250
Written Fee Schedule: Yes
Min Charge for Deps: No
Min Charge for Trial: No
Cancellation Charge for Deps/Trial: No
Retainer Required: Yes, Depends on case (Partially Refundable, One Time)
Procedure When Dep Exceeds Paid Time: Get payment before proceeding further
Expenses Marked Up: No
Expenses Billed For: Airline Tickets, Photocopies, Telephone Calls, Lab/Testing, Photographs, Demonstrative Aids
Portal-to-Portal: Yes **1st-class Airfare:** No
Written Retainer Agreement: Yes
Terms: Lawyer is responsible for fee, not lawyer's client, Interest for delinquent accounts, Out-of-pocket expense policies, Retaining counsel pays all deposition charges, Fee schedules, Portal-to-portal travel time, Attorney's fees if forced to sue for collection, Payment for preparation time
Failure to Pay Bill Last 5 Years; Retaining Counsel: Yes **Opposing (Deps):** Yes

Vocational/Life Care Planning
Court: $150 **Review/Prep:** $150 **Deps:** $150
Years Testifying: 20
Written Fee Schedule: Yes
Min Charge for Deps: No
Min Charge for Trial: No
Cancellation Charge for Deps/Trial: Yes
Retainer Required: Yes, $2,000 (Refundable, One Time)
Expenses Marked Up: No
Expenses Billed For: Mileage, Airline Tickets, Telephone Calls
Portal-to-Portal: Yes **1st-class Airfare:** No
Written Retainer Agreement: No
Failure to Pay Bill Last 5 Years; Retaining Counsel: Yes **Opposing Counsel (Deps):** No

Vocational Rehabilitation
Court: $300 **Review/Prep:** $285 **Deps:** $285
Years Testifying: 1 **Majority:** Plaintiff
Written Fee Schedule: Yes
Min Charge for Deps: Yes **Hours:** 5
Min Charge for Trial: Yes **Hours:** 5
Cancellation Charge for Deps/Trial: Yes
Retainer Required: Yes, $1,250 (Refundable, One Time)
Procedure When Dep Exceeds Paid Time: Get payment before proceeding further
Expenses Marked Up: Yes
Expenses Billed For: Mileage, Airline Tickets, Photographs, Demonstrative Aids
Portal-to-Portal: Yes **1st-class Airfare:** No
Written Retainer Agreement: Yes
Terms: Out-of-pocket expense policies, In-court testimony minimums, Retaining counsel pays all deposition charges, Fee schedules, Attorney's fees if forced to sue for collection, Payment for preparation time
Failure to Pay Bill Last 5 Years; Retaining Counsel: No **Opposing Counsel (Deps):** No

North Carolina

Chiropractic
Court: $200 **Review/Prep:** $125 **Deps:** $175
Years Testifying: 32
Written Fee Schedule: Yes
Min Charge for Deps: No
Min Charge for Trial: No
Cancellation Charge for Deps/Trial: No
Retainer Required: Yes, $200 (Refundable, One Time)
Procedure When Dep Exceeds Paid Time: Proceed without immediate payment
Expenses Marked Up: No
Expenses Billed For: Mileage, Airline Tickets, Photocopies, Telephone Calls, Photographs
Portal-to-Portal: Yes **1st-class Airfare:** No
Written Retainer Agreement: No
Failure to Pay Bill Last 5 Years; Retaining Counsel: No **Opposing Counsel (Deps):** No

Emergency Medicine
Court: $600 **Review/Prep:** $275 **Deps:** $400
Years Testifying: 3
Written Fee Schedule: Yes
Min Charge for Deps: Yes **Hours:** 2
Min Charge for Trial: Yes **Hours:** 2
Cancellation Charge for Deps/Trial: Yes
Retainer Required: Yes, $550 (Refundable, Replenishable)
Expenses Marked Up: No
Portal-to-Portal: Yes **1st-class Airfare:** No
Written Retainer Agreement: No
Failure to Pay Bill Last 5 Years; Retaining Counsel: No **Opposing Counsel (Deps):** No

Engineering, Electrical
Court: $225 **Review/Prep:** $175 **Deps:** $225
Written Fee Schedule: Yes
Min Charge for Deps: Yes **Hours:** 4
Min Charge for Trial: Yes **Hours:** 4
Cancellation Charge for Deps/Trial: Yes
Retainer Required: Yes, $2,500 (Non-Refundable, One Time)
Expenses Marked Up: No
Expenses Billed For: Mileage, Airline Tickets, Photocopies, Telephone Calls, Lab/Testing, Photographs, Demonstrative Aids
Portal-to-Portal: Yes **1st-class Airfare:** No
Written Retainer Agreement: No
Failure to Pay Bill Last 5 Years; Retaining Counsel: Yes **Opposing Counsel (Deps):** No

Engineering, Mechanical/Product Liability
Court: $225 **Review/Prep:** $225 **Deps:** $225
Years Testifying: 14
Written Fee Schedule: Yes
Min Charge for Deps: Yes **Hours:** 7
Min Charge for Trial: Yes **Hours:** 7
Cancellation Charge for Deps/Trial: Yes
Retainer Required: Yes, $2,500 (Refundable, One Time)
Expenses Marked Up: Yes
Expenses Billed For: Mileage, Airline Tickets, Photocopies, Lab/Testing, Photographs, Demonstrative Aids
Portal-to-Portal: Yes **1st-class Airfare:** No
Written Retainer Agreement: Yes
Terms: Lawyer is responsible for fee, not lawyer's client, Interest for delinquent accounts, Out-of-pocket expense policies, Fee schedules
Failure to Pay Bill Last 5 Years; Retaining Counsel: Yes **Opposing (Deps):** Yes

Engineering, Transportation
Court: $175 **Review/Prep:** $130 **Deps:** $175
Years Testifying: 8
Written Fee Schedule: Yes
Min Charge for Deps: No
Min Charge for Trial: No
Cancellation Charge for Deps/Trial: No
Retainer Required: Yes, $1,500 (Refundable, One Time)
Expenses Marked Up: Yes
Expenses Billed For: Mileage, Airline Tickets, Photocopies, Telephone Calls, Lab/Testing, Photographs, Demonstrative Aids
Portal-to-Portal: Yes **1st-class Airfare:** No
Written Retainer Agreement: Yes
Terms: Lawyer is responsible for fee, not lawyer's client, Interest for delinquent accounts, Out-of-pocket expense policies, Retaining counsel pays all deposition charges, Fee schedules, Attorney's fees if forced to sue for collection
Failure to Pay Bill Last 5 Years; Retaining Counsel: Yes **Opposing Counsel (Deps):** No

Human Factors/Engineering/Safety
Court: $300 **Review/Prep:** $200 **Deps:** $300
Years Testifying: 23
Written Fee Schedule: Yes
Min Charge for Deps: Yes **Hours:** 1
Min Charge for Trial: Yes **Hours:** 1
Cancellation Charge for Deps/Trial: Yes
Retainer Required: Yes, $1,600 (Non-Refundable, One Time)
Procedure When Dep Exceeds Paid Time: Proceed without immediate payment
Expenses Marked Up: No
Expenses Billed For: Mileage, Airline

Tickets, Photocopies, Photographs
Portal-to-Portal: Yes **1st-class Airfare:** No
Written Retainer Agreement: Yes
Terms: Lawyer is responsible for fee, not lawyer's client, Interest for delinquent accounts, Out-of-pocket expense policies, In-court testimony minimums, Retaining counsel pays all deposition charges, Fee schedules, Portal-to-portal travel time, Attorney's fees if forced to sue for collection, Deposition minimum fee, Payment for preparation time
Failure to Pay Bill Last 5 Years; Retaining Counsel: Yes **Opposing Counsel (Deps):** No

Human Resources
Court: $150 **Review/Prep:** $150 **Deps:** $150
Years Testifying: 3 **Majority:** Defendant
Written Fee Schedule: No
Min Charge for Deps: Yes **Hours:** 1
Min Charge for Trial: Yes **Hours:** 1
Cancellation Charge for Deps/Trial: No
Retainer Required: No
Expenses Marked Up: Yes
Expenses Billed For: Mileage, Airline Tickets, Photocopies, Telephone Calls, Lab/Testing, Photographs, Demonstrative Aids
Portal-to-Portal: Yes **1st-class Airfare:** No
Written Retainer Agreement: Yes
Terms: Lawyer is responsible for fee, not lawyer's client, Interest for delinquent accounts, Out-of-pocket expense policies, In-court testimony minimums, Retaining counsel pays all deposition charges, Fee schedules, Portal-to-portal travel time, Attorney's fees if forced to sue for collection, Deposition minimum fee, Payment for preparation time
Failure to Pay Bill Last 5 Years; Retaining Counsel: No **Opposing Counsel (Deps):** No

Internal Medicine
Court: $600 **Review/Prep:** $300 **Deps:** $600
Years Testifying: 16
Written Fee Schedule: Yes
Min Charge for Deps: Yes **Hours:** 2
Min Charge for Trial: Yes **Hours:** 2
Cancellation Charge for Deps/Trial: Yes
Retainer Required: Yes, (Non-Refundable, Replenishable)
Procedure When Dep Exceeds Paid Time: Proceed without immediate payment
Expenses Marked Up: No
Expenses Billed For:
Portal-to-Portal: Yes **1st-class Airfare:** Yes
Written Retainer Agreement: Yes
Terms: Lawyer is responsible for fee, not lawyer's client
Failure to Pay Bill Last 5 Years; Retaining Counsel: Yes **Opposing (Deps):** Yes

Mental Health
Court: $250 **Review/Prep:** $125 **Deps:** $250
Years Testifying: 15
Written Fee Schedule: Yes
Min Charge for Deps: Yes **Hours:** 2
Min Charge for Trial: Yes **Hours:** 2
Cancellation Charge for Deps/Trial: Yes
Retainer Required: Yes, $1,000 (Non-Refundable, Replenishable)
Procedure When Dep Exceeds Paid Time: Proceed without immediate payment
Expenses Marked Up: No
Expenses Billed For: Airline Tickets, Telephone Calls, Lab/Testing, Demonstrative Aids
Portal-to-Portal: Yes **1st-class Airfare:** No
Written Retainer Agreement: Yes
Terms: In-court testimony minimums, Retaining counsel pays all deposition charges, Fee schedules, Payment for preparation time
Failure to Pay Bill Last 5 Years; Retaining Counsel: Yes **Opposing Counsel (Deps):** No

Orthopedics
Court: $250 **Review/Prep:** $300 **Deps:** $300
Years Testifying: 30 **Majority:** Defendant
Written Fee Schedule: Yes
Min Charge for Deps: Yes **Hours:** 4
Min Charge for Trial: Yes **Hours:** 4
Cancellation Charge for Deps/Trial: No
Retainer Required: Yes, $2,500 (Refundable, One Time)
Procedure When Dep Exceeds Paid Time: Proceed without immediate payment
Expenses Marked Up: No
Expenses Billed For: Mileage, Airline Tickets, Photocopies, Telephone Calls, Lab/Testing, Photographs, Demonstrative Aids
Portal-to-Portal: Yes **1st-class Airfare:** No
Written Retainer Agreement: Yes
Terms: Lawyer is responsible for fee, not lawyer's client, Interest for delinquent accounts, Out-of-pocket expense policies, In-court testimony minimums, Retaining counsel pays all deposition charges, Fee schedules, Portal-to-portal travel time, Attorney's fees if forced to sue for collection, Deposition minimum fee, Payment for preparation time
Failure to Pay Bill Last 5 Years; Retaining Counsel: Yes **Opposing (Deps):** Yes

Otolaryngology
Court: $250 **Review/Prep:** $250 **Deps:** $250
Majority: Defendant
Written Fee Schedule: No
Min Charge for Deps: No
Min Charge for Trial: No
Cancellation Charge for Deps/Trial: No
Retainer Required: No
Expenses Marked Up: No
Expenses Billed For: Mileage, Airline Tickets, Photocopies, Lab/Testing
Portal-to-Portal: Yes **1st-class Airfare:** No
Written Retainer Agreement: No
Failure to Pay Bill Last 5 Years; Retaining Counsel: No **Opposing Counsel (Deps):** No

Physical Medicine & Rehabilitation
Court: $875 **Review/Prep:** $350 **Deps:** $500
Years Testifying: 5
Written Fee Schedule: Yes
Min Charge for Deps: Yes **Hours:** 4
Min Charge for Trial: Yes **Hours:** 4
Cancellation Charge for Deps/Trial: Yes
Retainer Required: Yes, $350 (Non-Refundable, One Time)
Procedure When Dep Exceeds Paid Time: Proceed without immediate payment
Expenses Marked Up: No
Expenses Billed For: Mileage, Airline Tickets, Photocopies, Demonstrative Aids
Portal-to-Portal: Yes **1st-class Airfare:** No
Written Retainer Agreement: No
Failure to Pay Bill Last 5 Years; Retaining Counsel: Yes **Opposing Counsel (Deps):** No

Pressure Vessels/Tankage
Court: $150 **Review/Prep:** $150 **Deps:** $150
Years Testifying: 8 **Majority:** Defendant
Written Fee Schedule: No
Min Charge for Deps: No
Min Charge for Trial: No
Cancellation Charge for Deps/Trial: No
Retainer Required: No
Procedure When Dep Exceeds Paid Time: Proceed without immediate payment
Expenses Marked Up: No
Expenses Billed For: Mileage, Airline Tickets, Photocopies, Telephone Calls, Demonstrative Aids
Portal-to-Portal: Yes **1st-class Airfare:** No
Written Retainer Agreement: No
Failure to Pay Bill Last 5 Years; Retaining Counsel: No **Opposing Counsel (Deps):** No

Psychiatry
Court: $320 **Review/Prep:** $320 **Deps:** $320
Years Testifying: 10
Written Fee Schedule: Yes
Min Charge for Deps: Yes
Min Charge for Trial: No
Cancellation Charge for Deps/Trial: Yes
Retainer Required: No
Expenses Marked Up: No
Expenses Billed For: Mileage, Airline Tickets, Telephone Calls, Lab/Testing, Demonstrative Aids
Portal-to-Portal: Yes **1st-class Airfare:** No
Written Retainer Agreement: No
Failure to Pay Bill Last 5 Years; Retaining Counsel: Yes **Opposing Counsel (Deps):** No

Risk Management

Court: $150 **Review/Prep:** $150 **Deps:** $150
Years Testifying: 10
Written Fee Schedule: No
Min Charge for Deps: No
Min Charge for Trial: No
Cancellation Charge for Deps/Trial: No
Retainer Required: Yes, $1,500 (Non-Refundable, One Time)
Procedure When Dep Exceeds Paid Time: Proceed without immediate payment
Expenses Marked Up: No
Expenses Billed For: Mileage, Airline Tickets, Photocopies, Telephone Calls, Photographs
Portal-to-Portal: Yes **1st-class Airfare:** No
Written Retainer Agreement: No
Failure to Pay Bill Last 5 Years; Retaining Counsel: Yes **Opposing Counsel (Deps):** No

Security/Human Resources

Court: $250 **Review/Prep:** $185 **Deps:** $250
Years Testifying: 10
Written Fee Schedule: Yes
Min Charge for Deps: Yes **Hours:** 10
Min Charge for Trial: Yes **Hours:** 10
Cancellation Charge for Deps/Trial: Yes
Retainer Required: Yes, $3,000 (Non-Refundable, Replenishable)
Expenses Marked Up: No
Expenses Billed For: Mileage, Airline Tickets, Photocopies, Telephone Calls
Portal-to-Portal: Yes **1st-class Airfare:** No
Written Retainer Agreement: Yes
Terms: Lawyer is responsible for fee, not lawyer's client, Interest for delinquent accounts, Out-of-pocket expense policies, In-court testimony minimums, Retaining counsel pays all deposition charges, Fee schedules, Portal-to-portal travel time, Attorney's fees if forced to sue for collection, Deposition minimum fee
Failure to Pay Bill Last 5 Years; Retaining Counsel: Yes **Opposing Counsel (Deps):** No

Statistics, Sampling

Court: $200 **Review/Prep:** $150 **Deps:** $200
Years Testifying: 8 **Majority:** Plaintiff
Written Fee Schedule: Yes
Min Charge for Deps: Yes **Hours:** 4
Min Charge for Trial: Yes **Hours:** 4
Cancellation Charge for Deps/Trial: No
Retainer Required: Yes, $1,500 (Refundable, Replenishable)
Procedure When Dep Exceeds Paid Time: Proceed without immediate payment
Expenses Marked Up: No
Expenses Billed For: Mileage, Airline Tickets, Photocopies, Telephone Calls, Lab/Testing, Photographs
Portal-to-Portal: Yes **1st-class Airfare:** No
Written Retainer Agreement: Yes
Terms: Out-of-pocket expense policies, In-court testimony minimums, Retaining counsel pays all deposition charges, Fee schedules, Portal-to-portal travel time, Attorney's fees if forced to sue for collection, Payment for preparation time
Failure to Pay Bill Last 5 Years; Retaining Counsel: Yes **Opposing Counsel (Deps):** No

Toxicology

Court: $250 **Review/Prep:** $250 **Deps:** $250
Years Testifying: 11 **Majority:** Defendant
Written Fee Schedule: Yes
Min Charge for Deps: No
Min Charge for Trial: No
Cancellation Charge for Deps/Trial: No
Retainer Required: Yes, $2,500 (Non-Refundable, One Time)
Expenses Marked Up: No
Expenses Billed For: Mileage, Airline Tickets
Portal-to-Portal: Yes **1st-class Airfare:** No
Written Retainer Agreement: No
Failure to Pay Bill Last 5 Years; Retaining Counsel: No **Opposing Counsel (Deps):** Yes

Vocational Rehabilitation/Life Care Planning

Court: $165 **Review/Prep:** $165 **Deps:** $165
Years Testifying: 15 **Majority:** Plaintiff
Written Fee Schedule: Yes
Min Charge for Deps: No
Min Charge for Trial: No
Cancellation Charge for Deps/Trial: Yes
Retainer Required: Yes, $1,500 (One Time)
Procedure When Dep Exceeds Paid Time: Proceed without immediate payment
Expenses Marked Up: No
Expenses Billed For: Mileage, Airline Tickets, Telephone Calls
Portal-to-Portal: Yes **1st-class Airfare:** No
Written Retainer Agreement: Yes
Terms: Lawyer is responsible for fee, not lawyer's client, Interest for delinquent accounts, Out-of-pocket expense policies, In-court testimony minimums, Retaining counsel pays all deposition charges, Fee schedules, Portal-to-portal travel time, Attorney's fees if forced to sue for collection, Payment for preparation time
Failure to Pay Bill Last 5 Years; Retaining Counsel: No **Opposing Counsel (Deps):** Yes

North Dakota

Damages, Business

Court: $225 **Review/Prep:** $225 **Deps:** $225
Years Testifying: 15
Written Fee Schedule: No
Min Charge for Deps: No
Min Charge for Trial: No
Cancellation Charge for Deps/Trial: No
Retainer Required: Yes, Depends on case (Refundable, One Time)
Expenses Marked Up: No
Expenses Billed For: Mileage, Airline Tickets, Photocopies, Telephone Calls, Lab/Testing, Photographs, Demonstrative Aids
Portal-to-Portal: Yes **1st-class Airfare:** No
Written Retainer Agreement: Yes
Terms: Lawyer is responsible for fee, not lawyer's client, Interest for delinquent accounts, Out-of-pocket expense policies, Retaining counsel pays all deposition charges, Fee schedules, Portal-to-portal travel time, Attorney's fees if forced to sue for collection, Payment for preparation time
Failure to Pay Bill Last 5 Years; Retaining Counsel: Yes **Opposing Counsel (Deps):** No

Surgery, General

Review/Prep: $250 **Deps:** $350
Written Fee Schedule: No
Min Charge for Deps: No
Min Charge for Trial: No
Cancellation Charge for Deps/Trial: Yes
Retainer Required: No
Expenses Marked Up: No
Expenses Billed For: Mileage
Portal-to-Portal: Yes **1st-class Airfare:** No
Written Retainer Agreement: No
Failure to Pay Bill Last 5 Years; Retaining Counsel: No **Opposing Counsel (Deps):** No

Ohio

Chiropractic

Court: $525 **Review/Prep:** $225 **Deps:** $525
Years Testifying: 25 **Majority:** Defendant
Written Fee Schedule: Yes
Min Charge for Deps: Yes **Hours:** 2
Min Charge for Trial: Yes **Hours:** 2
Cancellation Charge for Deps/Trial: Yes
Retainer Required: Yes, $525 (Refundable, One Time)
Procedure When Dep Exceeds Paid Time: Get payment before proceeding further
Expenses Marked Up: No
Expenses Billed For: Mileage, Airline Tickets, Photocopies, Telephone Calls, Demonstrative Aids
Portal-to-Portal: Yes **1st-class Airfare:** No
Written Retainer Agreement: Yes
Terms: Out-of-pocket expense policies, In-court testimony minimums, Retaining counsel pays all deposition charges, Fee schedules, Attorney's fees if forced to sue for collection, Deposition minimum fee, Payment for preparation time

Failure to Pay Bill Last 5 Years; Retaining Counsel: Yes **Opposing Counsel (Deps):** No

Electrical, Power Systems
Court: $250 **Review/Prep:** $150 **Deps:** $250
Years Testifying: 6 **Majority:** Plaintiff
Written Fee Schedule: No
Min Charge for Deps: No
Min Charge for Trial: No
Cancellation Charge for Deps/Trial: No
Retainer Required: Yes, $750 (Refundable, One Time)
Procedure When Dep Exceeds Paid Time: Proceed without immediate payment
Expenses Billed For: Airline Tickets, Photocopies, Lab/Testing, Photographs, Demonstrative Aids
Portal-to-Portal: Yes **1st-class Airfare:** No
Written Retainer Agreement: Yes
Failure to Pay Bill Last 5 Years; Retaining Counsel: No **Opposing Counsel (Deps):** No

Emergency Medicine
Court: $1,000 **Review/Prep:** $300 **Deps:** $400
Years Testifying: 15
Written Fee Schedule: Yes
Min Charge for Deps: Yes **Hours:** 4
Min Charge for Trial: Yes **Hours:** 4
Cancellation Charge for Deps/Trial: No
Retainer Required: Yes, $1,200 (Refundable, Replenishable)
Expenses Marked Up: No
Expenses Billed For: Airline Tickets, Photocopies, Telephone Calls
Portal-to-Portal: No **1st-class Airfare:** No
Written Retainer Agreement: No
Failure to Pay Bill Last 5 Years; Retaining Counsel: Yes **Opposing Counsel (Deps):** No

Emergency Medicine
Court: $350 **Review/Prep:** $350 **Deps:** $350
Years Testifying: 15 **Majority:** Defendant
Written Fee Schedule: No
Min Charge for Deps: No
Min Charge for Trial: No
Cancellation Charge for Deps/Trial: No
Retainer Required: No
Expenses Marked Up: No
Expenses Billed For: Airline Tickets
Portal-to-Portal: Yes **1st-class Airfare:** No
Written Retainer Agreement: No
Failure to Pay Bill Last 5 Years; Retaining Counsel: Yes **Opposing Counsel (Deps):** No

Engineering, Civil
Court: $195 **Review/Prep:** $195 **Deps:** $195
Years Testifying: 8
Written Fee Schedule: Yes
Min Charge for Deps: No
Min Charge for Trial: No
Cancellation Charge for Deps/Trial: No
Retainer Required: Yes, Depends on case (Refundable, Replenishable)
Expenses Marked Up: No
Expenses Billed For: Mileage, Airline Tickets, Photocopies, Telephone Calls, Lab/Testing, Photographs, Demonstrative Aids
Portal-to-Portal: Yes **1st-class Airfare:** No
Written Retainer Agreement: No
Failure to Pay Bill Last 5 Years; Retaining Counsel: Yes **Opposing Counsel (Deps):** No

Engineering, Mechanical
Court: $150 **Review/Prep:** $150 **Deps:** $150
Years Testifying: 15
Written Fee Schedule: Yes
Min Charge for Deps: Yes **Hours:** 3
Min Charge for Trial: Yes **Hours:** 3
Cancellation Charge for Deps/Trial: No
Retainer Required: Yes, Depends on case (Non-Refundable, Replenishable)
Procedure When Dep Exceeds Paid Time: Proceed without immediate payment
Expenses Marked Up: No
Expenses Billed For: Mileage, Airline Tickets, Photocopies, Telephone Calls, Lab/Testing, Photographs, Demonstrative Aids
Portal-to-Portal: Yes **1st-class Airfare:** No
Written Retainer Agreement: No
Failure to Pay Bill Last 5 Years; Retaining Counsel: No **Opposing Counsel (Deps):** No

Engineering, Petroleum
Court: $125 **Review/Prep:** $125 **Deps:** $125
Years Testifying: 15 **Majority:** Defendant
Written Fee Schedule: Yes
Min Charge for Deps: No
Min Charge for Trial: No
Cancellation Charge for Deps/Trial: No
Retainer Required: No
Expenses Marked Up: No
Expenses Billed For: Mileage, Airline Tickets, Photocopies, Telephone Calls, Lab/Testing, Photographs, Demonstrative Aids
Portal-to-Portal: Yes **1st-class Airfare:** No
Written Retainer Agreement: No
Failure to Pay Bill Last 5 Years; Retaining Counsel: No **Opposing Counsel (Deps):** No

Environmental Medicine
Court: $600 **Review/Prep:** $400 **Deps:** $500
Years Testifying: 20
Written Fee Schedule: Yes
Min Charge for Deps: No
Min Charge for Trial: No
Cancellation Charge for Deps/Trial: Yes
Retainer Required: No
Expenses Marked Up: No
Expenses Billed For: Mileage, Airline Tickets, Photocopies, Lab/Testing, Photographs, Demonstrative Aids
Written Retainer Agreement: No
Failure to Pay Bill Last 5 Years; Retaining Counsel: No **Opposing Counsel (Deps):** No

Family Practice
Court: $500 **Review/Prep:** $125 **Deps:** $500
Years Testifying: 5
Written Fee Schedule: Yes
Min Charge for Deps: Yes **Hours:** 1
Min Charge for Trial: Yes **Hours:** 1
Retainer Required: Yes, $500 (Non-Refundable, Replenishable)
Procedure When Dep Exceeds Paid Time: Proceed without immediate payment
Expenses Marked Up: No
Expenses Billed For: Mileage
Portal-to-Portal: Yes **1st-class Airfare:** No
Written Retainer Agreement: Yes
Terms: Lawyer is responsible for fee, not lawyer's client
Failure to Pay Bill Last 5 Years; Retaining Counsel: No **Opposing Counsel (Deps):** No

Fire
Court: $100 **Review/Prep:** $100 **Deps:** $100
Years Testifying: 28
Written Fee Schedule: Yes
Min Charge for Deps: Yes **Hours:** 8
Min Charge for Trial: Yes **Hours:** 8
Cancellation Charge for Deps/Trial: No
Retainer Required: Yes, $800 (Refundable, One Time)
Procedure When Dep Exceeds Paid Time: Proceed without immediate payment
Expenses Marked Up: No
Expenses Billed For: Mileage, Airline Tickets, Lab/Testing, Photographs, Demonstrative Aids
Portal-to-Portal: Yes **1st-class Airfare:** No
Written Retainer Agreement: Yes
Terms: Lawyer is responsible for fee, not lawyer's client, Out-of-pocket expense policies, In-court testimony minimums, Retaining counsel pays all deposition charges, Fee schedules, Portal-to-portal travel time, Deposition minimum fee, Payment for preparation time
Failure to Pay Bill Last 5 Years; Retaining Counsel: No **Opposing Counsel (Deps):** No

Force Dynamics
Court: $395 **Review/Prep:** $295 **Deps:** $395
Years Testifying: 22 **Majority:** Plaintiff
Written Fee Schedule: Yes
Min Charge for Deps: No
Min Charge for Trial: No
Cancellation Charge for Deps/Trial: No
Retainer Required: Yes, $5,000

(Refundable, Replenishable)
Procedure When Dep Exceeds Paid Time: Proceed without immediate payment
Expenses Marked Up: No
Expenses Billed For: Mileage, Airline Tickets, Photocopies, Lab/Testing, Photographs, Demonstrative Aids
Portal-to-Portal: Yes **1st-class Airfare:** No
Written Retainer Agreement: Yes
Terms: Lawyer is responsible for fee, not lawyer's client, Interest for delinquent accounts, Out-of-pocket expense policies, Retaining counsel pays all deposition charges, Fee schedules, Portal-to-portal travel time, Attorney's fees if forced to sue for collection
Failure to Pay Bill Last 5 Years; Retaining Counsel: Yes **Opposing Counsel (Deps):** No

Healthcare, Operations/Finance
Court: $275 **Review/Prep:** $185 **Deps:** $225
Years Testifying: 14 **Majority:** Plaintiff
Written Fee Schedule: No
Min Charge for Deps: No
Min Charge for Trial: No
Cancellation Charge for Deps/Trial: No
Retainer Required: Yes, $8,750 (Refundable, Replenishable)
Expenses Marked Up: No
Expenses Billed For: Mileage, Airline Tickets, Photocopies, Photographs, Demonstrative Aids
Portal-to-Portal: Yes **1st-class Airfare:** No
Written Retainer Agreement: Yes
Terms: Lawyer is responsible for fee, not lawyer's client, Out-of-pocket expense policies, In-court testimony minimums, Retaining counsel pays all deposition charges, Portal-to-portal travel time, Attorney's fees if forced to sue for collection, Payment for preparation time
Failure to Pay Bill Last 5 Years; Retaining Counsel: No **Opposing Counsel (Deps):** No

Law, Legal Malpractice
Court: $325 **Review/Prep:** $325 **Deps:** $325
Years Testifying: 6
Written Fee Schedule: No
Min Charge for Deps: No
Min Charge for Trial: No
Cancellation Charge for Deps/Trial: No
Retainer Required: Yes, $5,000 (Refundable, One Time)
Expenses Marked Up: No
Expenses Billed For: Mileage, Airline Tickets, Photocopies, Telephone Calls, Lab/Testing, Photographs, Demonstrative Aids
Portal-to-Portal: Yes **1st-class Airfare:** No
Written Retainer Agreement: No
Failure to Pay Bill Last 5 Years; Retaining Counsel: No **Opposing Counsel (Deps):** No

Medical Doctor
Court: $2,500 **Review/Prep:** $400 **Deps:** $400
Years Testifying: 15
Written Fee Schedule: No
Min Charge for Deps: No
Min Charge for Trial: No
Cancellation Charge for Deps/Trial: Yes
Retainer Required: Yes, $1,800 (Non-Refundable, One Time)
Expenses Marked Up: Yes
Expenses Billed For: Airline Tickets, Telephone Calls
Portal-to-Portal: No **1st-class Airfare:** No
Written Retainer Agreement: No
Failure to Pay Bill Last 5 Years; Retaining Counsel: Yes **Opposing (Deps):** Yes

Nursing
Court: $150 **Review/Prep:** $100 **Deps:** $150
Years Testifying: 7 **Majority:** Defendant
Written Fee Schedule: No
Min Charge for Deps: No
Min Charge for Trial: No
Cancellation Charge for Deps/Trial: Yes
Retainer Required: Yes, $1,500 (Refundable, One Time)
Expenses Marked Up: No
Expenses Billed For: Mileage, Airline Tickets, Demonstrative Aids
Portal-to-Portal: Yes **1st-class Airfare:** No
Written Retainer Agreement: No
Failure to Pay Bill Last 5 Years; Retaining Counsel: Yes **Opposing Counsel (Deps):** No

Obstetrics & Gynecology
Court: $500 **Review/Prep:** $300 **Deps:** $500
Years Testifying: 1 **Majority:** Plaintiff
Written Fee Schedule: Yes
Min Charge for Deps: Yes **Hours:** 4
Min Charge for Trial: Yes **Hours:** 4
Cancellation Charge for Deps/Trial: Yes
Retainer Required: Yes, $900 (Non-Refundable, One Time)
Procedure When Dep Exceeds Paid Time: Get payment before proceeding further
Expenses Marked Up: No
Portal-to-Portal: Yes **1st-class Airfare:** Yes
Written Retainer Agreement: Yes
Terms: Lawyer is responsible for fee, not lawyer's client, In-court testimony minimums, Retaining counsel pays all deposition charges, Fee schedules, Portal-to-portal travel time, Deposition minimum fee, Payment for preparation time, First class air travel
Failure to Pay Bill Last 5 Years; Retaining Counsel: Yes **Opposing Counsel (Deps):** No

Obstetrics & Gynecology
Court: $300 **Review/Prep:** $300 **Deps:** $300
Years Testifying: 5
Written Fee Schedule: Yes
Min Charge for Deps: Yes **Hours:** 4
Min Charge for Trial: Yes **Hours:** 4
Cancellation Charge for Deps/Trial: Yes
Retainer Required: No
Procedure When Dep Exceeds Paid Time: Proceed without immediate payment
Expenses Marked Up: No
Expenses Billed For: Airline Tickets
Portal-to-Portal: Yes **1st-class Airfare:** No
Written Retainer Agreement: No
Failure to Pay Bill Last 5 Years; Retaining Counsel: No **Opposing Counsel (Deps):** No

Occupational Medicine
Court: $1,000 **Review/Prep:** $150 **Deps:** $500
Years Testifying: 1 **Majority:** Defendant
Written Fee Schedule: Yes
Min Charge for Deps: Yes **Hours:** 4
Min Charge for Trial: Yes **Hours:** 4
Cancellation Charge for Deps/Trial: Yes
Retainer Required: Yes, $500 (Non-Refundable, One Time)
Expenses Marked Up: Yes
Expenses Billed For: Mileage, Airline Tickets
Portal-to-Portal: Yes **1st-class Airfare:** No
Written Retainer Agreement: No
Failure to Pay Bill Last 5 Years; Retaining Counsel: No **Opposing Counsel (Deps):** No

Ophthalmology
Court: $1,000 **Review/Prep:** $400 **Deps:** $800
Years Testifying: 17
Written Fee Schedule: No
Min Charge for Deps: Yes **Hours:** 2
Min Charge for Trial: Yes **Hours:** 2
Cancellation Charge for Deps/Trial: Yes
Retainer Required: No
Procedure When Dep Exceeds Paid Time: Proceed without immediate payment
Expenses Marked Up: No
Expenses Billed For: Mileage, Airline Tickets, Telephone Calls
Portal-to-Portal: Yes
Written Retainer Agreement: No
Failure to Pay Bill Last 5 Years; Retaining Counsel: No **Opposing Counsel (Deps):** No

Orthopedics
Court: $2,500 **Review/Prep:** $400 **Deps:** $1,250
Written Fee Schedule: No
Min Charge for Deps: Yes **Hours:** 1
Min Charge for Trial: Yes **Hours:** 1
Cancellation Charge for Deps/Trial: Yes

Retainer Required: Yes, $1,700 (Non-Refundable, Replenishable)
Procedure When Dep Exceeds Paid Time: Proceed without immediate payment
Expenses Marked Up: No
Expenses Billed For: Mileage, Airline Tickets, Photocopies, Telephone Calls, Demonstrative Aids
Portal-to-Portal: Yes **1st-class Airfare:** No
Written Retainer Agreement: No
Failure to Pay Bill Last 5 Years; Retaining Counsel: No **Opposing Counsel (Deps):** No

Orthopedics
Court: $600 **Review/Prep:** $600 **Deps:** $600
Years Testifying: 3 **Majority:** Defendant
Written Fee Schedule: Yes
Min Charge for Deps: Yes **Hours:** 4
Min Charge for Trial: Yes **Hours:** 4
Cancellation Charge for Deps/Trial: Yes
Retainer Required: Yes, $1,200 (Refundable, One Time)
Procedure When Dep Exceeds Paid Time: Proceed without immediate payment
Expenses Marked Up: No
Expenses Billed For: Mileage, Airline Tickets
Portal-to-Portal: No **1st-class Airfare:** No
Written Retainer Agreement: Yes
Terms: Lawyer is responsible for fee, not lawyer's client, Interest for delinquent accounts, Out-of-pocket expense policies, In-court testimony minimums, Retaining counsel pays all deposition charges, Fee schedules, Attorney's fees if forced to sue for collection, Deposition minimum fee, Payment for preparation time
Failure to Pay Bill Last 5 Years; Retaining Counsel: Yes **Opposing (Deps):** Yes

Orthopedics
Court: $850 **Review/Prep:** $400 **Deps:** $600
Years Testifying: 20 **Majority:** Defendant
Written Fee Schedule: Yes
Min Charge for Deps: Yes **Hours:** 1
Min Charge for Trial: Yes **Hours:** 1
Cancellation Charge for Deps/Trial: Yes
Retainer Required: No
Expenses Marked Up: No
Expenses Billed For: Mileage, Airline Tickets, Photocopies, Telephone Calls
Portal-to-Portal: Yes **1st-class Airfare:** No
Written Retainer Agreement: No
Failure to Pay Bill Last 5 Years; Retaining Counsel: No **Opposing Counsel (Deps):** No

Pediatrics
Court: $650 **Review/Prep:** $395 **Deps:** $650
Years Testifying: 8
Written Fee Schedule: Yes
Min Charge for Deps: Yes **Hours:** 10
Min Charge for Trial: Yes **Hours:** 10
Cancellation Charge for Deps/Trial: Yes
Retainer Required: Yes, $1,500 (Non-Refundable, One Time)
Procedure When Dep Exceeds Paid Time: Proceed without immediate payment
Expenses Billed For: Mileage, Airline Tickets, Photocopies, Telephone Calls
Portal-to-Portal: Yes **1st-class Airfare:** No
Written Retainer Agreement: No
Failure to Pay Bill Last 5 Years; Retaining Counsel: Yes **Opposing (Deps):** Yes

Physical Therapy
Court: $275 **Review/Prep:** $225 **Deps:** $275
Years Testifying: 10
Written Fee Schedule: Yes
Min Charge for Deps: Yes **Hours:** 2
Min Charge for Trial: Yes **Hours:** 2
Cancellation Charge for Deps/Trial: Yes
Retainer Required: Yes, $525 (Non-Refundable, One Time)
Expenses Marked Up: No
Expenses Billed For: Mileage, Airline Tickets
Portal-to-Portal: Yes **1st-class Airfare:** No
Written Retainer Agreement: No
Failure to Pay Bill Last 5 Years; Retaining Counsel: Yes **Opposing (Deps):** Yes

Psychology
Court: $175 **Review/Prep:** $125 **Deps:** $175
Years Testifying: 20
Written Fee Schedule: No
Min Charge for Deps: Yes **Hours:** 4
Min Charge for Trial: Yes **Hours:** 4
Cancellation Charge for Deps/Trial: Yes
Retainer Required: Yes, $500 (Refundable, One Time)
Expenses Marked Up: No
Expenses Billed For: Mileage, Airline Tickets, Photocopies, Telephone Calls
Portal-to-Portal: Yes **1st-class Airfare:** No
Written Retainer Agreement: Yes
Terms: Lawyer is responsible for fee, not lawyer's client, Out-of-pocket expense policies, In-court testimony minimums, Retaining counsel pays all deposition charges, Portal-to-portal travel time, Attorney's fees if forced to sue for collection, Deposition minimum fee, Payment for preparation time
Failure to Pay Bill Last 5 Years; Retaining Counsel: Yes **Opposing Counsel (Deps):** No

Pulmonology
Court: $600 **Review/Prep:** $500 **Deps:** $500
Years Testifying: 20 **Majority:** Defendant
Written Fee Schedule: No
Min Charge for Deps: No
Min Charge for Trial: No
Cancellation Charge for Deps/Trial: Yes
Retainer Required: No
Expenses Marked Up: No
Portal-to-Portal: Yes **1st-class Airfare:** No
Written Retainer Agreement: No
Failure to Pay Bill Last 5 Years; Retaining Counsel: No **Opposing Counsel (Deps):** No

Railroads
Court: $125 **Review/Prep:** $125 **Deps:** $125
Years Testifying: 15 **Majority:** Plaintiff
Written Fee Schedule: No
Min Charge for Deps: Yes
Min Charge for Trial: No
Cancellation Charge for Deps/Trial: No
Retainer Required: Yes, $650 (Non-Refundable, One Time)
Procedure When Dep Exceeds Paid Time: Proceed without immediate payment
Expenses Billed For: Mileage, Airline Tickets, Photocopies, Telephone Calls
Portal-to-Portal: Yes **1st-class Airfare:** No
Written Retainer Agreement: No
Failure to Pay Bill Last 5 Years; Retaining Counsel: No **Opposing Counsel (Deps):** No

Real Estate/Environmental
Court: $500 **Review/Prep:** $350 **Deps:** $500
Years Testifying: 5 **Majority:** Plaintiff
Written Fee Schedule: Yes
Min Charge for Deps: Yes **Hours:** 8
Min Charge for Trial: Yes **Hours:** 8
Cancellation Charge for Deps/Trial: No
Retainer Required: Yes, $4,000 (Non-Refundable, One Time)
Expenses Marked Up: No
Expenses Billed For: Mileage, Airline Tickets, Photocopies, Telephone Calls
Portal-to-Portal: Yes **1st-class Airfare:** No
Written Retainer Agreement: Yes
Terms: Out-of-pocket expense policies, In-court testimony minimums, Retaining counsel pays all deposition charges, Fee schedules, Deposition minimum fee, Payment for preparation time
Failure to Pay Bill Last 5 Years; Retaining Counsel: Yes **Opposing Counsel (Deps):** No

Safety, Pipeline
Court: $200 **Review/Prep:** $175 **Deps:** $200
Years Testifying: 25 **Majority:** Defendant
Written Fee Schedule: No
Min Charge for Deps: No
Min Charge for Trial: No
Cancellation Charge for Deps/Trial: No
Retainer Required: Yes, $5,000 (Refundable, One Time)
Expenses Marked Up: No
Expenses Billed For: Mileage, Airline Tickets, Photocopies, Lab/Testing, Photographs, Demonstrative Aids
Portal-to-Portal: Yes **1st-class Airfare:** No

Written Retainer Agreement: Yes
Failure to Pay Bill Last 5 Years; Retaining Counsel: Yes **Opposing Counsel (Deps):** No

Security
Court: $250 **Review/Prep:** $250 **Deps:** $250
Years Testifying: 10
Written Fee Schedule: Yes
Min Charge for Deps: Yes **Hours:** 8
Min Charge for Trial: Yes **Hours:** 8
Cancellation Charge for Deps/Trial: No
Retainer Required: Yes, $2,500 (Non-Refundable, Replenishable)
Procedure When Dep Exceeds Paid Time: Retaining Counsel
Expenses Marked Up: No
Expenses Billed For: Mileage, Airline Tickets, Photocopies, Telephone Calls
Portal-to-Portal: Yes **1st-class Airfare:** No
Written Retainer Agreement: Yes
Terms: Lawyer is responsible for fee, not lawyer's client, Out-of-pocket expense policies, Retaining counsel pays all deposition charges, Deposition minimum fee, Payment for preparation time
Failure to Pay Bill Last 5 Years; Retaining Counsel: Yes **Opposing (Deps):** Yes

Surgery, Colon & Rectal
Court: $750 **Review/Prep:** $300 **Deps:** $500
Years Testifying: 15 **Majority:** Defendant
Written Fee Schedule: Yes
Min Charge for Deps: Yes **Hours:** 4
Min Charge for Trial: Yes **Hours:** 4
Cancellation Charge for Deps/Trial: Yes
Retainer Required: No
Expenses Marked Up: No
Expenses Billed For: Mileage, Airline Tickets, Photocopies, Telephone Calls, Photographs
Portal-to-Portal: Yes **1st-class Airfare:** No
Written Retainer Agreement: No
Failure to Pay Bill Last 5 Years; Retaining Counsel: No **Opposing Counsel (Deps):** No

Surgery, Neurological
Court: $600 **Review/Prep:** $400 **Deps:** $400
Years Testifying: 20 **Majority:** Defendant
Written Fee Schedule: Yes
Min Charge for Deps: No **Hours:** 5
Min Charge for Trial: Yes **Hours:** 5
Cancellation Charge for Deps/Trial: Yes
Retainer Required: Yes, $1,000 (Refundable, One Time)
Expenses Marked Up: No
Expenses Billed For: Mileage, Airline Tickets
Portal-to-Portal: Yes **1st-class Airfare:** Yes
Written Retainer Agreement: Yes
Terms: Lawyer is responsible for fee, not lawyer's client, Out-of-pocket expense policies, In-court testimony minimums, Retaining counsel pays all deposition charges, Fee schedules, Portal-to-portal travel time, Attorney's fees if forced to sue for collection, Deposition minimum fee, Payment for preparation time, First class air travel
Failure to Pay Bill Last 5 Years; Retaining Counsel: No **Opposing Counsel (Deps):** No

Surgery, Plastic
Court: $1,062 **Review/Prep:** $1,000 **Deps:** $1,000
Years Testifying: 10 **Majority:** Defendant
Written Fee Schedule: Yes
Min Charge for Deps: Yes **Hours:** 1
Min Charge for Trial: Yes **Hours:** 1
Cancellation Charge for Deps/Trial: Yes
Retainer Required: Yes, $1,000 (Non-Refundable, One Time)
Procedure When Dep Exceeds Paid Time: Proceed without immediate payment
Expenses Marked Up: No
Expenses Billed For: Mileage, Airline Tickets, Photographs
Portal-to-Portal: Yes **1st-class Airfare:** No
Written Retainer Agreement: No
Failure to Pay Bill Last 5 Years; Retaining Counsel: No **Opposing Counsel (Deps):** No

Traffic/Accident Reconstruction, Collisions
Court: $100 **Review/Prep:** $75 **Deps:** $100
Years Testifying: 12 **Majority:** Defendant
Written Fee Schedule: Yes
Min Charge for Deps: No
Min Charge for Trial: No
Cancellation Charge for Deps/Trial: Yes
Retainer Required: No
Expenses Marked Up: No
Expenses Billed For: Mileage, Photocopies, Telephone Calls, Lab/Testing, Photographs
Portal-to-Portal: Yes
Written Retainer Agreement: Yes
Terms: Lawyer is responsible for fee, not lawyer's client, Interest for delinquent accounts, Out-of-pocket expense policies, In-court testimony minimums, Portal-to-portal travel time, Payment for preparation time
Failure to Pay Bill Last 5 Years; Retaining Counsel: No **Opposing Counsel (Deps):** No

Valuation, Business/Damages, Economic
Court: $400 **Review/Prep:** $125 **Deps:** $250
Years Testifying: 6
Written Fee Schedule: No
Min Charge for Deps: Yes **Hours:** 4
Min Charge for Trial: Yes **Hours:** 4
Cancellation Charge for Deps/Trial: Yes
Retainer Required: Yes, (Non-Refundable, Replenishable)
Procedure When Dep Exceeds Paid Time: Varies depending on case
Expenses Marked Up: No
Expenses Billed For: Mileage, Airline Tickets, Photocopies, Telephone Calls, Lab/Testing, Photographs, Demonstrative Aids
Portal-to-Portal: No **1st-class Airfare:** Yes
Written Retainer Agreement: No
Failure to Pay Bill Last 5 Years; Retaining Counsel: No **Opposing Counsel (Deps):** No

Vocational Rehabilitation
Court: $200 **Review/Prep:** $150 **Deps:** $200
Years Testifying: 25
Written Fee Schedule: Yes
Min Charge for Deps: Yes
Min Charge for Trial: No
Cancellation Charge for Deps/Trial: No
Retainer Required: Yes, $1,000 (Refundable, One Time)
Procedure When Dep Exceeds Paid Time: Proceed without immediate payment
Expenses Marked Up: No
Expenses Billed For: Mileage, Airline Tickets, Photocopies, Telephone Calls
Portal-to-Portal: Yes **1st-class Airfare:** No
Written Retainer Agreement: Yes
Terms: Lawyer is responsible for fee, not lawyer's client, Out-of-pocket expense policies, In-court testimony minimums, Retaining counsel pays all deposition charges, Fee schedules, Portal-to-portal travel time, Deposition minimum fee, Payment for preparation time
Failure to Pay Bill Last 5 Years; Retaining Counsel: Yes **Opposing Counsel (Deps):** No

Vocational Rehabilitation
Court: $150 **Review/Prep:** $150 **Deps:** $125
Years Testifying: 21
Written Fee Schedule: No
Min Charge for Deps: Yes **Hours:** 2
Min Charge for Trial: Yes **Hours:** 2
Cancellation Charge for Deps/Trial: Yes
Retainer Required: Yes, $250 (Non-Refundable, Replenishable)
Expenses Marked Up: No
Expenses Billed For: Mileage, Airline Tickets, Telephone Calls
Portal-to-Portal: Yes **1st-class Airfare:** No
Written Retainer Agreement: No
Failure to Pay Bill Last 5 Years; Retaining Counsel: No **Opposing Counsel (Deps):** No

Vocational Rehabilitation
Court: $250 **Review/Prep:** $150 **Deps:** $250
Years Testifying: 12
Written Fee Schedule: Yes
Min Charge for Deps: Yes **Hours:** 2
Min Charge for Trial: Yes **Hours:** 2

Cancellation Charge for Deps/Trial: Yes
Retainer Required: No
Expenses Marked Up: No
Expenses Billed For: Mileage, Airline Tickets, Demonstrative Aids
Portal-to-Portal: Yes **1st-class Airfare:** No
Written Retainer Agreement: No
Failure to Pay Bill Last 5 Years; Retaining Counsel: No **Opposing Counsel (Deps):** No

Oklahoma

Appraisal, Real Estate
Court: $100 **Review/Prep:** $65 **Deps:** $100
Years Testifying: 20 **Majority:** Defendant
Written Fee Schedule: No
Min Charge for Deps: No
Min Charge for Trial: No
Cancellation Charge for Deps/Trial: No
Retainer Required: No
Expenses Marked Up: No
Expenses Billed For: Mileage, Airline Tickets, Photocopies, Photographs, Demonstrative Aids
1st-class Airfare: No
Written Retainer Agreement: No
Failure to Pay Bill Last 5 Years; Retaining Counsel: No **Opposing Counsel (Deps):** No

Engineering/Accident Reconstruction
Court: $150 **Review/Prep:** $150 **Deps:** $150
Years Testifying: 5
Written Fee Schedule: Yes
Min Charge for Deps: No
Min Charge for Trial: No
Cancellation Charge for Deps/Trial: No
Retainer Required: No
Expenses Marked Up: No
Expenses Billed For: Mileage, Airline Tickets, Lab/Testing, Photographs
Portal-to-Portal: Yes **1st-class Airfare:** No
Written Retainer Agreement: No
Failure to Pay Bill Last 5 Years; Retaining Counsel: No **Opposing Counsel (Deps):** No

Engineering, Structural
Court: $150 **Review/Prep:** $150 **Deps:** $150
Years Testifying: 23
Written Fee Schedule: Yes
Min Charge for Deps: No
Min Charge for Trial: No
Cancellation Charge for Deps/Trial: No
Retainer Required: Depends
Expenses Marked Up: Yes
Expenses Billed For: Mileage, Airline Tickets, Photocopies, Telephone Calls, Lab/Testing, Photographs, Demonstrative Aids
Portal-to-Portal: Yes **1st-class Airfare:** No
Written Retainer Agreement: Yes
Terms: Lawyer is responsible for fee, not lawyer's client, Interest for delinquent accounts, Out-of-pocket expense policies, Retaining counsel pays all deposition charges, Fee schedules, Attorney's fees if forced to sue for collection
Failure to Pay Bill Last 5 Years; Retaining Counsel: Yes **Opposing (Deps):** Yes

Family Practice
Court: $750 **Review/Prep:** $350 **Deps:** $500
Years Testifying: 2
Written Fee Schedule: Yes
Min Charge for Deps: No **Hours:** 4
Min Charge for Trial: Yes **Hours:** 4
Cancellation Charge for Deps/Trial: Yes
Retainer Required: No
Procedure When Dep Exceeds Paid Time: Proceed without immediate payment
Expenses Marked Up: No
Expenses Billed For: Mileage, Airline Tickets, Photocopies, Telephone Calls, Lab/Testing, Photographs, Demonstrative Aids
Portal-to-Portal: Yes **1st-class Airfare:** No
Written Retainer Agreement: No
Failure to Pay Bill Last 5 Years; Retaining Counsel: No **Opposing Counsel (Deps):** Yes

Fire Investigation
Court: $125 **Review/Prep:** $125 **Deps:** $125
Years Testifying: 25 **Majority:** Defendant
Written Fee Schedule: Yes
Min Charge for Deps: No
Min Charge for Trial: No
Cancellation Charge for Deps/Trial: No
Retainer Required: No
Expenses Marked Up: No
Expenses Billed For: Mileage, Airline Tickets, Photocopies, Telephone Calls, Photographs, Demonstrative Aids
Portal-to-Portal: Yes **1st-class Airfare:** No
Written Retainer Agreement: No
Failure to Pay Bill Last 5 Years; Retaining Counsel: Yes **Opposing Counsel (Deps):** No

Law Enforcement/Security
Court: $250 **Review/Prep:** $200 **Deps:** $250
Years Testifying: 10
Written Fee Schedule: Yes
Min Charge for Deps: Yes **Hours:** 4
Min Charge for Trial: Yes **Hours:** 4
Cancellation Charge for Deps/Trial: Yes
Retainer Required: Yes, $2,000 (Non-Refundable, Replenishable)
Procedure When Dep Exceeds Paid Time: Get payment before proceeding further
Expenses Marked Up: Yes
Expenses Billed For: Mileage, Airline Tickets, Photocopies, Lab/Testing, Photographs, Demonstrative Aids
Portal-to-Portal: Yes **1st-class Airfare:** Yes
Written Retainer Agreement: Yes
Terms: Lawyer is responsible for fee, not lawyer's client, Interest for delinquent accounts, Out-of-pocket expense policies, In-court testimony minimums, Retaining counsel pays all deposition charges, Fee schedules, Portal-to-portal travel time, Attorney's fees if forced to sue for collection, Deposition minimum fee, Payment for preparation time, First class air travel
Failure to Pay Bill Last 5 Years; Retaining Counsel: Yes **Opposing Counsel (Deps):** No

Toxicology
Court: $250 **Review/Prep:** $300 **Deps:** $300
Years Testifying: 50
Written Fee Schedule: Yes
Min Charge for Deps: Yes **Hours:** 8
Min Charge for Trial: Yes **Hours:** 8
Cancellation Charge for Deps/Trial: Yes
Retainer Required: Yes, $6,000 (Refundable, Replenishable)
Procedure When Dep Exceeds Paid Time: Proceed without immediate payment
Expenses Marked Up: No
Expenses Billed For: Mileage, Airline Tickets, Telephone Calls, Lab/Testing, Photographs, Demonstrative Aids
Portal-to-Portal: No **1st-class Airfare:** Yes
Written Retainer Agreement: Yes
Terms: Lawyer is responsible for fee, not lawyer's client, Interest for delinquent accounts, Out-of-pocket expense policies, In-court testimony minimums, Retaining counsel pays all deposition charges, Fee schedules, Attorney's fees if forced to sue for collection, Deposition minimum fee, Payment for preparation time, First class air travel
Failure to Pay Bill Last 5 Years; Retaining Counsel: No **Opposing Counsel (Deps):** No

Oregon

Accident Reconstruction/Failure Analysis
Court: $250 **Review/Prep:** $250 **Deps:** $250
Years Testifying: 25
Written Fee Schedule: Yes
Min Charge for Deps: No
Min Charge for Trial: No
Cancellation Charge for Deps/Trial: No
Retainer Required: New Client
Expenses Marked Up: No
Expenses Billed For: Mileage, Airline Tickets, Photocopies, Telephone Calls, Lab/Testing, Photographs, Demonstrative Aids
Portal-to-Portal: Yes **1st-class Airfare:** No
Written Retainer Agreement: Yes

Failure to Pay Bill Last 5 Years; Retaining Counsel: Yes **Opposing Counsel (Deps):** No

Accounting
Court: $260 **Review/Prep:** $260 **Deps:** $260
Years Testifying: 20
Written Fee Schedule: Yes
Min Charge for Deps: No
Min Charge for Trial: No
Cancellation Charge for Deps/Trial: No
Retainer Required: Yes, $7,500 (Refundable, One Time)
Expenses Marked Up: No
Expenses Billed For: Mileage, Airline Tickets, Photocopies, Telephone Calls, Lab/Testing, Photographs, Demonstrative Aids
Portal-to-Portal: Yes **1st-class Airfare:** No
Written Retainer Agreement: Yes
Terms: Lawyer is responsible for fee, not lawyer's client, Interest for delinquent accounts, Out-of-pocket expense policies, Retaining counsel pays all deposition charges, Fee schedules, Attorney's fees if forced to sue for collection, Payment for preparation time
Failure to Pay Bill Last 5 Years; Retaining Counsel: No **Opposing Counsel (Deps):** No

Document Examiner
Court: $100 **Review/Prep:** $150 **Deps:** $100
Years Testifying: 12
Written Fee Schedule: Yes
Min Charge for Deps: No
Min Charge for Trial: No
Cancellation Charge for Deps/Trial: Yes
Retainer Required: Yes, $500 (Non-Refundable, Replenishable)
Procedure When Dep Exceeds Paid Time: Proceed without immediate payment
Expenses Marked Up: No
Expenses Billed For: Mileage, Airline Tickets, Demonstrative Aids
Portal-to-Portal: Yes **1st-class Airfare:** No
Written Retainer Agreement: No
Failure to Pay Bill Last 5 Years; Retaining Counsel: No **Opposing Counsel (Deps):** No

Emergency Medicine
Court: $250 **Review/Prep:** $250 **Deps:** $200
Majority: Defendant
Written Fee Schedule: Yes
Min Charge for Deps: Yes **Hours:** 8
Min Charge for Trial: Yes **Hours:** 8
Cancellation Charge for Deps/Trial: No
Retainer Required: No
Expenses Marked Up: No
Expenses Billed For: Airline Tickets
Portal-to-Portal: No **1st-class Airfare:** No
Written Retainer Agreement: No
Failure to Pay Bill Last 5 Years; Retaining Counsel: No **Opposing Counsel (Deps):** No

Engineering, Civil/Engineering, Mechanical
Court: $315 **Review/Prep:** $250 **Deps:** $315
Years Testifying: 40
Written Fee Schedule: Yes
Min Charge for Deps: No
Min Charge for Trial: No
Cancellation Charge for Deps/Trial: No
Retainer Required: Yes, 25% est. fee (Refundable, One Time)
Expenses Marked Up: Yes
Expenses Billed For: Mileage, Airline Tickets, Photocopies, Lab/Testing, Photographs, Demonstrative Aids
Portal-to-Portal: Yes **1st-class Airfare:** No
Written Retainer Agreement: Yes
Terms: Lawyer is responsible for fee, not lawyer's client, Interest for delinquent accounts, Out-of-pocket expense policies, Retaining counsel pays all deposition charges, Fee schedules, Portal-to-portal travel time, Attorney's fees if forced to sue for collection, Payment for preparation time
Failure to Pay Bill Last 5 Years; Retaining Counsel: Yes **Opposing Counsel (Deps):** No

Fire Investigation
Court: $175 **Review/Prep:** $100 **Deps:** $175
Years Testifying: 24
Written Fee Schedule: Yes
Min Charge for Deps: Yes **Hours:** 4
Min Charge for Trial: Yes **Hours:** 4
Cancellation Charge for Deps/Trial: No
Retainer Required: Depends, Depends on case
Expenses Marked Up: No
Expenses Billed For: Mileage, Airline Tickets, Photocopies, Telephone Calls, Lab/Testing, Photographs, Demonstrative Aids
Portal-to-Portal: Yes **1st-class Airfare:** No
Written Retainer Agreement: No
Failure to Pay Bill Last 5 Years; Retaining Counsel: Yes **Opposing Counsel (Deps):** No

Forensics
Court: $350 **Review/Prep:** $350 **Deps:** $350
Years Testifying: 40 **Majority:** Plaintiff
Written Fee Schedule: Yes
Min Charge for Deps: No
Min Charge for Trial: No
Cancellation Charge for Deps/Trial: No
Retainer Required: Yes, $4,250 (Refundable, Replenishable)
Expenses Marked Up: No
Expenses Billed For: Mileage, Airline Tickets, Photocopies, Lab/Testing, Photographs, Demonstrative Aids
Portal-to-Portal: Yes **1st-class Airfare:** No
Written Retainer Agreement: No
Failure to Pay Bill Last 5 Years; Retaining Counsel: No **Opposing Counsel (Deps):** No

Occupational Medicine
Court: $500 **Review/Prep:** $100 **Deps:** $500
Years Testifying: 24
Written Fee Schedule: Yes
Min Charge for Deps: No
Min Charge for Trial: No
Cancellation Charge for Deps/Trial: Yes
Retainer Required: Yes, $500 (Refundable, One Time)
Procedure When Dep Exceeds Paid Time: Proceed without immediate payment
Expenses Marked Up: No
Portal-to-Portal: Yes **1st-class Airfare:** No
Written Retainer Agreement: No
Failure to Pay Bill Last 5 Years; Retaining Counsel: No **Opposing Counsel (Deps):** No

Orthopedics
Court: $250 **Review/Prep:** $250 **Deps:** $250
Years Testifying: 11
Written Fee Schedule: No
Min Charge for Deps: Yes **Hours:** 8
Min Charge for Trial: Yes **Hours:** 8
Cancellation Charge for Deps/Trial: Yes
Retainer Required: No
Expenses Marked Up: No
Expenses Billed For: Airline Tickets
Portal-to-Portal: No **1st-class Airfare:** No
Written Retainer Agreement: No
Failure to Pay Bill Last 5 Years; Retaining Counsel: Yes **Opposing Counsel (Deps):** No

Pathology
Court: $300 **Review/Prep:** $300 **Deps:** $300
Years Testifying: 31
Written Fee Schedule: Yes
Min Charge for Deps: Yes **Hours:** 4
Min Charge for Trial: Yes **Hours:** 4
Cancellation Charge for Deps/Trial: Yes
Retainer Required: Yes, Depends on case (Non-Refundable)
Procedure When Dep Exceeds Paid Time: Proceed without immediate payment
Expenses Marked Up: No
Expenses Billed For: Lab/Testing, Demonstrative Aids
Portal-to-Portal: Yes **1st-class Airfare:** No
Written Retainer Agreement: No
Failure to Pay Bill Last 5 Years; Retaining Counsel: No **Opposing Counsel (Deps):** No

Surgery, General
Court: $500 **Review/Prep:** $500 **Deps:** $500
Years Testifying: 3 **Majority:** Defendant
Written Fee Schedule: Yes
Min Charge for Deps: Yes **Hours:** 4
Min Charge for Trial: Yes **Hours:** 4
Cancellation Charge for Deps/Trial: Yes

Retainer Required: No
Expenses Marked Up: No
Expenses Billed For: Mileage, Airline Tickets, Photocopies, Telephone Calls, Lab/Testing, Photographs, Demonstrative Aids
Portal-to-Portal: Yes **1st-class Airfare:** No
Written Retainer Agreement: No
Failure to Pay Bill Last 5 Years; Retaining Counsel: No **Opposing Counsel (Deps):** No

Pennsylvania

Accident Reconstruction
Court: $125 **Review/Prep:** $125 **Deps:** $125
Years Testifying: 32 **Majority:** Plaintiff
Min Charge for Deps: Yes **Hours:** 2
Min Charge for Trial: Yes **Hours:** 2
Cancellation Charge for Deps/Trial: No
Retainer Required: Yes, $1,000 (Refundable)
Expenses Marked Up: No
Expenses Billed For: Mileage, Airline Tickets, Lab/Testing, Photographs, Demonstrative Aids
Portal-to-Portal: Yes **1st-class Airfare:** No
Written Retainer Agreement: Yes
Terms: Lawyer is responsible for fee, not lawyer's client, Out-of-pocket expense policies, In-court testimony minimums, Retaining counsel pays all deposition charges, Fee schedules, Portal-to-portal travel time, Deposition minimum fee
Failure to Pay Bill Last 5 Years; Retaining Counsel: Yes **Opposing (Deps):** Yes

Accounting/Damages, Economic
Court: $315 **Review/Prep:** $315 **Deps:** $315
Years Testifying: 25
Written Fee Schedule: Yes
Min Charge for Deps: Yes **Hours:** 4
Min Charge for Trial: Yes **Hours:** 4
Cancellation Charge for Deps/Trial: No
Retainer Required: Yes, Depends on case (Refundable, Replenishable)
Expenses Marked Up: No
Expenses Billed For: Mileage, Airline Tickets
Portal-to-Portal: Yes **1st-class Airfare:** No
Written Retainer Agreement: Yes
Terms: Interest for delinquent accounts, Out-of-pocket expense policies, In-court testimony minimums, Retaining counsel pays all deposition charges, Fee schedules, Attorney's fees if forced to sue for collection, Payment for preparation time
Failure to Pay Bill Last 5 Years; Retaining Counsel: No **Opposing Counsel (Deps):** No

Accounting
Court: $210 **Review/Prep:** $210 **Deps:** $210
Years Testifying: 9 **Majority:** Plaintiff
Written Fee Schedule: Yes
Min Charge for Deps: No
Min Charge for Trial: No
Cancellation Charge for Deps/Trial: No
Retainer Required: Yes, $1,500 (Non-Refundable, Replenishable)
Expenses Marked Up: No
Expenses Billed For: Mileage, Airline Tickets, Telephone Calls
Portal-to-Portal: Yes **1st-class Airfare:** No
Written Retainer Agreement: Yes
Terms: Out-of-pocket expense policies, In-court testimony minimums, Retaining counsel pays all deposition charges, Fee schedules, Portal-to-portal travel time, Payment for preparation time
Failure to Pay Bill Last 5 Years; Retaining Counsel: No **Opposing Counsel (Deps):** No

Anesthesiology/Pain Management/ Medicine
Court: $750 **Review/Prep:** $275 **Deps:** $500
Years Testifying: 5 **Majority:** Plaintiff
Written Fee Schedule: Yes
Min Charge for Deps: Yes **Hours:** 4
Min Charge for Trial: Yes **Hours:** 4
Cancellation Charge for Deps/Trial: No
Retainer Required: Yes, $1,100 (Refundable, Replenishable)
Procedure When Dep Exceeds Paid Time: Get payment before proceeding further
Expenses Marked Up: No
Expenses Billed For: Mileage, Airline Tickets
Portal-to-Portal: Yes **1st-class Airfare:** No
Written Retainer Agreement: No
Failure to Pay Bill Last 5 Years; Retaining Counsel: Yes **Opposing Counsel (Deps):** No

Arborist
Court: $110 **Deps:** $350
Years Testifying: 10
Written Fee Schedule: No
Min Charge for Deps: Yes **Hours:** 2
Min Charge for Trial: Yes **Hours:** 2
Cancellation Charge for Deps/Trial: Yes
Retainer Required: Yes, $650 (Non-Refundable, One Time)
Procedure When Dep Exceeds Paid Time: Proceed without immediate payment
Expenses Marked Up: Yes
Expenses Billed For: Mileage, Airline Tickets, Lab/Testing, Photographs, Demonstrative Aids
Portal-to-Portal: Yes **1st-class Airfare:** No
Written Retainer Agreement: Yes
Terms: Lawyer is responsible for fee, not lawyer's client, Out-of-pocket expense policies, In-court testimony minimums, Retaining counsel pays all deposition charges, Fee schedules, Portal-to-portal travel time, Deposition minimum fee, Payment for preparation time, Fees, specific to assignment
Failure to Pay Bill Last 5 Years; Retaining Counsel: No **Opposing Counsel (Deps):** No

Chemicals, Environmental
Court: $450 **Review/Prep:** $225 **Deps:** $225
Years Testifying: 20
Written Fee Schedule: Yes
Min Charge for Deps: No
Min Charge for Trial: No
Cancellation Charge for Deps/Trial: No
Retainer Required: No
Expenses Marked Up: No
Expenses Billed For: Mileage, Airline Tickets, Photocopies, Telephone Calls, Lab/Testing, Photographs, Demonstrative Aids
Portal-to-Portal: No **1st-class Airfare:** No
Written Retainer Agreement: Yes
Terms: Interest for delinquent accounts, Out-of-pocket expense policies, Fee schedules, Payment for preparation time
Failure to Pay Bill Last 5 Years; Retaining Counsel: Yes **Opposing (Deps):** Yes

Child Custody
Court: $250 **Review/Prep:** $250 **Deps:** $250
Years Testifying: 10
Written Fee Schedule: Yes
Min Charge for Deps: Yes **Hours:** 4
Min Charge for Trial: Yes **Hours:** 4
Cancellation Charge for Deps/Trial: Yes
Retainer Required: Yes, $5,000 (Refundable, Replenishable)
Procedure When Dep Exceeds Paid Time: Proceed without immediate payment
Expenses Marked Up: No
Expenses Billed For: Mileage, Airline Tickets, Photocopies, Telephone Calls
Portal-to-Portal: Yes **1st-class Airfare:** No
Written Retainer Agreement: Yes
Terms: Out-of-pocket expense policies, In-court testimony minimums, Retaining counsel pays all deposition charges, Fee schedules, Deposition minimum fee, Payment for preparation time
Failure to Pay Bill Last 5 Years; Retaining Counsel: Yes **Opposing (Deps):** Yes

Construction/Premises Liability
Court: $350 **Review/Prep:** $250 **Deps:** $350
Years Testifying: 18 **Majority:** Plaintiff
Written Fee Schedule: Yes
Min Charge for Deps: Yes **Hours:** 4
Min Charge for Trial: Yes **Hours:** 4

Cancellation Charge for Deps/Trial: No
Retainer Required: Yes, $2,000 (Non-Refundable, One Time)
Expenses Marked Up: No
Expenses Billed For: Airline Tickets, Demonstrative Aids
Portal-to-Portal: Yes **1st-class Airfare:** No
Written Retainer Agreement: Yes
Terms: Lawyer is responsible for fee, not lawyer's client, Interest for delinquent accounts, Out-of-pocket expense policies, In-court testimony minimums, Retaining counsel pays all deposition charges, Fee schedules, Portal-to-portal travel time, Deposition minimum fee, Payment for preparation time
Failure to Pay Bill Last 5 Years; Retaining Counsel: Yes **Opposing (Deps):** Yes

Construction
Court: $550 **Review/Prep:** $335 **Deps:** $550
Years Testifying: 15
Written Fee Schedule: Yes
Min Charge for Deps: Yes **Hours:** 4
Min Charge for Trial: Yes **Hours:** 4
Cancellation Charge for Deps/Trial: No
Retainer Required: Yes, Depends on case (Refundable, One Time)
Expenses Marked Up: No
Expenses Billed For: Mileage, Airline Tickets, Photocopies, Telephone Calls, Lab/Testing, Photographs, Demonstrative Aids
Portal-to-Portal: No **1st-class Airfare:** No
Written Retainer Agreement: Yes
Terms: Interest for delinquent accounts, Out-of-pocket expense policies, In-court testimony minimums, Retaining counsel pays all deposition charges, Fee schedules, Attorney's fees if forced to sue for collection, Payment for preparation time
Failure to Pay Bill Last 5 Years; Retaining Counsel: No **Opposing Counsel (Deps):** No

Damages, Business
Court: $300 **Review/Prep:** $200 **Deps:** $300
Years Testifying: 27 **Majority:** Plaintiff
Written Fee Schedule: Yes
Min Charge for Deps: Yes **Hours:** 1
Min Charge for Trial: Yes **Hours:** 1
Cancellation Charge for Deps/Trial: Yes
Retainer Required: Yes, $1,000 (Non-Refundable, One Time)
Expenses Marked Up: No
Expenses Billed For: Airline Tickets
Portal-to-Portal: Yes **1st-class Airfare:** No
Written Retainer Agreement: Yes
Terms: Lawyer is responsible for fee, not lawyer's client, Out-of-pocket expense policies, In-court testimony minimums, Retaining counsel pays all deposition charges, Fee schedules, Portal-to-portal travel time, Attorney's fees if forced to sue for collection, Deposition minimum fee, Payment for preparation time
Failure to Pay Bill Last 5 Years; Retaining Counsel: No **Opposing Counsel (Deps):** No

Dentistry
Court: $200 **Review/Prep:** $150 **Deps:** $200
Years Testifying: 10 **Majority:** Plaintiff
Written Fee Schedule: Yes
Min Charge for Deps: Yes **Hours:** 1
Min Charge for Trial: Yes **Hours:** 1
Cancellation Charge for Deps/Trial: Yes
Retainer Required: Yes, $200 (Non-Refundable, One Time)
Expenses Marked Up: No
Expenses Billed For: Mileage, Airline Tickets
Portal-to-Portal: No **1st-class Airfare:** No
Written Retainer Agreement: No
Failure to Pay Bill Last 5 Years; Retaining Counsel: No **Opposing Counsel (Deps):** No

Engineering
Court: $180 **Review/Prep:** $150 **Deps:** $180
Years Testifying: 15
Written Fee Schedule: Yes
Min Charge for Deps: Yes
Min Charge for Trial: No
Cancellation Charge for Deps/Trial: No
Retainer Required: No
Expenses Marked Up: No
Expenses Billed For: Mileage, Airline Tickets, Photographs
Portal-to-Portal: No **1st-class Airfare:** No
Written Retainer Agreement: Yes
Terms: Interest for delinquent accounts, Fee schedules, Portal-to-portal travel time
Failure to Pay Bill Last 5 Years; Retaining Counsel: No **Opposing Counsel (Deps):** No

Engineering
Court: $225 **Review/Prep:** $225 **Deps:** $225
Years Testifying: 30
Written Fee Schedule: Yes
Min Charge for Deps: No
Min Charge for Trial: No
Cancellation Charge for Deps/Trial: No
Retainer Required: No
Expenses Marked Up: No
Expenses Billed For: Mileage, Airline Tickets, Lab/Testing, Photographs, Demonstrative Aids
Portal-to-Portal: Yes **1st-class Airfare:** No
Written Retainer Agreement: No
Failure to Pay Bill Last 5 Years; Retaining Counsel: No **Opposing Counsel (Deps):** No

Engineering/Accident Reconstruction
Court: $125 **Review/Prep:** $125 **Deps:** $125
Years Testifying: 30 **Majority:** Plaintiff
Written Fee Schedule: Yes
Min Charge for Deps: Yes **Hours:** 8
Min Charge for Trial: Yes **Hours:** 8
Cancellation Charge for Deps/Trial: Yes
Retainer Required: Yes, $1,000 (Refundable, One Time)
Procedure When Dep Exceeds Paid Time: Get payment before proceeding further
Expenses Marked Up: No
Expenses Billed For: Mileage, Airline Tickets, Lab/Testing, Demonstrative Aids
Portal-to-Portal: Yes **1st-class Airfare:** No
Written Retainer Agreement: Yes
Terms: Lawyer is responsible for fee, not lawyer's client, Interest for delinquent accounts, In-court testimony minimums, Retaining counsel pays all deposition charges, Fee schedules, Deposition minimum fee, Payment for preparation time, Review time for pertinent documents
Failure to Pay Bill Last 5 Years; Retaining Counsel: Yes **Opposing Counsel (Deps):** No

Engineering, Civil/Engineering, Structural
Court: $225 **Review/Prep:** $150 **Deps:** $225
Written Fee Schedule: No
Min Charge for Deps: Yes **Hours:** 4
Min Charge for Trial: Yes **Hours:** 4
Cancellation Charge for Deps/Trial: No
Retainer Required: No
Expenses Marked Up: No
Expenses Billed For: Mileage, Airline Tickets, Photocopies, Lab/Testing, Photographs, Demonstrative Aids
Portal-to-Portal: Yes **1st-class Airfare:** No
Written Retainer Agreement: Yes
Terms: Interest for delinquent accounts, Out-of-pocket expense policies, Retaining counsel pays all deposition charges, Fee schedules, Portal-to-portal travel time, Attorney's fees if forced to sue for collection, Deposition minimum fee, Payment for preparation time
Failure to Pay Bill Last 5 Years; Retaining Counsel: No **Opposing Counsel (Deps):** Yes

Engineering, Electrical
Court: $140 **Review/Prep:** $140 **Deps:** $140
Years Testifying: 23
Written Fee Schedule: Yes
Min Charge for Deps: Yes **Hours:** 8
Min Charge for Trial: Yes **Hours:** 8
Cancellation Charge for Deps/Trial: No
Retainer Required: Yes, $1,000 (Refundable, One Time)
Procedure When Dep Exceeds Paid Time: Proceed without immediate payment

Expenses Marked Up: No
Expenses Billed For: Mileage, Airline Tickets, Photocopies, Telephone Calls, Lab/Testing, Photographs, Demonstrative Aids
Portal-to-Portal: Yes **1st-class Airfare:** No
Written Retainer Agreement: Yes
Terms: Lawyer is responsible for fee, not lawyer's client, Interest for delinquent accounts, Out-of-pocket expense policies, In-court testimony minimums, Retaining counsel pays all deposition charges, Fee schedules, Deposition minimum fee, Payment for preparation time
Failure to Pay Bill Last 5 Years; Retaining Counsel: Yes **Opposing Counsel (Deps):** No

Engineering, Electrical/ Engineering, Mechanical/Fire
Court: $200 **Review/Prep:** $200 **Deps:** $200
Years Testifying: 20
Written Fee Schedule: Yes
Min Charge for Deps: Yes
Min Charge for Trial: No
Cancellation Charge for Deps/Trial: Yes
Retainer Required: Yes, $2,500 (Refundable, One Time)
Expenses Marked Up: Yes
Expenses Billed For: Mileage, Airline Tickets, Photocopies, Telephone Calls, Lab/Testing, Photographs, Demonstrative Aids
Portal-to-Portal: Yes **1st-class Airfare:** Yes
Written Retainer Agreement: No
Failure to Pay Bill Last 5 Years; Retaining Counsel: Yes **Opposing Counsel (Deps):** No

Engineering, Mechanical/Safety, Machine/Product Liability
Court: $150 **Review/Prep:** $150 **Deps:** $150
Years Testifying: 36 **Majority:** Plaintiff
Written Fee Schedule: Yes
Min Charge for Deps: Yes **Hours:** 4
Min Charge for Trial: Yes **Hours:** 4
Cancellation Charge for Deps/Trial: Yes
Retainer Required: Yes, $600 (Non-Refundable, Replenishable)
Procedure When Dep Exceeds Paid Time: Proceed without immediate payment
Expenses Marked Up: No
Expenses Billed For: Airline Tickets
Portal-to-Portal: Yes **1st-class Airfare:** No
Written Retainer Agreement: No
Failure to Pay Bill Last 5 Years; Retaining Counsel: Yes **Opposing Counsel (Deps):** No

Engineering, Safety
Court: $150 **Review/Prep:** $150 **Deps:** $150
Years Testifying: 28 **Majority:** Plaintiff
Written Fee Schedule: Yes
Min Charge for Deps: Yes **Hours:** 4
Min Charge for Trial: Yes **Hours:** 4
Cancellation Charge for Deps/Trial: No
Retainer Required: Yes, $1,000 (Refundable, One Time)
Expenses Marked Up: No
Expenses Billed For: Mileage, Airline Tickets, Lab/Testing, Demonstrative Aids
Portal-to-Portal: Yes **1st-class Airfare:** No
Written Retainer Agreement: No
Failure to Pay Bill Last 5 Years; Retaining Counsel: No **Opposing Counsel (Deps):** No

Engineering, Structural
Court: $250 **Review/Prep:** $250 **Deps:** $250
Years Testifying: 30 **Majority:** Defendant
Written Fee Schedule: No
Min Charge for Deps: Yes **Hours:** 8
Min Charge for Trial: Yes **Hours:** 8
Cancellation Charge for Deps/Trial: No
Retainer Required: No
Expenses Marked Up: No
Expenses Billed For: Mileage, Airline Tickets, Lab/Testing, Photographs, Demonstrative Aids
Portal-to-Portal: Yes **1st-class Airfare:** No
Written Retainer Agreement: No
Failure to Pay Bill Last 5 Years; Retaining Counsel: Yes **Opposing (Deps):** Yes

Environmental Health
Court: $250 **Review/Prep:** $250 **Deps:** $250
Years Testifying: 3 **Majority:** Defendant
Written Fee Schedule: Yes
Min Charge for Deps: No
Min Charge for Trial: No
Cancellation Charge for Deps/Trial: No
Retainer Required: No
Expenses Marked Up: No
Expenses Billed For: Mileage, Airline Tickets, Photocopies, Lab/Testing, Photographs, Demonstrative Aids
Portal-to-Portal: Yes **1st-class Airfare:** No
Written Retainer Agreement: No

Environmental, Contaminated Soil/Environmental, Groundwater
Court: $170 **Review/Prep:** $170 **Deps:** $170
Years Testifying: 7
Written Fee Schedule: Yes
Min Charge for Deps: No
Min Charge for Trial: No
Cancellation Charge for Deps/Trial: No
Retainer Required: No
Expenses Marked Up: Yes
Expenses Billed For: Mileage, Airline Tickets, Photocopies, Lab/Testing, Photographs, Demonstrative Aids
Portal-to-Portal: Yes **1st-class Airfare:** No
Written Retainer Agreement: No
Failure to Pay Bill Last 5 Years; Retaining Counsel: No **Opposing Counsel (Deps):** No

Family Practice
Court: $350 **Review/Prep:** $200 **Deps:** $350
Years Testifying: 15
Written Fee Schedule: Yes
Min Charge for Deps: Yes **Hours:** 4
Min Charge for Trial: Yes **Hours:** 4
Cancellation Charge for Deps/Trial: Yes
Retainer Required: Yes, $1,000 (Refundable, One Time)
Procedure When Dep Exceeds Paid Time: Proceed without immediate payment
Expenses Marked Up: No
Expenses Billed For: Airline Tickets
Portal-to-Portal: Yes **1st-class Airfare:** No
Written Retainer Agreement: No
Failure to Pay Bill Last 5 Years; Retaining Counsel: Yes **Opposing (Deps):** Yes

Geriatrics
Court: $300 **Review/Prep:** $250 **Deps:** $300
Years Testifying: 4 **Majority:** Plaintiff
Written Fee Schedule: Yes
Min Charge for Deps: Yes **Hours:** 10
Min Charge for Trial: Yes **Hours:** 10
Cancellation Charge for Deps/Trial: Yes
Retainer Required: Yes, $1,000 (Non-Refundable, One Time)
Procedure When Dep Exceeds Paid Time: Get payment before proceeding further
Expenses Marked Up: No
Portal-to-Portal: Yes **1st-class Airfare:** No
Written Retainer Agreement: Yes
Terms: Lawyer is responsible for fee, not lawyer's client, Out-of-pocket expense policies, In-court testimony minimums, Retaining counsel pays all deposition charges, Fee schedules, Portal-to-portal travel time, Deposition minimum fee
Failure to Pay Bill Last 5 Years; Retaining Counsel: No **Opposing Counsel (Deps):** No

Hospitality, Hotels
Court: $350 **Review/Prep:** $300 **Deps:** $350
Years Testifying: 17
Written Fee Schedule: No
Min Charge for Deps: Yes **Hours:** 2
Min Charge for Trial: Yes **Hours:** 2
Cancellation Charge for Deps/Trial: No
Retainer Required: Yes, $4,000 (Partially Refundable, One Time)
Procedure When Dep Exceeds Paid Time: Proceed without immediate payment
Expenses Marked Up: No
Expenses Billed For: Airline Tickets, Photocopies, Telephone Calls, Photographs, Demonstrative Aids
Portal-to-Portal: Yes **1st-class Airfare:** No
Written Retainer Agreement: Yes
Terms: Lawyer is responsible for fee, not lawyer's client, Out-of-pocket expense

policies, In-court testimony minimums, Retaining counsel pays all deposition charges, Fee schedules, Deposition minimum fee
Failure to Pay Bill Last 5 Years; Retaining Counsel: Yes **Opposing Counsel (Deps):** No

Human Factors
Court: $250 **Review/Prep:** $250 **Deps:** $250
Years Testifying: 16 **Majority:** Defendant
Written Fee Schedule: Yes
Min Charge for Deps: No
Min Charge for Trial: No
Cancellation Charge for Deps/Trial: No
Retainer Required: Yes, $2,000 (Refundable, One Time)
Expenses Billed For: Airline Tickets, Photocopies, Demonstrative Aids
Portal-to-Portal: Yes **1st-class Airfare:** No
Written Retainer Agreement: No
Failure to Pay Bill Last 5 Years; Retaining Counsel: Yes **Opposing Counsel (Deps):** No

Insurance
Court: $150 **Review/Prep:** $125 **Deps:** $150
Years Testifying: 4
Written Fee Schedule: Yes
Min Charge for Deps: No
Min Charge for Trial: No
Cancellation Charge for Deps/Trial: No
Retainer Required: Yes, $1,000 (Non-Refundable, One Time)
Expenses Marked Up: No
Expenses Billed For: Mileage, Airline Tickets, Photocopies, Telephone Calls, Photographs
Portal-to-Portal: Yes **1st-class Airfare:** No
Written Retainer Agreement: No
Failure to Pay Bill Last 5 Years; Retaining Counsel: No **Opposing Counsel (Deps):** No

Law, Employment/Employment, Earning Capacity
Court: $180 **Review/Prep:** $180 **Deps:** $180
Years Testifying: 19 **Majority:** Plaintiff
Written Fee Schedule: No
Min Charge for Deps: No
Min Charge for Trial: No
Cancellation Charge for Deps/Trial: No
Retainer Required: No
Expenses Marked Up: No
Expenses Billed For: Demonstrative Aids
Portal-to-Portal: Yes **1st-class Airfare:** No
Written Retainer Agreement: No
Failure to Pay Bill Last 5 Years; Retaining Counsel: No **Opposing Counsel (Deps):** No

Medical Doctor
Court: $600 **Review/Prep:** $250 **Deps:** $750
Years Testifying: 25
Written Fee Schedule: Yes
Min Charge for Deps: Yes **Hours:** 6
Min Charge for Trial: Yes **Hours:** 6
Cancellation Charge for Deps/Trial: Yes
Retainer Required: Yes, $5,000 (Non-Refundable, Replenishable)
Expenses Marked Up: No
Expenses Billed For: Mileage, Airline Tickets, Photocopies, Telephone Calls, Lab/Testing, Photographs, Demonstrative Aids
Portal-to-Portal: Yes **1st-class Airfare:** No
Written Retainer Agreement: Yes
Terms: Lawyer is responsible for fee, not lawyer's client, Out-of-pocket expense policies, In-court testimony minimums, Retaining counsel pays all deposition charges, Fee schedules, Portal-to-portal travel time, Deposition minimum fee, Payment for preparation time
Failure to Pay Bill Last 5 Years; Retaining Counsel: Yes **Opposing (Deps):** Yes

Neurology
Court: $1,250 **Review/Prep:** $600 **Deps:** $625
Years Testifying: 20
Written Fee Schedule: Yes
Min Charge for Deps: Yes **Hours:** 8
Min Charge for Trial: Yes **Hours:** 8
Cancellation Charge for Deps/Trial: Yes
Retainer Required: Yes, Total est. fee (Refundable)
Expenses Marked Up: Yes
Portal-to-Portal: No **1st-class Airfare:** No
Written Retainer Agreement: No
Failure to Pay Bill Last 5 Years; Retaining Counsel: No **Opposing Counsel (Deps):** No

Obstetrics & Gynecology
Court: $300 **Review/Prep:** $300 **Deps:** $300
Years Testifying: 8 **Majority:** Defendant
Written Fee Schedule: Yes
Min Charge for Deps: No **Hours:** 8
Min Charge for Trial: Yes **Hours:** 8
Cancellation Charge for Deps/Trial: No
Retainer Required: No
Expenses Marked Up: No
Expenses Billed For: Mileage, Airline Tickets, Telephone Calls
Portal-to-Portal: Yes **1st-class Airfare:** No
Written Retainer Agreement: No
Failure to Pay Bill Last 5 Years; Retaining Counsel: No **Opposing Counsel (Deps):** No

Obstetrics & Gynecology
Court: $600 **Review/Prep:** $300 **Deps:** $600
Years Testifying: 5 **Majority:** Defendant
Written Fee Schedule: No
Min Charge for Deps: No
Min Charge for Trial: No
Cancellation Charge for Deps/Trial: No
Retainer Required: No
Expenses Marked Up: No
Expenses Billed For: Mileage, Telephone Calls, Photographs, Demonstrative Aids
Portal-to-Portal: Yes
Written Retainer Agreement: No
Failure to Pay Bill Last 5 Years; Retaining Counsel: No **Opposing Counsel (Deps):** No

Ophthalmology
Court: $1,000 **Review/Prep:** $500 **Deps:** $750
Years Testifying: 10 **Majority:** Defendant
Written Fee Schedule: Yes
Min Charge for Deps: Yes **Hours:** 3
Min Charge for Trial: Yes **Hours:** 3
Cancellation Charge for Deps/Trial: Yes
Retainer Required: Yes, (Non-Refundable)
Procedure When Dep Exceeds Paid Time: Get payment before proceeding further
Expenses Marked Up: Yes
Expenses Billed For: Mileage, Airline Tickets, Photocopies, Photographs, Demonstrative Aids
Portal-to-Portal: Yes **1st-class Airfare:** No
Written Retainer Agreement: No
Failure to Pay Bill Last 5 Years; Retaining Counsel: Yes **Opposing (Deps):** Yes

Orthopedics/Disability
Court: $1,450 **Deps:** $1,250
Years Testifying: 30 **Majority:** Plaintiff
Written Fee Schedule: No
Min Charge for Deps: No
Min Charge for Trial: No
Cancellation Charge for Deps/Trial: Yes
Retainer Required: No
Expenses Marked Up: No
Expenses Billed For: Mileage, Airline Tickets
Portal-to-Portal: No **1st-class Airfare:** No
Written Retainer Agreement: No
Failure to Pay Bill Last 5 Years; Retaining Counsel: No **Opposing Counsel (Deps):** No

Orthopedics
Court: $1,000 **Review/Prep:** $500 **Deps:** $1,167
Years Testifying: 18 **Majority:** Defendant
Written Fee Schedule: Yes
Min Charge for Deps: Yes **Hours:** 5
Min Charge for Trial: Yes **Hours:** 5
Cancellation Charge for Deps/Trial: Yes
Retainer Required: Yes, $3,500
Expenses Marked Up: No
Expenses Billed For: Mileage, Airline Tickets
Portal-to-Portal: Yes **1st-class Airfare:** No
Written Retainer Agreement: Yes
Terms: Lawyer is responsible for fee, not lawyer's client, Interest for delinquent accounts, Out-of-pocket expense policies,

In-court testimony minimums, Retaining counsel pays all deposition charges, Fee schedules, Portal-to-portal travel time, Attorney's fees if forced to sue for collection, Deposition minimum fee, Payment for preparation time
Failure to Pay Bill Last 5 Years; Retaining Counsel: No **Opposing Counsel (Deps):** No

Pain Management/Medicine
Court: $2,500 **Review/Prep:** $350 **Deps:** $2,500
Years Testifying: 20 **Majority:** Plaintiff
Written Fee Schedule: Yes
Min Charge for Deps: Yes **Hours:** 1
Min Charge for Trial: Yes **Hours:** 1
Cancellation Charge for Deps/Trial: Yes
Retainer Required: Yes, $2,500 (Refundable)
Procedure When Dep Exceeds Paid Time: Proceed without immediate payment
Expenses Marked Up: No
Expenses Billed For: Mileage, Airline Tickets
Portal-to-Portal: Yes **1st-class Airfare:** No
Written Retainer Agreement: No
Failure to Pay Bill Last 5 Years; Retaining Counsel: No **Opposing Counsel (Deps):** No

Pharmacology/Nursing/Healthcare
Court: $125 **Review/Prep:** $125 **Deps:** $125
Years Testifying: 11 **Majority:** Plaintiff
Written Fee Schedule: Yes
Min Charge for Deps: No
Min Charge for Trial: No
Cancellation Charge for Deps/Trial: No
Retainer Required: Yes, $500 (Refundable, One Time)
Expenses Marked Up: No
Expenses Billed For: Mileage, Airline Tickets, Telephone Calls
Portal-to-Portal: Yes **1st-class Airfare:** No
Written Retainer Agreement: No
Failure to Pay Bill Last 5 Years; Retaining Counsel: Yes **Opposing Counsel (Deps):** No

Physical Medicine & Rehabilitation
Court: $850 **Review/Prep:** $250 **Deps:** $500
Years Testifying: 10
Written Fee Schedule: Yes
Min Charge for Deps: Yes **Hours:** 5
Min Charge for Trial: Yes **Hours:** 5
Cancellation Charge for Deps/Trial: Yes
Retainer Required: No
Expenses Marked Up: No
Expenses Billed For:
Portal-to-Portal: No
Written Retainer Agreement: No
Failure to Pay Bill Last 5 Years; Retaining Counsel: No **Opposing Counsel (Deps):** No

Safety/Environmental
Court: $150 **Review/Prep:** $150 **Deps:** $150
Years Testifying: 6
Written Fee Schedule: Yes
Min Charge for Deps: No **Hours:** 10
Min Charge for Trial: Yes **Hours:** 10
Cancellation Charge for Deps/Trial: Yes
Retainer Required: Yes, $1,500 (Non-Refundable)
Expenses Marked Up: No
Expenses Billed For: Mileage, Airline Tickets, Photographs
Portal-to-Portal: Yes
Written Retainer Agreement: No
Failure to Pay Bill Last 5 Years; Retaining Counsel: No **Opposing Counsel (Deps):** No

Safety, Radiation/Safety, Particle Acceleratory
Court: $200 **Review/Prep:** $150 **Deps:** $200
Years Testifying: 2
Written Fee Schedule: No
Min Charge for Deps: No
Min Charge for Trial: No
Cancellation Charge for Deps/Trial: No
Retainer Required: Yes, $2,000 (Refundable, Replenishable)
Procedure When Dep Exceeds Paid Time: Get payment before proceeding further
Expenses Marked Up: No
Expenses Billed For: Mileage, Airline Tickets, Lab/Testing, Photographs, Demonstrative Aids
Portal-to-Portal: No **1st-class Airfare:** No
Written Retainer Agreement: No
Failure to Pay Bill Last 5 Years; Retaining Counsel: No **Opposing Counsel (Deps):** No

Slip, Trip & Fall
Court: $300 **Review/Prep:** $150 **Deps:** $200
Years Testifying: 30
Written Fee Schedule: Yes
Min Charge for Deps: Yes **Hours:** 2
Min Charge for Trial: Yes **Hours:** 2
Cancellation Charge for Deps/Trial: No
Retainer Required: No
Procedure When Dep Exceeds Paid Time: Proceed without immediate payment
Expenses Marked Up: Yes
Expenses Billed For: Mileage, Lab/Testing, Photographs
Portal-to-Portal: No **1st-class Airfare:** No
Written Retainer Agreement: No
Failure to Pay Bill Last 5 Years; Retaining Counsel: No **Opposing Counsel (Deps):** No

Statistics
Court: $350 **Review/Prep:** $350 **Deps:** $350
Years Testifying: 24
Written Fee Schedule: Yes
Min Charge for Deps: No
Min Charge for Trial: No
Cancellation Charge for Deps/Trial: No
Retainer Required: No
Expenses Marked Up: No
Expenses Billed For: Mileage, Airline Tickets, Demonstrative Aids
Portal-to-Portal: Yes **1st-class Airfare:** No
Written Retainer Agreement: No
Failure to Pay Bill Last 5 Years; Retaining Counsel: No **Opposing Counsel (Deps):** No

Surgery, General
Review/Prep: $400 **Deps:** $1,750
Years Testifying: 40 **Majority:** Plaintiff
Written Fee Schedule: Yes
Min Charge for Deps: Yes
Min Charge for Trial: No
Cancellation Charge for Deps/Trial: Yes
Retainer Required: Yes, 50% of est. fee (Refundable)
Procedure When Dep Exceeds Paid Time: Get payment before proceeding further
Expenses Marked Up: No
Expenses Billed For: Airline Tickets, Photocopies, Lab/Testing, Photographs, Demonstrative Aids
Portal-to-Portal: Yes **1st-class Airfare:** No
Written Retainer Agreement: Yes
Terms: Lawyer is responsible for fee, not lawyer's client, Out-of-pocket expense policies, In-court testimony minimums, Retaining counsel pays all deposition charges, Fee schedules, Portal-to-portal travel time, Attorney's fees if forced to sue for collection, Deposition minimum fee, Payment for preparation time
Failure to Pay Bill Last 5 Years; Retaining Counsel: Yes **Opposing Counsel (Deps):** No

Surgery, General
Court: $250 **Review/Prep:** $250 **Deps:** $250
Years Testifying: 10 **Majority:** Defendant
Written Fee Schedule: Yes
Min Charge for Deps: No **Hours:** 8
Min Charge for Trial: Yes **Hours:** 8
Cancellation Charge for Deps/Trial: Yes
Retainer Required: No
Expenses Marked Up: No
Expenses Billed For: Telephone Calls
Portal-to-Portal: No **1st-class Airfare:** No
Written Retainer Agreement: No
Failure to Pay Bill Last 5 Years; Retaining Counsel: No **Opposing Counsel (Deps):** No

Surgery, Neurological
Court: $1,500 **Review/Prep:** $800 **Deps:** $3,000
Years Testifying: 20
Written Fee Schedule: Yes
Min Charge for Deps: Yes **Hours:** 1
Min Charge for Trial: Yes **Hours:** 1

Cancellation Charge for Deps/Trial: Yes
Retainer Required: Yes, 50% est. fee (Refundable, Replenishable)
Expenses Marked Up: No
Expenses Billed For: Mileage, Airline Tickets, Photocopies
Portal-to-Portal: Yes **1st-class Airfare:** No
Written Retainer Agreement: No
Failure to Pay Bill Last 5 Years; Retaining Counsel: Yes **Opposing Counsel (Deps):** No

Surgery, Neurological
Review/Prep: $500 **Deps:** $1,200
Years Testifying: 15 **Majority:** Plaintiff
Written Fee Schedule: Yes
Min Charge for Deps: No
Min Charge for Trial: No
Cancellation Charge for Deps/Trial: Yes
Retainer Required: Yes, (Refundable)
Expenses Marked Up: No
Expenses Billed For: Mileage, Airline Tickets
1st-class Airfare: No
Written Retainer Agreement: No
Failure to Pay Bill Last 5 Years; Retaining Counsel: No **Opposing Counsel (Deps):** No

Surgery, Plastic
Court: $1,000 **Review/Prep:** $350 **Deps:** $800
Majority: Defendant
Written Fee Schedule: Yes
Min Charge for Deps: Yes **Hours:** 2
Min Charge for Trial: Yes **Hours:** 2
Cancellation Charge for Deps/Trial: Yes
Retainer Required: Yes, 100% est. fee (Non-Refundable)
Procedure When Dep Exceeds Paid Time: Proceed without immediate payment
Expenses Marked Up: No
Expenses Billed For: Mileage, Airline Tickets
Portal-to-Portal: Yes **1st-class Airfare:** Yes
Written Retainer Agreement: Yes
Terms: Lawyer is responsible for fee, not lawyer's client, Out-of-pocket expense policies, In-court testimony minimums, Retaining counsel pays all deposition charges, Fee schedules, Portal-to-portal travel time
Failure to Pay Bill Last 5 Years; Retaining Counsel: No **Opposing Counsel (Deps):** No

Surgery, Thoracic
Court: $500 **Review/Prep:** $200 **Deps:** $400
Years Testifying: 15
Written Fee Schedule: Yes
Min Charge for Deps: No
Min Charge for Trial: No
Cancellation Charge for Deps/Trial: Yes
Retainer Required: Yes, $1,000 (Non-Refundable)
Procedure When Dep Exceeds Paid Time: Proceed without immediate payment
Expenses Marked Up: Yes
Expenses Billed For: Mileage, Airline Tickets, Photocopies, Telephone Calls, Photographs, Demonstrative Aids
Portal-to-Portal: No **1st-class Airfare:** No
Written Retainer Agreement: No
Failure to Pay Bill Last 5 Years; Retaining Counsel: No **Opposing Counsel (Deps):** No

Vocational Economics
Court: $190 **Review/Prep:** $100 **Deps:** $200
Years Testifying: 12
Min Charge for Deps: Yes **Hours:** 8
Min Charge for Trial: Yes **Hours:** 8
Cancellation Charge for Deps/Trial: Yes
Retainer Required: Yes, Depends on case (One Time)
Procedure When Dep Exceeds Paid Time: Varies depending on case
Expenses Marked Up: No
Portal-to-Portal: No
Written Retainer Agreement: No
Failure to Pay Bill Last 5 Years; Retaining Counsel: No **Opposing Counsel (Deps):** No

Puerto Rico

Construction/Damages
Court: $150 **Review/Prep:** $125 **Deps:** $150
Years Testifying: 15
Written Fee Schedule: Yes
Min Charge for Deps: Yes **Hours:** 3
Min Charge for Trial: Yes **Hours:** 3
Cancellation Charge for Deps/Trial: No
Retainer Required: Yes, $7,500 (Refundable, One Time)
Procedure When Dep Exceeds Paid Time: Proceed without immediate payment
Expenses Marked Up: No
Expenses Billed For: Mileage, Airline Tickets, Telephone Calls
Portal-to-Portal: Yes **1st-class Airfare:** No
Written Retainer Agreement: Yes
Terms: Retaining counsel pays all deposition charges, Fee schedules
Failure to Pay Bill Last 5 Years; Retaining Counsel: No **Opposing Counsel (Deps):** No

Document Examiner
Court: $75 **Review/Prep:** $50 **Deps:** $600
Years Testifying: 21 **Majority:** Plaintiff
Written Fee Schedule: No
Min Charge for Deps: Yes **Hours:** 1
Min Charge for Trial: Yes **Hours:** 1
Cancellation Charge for Deps/Trial: Yes
Retainer Required: Yes, 50% est. fee (Non-Refundable, One Time)
Procedure When Dep Exceeds Paid Time: Proceed without immediate payment
Expenses Marked Up: Yes
Expenses Billed For: Lab/Testing, Photographs
Portal-to-Portal: No **1st-class Airfare:** No
Written Retainer Agreement: No
Failure to Pay Bill Last 5 Years; Retaining Counsel: Yes **Opposing Counsel (Deps):** No

Economics/Finance
Court: $250 **Review/Prep:** $200 **Deps:** $250
Years Testifying: 28 **Majority:** Plaintiff
Written Fee Schedule: No
Min Charge for Deps: No
Min Charge for Trial: No
Cancellation Charge for Deps/Trial: No
Retainer Required: Yes, $5,000 (Non-Refundable, Replenishable)
Expenses Marked Up: No
Expenses Billed For: Photocopies, Telephone Calls
Portal-to-Portal: Yes **1st-class Airfare:** No
Written Retainer Agreement: Yes
Terms: Out-of-pocket expense policies, In-court testimony minimums, Retaining counsel pays all deposition charges, Fee schedules, Deposition minimum fee, Payment for preparation time
Failure to Pay Bill Last 5 Years; Retaining Counsel: No **Opposing Counsel (Deps):** No

Neurology
Court: $200 **Review/Prep:** $200 **Deps:** $200
Years Testifying: 10
Written Fee Schedule: Yes
Min Charge for Deps: Yes
Min Charge for Trial: No
Cancellation Charge for Deps/Trial: Yes
Retainer Required: Yes, $600 (Non-Refundable, One Time)
Expenses Marked Up: No
Expenses Billed For: Airline Tickets
Portal-to-Portal: No **1st-class Airfare:** No
Written Retainer Agreement: Yes
Terms: Lawyer is responsible for fee, not lawyer's client, In-court testimony minimums, Retaining counsel pays all deposition charges, Fee schedules, Deposition minimum fee, Payment for preparation time
Failure to Pay Bill Last 5 Years; Retaining Counsel: Yes **Opposing (Deps):** Yes

Orthopedics
Court: $200 **Review/Prep:** $200 **Deps:** $200
Years Testifying: 25 **Majority:** Defendant
Written Fee Schedule: Yes
Min Charge for Deps: Yes **Hours:** 5
Min Charge for Trial: Yes **Hours:** 5
Cancellation Charge for Deps/Trial: Yes
Retainer Required: Yes, 50% of est. fee (One Time)

Procedure When Dep Exceeds Paid Time: Proceed without immediate payment
Expenses Marked Up: No
Portal-to-Portal: No **1st-class Airfare:** No
Written Retainer Agreement: No
Failure to Pay Bill Last 5 Years; Retaining Counsel: Yes **Opposing (Deps):** Yes

Physical Medicine & Rehabilitation
Court: $450 **Review/Prep:** $125 **Deps:** $450
Years Testifying: 10 **Majority:** Defendant
Written Fee Schedule: Yes
Min Charge for Deps: Yes **Hours:** 8
Min Charge for Trial: Yes **Hours:** 8
Cancellation Charge for Deps/Trial: Yes
Retainer Required: No
Expenses Marked Up: No
Expenses Billed For: Photocopies, Lab/Testing
Portal-to-Portal: Yes **1st-class Airfare:** No
Written Retainer Agreement: No
Failure to Pay Bill Last 5 Years; Retaining Counsel: No **Opposing Counsel (Deps):** No

Psychiatry
Court: $200 **Review/Prep:** $200 **Deps:** $200
Years Testifying: 15 **Majority:** Defendant
Written Fee Schedule: Yes
Min Charge for Deps: No
Min Charge for Trial: No
Cancellation Charge for Deps/Trial: No
Retainer Required: Yes, $1,500 (Non-Refundable, One Time)
Procedure When Dep Exceeds Paid Time: Proceed without immediate payment
Expenses Marked Up: No
Expenses Billed For: Airline Tickets, Lab/Testing
Portal-to-Portal: Yes **1st-class Airfare:** No
Written Retainer Agreement: No
Failure to Pay Bill Last 5 Years; Retaining Counsel: No **Opposing Counsel (Deps):** No

Psychiatry
Court: $200 **Review/Prep:** $200 **Deps:** $200
Years Testifying: 30
Written Fee Schedule: Yes
Min Charge for Deps: Yes **Hours:** 4
Min Charge for Trial: Yes **Hours:** 4
Cancellation Charge for Deps/Trial: Yes
Retainer Required: Yes, $600 (Non-Refundable, One Time)
Expenses Marked Up: No
Portal-to-Portal: Yes **1st-class Airfare:** No
Written Retainer Agreement: Yes
Terms: Lawyer is responsible for fee, not lawyer's client, In-court testimony minimums, Retaining counsel pays all deposition charges, Fee schedules, Portal-to-portal travel time, Deposition minimum fee, Payment for preparation time
Failure to Pay Bill Last 5 Years; Retaining Counsel: Yes **Opposing Counsel (Deps):** No

Psychology
Court: $120 **Review/Prep:** $120 **Deps:** $120
Years Testifying: 10
Written Fee Schedule: Yes
Min Charge for Deps: Yes **Hours:** 8
Min Charge for Trial: Yes **Hours:** 8
Cancellation Charge for Deps/Trial: Yes
Retainer Required: Yes, $1,000 (One Time)
Expenses Marked Up: No
Expenses Billed For: Mileage, Airline Tickets
Portal-to-Portal: Yes **1st-class Airfare:** No
Written Retainer Agreement: Yes
Terms: Out-of-pocket expense policies, In-court testimony minimums, Retaining counsel pays all deposition charges, Fee schedules, Portal-to-portal travel time, Deposition minimum fee
Failure to Pay Bill Last 5 Years; Retaining Counsel: No **Opposing Counsel (Deps):** No

Rhode Island

Damages, Business
Court: $300 **Review/Prep:** $200 **Deps:** $300
Years Testifying: 12
Written Fee Schedule: No
Min Charge for Deps: Yes **Hours:** 4
Min Charge for Trial: Yes **Hours:** 4
Cancellation Charge for Deps/Trial: Yes
Retainer Required: Yes, 50% est. fee (Non-Refundable, Replenishable)
Procedure When Dep Exceeds Paid Time: Proceed without immediate payment
Expenses Marked Up: No
Expenses Billed For: Mileage, Airline Tickets, Photocopies, Telephone Calls, Demonstrative Aids
Portal-to-Portal: No **1st-class Airfare:** No
Written Retainer Agreement: Yes
Terms: Interest for delinquent accounts, Out-of-pocket expense policies, In-court testimony minimums, Retaining counsel pays all deposition charges, Fee schedules, Attorney's fees if forced to sue for collection, Deposition minimum fee
Failure to Pay Bill Last 5 Years; Retaining Counsel: Yes **Opposing (Deps):** Yes

Occupational Medicine
Court: $350 **Review/Prep:** $350 **Deps:** $350
Years Testifying: 11
Written Fee Schedule: No
Min Charge for Deps: Yes
Min Charge for Trial: No
Cancellation Charge for Deps/Trial: Yes
Retainer Required: No
Expenses Marked Up: No
Portal-to-Portal: Yes
Opposing Counsel (Deps): No

Pathology
Court: $400 **Review/Prep:** $400 **Deps:** $400
Years Testifying: 15 **Majority:** Defendant
Written Fee Schedule: No
Min Charge for Deps: No
Min Charge for Trial: No
Cancellation Charge for Deps/Trial: No
Retainer Required: No
Expenses Billed For: Airline Tickets, Lab/Testing, Photographs, Demonstrative Aids
1st-class Airfare: No
Written Retainer Agreement: No
Failure to Pay Bill Last 5 Years; Retaining Counsel: Yes **Opposing Counsel (Deps):** No

Psychiatry
Court: $400 **Review/Prep:** $250 **Deps:** $300
Years Testifying: 12 **Majority:** Defendant
Written Fee Schedule: Yes
Min Charge for Deps: Yes **Hours:** 3
Min Charge for Trial: Yes **Hours:** 3
Cancellation Charge for Deps/Trial: Yes
Retainer Required: Yes, 50% est. fee (Refundable, Replenishable)
Procedure When Dep Exceeds Paid Time: Proceed without immediate payment
Expenses Marked Up: No
Expenses Billed For: Airline Tickets
Portal-to-Portal: Yes **1st-class Airfare:** Yes
Written Retainer Agreement: Yes
Terms: Lawyer is responsible for fee, not lawyer's client, Interest for delinquent accounts, Out-of-pocket expense policies, In-court testimony minimums, Retaining counsel pays all deposition charges, Fee schedules, Portal-to-portal travel time, Attorney's fees if forced to sue for collection, Deposition minimum fee, Payment for preparation time, First class air travel
Failure to Pay Bill Last 5 Years; Retaining Counsel: Yes **Opposing (Deps):** Yes

South Carolina

Chiropractic
Court: $437 **Review/Prep:** $150 **Deps:** $350
Years Testifying: 20 **Majority:** Plaintiff
Written Fee Schedule: Yes
Min Charge for Deps: Yes **Hours:** 4
Min Charge for Trial: Yes **Hours:** 4
Cancellation Charge for Deps/Trial: Yes
Retainer Required: Yes, $3,500 (Non-Refundable, One Time)
Procedure When Dep Exceeds Paid Time: Get payment before proceeding further
Expenses Marked Up: No
Expenses Billed For: Mileage, Airline

Tickets, Photocopies, Telephone Calls, Lab/Testing, Photographs, Demonstrative Aids
Portal-to-Portal: Yes **1st-class Airfare:** Yes
Written Retainer Agreement: Yes
Terms: Interest for delinquent accounts, Out-of-pocket expense policies, In-court testimony minimums, Retaining counsel pays all deposition charges, Fee schedules, Portal-to-portal travel time, Attorney's fees if forced to sue for collection, Deposition minimum fee, Payment for preparation time, First class air travel
Failure to Pay Bill Last 5 Years; Retaining Counsel: No **Opposing Counsel (Deps):** No

Engineering, Mechanical
Court: $200 **Review/Prep:** $200 **Deps:** $200
Years Testifying: 15
Written Fee Schedule: Yes
Min Charge for Deps: No
Min Charge for Trial: No
Cancellation Charge for Deps/Trial: No
Retainer Required: No
Expenses Marked Up: Yes
Expenses Billed For: Mileage, Airline Tickets, Photocopies, Telephone Calls, Lab/Testing, Photographs, Demonstrative Aids
Portal-to-Portal: Yes **1st-class Airfare:** No
Written Retainer Agreement: No
Failure to Pay Bill Last 5 Years; Retaining Counsel: Yes **Opposing (Deps):** Yes

Engineering, Mechanical
Court: $250 **Review/Prep:** $250 **Deps:** $250
Years Testifying: 25 **Majority:** Plaintiff
Written Fee Schedule: Yes
Min Charge for Deps: Yes
Min Charge for Trial: No
Cancellation Charge for Deps/Trial: No
Retainer Required: Yes, $2,000 (Non-Refundable, Replenishable)
Procedure When Dep Exceeds Paid Time: Proceed without immediate payment
Expenses Marked Up: Yes
Expenses Billed For: Mileage, Airline Tickets, Photocopies, Lab/Testing, Photographs, Demonstrative Aids
Portal-to-Portal: Yes **1st-class Airfare:** No
Written Retainer Agreement: Yes
Terms: Lawyer is responsible for fee, not lawyer's client, Interest for delinquent accounts, Out-of-pocket expense policies, Retaining counsel pays all deposition charges, Fee schedules, Attorney's fees if forced to sue for collection, Deposition minimum fee
Failure to Pay Bill Last 5 Years; Retaining Counsel: No **Opposing Counsel (Deps):** No

Finance
Court: $250 **Review/Prep:** $250 **Deps:** $200
Majority: Plaintiff
Written Fee Schedule: Yes
Min Charge for Deps: No
Min Charge for Trial: No
Cancellation Charge for Deps/Trial: No
Retainer Required: No
Expenses Marked Up: Yes
Expenses Billed For: Mileage, Airline Tickets, Lab/Testing, Photographs
Portal-to-Portal: No **1st-class Airfare:** No
Written Retainer Agreement: No
Failure to Pay Bill Last 5 Years; Retaining Counsel: No **Opposing Counsel (Deps):** No

Healthcare
Court: $250 **Review/Prep:** $150 **Deps:** $250
Years Testifying: 7 **Majority:** Defendant
Written Fee Schedule: Yes
Min Charge for Deps: No
Min Charge for Trial: No
Cancellation Charge for Deps/Trial: Yes
Retainer Required: Yes, $3,000 (Refundable, Replenishable)
Expenses Marked Up: No
Expenses Billed For: Mileage, Airline Tickets, Photocopies, Telephone Calls, Lab/Testing, Photographs, Demonstrative Aids
Portal-to-Portal: Yes **1st-class Airfare:** No
Written Retainer Agreement: No
Failure to Pay Bill Last 5 Years; Retaining Counsel: No **Opposing Counsel (Deps):** No

Insurance, Health
Court: $175 **Review/Prep:** $175 **Deps:** $175
Years Testifying: 14 **Majority:** Plaintiff
Written Fee Schedule: No
Min Charge for Deps: No
Min Charge for Trial: No
Cancellation Charge for Deps/Trial: No
Retainer Required: No
Expenses Marked Up: No
Expenses Billed For: Mileage, Airline Tickets
Portal-to-Portal: No **1st-class Airfare:** No
Written Retainer Agreement: No
Failure to Pay Bill Last 5 Years; Retaining Counsel: No **Opposing Counsel (Deps):** No

Long Term Care
Court: $250 **Review/Prep:** $150 **Deps:** $150
Years Testifying: 2 **Majority:** Defendant
Written Fee Schedule: Yes
Min Charge for Deps: No
Min Charge for Trial: No
Cancellation Charge for Deps/Trial: No
Retainer Required: Yes, $1,000 (Refundable, One Time)
Procedure When Dep Exceeds Paid Time: Proceed without immediate payment
Expenses Marked Up: No
Expenses Billed For: Mileage, Airline Tickets, Photocopies
Portal-to-Portal: Yes **1st-class Airfare:** No
Written Retainer Agreement: No
Failure to Pay Bill Last 5 Years; Retaining Counsel: No **Opposing Counsel (Deps):** No

Long Term Care
Court: $300 **Review/Prep:** $200 **Deps:** $300
Years Testifying: 5 **Majority:** Plaintiff
Written Fee Schedule: Yes
Min Charge for Deps: Yes **Hours:** 8
Min Charge for Trial: Yes **Hours:** 8
Cancellation Charge for Deps/Trial: Yes
Retainer Required: Yes, $1,200 (Non-Refundable, One Time)
Procedure When Dep Exceeds Paid Time: Get payment before proceeding further
Expenses Marked Up: Yes
Expenses Billed For: Mileage, Airline Tickets, Photocopies
Portal-to-Portal: Yes
Written Retainer Agreement: No
Failure to Pay Bill Last 5 Years; Retaining Counsel: No **Opposing Counsel (Deps):** No

Obstetrics & Gynecology
Court: $375 **Review/Prep:** $350 **Deps:** $350
Years Testifying: 15
Written Fee Schedule: No
Min Charge for Deps: No **Hours:** 4
Min Charge for Trial: Yes **Hours:** 4
Cancellation Charge for Deps/Trial: No
Retainer Required: Yes, $700 (Refundable, One Time)
Expenses Marked Up: No
Expenses Billed For: Mileage, Airline Tickets
Portal-to-Portal: Yes **1st-class Airfare:** No
Written Retainer Agreement: No
Failure to Pay Bill Last 5 Years; Retaining Counsel: No **Opposing Counsel (Deps):** No

Psychology
Court: $200 **Review/Prep:** $200 **Deps:** $200
Years Testifying: 10 **Majority:** Plaintiff
Written Fee Schedule: Yes
Min Charge for Deps: Yes **Hours:** 8
Min Charge for Trial: Yes **Hours:** 8
Cancellation Charge for Deps/Trial: No
Retainer Required: Yes, $2,000 (Non-Refundable, Replenishable)
Expenses Marked Up: No
Expenses Billed For: Mileage, Airline Tickets
Portal-to-Portal: Yes **1st-class Airfare:** Yes
Written Retainer Agreement: No

Failure to Pay Bill Last 5 Years; Retaining Counsel: No **Opposing Counsel (Deps):** No

Safety/Risk Management

Court: $165 **Review/Prep:** $165 **Deps:** $165
Years Testifying: 3
Written Fee Schedule: Yes
Min Charge for Deps: Yes
Min Charge for Trial: No
Cancellation Charge for Deps/Trial: No
Retainer Required: Yes, $2,000 (Non-Refundable, Replenishable)
Procedure When Dep Exceeds Paid Time: Proceed without immediate payment
Expenses Marked Up: No
Expenses Billed For: Mileage, Airline Tickets, Photocopies, Lab/Testing, Photographs, Demonstrative Aids
Portal-to-Portal: Yes **1st-class Airfare:** No
Written Retainer Agreement: Yes
Terms: Lawyer is responsible for fee, not lawyer's client, Interest for delinquent accounts, Out-of-pocket expense policies, Retaining counsel pays all deposition charges, Fee schedules, Attorney's fees if forced to sue for collection, Deposition minimum fee
Failure to Pay Bill Last 5 Years; Retaining Counsel: No **Opposing Counsel (Deps):** No

Vocational Rehabilitation

Court: $150 **Review/Prep:** $150 **Deps:** $150
Years Testifying: 20
Written Fee Schedule: Yes
Min Charge for Deps: Yes **Hours:** 4
Min Charge for Trial: Yes **Hours:** 4
Cancellation Charge for Deps/Trial: Yes
Retainer Required: Yes, $2,000 (Non-Refundable, One Time)
Procedure When Dep Exceeds Paid Time: Get payment before proceeding further
Expenses Marked Up: No
Expenses Billed For: Mileage, Airline Tickets, Photocopies, Telephone Calls, Photographs, Demonstrative Aids
Portal-to-Portal: Yes **1st-class Airfare:** No
Written Retainer Agreement: Yes
Terms: Lawyer is responsible for fee, not lawyer's client, Interest for delinquent accounts, Out-of-pocket expense policies, In-court testimony minimums, Retaining counsel pays all deposition charges, Fee schedules, Portal-to-portal travel time, Deposition minimum fee, Payment for preparation time
Failure to Pay Bill Last 5 Years; Retaining Counsel: Yes **Opposing Counsel (Deps):** No

South Dakota

Crime

Court: $275 **Review/Prep:** $275 **Deps:** $275
Years Testifying: 25
Written Fee Schedule: Yes
Min Charge for Deps: Yes **Hours:** 8
Min Charge for Trial: Yes **Hours:** 8
Retainer Required: No
Expenses Marked Up: No
Expenses Billed For: Mileage, Airline Tickets, Telephone Calls
Portal-to-Portal: Yes **1st-class Airfare:** No
Written Retainer Agreement: Yes
Terms: Lawyer is responsible for fee, not lawyer's client, Out-of-pocket expense policies, Fee schedules, Portal-to-portal travel time, Payment for preparation time
Failure to Pay Bill Last 5 Years; Retaining Counsel: Yes **Opposing Counsel (Deps):** No

Occupational Medicine

Court: $400 **Review/Prep:** $250 **Deps:** $400
Years Testifying: 10
Written Fee Schedule: Yes
Min Charge for Deps: Yes **Hours:** 2
Min Charge for Trial: Yes **Hours:** 2
Cancellation Charge for Deps/Trial: Yes
Retainer Required: No
Expenses Marked Up: Yes
Expenses Billed For: Airline Tickets, Telephone Calls, Demonstrative Aids
Portal-to-Portal: Yes **1st-class Airfare:** No
Written Retainer Agreement: No
Failure to Pay Bill Last 5 Years; Retaining Counsel: No **Opposing Counsel (Deps):** No

Psychiatry

Court: $275 **Review/Prep:** $275 **Deps:** $275
Years Testifying: 25
Written Fee Schedule: Yes
Min Charge for Deps: No
Min Charge for Trial: No
Retainer Required: No
Expenses Marked Up: No
Expenses Billed For: Mileage, Telephone Calls
Portal-to-Portal: Yes **1st-class Airfare:** No
Written Retainer Agreement: Yes
Terms: Lawyer is responsible for fee, not lawyer's client, Out-of-pocket expense policies, Fee schedules, Portal-to-portal travel time, Payment for preparation time
Failure to Pay Bill Last 5 Years; Retaining Counsel: Yes **Opposing Counsel (Deps):** No

Tennessee

Emergency Medicine

Court: $500 **Review/Prep:** $250 **Deps:** $300
Years Testifying: 8 **Majority:** Defendant
Written Fee Schedule: No
Min Charge for Deps: Yes **Hours:** 1
Min Charge for Trial: Yes **Hours:** 1
Cancellation Charge for Deps/Trial: No
Retainer Required: No
Expenses Marked Up: No
Portal-to-Portal: Yes **1st-class Airfare:** No
Written Retainer Agreement: No
Opposing Counsel (Deps): No

Engineering, Electrical

Court: $175 **Review/Prep:** $175 **Deps:** $175
Years Testifying: 41
Written Fee Schedule: No
Min Charge for Deps: No **Hours:** 10
Min Charge for Trial: Yes **Hours:** 10
Cancellation Charge for Deps/Trial: No
Retainer Required: No
Expenses Marked Up: No
Expenses Billed For: Mileage, Airline Tickets, Telephone Calls, Demonstrative Aids
Portal-to-Portal: Yes **1st-class Airfare:** Yes
Written Retainer Agreement: No
Failure to Pay Bill Last 5 Years; Retaining Counsel: Yes **Opposing Counsel (Deps):** No

Engineering, Mechanical

Court: $175 **Review/Prep:** $160 **Deps:** $175
Years Testifying: 36 **Majority:** Plaintiff
Min Charge for Deps: Yes **Hours:** 5
Min Charge for Trial: Yes **Hours:** 5
Cancellation Charge for Deps/Trial: Yes
Retainer Required: No
Expenses Billed For: Mileage, Airline Tickets, Photocopies, Telephone Calls, Lab/Testing, Photographs, Demonstrative Aids
Portal-to-Portal: Yes **1st-class Airfare:** No
Written Retainer Agreement: No
Failure to Pay Bill Last 5 Years; Retaining Counsel: No **Opposing Counsel (Deps):** No

Finance

Court: $300 **Review/Prep:** $300 **Deps:** $300
Years Testifying: 1
Written Fee Schedule: Yes
Min Charge for Deps: Yes **Hours:** 10
Min Charge for Trial: Yes **Hours:** 10
Cancellation Charge for Deps/Trial: Yes
Retainer Required: Yes, $5,000 (Non-Refundable, One Time)
Expenses Marked Up: No
Expenses Billed For: Mileage, Airline Tickets, Demonstrative Aids
Portal-to-Portal: Yes **1st-class Airfare:** No

Written Retainer Agreement: Yes
Terms: Interest for delinquent accounts, Out-of-pocket expense policies, In-court testimony minimums, Retaining counsel pays all deposition charges, Fee schedules, Portal-to-portal travel time, Attorney's fees if forced to sue for collection, Deposition minimum fee, Payment for preparation time
Failure to Pay Bill Last 5 Years; Retaining Counsel: No **Opposing Counsel (Deps):** No

Orthopedics
Court: $750 **Review/Prep:** $250 **Deps:** $500
Years Testifying: 7 **Majority:** Defendant
Written Fee Schedule: No
Min Charge for Deps: Yes **Hours:** 1
Min Charge for Trial: Yes **Hours:** 1
Cancellation Charge for Deps/Trial: No
Retainer Required: No
Procedure When Dep Exceeds Paid Time: Proceed without immediate payment
Expenses Marked Up: Yes
Expenses Billed For: Photocopies, Telephone Calls
Portal-to-Portal: Yes
Written Retainer Agreement: No
Failure to Pay Bill Last 5 Years; Retaining Counsel: No **Opposing Counsel (Deps):** No

Psychiatry
Court: $400 **Review/Prep:** $250 **Deps:** $400
Years Testifying: 5
Written Fee Schedule: Yes
Min Charge for Deps: Yes **Hours:** 4
Min Charge for Trial: Yes **Hours:** 4
Cancellation Charge for Deps/Trial: Yes
Retainer Required: Yes, $1,200 (Non-Refundable, One Time)
Expenses Marked Up: No
Expenses Billed For: Airline Tickets, Lab/Testing
Portal-to-Portal: Yes **1st-class Airfare:** No
Written Retainer Agreement: No
Failure to Pay Bill Last 5 Years; Retaining Counsel: Yes **Opposing (Deps):** Yes

Psychology/Vocational
Court: $250 **Review/Prep:** $120 **Deps:** $250
Years Testifying: 20
Written Fee Schedule: Yes
Min Charge for Deps: Yes **Hours:** 1
Min Charge for Trial: Yes **Hours:** 1
Cancellation Charge for Deps/Trial: Yes
Retainer Required: Depends, Total est. fee
Procedure When Dep Exceeds Paid Time: Re-Schedule
Expenses Marked Up: No
Expenses Billed For: Airline Tickets
Portal-to-Portal: Yes **1st-class Airfare:** No
Written Retainer Agreement: No
Failure to Pay Bill Last 5 Years; Retaining Counsel: No **Opposing Counsel (Deps):** No

Railroads
Court: $250 **Review/Prep:** $150 **Deps:** $250
Years Testifying: 8 **Majority:** Plaintiff
Written Fee Schedule: Yes
Min Charge for Deps: Yes **Hours:** 3
Min Charge for Trial: Yes **Hours:** 3
Cancellation Charge for Deps/Trial: No
Retainer Required: No
Expenses Marked Up: No
Expenses Billed For: Mileage, Airline Tickets, Photocopies, Photographs, Demonstrative Aids
Portal-to-Portal: No **1st-class Airfare:** No
Written Retainer Agreement: Yes
Terms: Lawyer is responsible for fee, not lawyer's client, Out-of-pocket expense policies, In-court testimony minimums, Fee schedules, Attorney's fees if forced to sue for collection, Deposition minimum fee, Payment for preparation time
Failure to Pay Bill Last 5 Years; Retaining Counsel: Yes **Opposing (Deps):** Yes

Surgery, Neurological
Court: $1,000 **Review/Prep:** $500 **Deps:** $1,000
Years Testifying: 39
Written Fee Schedule: Yes
Min Charge for Deps: Yes **Hours:** 5
Min Charge for Trial: Yes **Hours:** 5
Cancellation Charge for Deps/Trial: Yes
Retainer Required: Yes, $1,500 (Refundable)
Expenses Marked Up: No
Expenses Billed For: Mileage, Airline Tickets
Portal-to-Portal: Yes **1st-class Airfare:** No
Written Retainer Agreement: No
Failure to Pay Bill Last 5 Years; Retaining Counsel: Yes **Opposing Counsel (Deps):** No

Vocational Rehabilitation/ Employment, Earning Capacity
Court: $250 **Review/Prep:** $85 **Deps:** $250
Years Testifying: 7 **Majority:** Plaintiff
Written Fee Schedule: Yes
Min Charge for Deps: Yes **Hours:** 1
Min Charge for Trial: Yes **Hours:** 1
Cancellation Charge for Deps/Trial: Yes
Retainer Required: Yes, $250 (Non-Refundable, One Time)
Procedure When Dep Exceeds Paid Time: Proceed without immediate payment
Expenses Marked Up: No
Expenses Billed For: Mileage, Airline Tickets, Photographs, Demonstrative Aids
Portal-to-Portal: Yes **1st-class Airfare:** No
Written Retainer Agreement: Yes
Terms: Lawyer is responsible for fee, not lawyer's client, Interest for delinquent accounts, Out-of-pocket expense policies, In-court testimony minimums, Retaining counsel pays all deposition charges, Fee schedules, Deposition minimum fee
Failure to Pay Bill Last 5 Years; Retaining Counsel: No **Opposing Counsel (Deps):** No

Texas

Accounting
Court: $250 **Review/Prep:** $250 **Deps:** $250
Years Testifying: 4 **Majority:** Defendant
Written Fee Schedule: Yes
Min Charge for Deps: No
Min Charge for Trial: No
Cancellation Charge for Deps/Trial: No
Retainer Required: Yes, $5,000 (Refundable, Replenishable)
Procedure When Dep Exceeds Paid Time: Proceed without immediate payment
Expenses Marked Up: No
Expenses Billed For: Mileage, Airline Tickets, Photocopies, Telephone Calls, Lab/Testing, Photographs, Demonstrative Aids
Portal-to-Portal: Yes **1st-class Airfare:** No
Written Retainer Agreement: Yes
Terms: Interest for delinquent accounts, Out-of-pocket expense policies, Retaining counsel pays all deposition charges, Fee schedules, Portal-to-portal travel time, Payment for preparation time
Failure to Pay Bill Last 5 Years; Retaining Counsel: Yes **Opposing Counsel (Deps):** No

Accounting
Court: $250 **Review/Prep:** $200 **Deps:** $250
Years Testifying: 3
Written Fee Schedule: Yes
Min Charge for Deps: No
Min Charge for Trial: No
Cancellation Charge for Deps/Trial: No
Retainer Required: Yes, $6,250 (Refundable, Replenishable)
Procedure When Dep Exceeds Paid Time: Proceed without immediate payment
Expenses Marked Up: No
Expenses Billed For: Mileage, Airline Tickets, Photocopies, Telephone Calls, Demonstrative Aids
Portal-to-Portal: Yes **1st-class Airfare:** No
Written Retainer Agreement: Yes
Terms: Out-of-pocket expense policies, Retaining counsel pays all deposition charges, Fee schedules, Portal-to-portal travel time, Payment for preparation time
Failure to Pay Bill Last 5 Years; Retaining Counsel: Yes **Opposing Counsel (Deps):** No

Accounting
Court: $400 **Review/Prep:** $400 **Deps:** $400
Years Testifying: 15
Written Fee Schedule: No
Min Charge for Deps: No
Min Charge for Trial: No
Cancellation Charge for Deps/Trial: No
Retainer Required: Depends, $8,000
Expenses Marked Up: No
Expenses Billed For: Mileage, Airline Tickets, Photocopies, Telephone Calls
Portal-to-Portal: Yes **1st-class Airfare:** Yes
Written Retainer Agreement: Yes
Terms: Interest for delinquent accounts, Out-of-pocket expense policies, Retaining counsel pays all deposition charges, Portal-to-portal travel time, Attorney's fees if forced to sue for collection, Payment for preparation time, Mediation clause
Failure to Pay Bill Last 5 Years; Retaining Counsel: Yes

Animation
Court: $225 **Review/Prep:** $175 **Deps:** $225
Years Testifying: 15 **Majority:** Defendant
Written Fee Schedule: Yes
Min Charge for Deps: Yes **Hours:** 4
Min Charge for Trial: Yes **Hours:** 4
Cancellation Charge for Deps/Trial: Yes
Retainer Required: Yes, $3,000 (Refundable, One Time)
Procedure When Dep Exceeds Paid Time: Proceed without immediate payment
Expenses Marked Up: Yes
Expenses Billed For: Mileage, Airline Tickets, Lab/Testing, Photographs, Demonstrative Aids
Portal-to-Portal: No **1st-class Airfare:** No
Written Retainer Agreement: Yes
Terms: Lawyer is responsible for fee, not lawyer's client, Interest for delinquent accounts, Out-of-pocket expense policies, In-court testimony minimums, Retaining counsel pays all deposition charges
Failure to Pay Bill Last 5 Years; Retaining Counsel: Yes **Opposing Counsel (Deps):** No

Annuitist
Court: $275 **Review/Prep:** $275 **Deps:** $275
Years Testifying: 11 **Majority:** Defendant
Written Fee Schedule: No
Min Charge for Deps: Yes
Min Charge for Trial: No
Cancellation Charge for Deps/Trial: No
Retainer Required: No
Expenses Marked Up: No
Expenses Billed For: Airline Tickets
Portal-to-Portal: Yes **1st-class Airfare:** No
Written Retainer Agreement: No
Failure to Pay Bill Last 5 Years; Retaining Counsel: No **Opposing Counsel (Deps):** No

Architecture
Court: $270 **Review/Prep:** $200 **Deps:** $270
Years Testifying: 13
Written Fee Schedule: Yes
Min Charge for Deps: No
Min Charge for Trial: No
Cancellation Charge for Deps/Trial: No
Retainer Required: Yes, $3,000 (Non-Refundable, Replenishable)
Procedure When Dep Exceeds Paid Time: Proceed without immediate payment
Expenses Marked Up: Yes
Expenses Billed For: Mileage, Airline Tickets, Lab/Testing, Photographs, Demonstrative Aids
Portal-to-Portal: Yes **1st-class Airfare:** No
Written Retainer Agreement: Yes
Terms: Lawyer is responsible for fee, not lawyer's client, Interest for delinquent accounts, Out-of-pocket expense policies, Retaining counsel pays all deposition charges, Fee schedules, Portal-to-portal travel time, Deposition minimum fee, Payment for preparation time
Failure to Pay Bill Last 5 Years; Retaining Counsel: Yes **Opposing Counsel (Deps):** No

Automotive
Court: $200 **Review/Prep:** $200 **Deps:** $200
Years Testifying: 10
Written Fee Schedule: Yes
Min Charge for Deps: No
Min Charge for Trial: No
Cancellation Charge for Deps/Trial: No
Retainer Required: Yes, $2,000 (Refundable, Replenishable)
Expenses Marked Up: No
Expenses Billed For: Airline Tickets, Photocopies, Telephone Calls, Lab/Testing, Photographs, Demonstrative Aids
Portal-to-Portal: Yes **1st-class Airfare:** No
Written Retainer Agreement: Yes
Terms: Interest for delinquent accounts, Out-of-pocket expense policies, Retaining counsel pays all deposition charges, Fee schedules, Portal-to-portal travel time
Failure to Pay Bill Last 5 Years; Retaining Counsel: Yes **Opposing Counsel (Deps):** No

Aviation/Aviation, Air Traffic Control
Court: $150 **Review/Prep:** $150 **Deps:** $150
Years Testifying: 9 **Majority:** Plaintiff
Written Fee Schedule: Yes
Min Charge for Deps: Yes **Hours:** 8
Min Charge for Trial: Yes **Hours:** 8
Cancellation Charge for Deps/Trial: No
Retainer Required: No
Expenses Marked Up: No
Expenses Billed For: Mileage, Airline Tickets
Portal-to-Portal: Yes **1st-class Airfare:** No
Written Retainer Agreement: No
Failure to Pay Bill Last 5 Years; Retaining Counsel: No **Opposing Counsel (Deps):** No

Aviation
Court: $150 **Review/Prep:** $125 **Deps:** $150
Years Testifying: 3 **Majority:** Plaintiff
Written Fee Schedule: Yes
Min Charge for Deps: No
Min Charge for Trial: No
Cancellation Charge for Deps/Trial: No
Retainer Required: No
Expenses Marked Up: No
Expenses Billed For: Mileage, Airline Tickets, Photocopies, Photographs
Portal-to-Portal: Yes **1st-class Airfare:** No
Written Retainer Agreement: No
Failure to Pay Bill Last 5 Years; Retaining Counsel: No **Opposing Counsel (Deps):** No

Banking
Court: $450 **Review/Prep:** $350 **Deps:** $450
Years Testifying: 5
Written Fee Schedule: Yes
Min Charge for Deps: Yes **Hours:** 4
Min Charge for Trial: Yes **Hours:** 4
Cancellation Charge for Deps/Trial: No
Retainer Required: Yes, $5,000 (Non-Refundable, One Time)
Expenses Marked Up: No
Expenses Billed For: Mileage, Airline Tickets, Photocopies, Telephone Calls, Demonstrative Aids
Portal-to-Portal: Yes **1st-class Airfare:** No
Written Retainer Agreement: Yes
Terms: Lawyer is responsible for fee, not lawyer's client, Interest for delinquent accounts, Out-of-pocket expense policies, In-court testimony minimums, Retaining counsel pays all deposition charges, Fee schedules, Portal-to-portal travel time, Deposition minimum fee, Payment for preparation time
Failure to Pay Bill Last 5 Years; Retaining Counsel: No **Opposing Counsel (Deps):** Yes

Cardiology
Court: $375 **Review/Prep:** $300 **Deps:** $500
Years Testifying: 10 **Majority:** Defendant
Written Fee Schedule: No
Min Charge for Deps: No
Min Charge for Trial: No
Cancellation Charge for Deps/Trial: No
Retainer Required: No
Expenses Marked Up: No
Expenses Billed For: Mileage, Airline Tickets, Demonstrative Aids
Portal-to-Portal: No **1st-class Airfare:** No
Written Retainer Agreement: No
Failure to Pay Bill Last 5 Years; Retaining Counsel: Yes **Opposing Counsel (Deps):** No

Chemicals/Plastics
Court: $250 **Review/Prep:** $175 **Deps:** $250
Years Testifying: 25
Written Fee Schedule: No
Min Charge for Deps: No
Min Charge for Trial: No
Cancellation Charge for Deps/Trial: No
Retainer Required: No
Expenses Marked Up: No
Expenses Billed For: Lab/Testing
Portal-to-Portal: Yes **1st-class Airfare:** No
Written Retainer Agreement: No
Failure to Pay Bill Last 5 Years; Retaining Counsel: No **Opposing Counsel (Deps):** No

Chiropractic
Court: $400 **Review/Prep:** $350 **Deps:** $400
Years Testifying: 13
Written Fee Schedule: Yes
Min Charge for Deps: Yes **Hours:** 4
Min Charge for Trial: Yes **Hours:** 4
Cancellation Charge for Deps/Trial: Yes
Retainer Required: Yes, $1,000 (Refundable, One Time)
Procedure When Dep Exceeds Paid Time: Get payment before proceeding further
Expenses Marked Up: No
Expenses Billed For: Airline Tickets, Demonstrative Aids
Portal-to-Portal: Yes **1st-class Airfare:** No
Written Retainer Agreement: Yes
Failure to Pay Bill Last 5 Years; Retaining Counsel: No **Opposing Counsel (Deps):** No

Computers
Court: $200 **Review/Prep:** $150 **Deps:** $200
Years Testifying: 15
Written Fee Schedule: No
Min Charge for Deps: No
Min Charge for Trial: No
Cancellation Charge for Deps/Trial: No
Retainer Required: Yes, $1,500 (Refundable, One Time)
Procedure When Dep Exceeds Paid Time: Proceed without immediate payment
Expenses Marked Up: No
Expenses Billed For: Airline Tickets, Photocopies, Telephone Calls, Lab/Testing
Portal-to-Portal: Yes **1st-class Airfare:** No
Written Retainer Agreement: No
Failure to Pay Bill Last 5 Years; Retaining Counsel: Yes **Opposing Counsel (Deps):** No

Construction
Court: $200 **Review/Prep:** $200 **Deps:** $200
Years Testifying: 25 **Majority:** Defendant
Written Fee Schedule: Yes
Min Charge for Deps: Yes **Hours:** 10
Min Charge for Trial: Yes **Hours:** 10
Cancellation Charge for Deps/Trial: No
Retainer Required: Yes, $2,000 (Non-Refundable, One Time)
Procedure When Dep Exceeds Paid Time: Proceed without immediate payment
Expenses Marked Up: No
Expenses Billed For: Mileage, Airline Tickets, Photocopies, Telephone Calls, Lab/Testing, Photographs, Demonstrative Aids
Portal-to-Portal: No **1st-class Airfare:** No
Written Retainer Agreement: Yes
Terms: Out-of-pocket expense policies, In-court testimony minimums, Retaining counsel pays all deposition charges, Fee schedules, Deposition minimum fee, Payment for preparation time
Failure to Pay Bill Last 5 Years; Retaining Counsel: Yes **Opposing Counsel (Deps):** No

Damages
Court: $350 **Review/Prep:** $350 **Deps:** $350
Years Testifying: 21
Written Fee Schedule: Yes
Min Charge for Deps: No
Min Charge for Trial: No
Cancellation Charge for Deps/Trial: No
Retainer Required: Yes, Varies (Refundable, Replenishable)
Expenses Marked Up: No
Expenses Billed For: Airline Tickets, Photocopies, Photographs, Demonstrative Aids
Portal-to-Portal: No **1st-class Airfare:** No
Written Retainer Agreement: Yes
Terms: Interest for delinquent accounts, Out-of-pocket expense policies, Retaining counsel pays all deposition charges, Fee schedules, Attorney's fees if forced to sue for collection
Failure to Pay Bill Last 5 Years; Retaining Counsel: Yes **Opposing (Deps):** Yes

Damages, Business
Court: $250 **Review/Prep:** $250 **Deps:** $250
Years Testifying: 25 **Majority:** Plaintiff
Written Fee Schedule: No
Min Charge for Deps: No
Min Charge for Trial: No
Cancellation Charge for Deps/Trial: No
Retainer Required: Yes, $3,500 (Refundable, One Time)
Expenses Marked Up: No
Expenses Billed For: Airline Tickets
Portal-to-Portal: No **1st-class Airfare:** No
Written Retainer Agreement: No
Failure to Pay Bill Last 5 Years; Retaining Counsel: Yes **Opposing Counsel (Deps):** No

Demolition
Court: $350 **Review/Prep:** $350 **Deps:** $350
Years Testifying: 10
Written Fee Schedule: Yes
Min Charge for Deps: Yes **Hours:** 4
Min Charge for Trial: Yes **Hours:** 4
Cancellation Charge for Deps/Trial: No
Retainer Required: Yes, $3,000 (One Time)
Expenses Marked Up: No
Expenses Billed For: Airline Tickets, Photographs
Portal-to-Portal: Yes **1st-class Airfare:** No
Written Retainer Agreement: No
Failure to Pay Bill Last 5 Years; Retaining Counsel: No **Opposing Counsel (Deps):** No

Economics
Court: $300 **Review/Prep:** $300 **Deps:** $300
Years Testifying: 14 **Majority:** Plaintiff
Written Fee Schedule: Yes
Min Charge for Deps: Yes **Hours:** 4
Min Charge for Trial: Yes **Hours:** 4
Cancellation Charge for Deps/Trial: No
Retainer Required: Yes, 100% est. fee (Non-Refundable, One Time)
Procedure When Dep Exceeds Paid Time: Get payment before proceeding further
Expenses Marked Up: No
Portal-to-Portal: Yes **1st-class Airfare:** No
Written Retainer Agreement: Yes
Terms: Lawyer is responsible for fee, not lawyer's client, In-court testimony minimums, Retaining counsel pays all deposition charges, Fee schedules, Portal-to-portal travel time, Attorney's fees if forced to sue for collection, Deposition minimum fee, Payment for preparation time
Failure to Pay Bill Last 5 Years; Retaining Counsel: Yes **Opposing (Deps):** Yes

Economics
Court: $200 **Review/Prep:** $200 **Deps:** $200
Years Testifying: 25 **Majority:** Plaintiff
Written Fee Schedule: No
Min Charge for Deps: No
Min Charge for Trial: No
Cancellation Charge for Deps/Trial: No
Retainer Required: Yes, $500 (Non-Refundable, One Time)
Expenses Marked Up: No
Expenses Billed For: Mileage, Airline Tickets
Portal-to-Portal: Yes **1st-class Airfare:** No
Written Retainer Agreement: No
Failure to Pay Bill Last 5 Years; Retaining Counsel: Yes **Opposing Counsel (Deps):** No

Engineering
Court: $250 **Review/Prep:** $250 **Deps:** $250
Years Testifying: 20 **Majority:** Plaintiff
Written Fee Schedule: Yes
Min Charge for Deps: No
Min Charge for Trial: No
Cancellation Charge for Deps/Trial: No
Retainer Required: Yes, $2,000 (Non-Refundable, One Time)

Expenses Marked Up: No
Expenses Billed For: Mileage, Airline Tickets, Photocopies, Lab/Testing, Photographs
Portal-to-Portal: Yes **1st-class Airfare:** No
Written Retainer Agreement: Yes
Terms: Lawyer is responsible for fee, not lawyer's client, Interest for delinquent accounts, Out-of-pocket expense policies, In-court testimony minimums, Retaining counsel pays all deposition charges, Fee schedules, Portal-to-portal travel time, Attorney's fees if forced to sue for collection, Payment for preparation time
Failure to Pay Bill Last 5 Years; Retaining Counsel: Yes **Opposing Counsel (Deps):** No

Engineering
Court: $180 **Review/Prep:** $180 **Deps:** $0
Years Testifying: 7 **Majority:** Defendant
Written Fee Schedule: Yes
Min Charge for Deps: No
Min Charge for Trial: No
Cancellation Charge for Deps/Trial: No
Retainer Required: No
Expenses Marked Up: No
Expenses Billed For: Mileage, Airline Tickets
Portal-to-Portal: Yes **1st-class Airfare:** No
Written Retainer Agreement: Yes
Terms: Out-of-pocket expense policies, Fee schedules
Failure to Pay Bill Last 5 Years; Retaining Counsel: No **Opposing Counsel (Deps):** No

Engineering, Biomedical
Court: $350 **Review/Prep:** $300 **Deps:** $325
Years Testifying: 25 **Majority:** Plaintiff
Written Fee Schedule: Yes
Min Charge for Deps: No
Min Charge for Trial: No
Cancellation Charge for Deps/Trial: Yes
Retainer Required: Yes, $2,000 (Refundable, One Time)
Procedure When Dep Exceeds Paid Time: Proceed without immediate payment
Expenses Marked Up: No
Expenses Billed For: Mileage, Airline Tickets, Lab/Testing, Photographs, Demonstrative Aids
Portal-to-Portal: Yes **1st-class Airfare:** No
Written Retainer Agreement: No
Failure to Pay Bill Last 5 Years; Retaining Counsel: No **Opposing Counsel (Deps):** No

Engineering, Chemical
Court: $250 **Review/Prep:** $125 **Deps:** $250
Years Testifying: 5
Written Fee Schedule: No
Min Charge for Deps: No
Min Charge for Trial: No
Cancellation Charge for Deps/Trial: No
Retainer Required: Yes, $2,000 (Refundable, One Time)
Procedure When Dep Exceeds Paid Time: Proceed without immediate payment
Expenses Marked Up: Yes
Expenses Billed For: Lab/Testing, Demonstrative Aids
Portal-to-Portal: Yes **1st-class Airfare:** No
Written Retainer Agreement: No
Failure to Pay Bill Last 5 Years; Retaining Counsel: Yes **Opposing (Deps):** Yes

Engineering, Civil/Engineering, Structural
Court: $220 **Review/Prep:** $220 **Deps:** $220
Years Testifying: 12
Written Fee Schedule: No
Min Charge for Deps: No
Min Charge for Trial: No
Cancellation Charge for Deps/Trial: No
Retainer Required: Yes, $3,000 (Non-Refundable, One Time)
Expenses Marked Up: No
Expenses Billed For: Mileage, Airline Tickets
Portal-to-Portal: Yes **1st-class Airfare:** No
Written Retainer Agreement: No
Failure to Pay Bill Last 5 Years; Retaining Counsel: No **Opposing Counsel (Deps):** No

Engineering, Civil
Court: $235 **Review/Prep:** $235 **Deps:** $235
Years Testifying: 8 **Majority:** Defendant
Written Fee Schedule: No
Min Charge for Deps: Yes **Hours:** 4
Min Charge for Trial: Yes **Hours:** 4
Cancellation Charge for Deps/Trial: No
Retainer Required: Yes, Depends on case (Refundable, One Time)
Expenses Marked Up: Yes
Expenses Billed For: Photocopies, Telephone Calls, Lab/Testing, Photographs, Demonstrative Aids
Portal-to-Portal: Yes **1st-class Airfare:** No
Written Retainer Agreement: No
Failure to Pay Bill Last 5 Years; Retaining Counsel: Yes **Opposing Counsel (Deps):** No

Engineering, Electrical
Court: $150 **Review/Prep:** $125 **Deps:** $150
Years Testifying: 11 **Majority:** Plaintiff
Written Fee Schedule: Yes
Min Charge for Deps: No
Min Charge for Trial: No
Cancellation Charge for Deps/Trial: No
Retainer Required: Yes, $750 (Refundable, One Time)
Expenses Marked Up: No
Expenses Billed For: Mileage, Airline Tickets, Photocopies, Telephone Calls, Lab/Testing, Photographs, Demonstrative Aids
Portal-to-Portal: Yes **1st-class Airfare:** No
Written Retainer Agreement: No
Failure to Pay Bill Last 5 Years; Retaining Counsel: No **Opposing Counsel (Deps):** No

Engineering, Industrial
Court: $200 **Review/Prep:** $200 **Deps:** $200
Years Testifying: 2
Written Fee Schedule: Yes
Min Charge for Deps: Yes **Hours:** 8
Min Charge for Trial: Yes **Hours:** 8
Cancellation Charge for Deps/Trial: No
Retainer Required: Yes, $1,600 (Non-Refundable, One Time)
Expenses Marked Up: No
Expenses Billed For: Mileage, Airline Tickets, Lab/Testing, Photographs, Demonstrative Aids
Portal-to-Portal: Yes **1st-class Airfare:** No
Written Retainer Agreement: Yes
Terms: Lawyer is responsible for fee, not lawyer's client, Interest for delinquent accounts, Out-of-pocket expense policies, In-court testimony minimums, Retaining counsel pays all deposition charges, Fee schedules, Attorney's fees if forced to sue for collection, Deposition minimum fee, Payment for preparation time
Failure to Pay Bill Last 5 Years; Retaining Counsel: Yes

Engineering, Structural
Court: $250 **Review/Prep:** $150 **Deps:** $175
Years Testifying: 5 **Majority:** Plaintiff
Written Fee Schedule: Yes
Min Charge for Deps: No **Hours:** 4
Min Charge for Trial: Yes **Hours:** 4
Cancellation Charge for Deps/Trial: No
Retainer Required: Yes, $4,000 (Refundable, One Time)
Expenses Marked Up: Yes
Expenses Billed For: Mileage, Airline Tickets, Lab/Testing, Photographs, Demonstrative Aids
Portal-to-Portal: Yes **1st-class Airfare:** No
Written Retainer Agreement: Yes
Terms: Lawyer is responsible for fee, not lawyer's client, Interest for delinquent accounts, Out-of-pocket expense policies, In-court testimony minimums, Retaining counsel pays all deposition charges, Fee schedules, Portal-to-portal travel time, Payment for preparation time
Failure to Pay Bill Last 5 Years; Retaining Counsel: Yes **Opposing Counsel (Deps):** No

Engineering, Structural/ Architecture
Court: $200 **Review/Prep:** $150 **Deps:** $200
Years Testifying: 10
Written Fee Schedule: Yes
Min Charge for Deps: No **Hours:** 4
Min Charge for Trial: Yes **Hours:** 4
Cancellation Charge for Deps/Trial: No
Retainer Required: Yes, $1,250 (Refundable, One Time)
Expenses Marked Up: No
Expenses Billed For: Mileage, Airline Tickets, Photographs
Portal-to-Portal: Yes **1st-class Airfare:** No
Written Retainer Agreement: Yes
Terms: Lawyer is responsible for fee, not lawyer's client, Interest for delinquent accounts, Out-of-pocket expense policies, In-court testimony minimums, Retaining counsel pays all deposition charges, Fee schedules, Portal-to-portal travel time, Attorney's fees if forced to sue for collection
Failure to Pay Bill Last 5 Years; Retaining Counsel: Yes

Engineering, Traffic
Court: $250 **Review/Prep:** $250 **Deps:** $250
Years Testifying: 15 **Majority:** Defendant
Written Fee Schedule: Yes
Min Charge for Deps: No
Min Charge for Trial: No
Cancellation Charge for Deps/Trial: No
Retainer Required: Yes, $1,500 (Non-Refundable, One Time)
Expenses Billed For: Mileage, Airline Tickets
Portal-to-Portal: Yes **1st-class Airfare:** No
Written Retainer Agreement: No
Failure to Pay Bill Last 5 Years; Retaining Counsel: Yes **Opposing Counsel (Deps):** No

Environmental
Court: $180 **Review/Prep:** $180 **Deps:** $180
Years Testifying: 10
Written Fee Schedule: Yes
Min Charge for Deps: No
Min Charge for Trial: No
Cancellation Charge for Deps/Trial: No
Retainer Required: Yes, $4,000 (Non-Refundable, Replenishable)
Expenses Marked Up: Yes
Expenses Billed For: Mileage, Airline Tickets, Lab/Testing, Photographs, Demonstrative Aids
Portal-to-Portal: Yes **1st-class Airfare:** No
Written Retainer Agreement: Yes
Terms: Interest for delinquent accounts, Out-of-pocket expense policies, Retaining counsel pays all deposition charges, Fee schedules, Payment for preparation time
Failure to Pay Bill Last 5 Years; Retaining Counsel: No **Opposing Counsel (Deps):** No

Environmental, Air Pollution
Court: $150 **Review/Prep:** $100 **Deps:** $150
Years Testifying: 20 **Majority:** Plaintiff
Written Fee Schedule: Yes
Min Charge for Deps: Yes **Hours:** 8
Min Charge for Trial: Yes **Hours:** 8
Cancellation Charge for Deps/Trial: No
Retainer Required: No
Expenses Marked Up: Yes
Expenses Billed For: Mileage, Airline Tickets, Lab/Testing
Portal-to-Portal: No **1st-class Airfare:** No
Written Retainer Agreement: No
Failure to Pay Bill Last 5 Years; Retaining Counsel: No **Opposing Counsel (Deps):** No

Ergonomics/Biomechanics
Court: $150 **Review/Prep:** $150 **Deps:** $150
Years Testifying: 10 **Majority:** Defendant
Written Fee Schedule: Yes
Min Charge for Deps: No
Min Charge for Trial: No
Cancellation Charge for Deps/Trial: No
Retainer Required: Yes, $2,000 (Refundable, One Time)
Procedure When Dep Exceeds Paid Time: Proceed without immediate payment
Expenses Marked Up: No
Expenses Billed For: Airline Tickets, Lab/Testing
Portal-to-Portal: Yes **1st-class Airfare:** No
Written Retainer Agreement: No
Failure to Pay Bill Last 5 Years; Retaining Counsel: No **Opposing Counsel (Deps):** No

Family Practice/Occupational Medicine
Court: $500 **Review/Prep:** $500 **Deps:** $500
Years Testifying: 12
Written Fee Schedule: Yes
Min Charge for Deps: No
Min Charge for Trial: No
Cancellation Charge for Deps/Trial: Yes
Retainer Required: Yes, $1,000 (Refundable, One Time)
Procedure When Dep Exceeds Paid Time: Proceed without immediate payment
Expenses Marked Up: No
Expenses Billed For: Airline Tickets
Portal-to-Portal: Yes **1st-class Airfare:** No
Written Retainer Agreement: No
Failure to Pay Bill Last 5 Years; Retaining Counsel: Yes **Opposing (Deps):** Yes

Gastroenterology
Court: $500 **Review/Prep:** $400 **Deps:** $500
Years Testifying: 15
Written Fee Schedule: No
Min Charge for Deps: No
Min Charge for Trial: No
Cancellation Charge for Deps/Trial: No
Retainer Required: Yes, (Non-Refundable, One Time)
Expenses Marked Up: No
Expenses Billed For: Mileage, Airline Tickets, Telephone Calls
Portal-to-Portal: Yes **1st-class Airfare:** No
Written Retainer Agreement: No
Failure to Pay Bill Last 5 Years; Retaining Counsel: No **Opposing Counsel (Deps):** No

Gerontology/Nursing Homes
Court: $150 **Review/Prep:** $125 **Deps:** $150
Years Testifying: 1
Min Charge for Deps: No
Min Charge for Trial: No
Cancellation Charge for Deps/Trial: No
Retainer Required: No
Expenses Marked Up: No
Expenses Billed For: Airline Tickets
Portal-to-Portal: No **1st-class Airfare:** No
Written Retainer Agreement: No
Failure to Pay Bill Last 5 Years; Retaining Counsel: No **Opposing Counsel (Deps):** No

Handwriting/Document Examiner
Court: $125 **Review/Prep:** $125 **Deps:** $125
Years Testifying: 4
Written Fee Schedule: Yes
Min Charge for Deps: Yes **Hours:** 4
Min Charge for Trial: Yes **Hours:** 4
Cancellation Charge for Deps/Trial: No
Retainer Required: Yes, $500 (Non-Refundable, Replenishable)
Procedure When Dep Exceeds Paid Time: Proceed without immediate payment
Expenses Marked Up: No
Expenses Billed For: Mileage, Airline Tickets, Photocopies, Telephone Calls, Lab/Testing, Photographs, Demonstrative Aids
Portal-to-Portal: Yes **1st-class Airfare:** No
Written Retainer Agreement: Yes
Terms: Interest for delinquent accounts, Out-of-pocket expense policies, Retaining counsel pays all deposition charges, Fee schedules, Attorney's fees if forced to sue for collection
Failure to Pay Bill Last 5 Years; Retaining Counsel: No **Opposing Counsel (Deps):** No

Insurance
Court: $250 **Review/Prep:** $250 **Deps:** $250
Years Testifying: 12
Written Fee Schedule: No
Min Charge for Deps: No
Min Charge for Trial: No
Cancellation Charge for Deps/Trial: No
Retainer Required: Yes, $2,500 (Non-Refundable, One Time)

Expenses Marked Up: No
Expenses Billed For: Mileage, Airline Tickets, Photocopies, Telephone Calls, Demonstrative Aids
Portal-to-Portal: Yes **1st-class Airfare:** No
Written Retainer Agreement: No
Failure to Pay Bill Last 5 Years; Retaining Counsel: No **Opposing Counsel (Deps):** No

Internal Medicine/Occupational Medicine
Review/Prep: $250 **Deps:** $250
Years Testifying: 25
Written Fee Schedule: No
Min Charge for Deps: No
Min Charge for Trial: No
Cancellation Charge for Deps/Trial: No
Retainer Required: No
Expenses Marked Up: No
Expenses Billed For: Mileage, Airline Tickets
Portal-to-Portal: Yes
Written Retainer Agreement: No
Failure to Pay Bill Last 5 Years; Retaining Counsel: No **Opposing Counsel (Deps):** No

Jewelry
Court: $250 **Review/Prep:** $250 **Deps:** $250
Years Testifying: 10
Written Fee Schedule: No
Min Charge for Deps: Yes **Hours:** 12
Min Charge for Trial: Yes **Hours:** 12
Cancellation Charge for Deps/Trial: Yes
Retainer Required: Yes, $1,000 (Non-Refundable, Replenishable)
Procedure When Dep Exceeds Paid Time: Get payment before proceeding further
Expenses Marked Up: Yes
Expenses Billed For: Mileage, Airline Tickets, Photocopies, Telephone Calls, Lab/Testing, Photographs, Demonstrative Aids
Portal-to-Portal: Yes **1st-class Airfare:** No
Written Retainer Agreement: Yes
Terms: Lawyer is responsible for fee, not lawyer's client, Interest for delinquent accounts, Out-of-pocket expense policies, In-court testimony minimums, Retaining counsel pays all deposition charges, Portal-to-portal travel time, Attorney's fees if forced to sue for collection, Deposition minimum fee, Payment for preparation time
Failure to Pay Bill Last 5 Years; Retaining Counsel: No **Opposing Counsel (Deps):** No

Law, Family
Court: $450 **Review/Prep:** $450
Years Testifying: 19
Written Fee Schedule: Yes
Min Charge for Deps: Yes **Hours:** 3
Min Charge for Trial: Yes **Hours:** 3
Cancellation Charge for Deps/Trial: Yes
Retainer Required: Yes, Based on est. time (Refundable, Replenishable)
Expenses Marked Up: No
Expenses Billed For: Airline Tickets, Demonstrative Aids
1st-class Airfare: No
Written Retainer Agreement: Yes
Terms: Out-of-pocket expense policies, In-court testimony minimums, Retaining counsel pays all deposition charges, Fee schedules, Attorney's fees if forced to sue for collection, Payment for preparation time
Failure to Pay Bill Last 5 Years; Retaining Counsel: No **Opposing Counsel (Deps):** No

Life Care Planning
Court: $400 **Review/Prep:** $250 **Deps:** $300
Years Testifying: 15 **Majority:** Plaintiff
Written Fee Schedule: Yes
Min Charge for Deps: Yes **Hours:** 4
Min Charge for Trial: Yes **Hours:** 4
Cancellation Charge for Deps/Trial: Yes
Retainer Required: Yes, $2,000 (Refundable, One Time)
Procedure When Dep Exceeds Paid Time: Proceed without immediate payment
Expenses Marked Up: No
Expenses Billed For: Mileage, Airline Tickets
Portal-to-Portal: Yes **1st-class Airfare:** No
Written Retainer Agreement: Yes
Terms: Lawyer is responsible for fee, not lawyer's client, In-court testimony minimums, Retaining counsel pays all deposition charges, Fee schedules, Deposition minimum fee
Failure to Pay Bill Last 5 Years; Retaining Counsel: Yes **Opposing Counsel (Deps):** No

Marine
Court: $175 **Review/Prep:** $150 **Deps:** $175
Years Testifying: 20
Written Fee Schedule: Yes
Min Charge for Deps: No
Min Charge for Trial: No
Cancellation Charge for Deps/Trial: Yes
Retainer Required: Yes, $2,500 (Non-Refundable, One Time)
Procedure When Dep Exceeds Paid Time: Proceed without immediate payment
Expenses Marked Up: No
Expenses Billed For: Mileage, Airline Tickets, Photocopies, Telephone Calls, Lab/Testing, Photographs, Demonstrative Aids
Portal-to-Portal: Yes **1st-class Airfare:** No
Written Retainer Agreement: Yes
Terms: Lawyer is responsible for fee, not lawyer's client, Interest for delinquent accounts, Out-of-pocket expense policies, In-court testimony minimums, Retaining counsel pays all deposition charges, Fee schedules, Portal-to-portal travel time, Attorney's fees if forced to sue for collection, Deposition minimum fee, Payment for preparation time
Failure to Pay Bill Last 5 Years; Retaining Counsel: Yes **Opposing Counsel (Deps):** No

Marketing/Advertising
Court: $350 **Review/Prep:** $350 **Deps:** $350
Years Testifying: 5
Written Fee Schedule: No
Min Charge for Deps: No
Min Charge for Trial: No
Cancellation Charge for Deps/Trial: No
Retainer Required: No
Expenses Marked Up: No
Expenses Billed For: Mileage, Airline Tickets
Portal-to-Portal: No **1st-class Airfare:** No
Written Retainer Agreement: No
Failure to Pay Bill Last 5 Years; Retaining Counsel: No **Opposing Counsel (Deps):** No

Materials/Failure Analysis
Court: $225 **Review/Prep:** $150 **Deps:** $225
Years Testifying: 15 **Majority:** Plaintiff
Written Fee Schedule: Yes
Min Charge for Deps: Yes **Hours:** 2
Min Charge for Trial: Yes **Hours:** 2
Cancellation Charge for Deps/Trial: Yes
Retainer Required: Yes, $1,500 (Refundable, One Time)
Expenses Marked Up: No
Expenses Billed For: Mileage, Airline Tickets, Photocopies, Telephone Calls, Lab/Testing, Photographs, Demonstrative Aids
Portal-to-Portal: Yes **1st-class Airfare:** No
Written Retainer Agreement: Yes
Terms: Lawyer is responsible for fee, not lawyer's client, Out-of-pocket expense policies, In-court testimony minimums, Retaining counsel pays all deposition charges, Fee schedules, Portal-to-portal travel time, Deposition minimum fee, Payment for preparation time
Failure to Pay Bill Last 5 Years; Retaining Counsel: Yes **Opposing Counsel (Deps):** No

Medical Doctor
Court: $250 **Review/Prep:** $250 **Deps:** $250
Years Testifying: 20
Written Fee Schedule: Yes
Min Charge for Deps: Yes
Min Charge for Trial: No
Cancellation Charge for Deps/Trial: Yes
Retainer Required: Yes, $1,000 (Non-Refundable, One Time)
Procedure When Dep Exceeds Paid Time: Proceed without immediate payment
Expenses Marked Up: No

Expenses Billed For: Mileage, Airline Tickets
Portal-to-Portal: Yes **1st-class Airfare:** No
Written Retainer Agreement: Yes
Terms: Interest for delinquent accounts, Out-of-pocket expense policies, Retaining counsel pays all deposition charges, Fee schedules, Portal-to-portal travel time, Deposition minimum fee
Failure to Pay Bill Last 5 Years; Retaining Counsel: No **Opposing Counsel (Deps):** No

Mold
Court: $300 **Review/Prep:** $150 **Deps:** $300
Years Testifying: 10 **Majority:** Plaintiff
Written Fee Schedule: Yes
Min Charge for Deps: No
Min Charge for Trial: No
Cancellation Charge for Deps/Trial: No
Retainer Required: No
Expenses Marked Up: No
Expenses Billed For: Airline Tickets, Lab/Testing
Portal-to-Portal: Yes **1st-class Airfare:** No
Written Retainer Agreement: No
Failure to Pay Bill Last 5 Years; Retaining Counsel: Yes **Opposing Counsel (Deps):** No

Nursing
Court: $500 **Review/Prep:** $200 **Deps:** $400
Years Testifying: 2
Written Fee Schedule: Yes
Min Charge for Deps: No
Min Charge for Trial: No
Cancellation Charge for Deps/Trial: No
Retainer Required: Yes, $400 (Non-Refundable, Replenishable)
Expenses Marked Up: No
Expenses Billed For: Airline Tickets, Telephone Calls
Portal-to-Portal: No **1st-class Airfare:** No
Written Retainer Agreement: No
Failure to Pay Bill Last 5 Years; Retaining Counsel: No **Opposing Counsel (Deps):** No

Nursing
Court: $200 **Review/Prep:** $125 **Deps:** $200
Majority: Plaintiff
Written Fee Schedule: Yes
Min Charge for Deps: No
Min Charge for Trial: No
Cancellation Charge for Deps/Trial: No
Retainer Required: Yes, $500 (Non-Refundable, One Time)
Expenses Marked Up: No
Expenses Billed For: Mileage, Airline Tickets, Demonstrative Aids
Portal-to-Portal: Yes **1st-class Airfare:** No
Written Retainer Agreement: No
Failure to Pay Bill Last 5 Years; Retaining Counsel: No

Nursing
Court: $200 **Review/Prep:** $125 **Deps:** $200
Years Testifying: 2 **Majority:** Plaintiff
Written Fee Schedule: Yes
Min Charge for Deps: No
Min Charge for Trial: No
Cancellation Charge for Deps/Trial: No
Retainer Required: Yes, $500 (Non-Refundable, One Time)
Expenses Marked Up: No
Expenses Billed For: Mileage, Airline Tickets, Demonstrative Aids
Portal-to-Portal: Yes **1st-class Airfare:** No
Written Retainer Agreement: No
Failure to Pay Bill Last 5 Years; Retaining Counsel: Yes **Opposing Counsel (Deps):** No

Obstetrics & Gynecology
Court: $500 **Review/Prep:** $250 **Deps:** $500
Years Testifying: 3 **Majority:** Plaintiff
Written Fee Schedule: No
Min Charge for Deps: Yes **Hours:** 6
Min Charge for Trial: Yes **Hours:** 6
Cancellation Charge for Deps/Trial: Yes
Retainer Required: Yes, $2,000 (Non-Refundable, One Time)
Procedure When Dep Exceeds Paid Time: Proceed without immediate payment
Expenses Marked Up: No
Expenses Billed For: Mileage, Airline Tickets, Photocopies, Telephone Calls, Lab/Testing, Photographs, Demonstrative Aids
Portal-to-Portal: Yes **1st-class Airfare:** Yes
Written Retainer Agreement: No
Failure to Pay Bill Last 5 Years; Retaining Counsel: Yes **Opposing Counsel (Deps):** No

Obstetrics & Gynecology
Court: $500 **Review/Prep:** $300 **Deps:** $500
Years Testifying: 8
Written Fee Schedule: Yes
Min Charge for Deps: Yes **Hours:** 8
Min Charge for Trial: Yes **Hours:** 8
Cancellation Charge for Deps/Trial: Yes
Retainer Required: Yes, $1,000 (Refundable, One Time)
Procedure When Dep Exceeds Paid Time: Proceed without immediate payment
Expenses Marked Up: No
Expenses Billed For: Mileage, Airline Tickets
Portal-to-Portal: No **1st-class Airfare:** No
Written Retainer Agreement: No
Failure to Pay Bill Last 5 Years; Retaining Counsel: Yes **Opposing Counsel (Deps):** No

Oil & Gas
Court: $175 **Review/Prep:** $175 **Deps:** $175
Years Testifying: 10
Written Fee Schedule: Yes
Min Charge for Deps: No
Min Charge for Trial: No
Cancellation Charge for Deps/Trial: Yes
Retainer Required: Yes, $5,000 (Non-Refundable, One Time)
Expenses Marked Up: No
Expenses Billed For: Mileage, Airline Tickets, Lab/Testing, Photographs, Demonstrative Aids
Portal-to-Portal: Yes **1st-class Airfare:** No
Written Retainer Agreement: No
Failure to Pay Bill Last 5 Years; Retaining Counsel: Yes **Opposing Counsel (Deps):** No

Oil & Gas/Chemicals
Court: $175 **Review/Prep:** $175 **Deps:** $175
Written Fee Schedule: Yes
Min Charge for Deps: No
Min Charge for Trial: No
Cancellation Charge for Deps/Trial: No
Retainer Required: Yes, $2,000 (Refundable, One Time)
Expenses Marked Up: No
Expenses Billed For: Mileage, Airline Tickets, Photocopies, Telephone Calls, Lab/Testing, Photographs, Demonstrative Aids
Portal-to-Portal: Yes **1st-class Airfare:** No
Written Retainer Agreement: Yes
Terms: Lawyer is responsible for fee, not lawyer's client, Fee schedules
Failure to Pay Bill Last 5 Years; Retaining Counsel: No **Opposing Counsel (Deps):** No

Oil & Gas
Court: $225 **Review/Prep:** $225 **Deps:** $225
Years Testifying: 25 **Majority:** Defendant
Written Fee Schedule: Yes
Min Charge for Deps: No
Min Charge for Trial: No
Cancellation Charge for Deps/Trial: No
Retainer Required: Yes, $2,000 (Non-Refundable, Replenishable)
Expenses Marked Up: No
Expenses Billed For: Mileage, Airline Tickets, Photocopies, Telephone Calls, Lab/Testing, Photographs, Demonstrative Aids
Portal-to-Portal: Yes **1st-class Airfare:** No
Written Retainer Agreement: No
Failure to Pay Bill Last 5 Years; Retaining Counsel: Yes **Opposing Counsel (Deps):** No

Ophthalmology
Court: $725 **Review/Prep:** $750 **Deps:** $750
Years Testifying: 43 **Majority:** Plaintiff
Written Fee Schedule: Yes
Min Charge for Deps: Yes **Hours:** 1
Min Charge for Trial: Yes **Hours:** 1
Cancellation Charge for Deps/Trial: Yes

Retainer Required: Yes, $750 (Non-Refundable, Replenishable)
Expenses Marked Up: No
Expenses Billed For: Mileage, Airline Tickets
Portal-to-Portal: Yes **1st-class Airfare:** No
Written Retainer Agreement: No
Failure to Pay Bill Last 5 Years; Retaining Counsel: No **Opposing Counsel (Deps):** No

Ophthalmology
Court: $250 **Review/Prep:** $250 **Deps:** $250
Years Testifying: 10 **Majority:** Defendant
Written Fee Schedule: No
Min Charge for Deps: No
Min Charge for Trial: No
Cancellation Charge for Deps/Trial: No
Retainer Required: No
Expenses Marked Up: No
Expenses Billed For: Airline Tickets, Demonstrative Aids
Portal-to-Portal: Yes **1st-class Airfare:** No
Written Retainer Agreement: No
Failure to Pay Bill Last 5 Years; Retaining Counsel: Yes **Opposing Counsel (Deps):** No

Ophthalmology
Court: $500 **Review/Prep:** $200 **Deps:** $300
Years Testifying: 3 **Majority:** Plaintiff
Written Fee Schedule: Yes
Min Charge for Deps: Yes
Min Charge for Trial: No
Cancellation Charge for Deps/Trial: Yes
Retainer Required: No
Procedure When Dep Exceeds Paid Time: Proceed without immediate payment
Expenses Marked Up: No
Expenses Billed For: Mileage, Airline Tickets, Photocopies, Telephone Calls, Photographs, Demonstrative Aids
Portal-to-Portal: Yes **1st-class Airfare:** No
Written Retainer Agreement: No
Failure to Pay Bill Last 5 Years; Retaining Counsel: No **Opposing Counsel (Deps):** No

Orthopedics
Court: $600 **Review/Prep:** $250 **Deps:** $600
Years Testifying: 10
Written Fee Schedule: Yes
Min Charge for Deps: Yes **Hours:** 4
Min Charge for Trial: Yes **Hours:** 4
Cancellation Charge for Deps/Trial: Yes
Retainer Required: No
Procedure When Dep Exceeds Paid Time: Proceed without immediate payment
Expenses Marked Up: No
Expenses Billed For: Mileage, Airline Tickets, Photographs, Demonstrative Aids
Portal-to-Portal: Yes **1st-class Airfare:** No
Written Retainer Agreement: No
Failure to Pay Bill Last 5 Years; Retaining Counsel: No **Opposing Counsel (Deps):** No

Orthopedics
Court: $2,000 **Review/Prep:** $200 **Deps:** $1,000
Years Testifying: 15
Written Fee Schedule: Yes
Min Charge for Deps: No **Hours:** 1
Min Charge for Trial: Yes **Hours:** 1
Cancellation Charge for Deps/Trial: Yes
Retainer Required: Yes, $200 (Non-Refundable, One Time)
Expenses Marked Up: No
Expenses Billed For: Airline Tickets, Photocopies
Portal-to-Portal: Yes **1st-class Airfare:** No
Written Retainer Agreement: No
Failure to Pay Bill Last 5 Years; Retaining Counsel: Yes **Opposing (Deps):** Yes

Physical Medicine & Rehabilitation
Court: $400 **Review/Prep:** $400 **Deps:** $400
Years Testifying: 15
Written Fee Schedule: Yes
Min Charge for Deps: Yes **Hours:** 4
Min Charge for Trial: Yes **Hours:** 4
Cancellation Charge for Deps/Trial: Yes
Retainer Required: No
Procedure When Dep Exceeds Paid Time: Proceed without immediate payment
Expenses Marked Up: No
Expenses Billed For: Airline Tickets, Photocopies, Telephone Calls, Lab/Testing, Photographs, Demonstrative Aids
Portal-to-Portal: Yes **1st-class Airfare:** Yes
Written Retainer Agreement: Yes
Terms: Out-of-pocket expense policies, In-court testimony minimums, Retaining counsel pays all deposition charges, Fee schedules, Portal-to-portal travel time, Deposition minimum fee, Payment for preparation time, First class air travel
Failure to Pay Bill Last 5 Years; Retaining Counsel: Yes **Opposing Counsel (Deps):** No

Physical Medicine & Rehabilitation
Court: $350 **Review/Prep:** $350 **Deps:** $350
Years Testifying: 2
Written Fee Schedule: No
Min Charge for Deps: No
Min Charge for Trial: No
Cancellation Charge for Deps/Trial: No
Retainer Required: No
Expenses Marked Up: No
Expenses Billed For: Mileage, Airline Tickets, Photocopies, Lab/Testing
Portal-to-Portal: Yes **1st-class Airfare:** No
Written Retainer Agreement: No
Failure to Pay Bill Last 5 Years; Retaining Counsel: No **Opposing Counsel (Deps):** No

Podiatry
Court: $1,500 **Review/Prep:** $375 **Deps:** $1,500
Years Testifying: 8 **Majority:** Defendant
Written Fee Schedule: No
Min Charge for Deps: Yes **Hours:** 5
Min Charge for Trial: Yes **Hours:** 5
Cancellation Charge for Deps/Trial: No
Retainer Required: Yes, $2,500 (Refundable, One Time)
Procedure When Dep Exceeds Paid Time: Proceed without immediate payment
Expenses Marked Up: No
Expenses Billed For: Airline Tickets, Demonstrative Aids
Portal-to-Portal: Yes **1st-class Airfare:** No
Written Retainer Agreement: No
Failure to Pay Bill Last 5 Years; Retaining Counsel: Yes **Opposing (Deps):** Yes

Psychiatry
Court: $500 **Review/Prep:** $300 **Deps:** $500
Years Testifying: 30
Written Fee Schedule: No
Min Charge for Deps: No
Min Charge for Trial: No
Cancellation Charge for Deps/Trial: No
Retainer Required: No
Expenses Marked Up: No
Expenses Billed For: Airline Tickets, Lab/Testing
Portal-to-Portal: No **1st-class Airfare:** Yes
Written Retainer Agreement: No
Failure to Pay Bill Last 5 Years; Retaining Counsel: No **Opposing Counsel (Deps):** No

Psychiatry
Court: $350 **Review/Prep:** $300 **Deps:** $350
Years Testifying: 13 **Majority:** Plaintiff
Written Fee Schedule: Yes
Min Charge for Deps: No
Min Charge for Trial: No
Cancellation Charge for Deps/Trial: No
Retainer Required: Yes, $1,500 (Refundable, One Time)
Expenses Marked Up: No
Expenses Billed For: Airline Tickets
Portal-to-Portal: Yes **1st-class Airfare:** No
Written Retainer Agreement: No
Failure to Pay Bill Last 5 Years; Retaining Counsel: No **Opposing Counsel (Deps):** No

Railroads
Court: $175 **Review/Prep:** $175 **Deps:** $175
Years Testifying: 33 **Majority:** Plaintiff
Written Fee Schedule: Yes
Min Charge for Deps: No
Min Charge for Trial: No
Cancellation Charge for Deps/Trial: No
Retainer Required: No
Expenses Marked Up: No

Expenses Billed For: Mileage, Airline Tickets, Photocopies, Telephone Calls, Lab/Testing, Photographs, Demonstrative Aids
Portal-to-Portal: No **1st-class Airfare:** No
Written Retainer Agreement: Yes
Terms: Lawyer is responsible for fee, not lawyer's client, Out-of-pocket expense policies, In-court testimony minimums, Fee schedules, Attorney's fees if forced to sue for collection, Payment for preparation time
Failure to Pay Bill Last 5 Years; Retaining Counsel: Yes **Opposing Counsel (Deps):** No

Real Estate
Court: $100 **Review/Prep:** $100 **Deps:** $100
Years Testifying: 10
Written Fee Schedule: Yes
Min Charge for Deps: No
Min Charge for Trial: No
Cancellation Charge for Deps/Trial: No
Retainer Required: No
Expenses Marked Up: No
Expenses Billed For: Mileage, Airline Tickets, Photocopies, Telephone Calls, Lab/Testing, Photographs, Demonstrative Aids
Portal-to-Portal: Yes **1st-class Airfare:** No
Written Retainer Agreement: Yes
Terms: Lawyer is responsible for fee, not lawyer's client, Interest for delinquent accounts, Out-of-pocket expense policies, In-court testimony minimums, Fee schedules, Portal-to-portal travel time, Attorney's fees if forced to sue for collection, Payment for preparation time
Failure to Pay Bill Last 5 Years; Retaining Counsel: Yes **Opposing Counsel (Deps):** No

Real Estate
Court: $295 **Review/Prep:** $195 **Deps:** $295
Years Testifying: 17
Written Fee Schedule: No
Min Charge for Deps: No
Min Charge for Trial: No
Cancellation Charge for Deps/Trial: No
Retainer Required: Yes, $4,000 (Refundable, Replenishable)
Procedure When Dep Exceeds Paid Time: Varies depending on case
Expenses Marked Up: No
Expenses Billed For: Mileage, Airline Tickets, Photocopies, Telephone Calls, Lab/Testing, Photographs, Demonstrative Aids
Portal-to-Portal: Yes **1st-class Airfare:** No
Written Retainer Agreement: Yes
Terms: Out-of-pocket expense policies, In-court testimony minimums, Retaining counsel pays all deposition charges, Portal-to-portal travel time, Deposition minimum fee
Failure to Pay Bill Last 5 Years; Retaining Counsel: Yes

Safety, Highway
Court: $300 **Review/Prep:** $250 **Deps:** $300
Years Testifying: 17 **Majority:** Plaintiff
Written Fee Schedule: Yes
Min Charge for Deps: Yes **Hours:** 5
Min Charge for Trial: Yes **Hours:** 5
Cancellation Charge for Deps/Trial: No
Retainer Required: Yes, $1,500 (Non-Refundable)
Expenses Marked Up: No
Expenses Billed For: Mileage, Airline Tickets, Lab/Testing, Photographs, Demonstrative Aids
Portal-to-Portal: No **1st-class Airfare:** No
Written Retainer Agreement: No
Failure to Pay Bill Last 5 Years; Retaining Counsel: No **Opposing Counsel (Deps):** Yes

Security
Court: $150 **Review/Prep:** $150 **Deps:** $150
Years Testifying: 12
Written Fee Schedule: Yes
Min Charge for Deps: No
Min Charge for Trial: No
Cancellation Charge for Deps/Trial: No
Retainer Required: Yes, $3,000 (Non-Refundable, Replenishable)
Expenses Marked Up: No
Expenses Billed For: Mileage, Airline Tickets, Telephone Calls, Lab/Testing, Photographs, Demonstrative Aids
Portal-to-Portal: Yes **1st-class Airfare:** No
Written Retainer Agreement: Yes
Terms: Lawyer is responsible for fee, not lawyer's client, Interest for delinquent accounts, Out-of-pocket expense policies, Fee schedules, Attorney's fees if forced to sue for collection, Payment for preparation time
Failure to Pay Bill Last 5 Years; Retaining Counsel: Yes **Opposing Counsel (Deps):** No

Slip, trip & fall
Court: $150 **Review/Prep:** $100 **Deps:** $100
Years Testifying: 17 **Majority:** Defendant
Written Fee Schedule: Yes
Min Charge for Deps: No
Min Charge for Trial: No
Cancellation Charge for Deps/Trial: No
Retainer Required: Yes, Depends on case
Expenses Marked Up: No
Expenses Billed For: Mileage, Airline Tickets, Photocopies, Telephone Calls, Lab/Testing, Photographs, Demonstrative Aids
Portal-to-Portal: Yes **1st-class Airfare:** No
Written Retainer Agreement: Yes
Terms: Lawyer is responsible for fee, not lawyer's client, Out-of-pocket expense policies, Fee schedules, Portal-to-portal travel time, Deposition minimum fee, Payment for preparation time
Failure to Pay Bill Last 5 Years; Retaining Counsel: No **Opposing Counsel (Deps):** No

Surgery, General
Court: $500 **Review/Prep:** $200 **Deps:** $350
Years Testifying: 15 **Majority:** Defendant
Written Fee Schedule: No
Min Charge for Deps: Yes **Hours:** 2
Min Charge for Trial: Yes **Hours:** 2
Cancellation Charge for Deps/Trial: Yes
Retainer Required: No
Expenses Marked Up: No
Expenses Billed For: Mileage, Airline Tickets, Photocopies, Telephone Calls, Demonstrative Aids
Portal-to-Portal: Yes **1st-class Airfare:** No
Written Retainer Agreement: No
Failure to Pay Bill Last 5 Years; Retaining Counsel: No **Opposing Counsel (Deps):** No

Surgery, General
Court: $400 **Review/Prep:** $400 **Deps:** $400
Years Testifying: 4
Written Fee Schedule: Yes
Min Charge for Deps: Yes **Hours:** 8
Min Charge for Trial: Yes **Hours:** 8
Cancellation Charge for Deps/Trial: Yes
Retainer Required: Yes, $4,000 (Non-Refundable, One Time)
Procedure When Dep Exceeds Paid Time: Proceed without immediate payment
Expenses Marked Up: No
Expenses Billed For: Airline Tickets
Portal-to-Portal: Yes **1st-class Airfare:** Yes
Written Retainer Agreement: No
Failure to Pay Bill Last 5 Years; Retaining Counsel: No **Opposing Counsel (Deps):** No

Surgery, Neurological
Court: $750 **Review/Prep:** $250 **Deps:** $500
Years Testifying: 4
Written Fee Schedule: Yes
Min Charge for Deps: Yes **Hours:** 2
Min Charge for Trial: Yes **Hours:** 2
Cancellation Charge for Deps/Trial: Yes
Retainer Required: Yes, $1,500 (Non-Refundable, One Time)
Expenses Marked Up: No
Expenses Billed For: Mileage, Airline Tickets, Photocopies, Telephone Calls
Portal-to-Portal: Yes
Failure to Pay Bill Last 5 Years; Retaining Counsel: No **Opposing Counsel (Deps):** No

Trucking
Court: $250 **Review/Prep:** $175 **Deps:** $250
Years Testifying: 5 **Majority:** Plaintiff
Written Fee Schedule: Yes

Min Charge for Deps: Yes **Hours:** 4
Min Charge for Trial: Yes **Hours:** 4
Cancellation Charge for Deps/Trial: Yes
Retainer Required: Yes, $2,500 (Refundable, Replenishable)
Expenses Marked Up: No
Expenses Billed For: Mileage, Airline Tickets, Photocopies, Lab/Testing, Photographs, Demonstrative Aids
Portal-to-Portal: Yes **1st-class Airfare:** No
Written Retainer Agreement: Yes
Terms: Lawyer is responsible for fee, not lawyer's client, Interest for delinquent accounts, Out-of-pocket expense policies, In-court testimony minimums, Retaining counsel pays all deposition charges, Portal-to-portal travel time, Attorney's fees if forced to sue for collection, Deposition minimum fee, Payment for preparation time
Failure to Pay Bill Last 5 Years; Retaining Counsel: Yes **Opposing Counsel (Deps):** No

Trusts & Estates/Taxation
Court: $350 **Review/Prep:** $250 **Deps:** $350
Years Testifying: 30 **Majority:** Plaintiff
Written Fee Schedule: No
Min Charge for Deps: Yes **Hours:** 3
Min Charge for Trial: Yes **Hours:** 3
Cancellation Charge for Deps/Trial: Yes
Retainer Required: Yes, $2,500 (Non-Refundable, Replenishable)
Procedure When Dep Exceeds Paid Time: Proceed without immediate payment
Expenses Marked Up: No
Expenses Billed For: Mileage, Airline Tickets, Photocopies, Telephone Calls
Portal-to-Portal: Yes **1st-class Airfare:** No
Written Retainer Agreement: Yes
Terms: Lawyer is responsible for fee, not lawyer's client, Out-of-pocket expense policies, In-court testimony minimums, Retaining counsel pays all deposition charges, Portal-to-portal travel time, Attorney's fees if forced to sue for collection, Deposition minimum fee, Payment for preparation time
Failure to Pay Bill Last 5 Years; Retaining Counsel: No **Opposing Counsel (Deps):** No

Valuation, Business
Court: $300 **Review/Prep:** $200 **Deps:** $300
Years Testifying: 25
Written Fee Schedule: No
Min Charge for Deps: No **Hours:** 4
Min Charge for Trial: Yes **Hours:** 4
Cancellation Charge for Deps/Trial: Yes
Retainer Required: Yes, 50% Report Fee (Refundable, One Time)
Expenses Marked Up: No
Expenses Billed For: Mileage, Airline Tickets
Portal-to-Portal: Yes **1st-class Airfare:** No
Written Retainer Agreement: Yes
Terms: Out-of-pocket expense policies, In-court testimony minimums, Retaining counsel pays all deposition charges, Fee schedules, Portal-to-portal travel time, Deposition minimum fee, Payment for preparation time
Failure to Pay Bill Last 5 Years; Retaining Counsel: No **Opposing Counsel (Deps):** No

Valuation, Business
Court: $200 **Review/Prep:** $200 **Deps:** $200
Years Testifying: 25
Written Fee Schedule: No
Min Charge for Deps: No
Min Charge for Trial: No
Cancellation Charge for Deps/Trial: No
Retainer Required: Yes, $3,750 (Refundable, One Time)
Expenses Marked Up: No
Expenses Billed For: Airline Tickets, Photocopies, Telephone Calls
Portal-to-Portal: Yes **1st-class Airfare:** No
Written Retainer Agreement: No
Failure to Pay Bill Last 5 Years; Retaining Counsel: No **Opposing Counsel (Deps):** No

Valuation, Business
Court: $300 **Review/Prep:** $300 **Deps:** $300
Years Testifying: 5
Written Fee Schedule: Yes
Min Charge for Deps: No
Min Charge for Trial: No
Cancellation Charge for Deps/Trial: No
Retainer Required: Yes, $7,500 (Refundable, One Time)
Expenses Marked Up: No
Expenses Billed For: Mileage, Airline Tickets, Photocopies, Demonstrative Aids
Portal-to-Portal: Yes **1st-class Airfare:** No
Written Retainer Agreement: Yes
Terms: Interest for delinquent accounts, Out-of-pocket expense policies, Retaining counsel pays all deposition charges, Fee schedules, Attorney's fees if forced to sue for collection, Arbitration clause
Failure to Pay Bill Last 5 Years; Retaining Counsel: Yes **Opposing Counsel (Deps):** No

Vocational Rehabilitation
Court: $200 **Review/Prep:** $200 **Deps:** $200
Years Testifying: 30 **Majority:** Defendant
Written Fee Schedule: Yes
Min Charge for Deps: No
Min Charge for Trial: No
Cancellation Charge for Deps/Trial: No
Retainer Required: No
Expenses Marked Up: No
Expenses Billed For: Airline Tickets
Portal-to-Portal: Yes **1st-class Airfare:** No
Written Retainer Agreement: No
Failure to Pay Bill Last 5 Years; Retaining Counsel: No **Opposing Counsel (Deps):** No

Utah

Accident Reconstruction/ Biomechanics
Court: $210 **Review/Prep:** $160 **Deps:** $210
Years Testifying: 7 **Majority:** Defendant
Written Fee Schedule: Yes
Min Charge for Deps: No
Min Charge for Trial: No
Cancellation Charge for Deps/Trial: Yes
Retainer Required: Yes, $750 (Refundable, One Time)
Procedure When Dep Exceeds Paid Time: Proceed without immediate payment
Expenses Marked Up: Yes
Expenses Billed For: Mileage, Airline Tickets, Photographs, Demonstrative Aids
Portal-to-Portal: No **1st-class Airfare:** No
Written Retainer Agreement: No
Failure to Pay Bill Last 5 Years; Retaining Counsel: No **Opposing Counsel (Deps):** No

Engineering, Geotechnical
Court: $150 **Review/Prep:** $120 **Deps:** $150
Years Testifying: 10
Written Fee Schedule: No
Min Charge for Deps: No
Min Charge for Trial: No
Cancellation Charge for Deps/Trial: No
Retainer Required: No
Expenses Marked Up: Yes
Expenses Billed For: Mileage, Airline Tickets, Photocopies, Lab/Testing, Photographs
Portal-to-Portal: Yes **1st-class Airfare:** No
Written Retainer Agreement: Yes
Terms: Lawyer is responsible for fee, not lawyer's client, Interest for delinquent accounts, Out-of-pocket expense policies, Portal-to-portal travel time, Attorney's fees if forced to sue for collection, Payment for preparation time
Failure to Pay Bill Last 5 Years; Retaining Counsel: Yes **Opposing (Deps):** Yes

Occupational Medicine/ Environmental Toxicology
Court: $500 **Review/Prep:** $500 **Deps:** $500
Years Testifying: 5
Written Fee Schedule: No
Min Charge for Deps: Yes **Hours:** 4
Min Charge for Trial: Yes **Hours:** 4
Cancellation Charge for Deps/Trial: Yes
Retainer Required: Yes, Depends on case (Refundable, One Time)

Procedure When Dep Exceeds Paid Time: Proceed without immediate payment
Expenses Marked Up: No
Expenses Billed For: Mileage, Airline Tickets, Photocopies, Telephone Calls, Lab/Testing, Photographs
Portal-to-Portal: Yes **1st-class Airfare:** No
Written Retainer Agreement: Yes
Terms: In-court testimony minimums, Retaining counsel pays all deposition charges, Fee schedules, Deposition minimum fee, Payment for preparation time
Failure to Pay Bill Last 5 Years; Retaining Counsel: Yes **Opposing Counsel (Deps):** No

Orthopedics
Court: $1,000 **Review/Prep:** $250 **Deps:** $300
Years Testifying: 10 **Majority:** Defendant
Written Fee Schedule: No
Min Charge for Deps: Yes
Min Charge for Trial: No
Cancellation Charge for Deps/Trial: Yes
Retainer Required: No
Expenses Marked Up: No
Expenses Billed For: Mileage, Airline Tickets
1st-class Airfare: No
Written Retainer Agreement: No
Failure to Pay Bill Last 5 Years; Retaining Counsel: No **Opposing Counsel (Deps):** No

Physical Medicine & Rehabilitation
Court: $350 **Review/Prep:** $350 **Deps:** $350
Years Testifying: 15
Written Fee Schedule: No
Min Charge for Deps: Yes **Hours:** 1
Min Charge for Trial: Yes **Hours:** 1
Cancellation Charge for Deps/Trial: Yes
Retainer Required: No
Expenses Marked Up: Yes
Expenses Billed For: Photocopies, Telephone Calls
Portal-to-Portal: Yes **1st-class Airfare:** No
Written Retainer Agreement: No
Failure to Pay Bill Last 5 Years; Retaining Counsel: No **Opposing Counsel (Deps):** No

Vermont

Accounting
Court: $85 **Review/Prep:** $85 **Deps:** $85
Years Testifying: 30 **Majority:** Plaintiff
Written Fee Schedule: No
Min Charge for Deps: No
Min Charge for Trial: No
Cancellation Charge for Deps/Trial: No
Retainer Required: No
Expenses Marked Up: No
Expenses Billed For: Mileage, Airline Tickets, Lab/Testing, Photographs
Portal-to-Portal: Yes **1st-class Airfare:** No
Written Retainer Agreement: No
Failure to Pay Bill Last 5 Years; Retaining Counsel: No **Opposing Counsel (Deps):** No

Appraisal, Real Estate
Court: $175 **Review/Prep:** $175 **Deps:** $175
Years Testifying: 35
Written Fee Schedule: No
Min Charge for Deps: Yes **Hours:** 4
Min Charge for Trial: Yes **Hours:** 4
Cancellation Charge for Deps/Trial: No
Retainer Required: Yes, Depends on case (Refundable, One Time)
Expenses Marked Up: No
Expenses Billed For: Airline Tickets, Photocopies, Photographs, Demonstrative Aids
Portal-to-Portal: Yes **1st-class Airfare:** No
Written Retainer Agreement: No
Failure to Pay Bill Last 5 Years; Retaining Counsel: No **Opposing Counsel (Deps):** No

Chiropractic
Court: $400 **Review/Prep:** $300 **Deps:** $400
Years Testifying: 20
Written Fee Schedule: Yes
Min Charge for Deps: Yes **Hours:** 1
Min Charge for Trial: Yes **Hours:** 1
Cancellation Charge for Deps/Trial: Yes
Retainer Required: No
Procedure When Dep Exceeds Paid Time: Proceed without immediate payment
Expenses Marked Up: No
Expenses Billed For: Airline Tickets, Photocopies, Telephone Calls, Photographs
Portal-to-Portal: Yes **1st-class Airfare:** No
Written Retainer Agreement: Yes
Terms: Lawyer is responsible for fee, not lawyer's client, Interest for delinquent accounts, In-court testimony minimums, Retaining counsel pays all deposition charges, Fee schedules, Portal-to-portal travel time, Deposition minimum fee, Payment for preparation time
Failure to Pay Bill Last 5 Years; Retaining Counsel: No **Opposing Counsel (Deps):** No

Neuropsychology/Psychology
Court: $250 **Review/Prep:** $250 **Deps:** $250
Years Testifying: 10
Written Fee Schedule: Yes
Min Charge for Deps: Yes **Hours:** 8
Min Charge for Trial: Yes **Hours:** 8
Cancellation Charge for Deps/Trial: Yes
Retainer Required: Yes, Depends on case (Refundable, Replenishable)
Procedure When Dep Exceeds Paid Time: Get payment before proceeding further
Expenses Marked Up: Yes
Expenses Billed For: Mileage, Airline Tickets, Photocopies, Telephone Calls, Lab/Testing, Photographs, Demonstrative Aids
Portal-to-Portal: Yes
Written Retainer Agreement: No
Failure to Pay Bill Last 5 Years; Retaining Counsel: No **Opposing Counsel (Deps):** No

Occupational Medicine
Court: $500 **Review/Prep:** $300 **Deps:** $500
Years Testifying: 3 **Majority:** Defendant
Written Fee Schedule: Yes
Min Charge for Deps: Yes **Hours:** Varies
Min Charge for Trial: Yes **Hours:** Varies
Retainer Required: Yes,
Procedure When Dep Exceeds Paid Time: Varies depending on case
Expenses Marked Up: No
Portal-to-Portal: Yes
Written Retainer Agreement: No
Failure to Pay Bill Last 5 Years; Retaining Counsel: No **Opposing Counsel (Deps):**

Psychology
Court: $300 **Review/Prep:** $150 **Deps:** $300
Years Testifying: 10 **Majority:** Plaintiff
Written Fee Schedule: Yes
Min Charge for Deps: Yes **Hours:** 4
Min Charge for Trial: Yes **Hours:** 4
Cancellation Charge for Deps/Trial: Yes
Retainer Required: Yes, $1,500 (Refundable, One Time)
Procedure When Dep Exceeds Paid Time: Proceed without immediate payment
Expenses Marked Up: No
Expenses Billed For: Mileage, Photocopies, Telephone Calls, Lab/Testing
Portal-to-Portal: Yes **1st-class Airfare:** Yes
Written Retainer Agreement: Yes
Terms: Lawyer is responsible for fee, not lawyer's client, Interest for delinquent accounts, Out-of-pocket expense policies, Retaining counsel pays all deposition charges, Fee schedules, Portal-to-portal travel time, Deposition minimum fee, Payment for preparation time
Failure to Pay Bill Last 5 Years; Retaining Counsel: No **Opposing Counsel (Deps):** No

Virginia

Document Examiner
Court: $200 **Review/Prep:** $200 **Deps:** $200
Years Testifying: 37
Written Fee Schedule: Yes
Min Charge for Deps: No
Min Charge for Trial: No
Cancellation Charge for Deps/Trial: Yes
Retainer Required: Yes, $500 (Non-Refundable, One Time)

Procedure When Dep Exceeds Paid Time: Proceed without immediate payment
Expenses Marked Up: No
Expenses Billed For: Mileage, Airline Tickets, Lab/Testing, Photographs, Demonstrative Aids
Portal-to-Portal: Yes **1st-class Airfare:** No
Written Retainer Agreement: No
Failure to Pay Bill Last 5 Years; Retaining Counsel: No **Opposing Counsel (Deps):** Yes

Engineering, Civil/Engineering, Railway
Court: $250 **Review/Prep:** $170 **Deps:** $250
Years Testifying: 15 **Majority:** Plaintiff
Written Fee Schedule: Yes
Min Charge for Deps: Yes **Hours:** 4
Min Charge for Trial: Yes **Hours:** 4
Cancellation Charge for Deps/Trial: Yes
Retainer Required: Yes, $4,000 (One Time)
Procedure When Dep Exceeds Paid Time: Get payment before proceeding further
Expenses Marked Up: Yes
Expenses Billed For: Mileage, Airline Tickets, Photocopies, Telephone Calls, Lab/Testing, Photographs, Demonstrative Aids
Portal-to-Portal: Yes **1st-class Airfare:** Yes
Written Retainer Agreement: Yes
Terms: Lawyer is responsible for fee, not lawyer's client, Interest for delinquent accounts, Out-of-pocket expense policies, In-court testimony minimums, Retaining counsel pays all deposition charges, Fee schedules, Portal-to-portal travel time, Attorney's fees if forced to sue for collection, Deposition minimum fee, Payment for preparation time, First class air travel, Right to increase fees after 1 yr., Payment for review/correction of depo transcripts
Failure to Pay Bill Last 5 Years; Retaining Counsel: Yes **Opposing (Deps):** Yes

Engineering, Electrical
Court: $200 **Review/Prep:** $200 **Deps:** $200
Years Testifying: 12
Written Fee Schedule: No
Min Charge for Deps: No
Min Charge for Trial: No
Cancellation Charge for Deps/Trial: No
Retainer Required: Yes, $3,000 (Refundable, One Time)
Expenses Marked Up: No
Expenses Billed For: Mileage, Airline Tickets, Photocopies, Lab/Testing, Photographs, Demonstrative Aids
Portal-to-Portal: Yes **1st-class Airfare:** No
Written Retainer Agreement: Yes
Terms: Lawyer is responsible for fee, not lawyer's client, Interest for delinquent accounts, Out-of-pocket expense policies, Retaining counsel pays all deposition charges, Attorney's fees if forced to sue for collection, Payment for preparation time
Failure to Pay Bill Last 5 Years; Retaining Counsel: Yes **Opposing Counsel (Deps):** No

Environmental/Geology, Hydro
Court: $250 **Review/Prep:** $150 **Deps:** $250
Years Testifying: 5 **Majority:** Plaintiff
Written Fee Schedule: Yes
Min Charge for Deps: No
Min Charge for Trial: No
Cancellation Charge for Deps/Trial: No
Retainer Required: No
Expenses Marked Up: Yes
Expenses Billed For: Mileage, Airline Tickets, Photocopies, Telephone Calls, Lab/Testing, Photographs, Demonstrative Aids
Portal-to-Portal: Yes **1st-class Airfare:** No
Written Retainer Agreement: No
Failure to Pay Bill Last 5 Years; Retaining Counsel: No **Opposing Counsel (Deps):** No

Family Practice
Court: $200 **Review/Prep:** $200 **Deps:** $200
Years Testifying: 11
Written Fee Schedule: Yes
Min Charge for Deps: Yes **Hours:** 1
Min Charge for Trial: Yes **Hours:** 1
Cancellation Charge for Deps/Trial: Yes
Retainer Required: No
Procedure When Dep Exceeds Paid Time: Proceed without immediate payment
Expenses Marked Up: No
Expenses Billed For: Mileage, Airline Tickets, Photocopies, Telephone Calls, Lab/Testing
Portal-to-Portal: Yes **1st-class Airfare:** No
Written Retainer Agreement: Yes
Failure to Pay Bill Last 5 Years; Retaining Counsel: No **Opposing Counsel (Deps):** No

Gastroenterology
Court: $500 **Review/Prep:** $300 **Deps:** $400
Years Testifying: 4 **Majority:** Defendant
Written Fee Schedule: Yes
Min Charge for Deps: No **Hours:** 4
Min Charge for Trial: Yes **Hours:** 4
Cancellation Charge for Deps/Trial: No
Retainer Required: Yes, $600 (Non-Refundable, One Time)
Expenses Marked Up: No
Expenses Billed For: Mileage, Airline Tickets
Portal-to-Portal: Yes **1st-class Airfare:** No
Written Retainer Agreement: No
Failure to Pay Bill Last 5 Years; Retaining Counsel: Yes **Opposing Counsel (Deps):** No

Neurology
Court: $450 **Review/Prep:** $350 **Deps:** $450
Years Testifying: 10
Written Fee Schedule: Yes
Min Charge for Deps: Yes **Hours:** 4
Min Charge for Trial: Yes **Hours:** 4
Cancellation Charge for Deps/Trial: Yes
Retainer Required: Yes, $7,500 (Refundable, One Time)
Procedure When Dep Exceeds Paid Time: Proceed without immediate payment
Expenses Marked Up: Yes
Expenses Billed For: Mileage, Airline Tickets, Photocopies, Telephone Calls, Photographs
Portal-to-Portal: Yes **1st-class Airfare:** No
Written Retainer Agreement: Yes
Terms: Lawyer is responsible for fee, not lawyer's client, Interest for delinquent accounts, Out-of-pocket expense policies, Retaining counsel pays all deposition charges, Fee schedules, Attorney's fees if forced to sue for collection
Failure to Pay Bill Last 5 Years; Retaining Counsel: Yes **Opposing Counsel (Deps):** No

Neurology
Review/Prep: $375 **Deps:** $600
Years Testifying: 25
Written Fee Schedule: Yes
Min Charge for Deps: Yes **Hours:** 6
Min Charge for Trial: Yes **Hours:** 6
Cancellation Charge for Deps/Trial: No
Retainer Required: Yes, $750 (Non-Refundable)
Procedure When Dep Exceeds Paid Time: Proceed without immediate payment
Expenses Marked Up: No
Expenses Billed For: Mileage, Airline Tickets
Portal-to-Portal: Yes **1st-class Airfare:** No
Written Retainer Agreement: Yes
Terms: Out-of-pocket expense policies, In-court testimony minimums, Retaining counsel pays all deposition charges, Fee schedules, Deposition minimum fee
Failure to Pay Bill Last 5 Years; Retaining Counsel: No **Opposing Counsel (Deps):** No

Neuropsychology
Court: $500 **Review/Prep:** $400 **Deps:** $500
Years Testifying: 12
Written Fee Schedule: Yes
Min Charge for Deps: Yes **Hours:** 2
Min Charge for Trial: Yes **Hours:** 2
Cancellation Charge for Deps/Trial: Yes
Retainer Required: Yes, $2,500 (Refundable, One Time)
Procedure When Dep Exceeds Paid Time: Get payment before proceeding further
Expenses Marked Up: Yes

Expenses Billed For: Mileage, Airline Tickets, Photocopies, Telephone Calls, Lab/Testing, Photographs, Demonstrative Aids
Portal-to-Portal: Yes **1st-class Airfare:** No
Written Retainer Agreement: Yes
Terms: Lawyer is responsible for fee, not lawyer's client, Out-of-pocket expense policies, In-court testimony minimums, Retaining counsel pays all deposition charges, Fee schedules, Portal-to-portal travel time, Deposition minimum fee, Payment for preparation time
Failure to Pay Bill Last 5 Years; Retaining Counsel: Yes **Opposing (Deps):** Yes

Neuropsychology
Court: $500 **Review/Prep:** $400 **Deps:** $500
Years Testifying: 12
Written Fee Schedule: Yes
Min Charge for Deps: Yes **Hours:** 2
Min Charge for Trial: Yes **Hours:** 2
Cancellation Charge for Deps/Trial: Yes
Retainer Required: Yes, $2,500 (Refundable, One Time)
Procedure When Dep Exceeds Paid Time: Get payment before proceeding further
Expenses Marked Up: Yes
Expenses Billed For: Mileage, Airline Tickets, Photocopies, Telephone Calls, Lab/Testing, Photographs, Demonstrative Aids
Portal-to-Portal: Yes **1st-class Airfare:** No
Written Retainer Agreement: Yes
Terms: Lawyer is responsible for fee, not lawyer's client, Out-of-pocket expense policies, In-court testimony minimums, Retaining counsel pays all deposition charges, Fee schedules, Portal-to-portal travel time, Deposition minimum fee, Payment for preparation time
Failure to Pay Bill Last 5 Years; Retaining Counsel: Yes **Opposing (Deps):** Yes

Neuroradiology
Court: $700 **Review/Prep:** $350 **Deps:** $700
Years Testifying: 20
Written Fee Schedule: No
Min Charge for Deps: Yes **Hours:** 2
Min Charge for Trial: Yes **Hours:** 2
Cancellation Charge for Deps/Trial: No
Retainer Required: No
Expenses Marked Up: No
Expenses Billed For: Mileage, Airline Tickets, Photocopies, Telephone Calls, Lab/Testing, Photographs, Demonstrative Aids
Portal-to-Portal: Yes **1st-class Airfare:** No
Written Retainer Agreement: No
Failure to Pay Bill Last 5 Years; Retaining Counsel: Yes **Opposing Counsel (Deps):** No

Ophthalmology
Court: $7,500 **Review/Prep:** $350 **Deps:** $350
Years Testifying: 15 **Majority:** Plaintiff
Written Fee Schedule: Yes
Min Charge for Deps: No **Hours:** 1
Min Charge for Trial: Yes **Hours:** 1
Cancellation Charge for Deps/Trial: Yes
Retainer Required: No
Expenses Marked Up: Yes
Expenses Billed For: Mileage, Airline Tickets, Photocopies, Telephone Calls, Lab/Testing, Photographs, Demonstrative Aids
Portal-to-Portal: No **1st-class Airfare:** No
Written Retainer Agreement: No
Failure to Pay Bill Last 5 Years; Retaining Counsel: Yes **Opposing Counsel (Deps):** No

Physical Medicine & Rehabilitation
Court: $350 **Review/Prep:** $300 **Deps:** $350
Years Testifying: 16
Written Fee Schedule: Yes
Min Charge for Deps: Yes **Hours:** 4
Min Charge for Trial: Yes **Hours:** 4
Cancellation Charge for Deps/Trial: Yes
Retainer Required: No
Expenses Marked Up: No
Portal-to-Portal: Yes **1st-class Airfare:** No
Written Retainer Agreement: Yes
Terms: In-court testimony minimums, Retaining counsel pays all deposition charges, Fee schedules, Portal-to-portal travel time, Deposition minimum fee
Failure to Pay Bill Last 5 Years; Retaining Counsel: Yes **Opposing (Deps):** Yes

Podiatry
Court: $400 **Review/Prep:** $200 **Deps:** $300
Years Testifying: 3 **Majority:** Plaintiff
Written Fee Schedule: Yes
Min Charge for Deps: Yes **Hours:** 6
Min Charge for Trial: Yes **Hours:** 6
Cancellation Charge for Deps/Trial: Yes
Retainer Required: Yes, $800 (Non-Refundable, One Time)
Expenses Marked Up: No
Expenses Billed For: Mileage, Airline Tickets, Photocopies, Telephone Calls
Portal-to-Portal: Yes **1st-class Airfare:** No
Written Retainer Agreement: Yes
Terms: In-court testimony minimums, Retaining counsel pays all deposition charges, Fee schedules, Deposition minimum fee
Failure to Pay Bill Last 5 Years; Retaining Counsel: Yes **Opposing Counsel (Deps):** No

Product Liability
Court: $300 **Review/Prep:** $300 **Deps:** $300
Years Testifying: 16 **Majority:** Plaintiff
Written Fee Schedule: Yes
Min Charge for Deps: Yes **Hours:** 11
Min Charge for Trial: Yes **Hours:** 11
Cancellation Charge for Deps/Trial: No
Retainer Required: Yes, $2,000 (Non-Refundable, One Time)
Expenses Marked Up: Yes
Expenses Billed For: Mileage, Airline Tickets, Photographs, Demonstrative Aids
Portal-to-Portal: Yes **1st-class Airfare:** No
Written Retainer Agreement: No
Failure to Pay Bill Last 5 Years; Retaining Counsel: Yes **Opposing Counsel (Deps):** No

Psychology
Court: $225 **Review/Prep:** $175 **Deps:** $225
Years Testifying: 15
Written Fee Schedule: Yes
Min Charge for Deps: Yes **Hours:** 2
Min Charge for Trial: Yes **Hours:** 2
Cancellation Charge for Deps/Trial: Yes
Retainer Required: Yes, $1,500 (Refundable, One Time)
Procedure When Dep Exceeds Paid Time: Proceed without immediate payment
Expenses Marked Up: No
Expenses Billed For: Airline Tickets, Lab/Testing
Portal-to-Portal: Yes **1st-class Airfare:** No
Written Retainer Agreement: Yes
Terms: Lawyer is responsible for fee, not lawyer's client, Interest for delinquent accounts, Out-of-pocket expense policies, In-court testimony minimums, Retaining counsel pays all deposition charges, Fee schedules, Portal-to-portal travel time, Attorney's fees if forced to sue for collection, Deposition minimum fee, Payment for preparation time
Failure to Pay Bill Last 5 Years; Retaining Counsel: Yes **Opposing Counsel (Deps):** No

Surgery, Neurological
Court: $750 **Review/Prep:** $450 **Deps:** $500
Years Testifying: 3
Written Fee Schedule: Yes
Min Charge for Deps: Yes **Hours:** 4
Min Charge for Trial: Yes **Hours:** 4
Cancellation Charge for Deps/Trial: Yes
Retainer Required: Yes, $1,800 (Refundable, One Time)
Procedure When Dep Exceeds Paid Time: Proceed without immediate payment
Expenses Marked Up: No
Expenses Billed For: Mileage, Airline Tickets, Photocopies, Telephone Calls
Portal-to-Portal: Yes **1st-class Airfare:** No
Written Retainer Agreement: Yes
Terms: Lawyer is responsible for fee, not lawyer's client, Interest for delinquent accounts, Out-of-pocket expense policies, In-court testimony minimums, Retaining counsel pays all deposition charges, Fee schedules,

Portal-to-portal travel time, Attorney's fees if forced to sue for collection, Deposition minimum fee, Payment for preparation time
Failure to Pay Bill Last 5 Years; Retaining Counsel: Yes **Opposing (Deps):** Yes

Vocational Rehabilitation
Court: $150 **Review/Prep:** $100 **Deps:** $150
Years Testifying: 20
Written Fee Schedule: Yes
Min Charge for Deps: No
Min Charge for Trial: No
Cancellation Charge for Deps/Trial: Yes
Retainer Required: No
Expenses Marked Up: No
Expenses Billed For: Mileage, Airline Tickets
Portal-to-Portal: Yes **1st-class Airfare:** No
Written Retainer Agreement: No
Failure to Pay Bill Last 5 Years; Retaining Counsel: Yes **Opposing Counsel (Deps):** No

Washington

Accident Reconstruction/ Engineering
Court: $135 **Review/Prep:** $135 **Deps:** $200
Years Testifying: 30
Written Fee Schedule: No
Min Charge for Deps: No
Min Charge for Trial: No
Cancellation Charge for Deps/Trial: No
Retainer Required: No
Expenses Marked Up: No
Expenses Billed For: Mileage, Airline Tickets, Lab/Testing, Photographs, Demonstrative Aids
Portal-to-Portal: Yes **1st-class Airfare:** No
Written Retainer Agreement: No
Failure to Pay Bill Last 5 Years; Retaining Counsel: No **Opposing Counsel (Deps):** No

Accident Reconstruction, Aircraft
Court: $150 **Review/Prep:** $150 **Deps:** $150
Years Testifying: 20
Written Fee Schedule: No
Min Charge for Deps: No
Min Charge for Trial: No
Cancellation Charge for Deps/Trial: No
Retainer Required: Yes, $1,500 (Refundable, Replenishable)
Expenses Marked Up: No
Expenses Billed For: Mileage, Airline Tickets, Lab/Testing, Photographs, Demonstrative Aids
Portal-to-Portal: No
Failure to Pay Bill Last 5 Years; Retaining Counsel: No **Opposing Counsel (Deps):** No

Appraisal, Gem & Jewelry
Court: $200 **Review/Prep:** $150 **Deps:** $200
Written Fee Schedule: Yes
Min Charge for Deps: No
Min Charge for Trial: No
Cancellation Charge for Deps/Trial: No
Retainer Required: Yes, 50% est. fee (Non-Refundable, Replenishable)
Procedure When Dep Exceeds Paid Time: Proceed without immediate payment
Expenses Marked Up: No
Expenses Billed For: Mileage, Airline Tickets, Photocopies, Telephone Calls, Lab/Testing
Portal-to-Portal: Yes **1st-class Airfare:** No
Written Retainer Agreement: No
Failure to Pay Bill Last 5 Years; Retaining Counsel: No **Opposing Counsel (Deps):** No

Dermatology/Surgery, Cosmetic
Court: $500 **Review/Prep:** $300 **Deps:** $300
Years Testifying: 5
Written Fee Schedule: No
Min Charge for Deps: Yes **Hours:** 4
Min Charge for Trial: Yes **Hours:** 4
Cancellation Charge for Deps/Trial: Yes
Retainer Required: No
Expenses Marked Up: Yes
Expenses Billed For: Mileage, Airline Tickets, Photocopies, Telephone Calls, Photographs, Demonstrative Aids
Portal-to-Portal: Yes **1st-class Airfare:** No
Written Retainer Agreement: No
Failure to Pay Bill Last 5 Years; Retaining Counsel: No **Opposing Counsel (Deps):** No

Engineering, Civil
Court: $100 **Review/Prep:** $94 **Deps:** $94
Years Testifying: 20 **Majority:** Defendant
Written Fee Schedule: Yes
Min Charge for Deps: No **Hours:** 8
Min Charge for Trial: Yes **Hours:** 8
Cancellation Charge for Deps/Trial: No
Retainer Required: Yes, $1,000 (Non-Refundable, One Time)
Expenses Marked Up: Yes
Expenses Billed For: Mileage, Airline Tickets, Photocopies, Telephone Calls, Lab/Testing, Photographs, Demonstrative Aids
Portal-to-Portal: Yes **1st-class Airfare:** No
Written Retainer Agreement: Yes
Terms: Lawyer is responsible for fee, not lawyer's client, Interest for delinquent accounts, Out-of-pocket expense policies, In-court testimony minimums, Retaining counsel pays all deposition charges, Fee schedules, Portal-to-portal travel time, Payment for preparation time
Failure to Pay Bill Last 5 Years; Retaining Counsel: No **Opposing Counsel (Deps):** No

Engineering, Geotechnical
Court: $175 **Review/Prep:** $175 **Deps:** $175
Years Testifying: 10 **Majority:** Defendant
Written Fee Schedule: Yes
Min Charge for Deps: No
Min Charge for Trial: No
Cancellation Charge for Deps/Trial: No
Retainer Required: Yes, Depends on case (Refundable, One Time)
Expenses Marked Up: Yes
Expenses Billed For: Mileage, Airline Tickets, Photocopies, Telephone Calls, Lab/Testing, Photographs, Demonstrative Aids
Portal-to-Portal: Yes **1st-class Airfare:** No
Written Retainer Agreement: Yes
Terms: Lawyer is responsible for fee, not lawyer's client, Interest for delinquent accounts, Out-of-pocket expense policies, Retaining counsel pays all deposition charges, Fee schedules, Portal-to-portal travel time
Failure to Pay Bill Last 5 Years; Retaining Counsel: Yes **Opposing (Deps):** Yes

Neurology
Court: $450 **Review/Prep:** $300 **Deps:** $450
Years Testifying: 20
Written Fee Schedule: Yes
Min Charge for Deps: Yes **Hours:** 1
Min Charge for Trial: Yes **Hours:** 1
Cancellation Charge for Deps/Trial: Yes
Retainer Required: No
Procedure When Dep Exceeds Paid Time: Proceed without immediate payment
Expenses Marked Up: No
Portal-to-Portal: Yes
Written Retainer Agreement: Yes
Terms: Lawyer is responsible for fee, not lawyer's client, Retaining counsel pays all deposition charges, Fee schedules, Portal-to-portal travel time, Payment for preparation time
Failure to Pay Bill Last 5 Years; Retaining Counsel: No **Opposing Counsel (Deps):** No

Neurology
Court: $500 **Review/Prep:** $250 **Deps:** $350
Years Testifying: 4 **Majority:** Plaintiff
Written Fee Schedule: Yes
Min Charge for Deps: Yes **Hours:** 1
Min Charge for Trial: No **Hours:** 1
Cancellation Charge for Deps/Trial: No
Retainer Required: No
Expenses Marked Up: Yes
Expenses Billed For: Mileage, Airline Tickets, Photocopies, Telephone Calls
Portal-to-Portal: Yes **1st-class Airfare:** No
Written Retainer Agreement: No
Failure to Pay Bill Last 5 Years; Retaining Counsel: No **Opposing Counsel (Deps):** No

Neurology
Court: $750 **Review/Prep:** $300 **Deps:** $700
Years Testifying: 20
Written Fee Schedule: Yes
Min Charge for Deps: Yes **Hours:** 1
Min Charge for Trial: Yes **Hours:** 1
Cancellation Charge for Deps/Trial: Yes
Retainer Required: Yes, $750 (Refundable)
Expenses Marked Up: No
Expenses Billed For: Airline Tickets, Demonstrative Aids
Portal-to-Portal: Yes **1st-class Airfare:** No
Written Retainer Agreement: No
Failure to Pay Bill Last 5 Years; Retaining Counsel: No **Opposing Counsel (Deps):** No

Orthopedics
Court: $500 **Review/Prep:** $400 **Deps:** $450
Years Testifying: 20 **Majority:** Defendant
Written Fee Schedule: Yes
Min Charge for Deps: Yes
Min Charge for Trial: Yes
Cancellation Charge for Deps/Trial: Yes
Retainer Required: No
Expenses Marked Up: No
Portal-to-Portal: No **1st-class Airfare:** No
Written Retainer Agreement: No
Failure to Pay Bill Last 5 Years; Retaining Counsel: No **Opposing Counsel (Deps):** Yes

Orthopedics
Court: $550 **Review/Prep:** $350 **Deps:** $550
Years Testifying: 6 **Majority:** Defendant
Written Fee Schedule: No
Min Charge for Deps: Yes **Hours:** 1
Min Charge for Trial: Yes **Hours:** 1
Cancellation Charge for Deps/Trial: Yes
Retainer Required: Yes, $2,000 (Refundable, One Time)
Procedure When Dep Exceeds Paid Time: Proceed without immediate payment
Expenses Marked Up: No
Expenses Billed For: Telephone Calls, Demonstrative Aids
Portal-to-Portal: Yes **1st-class Airfare:** No
Written Retainer Agreement: No
Failure to Pay Bill Last 5 Years; Retaining Counsel: Yes **Opposing (Deps):** Yes

Psychiatry
Court: $400 **Review/Prep:** $140 **Deps:** $350
Years Testifying: 33
Written Fee Schedule: Yes
Min Charge for Deps: No
Min Charge for Trial: No
Cancellation Charge for Deps/Trial: No
Retainer Required: No
Expenses Marked Up: No
Expenses Billed For: Photocopies, Telephone Calls
Portal-to-Portal: Yes **1st-class Airfare:** Yes
Written Retainer Agreement: No
Failure to Pay Bill Last 5 Years; Retaining Counsel: No **Opposing Counsel (Deps):** No

Psychology
Court: $300 **Review/Prep:** $200 **Deps:** $300
Years Testifying: 22 **Majority:** Plaintiff
Written Fee Schedule: Yes
Min Charge for Deps: Yes **Hours:** 2
Min Charge for Trial: Yes **Hours:** 2
Cancellation Charge for Deps/Trial: Yes
Retainer Required: Yes, $2,500 (Non-Refundable, One Time)
Procedure When Dep Exceeds Paid Time: Proceed without immediate payment
Expenses Marked Up: No
Expenses Billed For: Mileage, Airline Tickets, Photocopies, Telephone Calls, Lab/Testing
Portal-to-Portal: Yes **1st-class Airfare:** No
Written Retainer Agreement: Yes
Terms: Out-of-pocket expense policies, In-court testimony minimums, Retaining counsel pays all deposition charges, Fee schedules, Portal-to-portal travel time, Deposition minimum fee
Failure to Pay Bill Last 5 Years; Retaining Counsel: Yes **Opposing (Deps):** Yes

Psychology
Court: $300 **Review/Prep:** $200 **Deps:** $200
Years Testifying: 15
Written Fee Schedule: No
Min Charge for Deps: Yes **Hours:** 2
Min Charge for Trial: Yes **Hours:** 2
Cancellation Charge for Deps/Trial: Yes
Retainer Required: Yes, $1,000 (Partially Refundable, Replenishable)
Expenses Marked Up: No
Expenses Billed For: Mileage, Airline Tickets, Telephone Calls, Photographs, Demonstrative Aids
Portal-to-Portal: Yes **1st-class Airfare:** No
Written Retainer Agreement: No
Failure to Pay Bill Last 5 Years; Retaining Counsel: No **Opposing Counsel (Deps):** No

Valuation, Business
Court: $145 **Review/Prep:** $125 **Deps:** $145
Years Testifying: 5
Written Fee Schedule: No
Min Charge for Deps: Yes **Hours:** 5
Min Charge for Trial: Yes **Hours:** 5
Cancellation Charge for Deps/Trial: Yes
Retainer Required: Yes, $725 (Non-Refundable, One Time)
Procedure When Dep Exceeds Paid Time: Proceed without immediate payment
Expenses Marked Up: No
Expenses Billed For: Mileage, Airline Tickets, Photocopies, Telephone Calls, Lab/Testing, Photographs, Demonstrative Aids
Portal-to-Portal: Yes **1st-class Airfare:** No
Written Retainer Agreement: Yes
Terms: Lawyer is responsible for fee, not lawyer's client, Interest for delinquent accounts, Out-of-pocket expense policies, In-court testimony minimums, Retaining counsel pays all deposition charges, Portal-to-portal travel time, Attorney's fees if forced to sue for collection, Deposition minimum fee, Payment for preparation time
Failure to Pay Bill Last 5 Years; Retaining Counsel: No **Opposing Counsel (Deps):** No

Vocational
Court: $115 **Review/Prep:** $100 **Deps:** $100
Years Testifying: 11
Written Fee Schedule: Yes
Min Charge for Deps: No
Min Charge for Trial: No
Cancellation Charge for Deps/Trial: No
Retainer Required: Yes, $750 (Refundable)
Expenses Billed For: Mileage, Photocopies
Portal-to-Portal: Yes **1st-class Airfare:** No
Written Retainer Agreement: No
Failure to Pay Bill Last 5 Years; Retaining Counsel: Yes **Opposing Counsel (Deps):** No

Vocational Rehabilitation
Court: $230 **Review/Prep:** $145 **Deps:** $230
Years Testifying: 8 **Majority:** Plaintiff
Written Fee Schedule: Yes
Min Charge for Deps: Yes **Hours:** 1
Min Charge for Trial: Yes **Hours:** 1
Cancellation Charge for Deps/Trial: Yes
Retainer Required: Yes, $500 (Non-Refundable, One Time)
Expenses Marked Up: No
Expenses Billed For: Mileage, Airline Tickets, Photocopies
Portal-to-Portal: Yes **1st-class Airfare:** No
Written Retainer Agreement: No
Failure to Pay Bill Last 5 Years; Retaining Counsel: Yes **Opposing (Deps):** Yes

Vocational Rehabilitation
Court: $250 **Review/Prep:** $150 **Deps:** $250
Years Testifying: 22
Written Fee Schedule: Yes
Min Charge for Deps: No
Min Charge for Trial: No
Cancellation Charge for Deps/Trial: No
Retainer Required: Yes, $1,500 (Refundable, One Time)
Expenses Marked Up: No
Expenses Billed For: Photocopies, Telephone Calls, Lab/Testing
Portal-to-Portal: Yes **1st-class Airfare:** No
Written Retainer Agreement: No

Failure to Pay Bill Last 5 Years; Retaining Counsel: No **Opposing Counsel (Deps):** Yes

West Virginia

Cardiology/Internal Medicine
Court: $500 **Review/Prep:** $350 **Deps:** $350
Years Testifying: 20 **Majority:** Defendant
Written Fee Schedule: Yes
Min Charge for Deps: Yes **Hours:** 4
Min Charge for Trial: Yes **Hours:** 4
Cancellation Charge for Deps/Trial: No
Retainer Required: No
Procedure When Dep Exceeds Paid Time: Proceed without immediate payment
Expenses Marked Up: No
Expenses Billed For: Airline Tickets, Photographs, Demonstrative Aids
Portal-to-Portal: Yes **1st-class Airfare:** No
Written Retainer Agreement: No
Failure to Pay Bill Last 5 Years; Retaining Counsel: No **Opposing Counsel (Deps):** No

Engineering/Construction
Court: $135 **Review/Prep:** $135 **Deps:** $135
Years Testifying: 10
Written Fee Schedule: Yes
Min Charge for Deps: No
Min Charge for Trial: No
Cancellation Charge for Deps/Trial: No
Retainer Required: Depends, $2,000
Expenses Marked Up: No
Expenses Billed For: Mileage, Airline Tickets, Photocopies, Telephone Calls, Lab/Testing, Photographs, Demonstrative Aids
Portal-to-Portal: Yes **1st-class Airfare:** No
Written Retainer Agreement: No
Failure to Pay Bill Last 5 Years; Retaining Counsel: No **Opposing Counsel (Deps):** No

Pharmacy/Pharmacology
Court: $300 **Review/Prep:** $250 **Deps:** $300
Years Testifying: 3 **Majority:** Plaintiff
Written Fee Schedule: Yes
Min Charge for Deps: Yes **Hours:** 5
Min Charge for Trial: Yes **Hours:** 5
Cancellation Charge for Deps/Trial: Yes
Retainer Required: Yes, $2,000 (Refundable, One Time)
Procedure When Dep Exceeds Paid Time: Proceed without immediate payment
Expenses Marked Up: No
Expenses Billed For: Mileage, Airline Tickets, Photocopies, Telephone Calls, Lab/Testing, Photographs, Demonstrative Aids
Portal-to-Portal: No **1st-class Airfare:** No
Written Retainer Agreement: Yes
Terms: Lawyer is responsible for fee, not lawyer's client, Interest for delinquent accounts, Out-of-pocket expense policies, In-court testimony minimums, Retaining counsel pays all deposition charges, Fee schedules, Attorney's fees if forced to sue for collection, Deposition minimum fee, Payment for preparation time
Failure to Pay Bill Last 5 Years; Retaining Counsel: No **Opposing Counsel (Deps):** No

Science
Court: $125 **Review/Prep:** $125 **Deps:** $125
Years Testifying: 40
Written Fee Schedule: Yes
Min Charge for Deps: Yes **Hours:** 3
Min Charge for Trial: Yes **Hours:** 3
Cancellation Charge for Deps/Trial: No
Retainer Required: Yes, $750 (Refundable, Replenishable)
Expenses Marked Up: No
Expenses Billed For: Airline Tickets, Lab/Testing
Portal-to-Portal: Yes **1st-class Airfare:** No
Written Retainer Agreement: No
Failure to Pay Bill Last 5 Years; Retaining Counsel: Yes **Opposing Counsel (Deps):** No

Surgery, Cardiothoracic
Court: $600 **Review/Prep:** $450 **Deps:** $450
Years Testifying: 8 **Majority:** Defendant
Written Fee Schedule: No
Min Charge for Deps: No **Hours:** 10
Min Charge for Trial: Yes **Hours:** 10
Cancellation Charge for Deps/Trial: No
Retainer Required: Yes, $900 (Refundable, One Time)
Expenses Marked Up: No
Expenses Billed For: Airline Tickets, Photocopies, Lab/Testing, Photographs, Demonstrative Aids
Portal-to-Portal: Yes **1st-class Airfare:** No
Written Retainer Agreement: No
Failure to Pay Bill Last 5 Years; Retaining Counsel: No **Opposing Counsel (Deps):** No

Transportation/Engineering, Civil
Court: $200 **Review/Prep:** $200 **Deps:** $200
Years Testifying: 20 **Majority:** Plaintiff
Written Fee Schedule: Yes
Min Charge for Deps: No
Min Charge for Trial: No
Cancellation Charge for Deps/Trial: No
Retainer Required: Yes, $500 (Refundable, One Time)
Expenses Marked Up: No
Expenses Billed For: Mileage, Airline Tickets, Photocopies, Telephone Calls, Lab/Testing, Photographs, Demonstrative Aids
Portal-to-Portal: Yes **1st-class Airfare:** No
Written Retainer Agreement: No
Failure to Pay Bill Last 5 Years; Retaining Counsel: Yes **Opposing (Deps):** Yes

Wisconsin

Accident Reconstruction
Court: $300 **Review/Prep:** $200 **Deps:** $300
Years Testifying: 10
Written Fee Schedule: Yes
Min Charge for Deps: No
Min Charge for Trial: No
Cancellation Charge for Deps/Trial: No
Retainer Required: Yes, $1,000 (Refundable, One Time)
Expenses Marked Up: No
Expenses Billed For: Mileage, Airline Tickets, Photographs, Demonstrative Aids
Portal-to-Portal: Yes **1st-class Airfare:** No
Written Retainer Agreement: No
Failure to Pay Bill Last 5 Years; Retaining Counsel: No **Opposing Counsel (Deps):** No

Accident Reconstruction
Court: $145 **Review/Prep:** $145 **Deps:** $145
Years Testifying: 30 **Majority:** Defendant
Written Fee Schedule: Yes
Min Charge for Deps: Yes
Min Charge for Trial: No
Cancellation Charge for Deps/Trial: No
Retainer Required: Yes, $1,000 (Refundable, One Time)
Expenses Marked Up: Yes
Expenses Billed For: Mileage, Airline Tickets, Photocopies, Photographs
Portal-to-Portal: Yes **1st-class Airfare:** No
Written Retainer Agreement: No
Failure to Pay Bill Last 5 Years; Retaining Counsel: Yes **Opposing (Deps):** Yes

Engineering/Safety
Court: $170 **Review/Prep:** $85 **Deps:** $170
Years Testifying: 40
Written Fee Schedule: Yes
Min Charge for Deps: Yes **Hours:** 4
Min Charge for Trial: Yes **Hours:** 4
Cancellation Charge for Deps/Trial: No
Retainer Required: Yes, Depends on case (Refundable, One Time)
Procedure When Dep Exceeds Paid Time: Proceed without immediate payment
Expenses Marked Up: No
Expenses Billed For: Airline Tickets, Lab/Testing
Portal-to-Portal: Yes **1st-class Airfare:** No
Written Retainer Agreement: Yes
Terms: Lawyer is responsible for fee, not lawyer's client, Interest for delinquent accounts, Out-of-pocket expense policies, In-court testimony minimums, Retaining counsel

pays all deposition charges, Fee schedules, Portal-to-portal travel time, Payment for preparation time
Failure to Pay Bill Last 5 Years; Retaining Counsel: No **Opposing Counsel (Deps):** No

Geriatrics
Court: $375 **Review/Prep:** $250 **Deps:** $375
Years Testifying: 5
Written Fee Schedule: No
Min Charge for Deps: No
Min Charge for Trial: No
Cancellation Charge for Deps/Trial: No
Retainer Required: No
Expenses Marked Up: No
Portal-to-Portal: No **1st-class Airfare:** No
Written Retainer Agreement: No
Failure to Pay Bill Last 5 Years; Retaining Counsel: No **Opposing Counsel (Deps):** No

Machinery/Appraisal, Equipment
Court: $200 **Review/Prep:** $100 **Deps:** $200
Years Testifying: 20 **Majority:** Plaintiff
Written Fee Schedule: No
Min Charge for Deps: Yes **Hours:** 3
Min Charge for Trial: Yes **Hours:** 3
Cancellation Charge for Deps/Trial: Yes
Retainer Required: Yes, $350 (Refundable, One Time)
Expenses Marked Up: No
Expenses Billed For: Mileage, Airline Tickets, Photocopies, Telephone Calls
Portal-to-Portal: Yes **1st-class Airfare:** No
Written Retainer Agreement: No
Failure to Pay Bill Last 5 Years; Retaining Counsel: No **Opposing Counsel (Deps):** No

Neurology
Court: $600 **Review/Prep:** $360 **Deps:** $500
Years Testifying: 35 **Majority:** Defendant
Written Fee Schedule: Yes
Min Charge for Deps: No
Min Charge for Trial: No
Cancellation Charge for Deps/Trial: Yes
Retainer Required: No
Expenses Marked Up: No
Expenses Billed For: Mileage, Airline Tickets
Portal-to-Portal: Yes **1st-class Airfare:** No
Written Retainer Agreement: No
Failure to Pay Bill Last 5 Years; Retaining Counsel: No **Opposing Counsel (Deps):** Yes

Obstetrics & Gynecology
Court: $500 **Review/Prep:** $350 **Deps:** $400
Years Testifying: 15
Written Fee Schedule: No
Min Charge for Deps: Yes **Hours:** 4
Min Charge for Trial: Yes **Hours:** 4
Cancellation Charge for Deps/Trial: No
Retainer Required: No
Expenses Marked Up: No
Expenses Billed For: Mileage, Airline Tickets
Portal-to-Portal: Yes **1st-class Airfare:** No
Written Retainer Agreement: No
Failure to Pay Bill Last 5 Years; Retaining Counsel: No **Opposing Counsel (Deps):** No

Orthopedics
Court: $850 **Review/Prep:** $350 **Deps:** $850
Years Testifying: 30
Written Fee Schedule: Yes
Min Charge for Deps: Yes **Hours:** 1
Min Charge for Trial: Yes **Hours:** 1
Cancellation Charge for Deps/Trial: Yes
Retainer Required: Yes, $1,600 (Refundable, One Time)
Procedure When Dep Exceeds Paid Time: Proceed without immediate payment
Expenses Marked Up: No
Expenses Billed For: Mileage, Airline Tickets, Photocopies, Telephone Calls, Lab/Testing
Portal-to-Portal: No **1st-class Airfare:** Yes
Written Retainer Agreement: No
Failure to Pay Bill Last 5 Years; Retaining Counsel: No **Opposing Counsel (Deps):** No

Orthopedics
Court: $1,500 **Review/Prep:** $300 **Deps:** $1,000
Years Testifying: 20 **Majority:** Defendant
Written Fee Schedule: Yes
Min Charge for Deps: Yes **Hours:** 1
Min Charge for Trial: Yes **Hours:** 1
Cancellation Charge for Deps/Trial: Yes
Retainer Required: No
Expenses Marked Up: No
Expenses Billed For: Mileage
Portal-to-Portal: Yes **1st-class Airfare:** No
Written Retainer Agreement: No
Failure to Pay Bill Last 5 Years; Retaining Counsel: No **Opposing Counsel (Deps):** Yes

Physics
Court: $230 **Review/Prep:** $230 **Deps:** $230
Years Testifying: 30 **Majority:** Defendant
Written Fee Schedule: No
Min Charge for Deps: No
Min Charge for Trial: No
Cancellation Charge for Deps/Trial: No
Retainer Required: No
Expenses Marked Up: No
Expenses Billed For: Mileage, Airline Tickets, Photocopies, Telephone Calls, Lab/Testing, Photographs, Demonstrative Aids
Portal-to-Portal: Yes **1st-class Airfare:** No
Written Retainer Agreement: No
Failure to Pay Bill Last 5 Years; Retaining Counsel: No **Opposing Counsel (Deps):** No

Psychiatry
Court: $400 **Review/Prep:** $400 **Deps:** $400
Years Testifying: 15 **Majority:** Defendant
Written Fee Schedule: No
Min Charge for Deps: No
Min Charge for Trial: No
Cancellation Charge for Deps/Trial: No
Retainer Required: No
Expenses Marked Up: No
Expenses Billed For: Mileage, Airline Tickets, Lab/Testing, Photographs
Portal-to-Portal: Yes **1st-class Airfare:** No
Written Retainer Agreement: No
Failure to Pay Bill Last 5 Years; Retaining Counsel: No **Opposing Counsel (Deps):** No

Urology
Court: $450 **Review/Prep:** $375 **Deps:** $450
Years Testifying: 35 **Majority:** Defendant
Written Fee Schedule: Yes
Min Charge for Deps: Yes
Min Charge for Trial: No
Cancellation Charge for Deps/Trial: No
Retainer Required: Yes, $500 (Non-Refundable, One Time)
Expenses Billed For: Mileage, Demonstrative Aids
Portal-to-Portal: Yes **1st-class Airfare:** No
Written Retainer Agreement: Yes
Terms: Lawyer is responsible for fee, not lawyer's client, In-court testimony minimums, Retaining counsel pays all deposition charges, Fee schedules, Portal-to-portal travel time, Deposition minimum fee, Payment for preparation time
Failure to Pay Bill Last 5 Years; Retaining Counsel: Yes **Opposing Counsel (Deps):** No

Wyoming

Urology
Court: $400 **Review/Prep:** $400 **Deps:** $400
Written Fee Schedule: Yes
Min Charge for Deps: Yes **Hours:** 1
Min Charge for Trial: Yes **Hours:** 1
Cancellation Charge for Deps/Trial: Yes
Retainer Required: Yes, $400 (Non-Refundable, Replenishable)
Procedure When Dep Exceeds Paid Time: Proceed without immediate payment
Expenses Marked Up: No
Expenses Billed For: Mileage, Photocopies, Telephone Calls
Portal-to-Portal: Yes **1st-class Airfare:** No
Written Retainer Agreement: No
Failure to Pay Bill Last 5 Years; Retaining Counsel: No **Opposing Counsel (Deps):** No

Urology
Court: $400 **Review/Prep:** $400 **Deps:** $400
Years Testifying: 1
Written Fee Schedule: Yes
Min Charge for Deps: Yes
Min Charge for Trial: No
Cancellation Charge for Deps/Trial: Yes
Retainer Required: Yes, $800 (Non-Refundable, Replenishable)
Procedure When Dep Exceeds Paid Time: Get payment before proceeding further
Expenses Marked Up: Yes
Expenses Billed For: Mileage, Airline Tickets, Lab/Testing, Photographs, Demonstrative Aids
Portal-to-Portal: Yes **1st-class Airfare:** Yes
Written Retainer Agreement: Yes
Terms: Lawyer is responsible for fee, not lawyer's client, Interest for delinquent accounts, Out-of-pocket expense policies, Retaining counsel pays all deposition charges, Fee schedules, Portal-to-portal travel time, Attorney's fees if forced to sue for collection, Deposition minimum fee, Payment for preparation time, First class air travel
Failure to Pay Bill Last 5 Years; Retaining Counsel: No **Opposing Counsel (Deps):** No

Index

T

U

V

W

Y